D. Bethune Duffield

MISCELLANIES;

EMBRACING

REVIEWS, ESSAYS, AND ADDRESSES.

BY THE LATE

THOMAS CHALMERS, D.D. & LL.D.

NEW YORK:
ROBERT CARTER & BROTHERS,
No. 285 BROADWAY.

1851.

CONTENTS.

BRIEF MEMOIR OF DR. CHALMERS.

Thomas Chalmers was born at Anstruther, in Fife, on the 17th of March, 1780, and was early sent to study at St. Andrew's University. From traditions still plentiful in the North, his college career must have been distinguished by some of his subsequent peculiarities—energy, good humor, companionableness, and ascendency over others. And it was then that his passion for the physical sciences was first developed. He studied mathematics, chemistry, and some branches of natural history, with more than youthful enthusiasm, and with such success, that besides assisting his own professor he made a narrow escape from the mathematical chair in Edinburgh. For these early pursuits he never lost a lingering taste, and in the summer holidays of his mellow age, it was his delight to give lectures to youthful audiences on electricity and the laws of chemical combination. His attainments in these fields of knowledge were not those of a mere amateur; but in earlier life had all the system and security of an accomplished philosopher. And though for some years they engrossed him too much, they afterwards helped him amazingly. Mathematics especially, gave him the power of severe and continuous thinking; and enabled him, unseduced by a salient fancy, to follow each recondite speculation to its curious landing-place, and each high argument to its topmost stronghold. And whilst this stern discipline gave a stability to his judgment and a steadiness to his intellect, such as few men of exuberant imagination have ever enjoyed, the facts and laws of the natural sciences furnished that imagination with its appropriate wealth. They supplied the imagery often gorgeous and august, sometimes brilliant and dazzling, by which in after days he made familiar truths grander or clearer than they had ever been before; and, linked together by a genius mighty in analogies, they formed the rope-ladder by which he scaled pinnacles of dazzling elevation, and told down to wondering listeners, the new panorama which stretched around him. Consecrated and Christianized, his youthful science reappeared and was laid on the altar of religion in the Astronomical Discourses and Natural Theology.

The first place where he exercised his ministry was Cavers, in the South of Scotland, where he was helper to the aged minister. It was here that he made the acquaintance of Charters of Wilton—a minister remarkable for this, that he did not preach anything which he did not understand. He did not fully understand the Gospel, and he did not fully preach it; but those moral truths and personal duties which he did comprehend, he enforced with a downrightness, a simplicity and minuteness which cannot be sufficiently admired. To latest existence Dr. Chalmers retained a profound respect for the practical wisdom and lively sense of this Scottish Epictetus; and though it is comparing the greater with the less, those who have heard him in his more familiar sermons—discoursing the matter with a village audience, or breaking it down to the unlettered hearers of the West Port or the Dean—were just listening to old Charters of Wilton, revived in a more affectionate and evangelical version.

In May, 1803, he was settled in the rural parish of Kilmany. This was to his heart's content. It brought him back to his native county. It gave him an abundance of leisure. It brought him near the manse of Flisk, and beside a congenial and distinguished naturalist. It was the country, with the clear stars above and the glorious hills around him; and it allowed him to wander all day long, hammer in hand and botanical box on his shoulders, chipping the rocks, and ransacking the glens, and cultivating a kindly acquaintance with the outlandish peasantry. But all this while, though a minister, he was ignorant of essential Christianity. There was in nature much that pleased his taste, and he knew very well the quickened step and the glistening eye of the eagle collector, as he pounces on some rare crystal or quaint and novel flower. But as yet no Bible text had made his bosom flutter, and he had not hidden in his heart sayings which he had detected with delight and treasured up like pearls. And though his nature was genial and benevolent—though he had his chosen friends and longed to elevate his parishioners to a higher level of intelligence, and domestic comfort, and virtuous enjoyment—he had not discovered any Being possessed of such paramount claims and overwhelming attractions as to make it end enough to live and labor for His sake. But that discovery he made while writing for an Encyclopædia an article on Christianity. The death of a relation is said to have saddened his mind into more than usual thoughtfulness, and whilst engaged in the researches which his task demanded, the scheme of God was manifested to his astonished understanding, and the Son of God was revealed to his admiring and adoring affections. The Godhead imbodied in the person and exemplified in the life of the Saviour, the remarkable arrangement for the removal and annihilation of sin, a gratuitous pardon as the germ of piety and the secret of spiritual peace—these truths flung a brightness over his field of view, and accumulated in wonder and endearment round the Redeemer's person. He found himself in sudden possession of an instrument potent to touch, and, in certain circumstances, omnipotent to transform the hearts of men; and exulted to discover a Friend all-worthy and divine, to whom he might dedicate his every faculty, and in serving whom he would most effectually subserve the widest good of man. And ignorant of their peculiar phraseology, almost ignorant of their history, by the direct door of the Bible itself he landed on the theology of the Reformers and the Puritans; and ere ever he was aware, his quickened and concentrated faculties were intent on reviving and ennobling the old Evangelism.

The heroism with which he avowed his change, and the fervor with which he proclaimed the newly-discovered Gospel, made a mighty stir in the quiet country around Kilmany; and at last the renown of this upland Boanerges began to spread over Scotland, till, in 1815, the Town Council of Glasgow invited him to come and be the minister of their Tron Church and parish. He came, and in that city for eight years sustained a series of the most brilliant arguments and overpowering appeals in behalf of vital godliness which devotion has ever kindled or eloquence ever launched into the flaming atmosphere of human thought. And though the burning words and meteor fancies were to many no more than a spectacle—the crash and sparkle of an illumination which exploded weekly, and lit up the Tron Church into a dome of colored fire—they were designed by their author, and they told like a weekly bombardment. Into the fastnesses of aristocratic *hauteur* and commercial self-sufficiency—into the airy battlements of elegant morality and irreligious respectability, they sent showering the junipers of hot conviction; and in hundreds of consciences were mighty to the pulling down of strong-holds. And though the effort was awful—though in each paroxysmal climax, as his aim pointed more and yet more loftily, he poured forth his very soul—for the Gospel, and love to men, and zeal for God now mingled with his being, and formed his temperament, his genius, and his passion—though he himself was his own artillery, and in these self-consuming sermons was rapidly blazing away that holocaust—himself—the effort was sublimely successful. In the cold philosophy of the Eastern capital and the coarse earthliness of the Western a breach was effected, and in its Bible dimensions and its sovereign insignia the Gospel triumphant went through. Though the labors of Love and Balfour had been blessed to the winning of many, it was not till in the might of commanding intellect and consecrated reason Chalmers came up—it was not till then that the citadel yielded, and evangelical doctrine effected its lodgment in the meditative and active mind of modern Scotland; and whatever other influences may have worked together,. it was then and there that the battle of a vitalized Christianity was fought and won. Patrons converted or overawed, evangelical majorities in Synods and Assemblies, Church of Scotland Missions, the two hundred additional chapels, the Disruption, the Free Church, an earnest ministry and a liberal laity, are the trophies of this good soldier, and the splendid results of that Glasgow campaign.

From that high service, worn, but not weary, he was fain to seek relief in an academic retreat. Again his native county offered an asylum, and in the University of St. Andrew's, and its chair of Moral Philosophy, he spent five years of calmer but not inglorious toil. Omitting that psychology, which in Scottish colleges is the great staple of moral philosophy lectures, with his characteristic intentness he advanced direct to those prime questions which affect man as a responsible being, and instead of dried specimens from ancient cabinets, instead of those smoked and dusty virtues which have lain about since the time of Socrates and Seneca—instead of withered maxims from a pagan text, he took his code of morals fresh from Heaven's statute-book. It is not enough to say, that into his system of morality he flung all his heart and soul. He threw in himself—but he threw something better—he threw the Gospel, and for the first time in a Northern University was taught an evangelized ethics—a system with a motive as well as a rule—a system instinct with the love of God, and buoyant with noble purposes. And in the warm atmosphere of his crowded class-room—caught up by enthusiastic and admiring listeners the contagion spread; and as they passed from before his chair, the *elite* of Scottish youth, Urquhart, Duff, and Adam, issued forth on the world, awake to the chief end of man, and sworn to life-long labors in the cause of Christ. Too often a school for sceptics—when Chalmers was professor, the ethic class became a mission college—the citadel of living faith, and the metropolis of active philanthrophy; and whilst every intellect expanded to the vastness and grandeur of his views, every susceptible spirit carried away a holy and generous impulse from his own noble and transfusive nature.

And then they took him to Edinburgh College, and made him Professor of Theology. In the old-established times this was the top of the pyramid—the highest post which Presbyterian Scotland knew—and like Newton to the Mathematic chair in Cambridge, his pre-eminent fitness bore Chalmers into the Edinburgh chair of divinity. And perhaps that Faculty never owned such a combination as the colleagues, Welsh and Chalmers. Alike men of piety—alike men of lofty integrity, and in their public career distinguished by immaculate purity—the genius and talents of the one were a supplement to those of the other. Popular and impassioned—a declaimer in the desk, and often causing his class-room to ring again with the fine phrensy of his eloquence, Chalmers was the man of power. Academic and reserved—adhering steadfastly to the severe succession of his subjects, and handling them earnestly but calmly—Welsh was the man of system.

Ideal and impetuous, the one beheld the truth imbodied in some glorious fancy, and as the best and briefest argument tore the curtain and bade you look and see. Contemplative and cautious, the other was constantly rejecting the illustrations which pass for arguments, and putting the staff of his remorseless logic through the illusions of poetry when substituted for the deductions of reason or the statements of history. Sanguine and strenuous, the one was impatient of doubts and delays; and if reasoning failed had recourse to rhetoric;—if the regular passage-boat refused his dispatches, he at once bound them to a rocket and sent them right over the river. Patient and acute, the other was willing to wait, and was confident that truth if understood must sooner or later win the day. Ardent and generous, the panegyric of the one was an inspiring cordial; vigilant and faithful, the criticism of the other was a timely caveat. A man of might, the one sought to deposit great principles, and was himself the example of great exploits. A man of method, the other was minute in his directions, and painstaking in his lessons, and frequent in his rehearsals and reviews. The one was the man of grandeur; the other the man of grace. The one was the valcano; the other was the verdure on its side. The one was the burning light; the other the ground-glass which made it softer shine. Each had his own tint and magnitude; but the two close-united made a double star, which looked like one; and now that they have set together, who will venture to predict the rising of such another?

For thirty years it had been the great labor of Dr. Chalmers to popularize the Scottish Establishment. A religion truly national, enthroned in the highest places, and a beatific inmate in the humblest homes—a Church which all the people loved, and which provided for them all—a Church with a king for its nursing father, and a nation for its members—this was the splendid vision which he had once seen in Isaiah, and longed to behold in Scotland. It was to this that the herculean exertions of the pastor, and anon the professor, tended. By his great ascendency he converted the populous and plebeian parish of St. John's into an isolated district—with an elder and a deacon to every family, and a Sabbath school for every child—and had well nigh banished pauperism from within its borders. And though it stood a reproachful oasis, only shaming the wastes around it, his hope and prayer had been that its order and beauty would have said to other ministers and sessions, Go ye and do likewise. And then the whole drift of his prelections was to send his students forth upon the country ardent evangelists and affectionate pastors—indoctrinated with his own extensive plans, and inflamed with his own benevolent purposes. And then, when for successive years he crusaded the country, begging from the rich 200 churches for the poor, and went up to London to lecture on the establishment and extension of Christian Churches, it was still the same golden future—a Church national but Christian, endowed but independent, established but free—which inspirited his efforts, and awoke from beneath their ashes the fires of earlier days. And when at last the delusion of a century was dissolved—when the courts of law changed their own mind, and revoked the liberty of the Scottish Church—much as he loved its old establishment—much as he loved his Edinburgh professorship, and much more as he loved his 200 churches—with a single movement of his pen he signed them all away. He had reached his grand climacteric, and many thought that, smitten down by the shock, his gray hairs would descend in sorrow to the grave. It was time for him "to break his mighty heart and die." But they little knew the man. They forgot that spirit which, like the trodden palm, had so often sprung erect and stalwart from a crushing overthrow. We saw him that November. We saw him in its Convocation—the sublimest aspect in which we ever saw the noble man. The ship was fast aground, and as they looked over the bulwarks, through the mist and the breakers, all on board seemed anxious and sad. Never had they felt prouder of their old first-rate, and never had she ploughed a braver path than when—contrary to all the markings in the chart, and all the experience of former voyages—she dashed on this fatal bar. The stoutest were dismayed, and many talked of taking to the fragments, and, one by one, trying for the nearest shore; when calmer because of the turmoil, and with the exultation of one who saw safety ahead, the voice of this dauntless veteran was heard propounding his confident scheme. Cheered by his assurance, and inspired by his example, they set to work, and that dreary winter was spent in constructing a vessel with a lighter draught and a simpler rigging, but large enough to carry every true-hearted man who ever trod the old ship's timbers. Never did he work more blithely, and never was there more of athletic ardor in his looks than during the six months that this ark was a building—though every stroke of the mallet told of blighted hopes and defeated toil, and the unknown sea before him. And when the signal-psalm announced the new vessel launched, and leaving the old galley high and dry on the breakers, the banner unfurled, and showed the covenanting blue still spotless, and the symbolic bush still burning, few will forget the renovation of his youth and the joyful omen of his shining countenance. It was not only the rapture of his prayers, but the radiance of his spirit which repeated "God is our Refuge."* It is something heart-stirring to see the old soldier take the field, or the old trader exerting every energy to retrieve his shattered fortunes; but far the finest spectacle of the moulting eagle was Chalmers with his hoary locks beginning life anew. But indeed he was not old. They who

* The psalm with which the Free Assembly opened.

can fill their veins with every hopeful healthful thing around them—those who can imbibe the sunshine of the future, and transfuse life from realities not come as yet—their blood need never freeze. And his bosom heaved with all the newness of the Church's life and all the bigness of the Church's plans. And, best of all, those who wait upon the Lord are always young. This was the reason why, on the morning of that Exodus, he did not totter forth from the old Establishment a blank and palsy-stricken man; but with flashing eye snatched up his palmer-staff, and as he stamped it on the ground all Scotland shook, and answered with a deep God-speed to the giant gone on pilgrimage.

From that period till he finished his course, there was no fatigue in his spirit and no hesitation in his gait. Relieved from hollow plaudits and from hampering patronage, far ahead of the sycophants who used to raise the worldly dust around him, and surrounded by men in whose sincerity and intelligent sympathy his spirit was refreshed, and in whose wisdom and affection he confided and rejoiced, he advanced along his brightening path, with uprightness and consistency in his even mien, and the peace of God in his cheerful countenance. His eye was not dim nor his force abated. On the 14th of May we passed our last morning with him. It was his first visit to London after the Hanover Square Ovation, nine years ago. But there were now no coronets nor mitres at the door. Besides one or two of his own family, J. D. Morell, Baptist Noel, and Isaac Taylor were his guests. And he was happy. There was neither the exhaustion of past excitement nor the pressure of future engagements and anxieties in his look. It was a serene and restful morning, and little else than earnest kindness looked through the summer of his eyes. The day before, he had given his evidence before the Sites' Committee of the House of Commons, and, reminded that, according to the days of the week, it was twenty years that day since he had opened Edward Irving's church, most of the conversation reverted to his early friend. There was a mildness in his tone and a sweetness in his manner, and we could now almost fancy a halo around his head which might have warned us of what was coming. He preached all the Sabbaths of his sojourn in England, willingly and powerfully, and on the last Sabbath of May he was again at home. That evening he is said to have remarked to a friend that he thought his public work completed. He had seen the Disruption students through the four years of their course. He had seen the Sustentation Fund organized. He had been to Parliament and borne his testimony in high places. To-morrow he would give in the College Report to the Free Assembly; and after that he hoped to be permitted to retire and devote to the West Port poor his remaining days. He was willing to decrease, and close his career as a city missionary. But just as he was preparing to take the lower room, the Master said, "Come up hither," and took him up beside himself. Next morning all that met the gaze of love was the lifeless form—in stately repose on the pillow, as one who beheld it said, "a brow not cast in the mould o the sons of men." Like his friends, Thomson, M'Crie, Welsh, and Abercrombie, that stout heart which had worked so hard and swelled with so many vast emotions, had gently yielded, and to his ransomed spirit opened heaven's nearest portal.

He possessed in highest measure that divinest faculty of spirit, the power of creating its own world; but it was not a poet creating worlds to look at: it was the reformer and philanthropist in haste to people and possess them. His was the working earnestness which is impatient till its conceptions are realities and its hopes imbodied in results. For example, he took his idea of Christianity, not from books, nor from its living specimens; for the Christianity of books is often trite, and the Christianity of living men is often arrogant and vulgar; but he took his type of Christianity from his Divine Original—benignant, majestic, and God-like as he found it in the Bible—and gave this refined and lofty idea perpetual presidency in his congenial Imagination. And what sort of place was that? Why, it was quite peculiar. It was not like Jeremy Taylor's—a fairy grotto where you looked up through the woodbine ceiling and saw the sky with its moonlit clouds and the angels moving among them; or listed the far-off waterfall now dying like an old-world melody, or swelling powerfully like a prophecy when the end is near. Nor was it like Foster's—a donjon on a frowning steep—where the moat was black, and the winds were cold, and the sounds were not of earth, and iron gauntlets clanged on the deaf unheeding door. Nor was it his favorite Cowper's—a cottage with its summer joy, where the swallow nestled in the eaves and the leveret sported on the floor—where the sunbeam kissed the open Bible, and Homer lay below the table till the morning hymn was sung. Nor was it the Imagination of his dear companion, Edward Irving—a mountain-sanctuary at even-tide, where the spirits of his sainted sires would come to him, and martyr tunes begin to float through the duskier aisles, and giant worthies enter from the mossy graves and fill with reverend mien the ancient pews. More real than the first—more happy than the second—more lordly than the third, it was more modern and more lightsome than the last. It was a mansion airy, vast, and elegant—an open country all round it and sunshine all through it—not crowded with curiosities nor strewed with trinkets and toys—but massy in its proportions and stately in its ornaments—the lofty dwelling of a princely mind. And into this imagination its happy owner took the Gospel and inshrined and enthroned it. That Gospel was soon the better Genius of the place. It gave the aspect of broad welcome and bright expectation to its threshold. It shed a rose-tint on its marble and breathed the air of heaven through its halls. And like an Alhambra with a seraph for its occupant, it looked forth from the lattice brighter than the noon that looked in. Yes, it was no common home which the Gospel found when it first consecrated that lofty mind; and it was no common day in the history of the Church when that spirit first felt the dignity and gladness of this celestial inmate. Powers and resources were devoted to his service—not needed by that Gospel, but much needed by Gospel-rejecting man. And, not to specify the successive offerings laid at its feet by one of the most gifted as well as grateful of devotees, we would mention his Parochial Sermons and his Astronomical Discourses. In the one we have the Gospel made so palpable that the simplest and slowest hardly can miss it; in the other we find it made so majestic that the most intellectual and learned cannot but admire it. In the one we have Christianity brought down to the common affairs of life; in the other we have it exalted above the heavens. In the one we see the Gospel in its world-ward direction, and starting from the cradle at Bethlehem, follow it to the school and the fireside and the dying bed; in the other we view it in its God-ward direction, and following its fiery chariot far beyond the galaxy, lose it in the light inaccessible. In the one we have existence evangelized; in the other we have the Gospel glorified. The one is the primer of Christianity; the other is its epic.

But it was not in mere sermons that his imagination burned and shone. His schemes of beneficence—his plans for the regeneration of his country took their vastness and freshness from the idealism of a creative mind. At first sight they had all the look of a romance—impossible, transcendental, and unreal. And had the inventive talent been his only faculty, they would have continued romantic projects and nothing more;—a new Atlantis, a happy valley, or a fairy-land. And if he had been like most men of poetic mood, he would have deprecated any attempt to reduce his gorgeous abstractions to dull actualities. But Chalmers was never haunted by this fear. He had no fear of carnalizing his conceptions, but longed to see them clothed in flesh and blood. He had no tenderness for his day-dreams, but would rather see them melt away, and leave in their place a waking world as good and lovely as themselves. Vivid as was his fancy, his working faculty was no less vehement; and his constructive instinct compelled him to set to work as soon as the idea of an institution or an effort had once fairly filled his soul. And these exertions he made with an intensity as irresistible as it was contagious. Like the statesman who, in the union of a large philosophy and a gorgeous fancy, was his parallel*—he might have divided his active career into successive "fits," or "manias,"—a preaching fit, a pastoral fit, a fit of Church-reforming, a fit of Church-extending. And such transforming possessions were these fits—so completely did they change his whole nature into the image of the object at which he aimed, that the Apostle's words, "this one thing I do," he might have altered to, "this one thing I am." There was no division of his strength—no division of his mind; but with a concentration of mighty powers which made the spectacle sublime, he moved to the onset with lip compressed and massy tread, and victory foreseen in the glance of his eagle eye. And like all men of overmastering energy—like all men of clear conception and valiant purpose—like Nelson and Napoleon, and others born to be commanders—over and above the assurance given by his frequent success, there was a spell in his audacity—a fascination in his sanguine chivalry. Many were drawn after him, carried helpless captives by his force of character; and though, at first,

* Edmund Burke.

many found that it required some faith to follow him, like the great genius of modern warfare, experience showed that for moral as well as military conquests, there may be the deepest wisdom in dazzling projects, and rapid movements, and reckless daring. It was owing to the width of his field, and the extent of his future, and, above all, the greatness of his faith, that he was the most venturesome of philanthropists, and also the most victorious. The width of his field—for if he was operating on St. John's, he had his eye to Scotland—if he was making an effort on his own Establishment, he had an eye to Christendom. And the extent of his future—for every man who is greater than his coevals is a vaticination of some age to come—and, with Chalmers, the struggle was to speed this generation on and bring it abreast of that wiser and holier epoch of which he himself was the precocious denizen. And the greatness of his faith—for he believed that whatever is scriptural is politic. He believed that whatever is in the Bible will yet be in the world. And he believed that all things were coming which God has promised, and that all things are practicable which God bids us perform.

But we shall misrepresent the man, unless the prime feature in our memory's picture be his wondrous goodness. It was not so much in his capacious intellect, or his soaring fancy, that he surpassed all his fellows, as in his mighty heart. Big to begin with, the Gospel made it expand till it took in the human family. "Good-will to man" was the inscription on his serene and benignant countenance; and if at times the shadow of some inward anxiety darkened it, or the cloud of a momentary displeasure lowered over it, all that was needful to brighten it into its wonted benignity, was the sight of something human. Deeply impressed with our nature's wrong estate —a firm and sorrowful believer in its depravity and desperate wickedness—the sadness of his creed gave nothing bitter to his spirit and nothing sombre to his bearing. Like Him who best knew what was in man, but who was so bent on making him better, that the kindness of his errand counteracted the keenness of his intuition, and filled his mouth with gracious words—there was so much inherent warmth in his temperament, and so much of heaven-imparted kindliness in his Christianity, that love to man was his vital air, and good offices to man his daily bread. And how was his ruling passion—how was his philanthropy displayed? Not in phrases of ecstatic fondness—for though a citizen of the world he was also a Scotchman—in the region of the softer feelings sequestered, proud and shy—and, except the "my dear sir," of friendly talk, and the cordial shake of eager recognition, he was saving of the commonplace expressions of endearment, and did not depreciate friendship's currency by too lavish employment of its smaller coin. He must have been a special friend to whom he subscribed himself as anything more addicted than "Yours very truly." Nor did his warmth come out in tears of tenderness and the usual utterances of wounded feeling; for in these he was not so profuse and prompt as many. How did it appear? On a wintry day, how do we know that the hidden stove is lit, but because the frost on the panes is thawing, and life is tingling back into our dead fingers and leaden feet? And it was by the glow that spread around wherever Dr. Chalmers entered,—by the gayety which sparkled in every eye and the happiness which bounded in every breast,—by the mellow temperature to which the atmosphere suddenly ascended,—it was by this that you recognized your nearness to a focus of philanthropy. How did it appear? How do we know that that huge Newfoundland, pacing leisurely about the lawn, has a propensity for saving drowning people, but just because the moment yon playing child capsizes into the garden pond, he plunges after, and lands him dripping on the gravel? And it was by the instinctive bound with which he sprang to the relief of misery,—the importunity with which, despite his population and his pauper theories, he entreated for such emergencies as the Highland distress, and the liberality with which he relieved the successive cases of poverty and woe that came to his private ear and eye,—it was because wherever grief or suffering was, there was Dr. Chalmers, that you knew him to be a man of sympathies. But you might know it in other ways. Read the five-and-twenty volumes of his works, and say what are they but a magazine of generous thoughts for the elevation, and genial thoughts for the comfort of mankind? What are they but a collection of pleadings with power on the behalf of weakness; with opulence on the behalf of penury; with Christian intelligence on the behalf of outcast ignorance and home-grown paganism?—What are they but a series of the most skilful prescriptions for moral misery,—a good and wise physician's legacy to a disordered world, which he dearly loved and did his best to heal? And what was the succession of his services during the last thirty years? For what, short of God's glory, but the good of man, was he spending his intellect, his ascendency over others, his constitution, and his time? We have spoken of his colossal strength and his flaming energy; and the idea we now retain of his life-long career is just an engine of highest pressure pursuing the iron path of an inflexible philanthropy, and speeding to the terminus of a happier clime a lengthy train, of the poor, the halt, the blind; and we pity those who, in the shriek, the hurry, and the thunder of the transit—the momentary warmth and passing indignation of the man, forget the matchless prowess of the Christian, and the splendid purpose of his living sacrifice. And yet our wonder is, that with such a weight upon his thoughts, and such a work on his hands, he found so much time for specific kindness, and took such care to rule his spirit. Like the apostle on whom devolved the care of all the churches, but who in one letter sends messages to or from six-and-thirty friends, there was no favor so little, and no friend so obscure, that he ever forgot him. If, in a moment of absence, he omitted some wonted civility, or, by an untimely interruption, was betrayed into a word of sharpness, he showed an excessive anxiety to redress the wrong, and heal the unwilling wound. And glorious as it was to see him on the Parnassus of some transcendent inspiration, or rather on the Pisgah of some sacred and enraptured survey, it was more delightful to behold him in self-unconscious lowliness—still great, but forgetful of his greatness—by the hearth of some quiet neighbor, or in the bosom of his own family, or among friends who did not make an open show of him, out of the good treasure of his heart bringing forth nothing but good things. With all the puissant combativeness and intellectual prowess essential to such a lofty reason, it was lovely to see the gentle play of the lion-hearted man. With all his optimism—his longings after a higher scale of piety, and a nobler style of Christianity, it was beautiful to see how contented he was with every friend as he is, and with what magnetic alertness all that was Christian in himself darted forth to all that was Christian in a brother. And above all, with his wholesale beneficence, the abundance of his labors, the extent of his regards, and the vastness of his projects, it was instructive to see his affections so tender, his friendships so firm, and his kind offices so thoughtful and untiring.

Perhaps there never was a theologian who approached a given text with less appearance of system or pre-conception. No passage wore to him a suspicious or precarious look, and instead of handling it uneasily, as if it were some deadly thing, he took it up securely and frankly, and dealt with it in all the confidence of a good understanding. Some Scripture interpreters have no system. To them all texts are isolated, and none interprets another. And the system of others is too scanty. It is not co-extensive with the whole counsel of God. It interprets some passages, but leaves others unexplained. In the highest sense, Dr. Chalmers was systematic. He justly assumed that a revelation from God must be pervaded by some continuous truth; and that a clue to its general meaning must be sought in some ultimate fact, some self-consistent and all-reconciling principle. To him the Gospel was a REVELATION of RIGHTEOUSNESS; and MAN'S NEED and GOD'S GIFT were the simple elements into which his theology resolved itself. In the various forms of man's vacuity and God's fulness, man's blindness and the Spirit's enlightening, the carnal enmity and the supplanting power of a new affection, the hollowness of a morality without godliness, and the purifying influence of the Christian faith, these primary truths were constantly re-appearing; and just because his first principles were so few, they suited every case, and because his system was so simple, he felt it perfectly secure. Instead of forcing locks, he had found the master-key, and went freely out and in. And in this we believe that he was right. From want of spirituality, from want of study or capacity, we may fail to catch it; but there is a Scriptural unity. So far as the Bible is a record, its main fact is *one;* so far as it is a revelation, its chief doctrine is *one;* so far as it is the mind of God exhibited to fallen man, its prevailing tone and feeling are *one.* And having in comprehension of mind ascertained, and in simplicity of faith accepted this unity—the revealed truth and the Scriptural temperament, Dr. Chalmers walked at liberty. It was his systematic strength which gave him textual freedom; and if for one forenoon he would dilate on a single duty till it seemed to expand into the whole of man, or on one doctrine till it bulked into a Bible, it was only a portion of the grand scheme passing under the evangelic microscope. It was the lamp of the one cardinal truth lighting up a particular topic. And those who, on the other hand, objected to his preaching as not sufficiently evangelical, were only less evangelical than he. With many the Gospel is a tenet; with Dr. Chalmers the Gospel was a pervasion. The sermons of Dr. Chalmers were not stuck over with quoted texts, but every paragraph had its Scriptural seasoning. His whole being held the Gospel in solution, and beyond most text-reciters, it was his anxiety to saturate with its purest truth ethical philosophy and political economy, daily life and personal conduct, as well as retired meditation and Sabbath-day religion.

We would only, in conclusion, commemorate the Lord's great goodness to his servant in allowing him such a completed work and finished course. Many a great man has had a good thing in his heart; a temple, or some august undertaking; but it was still in his heart when he died. And many more have just put to their hand, when death struck them down, and a stately fragment is all their monument. But there is a sublime and affecting conclusiveness in the work of Dr. Chalmers. What more could the Church or the world have asked from him? It will take the Church a generation to learn all that he has taught it, and the world a century to reach that point from which he was translated. And yet he has left all his meaning clear, and all his plans complete. And all that completed work is of the best kind; all gold and silver and precious stones. To activity and enterprise he has read a new lesson. To disinterested but foreseen goodness he has supplied a new motive. To philanthropy he has given new impulse, and to the pulpit new inspiration. And whilst he has added another to the short catalogue of this world's great men, he has gone up another and a majestic onlooker to the Cloud of Witnesses.

A SERMON,

BY

REV. JOHN BRUCE, A.M.,

FREE ST. ANDREW'S CHURCH, EDINBURGH.

[*Preached in Moringside Free Church, June 6, 1847, being the Sabbath immediately after the funeral of* THOMAS CHALMERS, *D. D., LL. D., &c., &c., &c.*]

ON the morning of Monday the 31st of May, there died, and on the afternoon of Friday the 4th of June, there was buried, the greatest and most noted man in Scotland. It is nearly three centuries since she knew one equally great and honored,—one more revered when living, more mourned when gone. In love to Scotland God gave her Knox; and when his work was done, He gave him a peaceful death-bed, an honored tomb, and a place in the memory of every true Scottish heart for many generations. In love to Scotland, in these later days, God raised up Chalmers to do a mighty work and wage a glorious warfare; and when his work was ended, he gave him as calm a dismissal, as hallowed a grave, and as deep a place in the heart of his country,—in the memory of his race.

Over neither do we sorrow as those who have no hope. They are not dead, they have but entered on their better life; they have not withered up and passed away, they are putting on new blossoms in a more genial clime, preparing for the day of the great fruit-bearing, when the resurrection-sun shall rise. They rest from their labors, and their works do follow them. What a meeting must that have been which has now taken place between these two mighty souls!—what a fellowship must that be which is now enjoyed as they sit together under the shade of the tree of life, or climb the bright slopes of the everlasting hills! Forever with each other, and forever with the Lord.

Summoned away at midnight in a moment, Dr. Chalmers has left us no death-bed testimony, has bequeathed us no parting counsels. But his counsels had been fully spoken and written long before; and his whole life was one grand testimony. What a testimony! From the day that he knew the grace of God in truth, his life became a consecrated thing,—himself a "living sacrifice." It was "Corban,"—a gift,—the life of one who knew that he was not his own, that he had been purchased by another for his service. The whole energy of his mighty spirit, the whole capacities of his gifted mind, the whole warmth of his loving heart, were gladly dedicated to his new and better Master—thrown unreservedly into his cause. His days were days of labor, unintermitted and untiring. His was a lifetime of care and toil and conflict; yet it was well-laid-out care, fruit-bearing toil, and successful conflict. There was a strength and untiringness of energy about him that seemed almost superhuman. His enthusiasm was of the fearless kind; his zeal never flagged; it remained as fresh in age as in the days of his fervent manhood. The chill of years was not on him; the innate fire of his spirit seemed to charm it away. The activity of the ever-moving power in him was only equalled by its steadiness and depth. It was constant, not fitful. It was vast, yet it was strangely equable. It had in it the strength of the torrent, but the depth of the wave.

He was a man of many thoughts, of many schemes, of many deeds,—all of them large and lofty. Their circle was of no common stretch. They ranged wide and far. Beyond the blue hills of Scotland; beyond the ocean-girdle that hems Britain in his soul went abroad and his sympathies spread themselves out over the wide compass of earth. In his views there was no narrowness. In his nature there was no littleness. All was massive and kingly. He was not like one looking upward from the bottom of some deep glen upon the sunny slopes around him, thinking nought of anything beyond their limit; but like one looking downward from some Alpine eminence upon a whole world beneath him; and this not simply as one admiring what he saw, but as one who was a part of it, who was knit to every atom of it, who felt himself "a debtor" to all who dwelt upon its surface,—Jew or Greek, Barbarian, Scythian, bond or free.

There was a wonderful fruitfulness and elasticity about him, so that nothing could shut him up or lead him to despair. He was rich in resources. His spirit knew no dearth. Nor was this mere ingenuity. It was more, it was something higher and more commanding. It was fruitfulness, it was depth, it was power. Nay more, it was bravery. For a fearless spirit was in him, and an indomitable tenacity, that no unlikelihood could discourage nor difficulty baffle. There was a quiet but resolute purpose about him, from which he turned not aside, and in the execution of which he never wearied. True representative of our ancient Scottish chiefs, true descendant of Reformers and Covenanters, he refused to swerve from his mark or give up the object of his pursuit. Like Knox, his eye went over Scotland,—all Scotland,—its cities and its villages, its plains and its moors. His heart took in all its families,—its rich and its poor, its old, its young. Towards every dweller in it, his desires flowed forth as to a brother or a child, with a true longing to bless them, and with profound commiseration for whatever he was unable to rectify or relieve. During last winter's famine, his sympathy for the suffering was most tender; he eagerly caught at each day's intelligence to learn whether there were any signs of amelioration appearing or sufficiency of relief administered.

Over all his fellow-men his heart most truly yearned. But it was towards the poor especially that his thoughts seemed ever to go forth. For them he toiled and wrote, and pleaded, and planned, and prayed. And the last great work of his life was to provide a church and a minister, a school and a teacher, for the poor.

He was permitted to see this completed, and to dispense the first communion in that new home of the gathered outcasts.

He had often expressed a longing to withdraw from public life, and spend the rest of his years in quiet and fellowship with God. This he was not allowed to carry into effect. He was taken up at once, and in the very midst of his labors. He was called to enter into rest, but it was a higher and more glorious rest than he had counted on. Yet his work was fully done. Of no one could this be more truly affirmed. It was a vast work to which he had been called, yet in the strength of his God he had done it; no part was left undone. What work is there which we could wish him to have undertaken that he has not accomplished? He might be said to have died working. He was to have addressed the General Assembly next day, and had made preparations for rising early to complete his work for that occasion. He was busy to the last. He had lost no time. He had laid out his life well,—therein leaving us an example that we should follow his steps,—an example of unconquerable energy, undecaying zeal, and faithful endurance to the end.

He was a marvellous compound of simplicity and greatness, of meekness and majesty, of modesty and manliness. He was the most unpretending, unassuming, unobtrusive, child-like of men. He had so much and yet so little of the child. There was nothing in him of frivolity or levity, yet was he one of the most brightly cheerful companions that could be met with. On his countenance there was thoughtfulness at all times, sometimes *absence* and abstraction, yet ever at the same time "an under-current of deep-running joy." No man delighted more in looking out upon the material world in its beauty or its grandeur. He was one of those who could say—

> "'Tis joy to move under the bended sky,
> To smell the pleasant earth and feel the winds go by."

He was so loving, so frank, so homely, so full of hope, so buoyant in his whole character, that no one who knew him could fail to be knit to him at once, soul to soul. All with him was thoroughly real and genuine, vital and full of vigorous strength, alike in the faculties of his mind and the feelings of his heart As one said of him, " he was the most lovable of all living men." How strong was the influence he exercised over other men and other minds! Yet it was a gentle and unconscious sway. It was not the control of the whirlwind over the billows of the deep—rude and wild in its exercise. It was the influence of the moon over the tides, wider and stronger than the other, yet imperceptible, the influence of overshadowing genius, yet still more the influence of his own placid and most paternal smile. The tenacity of his friendships and the warmth of his love were wonderful, considering the immense number and variety of his acquaintances. He seemed to forget no one, and delighted above all things to revisit the friends and scenes of other days. It was Beza, we think, who said when he heard of Calvin's death, " Now that Calvin is dead, life will be less sweet and death less bitter." How many are there in our Church and land who can at this time make these words most truly their own.

His love for divine truth was intense. His relish for the simple Gospel of the grace of God was one of the most striking features in his character. It was not only the theme of his sermons, but the subject of his letters and his conversation. No man ever preached it more freely or stated it more simply and beautifully than he. How touchingly is this brought out in one of the extracts given in Mr. Bruce's admirable sermon, from some of Dr. Chalmers' meditations. He thus writes, " What straining I have had after a right understanding of God and his ways! more especially the way of salvation! Give me greatness, clearness, fulness of understanding, O God."

He died, we may say, without a death-bed. His was not indeed the glorious ascension of Elijah in his blazing chariot, but it was even more sudden, more unforeseen. Yet not unprepared for. He knew in whom he had believed. To die was gain. As a shock of corn fully ripe he came to his end. Who would not die his death? A death without pain or weariness, without languishing or decay, an instantaneous passage from a happy family circle below to a far happier family circle above, where his large and loving heart can now get fullest vent to itself, and where his joy shall be forever full. Decay was not upon him, nor infirmity. Sickness did not waste him. His strength did not slowly ebb. His faculties did not wither up and fall into the imbecility of a second childhood. But in the fulness of his nature and unabated strength, in the undiminished vigor of his majestic mind, he passed up from among us, and took his seat in the general assembly and church of the first-born in Heaven.

He died alone. No eye but his Saviour's saw him die. No hand but his Saviour's took hold of his in the moment of departing. Like Moses, God led him aside that he might die alone; as if that were the most fitting as well as the most kind and gracious way of receiving him to himself. The bitterness of death he was not to taste; the "long day's dying" was not to "augment his pain." No tears were to be shed around him to discompose his parting hour. No farewells were to be heard around that solitary couch. No voice of sorrow, no sigh of the mourner was to fall upon his dying ear. All this his loving heart was spared. The advancing footsteps of death he was not to hear; only the quick summons to arise, so that he should not know that it was death till he had landed on the shore of life. In the silence of midnight, when all the loved ones of his circle were calmly sleeping, the great spirit shook off its mortal wrappings and went up to the spirits of the just made perfect. He had scarcely finished his earthly Sabbath, and come home from worshipping in the temple below, when he was summoned to begin the endless Sabbath in the bright courts above.

One of earth's mighty ones has gone. The loss is vast. It has made the world incalculably poorer. A standard-bearer has fallen. There is one star less in our darkening firmament. One by one the noble-minded are departing. The great souls of the earth are quitting it, taken away from the evil to come. For in

Dr. Chalmers, there was one out of the few exceptions to Dr. M'Crie's startling, but pregnant utterance, "in our day we have men of great minds, but no men of great souls."

God is striking away our human props. But he is offering us his own arm to lean upon. Woe be to us if we reject it. Thrice blessed if we read his meaning and betake ourselves to Him. Better than all earthly shields or weapons of war is he to the church that seeks refuge in Him.

Our loved father is only parted for a little. We shall see him again. We shall hear his voice again. We shall grasp his hand again. We shall be knit to his whole living man again, in the realms where there is no severance of bonds, where there comes no midnight messenger of death, where there is seen no shroud, no coffin, no funeral procession, no heaving turf, no mouldering grave ; but one perpetual living, an endless rejoicing, an eternal union, an unfading brightness, a day without a night, a sky without a cloud, a song without one note of sorrow to mar its perfect harmony.

THE EXAMPLE OF OUR SAVIOUR

A GUIDE AND AN UTHORITY

IN THE

ESTABLISHMENT OF CHARITABLE INSTITUTIONS.

"Then Jesus called his disciples unto him, and said, I have compassion on the multitude, because they continue with us now three days, and have nothing to eat: and I will not send them away fasting lest they faint in the way."—MATTHEW xv. 32.

"When the people therefore saw that Jesus was not there, neither his disciples, they also took shipping, and came to Capernaum, seeking for Jesus. And when they had found him on the other side of the sea, they said unto him, Rabbi, when camest thou hither? Jesus answered them, and said, Verily, verily, I say unto you, ye seek me, not because ye saw the miracles, but because ye did eat of the loaves, and were filled."—JOHN vi. 24—26.

"But when Jesus knew it, he withdrew himself from thence; and great multitudes followed him, and he healed them all."—MATTHEW xii. 15.

COMPASSION is that feeling which arises in the heart of a human being, when he looks to the misery of another—which, if unmixed with other feelings, keeps him restless and dissatisfied till the misery be done away—which prompts him to measures of relief;—and at length finds its ultimate gratification in the deliverance of its object, from that suffering which called forth the sensibility that we are now adverting to.

But there may be other feelings excited by the very same object, and which tend to modify or to suspend the exercise of compassion altogether. The misery in question may be the infliction of a punishment; and our sense of justice, if it do not prevent the existence of a sense of compassion, will at least so far keep it in check, as to restrain us from obeying the impulse of it. Or it may be the pain of a severe but salutary operation; and then the sensitive compassion which we would feel in common with children, we do not like children follow—and just because we put it under the control of a higher and more intelligent compassion. Or it may be the immediate suffering of a correction, administered for the moral good of him who is its object; and still there may be a moral rectitude in withstanding the dictate of compassion, while we feel the emotion of it. And thus while it goes to form a revolting unloveliness of character, to have a heart unmoved by even the slighter or more transient distresses of our common nature—yet it also goes not to impair but to perfect the character, when all these constitutional movements are brought under the guidance of principle, and of a virtuous and intelligent regard to the higher interests of our species.

In a matter of charity, a man may have the intelligence without the instinct; and we then look to him with something of the same dread and aversion that we do to one of those mutilated spirits among the infernal, who are permitted to retain the energies of their nature, after all its moralities have been extinguished. Yet that is no good reason why all our preferences should be directed to him, who has only the instinct without the intelligence—why the question should not be looked to with the eye of discernment, as well as with an eye of tearful sensibility—why thought and experience and wisdom should be banished from this department of human affairs—why the higher powers of the mind should not be admitted into the deliberations of charity—or, when sense is offered as well as sympathy upon the subject, why all the voices both of male and female sentimentalism should therefore be formed into one mighty effort to cry it down.

There is perhaps no one agony to which by our corporeal frame we are liable, that draws forth a readier compassion, or leads more surely to a consequent act of relief, than the agony of hunger. It is positively not in nature, to remain steeled against the look of despair, or the look of pining consumptiveness, with which it implores a relief to its cravings. There may be the suspicion of imposture, to shut and to harden the heart; and little do the poor among the people know, how their deadliest enemies by far, and they who have done most to shift the flood of liberality away from them, are to be found among those, who have counterfeited their sufferings, and handled their words and their sighs deceitfully. But let there be no deceit on the one side, and no imagination of it on the other; and it would argue a man to be a monster, could he withstand the piercing or the plaintive cry of a brother in the agonies of hunger. The law which would inflict such a suffering as this, even for the worst of crimes, would, in any humanized country, be reduced to a dead-letter for the want of agents to carry it into execution. There would not be found, even among the hardiest officers of a jail, men of nerve enough and sternness enough to be faithful to the barbarity that was assigned to them. The whole vicinity of such a place of torture, would itself be in torture, under the consciousness of any one portion of our nature being within its reach, and lingering under the inflictions of a calamity so exquisite. The very poorest of the people could not bear the thought of it; and they would be seen to elude the eye of half-conniving sentinels, and to cast a pittance of their own scanty fare through the gratings of this cell of anguish. Humanity would rise in rebellion against such a proceeding; and the law be trampled, as it ought, into utter inefficiency. So that, however man may blunder his arrangements for the anticipation of eventual hunger, man, if not an outcast from the general character of his fellows, never can listen unmoved to the claims of actual hunger. The speculation which would harden him into such indifference as this, deserves to have the seal of infamy set upon it—and no talent by which it is defended, no eloquence by which it is set forth to public acceptance, should go to shield it from the vengeance of public reprobation.

Nothing then can be more clearly imperative on the disciples of Christ, than to follow out those impulses of compassion, by which they are prompted to the redress of such sufferings as are presently before them. "If a brother or sister be actually naked, or actually destitute of daily food; and one of you say unto them, Depart in peace, be ye warmed and clothed, notwithstanding ye give them not those things which are needful for the body—what doth it profit? And whoso hath this world's goods, and seeth his brother have need, and shutteth up his bowels of compassion from him—how dwelleth the love of God in him?" And further, nothing is more thoroughly accordant with the whole spirit and character of our faith, than when, under the instigation of a more active and aspiring good-will, man, instead of waiting until distress presents itself before him, goeth forth on the errand of search and of discovery among its likely habitations—than when, with something more than a house and a heart open to the applications of the wretched, he maketh his own positive and personal aggressions on the territory of wretchedness—than when he not only consents to relieve, but offers to relieve; and not only welcomes the proposals of charity, but originates the proposals of charity—visiting the fatherless and the widow in their affliction; alive to all the actual distress that is within his reach; and holding the very existence of misery, whether seen or unseen, to be a claim upon his attentions and his services.

But what I think is egregiously wanted on the part of the benevolent public, is a clear and steady discernment of the difference that there is—between a proposal for the redress of present suffering, and a plan, which, additionally to this object, does, by the stability of its mechanism and the perpetuity of its operation, involve in it a proposal for the redress of future suffering. The object is altogether excellent. The desire that such distresses as are not yet in existence should be relieved when they arise, is just as much the natural and legitimate working of a principle of compassion, as the desire that the distresses now around us should be so relieved. Propose to compassion, either a suffering that now is, or a suffering that is certainly to be; and you in each case place before it the very object on which it fastens, and in which it finds matter for its proper and congenial exercise. In thus doing you make an appeal to the heart. But when you come forth with a plan, you come forth with an appeal to the understanding. A plan may, it is very possible, aggravate the distress which it proposes to do away. It may beget a delusive hope of its efficiency as a corrective to human suffering, and thus slacken the operation of all the preventatives of human suffering. Instead of drawing the rich into a closer and kindlier habit of intercourse with the poor, it may, through the intermedium of that body of management on which its execution is devolved, rise as a barrier of separation between them. It may be such a system of public and regulated charity, as goes to stifle and supersede the compassion of the heart instead of softening it; and, with the seemly apparatus of direct security which it has raised for the accommodation of the destitute —all it may ever do, is to force one great stream into an abyss that is bottomless; and to dry up or divert those innumerable lesser streams, which else would flow, in fruitful and refreshing circulation, among the many reservoirs of private society. All this may be a man's understanding; and, whether in error or not, it may be the understanding of one, who, along with the principle of intelligence in his bosom such as it is, may have room in its receptacles for lodging a compassionate heart. It may be the understanding of one, who feels compassion for all the misery that now is; and with whom it is the whole aim of his most strenuous philanthropy, to maintain among mankind the entireness and the efficacy of compassion, in unimpaired reserve for all the misery that is to come. It may be the understanding of one who partakes in all the sympathies of nature, and at the same time has such confidence in their wise and ready adaptation to the sufferings of nature, that he looks on the intermeddling, either of legislative or municipal wisdom, as pregnant with danger and disturbance to the best interests of humanity. It is not because he is hostile to commerce that he deprecates the interference of public regulation; but because he thinks that commerce thrives most prosperously, when left to the operation of her own unfettered principles on the wants and activities of the species. It is not because he is hostile to benevolence, that he protests against every attempt to turn a matter of kindness into a matter of compulsion; but because he thinks that benevolence, left to her own free and spontaneous energies, will shed a more abundant blessing upon the land, than benevolence moulded into the shape and lifelessness of a statue, by the hand of legislation. If he be wrong, he is only wrong in understanding; and for this error, let him be taken to the field of argument, and there let him endure all the severities of the contest, and, if so be, all the disgrace of an overthrow. But it ceases to be argument, and sours and blackens into calumny, when the impeachment is raised, not against his notions, but against his sensibilities—when denounced as the enemy of all benevolence, because, in resistance to modern inventions, he proclaims her authority in the way which he thinks to be coeval with the law of revelation and the law of the heart—when charged with the guilt of a rebel against the established maxims of charity, because he cannot bow the knee to the mandates of those courts and corporations of charity, which owe their title of established only to the perpetuity of error—when represented as a transgressor against nature, because he resists the deviations which have been made from her; and as trying by wisdom to school away all the sympathies of the human frame, only because he resists the encroachments, which the wisdom of man has made on the wisdom of Him, who, as the architect of the human frame, is also the alone rightful architect of all human morality. It is then that the poison of injustice enters into the controversy. It is then that the torch of truth is exchanged for the firebrand of discord; and her angry flash is all that remains to lighten up that field, where the war of argument has now become a war of recriminations. Let us cease to wonder, that, amid the thickenings of such a warfare, evil should be called good, or good should be called evil; that they should be traduced as having no heart, who have stood forth the most zealous champions of all its prerogatives—as having tried to extirpate humanity. who have done most to rescue her from thraldom—as having aimed by the weapon of an intellectual demonstration at the overthrow of benevolence—when their whole aim was the overthrow of those intellectual perversities, which have been gradually imbodied into the practice of the existing generation; and which have done so much to congeal benevolence, and to cramp all its feelings and all its generous aspirations among the entanglements of an artificial mechanism.

We now proceed to the direct consideration of the passages which have already been submitted to you.

I. From the first of them, do we learn the effect, which the exhibition of actual suffering had on the heart of Him, who, both in feeling and in morality, is held forth in Scripture as a pattern to us. Without any reference then to the origin of the suffering, was he immediately moved to compassion on his view of the existence of it. There may have been a culpability in the origin. There may have been a want of foresight, on the part of the people. There may, with some of them, have been the abandonment of their regular occupation for a few days on the impulse of an idle curiosity. There may, even at this earlier stage of their experience of Jesus Christ and of the rule of His proceedings, have been the sordid expectation of a miraculous supply from heaven, to relieve that hunger, against which they had failed to provide by their own industry. But no matter. Here is wretchedness in actual being, however it may have originated. Here is a multitude overtaken, and now in agony. Here a sense of their helplessness and of their danger and of their distance from food, is now spreading a visible alarm through this crowd of population. Here symptoms of increasing restlessness, and groups of busy consultation, and the evident awakenings of one topic and of one terror among them all, and a gathering hue of despair on the countenance of mothers, and the cries of famishing children—are now beginning to give authentic proclamation of nature in distress. And what was the effect we ask on Him, who took upon Him this nature; and that too, with the design of authorizing and exemplifying all the virtues of which it is capable? Did they suggest to him at the moment any calculation either of causes or of consequences? None, or none at least that we read of. Did they lead him to brood, in chilling thougtfulness, over either the habits of past improvidence, or the possibilities of future unbelief? No. Did he, in the conduct of relieving them, devise any line of separation betwixt the deserving and the undeserving? No. Did any one maxim of economy or of science, offer to lay an arrest upon his sensibilities, or to deafen the energy of that pleading voice, which now arose from the multitude before him? No. He looked to them, we are told; and He had compassion on them that they had nothing to eat; and He could not send them away fasting—lest they should faint on the way. He felt the urgency of the call, and He forthwith acted upon it. He provided for the whole extent of the present emergency; and, without delay or without discrimination, did He bring forward food for all, so that they did all eat and were filled.

And so may it happen in the present day. Distress may come at unawares; and this distress may extend to a multitude. By one unlooked for evolution in the mechanism of trade, a whole class of society may suddenly be overtaken; and, what with the actual misery of the present and the gloomy forebodings of the future, may realize the very sensations which drew out a miracle of loaves from the pitying Saviour. It is clearly our part to feel as he felt, and, as far as we are able, to do as He did. And were it possible to single out from the mass with which they are intermingled the verily destitute; and so to conduct the ministration that they should obtain all the benefit, without the encroachment of unworthy competitors; and so to pour in a stream of liberality on the one hand that it shall not be neutralized on the other, as it often is in the case of a public and combined movement of charity, by a consequent and a further depression in those very wages, the insufficiency of which is the cause and the essence of the whole disaster:—In a word, were it possible actually to know, as our Saviour knew, the whole length and breadth of the calamity—actually to bring it forth into a distinct place, as our Saviour did, and, by the might of an uplifted arm to crush it there into utter annihilation—actually to send forth such a flood of copious ness on this epidemic plague, as to quench and to overwhelm it—and so by some process that has not yet been discovered, to meet the recurring visitation, that instead of an invariable cry, sent forth as if from the devouring grave, that it is not yet enough, some fragments of the distribution were left and gathered up after all were satisfied:—If it be in the power of assembled men thus to surmount this evil, without the infliction of greater evil, both upon the character and interests of humanity—then, let the charities of all be formed into one great and visible aggregate, for the purpose of sweeping it away. But if this is not possible; if man cannot do with success by a combined effort upon the multitude, what every man might do, each with a measure of success, on his separate portion of it—Then does it not follow, that because the wisdom of man has failed, the will of God should fail—that because the contrivance of man should be abrogated, the commandment of God should be abrogated—that because the machinery of human concert has been found ineffectual and may therefore be dissolved, the morality of human conscience should also be dissolved. Compassion is still the unrepealed law of every individual heart, and that whether man by his laborious combinations has done more to aid or to impede the execution of its dictates. If a right economy of general and extended distribution, like one of the secret things of God, be above his skill, that is no reason, why any of the revealed things of God should be deemed beneath his submission—or why he who is rich in this world should not be rich in good works, and ready to distribute, and willing to communicate. O no, my brethren. Let men controvert, and calumniate, and strive with each other, in the contests of mutual vanity and intolerance, about plans—be assured that you will never lay hold on eternal life, unless you keep your firm and your fast hold upon principles—that compassion is a principle of uncancelled authority; nor can you expunge it from your bosom without expunging from it the resemblance of the Godhead, in one of the brightest of its lineaments—that in this, and in every season of general disaster, there is a louder call for its exercise; and each should now be looking with a wakeful and a pitying eye to the want and the wretchedness that multiply around him—that each should fill up his own little sphere of attention with the offices of kindness; and, in despite of cold speculation either about the origin or the result of our present suffering, should hold, even as our Saviour held, the existence of suffering to be in itself a claim upon his sympathies, to be in itself a call upon his services.

If any plan of wide and artificial co-operation shall be found effectual, then the advocate of compassion does not embarrass this plan—he only stimulates its formation, and puts more alacrity into all its movements. If again, with all the devices of a deep and variously exercised sagacity, no such plan can be adjusted—it is not he who is chargeable, but the impotency of human wisdom, or the uncontrollable difficulties with which it meets in the constitution of human society. This may be matter of regret, just as we regret any other evil for which there is no remedy. But if anything can alleviate this regret, or rather do it away altogether, it will be the discovery, that the remedy does not lie in the devisings of human wisdom at all, but in the simple doings of human obedience—that if each individual be left to the force of his own conceptions of duty, and the play of his own unsophisticated feelings, a better compound result will be obtained, than ever can be reached through the by-paths, and the intricacies of any great political contrivance—that there lie scattered through the mass of society such vigilance each for himself and such sympathy each for another, as if unmeddled with by legislation, will insure a better state of things, than legislation with all her powers ever can effectuate—that, even separate from Christianity, nature works too powerfully in the hearts of individuals—as that, if famine do not withhold the materials of subsistence, no human being ever will be permitted to perish for hunger in the sight of his fellows—that if to the compassionate instincts of nature in any given neighborhood, there be superadded the lights and the lessons of the Gospel, there will be placed in the way of an event so distressing, the barrier of a moral impossibility—that in such a state of things, abundance does find its way, in a thousand rills of unseen beneficence, among the habitations of the destitute; and comes into kindlier and more effective contact with human suffering, than ever can be reached by the unwieldy operations of a large and general superintendence—In other words, that a problem which is now exercising and baffling the ingenuity of many speculators, owes all its difficulty to the ambition of meddling with a matter that is too high for them—that if they would simply let it alone, and leave nature and Christianity to their own influence, they would do for the cause of philanthropy what parliament does for the interests of trade, when, repealing alike her restrictions and her encouragements, she withdraws that hand by which she meant to help, but has only embarrassed the operations of merchandise. In a word, we cease from our regret for the inefficiency of plans, when made to see that any mechanism of general and apparent distribution which art can devise, goes only to supersede the operations of a previous and a better mechanism—that, in spite of the prevalence of selfishness in our world, more is done for it even now, by each kind-hearted individual betaking himself in simplicity and in silence to his own separate walk of acquaintanceship among the poor, than by all the paraded charities of our land. And the delightful anticipation is before us, that, in proportion as Christians are multiplied; in proportion as Christian instruction is dealt out in larger quantities, among the families of a heretofore neglected population; in proportion as the mass of our assembled millions is broken down into manageable fragments and facilities are opened for the intercourse of wisdom and piety throughout the habitations; in proportion as men go forth amongst their fellows on the one errand of preparing them for heaven—in that very proportion will a mutual kindness be diffused through every neighborhood, to reduce and to sweeten all the hardships of the pilgrimage which leads to it—So that if any hearer among you is like to be lost in bewilderment among the intricacies of a plan, be assured that your best contribution to the good of society, is to submit your heart and conduct to the authority of a principle; and, while I proclaim the sanctions which the principle of compassion has gotten from the law of God, and the example of our Saviour—learn that your duty is, under the workings of this sensibility, never to hide yourself from your own flesh, but to devise liberal things in your heart, and to do with your hand and with all your might that which the hand findeth to do.

II. The next passage which I shall offer, is from John vi. 25–27. Here there is no miracle of loaves recorded, and it is likely that none was performed. We read only of two instances of such a miracle; and in each of them the multitude were overtaken with hunger. Even His own disciples, familiarized as they were to the supernatural achievements of their Master, were not, in either of these instances, counting on any miracle in their behalf, and far less, it is to be presumed, would the people be counting on it. He, in both these cases, felt a movement of compassion towards them, and He followed it. But when, instead of hunger overtaking them, they voluntarily courted hunger for the sake of the indolence which came before, and of the relief which they hoped would come after it—when, instead of being assailed by it in the shape of an unlooked-for visitation, they were actually drawing it upon themselves in the prospect of another compassionate interference—when dependence on the power and the kindness of another, was undermining the dependence they ought to have felt on the resources of their own care and their own industry—let us observe in this passage, how the discerning eye of the Saviour marked the first dawning of this sordid and mercenary expectation in their hearts, and how immediately he repressed it. There was room it would appear in His moral constitution, both for that softness of character, which is easily touched and awakened by the sight of human misery; and also for that firmness of character, which could promptly minister a wholesome correction, and set up a preventive stay to the progress of human worthlessness. Those philanthropists, who calculate as well as feel for the good of humanity, may take comfort under all the imputations of harshness and barbarity which are preferred against them—when thus made to understand, that calculation had its place, as well as feeling, with Him whose character was above every imputation—with Him in whose person all the graces were mixed and attempered with all the solidities of human virtue—with Him of whom it is recorded, that He both cast a weeping eye over the sufferings of our nature, and looked with the full scrutinizing gaze of an unclouded penetration on its sin and on its sordidness—who, on one occasion, put forth a miracle, that he might minister food to the actual hunger of the multitude around Him; and, on another occasion, withheld that miracle, lest it should minister food to the depravity of the same multitude. There is much to be gathered from the way in which He at one time relieved their necessities, and He at another time checked their expectations—And let this passage of our Saviour's history, while it may serve to guide, serve also to console every faithful disciple of His, who suffers under the execrations of a generous but mistaken sensibility; and that too, at the very time when laboriously toiling in all the duties of benevolence, and anxiously exploring a clear and conscientious path through all its difficulties.

Our Saviour could have ministered food to the destitute, with as great facility as He ministered health to the diseased; and it is a question worthy of being considered—why He was so sparing in the one, and so abundant and so indiscriminate and for anything we read so universal in the other ministration. We know not that He ever sent a petitioner for health uncured or disappointed away from Him; and we know not, at the same time, if He ever above twice in the whole course of His history upon earth, interposed with a miracle for the relief of hunger—while, in the passage before us, it appears, that, instead of meeting, He rebuked the expectations of those who were running after Him in the hope of such a miracle. The truth is, that our Saviour's progress in Judea had before this time become a path of public notoriety. The eye of general observation was upon all His footsteps; and the report of every transaction of His was now sure to circulate through the land. So that the operations of His beneficence were quite equivalent, in effect, to the operations of a proclaimed charity; and you have only to conceive the effect that it must have had on the habits of the people—did the Saviour, by an indefinite multiplication of loaves, hold out the assurance to all who followed Him, that they would also be fed by Him. It would, in fact, have deranged the whole mechanism of Jewish society; and the people, at large from the regularities of their wonted employment, would have carried a thickening and accumulating disorder along with them over the whole country. Every wholesome habit of industry would have been suspended—had the great teacher of moral righteousness been thus transformed into the almoner of assailing multitudes. And it would not only have brought a great civil and political mischief upon His countrymen. It would have also raised a subtle and unsurmountable barrier, in the way of every conversion from sin unto God. It would have marred the success of His own peculiar enterprise in the world. His object was to lead men on the path to heaven; but it is essential to the act of walking on this path, that there be the self-denial of every earth-born propensity—so that, from the very nature of the case, it ceases to be a movement heavenwards, when men are led to it by the bribery of this world's advantages. Godliness, by being turned into gain, ceases to be godliness. His undertaking was to accomplish in the person of every disciple, a triumph of the spiritual over the sensitive part of the human constitution; and to raise the affections of our degenerate nature, from the things which are beneath to the things which are above. Had He, in possession of the gift of multiplying loaves, done without measure and without consideration, what many of our scheming philanthropists would have counted so desirable, He in fact would have nullified His own errand. He would have stifled that principle which He wanted to implant, and nourished that principle which He wanted to destroy. He would only have deepened and confirmed that sunken debasement into which humanity had fallen; and, besides throwing the whole population among whom He expatiated into a state of restless and dissatisfied turbulence, the only other effect of His visit would have been, to have graven on the character of our species the traces of their selfishness and their sensuality, more indelibly than He had found them.

Something surely is to be learned from the caution, wherewith our Saviour put forth such miraculous powers, as might tempt the indigent away from their regular occupations. There was an unavoidable publicity in His proceedings; and there is a publicity equally unavoidable, in the proceedings of every corporate and combined charity. The lesson of the passage now under consideration, is not surely that any private individual should steel his heart against the sufferings of the poverty that is now in existence. I have attempted to draw an opposite lesson from the first of these passages. But it ought at least to make everybody of individuals, advert to that publicity which their doings have in common with the doings of the Saviour; and to be alike cautious with Him of the mischief which may flow from it. We are not to overlook the distinction which obtained in His practice, between miracles for the relief of hunger and miracles for the relief of disease. It may suggest a like distinction in our practice, between public measures for the relief of hunger and public measures for the relief of disease; and know, that, while it is the duty of each to carry in his bosom a heart most feelingly alive to all the sufferings of the poverty now in existence—it follows not, that it is therefore his duty, to enter into any scheme or any organization, which may have the effect of bringing more poverty into existence; of alluring men from their habits of self-dependence and self-respect; or, under the guise of liberality, of bringing a cruel disappointment on all its desires, and stamping an impotence and a folly on all its devices.

III. We now come to the third passage—from which, when taken in connection with the whole history of our Saviour's miracles, we infer that the caution which marked His proceedings when acting in the capacity of an almoner, He put altogether away from Him when acting in the capacity of a physician—that, whatever restraint he laid on His supernatural power of ministering to the necessities of indigence, He laid none whatever on His supernatural power of ministering to the necessities of disease—that, however fearful of mischief He seems to have been, had He expatiated with all the publicity, and all the dependence that might have attached to Him on the one walk of beneficence, He seems to have had no apprehenson of danger to the sufferers themselves by His expatiating with all publicity and freedom on the other walk of beneficence—healing every sickness and every disease amongst the people; leaving no recorded instance behind Him, of a single petitioner for a cure being sent disappointed away; and repeatedly, are we told, when surrounded by crowds of imploring sick, looking to them, and having compassion on them, and healing them all.

It may be right to advert shortly, to one great distinction in point of effect, between a public and indefinite system of operations for the relief of indigence, and the same system of operations for the relief of disease—as it may both serve to explain the conduct of our Saviour, and guide us in the paths of a wise and enlightened imitation.

The great cause of the distinction between these two cases is this.

To be an object for the one charity, a man has only to become poor; and though there be no charm in poverty itself, yet there are charms innumerable in the path of freedom and indolence and dissipation which leads to it. Poverty is the spectre, which stands at the termination of this path; and so frightful in aspect, that, when seen, though afar without mitigation and without disguise, it is able to scare away the great majority of the world from any wilful approximation. On the entrance of that descending avenue which leads to want, there lie a thousand temptations; but, such is the power of human foresight, that a view of the spectre at the other end is generally of force enough, and counteraction enough, to neutralize them. Now a public charity for the relief of want disarms this spectre. It relieves men of their present care, and of their present strenuousness; and so is it ever found, that, in proportion to the amplitude of such a charity, is the number of candidates for admission—and each having the real qualification too, of actual poverty to plead for them.

To be an object for the other charity, a man must be under disease; and, unless when disease is the effect of vicious indulgence, there is a strong and universal recoil on the part of nature, from the very first approaches of it. No man, generally speaking, will take on disease for the sake of its remedy—any more than he will put out his eyes for the benefit of a blind asylum; or will break a limb, for the sake of its amputation; or will inflict any wilful mutilation upon himself, for the benefit of admittance into an infirmary. Men find their way to the one charity by a transition of pleasure—they find their way to the other by the transition of pain. The one in this way multiplies its objects beyond its powers of relieving them; and thus adds, we believe, to the misery, as well as to the worthlessness of our species. The other does not so multiply its objects; and thus, by all the relief which it deals out on them, does it effectuate, without deterioration to the character, a clear abridgment on the sufferings of humanity.

In order to obscure the line of distinction between these two charities, it might be alleged, that, by exertion and economy on the part of individuals, each may render himself independent on charity for the relief of his wants; and that it is just by a higher degree of the same exertion and economy, that he renders himself independent on charity for the relief of his diseases. And certainly, as it does argue a higher independence in fact, when a man is able, on his own resources, to meet all the contingencies of his lot—so it does argue a higher independence of feeling, when a man aims, not merely at paying for himself what an hospital of poverty might otherwise offer to provide and to pay for him, but also to pay for himself what an hospital of disease might otherwise offer to provide and to pay for him. But still the one case does not melt into the other by a continuous gradation. There is a broad and immutable line of distinction between them. The one enlists the human will on the side of poverty; and therefore is sure to increase its ills, up to and beyond the measure of its own alleviations. The other never can enlist the human will on the side of disease; and therefore effectuates an unqualified good, by every inroad that it makes on the mass of involuntary wretchedness. Open the door of any public receptacle for indigence; and let the whole of his argument fall to the ground, if the invariable result of such an experiment has not been,—that the amount of poverty left out, swells instantaneously beyond the amount of all that poverty that was untouched and unrelieved at the outset of this operation. Open the door of a public receptacle for disease; and, by each patient who enters in, is the field of general humanity more delivered from the burden of that distress which lay upon it. There is, by a principle of our nature, a creative and multiplying process to fill up all the vacancies, which the hand of a public and permanent charity attempts to make on the territory of indigence. There is no such principle, and no such process for filling up the vacancies, which the hand of public charity makes on the territory of disease. By every shilling surrendered for the one object, you recede from its accomplishment. By every shilling surrendered for the other, you draw nearer to its accomplishment. Push the one to its uttermost; and you arrive at the result of a beggared population absorbing for its maintenance the whole wealth of the country, and the wealth of the country withering into decay from the decaying industry of its population. Push the other to its uttermost; and, with a small and definite fraction of the country's wealth, you accomplish all that can be accomplished for the mitigation of the evils, to which by nature and by providence the people of every country are liable. By every step in the progress of the one operation, you feed and inflame the mischief which you are vainly trying to extirpate. By every step in the progress of the other, you make a clear and satisfying advance towards an assignable fulfilment.

Doubtless the mind of an Icelandic native is sustained at a higher pitch of anticipation, and it may go to induce a habit of more virtuous economy—that, in addition to the cares of the men of other countries, he has to provide against the ravages of the impending volcano. Yet, if practicable, who would spare the combined expense, that could divert those fires to the bottom of the ocean? And it nerves and elevates the character of a northern peasantry, that they have to look forward to the severities of the coming winter; yet, if it could be purchased, who would not think it worthy of being so—that, by some mighty contribution, they obtained a softening of their climate and an everlasting exemption from its storms? And those men who live in a region of pestilence, would have a loftier cast of intelligence than their fellows, were they at all times wisely and carefully prepared for its periodic visitations. Yet what surrender of wealth would be counted extravagant, that could bring some healing stream to circulate through the land, and to chase forever the contagion away from it? And, in like manner, we, though we live at a distance from these extremes, have still the inflictions of nature and of necessity to contend with. And it doubtless argues a higher tone and state of a family—when, by the moral force of industry and care, it can not only provide for the ordinary accidents, but also for the accidents of blindness, and derangement, and dumbness, by which any of its members may be visited. Yet if nature could be bribed by money, tell me what would be the sum too large, to obtain from her in every district of the land, a medicinal well, of effect to cure and to alleviate each of these calamities? Would not such an accommodation as this, both of public notoriety and of permanent continuance, just translate our country into permanently better circumstances than before? The supposition is altogether fanciful. But it serves our purpose—if a public institution for any of these objects, formed out of the united sums of many contributors, is just, in its economic effect on the character and condition of our people, an equivalent to one of these wells. It is only, by the substitution of art for nature, translating our land into the condition of a more richly gifted country. By the money laid out on an asylum for indigence, you do not strike out a new fountain of abundance in the country—you do not purchase additional fertility to our fields—you do not obtain a larger proportion of food to the population—you only change the distribution of the food, and make it a worse distribution than before. By the money laid out on an asylum for disease, you strike out a new fountain of health in the country. You erect a Bethesda, out of which there may issue a refreshing stream on the sick and infirm of our population. And in all these ways, may it be proved, that there is indeed a firm barrier of distinction, between a public and indefinite system of relief for pauperism, and a public and indefinite system of relief for disease? The one, in truth, never can overtake the cases which its own operations tend to multiply. The other may be safely carried onwards, till, by the interest of a permanent capital, it becomes commensurate forever to all the demands which the country may make upon it.

There is not only wisdom, but a profoundness of wisdom, in the example of our Saviour. And in the matters of human charity, will it be seen, that, both by the actions of His history, and the admonitions of the greatest of His apostles, He not only provides in the best manner for the worth of individual character—but that He also provides in the best manner for the economic regulation of the largest and most complex societies.

He in the first instance gives us an example of the softest compassion at the sight of human misery; and He lets us know by it, that, if there be actual hunger within our reach, for which there appears no remedy—it is our part to give way to the sensibilities of our nature, and to stretch forth a helping hand for the purpose of relieving it. He would have spared the miracle, had other resources been at hand; but the people were far from the food of markets, or the food of their own habitations. He would have left the case to themselves, could they have supported the fatigue of reaching it themselves; but they would have fainted on the way—and therefore, as an example to us to give in such a predicament out of our abundance, did He call down a miracle from Heaven that the people before Him might eat and be filled.

In the second instance, what He granted to the urgent necessities of the people, He refused to their sordid expectations. It was not His habit to provide food for His followers in this extraordinary manner. He left poverty to the effect of its natural exhibition on the compassionate nature of those who were near it—and a nature which all His lessons are fitted to render more compassionate than before. He must have thought that it was better thus to leave it—than to bring out the clustering multitudes around Himself in the capacity of an almoner. All His doings were of public notoriety; and, in point of effect on the comfort and character of His countrymen, would they have been the same with the operations of a public charity. And we are not afraid to affirm—that generally it were better still, to leave the cause of indigence to the play of those innumerable sympathies, which are to be met with in manifold detail, and in deeply-extended diffusion, throughout every community of human beings—than that, by the existence of a great and widely-visible institution, either the recipients of charity should be tempted away from the resources of their own industry; or the dispensers of charity should be tempted away from the work of each cultivating his own province, and lavishing those generosities of character which adorn the man and are altogether indispensable to the Christian, on the walk of his own separate and familiar acquaintanceship.

But in the third instance, when he threw off all reserve, and stood publicly out to the eye of His countrymen in the capacity of a divine teacher—He also threw off all reserve, and stood as publicly out to the eye of His countrymen, in the capacity of one who healed all manner of sickness and all manner of diseases among the people. He did not bring down subsistence by miracle, and cast it abroad amongst them. But He brought down health by miracle, and cast it abroad amongst them. He did not encourage the people to forsake their callings and to riot after Him in trooping disorder through the country for food; but He laid no such prohibition on blameless and helpless disease. He did not choose that the report of His appearance, should be the signal for a jubilee of idleness and dissipation among His countrymen; but when it brought out the maimed, and the halt, and the dumb, and the lunatic, and those who were sick and sorely afflicted with various infirmities from the surrounding villages, He sent them not away. He saw a distinction between the one claim and the other, and He acted upon it. The restless philanthrophy of the day, ever scheming and ever intermeddling with the previous arrangements of nature, may gather some lessons from that peculiarity, which characterized the march of His wise and effective beneficence through the land of Judea. Whatever discouragements it may draw from His example in the erection of an asylum for indigence, it can draw none against the erection of an asylum for disease; and while the boding apprehension both of moral and physical disaster hangs over the one institution, do we infer, that, with the other, may its door be thrown open, and all its accommodations be widened and multiplied—till every imploring patient be taken in, and a harbor of sufficient amplitude be provided for all those sufferings, which an uncontrollable necessity has laid upon our species.

I shall conclude this argument, with three observations. First, we are quite aware of the advantage, which they, who contend for a public and proclaimed charity in behalf of indigence, appear to have over their antagonists. On the first blush of it, it looks like the contest of human sympathy against human selfishness—of kindness pressing a measure of positive beneficence, against steeled and hardened barbarity, laboring with all its strenuousness to put it down. We are aware of the apparent advantage which this gives to the combatants on the other side of this deeply interesting controversy; and we are equally aware of the uncandid and unmerciful use that they have made of it. Strange that the plea of compassion should be so vehemently urged, in defence of a system under which the virtue of compassion withers into lifelessness. Let it grow as a distinct plant in every heart, and be cherished among the privacies of kindly and familiar neighborhood; and then will it be sure to scatter its innumerable leaves in every quarter of society, for the healing of the population. But it loses all its succulence, and all its blossom, in the chilling atmosphere of an almshouse. Fostered there into a tree of leafless magnitude, it stands in monumental coldness—having the body without the breath of charity; and, for the support of its unwieldy materialism, is it now drying up all the native sensibilities of our land. If you wish to restore benevolence amongst us to its healthful circulation, this forced and factitious excrescence must finally be cleared away. Thus and thus alone will you bring back to compassion all the scope and all the excitement, by which she may break out again into the vigor and the efflorescence of liberty; and when so brought back, will there arise a thousand securities which are now dormant, against every one of those calamities, which law has only aggravated, in its vain attempts to combat and to reduce them. The lesson of our second passage, so far from counteracting, only affords space and encouragement for the lesson of our first. And in opposition to all that declamation has uttered, against the aggressions of the understanding upon the province of the heart, do we aver, that never were the powers of the one more directly engaged, in affirming the prerogatives and in vindicating the outraged sensibilities of the other—than when helping to release the business of human charity, from the grasp and the regulation of human power: And never will political philosophy have rendered so brilliant a service to the good and to the virtue of our species, as when she reinstates charity upon its original basis; and commits the cause of human suffering back again to those free sympathies of nature, from which it had been so unwisely wrested by the hand of legislation.

But secondly, whatever may have been said to damp or to deaden our regards towards a public institution for poverty, nothing has been said to alienate from a similar institution for disease. When charged with the desolating influences of speculation upon the heart, let it be understood, that there is an opportunity on which every economist may, by his ample contribution in behalf of a cause that is free from every exception, render to his own favorite science the most satisfying of all vindications. If the thought that indigence with all its ills, is fostered and augmented, just in proportion to the amount of that fund which is publicly provided for it—if this be the thought which restrained his liberality, let us see what is the style in which his liberality will expatiate, when this restraint is lifted away from it. In reference to the objects of a charity for disease, nature supplies him with a definite number of cases which no benevolence can increase; and let us therefore see, whether his benevolence will flag or whether it will persist with untired and undiminished energy, till the number be overtaken. If his reason told him that an asylum of one kind may be a vomitory of evil, both physical and moral, to the people of the land, and he therefore turned a deaf ear to all its applications—let us see what the sensibility and what the sacrifice will be, when his reason tells him that there is an asylum of another kind, which acts in every instance as an absorbent of human suffering, and in no instance as a fountain of mischievous emanation. We do not say it is wrong that the heart should be placed under the custody of the understanding; or that the one should lay its limitation on the feelings and exercises of the other. But we cannot know the character of the heart, till the time and the place occur when every limitation is removed, and so, when pleading for the relief of disease, instead of a forbidden glance from the intellectual power, she lends her full consent and smiles her approving testimony—when no voice of boding anticipation, is lifted up to deafen the solicitations of charity—when a path of safe and undoubted progress is opened, in which philanthropy may walk, till she reach the full achievement of her purposes—when she is moving on ground, where every step carries her forward in nearer approximation to a most complete and gratifying accomplishment—when a few of our brethren, whom the hand of nature hath mutilated of their faculties, are standing before us with the credentials of their impressive claim, stamped and authenticated upon their persons, and just as if Heaven had affixed a mark by which to select and to set them apart for the unqualified sympathy of all their fellows—when feeling urges us onwards in behalf of misfortune, so signalized and so privileged, and philosophy places no cold obstruction in her way—With all these favorable circumstances surrounding the cause, and all these incitements to bear us forward to its triumphant consummation, let us not cease to stimulate and to draw from the resources of the country, till every such institution be wide enough to take in all for whose relief it is adapted; and till it rise in the shape of a permanent endowment, among the most securely established and best provided charities of our land.

It is thus that an institution for disease, should stand before the eye of the public with a claim and a character which ought to secure it from every fluctuation. It should be brought out and peculiarized, from among the crowd of ambiguous and questionable charities. There are many other advantages in the combination and resources of a public society, formed for the mitigation of disease, on which I have no time to expatiate. And I shall only therefore remark of each such institution that, if not placed on the stable foundation of a sure and permanent capital, there ought at least to be a yearly subscription ample enough for the purpose of meeting every application. At all events it ought to have such an homage rendered to it, as to make it independent of any vindication which may be offered from the pulpit in its behalf; and it is a reproach to an intelligent public, that ministers have to descend so often from the higher walk of parochial and congregational usefulness, in order to stimulate their languid energies, in behalf of charities which ought long ago, to have been made productive enough for their interesting but limited necessities.

ON THE NECESSITY

OF

UNITING PRAYER WITH PERFORMANCE

FOR THE

SUCCESS OF MISSIONS.

Had the members of some school of philosophy, by dint of a skilful and laborious analysis, become profoundly conversant with the mysteries of the human spirit—Had they speculated with accuracy and effect, not merely on the progress of an individual mind from its first rude and unformed elements to the highest finish both of its moral and intellectual cultivation, but also on the progress of the collective mind in society—so as to trace all the continuous footsteps by which the transition is made from savage to civilized life—Had they, on the principles of their new system, devised a path of tuition, and instituted a method of discipline, and framed a book of elementary doctrine and scholarship, in virtue of which they held themselves prepared for a grand philanthropic experiment on some remote island of barbarians, yet in the ferocity and primitive ignorance of nature—Had they been able so to interest the public in their scheme, as to be upheld by them in all the cost of a benevolent expedition—and then set forth on the wide ocean of adventure, till they reached a far-distant and solitary shore, that was peopled by an untaught tribe of idolaters, where all the arts and habits and decencies of Europe were unknown, and where some hideous misshapen sculpture bespoke a paganism of the coarsest and most revolting character—Had they, in these circumstances, offered parley with the natives; and gained their confidence: and won such an ascendency, as that they could assemble and detain them at pleasure for the purposes of education; and furnished, as they were by an enlightened metaphysics with the best and fittest lessons for men in the infancy of understanding, brought their well-weighed processes to bear upon them—Had they got pupils from among all their families, and, in twenty years, wrought a change more marvellous, than twenty centuries, rolling over the head of many tribes and nations of our world, have been able to accomplish—In a word, had they transformed this horde of cannibals into a lettered and humanized peasantry; and, for the cruelties of their old and haggard superstition, trained them to the peaceful charities of this world and to the rejoicing hopes of another—Had they been further enabled to grace the whole of this exhibition by such pleasing and picturesque accompaniments, as those of newly-formed villages, and cultivated gardens, and prosperous industry, and the whole costume of industrious and well-regulated life—and all this on the part of a people who, but a few years before, were prowling in nakedness, and with fierce and untamed spirit, could assemble in delighted multitudes, around the agonies of a human sacrifice—An achievement so wonderful as this would have blazoned forth upon the world as one of the noblest triumphs of philosophy. It would have filled and dazzled the whole of our literary republic; and her academies would have vied with each other, in heaping their orders and their honorary titles on the men, who had found out that specific charm, by which to reclaim the wilds of humanity, and to quicken a hundred fold the march and improvement of our species.

Now it is not very many years ago, since such an enterprise was set on foot by the members of a certain college, though not a college of literati; and they carried out with them a certain book of instructions, though not one philosopher had to do with the composition of it; and they made the very attempt which we have now specified, on a territory removed by some thousands of miles from the outskirts of civilization; and through a severe ordeal of ridicule and of reverses did they ply their assiduous task, and have now brought their experiment to its termination. And, whatever the steps of their process may have been, there is many an eye-witness who can speak to the result of it. The island of Otaheite, which teemed with the worst abominations of savage passion and savage cruelty, was the selected arena on which they tried the virtue of their peculiar specific; and, whatever the *rationale* of its operation may have been, there is no doubt as to the certainty of the operation itself. The savages have been humanized. The rude and hideous characteristics of the savage state have all disappeared. A nation of gross and grovelling idolaters has become a nation of rational and kindred and companionable men; and, furnished now as they are with a written language, and having access by authorship and correspondence to other minds and other countries than their own—do the lights of Christendom now shine full upon their territory. And it is indeed a wondrous transformation—to look at their now modest attire, and their now sweet and comfortable habitations, and their village schools, and their well-ordered families, and their infant literature, and their new-formed alphabet, and a boyhood just taught and practised like our own in the various branches of scholarship; and, what perhaps poetry even though apart from religion would most fondly seize upon of all—the holiness of their sabbath-morn; and the chime of its worship-bell, now breaking for the first time on the ear of the delighted mariner who hovers upon their shore, and recognized by him as a sound that was before unheard, throughout the whole of that vast Pacific, in the solitude of whose mighty waters this island had lain buried and unknown for so many ages. Yes! all this has undoubtedly been done; but then a few Gospel missionaries had the doing of it; and they tell us that the whole charm and power of this marvellous translation are to be found in the Bible and in its cabalistic orthodoxy; and they talk moreover of prayers and outpourings and mystic influences from on high, which all the science of all our universities cannot lead us to comprehend or in any way to sympathize with—And thus, as the compound effect of this whole exhibition on many spirits, are there an incredulity; and a contempt; and at the same time an astonishment at a great moral phenomenon, the truth of which is forced upon them by the evidence of their senses; and withal, we fear, a still resolute determination to nauseate with all their might that peculiar evangelism, which has been the instrument of the most gigantic stride, that was ever made by barbarians on the road to civilization and virtue. And thus upon them do we perceive perhaps the most striking illustration of that text which can be given—who, "when God worketh a work in their days, will in no wise believe though a man should declare it unto them;" but what they would not believe they will be made to behold—though, still persisting in their contempt, it will be the beholding of despisers "who wonder and perish."

Now this appears to us the precise feeling of secular and merely scientific men in reference to Bible and missionary societies. These are the likely instruments under which the world will at length be christianized; and, by whose power we think, that there are a stir and an aspect and a sort of heaving even now towards millennium. The instance just quoted, is in itself a fine miniature exhibition of that which is destined at length to be universal—like the size of a man's hand on a very distant horizon; but the token of a general rain, the clouds and magazines of which will spread over the whole firmament of heaven, and descend in a universal shower on the thirsty world which is beneath it. The little stone is now distinctly visible to those who are looking for it; and from the visible it will rise into the conspicuous, so as to obtrude itself at length on the notice of the contemptuous and the careless; and at last will attain to the size of a mountain that shall fill the whole earth. Meanwhile Bible and missionary societies are now helping to build this spiritual Jerusalem; and much of most essential but unobserved ground-work must be done, ere the rising architecture shall be very discernible; and many are the laborers who must ply for years at the work of translations, and the work of scholarship, ere the Gospel shall be brought in its direct and naked force upon the consciences of the sinners in all nations; and assiduous must be the calls on the liberality of a Christian public, to uphold this work of faith and of patience; and during the whole of its progress, the resistance and the ridicule of despisers, are just what we should be prepared to look for. And accordingly, in spite of all the patronage that has descended on these institutions—still will we venture to affirm, that the great majority of the cultivated intellect in our land, is either in a state of contempt or in a state of hostility against them—that the charge of an obscure and ignoble fanaticism is still made to rest on the design and operation of these societies—that the example of success we have now quoted, which, had it been the success of a philosophical experiment, would have rung in high gratulation among all the *savans* of all the institutes in Europe, has from its being the success of a Christian experiment, scarcely ever reached them; or, if the report have fallen by accident upon their ears, it has been like the sound of a vague and distant something in which they had no concern. In short, there is an apathy about the whole enterprise—a cold and disdainful feeling towards the christianization of the world.

Now though much of this is to be ascribed to man's natural enmity against the Gospel of Jesus Christ, yet, along with the dislike, there is an incredulity, and an incredulity that can allege for itself a number of seemly arguments. The most plausible of these is, the utter inadequacy of the proposed means to the proposed end of the societies in question. It is to the spread of the Bible, and to the reading of the Bible, and to the charm of the preacher's voice when he urges home its lessons—it is apparently to these, that they look for a regenerated species. To means so utterly insignificant, the end appears to be out of all measure romantic and impracticable and hopeless. This goes a certain way to explain the contempt of adversaries for the Bible enterprise. They do not see how this book of antique phrase, and of hidden characters, is to work so miraculous a change on the spirit and the moral habitude of nations. They cannot see by what inexplicable charm it is, that the face of our whole world is to be so lightened and transformed by it. Like the enemies of Samson, they have not yet discovered wherein it is that the secret of its great strength lieth; and all their ideas of its powerlessness are abundantly confirmed by what they see of its slender efficacy among our home population. When they look to the palpable exhibition of this book, lying neglected and unopened on the shelves of almost all our habitations; and notice how very small a space in the system of human affairs, is taken up by the perusal of it; and estimate aright the wide distance which obtains between its spirit and the spirit of those who profess to own and to revere it; and see how, even in that very territory of Christendom where the silence originated, it tells with no practical or perceptible influence on the mass of families; and can shrewdly remark, after all, that humanity, even in England, takes very much its own spontaneous way, and that really there seems no distinct or satisfying proof of any sensible control, which the Bible has on its business or its morals or the general spirit and economy of its people—it is truly natural in these circumstances to ask, if the Bible have been of such minute and slender efficacy at home, by what inscrutable operation do we think that it is to achieve a transformation in every way so marvellous and so magical abroad? If after the residence and the reading of centuries amongst us, the aspect of our present British society is still as distant as possible from that which we conceive of the aspect of millennium—how do we imagine, that by the transportation of Bibles and missionaries into heathen lands, a new moral scenery is forthwith to emerge; and that the millennium of which we see no semblance immediately around us, is first to break forth on some distant and unknown wilderness? It is thus that among men of firm and secular understandings, there is a certain experimental feeling, as if the whole speculation were vain and visionary and most wildly extravagant. It is looked to as one of those delusive novelties, that will have its meteoric course, and then go into oblivion, among the other popular follies which had their day and are forgotten. While the cry and fashion of the thing last it is thought, money will be raised; and Bibles will be exported; and whole packages will be landed on the shores of idolatry; and missionaries will go forth and excite for a time a sort of marvel and interest among the natives, at the very unusual kind of wares in which they deal and the strange proposals which they have to offer—but that, in a few little years, all will vanish into impotency, and leave not one trace behind of that fantastic crusade which we are now called upon to succor and to sustain.

These are plausible discouragements, and they do operate with great force on nature and on the sagacity of natural men. They give a certain character of experimental wisdom to their opposition against that enterprise for which we are contending; and for the neutralizing of which, therefore, there is a peculiar importance in every fair example that can be quoted of missionary success. The experience of this success has greatly multiplied of late years; and meanwhile there are two distinct considerations that I would strongly urge, for the purpose of sustaining your faith and the constancy of your friendship to the cause.

The first consideration that I would urge, is the certain fitness of the Bible to that object for which it has been framed. You must not forget that this book of doubted and decried and disowned efficacy, is the word of God—that it is a message constructed by Him, and specially adapted by His wisdom to the special object of recalling a lost world from its state of exile and degeneracy—that such is declared to be the power of its doctrine, as that, whensoever it is received, there are received along with it the forgiveness of sin, and ability from on high to dethrone sin from its ascendency over our moral nature—that, with this chosen instrument of God for the recovery of our fallen race, there is a capacity for all those high and heavenly purposes which it is destined to accomplish—that we are not to despair, because of the long period of this world's resistance and this world's unconcern, for this is what the prophecies of the Bible itself have led us to anticipate—that meanwhile, and in the face of these prophecies, there is a precept of standing obligation to go and preach this Gospel unto all nations; and to go and carry this message to every creature under heaven—and, finally—as the fruit of a patience that must weather every discouragement, and of a perseverance that must be manfully sustained amid the revilings of a whole multitude of scorners, and of a faith which against hope will believe in hope that what God hath promised He is also able to perform, are we told of a latter-day glory which is to fill the whole earth; and that there is a veil which is to be lifted off from the eyes of all nations; and that another spirit will at length descend upon the world, than that by which it has so long been actuated; and that the obstinacy of the human heart will at length give way, under the assurances of redeeming mercy—So as that the Gospel, now so unproductive of any moral or spiritual harvest, shall at length find free course and be everywhere glorified—turning the earth into a well-watered garden, and causing it from one end to another to abound in all the fair and pleasant fruits of righteousness.

The second consideration that I would urge, for the purpose of sustaining our confidence in the future triumph and enlargement of this cause, is the efficacy of prayer. There is something in the whole temper and habit of philosophy, that leads us to distrust the virtue of this expedient. There is even something in the philanthropic activity of our age, that lures away the heart from its dependence upon God; and makes it confide to the powers of human agency alone, that which never will be made to prosper without the hand of the Almighty being both acknowledged and implored in it. When one sees so many societies, with the skilful mechanism of their various offices and appointments and committees; and sums up the contributions that are rendered to them; and looks to the train of their auxiliaries all over the land; and hears the annual eloquence, and peruses the annual reports which are issued forth from the fountain-heads of the whole operation; and further witnesses the spirit and agency and busy earnestness, wherewith all their proceedings are conducted—So goodly an apparatus as this, is apt to usurp the hope and the confidence which should be placed in God only. The instrument becomes an idol; and He who is jealous of His honor, and who will have the power of His divinity recognized throughout every step of that process which leads to the regeneration of our world, may choose to mortify the proud anticipations of those who calculate on their own strength and their own wisdom. The Christians who flourished in the days of Puritanism, that Augustan age of Christianity in England, were men of prayer but not men of missionary performance; and the Christians of our present day are men of performance, but need perhaps to be humbled by crosses and adversities into men of prayer. It is out of the happy combination of these two habits, that the evangelizing of the nations is to come. Both must go together, or no solid and enduring result will come forth of the experiment. It is by the neglect, either of the one or the other of these capabilities, that we explain the languid and stationary condition of the Gospel for so many ages; and as the suggestion of some new expedient, before unadverted to, like the breaking up of new ground or the opening of a tract before unexplored, raises the sinking hopes of a disappointed adventurer—so when the praying disciple is taught the necessity of labor, and the laborious disciple is taught the necessity of prayer—when these two elements meet together, and co-operate as they did in the days of the apostles—when our men of devotion become men of diligence, and our men of diligence become men of devotion—It is from this union of humble hearts with busy hands, that we would date the commencement of a new and a productive era in the Church's history upon earth: And we doubt not that what the old missionary Elliot reported and left on record of his own experience, will be found true of the collective missionary experience of all ages, that "it is in the power of pains and of prayers to do anything."

And we do look on the example already quoted as a verification of this. We are old enough to recollect the high-blown spirit of adventure in which the first mission to Otaheite was undertaken; and with what eclat the missionary vessel went forth upon her voyage, as if the flags and ensigns of victory were already streaming in the gale; and with what eloquence were pictured forth all the chances, if not all the certainties, of success. We doubt not that many were dazzled into an earthly confidence, when they looked to the complete equipment of all the human securities, that were so abundantly provided for the accomplishment of this great enterprise. And He, at whose disposal are all the elements of Nature, did carry it in safety to the shore. But He, at whose disposal also are all the elements of the moral world, taught, by humbling experience, that for these too He must be inquired after; and a cloud of disgrace and disaster hung for years over the enterprise; and the spirit, which worketh in the children of disobedience, stood its ground among the natives; and, more woful still, the spirit of apostasy made ravage among the missionaries themselves; and well can we remember the derision and the triumph of infidelity upon the misgiving of this sanguine speculation. We doubt not that many were effectually taught in the arts of patience and prayer by this fatherly correction; and led to look from the visible apparatus to the unseen Guide and mover of it; and that there was a busier ascent of importunities to heaven, and a louder knocking than before at the door of the upper sanctuary. And certain it is, that, after a season of severe but salutary chastisement, an influence, far too sudden and diffusive to be interpreted by any ordinary causes, came down upon the island; and, by a miracle as stupendous as if it had been newly summoned from the deep, do we now behold it a land of genial dwelling places—the quiet and lovely home of a christianized nation.

It were now a topic by far too unwieldy, did we attempt to state the philosophy of prayer—or to meet the antipathies of those who have explored nature, and, as far as the light of science can penetrate, have found in all her ways a constancy that is inflexible. But you can at least be made to understand how it is, that the study of this world's unvaried mechanism, should have put to flight that host of living and supernatural agencies wherewith at one time it was held to be actuated—how after such an abundant discovery as we now have of those trains and successions, that appear to be invariable and altogether to make up the history of our universe, the visions of the old mythology should all have been dissipated; because, instead of each department in nature being ruled by its own presiding divinity whom it is the part of superstition to implore, in each there are its own peculiar but steady and unchanging processes which it is the part of philosophy to investigate—that thus the spectres of a fabled imagery have now been swept away; and nature, instead of a haunted fairy-land, is now regarded as the stable and everlasting repository of innumerable sequences, in whose rigid uniformity we see nought of the caprice of will but all the certainty of mechanism. And so in this our enlightened day, there is no account taken of a spirit that resides in the thunder; or of a spirit in the air, at whose bidding the storm might either be hushed or awakened; or of a spirit in the angry deep, who might add to the wild uproar of the tempest by mixing his own element with that which is wielded by another potentate. The earth is now unpeopled of its demigods; and the substitution of the laws of nature in their place, has often been extolled as the best service which philosophy has rendered to our species.

You may now perhaps see, by how likely and continuous a transition it is, that men may pass from the extreme of superstition to the extreme of philosophical impiety. After that nature has been rescued by philosophy from the dominion of separate and subordinate deities, it may be placed by the same philosophy under the absolute and irreversible dominion of secondary causes. To guard this new dominion and make it inflexible, a supreme and eternal spirit may even be disowned; or, at all events, it might be reckoned indispensable, that He never should put forth His hand on the regularities of that universe which He Himself has established. It might be difficult to assign the place or the pre-eminence of such a God over His own workmanship; or to understand how He is admitted to a share in the government of His own world. But it is at least the imagination of many a philosopher, that all must give way to the omnipotence and the certainty of nature's laws. The interposition of the divine will with these is utterly excluded from his creed; and the efficacy of prayer would be deemed by him a monstrous inroad on that constancy, which he holds to be unalterable. It is thus, that, along with the mythology of Paganism, the Theism of Christianity is apt to be swept away; and the system of nature is reduced to an economy of blind and unconscious fatalism.

We are obviously on the confines of a subject, that is greatly too ponderous for a single essay; and there is imperious necessity for limiting ourselves. Let us only then say further, that it does not appear why an answer to prayer might not be given; and yet all the established sequences of our world be maintained in their wonted order, as far back as philosophy can discover them. Instead of God dispensing with the secondary causes, when He meets and satisfies our prayers, they may be the very instruments by which He fulfils them. When He hearkens to the supplication that ascends for a prosperous missionary voyage—He does not send forth a miraculous impulse upon the vessel, but causes the very wind to arise, which, by the laws of motion, should bear her onward to the destined haven. Even this wind might not be originated by miracle, but spring up from that previous condition of the air and the vapor and the heat, which, by the laws of meteorology, should cause that very gale to blow by which the service has been accomplished. And so to the uttermost limits of science, to the full extent of her possible observations, all might appear to move in strictly undeviating order. But still ulterior to this—and between the widest confines of all which nature can see upon the one hand, and that throne whence the Author of nature issues forth His mandates upon the other—there is a hidden intermediate process, which connects the purposes of the divine mind, with the visible phenomena of that universe which He has created: And, not among the palpable things which lie in the region of observation, but among the secret things which lie in the dark and the deep abyss that is between the farthest reach of man's discovery and the forthgoings of God's will—it is among these, where that responsive touch may be given by the finger of the Almighty, which shall guide the mechanism of our world and without thwarting any one of its laws. He moves those springs which be placed behind the curtain of sense and observation : and as He may thus, in subserviency to our prayers for the success of a missionary voyage, direct the processes of meteorology without deranging them—so, in subserviency to our prayers for the success of misssionary work, he may so direct the metaphysics of the human spirit in the whole business of conversion, as not to violate any one of the laws or the processes of human thought. It is thus that we may live under the canopy of a special providence, even on that platform of sensible things where all the trains and successions are invariable. It is thus, that, at one and the same time, we may be under the care of a presiding God, and among the regularities of a harmonious Universe.

But after all, this contempt for prayer and for the doctrine of its efficacy, is not more resolvable into a perverse philosophy, than it is resolvable into irreligion—into that spirit of inveterate worldliness, which is satisfied with things as they are and cares not for any transformation; which wants not the repose of nations to be disturbed, by this restless and aggressive proselytism ; and would rather that Paganism were left to remain fixed as it has been for countlsss generations, in its own deep and rooted antiquity. They hate all innovation on the existing state of things; and, as men will shut their eyes to avoid the spectacle of that which they dislike, so will they close their understandings against the light of that evidence, by which it now becomes every day more manifest, that we are on the eve of great moral and spiritual changes—that the world is heaving in fact towards some mighty and wondrous renovation—and that on the ruins of its present depravity, there will at length be established an order of truth and charity and righteousness. This is all romance to the eye of their earthly understanding, and they will in no wise believe though a man declare it unto them ; and, despising as they do the Gospel at bottom, they despise every account which reaches them of its progress—So that, when, instead of a report heard with the hearing of the ear, it reaches them in characters of nearness and authenticity—still, without the sympathy and without the discernment of its principles, they only marvel at what they cannot comprehend, and, looking on to a conversion of multitudes in which they do not partake, they wonder and they perish.

Let me conclude with one or two brief sentences of personal application. Those who dislike any inroad to be made on the deep repose of heathenism, we would warn to be careful, that they have not a dislike as violent to any inroad being made on the deep lethargy of their own souls. Those who think of friendly islanders and mild or peaceful Hindoos, that they stand in need of no transformation—let them tell whether they do not think the very same thing of themselves. They would rather that the heathen were let alone ; and would they not rather that themselves were let alone also? and are they not as incredulous about the need of a regeneration for themselves as individuals, as they are about the regeneration of a whole people? Is there not about them a general distrust of the whole matter?—and would they not nauseate the ministers who speak to them of the conversion of their own spirit, just as honestly and heartily as they nauseate the missionaries who go forth to the conversion of idolaters and savages? Then let them know, that life is passing away; and that, in their state of nature, there is a load of guilt unexpiated, of pollution unremoved—that there is but one specific for this disease all over the globe, and we invite them now to the Spirit who renews and to the Saviour who died for them. He is set forth a propitiation for all sin, and God through Him beseeches them to be reconciled. Let them persist, in contempt and unconcern no longer—for there is an event that will soon and surely overtake us; and which, if it find us unprepared, will excite, not the wonder of curiosity, but the amazement of terror. Death is at our door; and let us not despise the Saviour who came to destroy him—lest when we hear His approaching footsteps, and receive His last and awful summons, we grow pale and tremble and perish.

THE

INFLUENCE OF PAROCHIAL ASSOCIATIONS

FOR THE

MORAL AND SPIRITUAL GOOD OF MANKIND

THE INFLUENCE

OF

PAROCHIAL ASSOCIATIONS

FOR THE

MORAL AND SPIRITUAL GOOD OF MANKIND.*

ARGUMENT.

1. The Objection stated.—2. The Radical Answer to it.—3. But the Objection is not true in point of fact.—4. A former act of charity does not exempt from the obligation of a new act, if it can be afforded.—5. Estimate of the encroachment made by a Religious Society upon the funds of the country.—6. A Subscriber to a Parochial Society does not give less to the Poor on that account.—7. Evidence for the truth of this assertion.—8. And explanation of its principle. (1.) The ability for other acts of charity nearly as entire as before.—9. (2.) And the disposition greater.—10. Poverty is better kept under by a preventive, than by a positive treatment.—11. Exemplified in Scotland.—12. A Parochial Society has a strong preventive operation.—13. And therefore promotes the secular interests of the Poor.—14. The argument carried down to the case of Penny Societies.—15. Difficulty in the exposition of the argument.—16. The effects of a charitable endowment in a Parish pernicious to the Poor.—17. By inducing a dependence upon it.—18. And stripping them of their industrious habits.—19. The effects of a Parochial Association, such as we plead for, are in an opposite direction to those of a charitable endowment.—20. And it stands completely free of all the objections to which a tax is liable.—21. Such an Association gives dignity to the Poor.—22. And a delicate reluctance to pauperism.—23. The shame of pauperism is the best defence against it.—24. How a Bible Association augments this feeling.—25. By dignifying the Poor.—26. And adding to the Influence of Bible Principles.—27. Exemplified in the humblest situation.—28. The progress of these Associations in the country.—29. Compared with other Associations for the relief of temporal necessities.—30. The more salutary influence of Parochial Associations.—31. And how they counteract the pernicious influence of other charities.—32. It is best to confide the secular relief of the Poor to individual benevolence.—33. And a Parochial Association both augments and enlightens this principle.

1. Without entering into the positive claims of the Bible Society, or of any similar Association, upon the generosity of the public, I shall endeavor to do away an objection which meets us

* This pamphlet was originally published in 1814. It must be obvious of its reasonings that they apply to every benevolent Association which has for its object the moral and spiritual well-being of our fellow-men, whether at home or abroad. We hope, therefore, that its republication will not be deemed unseasonable at the present moment, when attempts are being made to enlist the general population in the pecuniary support of Four Great Schemes, which have received the high sanction of the General Assembly of the Church of Scotland.

at the very outset of every attempt to raise a subscription, or to found an institution in its favor. The secular necessities of the poor are brought into competition with it, and every shilling given to such an Association is represented as an encroachment upon that fund which was before allocated to the relief of poverty.

2. Admitting the fact stated in the objection to be true, we have an answer in readiness for it. If the Bible Society accomplish its professed object, which is, to make those who were before ignorant of the Bible better acquainted with it, then the advantage given more than atones for the loss sustained. We stand upon the high ground, that eternity is longer than time, and the unfading enjoyments of the one a boon more valuable than the perishable enjoyments of the other. Money is sometimes expended, for the idle purpose of amusing the poor by the gratuitous exhibition of a spectacle or show. It is a far wiser distribution of the money, when it is transferred from this object to the higher and more useful objects of feeding those among them who are hungry, clothing those among them who are naked, and paying for medicine, or attendance, to those among them who are sick. We make bold to say, that if money for the purpose could be got from no other quarter, it would be a wiser distribution still to withdraw it from the objects last mentioned, to the supreme object of paying for the knowledge of religion to those among them who are ignorant; and, at the hazard of being execrated by many, we do not hesitate to affirm, that it is better for the poor to be worse fed and worse clothed, than that they should be left ignorant of those Scriptures, which are able to make them wise unto salvation through the faith that is in Christ Jesus.

3. But the statement contained in the objection is not true. It seems to go upon the supposition, that the fund for relieving the temporal wants of the poor is the only fund which exists in the country; and that when any new object of benevolence is started, there is no other fund to which we can repair for the requisite expenses. But there are other funds in the country. There is a prodigious fund for the maintenance of Government, nor do we wish that fund to be encroached upon by a single farthing. There is a fund, out of which the people of the land are provided in the necessaries of life; and before we incur the odium of trenching upon necessaries, let us first inquire, if there be no other fund in existence. Go then to all who are elevated above the class of mere laborers, and you will find in their possession a fund, out of which they are provided with what are commonly called the superfluities of life. We do not dispute their right to these superfluities, nor do we deny the quantity of pleasure which lies in the enjoyment of them. We only state the existence of such a fund, and that by a trifling act of self-denial, on the part of those who possess it, we could obtain all that we are pleading for. It is a little hard that the competition should be struck betwixt the

fund of a Parochial Association for the moral good of others, and the fund for relieving the temporal wants of the poor, while the far larger and more transferable fund for superfluities is left out of consideration entirely, and suffered to remain an untouched and unimpaired quantity. In this way the odium of hostility to the poor is fastened upon those who are laboring for their most substantial interests, while a set of men who neglect the immortality of the poor, and would leave their souls to perish, are suffered to sheer off with the credit of all the finer sympathies of our nature.

4. To whom much is given, of them much will be required. Whatever be your former liberalities in another direction, when a new and likely direction of benevolence is pointed out, the question still comes back upon you, What have you to spare? If there be a remainder left, it is by the extent of this remainder that you will be judged; and it is not right to set the claims of the Parochial Association against the secular necessities of the poor, while means so ample are left, that the true way of instituting the competition is, to set these claims against some personal gratification which it is in your power to abandon. Have a care, lest, with the language of philanthropy in your mouth, you shall be found guilty of the cruelest indifference to the true welfare of the species, and lest the discerner of your heart shall perceive how it prefers some sordid indulgence of its own to the dearest interests of those around you.

5. But let me not put to hazard the prosperity of our cause, by resting it on a standard of charity far too elevated for the general practice of the times. Let us now drop our abstract reasoning upon the respective funds, and come to an actual specification of their quantities. The truth is, that to take one example, the fund for the Bible Society is so very small, that it is not entitled to make its appearance in any abstract argument whatever; and were it not to do away even the shadow of an objection, we would have been ashamed to have thrown the argument into the language of general discussion. What shall we think of the objection when told, that the whole yearly revenue of the Bible Society, as derived from the contributions of those who support it, does not amount to a half penny per month from each householder in Britain and Ireland? Can this be considered as a serious invasion upon any one fund allotted to other destinations; and shall the most splendid and promising enterprise that ever benevolence was engaged in be arrested upon an objection so fanciful? We do not want to oppress any individual by the extravagance of our demands. It is not in great sums, but in the combination of littles, that our strength lies. It is the power of combination which resolves the mystery. Great has been the progress and activity of the Bible Society since its first institution. All we want is, that this rate of activity in favor of all good associations, be kept up

and extended. The above statement will convince the reader that there is ample room for the extension.* The whole fund for the secular wants of the poor may be left untouched, and, as to the fund for luxuries, the revenue of our Christian Societies may be augmented a hundred-fold before this fund is sensibly encroached upon. The veriest crumbs and sweepings of extravagance would suffice us; and it will be long, and very long, before any invasion of ours upon this fund shall give rise to any perceivable abridgment of luxury, or have the weight of a straw upon the general style and establishment of families.

6. But there is still another way of meeting the objection. Let us come immediately to a question upon the point of fact. Does a man, on becoming a subscriber to a Parochial Association, give less to the secular wants of the poor than he did formerly? It is true, there is a difficulty in the way of obtaining an answer to this question. He who knows best what answer to give, will be the last to proclaim it. In as far as the subscribers themselves are concerned, we must leave the answer to their own experience, and sure we are that that experience will not be against us. But it is not from this quarter that we can expect to obtain the wished-for information. The benevolence of an individual does not stand out to the eye of the public. The knowledge of its operations is confined to the little neighborhood within which it expatiates. It is often kept from the poor themselves; and then the information we are in quest of is shut up with the giver in the silent consciousness of his own bosom, and with God in the book of His remembrance.

7. But much good has been done of late years by the combined exertions of individuals; and benevolence, when operating in this way, is necessarily exposed to public observation. Subscriptions have been started for almost every one object which benevolence can devise, and the published lists may furnish us with data for a partial solution of the proposed question. In point of fact, then, those who subscribe for a religious object, subscribe with the greatest readiness and liberality for the relief of human affliction, under all the various forms in which it pleads for sympathy. This is quite notorious. The human mind, by singling out the eternity of others as the main object of its benevolence, does not withdraw itself from the care of sustaining them on the way which leads to eternity. It exerts an act of preference, but not an act of exclusion. A friend of mine has been indebted to an active and beneficent patron for a lucrative situation in a distant country. But he wants money to pay his travelling expenses. I commit every reader to his own experience of human nature, when I rest with him the assertion, that if real kindness lay at the bottom of this act of patronage, the patron himself is the likeliest quarter

* Could we obtain a penny a-week, not from each individual, but *from each family* in Scotland—this alone would yield a hundred thousand pounds in the year.

from which the assistance will come. The man who signalizes himself by his religious charities, is not the last but the first man to whom I would apply in behalf of the sick and the destitute. The two principles are not inconsistent. They give support and nourishment to each other, or, rather, they are exertions of the same principle. This will appear in full display on the day of judgment; and even in this dark and undiscerning world, enough of evidence is before us upon which the benevolence of the Christian stands nobly vindicated, and from which it may be shown, that, while its chief care is for the immortality of others, it casts a wide and a wakeful eye over all the necessities and sufferings of the species.

8. Nor have we far to look for the explanation. The two elements which combine to form an act of charity, are the ability and the disposition; and the question simply resolves itself into this, "In how far these elements will survive a donation to a Parochial Association for religious objects, so as to leave the other charities unimpaired by it?" It is certainly conceivable, that an individual may give every spare farthing of his income to this institution. In this case, there is a total extinction of the first element. But, in point of fact, this is never done, or done so rarely as not to be admited into any general argument. With by far the greater number of subscribers, the ability is not sensibly encroached upon. There is no visible retrenchment in the superfluities of life. A very slight and partial change in the direction of that fund which is familiarly known by the name of *pocket-money*, can, generally speaking, provide for the whole amount of the donation in question. There are a thousand floating and incidental expenses, which can be given up without almost the feeling of a sacrifice; and the diversion of a few of them to the charity we are pleading for, leaves the ability of the giver to all sense as entire as before.

9. But the second element is subject to other laws, and the formal calculations of arithmetic do not apply to it. The disposition is not like the ability, a given quantity which suffers an abstraction by every new exercise. The effect of a donation upon the purse of the giver, is not the same with the moral influence of that donation upon his heart. Yet the two are assimilated by our antagonists; and the pedantry of computation carries them to results which are in the face of all experience. It is not so easy to awaken the benevolent principle out of its sleep, as, when once awakened in behalf of one object, to excite and to interest it in behalf of another. When the bar of selfishness is broken down, and the flood-gates of the heart are once opened, the stream of beneficence can be turned into a thousand directions. It is true, that there can be no beneficence without wealth, as there can be no stream without water. It is conceivable, that the opening of the flood-gates may give rise to no flow, as the opening of the

poor man's heart to the distresses of those around him may give rise to no act of almsgiving. But we have already proved the abundance of wealth; (N. B. see 8.) It is the selfishness of the inaccessible heart which forms the mighty barrier; and if this could be done away, a thousand fertilizing streams would issue from it. Now, this is what our Parochial Associations, in many instances, have accomplished. They have unlocked the avenue to many a heart, which was before inaccessible. They have come upon them with all the energy of a popular and prevailing impulse. They have created in them a new taste and a new principle. They have opened the fountain, and we are sure that, in every district of the land where a Parochial Association exists, the general principle of benevolence is more active and more expanding than ever.

10. And after all, what is the best method of providing for the secular necessities of the poor? Is it by laboring to meet the necessity after it has occurred, or by laboring to establish a principle and a habit which would go far to prevent its existence? If you wish to get rid of a noxious stream, you may first try to intercept it by throwing across a barrier; but, in this way, you only spread the pestilential water over a greater extent of ground, and when the basin is filled, a stream as copious as before is formed out of its overflow. The most effectual method, were it possible to carry it into accomplishment, would be, to dry up the source. The parallel in a great measure holds. If you wish to extinguish poverty, combat with it in its first elements. If you confine your beneficence to the relief of actual poverty, you do nothing. Dry up, if possible, the spring of poverty, for every attempt to intercept the running stream has totally failed. The education and the religious principle of Scotland have not annihilated pauperism, but they have restrained it to a degree that is almost incredible to our neighbors of the south: they keep down the mischief in its principle; they impart a sobriety and a right sentiment of independence to the character of our peasantry; they operate as a check upon profligacy and idleness. The maintenance of parish schools is a burden upon the landed property of Scotland, but it is a cheap defence against the poor rates, a burden far heavier, and which is aggravating perpetually. The writer of this paper knows of a parish in Fife, the average maintenance of whose poor is defrayed by twenty-four pounds sterling a year; and of a parish, of the same population, in Somersetshire, where the annual assessments come to thirteen hundred pounds sterling. The preventive regimen of the one country does more than the positive applications of the other. In England, they have suffered poverty to rise to all the virulence of a formed and obstinate disease. But they may as well think of arresting the destructive progress of a torrent by throwing across an embankment, as think

that the mere positive administration of relief will put a stop to the accumulating mischiefs of poverty.

11. The exemption of Scotland from the miseries of pauperism, is due to the education which their people receive at schools, and to the Bible which their scholarship gives them access to. The man who subscribes to the divine authority of this simple saying, "If any would not work, neither should he eat," possesses, in the good treasure of his own heart, a far more effectual security against the hardships of indigence, than the man who is trained, by the legal provisions of his country, to sit in slothful dependence upon the liberalities of those around him. It is easy to be eloquent in the praise of those liberalities; but the truth is, that they may be carried to the mischievous extent of forming a depraved and beggarly population. The hungry expectations of the poor will ever keep pace with the assessments of the wealthy; and their eye will be averted from the exertion of their own industry, as the only right source of comfort and independence. It is quite in vain to think that positive relief will ever do away the wretchedness of poverty. Carry the relief beyond a certain limit, and you foster the diseased principle which gives birth to poverty. On this subject the people of England felt themselves of late to be in a state of almost inextricable helplessness; and they were not without their fears of some mighty convulsion, to come upon them with all the energy of a tempest, before this devouring mischief could be swept away from the face of their community.

12. The best thing to avert this calamity from England is the education of their peasantry; and this is a cause to which the Religious Societies are contributing their full share of influence. A zeal for the circulation of the Bible is inseparable from a zeal for extending among the people the capacity of reading it; and it is not to be conceived, that the very same individual can be eager for the introduction of this volume into our cottages, and sit inactive under the galling reflection, that it is still a sealed book to many thousands of the occupiers. Accordingly we find, that the two concerns are keeping pace with one another. The Bible Society does not overstep the simplicity of its assigned object; but the members of that Society receive an impulse from the cause, which carries them to promote the education of the poor, either by their individual exertions, or by giving their support to the Society for Schools. The two Societies move in concert. Each contributes an essential element in the business of enlightening the people. This one furnishes the book of knowledge, and the other furnishes the key to it. This division of employment, as in every other instance, facilitates the work, and renders it more effective. But it does not hinder the same individual from giving his countenance to both; and sure I am, that the man whose feelings have been already warmed, and whose purse has been already drawn in behalf of the one, is a likelier subject for an application

in behalf of the other, than he whose money is still untouched, but whose heart is untouched also.

13. It will be seen, then, that our Parochial Societies are not barely defensible, but may be plead for upon that ground on which their enemies have raised an opposition to them. Their immediate object is, neither to feed the hungry nor to clothe the naked but, in every country under the benefit of their exertions, there will be less hunger to feed, and less nakedness to clothe. They do not cure actual poverty, but they anticipate eventual poverty. They aim their decisive thrust at the heart and principle of the mischief; and, instead of suffering it to form into the obstinacy of an inextirpable disease, they smother and destroy it in the infancy of its first elements. The love which worketh no ill to his neighbor, will not suffer the true Christian to live in idleness upon another's bounty; and he will do as Paul did before him; he will labor with his hands rather than be burdensome. Could we reform the improvident habits of the people, and pour the healthful infusion of Scripture principle into their hearts, it would reduce the existing poverty of the land to a very humble fraction of its present extent. We make bold to say, that, in ordinary times, there is not one-tenth of the pauperism of England due to unavoidable misfortune. It has grown out of a vicious and impolitic system; and the millions which are raised every year have only served to nourish and extend it. Now, Religious Education is a prime agent in the work of counteracting this disorder. Its mode of proceeding carries in it all the cheapness and all the superior efficacy of a preventive operation. With a revenue not equal to the poor rates of many a county, it is doing more even for the secular interests of the poor than all the charities of England united; and while a puling and injudicious sympathy is pouring out its complaints against the Societies which support this education, it is sowing the seeds of character and independence. and rearing, for future days, the spectacle of a thriving, substantial, and well-conditioned peasantry.

14. I have hitherto been supposing, that the rich only are the givers, but I now call on the poor to be sharers in this work of charity. It is true, that of these poor there are some who depend on charity for their subsistence, and these have no right to give what they receive from others. And there are some who have not arrived at this state of dependence, but are on the very verge of it. Let us keep back no part of the truth from them. "If any provide not for his own, and especially for those of his own house, he hath denied the faith, and is worse than an infidel." There are others, again, and these I apprehend form by far the most numerous class of society, who can maintain themselves in humble but honest independence, who can spare a little, and not feel it; who can do what Paul advises,* lay aside their penny a-

* 1 Corinthians xvi. 2.

week as God hath prospered them; who can share that blessedness which the Saviour spoke of when he said, It is more blessed to give than to receive; who though they cannot equal their richer neighbors in the amount of their donation, can bestow their something, and can, at all events, carry in their bosom a heart as warm to the cause, and call down as precious a blessing from the God who witnesses it. A Parochial Society is opposed, on the ground of its diverting a portion of relief from the secular necessities of the poor, even when the rich only are called upon to support it. When the application for support is brought down to the poor themselves, and, instead of the recipients, it is proposed to make them the dispensers of charity, we may lay our account with the opposition being still more clamorous. We undertake to prove, that this opposition is founded on a fallacy, and that, by interesting the great mass of a parish in the objects of religious benevolence, and assembling them into a penny association for their support, you raise a defence against the extension of pauperism.

15. We feel a difficulty in this undertaking, not from any uncertainty which hangs over the principle, but from the difficulty of bringing forward a plain and popular exhibition of it. However familiar the principle may be to a student of political science, it carries in it an air of paradox to the multitude, and it were well if this air of paradox were the only obstacle to its reception. But to the children of poesy and fine sentiment, the principle in question carries in it an air of barbarity also, and all the rigor of a pure and impregnable argument has not been able to protect the conclusions of Malthus from their clamorous indignation. There is a kind of hurrying sensibility about them, which allows neither time nor temper for listening to any calculation on the subject; and there is not a more striking vanity under the sun, than that the substantial interests of the poor have suffered less from the maglignant and the unfeeling, than from those who give without wisdom, and who feel without consideration:

Blessed is he that *wisely* doth
The poor man's case *consider*.

16. Let me put the case of two parishes, in the one of which there is a known and public endowment, out of which an annual sum is furnished for the maintenance of the poor; and that in the other there is no such endowment. At the outset, the poor of the first parish may be kept in greater comfort than the poor of the second; but it is the lesson of all experience, that no annual sum, however great, will be able to keep them permanently in greater comfort. The certain effect of an established provision for the poor is, a relaxation of their economical habits, and an increased number of improvident marriages. When their claim to a provision is known, that claim is always counted upon, and it were

well, if to flatter their natural indolence, they did not carry the calculation beyond the actual benefit they can ever receive. But this is what they always do. When a public charity is known and counted upon, the relaxation of frugal and providential habits is carried to such an extent, as not only to absorb the whole produce of the charity, but to leave new wants unprovided for, and the effect of the benevolent institution is just to create a population more wretched and more clamorous than ever.

17. In the second parish, the economical habits of the people are kept unimpared, and just because their economy is forced to take a higher aim, and to persevere in it. The aim of the first people is, to provide for themselves a part of their maintenance; the aim of the second people is to provide for themselves their whole maintenance. We do not deny that even among the latter we will meet with distress and poverty, just such distress and such poverty as are to be found in the average of Scottish parishes. This finds its alleviation in private benevolence. To alleviate poverty is all that can be done for it: to extinguish it we fear is hopeless. Sure we are, that the known and regular provisions of England will never extinguish it, and that, in respect of the poor themselves, the second parish is under a better system than the first. The poor rates are liable to many exceptions, but there is none of them more decisive with him who cares for the eternity of the poor, than the temptation they hold out to positive guilt, the guilt of not working with their own hands, and so becoming burdensome to others.*

18. Let us conceive a political change in the circumstances of the country, and that the public charity of the first parish fell among the ruin of other institutions. Then its malignant influence would be felt in all its extent; and it would be seen, that it, in fact, had impoverished those whom it professed to sustain, that it had stript them of a possession far more valuable than all it had ever given; that it had stript them of industrious habits, and left those whom its influence never reached wealthier in the resources of their own superior industry, than the artificial provisions of an unwise and meddling benevolence could ever make them.

19. The comparison betwixt these two parishes paves the way for another comparison. Let me now put the case of a third parish, where a Parochial Association is instituted, and where the simple regulation of a penny a-week throws it open to the bulk of the people. What effect has this upon their economical habits? It just throws them at a greater distance from the thriftlessness which prevails in the first parish, and leads them to strike a higher aim in the way of economy than the people of the second. The general aim of economy, in humble life, is to keep even with the world; but it is known to every man at all familiar with that class of society, that the great majority may strike their aim a little

* Acts xx. 35. 1 Timothy v. 8.

higher, and, in point of fact, have it in their power to redeem an annual sum from the mere squanderings of mismanagement and carelessness. The unwise provisions in the first parish, have had the effect of sinking the income of the poor below their habits of expenditure, and they are brought, permanently and irrecoverably brought, into a state of pauperism. In the second parish, the income, generally speaking, is even with the habits of expenditure. In the third the income is above the habits of expenditure, and above it by the annual sum contributed to the Parochial Society. The circumstance of being members to such a Society throws them at a greater distance from pauperism than if they had not been members of it.

20. The effect on the economical habits of the people would just be the same in whatever way the stated annual sum was obtained from them, even though a compulsory tax were the instrument of raising it.* This assimilation of our plan to a tax, may give rise to a world of impetuous declamation; but let it ever be remembered, that the institution of a Parochial Society gives you the whole benefit of such a tax, without its odiousness. It brings up their economy to a higher pitch; but it does so, not in the way which they resist, but in the way which they choose. The single circumstance of its being a *voluntary* act, forms the defence and the answer to all the clamors of an affected sympathy. You take from the poor. No! they give.—You take beyond their ability. Of this they are the best judges.—You abridge their comforts! No! there is a comfort in the exercise of charity: there is a comfort in the act of lending a hand to a noble enterprise; there is a comfort in the contemplation of its progress; there is a comfort in rendering a service to a friend, and when that friend is the Saviour, and that service the circulation of the message he left behind him, it is a comfort which many of the poor are ambitious to share in. Leave them to judge of their comfort; and if, in point of fact, they do give their penny a-week to a Parochial Society, it just speaks them to have more comfort in this way of spending it, than in any other which occurs to them.

21. Perhaps it does not occur to those friends of the poor, while they are sitting in judgment on their circumstances and feelings, how unjustly and how unworthily they think of them. They do not conceive how truth and benevolence can be at all objects to them; and suppose, that after they have got the meat to feed, the house to shelter, the raiment to cover them, there is nothing else that they will bestow a penny upon. They may not be able to express their feelings on a suspicion so ungenerous, but I shall do it for them: "We have souls as well as you, and precious to our hearts is the Saviour who died for them. It is true, we have our distresses; but these have bound us more firmly to our Bibles,

* I must here suppose the sum to be a stated one, and a feeling of security on the part of the people, that the tax shall not be subject to variation, at the caprice of an arbitrary government.

and it is the desire of our hearts, that a gift so precious should be sent to the poor of other countries. The word of God is our hope and our rejoicing; we desire that it may be theirs also, that the wandering savage may know it and be glad, and the poor negro, under the lash of his master, may be told of a Master in heaven, who is full of pity and full of kindness. Do you think that sympathy for such as these is your peculiar attribute? Know, that our hearts are made of the same materials with your own; that we can feel as well as you; and out of the earnings of a hard and an honest industry, we shall give an offering to the cause; nor shall we cease our exertions till the message of salvation be carried round the globe, and made known to the countless millions who live in guilt, and who die in darkness."

22. And here it is obvious, that a superior habit of economy is not the only defence which a Parochial Society raises against pauperism. The smallness of the sum contributed may give a littleness to this argument; but not, let it be remembered, without giving an equal littleness to the objection of those who declaim against the institution, on the ground of its oppressiveness to the poor contributors. The great defence which such a Society establishes against pauperism, is, the superior tone of dignity and independence which it imparts to the character of him who supports it. He stands on the high ground of being a dispenser of charity; and before he can submit to become a recipient of charity, he must let himself farther down than a poor man in ordinary circumstances. To him the transition will be more violent; and the value of this principle will be acknowledged by all who perceive that it is reluctance on the part of the poor man to become a pauper, which forms the mighty barrier against the extension of pauperism. A man, by becoming the member of a benevolent association, puts himself into the situation of a giver. He stands at a greater distance than before from the situation of a receiver. He has a wider interval to traverse before he can reach this point. He will feel it a greater degradation; and to save himself from it, he will put forth all his powers of frugality and exertion. The idea of restraining pauperism by external administrations seems now to be generally abandoned. But could we thus enter into the hearts of the poor, we would get in at the root of the mischief, and by fixing there a habit of economy and independence, more would be done for them, than by all the liberalities of all the opulent.

23. In those districts of Scotland where poor rates are unknown, the descending avenue which leads to pauperism is powerfully guarded by the stigma which attaches to it. Remove this stigma, and our cottagers, now rich in the possession of contentment and industry, would resign their habits, and crowd into the avenue by thousands. The shame of descending, is the powerful stimulus which urges them to a manful contest with the difficulties

of their situation, and which bears them through in all the pride of honest independence. Talk of this to the people of the South, and it sounds in their ears like an Arcadian story. But there is not a clergyman amongst us who has not witnessed the operation of the principle in all its fineness, and in all its moral delicacy; and surely a testimony is due to those village heroes who so nobly struggle with the difficulties of pauperism, that they may shun and surmount its degradation.

24. A Parochial Association gives additional vigor and buoyancy to this elevated principle. The trifle which it exacts from its contributor is, in truth, never missed by him; but it puts him in the high attitude of a giver, and every feeling which it inspires is on the side of independence and delicacy. Go over each of these feelings separately, and you find that they are all fitted to fortify his dislike at the shame and dependence of pauperism. There is a consciousness of importance which unavoidably attaches to the share he has taken in the support and direction of a public charity. There is the expanding effect of the information which comes to him through the medium of the circulated Reports, which lays before him the mighty progress of an institution reaching to all countries, and embracing in its ample grasp, the men of all latitudes and all languages, which deeply interests him in the object, and perpetuates his desire of promoting it. A man with his heart so occupied, and his attention so directed, is not capable of a voluntary descent to pauperism. He has, in fact, become a more cultivated and intellectual being than formerly. His mind gathers an enlargement from the wide and animating contemplations which are set before him; and we appeal to the reflection of every reader, if such a man will descend as readily to a dependence on the charity of others, as he whose mind is void of information, and whose feelings are void of dignity.

25. In such associations, the rich and the poor meet together. They share in one object, and are united by the sympathy of one feeling, and of one interest. We have not to look far into human nature to be convinced of the happy and the harmonizing influence which this must have upon society; and how, in the glow of one common cordiality, all asperity and discontent must give way to the kindlier principles of our nature. The days have been, when the very name of an association carried terror and suspicion along with it. In a Parochial Association for religious objects there is nothing which our rulers need to be afraid of; and they may rest assured, that the moral influence of such institutions is all on the side of peace and loyalty. But to confine myself to the present argument. Who does not see that they exalt the general tone and character of our people; that they bring them nearer to the dignity of superior and cultivated life; and that, therefore, though their direct aim is not to mitigate poverty, they go a certain way to dry up the most abundant of its sources?

26. Let me add, that the direct influence of Bible principles is inseparable from a zeal for the circulation of the Bible. It is not to be conceived, that anxiety for sending it to others can exist, while there is no reverence for it among ourselves; and we appeal to those districts where such associations have been formed, if a more visible attention to the Bible, and a more serious impression of its authority, is not the consequence of them. Now the lessons of this Bible are all on the side of industry. They tell us, that it is more blessed to give than to receive, and that, therefore, a man who, by his own voluntary idleness, is brought under the necessity of receiving, has disinherited himself of a blessing. The poor must have bread, but the Bible commands and exhorts, that wherever it is possible, that bread should be *their own*, and that all who are able should make it their own by working for it.* No precept can be devised which bears more directly on the source of pauperism. The minister who, in his faithful exposition of the Bible, urged this precept successfully upon his people, would do much to extinguish pauperism amongst them. It is true, that he does not always urge successfully; but surely if success is to be more looked for in one quarter than in another, it is among the pious and intelligent peasantry whom he has assembled around him, whom he has formed into a little society for the circulation of the Bible, and whose feelings he has interested in this purest and worthiest of causes.

27. Nor is the operation of this principle confined to the actual contributor. We have no doubt that it has been beautifully exemplified, even among those, who, unable to give their penny a week, either stand on the very verge of pauperism, or have got within its limits. They are unable to give anything of their own, but they may be able at the same time to forego the wonted allowance which they received from another, or a part of it. The refusals of the poor to take an offered charity, or to take the whole amount of the offer, are quite familiar to a Scottish clergyman; and the plea on which they set the refusal, that it would be taking from others who are even needier than they, entitles them, when honestly advanced, to all the praise of benevolence. A spirit of pious attachment to the Bible would prompt a refusal of the same kind. "You have other and higher claims upon you—you have the spiritual necessities of the world to provide for, and, that you may be the more able to make the provision, leave me to the frugality of my own management.' In this way the principle descends, and carries its healthful influence into the very regions of pauperism. It is the only principle competent to its extirpation. The obvious expedient of a positive supply, to meet the wants of existing poverty, has failed, and the poor rates of England will ever be a standing testimony to the utter inefficiency of this expedient, which, instead of killing the disease, has rooted and con-

* 2 Thes. iii. 12.

firmed it. Try the other expedient, then. The remedy against the extension of pauperism does not lie in the liberalities of the rich. It lies in the hearts and habits of the poor. Plant in their bosoms a principle of independence. Give a higher tone of delicacy to their characters. Teach them to recoil from pauperism as a degradation. The degradation may at times be unavoidable; but the thing which gives such alarming extent to the mischief, is the debasing influence of the poor rates, whereby, in the vast majority of instances, the degradation is voluntary. But if there be an exalting influence in Parochial Associations to counteract this; if they foster a right spirit of importance; above all, if they secure a readier submission to the lessons of the volume which they are designed to circulate, who does not see, that in proportion as they are multiplied and extended over the face of the country, they carry along with them the most effectual regimen for preventing the extension of poverty?

28. And here it may be asked, if it be at all likely that these Associations will extend to such a degree, as to have a sensible influence upon the habits of the country? Nothing more likely. A single individual of influence in each parish, would make the system universal. In point of fact, it is making progress every month; and such is the wonderful spirit of exertion which is now abroad, that in a few years every little district of the land may become the seat of a Parochial Society. We are now upon the dawn of very high anticipations; and the wholesome effect upon the habits and principles of the people at home is not the least of them. That part of the controversy which relates to the direct merits of the objects of our Parochial Associations, may be looked upon as already exhausted; and could the objection, founded on their interference with the relief of the poor, be annihilated, or still more, could it be converted into a positive argument in their behalf, we are not aware of a single remaining plea, upon which a rational or benevolent man can refuse his concurrence to them.

29. And the plea of conceived injury to the poor deserves to be attended to. It wears an amiable complexion, and we believe, that, in some instances, a real sympathy with their distresses lies at the bottom of it. Let sympathy be guided by consideration. It is the part of a Christian to hail benevolence in all its forms; but when a plan is started for the relief of the destitute, is he to be the victim of a popular and sentimental indignation, because he ventures to take up the question whether the plan be really an effective one? We know that in various towns of Scotland, you meet with two distinct Penny Societies, one an Association for religious objects, the other for the relief of the indigent. It is to be regretted, that there should ever be any jealousy betwixt them; but we believe that, agreeably to what we have already said, it will often be found that the one suggested the other, and that the supporters of the former, are the most zealous, and active, and useful friends of the latter. We cannot however suppress the

fact, that there is now a growing apprehension lest the growth of the latter Societies should break down the delicacies of the lower orders, and pave the way for a permanent introduction of poor rates. There is a pretty general impression, that the system may be carried too far; and the uncertainty as to the precise limit, has given the feeling to many, who embarked with enthusiasm, that they are now engaged in a ticklish and questionable undertaking. I do not attempt either to confirm or to refute this impression, but I account it a piece of justice to the associations I am pleading for, to assert, that they stand completely free of every such exception. Our associations are making steady advances towards the attainment of their object, and the sure effect of multiplying the subscribers, is to conduct them in a shorter time to the end of their labors. A Society for the relief of temporal necessities, is grasping at an object that is completely unattainable; and the mischief is, that the more known, and the more extensive, and the more able it becomes, it is sure to be more counted on, and at last to create more poverty than it provides for. A Bible Society, for example, aims at making every land a land of Bibles; and this aim it will accomplish after it has translated the Bible into all languages, and distributed a sample large enough to create a native and a universal demand for them.* After the people of the world have acquired such a taste for the Bible, and such a sense of its value, as to purchase it for themselves, the Society terminates its career; and, instead of the corruptions and abuses which other charities scatter in their way, it leaves the poor to whom it gives, more enlightened, and the poor from whom it takes, more elevated than it found them.

30. "Charity," says Shakspeare, "is twice blest. It blesses him who gives, and him who takes." This is far from being universally true. There is a blessing annexed to the heart which deviseth liberal things. Perhaps the founder of the English poor rates acquired this blessing; but the indolence and depravity which they have been the instrument of spreading over the face of the country, are incalculable. If we wish to see the assertion of the Poet realized in its full extent, go to such a charity as we are now pleading for, where the very exercise of giving on the one hand, and the instruction received on the other, have the effect of narrowing the limits of pauperism, by creating a more virtuous and dignified population.

31. There is poverty to be met with in every land, and we are ready to admit, that a certain proportion of it is due to unavoidable misfortune. But it is no less true, that in those countries where there is a known and established provision for the necessities of the poor, the greater proportion of the poverty which

* But this native demand never will be created without the exertion of missionaries; and the above reasoning applies, in its most important parts, to Missionary Associations. See *Appendix*.

exists in them is due to the debasing influence of a public charity on the habits of the people. The institution we are pleading for counteracts this influence. It does not annihilate all poverty, but it tends to annihilate the greater part of it. It arrests the progress of the many who were making a voluntary descent to pauperism, and it leaves none to be provided for but the few who have honestly struggled against their distresses, and have struggled in vain.

32. And how shall they be provided for? You may erect a public institution. This, in fact, is the same with erecting a signal of invitation, and the voluntary and self-created poor will rush in, to the exclusion of those modest and unobtrusive poor who are the genuine objects of charity. This is the never-failing mischief of a known and established provision,* and it has been sadly exemplified in England. The only method of doing away the mischief is to confide the relief of the poor to individual benevolence. This draws no dependence along with it. It is not counted upon like a public and proclaimed charity. It brings the claims of the poor under the discriminating eye of a neighbor, who will make a difference betwixt a case of genuine helplessness, and a case of idleness or misconduct. It turns the tide of benevolence into its true channel; and it will ever be found, that under its operation, the poverty of misfortune is better seen to, and the poverty of improvidence and guilt is more effectually prevented.

33. My concluding observation then is, that the extension of Parochial Societies, while it counteracts in various directions the mischief of the poor rates, augments that principle of individual benevolence, which is the best substitute for poor rates. You add to the stock of individual benevolence, by adding to the number of benevolent individuals; and this is the genuine effect of a Parochial Association. Or, you add to the stock of individual benevolence in a country, by adding to the intensity of the benevolent principle; and this is the undoubted tendency of a Parochial Association.† And, what is of mighty importance in this argument, a Parochial Association for these higher objects not only awakens the benevolent principle, but it enlightens it. It establishes an intercourse betwixt the various orders of society; and, on no former occasion in the history of this country, have the rich and the poor come so often together upon a footing of good will. The kindly influence of this is incalculable. It brings the poor under the eye of their richer neighbors. The visits and inquiries connected with the objects of our Parochial Societies, bring them into contact with one another. The rich come to be more skilled in the wants and difficulties of the poor; and, by entering their

* We must here except all those institutions, the object of which is to provide for involuntary distress, such as hospitals and dispensaries, and asylums for the lunatic or the blind. A man may resign himself to idleness, and become wilfully poor, that he may eat of the public bread; but he will not become wilfully sick or maimed, that he may receive medicines from a dispensary, or undergo an operation in a hospital.

† See 9.

houses, and joining with them in conversation, they not only acquire a benevolence towards them, but they gather that knowledge which is so essential to guide and enlighten their benevolence.*

* There never perhaps was so minute and statistical a survey of the poor families in London, as by the friends and agents of the Bible Society. That this survey has given rise to many deeds of secular benevolence, I do not know from any positive information; but I assert it upon the confidence I repose in the above principles, and am willing to risk upon this assertion the credit of the whole argument.

APPENDIX.

It is evident, that the above reasoning applies, in its chief parts, to benevolent Associations instituted for any other religious purpose. It is not necessary for example to restrict the argument to the case of Bible Associations. I should be sorry if the Bible Society were to engross the religious benevolence of the public, and if, in the multiplication of its auxiliaries over the face of the country, it were to occupy the whole ground, and leave no room for the great and important claims of other institutions.

Of this I conceive that there is little danger. The revenue of each of these Societies is founded upon voluntary contributions, and what is voluntary may be withdrawn or transferred to other objects. I may give both to a Bible and a Missionary Society: or, if I can only afford to give to one, I may select either, according to my impression of their respective claims. In this way a vigilant and discerning public will suit its benevolence to the urgency of the case, and it is evident that each institution can employ the same methods for obtaining patronage and support. Each can, and does bring forward a yearly statement of its claims and necessities. Each has the same access to the public, through the medium of the pulpit or the press. Each can send its advocates over the face of the country; and every individual, forming his own estimate of their respective claims, will apportion his benevolence accordingly.

Now what is done by an individual, may be done by every such Association as I am now pleading for. Its members may sit in judgment on the various schemes of utility which are now in operation; and, though originally formed as an auxiliary to the Bible Society, it may keep itself open to other calls, and occasionally give of its funds to Missionaries, or Moravians, or the Society for Gaelic Schools, or the African Institution, or to the Jewish, and Baptist, and Hibernian, and Lancasterian Societies.

In point of fact, the subordinate Associations of the country are tending towards this arrangement, and it is a highly beneficial arrangement. It carries in it a most salutary control over all these various institutions, each laboring to maintain itself in reputation with the public, and to secure the countenance of this great patron. Indolence and corruption may lay hold of an endowed charity, but when the charity depends upon public favor, a few glaring examples of mismanagement would annihilate it.

During a few of the first years of the Bible Society, the members of other Societies were alarmed at the rapid extension of its popularity, and expressed their fears lest it should engross all the attention and benevolence of the religious public. But the reverse has happened, and a principle made use of in the body of this pamphlet may be well illustrated by the history of this matter.* The Bible Society has drawn a great yearly sum of money from the public; and the first impression was that it would exhaust the fund for religious charities. But while it drew money from the hand, it sent a fresh and powerful excitement of Christian benevolence into the heart; and, under the

* See 9.

influence of this creative principle, the fund has extended to such a degree, as not only to meet the demands of the new Society, but to yield a more abundant revenue to the older Societies than ever. We believe, that the excitement goes much further than this, and that many a deed of ordinary charity could be traced to the impulse of the cause we are pleading for. We hazard the assertion, that many thousands of those who contribute to the Bible Society, find in themselves a greater readiness to every good work,* since the period of their connection with it, and that in the wholesome channel of individual benevolence, more hunger is fed, and more nakedness clothed, throughout the land than at any period anterior to the formation of our Religious Societies.

The alarm, grounded upon the tendency of these Societies, with their vast revenues, to impoverish the country, is ridiculous. If ever their total revenue shall amount to a sum which can make it worthy of consideration to an enlightened economist at all, it may be proved that it trenches upon no national interest whatever; that it leaves population and Public Revenue on precisely the same footing of extent and prosperity in which it found them; and that it interferes with no one object which Patriot or Politician needs to care for. In the meantime it may suffice to state, that the Income of all the Bible and Missionary Societies in the Island, would not do more than defray the annual maintenance of one Ship of the Line.† When put by the side of the millions which are lavished without a sigh, on the enterprises of war, it is nothing; and shall this veriest trifle be grudged to the advancement of a cause, which, when carried to its accomplishment, will put an end to war, and banish all its passions and atrocities from the world?

I should be sorry if Penny Associations were to bind themselves down to the support of the Bible Society. I should like to see them exercising a judgment over the numerous claims which are now before the public, and giving occasionally of their funds to other religious institutions. The effect of this very exercise would be to create a liberal and well-informed peasantry; to open a wider sphere to their contemplations; and to raise the standard, not merely of piety, but of general intelligence amongst them. The diminution of pauperism is only part of the general effect which the multiplication of these Societies will bring about in the country; and if my limits allowed me I might expatiate on their certain influence in raising the tone and character of the British Population.‡

* Titus iii. 1.

† This calculation applies to the year 1814.

‡ It is thought by some that the assumption of the title "Bible Association," carries in it an obligation to devote all the funds to the Bible Society. The title may easily be modified so as to leave the most entire liberty to every Association to give of its funds to any Religious Society whatever.

ON THE CONSISTENCY

OF THE

LEGAL AND VOLUNTARY PRINCIPLES,

AND THE

JOINT SUPPORT WHICH THEY MIGHT RENDER

TO THE CAUSE BOTH OF

CHRISTIAN AND COMMON EDUCATION.

THERE is nothing more palpable on the face of Jewish history, than the connection which obtains between the personal character of the monarch and the general prosperity of the kingdom. And it is alike obvious, that the one stood related to the other in the way of cause and consequence, from the interest which the religion that sways the heart of the king led him to take in the religion of his people. It was at the direct charge or bidding of Jehoshaphat, and in his direct employment, that the Levites taught in Judea and had the book of the law of the Lord with them, and went about throughout all the cities of Judea and taught the people. And so also Hezekiah, as is said, "spake comfortably to all the Levites that taught the good knowledge of the Lord." And so also Nehemiah, who, if not the king, was at least the supreme magistrate, the representative and depositary of the civil power, gave the direct sanction of his authority to the Levites, when they taught the people, and read in the book, in the law of God distinctly, and gave the sense, and caused them to understand the reading.—All marking, that, in these days, it was held a duty and a propriety in the rulers of the state, to concern themselves with the religious knowledge of the people—to provide for which, they maintained and employed teachers, whose business it was to go over the land, and to serve and supply every city with instruction in the law of God—thus fulfilling the object of an ordination, given by Moses at the outset of the Jewish polity, when he bade "gather the people together, men and women and *children*, and the stranger that is within thy gates, that they may hear, and that they may learn, and fear the Lord your God, and observe to do all the words of this law, and that their children which had not known anything may hear and learn to fear the Lord your God."

But while such was esteemed the befitting duty of Government in these days, there were other parties who shared the duty and the obligation along with them. In particular, there seems to have been felt by all right-minded parents, a peculiar and solemn responsibility for the religious knowledge of their children. This, if we may judge from various passages, both in their books of history and books of devotion, must have been a great characteristic and national virtue among the children of Israel. We meet with it so early as in the person of Abraham, the great progenitor of the Hebrew people, of whom we read this illustrious testimony from the mouth of God Himself—"For I know him, that he will command his children and his household after him; and they shall keep the way of the Lord to do justice and judgment." We read of it in the covenant, which Joshua made with the people, when he bade them choose the part they would take—telling them that "for me and for my house we will serve the Lord;" and the people with one consent made promise, that this should be the habit and the observance of all their families. We would even infer it, from the awful tragedy which befell the house of Eli, in whose signal punishment for the neglect of family discipline, the people of the land would behold an impressive manifestation of the divine will, on the side of the religion of families. But, without resting on individual examples, we know that the task and the obligation of parents religiously to educate their children, held a conspicuous and a foremost place in the code of Jewish morality. The facts and the doctrines of their religion, were things which they heard and knew; and therefore, to make use of the language of the Psalmist, they did "not hide them from their children, showing to the generation to come the praises of the Lord, and His strength and His wonderful works that He hath done. For He established a testimony in Jacob, and appointed a law in Israel, which He commanded our fathers that they should make them known to their children, that the generation to come might know them—even the children which should be born, and should arise and declare them to their children, that they might set their hope in God, and not forget the works of God; but keep his commandments."

Here then we have the example of a great duty, and that for the fulfilment of a great object, even the maintenance and preservation of religion in the land—this duty we say not monopolized or exclusively engrossed by one party, but shared between two—It being held, in these Old Testament times, to be the rightful care of the king upon his throne, to look after and provide what in him lay for the religion of his subjects; and the no less rightful care of the parents of families, to provide what in them lay for the religion of their children. We are here presented with the example of two powers or two influences, blended together in friendly co-operation, for the accomplishment of one and the same design. There was no conflict, no contrariety between them. The one party did not fear to do too much, lest it should be left to the other party to do too little. Such a jealousy, we believe, was never once heard of in these days. On the one hand, it would have been held quite monstrous in the king to say, that the morality and religion of the young is not my affair, but that of their own parents; and I will therefore care for none of these things. And, on the other hand, it would have been held still more monstrous and unnatural for parents to say, that the education of our children is the duty of our rulers; and we shall take no part of a burden, which legitimately lies upon them. Such a contest as this, if it could be imagined, wherein each of the two parties strives, for its own exoneration, to cast as much of the weight as possible upon the other, were not the way of bringing about the result of a well-trained or well-taught boyhood in any land; but between them, we should behold the melancholy spectacle of a depraved and degenerate society. The utmost effort and vigilance of both will fall greatly short of perfection; and the neglect of either were of deadly and withering influence on the virtue of any commonwealth. With an irreligious population, even under a religious government, we should have many an exhibition of reckless defiance, both to the divine law and to human authority—as when good king Hezekiah sent his posts from city to city, through the country of Ephraim, and Manasseh, even to Zebulon, to invite the people to return to the Lord from whom they had revolted, and to keep his passover; and they laughed them to scorn, and they mocked them. And, on the other hand, with an irreligious government, though with the benefit at first of an orderly and religious population, we should witness the rapid declension and disappearance of all sound principle in the land as in the days of the idolatrous Ahab, when a hidden and unseen remnant of true worshippers, was all that continued steadfast with God among the many thousands of Israel. It is miserable work, this shifting of the responsibility backward and forward from one party to another. Both parties in this cause are responsible—parents to do all they can for the right and religious schooling of their children; and government to provide, in right institutions, all helps and facilities for the same object. And it is only when a common spirit actuates them both—when the influence of the Christian parent in his household, is backed by the paternal influence of a Christian government in the state, that the sacred cause of good education will prosper in any land: or that, as if by the circulation of a healthful life's blood from the heart to the extremities of the body politic, a people, now in the rude infancy both of character and civilization, will be matured into a nation of well-principled and well-conditioned families.

The records of the children of Israel, tell us what religious kings did for their people, and religious parents did for their children; but they tell us nothing of what religious philanthropists did for the cause of education in their respective neighborhoods. Confident we are, that if any such sprung up at that period, their number and their exertions, instead of deadening the zeal of any right-minded government in the same noble enterprise; would but stimulate their energies the more, by the ascent of a virtuous influence from the people to the throne. And, on the other hand, the munificence of the government would lay no check or discouragement on the liberality of private individuals. It is not conceivable, that the manifestation of such a spirit in the high places of the land, would cause that, throughout the community at large, the love of men for their fellows and acquaintances around them should therefore wax cold. The effect would be precisely opposite to this. The patriotism of statesmen, and the philanthropy of private citizens, would act and react with powerful and most salutary operation on each other. Both would flow in the same current; and their union is fitted to enrich a land with those institutes for the promotion of knowledge and virtue, which, when rightly conducted and rightly patronized, constitute the real wealth and well-being of a nation.

But though we know little respecting such a union of efforts and contributions between the prince and the people, during the subsistence of the Jewish monarchy, to promote schooling for behoof of the young—we know a great deal, for we read often in the Bible, of a union between these two parties, to uphold the services of religion for behoof of the community at large. There was, in the first instance, a legal provision for the maintenance of ecclesiastical men, which it would have been not only spoliation but sacrilege for the state to have invaded. But in the second instance, this did not supersede the free-will offerings of the pious and the well-disposed—both for an additional maintenance to the priest, and more particularly for the erection of ecclesiastical fabrics. The truth is, that, in the history of the Jews, notwithstanding the more express and explicit sanction of the divine authority for their Church establishment than for that of any of the nations in Christendom, yet, so far from the legal support of religion superseding the voluntary, the voluntary went before the legal. And accordingly, when they abode in the wilderness, we find that the costly tabernacle was reared, not by a tax but by a subscription from the produce, not of a compulsory assessment, but of spontaneous contributions from the generous and the willing-hearted of the children of Israel. And this way of it was distinctly authorized by God himself; for He commanded, not that the people should give—He did not thus overbear their inclinations; but He commanded Moses to take of every man that gave willingly with his heart, and Moses madé proclamation, that whosoever was of a willing heart should bring him an offering to the Lord; and such were the power and productiveness of this method, that the people, not only brought what was sufficient, but too much, so that they had to be restrained from bringing any more. Thus did the voluntary method precede the legal; and even after this method was established, it did not supersede the voluntary. For we afterwards find, that, as it was resorted to in the erection of the tabernacle, so it was resorted to in the erection of the temple—for the raising of which there was a composition of the legal and the voluntary. David gave of his treasure, and the people gave of theirs; and, under the impulse of a common enthusiasm, all jealousy between these two parties was given to the winds—for we read that the people rejoiced, for that they offered willingly, because with perfect heart they offered willingly to the Lord; and David the king also rejoiced with great joy. It is interesting to remark, how, in these days, instead of an arena of conflict, on which the two principles of the legal and the voluntary were placed in hostile array, as if the triumph of the one should lead to the extermination of the other—both subsisted, nay flourished contemporaneously, not as warring elements, but in friendly and most effective coadjutorship; when the free-will offerings of the people were superadded to the levies of Solomon, and the magnificent temple of Jerusalem was the result of this happy and harmonious combination. Nor does this twofold method of supporting the worship of the Lord, seem to have been lost sight of, even to the latest ages of the Jewish dispensation—as in the days of King Joash, when the temple needed repair, he quoted the example of Moses for a collection; and accordingly a chest with a hole bored in the middle of it, was made by his orders, and set out at the gate of the temple; and this authoritative commandment of the king, met with the willing cordiality of his subjects—for we read, that all the princes and all the people rejoiced, and brought and cast in until they had made an end, and thus they gathered money in abundance. And in the days of Hezekiah, when there was another revival from idolatry, we are informed of the people bringing in their tithes, their legally ordained tithes; but, along with these, that they also brought in their free-will offerings. And in the reign of Josiah, another bright and sunny period of the Jewish history, we are again told of a collection at the door of the temple, for the reparation of its fabric; but over and above this, of money gathered over the land, by men who went forth in deputations among the people of Manasseh and Ephraim, and of all the remnant of Israel, and of all Judah and Benjamin, and returned with their contributions to Jerusalem. Further onward, at the rebuilding of the temple, do we meet with the same composition of the legal and the voluntary; and with this remarkable peculiarity, that a heathen prince gave his authority to the one, while a believing people gave out of their abundance to the other—he commanding his own subjects to help the enterprise, with their silver and their gold and their goods and their beasts; they coming forth of their own accord, with their free-will offerings—he ordering a grant for the edifice, for we expressly read of money being expended on it "according to the grant which they had of Cyrus king of Persia;" and agreeably to the terms of the decree, that the expenses be given out of the king's house. Yet this did not supersede the "free-will offering of the people, and of the priests' offering willingly, for the house of their God which is in Jerusalem"—neither in the days of Cyrus, nor after him in the days of Artaxerxes, who decreed, that whatever more should be needful for the house of God, should be bestowed out of the king's treasure-house, and gave orders to his treasurers accordingly. In these days there was a perfect coalescence of those two elements, between which now we read of nothing but fiercest controversy. To the public treasures of the prince, and the legal tithes of the people, there were added the spontaneous offerings of both; and even in the days of the New Testament, while there still subsisted a priesthood, and that legal economy yet unrepealed by which their maintenance was secured to them—we can trace nevertheless the hand of private liberality, in furtherance and support of the same cause; as in the case of the Roman centurion, honored by the people of Judea among whom he was stationed, as a good man, because, in the language of their own approving testimony, he loved their nation and had built them a synagogue.

Even from this brief and rapid induction which we have now offered, it is impossible not to conclude, that, in the times of the older dispensation, the public and the private, the legal and the voluntary, coalesced in the support and service of religion; and that for the promotion of this glorious object, they worked as it were into each other's hands. If there was any contest between them, it was not, at least in the best days of the Jewish commonwealth, it was not which should contribute the least, but which should contribute the most to the maintenance of the worship of the God of Israel. In the full tide of a common and a rejoicing sympathy between the king and his people, they provoked each other to love and to good works; and, whatever rivalry was felt on either side, it was founded on a noble and generous emulation, that led each party to render the greatest possible offering to the cause of piety and the public weal. And if ever there was an approximation to the joy of heaven upon earth, it was at one of those great convocations, which took place under the good kings of the children of Israel—a moral festival, when the whole nation held jubilee; and the heart of the king upon his throne, beat in unison with the hosannahs of the multitude. The spirit which reigned over such an assemblage as this, is as unlike as possible, is removed by tne whole distance of the antipodes, from that spirit, cold and withering and heartless, which animates the paltry economics of the present day. The king, on the one hand, did not abandon the support of religion to the voluntary principle, or say that it was for the people alone to bear the expenses of their own ministrations: Neither did the people leave altogether this highest interest of themselves and their families to the legal principle; or say that it was for the state alone, to do all and provide all for the religion of the land. The two principles moved in harmony together; and we leave yourselves to judge, whether in their generous concurrence, or in their fretful and fiery opposition, we behold the best and happiest state of the commonwealth.

Now all this, instead of being a narrative of useless and exploded antiquarianism, admits of a close and practical application to the present times; and more especially to the present juncture in the state and history of our own nation. A lesson might be read out of it to each of the two parties, whose proceedings we have just been describing to you—that is, to the Government on the one hand, and to the people on the other. When the rare opportunity occurs of addressing the first, as, for example, in a public sermon to the two houses of Parliament, a considerable stress, when advocating a legal provision for the services of religion in a land, should be laid on the Jewish analogy—for, though not so absolutely conclusive as if a specific and express precept could be appealed to, requiring the same aid and countenance from the civil governor in the economy under which we now live, as was then rendered under an economy that is dissolved and passed away—it should ever be recollected, not only, that, having in one notable instance in past history, even that history of which the apostle tells us that it has been preserved and transmitted downward for our admonition on whom the latter ends of the world have come—not only, in that great and memorable instance, have we the distinct and declared sanction of the divine authority for the maintenance of the church by the state; and which therefore, as being in that instance an express appointment of God, can have nothing in its own nature that is morally or absolutely wrong —But we should further recollect, that what was thus commanded to Jewish kings in many passages of the Old Testament, has never been forbidden to Christian kings in a single passage of the New Testament; and therefore that there is nothing in Scripture to countervail, but rather everything to confirm that argument, by which the lawfulness, or rather the positive and bounden duty of every Government to provide for the religious education of the people, has, on every principle, as we think, of piety and sound patriotism, been made the subject of a resistless demonstration. But on this we expatiate no farther at present, for it is with the other party, with a certain portion of the people that we are now holding converse; and the more proper theme therefore of our present occasion, is the second lesson—the duty which lies, not merely on rulers, but on private citizens, to provide for the education of the community both in the things of sacredness and the things of ordinary scholarship.

The first consideration then which we offer is, that, if, even under the Jewish economy, it was the part and duty of the people to help onward from their own liberality the maintenance of religion in the land—there lies a still more distinct and palpable obligation on private individuals, under the economy of the present day. For recollect, there could be no mistake, as there rested no obscurity, on the duty of kings, or the duty of the Government in Judea, to provide for the same object—for these, of all others, were the times of the most palpable and declared connection between the church and the state, when the support of ecclesiastical institutions and ecclesiastical men, was interwoven with the whole jurisprudence and polity of the Israelitish nation. And yet, even during the subsistence of that theocracy, when God laid his immediate command on the rulers of the Hebrews, to look after and provide for the religion of the people; and not one step of reasoning was necessary, to make out the connection between this being the duty of the king and the promulgated will of Him who is the King of kings—yet, even then, when so express and intelligible an obligation lay upon the one party, that is on the monarch—this did not exonerate the other party, that is the people, or discharge them from all part or fellowship in the exercise of the same duty. In that land, where, of all the countries of the earth, there was the greatest amount of tithes—there also was there the greatest amount of free-will offerings; and, along with the immense property and firmly constituted rights of an established priesthood, there flourished at the same time, in the utmost exuberance and vigor the generosity of a willing people. The one party did not fear to give largely, lest the other party should give less. The people did not, on the maxim that it was the duty of the Government to support religion, decline, on that account, the farther support and extension of it themselves. It was at the best and brightest periods in the history of the nation, that both parties gave with the most unsparing hand; and if ever there was a time when the heart and the treasure-house of the king were most open to the necessities of religion—then also was the time when the hearts of the people, as if touched by responsive sympathy, were most alive to the same cause; and the fullest and freest contributions were made by the citizens, for perfecting the services, or repairing the wastes and the breaches, that had taken place in the worship of the God of Israel.

We have no doubt of its being the wisdom and the duty of a Christian, as well as of a Jewish monarch, to furnish all necessary expenses, for the instruction of his people in the knowledge of the true religion; and for the maintenance of the true worship of God in his dominions. But it must at the same time be admitted, that the obligation of the one is not so pointedly or so unequivocally told him in the Bible, as the obligation of the other is. A king of the Jewish nation, could not possibly shut his eyes against the express requisition laid upon him in Scripture, to provide for the services of the sanctuary; or, if this failed, he could not shut his ears against the rebuke of those living prophets, who were sent from time to time to denounce the wrath of heaven, against the neglect and abandonment of heaven's own ordinances. We believe the obligation of the king in a Christian nation, to be no less real; but then it is not so palpable. He is more left to find it out by a train of inference, which, though grounded on the truths and principles of revelation, often does not tell so powerfully on the consciences—as when the lesson is visibly given forth, and presented as it were to the intuition of the mind in the immediate characters and very words of revelation. A king in Christendom therefore, might more readily escape from the sense and conviction of his duty, than a king in Judea could; and we ask if this do not lay a greater responsibility on the people of Christendom—because it may often leave them more to do for the maintenance of religion in their respective lands, than fell to the share of the people in Judea. Nothing can be imagined more direct or peremptory, than that voice from the God of heaven, which devolved on every Jewish king the maintenance of the established religion, within the limits of his monarchy; and yet the Jewish people did not, on that account, hold themselves absolved from all participation in the good work—and so they lent a helping hand, and added their free-will offerings, both to the legal endowments that had been fixed at the original institution of their church, and to the grants that from time to time were issued by royal command from the public treasury. Now, if, in these days of perfect certainty about the duty of their kings, nevertheless the Jewish people over and above came forward and did so much—in our days of controversy and denial about the duty of our kings, and when it is contended by many that the Scripture giveth forth an uncertain or even an adverse sound upon the matter, are we the Christian people to stand by and to do nothing? In the Old Testament period, both parties joined their efforts and their sacrifices; and all proved little enough for the maintenance of the temple, and synagogues of the land. If in the New Testament period, the one party, or the Government, are beginning to sit loose to their duty, or even threatening to cast it off altogether—whether is that a reason for us the other party, sitting loose to our duty also, or binding it all the more firmly on our conscience and observation than heretofore? Should we imitate their example; or were it not all the more incumbent on us, that we should flee to the rescue of the church, when hostility lowered upon us from high places, and rumor was afloat that old friends were forsaking us, and the main earthly pillar of the edifice was on the eve of giving way? Is this of all others, we ask, the reason for adding one desertion or one act of abandonment to another; and what shall we think of those, who, when asked to do something either for schools or churches, plead absolved, on the aphorism of which they tell us in didactic phrase and with the cold metaphysical face of a jurist on the question, that it is the part of the Government to do all—and, on the pretext of shifting the duty to its proper quarter, always contrive to shift the burden of it away from themselves.

Be assured that the true principle, is for each party, as they have opportunity, to do all they can for the glory of God, and the good of their fellow-men. Though all others should do their part to the full, there is still a part left for each to do—as when the kings of Israel did most for the church, still there was ample room for the children of Israel to manifest their liberality in behalf of the same cause. And if we live in times when kings and governments are inclined to do little, this just leaves us all the more room, and lays upon us a greater weight of obligation, to support and extend as we may the Christianity of the world. And instead of looking only to the principle, let us look also to the effect, of such a true right and Christian policy on our parts; and we shall find it far the likeliest and most effectual method of recalling to their duty, those who for a time may seem to have abandoned it. In proof of this, we bid you look to the first ages of Christianity, when the kings of the earth were persecutors; and disciples had to fight the battles of the faith, not only unsupported and alone, but were resisted even to the blood—their goods spoiled, and their persons given up to martyrdom. Innumerable were the calls made in these days on the liberality of Christians, for the erection of churches, for the entertainment of ministers, and for the expense of those missionary journeys by which they leavened all the cities—though they did not, and indeed could not, not even after the zeal and enterprise of three centuries, fill up all the provinces of the Roman empire, with the lessons of the Gospel—which, in the retirements and fastnesses of the country, still remained, down to the reign of Constantine, in a state of Paganism. And how were these calls met? Were they resisted by the disciples on the ground that the maintenance of the Gospel, within the territory of the monarch under whom they lived, formed no part of their concern? Were they for shifting off the obligation from themselves, and laying it upon others? Least of all, were they for waiting till the eyes of a blind and hostile government should be opened, and those rulers who now plundered and persecuted the churches should see it their duty to uphold them? They did not leave undone the work of expounding the duty of governors. They reasoned, and they remonstrated, and they made every attempt to enlighten the great potentates of the earth on the merits and claims of the Gospel of Jesus Christ—as may be seen in the noble apologies which have come down to our times, addressed by the venerable fathers of the Christian Church to the emperors of Rome. But they did not stop here; nor were they satisfied with simply telling the duty of our civil and earthly superiors. That duty, while neglected by others, they took upon themselves; and out of their own property, as far as it survived the confiscations that had been made of it by the hand of power, did they plant churches, and maintain clergymen, and defray the expenses of a Christian ministration in many thousand places of the empire. Instead of waiting, which might have been forever, till all this was done by the Government, they took it up at their own hands; and this proved the very instrument or process, by which the eyes of the Government were opened, and their resistance was at length borne down, when, after the commencement of the fourth century, the lordly autocrat of his vast dominions, gave in to the energy of the public sentiment; and, whether from motives of piety and principle or from the motive of policy we know not, provided an entrance for the teachers of the Gospel to every little district of the then civilized world*—and so, bringing the church into contact with the plenteous harvest of a vineyard heretofore too mighty for its grasp, cleared a way for the message of the Gospel to all the families of all his population.

Now what was the process then should be the process still. In the first ages of our era, the church had no aid or protection whatever from the state; and so the whole territory was without the blessings of any legal provision, till the Christian people so multiplied both their places of worship and their worshippers, that the Government at length was carried, and Christianity became the established religion of the empire. But it is possible, nay it has become the actual condition of things amongst us, that, from the increase of population, the original establishment of the country may become so inadequate to the number of our families, that nearly half the territory may be without the benefits of an establishment; and, to obtain these benefits, the Christians of the present day, may have to do for this half of the territory, what the Christians of the three first centuries had to do for the whole of theirs. Even, however friendly the Government of a land were to such an enterprise, it is the whole tenor of my argument, that this ought not to supersede the exertions and the liberality of private Christians. But should the Government not be friendly to this extension of the church, then is it still more incumbent—as incumbent in fact on the faithful disciples of the Saviour now, to do the same for the waste and unprovided places of the land, as

* Were it necessary for the purposes of our argument, we should rather say that, in strict historical precision, only a beginning of this work was made by Constantine; and that it took a lengthened period of time to fill up the present territorial establishment of Christendom.

of old the disciples did for the vast and unfurnished domain that lay before them. When Christianity at its outset, went forth on the then unbroken heathenism of the Roman empire, the voluntary system was put into operation first; and, when it carried the Government, the legal or endowed system was put into operation afterwards. And when we proceed, not against an entire mass, but against numerous and scattered portions of heathenism, in the overcrowded towns and parishes of our own land—the voluntary now may still have to precede the legal, even as it did then. It is therefore most wretchedly preposterous, when application is made for the aid of private Christians in this enterprise of additional churches, in any of them to say, we shall wait to know what the Government does before we do anything. This is neither fair to the Government nor to the church, for the Government does not lead, but follows the march of public sentiment; and grant that it is reluctant, or not enlightened on the present question, the efforts and sacrifices of the people all over the land, constitute the very means by which to enlighten our rulers—the very instrument by which, with moral compulsion, their reluctance is at length done away. To fetch an example from our very doors. It is by the generosity of private Christians, or on the strength of their voluntary subscriptions alone, that, within these few years, one hundred and eighty additional churches have been built or are in process of erection in various places of Scotland. Thus much for the contributions of the one party; but, so far are they from superseding or being exclusive of the other party, they, in effect, form one hundred and eighty arguments for that aid which we seek from the Government, and by which alone these places of worship can be made fully available for the families of the laboring classes in their respective neighborhoods. In a little time, there will be the voice of one hundred and eighty congregations, the testimony and influence of one hundred and eighty neighborhoods all bent on such a provision from the state, as might enable us, not to sell the Gospel as now for those golden seat-rents which are so shamefully extorted, and can only be paid by the higher and middling classes—but, if possible, to preach the Gospel to our workmen, our artificers, to one and all of our toil-worn population, without money and without price. The case is becoming more palpable and stronger every day, and must at length prove irresistible. We have only to multiply these erections; and every new fabric will be a new stepping-stone, which shall bring us so much nearer to the wished-for consummation. Instead of you waiting for the Government, why it is all the other way—the Government are waiting for you. It is clear that if both parties wait, nothing will be done. And therefore it is, we call on you the one party to do your part; and this is the high way to insure the other party doing theirs. The united efforts of private Christians for this best and highest interest of the people, will at length gather into a moral force which can be withstood no longer—when, not without your contributions on the oft-repeated maxim that Government should do all; but by your contributions, or on your doing something, it is that Government will do the rest: Or, in other words, it is through the medium of the country that the Government will be carried.

We should not have detained you so long with this argument, had it not admitted of the strictest application to the object of our meeting this day. There could not be a wiser or more patriotic act in any Government, than to institute a system of schooling, that should provide a sound and good and cheap education for all the families of the land. But great bodies move slowly; and though the glaring deficiency of schools, more especially in towns, has been expatiated on for upwards of a quarter of a century—we know not, if, even yet, any desirable approximation has been made towards the remedying of so great an evil. We have done nothing by our reasonings; but we shall have done a great deal, once that you and others are so far prevailed upon, that you shall begin to act. Let but a process of school extension be entered on, and I think it would start with even a fairer prospect of ultimate success, than did the process of Church Extension at the first—however much our prospects have brightened of late, by the general and enthusiastic support which our scheme has met with in every quarter of the kingdom. Now in several places, a beginning of this sort has been actually made; nor do I know if a better parish could have been selected, for typifying or holding forth a good miniature exhibition of the whole argument, than that one for the educational interest of whose young I now stand before you. The College parish contains a population of upwards of four thousand, the immense majority of whom, indeed we may almost say all, are of the common people—or of that class in society, whom to enlighten and to elevate and every way to better both in character and comfort, and more especially by the lessons of the Gospel, were the very highest achievement which philanthropy can overtake, and the noblest boast of philanthropy did she succeed in the undertaking. Now a most natural question is, how much would be necessary fully to provide for the schooling of such a population. It is greatly beneath the common estimate on this subject, when we say that at least five hundred, out of four thousand, should be at all times under the process of their elementary education; and that at least four schools would be required for conducting this education, in a complete and effective manner. Were we living in the days of John Knox, we should certainly have contended for four schools. But living as we do in an age when private luxury is carried to an unexampled height, while the most wretched parsimony in public objects, and more especially in providing for those national institutes which might best subserve the intelligence and virtue of the people, is the order of the day—we will not venture to specify more than three schools, with the respective school-houses and district teachers, as the proper complement for such a parish. Well then, as there has been yet no legal provision for this necessity, the voluntary principle has put forth an effort and done something for the cause. And, when compared with what is doing in other places and other parishes, it has, in this parish, considering the almost unexcepted poverty of the great mass of its inhabitants, done nobly and well. But it is truly instructive to remark, that, though the exertion made here greatly outruns the average of private and philanthropic exertion all over Scotland, still it is greatly, very greatly beneath the exigencies of the parish. With a severe struggle, and in which it has been found impossible altogether to escape the burden of an oppressive arrear, they have managed to keep agoing one school, and to furnish an almost gratuitous education to about a hundred scholars—or, in other words, as regards the number of schools, they have not accomplished one third ; and, as regards the number of scholars, not one fifth of what would be required to support an adequate system of instruction for the boyhood of this parish. Even for but one school, the allowance is both a penurious and a precarious one; and while there is a general conviction among those who have engaged in this enterprise of benevolence, that they will not be able with all their efforts to do more—there is even a well-founded doubt, whether they will succeed in keeping the ground which they have gotten, or continue year after year to do as much. There cannot be a more vivid illustration of the inadequacy of private means, and of the indispensable necessity for a public and legal provision—ere a right economy for education in a parish, and still more for education over a whole country or congeries of many hundreds of parishes, can possibly be perfected.

But though the voluntary principle falls so immeasurably short of the completion of a right educational economy, it does admirably for the commencement of it. Though carried to its utmost extent, the voluntary system will never overtake what the endowed system alone is equal for ; but let it be carried to this extent, and, as forming the most effectual of all harbingers, it will be sure to usher in the endowed system at the last. The philanthropy of the citizens, is the most effectual instrument for awakening the patriotism of the government; and could we only see as much done by every congregation in our large towns for its corresponding parish, it would compose such a weight and body of influence in behalf of this cause, as would ultimately be felt in high places ; and it should not be long, ere we witnessed the espousal of it by our rulers, who at last would bring the means and the resources of the State to bear upon it. It is well that the voluntary principle should begin the cause ; but it will not end the cause. It may start under the auspices of the voluntary system ; but it will issue in the establishment of the endowed system. And we care not from what quarter the endowment comes. We rejoice to understand that the managers of one of the great public charities in this city, have resolved to apply a large portion of their funds to the planting of schools in various districts within the royalty; and it is our respectful but earnest suggestion, that in no section of the territory, will they meet with a field of greater promise, and at the same time of greater necessity, than in the parish attached to this church—or a fitter scene on which to prove the wisdom, as well as benevolence, of the application which they so rightly propose to make, of the wealth that has been intrusted to their charge.

We have one observation more to make on this subject, and we deem it an important one. The school for which I am pleading is a scriptural school, in the character and system of the good olden time—where the Bible and the Catechism are taught; and the minds of the children are brought into contact with those holy principles and truths, by which alone they can be made wise unto salvation. We trust you perceive a momentous interest involved in the support and multiplication, not merely of schools, but of such schools. If there be any soundness in our argument, it is the voluntary system which germinates the endowment; and they are the schools which the one originates, if only raised in sufficient number and with a sufficient force of public opinion, that the other will perpetuate and extend. Let these voluntary schools then be but carried far enough; and they will not only give birth at the last to a far greater progeny of endowed schools, but, what is of capital importance, of schools in their own likeness: And upon your support therefore of such schools as are taught scripturally and soundly, it depends, whether in the days of your posterity, the land in which we live is to be blessed with a right and a religious, in one word, a good healthful Protestant system of national education. To revert once more to our analogous example, we have raised, or are in the act of raising, a hundred and eighty new churches, and are making it at the same time our strenuous endeavor that we shall obtain an endowment for them; and not this only, but an endowment for as many more as might supply the whole ecclesiastical destitution of the land. Now were these Catholic or Unitarian churches, such a measure might have operated with a deadly blight on the spirit and principle of future generations; and it serves to demonstrate the prodigious importance of an extended voluntary support, not for churches generally, but for the right kind of churches—that on this the alternative hinges, whether a pure or a vicious and corrupt theology, shall emanate from the great mass and majority of the pulpits in our land. Now what is true of the kind of churches, is as true of the kind of schools. If it be important to anticipate the Government with a right kind of churches, it is also important to anticipate them with a right kind of schools.

Let there be a sufficient rallying around these two great objects, of all the leal-hearted and well-principled in our land; and we shall make sure both of a sound Protestant theology in our pulpits, and of a sound and entire Bible education in all our parishes. The national system, hereafter, will take on the form and the character which individuals now may choose to impress on it. I stand before you in behalf of one such school, having this guarantee both for its being well constituted and well administered—that it is conducted under the immediate eye, the governance and guardianship of one of the most zealous friends to the prosperity, and ablest champions for the purity of the Church of Scotland. Let but this school, and a sufficient number around it in its own likeness, be upholden for a few years amid the difficulties which now encompass them; and we have every reason to anticipate, that, with the blessing of heaven, the whole will expand into a general and well-organized system, for transmitting the knowledge of the pure word of God throughout the families of our people, from generation to generation.

CONSIDERATIONS

ON THE

SYSTEM OF PAROCHIAL SCHOOLS IN SCOTLAND,

AND ON THE

ADVANTAGE OF ESTABLISHING THEM

IN LARGE TOWNS.

There are three school systems for the education of a country, each of which is fitted to have its own peculiar influence on the general habit and improvement of the people among whom it operates.

There is first the wholly unendowed system. Education, instead of being in any shape patronized or instituted, may be left merely as an article of native and spontaneous demand, among the people of a country. Each who has a desire for it, might, in this case, purchase it, just as he would do any other object of desire. He would, of course, have to pay the full and natural price for the article: or, in other words, the fees of education must, under such a system, be adequate to the entire maintenance of the teachers.

This way of it has never been found effectual to the object of originating, in any country, a habit of general education. It does not call out the people. It in fact abandons them to the chance of their making a proper and original motion of their own, and this motion is never generally made. And, had we time for looking so far back as to first causes, the reason of this might be rendered abundantly obvious. The truth is, that there is a very wide distinction between the moral or intellectual wants of our nature, on the one hand, and the merely physical wants of our nature on the other. In the latter case, the want is always accompanied with a strong and urgent desire for relief; and, just in proportion to the greatness of the want, is the intensity of the desire. The want of food is accompanied with hunger, and the want of liquids with thirst, and the want of raiment with cold; and these form so many powerful appetites of demand, which, among a people, though left to themselves, will be fully commensurate to the whole extent of their physical necessities. And hence it is, that whatever call may exist for a national establishment of teachers, a national establishment of bakers, or butchers, or tailors, or shoemakers, is altogether superfluous.

But the reverse of all this holds true, of the moral or intellectual wants of our nature. The want of virtue, so far from sharpening, has the effect of extinguishing the desire for virtue. The same is true of the want of knowledge. The more destitute we are of these articles, the more dead we are as to any inclination for them. Under the mere operation of demand and supply, there are sufficient guarantees in the constitution of nature, that the people will themselves make a primary movement after food. But there is no such guarantee for their ever making a primary movement after instruction. It is not from the quarter of ignorance, that we can at all look for the first advance towards knowledge; nor can we ever expect, that, for this object, a people as yet untaught, will surrender, either for their own behalf, or that of their children, any sensible proportion of that money, which went to the purchase of their physical gratifications.

The night of ignorance is sure to be perpetuated in every land, where no extraneous attempts are made, on the part of the wealthy and enlightened, for the object of its dissipation. And if the wholly unendowed system be incompetent to the effect of planting a habit of education among a people, in the first instance, it cannot be the best system for upholding that habit, where it is already established; and far less can it be the best for arresting the declension of this habit in a country, where, if education be upon the decline, the desire for education will be sure to decline along with it.

The next system of education, is that of free schools. It is in every point diametrically the reverse of the former, and may therefore at first view be regarded as the best for shunning all the evils, and all the inefficiency of the former. It is a wholly endowed, instead of a wholly unendowed system. It both spares the population the necessity of making the first movement after scholarship for their children, and it spares them the necessity of surrendering for this object any portion of their subsistence. For the completion of such a system, it were enough that schools and school-houses should be built in every little district of the land, and such a salary provided for the teachers, as, without the exaction of any fee, would enable them to render a full supply of scholarship to the families, at the public expense. In this way, the people would be fully met with an apparatus, broadly and visibly obtruded upon their notice; and yet we are far from thinking, that it would either create a native and universal habit of education in a country,—or arrest the process of its degradation in learning,—or sustain the practice of parents sending their children to school, and so stimulating and watching over the progress of their scholarship, as would lead to the formation of a well-taught and a well-informed peasantry.

What is gotten for no value, is rated at no value. What may be obtained without cost in money, is often counted unworthy of any cost in pains. What parents do not pay for the acquirement of, children will not be so urged to toil for the acquirement of. To be away from school, or to be idle at school, when not a matter of pecuniary loss, will far more readily be a matter of connivance. There is no doubt a loss of other advantages; but these, under a loose and gratuitous system of education, will be but held in capricious demand, and in slender estimation. The only way of thoroughly incorporating the education of the young, with the habit of families, is to make it form part of the family expenditure, and thus to make the interest, and the watchfulness, and the jealousy of parents, so many guarantees for the diligence of their children. And, for these reasons, do we hold the establishment of free schools in a country, to be a frail and impolitic expedient, for the object of either upholding a high tone of scholarship among our laboring classes, or of rendering the habit at all general, or of perpetuating that habit from generation to generation.

And such a system has not a more adverse influence on the scholars, than it has upon the teachers. Let a man deal in any article whatever, and there is not a more effective security for the good quality of what he deals in, than the control and the guardianship of his own customers. The teacher of a free school is under no such dependence. It is true, that he may be paid according to the proficiency of the learners; but the parent who can instantly withdraw his children, is a far more jealous inquisitor into this matter, than the official examinator, on whose personal interest at least there is no such powerful or effectual a hold. And we repeat it, therefore, that carelessness on the part of the teacher, as well as a remiss and partial attendance on the part of the taught, is the likely fruit of that gratuitious system of education, the aspect and the tendency of which we are now employed in contemplating.

It reflects infinite credit on the founders of our Scottish reformation, that, by the tact of a wise and well-discerning skilfulness, they have devised a system, which dexterously shuns and puts at an equal distance from our peasantry, the evils and inconveniences of the two former. It may, for the sake of distinction, be called the medium system of education. It is about two centuries and a half ago since it had its origin in Scotland. The first advance was made, not by the people at large, but by the founders of this system; and in this way, they escaped the inefficiency of what may be called the unendowed method of education. They built schools and school-houses, and held them conspicuously forth to the view of the population, and they furnished such a salary to the teacher, as enabled him, not to deal out a free education among the surrounding families, but to deal it out to them upon certain regular and moderate allowances. In this way, they escaped the evils which we have just now ascribed to the gratuitous system of education. The people were not fully met. But they were met half-way. It was not a movement of demand upon their side, in the first instance, which it had been vain to look for. Neither was it a full and altogether gratuitous invitation on the other side. But it was the movement of a proposal from the latter, upon certain terms; and this was at length followed up, on the side of the people, by the movement of a wide, and general, and almost unexcepted compliance.

This result has nobly accredited the wisdom of our parochial institutions. The common people of England and Ireland, left to demand education for themselves, never demanded it; nor would they, if left to the impulse of their own desire, ever have emerged from the deep, and stationary, and unalleviated ignorance of the middle ages. A great, and, in part, a successful effort, is making now, in behalf of both these countries, by a set of active philanthropic societies. By the stir and the strenuousness of these institutions, the people have certainly, in some measure, awakened from the stillness of their unlettered repose; and many young have been called out to scholarship, who else would have persisted in the dormancy of their forefathers. Still we hold, that there is no security for a system, either of universal or perpetual operation, until it shall cease to be entirely gratuitous—until the people themselves be associated in the support of it by their own payments—until they are led to look on scholarship as worthy of its price, and that price is actually rendered—until learning be so prized by them as to be purchased by them—and this bond be established for its regular prosecution among all their families, that its cost is estimated among the regular outgoings of a family.

This is the way in the country parishes of Scotland. The surrender which they have to make for the education of their young, is much smaller than it would have been, had there been no school, or school-house, or salary, provided by the legislature. Still, however, it is well that they have to make some surrender. It is well that the care of parents over the progress of their children's education, should be stimulated by the price which they have to render for it. It is well, that by their inspection being thus sharpened, there should be a far closer and more effective security for the diligence of the young, than ever could obtain, were the education of the country turned into one great and universal charity. We read much of the abuses of chartered and endowed schools for the poor; and it is well that while our schools are so far endowed as to reduce the country price of learning to at least one-half of what it would be, under a totally unprovided system; it is still well, that a fraction should be left to be paid by the parents, and that the teacher should be thus far responsible to them, for the performance of his duty and the faithfulness of his public services.

The universality of the habit of education in our Lowland parishes, is certainly a very striking fact; nor do we think that the mere lowness of the price forms the whole explanation of it. There is more than may appear at first sight, in the very circumstance of a marked and separate edifice, standing visibly out to the eye of the people, with its familiar and oft-repeated designation. There is also much in the constant residence of a teacher, moving through the people of his locality, and of recognized office, and distinction amongst them. And perhaps there is most of all in the tie which binds the locality itself to the parochial seminary, that has long stood as the place of repair, for the successive young belonging to the parish; for it is thus that one family borrows its practice from another—and the example spreads from house to house, till it embrace the whole of the assigned neighborhood—and the act of sending their children to the school, passes at length into one of the tacit, but well understood proprieties of the vicinage—and new families just fall, as if by infection, into the habit of the old ones—so as, in fact, to give a kind of firm, mechanical certainty to the operation of a habit, from which it were violence and singularity to depart—and in virtue of which, education has acquired a universality in Scotland, which is unknown in the other countries of the world.

There has many a distinct attempt been made to supplement the defective education of our cities. But if it have either been in the way of gratuitous education, or in the way of a vast Lancasterian establishment, for the general behoof of a wide and scattered community, or in any way which did not bind, by the tie of a local relationship, the close and contiguous families of a given district, to a seminary raised within its limits, and to a fixed and stationary teacher at the head of that seminary—then let it be remembered, that some of the most essential elements of success have been wanting to the operation. Nor let us be discouraged by the failure of former expedients, which are not at all analogous to the one that we shall venture to recommend, and by which it is proposed to circulate throughout the mass of a crowded population, as powerful and pervading an influence, in behalf of scholarship, as that which has been diffused over the face of our Lowland provinces, and diffused so thoroughly, as scarcely to leave in our country parishes, the exception of a single individual, or a single family behind it.

But there is still another school system which falls to be considered—not a medium, but what may rather be called a compound system—because made up of the unendowed and the free systems together, though not put together into the constitution of any one single seminary. This compound system is realized in all those places where so many of the schools are wholly free, and all the rest of them are wholly unendowed. We have already stated our objections against such an establishment of free schools as would meet the whole population. It is a different arrangement from this, where there is such an establishment of free schools as might provide part of the population with gratuitous learning, and where the remaining part have to pay that full price which obtains in schools that are totally unendowed. This amounts nearly to the actual system which obtains in Glasgow.

Our objections to this way of ordering the matter, are, that as far as free education prevails, a careless estimate of its value, and a loose and negligent attendance, are apt to prevail along with it; and that many parents, who, under the medium system, could have upheld the habit of purchasing the scholarship of their children, are thereby degraded into an inferior habit; and that there is not a more public way of exposing our people as the subjects of charity, than by drawing out their families to a charity school; and that the difference to the comfort of a family is so great, between having to pay the full price which an unendowed teacher must exact, and having to pay no price at all, as to make a place in one of the charity schools an object to men, who else would be greatly above cherishing any expectation of charity, or preferring any demand for it; and that, as the result of all this, the competition for places is so great, as often to elbow out those neediest and most destitute, for whom the institution was originally framed—besides the incalculable mischief of bringing down men, who, but for this temptation, would have stood erect and independent, to the attitude of petitioners; or, in other words, the mischief of carrying the spirit and the desires of pauperism upward, by several steps, along the scale of society.

We affirm one consequence of charity schools with us, to have been a diminution in the quantity of education. It is familiar to us all, that the applications for admittance are greatly more numerous than the vacancies. In this way there are many parents who are constantly standing out in the capacity of expectants, and who, under the operation of a hope which turns out to be delusive, are keeping off their children from other schools. Their children are thus suffered to outgrow their opportunities; and many are the instances in which they have stood for years at that gate to which they have been allured by false or mistaken signals of invitation, till the urgent concerns of their trade or their profession at length hurried them away—and that too, to a condition of life, where it was as impossible for them to retrieve any portion of their time for the purposes of education, as it was to recall those years which they had so idly spent in ill-directed endeavors to obtain it.

In all these circumstances, we hold the medium system, which obtains in the country parishes of Scotland, to be also, in every way, the best for its city parishes. Not leaving education without any endowment, to the random operation of demand and supply—not so endowing it, as to hold out a gratuitous education to all who should require it—not even endowing a restricted number of schools to this extent, and leaving the rest to the necessity of exacting an unendowed price from the scholars who repair to them—but endowing schools so far as will enable the teachers to furnish education to our town families upon country prices—erecting the schools and the school-houses—and multiplying these erections till they met the demand, and were thoroughly familiarized to the habit of our whole population.

It is little known amongst us, how much the people of our city parishes have fallen behind the full influence and benefit of such a system. With the exception of schools for Latin, there are almost no vestiges of any such endowment. Instead of any public and parochial edifice for scholarship, held forth to the view of the people, and constantly reminding them, as it were, of their duty, through the avenue of the senses,—the only education for their children, which is accessible to them, is dealt out from the privacy of obscure garrets, or at most from the single hired apartment of a house, in no way signalized by its official destination, and deeply retired from observation amid the closeness and frequency of the poorest dwelling-places. These stations, too, whither children repair for their education, are constantly shifting; and the teachers, being often unconnected by any ties of residence or local vicinity with the parents, there is positively, in spite of the sacredness of their mutual trust, as little of the feeling of any moral relationship between them, as there is between an ordinary shopkeeper and his customers. The very circumstance, too, of drawing his scholars from the widely scattered families of a town, instead of drawing them from the contiguous families of one of its parishes, slackens, among these parishes, the operation of that principle, which operates so powerfully among the immediate neighbors of a small country village; and where, in virtue of each doing as he sees others do, we behold so sure and so unfailing a currency towards the established schoolmaster, on the part of all the population. It forms a mighty addition to all these obstacles, in the way of education, when such a price must be paid for it, as might enable the teacher to live on his fees alone. And thus it is, that the demand for schooling, which is kept up without abatement in our country parishes, has been most wofully abridged amongst the laboring classes in our towns. Not a few feel tempted, by the greatness of its expense, to evade the schooling of their families altogether, insomuch, that with them the cause of education is altogether extinct; and very many are the parents who feel tempted to reduce the quantity of schooling, insomuch, that with them the cause of education is rapidly and alarmingly on the decline.

It is a very low estimate of the average expense of good education for reading, alone, to state it at five shillings a quarter, or twenty shillings a year. This expense is, in many instances, shunned altogether: and there are hundreds of adults who are utterly incapable of reading; and the number of these is increasing rapidly. The expense is, in many more instances, not shunned: but the period of it is lamentably shortened, so as fully to account for the slovenly and imperfect reading of so many of our artizans, and laborers, and household servants. The case of these last is, that of ignorance under the disguise of education. Theirs is a mere semblance or apology for learning. The individual who, in reading to another, stops, and spells, and blunders at every short interval, can never read a passage to himself, so as readily to understand the subject. To read intelligently, he must read fluently. And, therefore it is, that there may be a partial scholarship, which, for every purpose of moral or literary improvement, is just as worthless as no scholarship at all. The shadow of the good old Scottish habit may be still perpetuated amongst us for one or two generations; and, perhaps, may be preserved, by the annual importations of this habit from the country, from ever passing into utter dissipation. But, though the shadow of it should remain, the substance of it will soon be dissipated. Insomuch, that, if vice and ignorance stand together in nearly perpetual association—if an uneducated people be more formidable in their discontent, and more loathsome in their profligacy, and more improvident in their economical habits, and more hardened in all the ways of wickedness and impious profanation, than a people possessed of the Bible, and capable of using it—then, we cannot look on the progress of that undoubted decay in scholarship, which is every day becoming more conspicuous in our towns, without inferring a commensurate progress in those various elements of mischief, which go to feed and to augment all our moral and all our political disorders.

To extend a right system of parochial education over the whole city, is an enterprise greatly too gigantic for any one body of management. The truth is, that, did we compute the expense of its full accomplishment, the magnitude of the sum would paralyze any number of philanthropists who could willingly and readily act together, for the purpose of bringing round such a consummation. From the vastness of the necessary resources on the one hand, and the unwieldiness which ever attaches to the movements of any very extended society, on the other, we are quite sure that nothing very effectual could be done under a combined plan of operations, and that the agents of such an undertaking, would either give it up in despair, or retire from it, satisfied that they had done much, when they had scarcely done anything—

pointing, it may be, to some showy, but superficial achievement, as the trophy of their success,—to the establishment, it is likely, of one school in each parish, which would only suffice for a very small fraction of the whole, and leave untouched and unprovided by any salutary influence whatever, the great mass of the community.

But what one body of management cannot do in the gross, several distinct and independent bodies of management might be able to do in the detail. One thing is certain, that any such smaller body will act with an impetus and a vigor, of which a vast general society is utterly incapable. This would be the first effect of a subdivision in the field of agency. Let it only be broken down into manageable sections, and the influence will be the same with that which comes upon a man's whole energy and spirit, when any concern with which he is associated, is so reduced, from the hopelessly and impracticably vast, as to be brought within the compass of his probable attainment; and when the limit of his enterprise, instead of lying at a distance from him, in the remote and fathomless unknown, is brought so near, as to be distinctly visible, and likely to be overtaken; and when, by every step in his progress, he feels himself to be approximating to a given termination. In such a state of things, he is cheered and stimulated onwards by every new accession to his means, and every new movement in the execution of his measures; and just because the conclusion of the whole does not stand at an obscure and indefinite interval away from him. And such would be the difference, in point both of present alacrity and ultimate success, between the operations of one Society for parochial schools, to the whole of Glasgow, and of distinct Societies for the same object, in each of the parishes of Glasgow. Each would have its own manageable task; and each would be freed from the distractions of too manifold and cumbersome an operation; and each would not only have less to do, but have more in proportion to do with: for, it is of importance to remark, that, by thus dividing the mighty field, and assigning its own separate locality to each separate agency, the interest is greatly heightened, and the activity is greatly promoted; and even the feeling of rivalship gives a laudable impulse to each of the distinct undertakings; and the solicitations for aid are carried through each parish and congregation, far more closely and productively, when the attention and desire are thus devoted to one small portion of the territory, instead of being weakened by dispersion over the face of the extended whole.

It is on these grounds, that the Committee of Education for the parish of St. John, have conceived the hope, that, by intent perseverance, and the use of all those legitimate means which are within their reach, they may at length succeed in the establishment of a right parochial apparatus; or, in other words, may arrive at the result of as many schools and school-houses, with permanent salaries to each of the teachers, as shall be commensurate to the object of a good elementary education, at reduced prices, to all the families in the parish.

This will be gradually arrived at, by the erection of successive fabrics, and the accumulation of as much capital, as shall afford, by its interest, the salaries of the different teachers.

Each fabric, it is conceived, may have two school-rooms in its lower story, and, in its upper stories, the two school-houses. When the schools cease to be filled to an overflow, this will serve as an indication that the parochial equipment for schooling is completed.

We should feel it a public injustice to monopolize for our parish, more in the way of aid than legitimately belongs to it; and we hold it necessary, on this account, to explain, how far we mean to extend our solicitations, and what are the resources which we leave untouched for other parishes.

All who are connected with the parish, either by residence or by property, we count ourselves free to apply to, for such contributions as they may be prevailed upon to render, in behalf of this strictly parochial object; nor do we deem this in any way capable of being construed into an interference with the claims and the fair expectations of other parishes.

But, further, it must be evident, that did each parish of Glasgow confine its attempts to obtain money, within the limits which we have just now assigned, the most needful of these parishes would also be the most restricted in their means of raising a right parochial system. And, on the other hand, the great majority of our wealthiest individuals, residing either in the best provided districts of the town, or without the limits of the royalty altogether, would escape the pressure, or rather what most of them would hold to be the privilege, of sharing in this dispensation of liberality. There are many such, whom the poorer of our parishes may look up to, as a kind of common patrons, and whose wealth may be regarded as a common fund, out of which it is fair to draw, in the way of candid statement, and respectful entreaty, as much as can be gained from their good-will, for this best of objects. And while we abstain from encroaching, by more than our fair share, upon this wide and flourishing domain of our community, do we leave it to other parishes to enter upon it as they please, and to cultivate it in any way they will, and to call forth its produce and its capabilities to the uttermost.

What we fear not to announce as our equitable share of this fund, is just as much as we can possibly raise, by means of a congregational subscription, as additional to, and distinct from, our parochial ones; or, in other words, it is our intention to solicit aid from those who, without residence or property in the parish. have nevertheless seats in the church of St. John.

Our firm and confident answer to every charge of unfair usurpation, on the means of general Glasgow, for the furtherance of an object connected with the peculiar good of only one of its parishes, is, that ours is among the poorest of the city parishes, and ours is not the wealthiest of the city congregations.

Should there be another parish poorer than ours, and with a congregation not so wealthy, we do not ask it to restrict its operations for aid, within the limits which we have prescribed for ourselves. After it has made the most of its parish and congregation, it will have a still untrodden field, among those most affluent of our citizens, who have no peculiar connection with either, but who, in extending their patronage to the schooling of an unprovided district of the town, will find an ample scope for one of the most promising and productive of all charities.

On this field, the Committee for Education in the parish of St. John, do not propose to enter. Insomuch, that if a wealthy individual, not a parishoner, not a proprietor, and not a sitter in the church of St. John, should offer ten guineas for the furtherance of our undertaking, we honestly affirm, that it were in far more delightful harmony with all our wishes, did he reserve his money, and augment it to the gift of a hundred guineas, in behalf of another district, still more needy and unprovided than our own. Nor would we feel such interest and alacrity in this our parochial undertaking, did we not believe, that the plan was equally competent, and equally effective, for all the other parishes of Glasgow; and that it thus admitted of being so multiplied and transferred to the other districts both of our city and suburb population, as to offer by far the likeliest method of rearing a permanent security for the good and Christian education of all our families.

It is in the power of any munificent individual to bring this matter to the test, so as to ascertain, in a few months, whether the charm which we have ascribed to locality, be of an ideal, or of a soundly experimental character. We do not suppose him to be either a sitter in the church of St. John, or at all connected, either by residence or property, with the parish. Let him dwell without the limits of the royalty, and have no congregational bond of alliance with any part of the city, excepting, perhaps the very wealthiest of its districts. Should he, in these circumstances, select the most destitute of its parishes, as his own chosen field, on which he might lavish all his influence, and all his liberality—should he, for this purpose, head an enterprise for schools, by his own princely donation; and interest his personal friends; and encourage by his example and exertions, any parochial committee that may be formed; and spirit on the undertaking to the erection of one fabric, and to a fresh exertion for another, and to the anticipation for a third, he will soon feel, how much more effective a hold of him, such a plan of operations for ten thousand people has, than a similar plan for one hundred thousand. He will thus try the comparison of strength, between a local and a universal interest, and find how greatly the former, by the constitution of our nature, predominates; and how, by concentrating his attentions upon one district, his whole heart and endeavor are far more rivited to the cause of its moral cultivation, than if he had merged himself among the generalities of a wider, but more hopeless undertaking. He will, after having planted the cause in this his adopted, and, on that very account, his favorite and beloved vineyard, continue to water it, just because he had planted it; nor will he feel it possible to cease from fostering his own parochial establishment, till he had brought it on to its full-grown maturity. All the members of that body of subscription with which he is associated, will just feel as he does; and the very same local interest, which does so much to stimulate the activity of the doer, will also stimulate, beyond all calculation, the liberality of the giver. The cause will be nobly seconded in the parish itself, which is the field of this operation; and its contribution for its own schools, will exceed, by many times, any contribution to which it could possibly be called out, for the more extended, but, to it, greatly less exciting cause of schools in Glasgow. This is not philanthropy bounding herself round with narrow and unsocial limitations. It is philanthropy devising the way in which the greatest amount of good may be rendered to our species; and, for this purpose, availing herself of a principle, which, however neglected and lying in unobserved concealment heretofore, will, we trust, be mightily instrumental in calling forth a great resurrection of all that is wise, and moral, and salutary in our land. Let one set of men foster the attentions and reiterate the labors of benevolence upon one assigned and overtakeable district. Let our great towns be localized into separate portions, and men be called out, for thoroughly pervading each of them, and laboriously doing in detail, what has long been so vainly and ambitiously attempted *en masse.* Let each separate agency link itself with a subject, that there is some hope of completely finishing, and thus suit the dimensions of the enterprise to the real mediocrity of human power; then, in this humbler, but sounder way of it, a universal result will be far more surely and speedily obtained, than it ever can be by the airy, unproductive magnificence, as impotent as it is imposing, of widely comprehending plans, and great national undertakings.

We have one remark to offer, for the purpose of acquitting ourselves in full of the imputation of monopoly. There are many sitters in the church of St. John's, who have also seats elsewhere. We shall apply to them for aid in our parochial undertaking. But we beg to assure them, that, instead of their entire offering to the cause, it would be far more consonant both to our views of justice, and to our desire of extending this benefit beyond the limit of our own parish, if we were only admitted to a proportional share of their liberality.

The extra-parochial sitters in the church of St. John's will forgive the following observation. They are not parishioners; but they occupy the place of parishioners. They get the Sabbath accommodation, which, but for them, parishioners would have gotten; and we assure them, that, by helping on the cause of week-day instruction in the parish, they will make the kindest and most suitable atonement for such a deprivation.

To have a sufficient conception of the style in which the cause that we are now pleading for, deserves to be supported, it should be considered, how much there is to be done, and how great the benefit is, that will accrue from the doing of it. Ever since the first institution of schools in Scotland, towns have grown, and the provision for education has not grown along with them. The population greatly outstrips the endowed schools, and the object now is, to establish as many schools as shall overtake the population. Thus, to recover the distance we have lost—thus, to repair the negligence of upwards of two centuries—thus, to do, in a few years, the work which should have been gradually advancing along the lapse of several generations—may well appear an enterprise so vast, as to border on the romantic; and it is not to be disguised, that it is only on the strength of large sums and large sacrifices, that we can at all look for its entire and speedy accomplishment. And yet we will not despair of this cause, when we think of its many recommendations; and that, with all its cost, it would still form the best and the cheapest defence of our nation, against the misrule of the fiercer and more untoward passions of our nature; and that the true secret for managing a people, is not so much to curb, as to enlighten them; and that a moral is a far mightier operation than a physical force, in controlling the elements of political disorder; and that to give a certainty to the habit of education in towns, is to do for them that which has visibly raised the whole peasantry of Scotland, both in intelligence and virtue, above the level of any other population.

There is one encouraging circumstance in this charity. It is not, like many others, interminable. An assignable sum of money will suffice for it, and suffice for it conclusively. Every mite of contribution, brings it nearer to its fulfilment. When schools and school-houses are built, and salaries are provided, and a sum is raised for the calculable object of repairing our edifices, or of so extending them, as to meet the growing exigencies of a growing population, the undertaking is done, and the parish, permanently translated into the condition of a country parish, as it regards schools, is upheld in a high tone of scholarship, throughout all its succeeding generations.

Under such a system as has now been proposed, the efforts of respectable and well-taught men, may, in the capacity of teachers, be brought to bear on the very humblest classes of society. Linked with the parish, by the ties both of residence and of office, they might bring a mighty contribution of good to its moral agency. They would occupy what at present is an unfilled gap between the higher and the lower orders; fitted for intercourse with the former, and familiarized to the latter, both by local and official relationship. Let them have an honest zeal on the side of Christianity; and the effect of their frequent and extensive minglings with the people, would be beyond the reach of our present calculation. Those apparently outcast and outlandish features, which have had such time to grow, and to gather, and to settle into obstinacy, on the aspect of a neglected race, would soften and give way under the influences of this blander and better arrangement. It would do more than reclaim a parish;—it would go far to domesticate it. Nor do we know how a readier method could be devised for consolidating the parochial system of our great cities, or for supplementing, till better and more liberal days, those woful deficiencies which obtain in our ecclesiastical establishment.

There are many gentlemen of our city, familiar with the spectacle of a public examination at our grammar-school; and who have frequently enjoyed the gratifying assemblage of parents, and children, and spectators, all occupied with their respective interests, in this busy scene of emulation and display; and who have witnessed, with benevolent pleasure, the honest pride of fathers, and the keen rivalship which obtains among the most eminent of the young, and the expression of holiday-delight which sits on the countenances of them all; and who must be sensible, that, during the mixture of public with domestic feeling, in this little republic, where no other supremacy is owned, but that of proficiency and talent, the differences of rank, and the asperities of the great world, are for a season forgotten. How far this may contribute to soften and humanize the system of human life out of doors, it were difficult to say. But certainly, there is nothing that we should desire more to see, than a parent, among the very humblest of our workmen, sharing, at periodic intervals, in this very exhibition—coming, in his Sabbath attire, to witness the proficiency of his children, on the day, and in the hall of their annual examination,—meeting there, with all that is respectable and virtuous in the parish, assembled to do homage to the cherished cause of education among its families—mingling with parents of the higher orders, even as their children mingle, and sharing along with them in the same delightful interests, and in the same pure and pacific triumphs—soothed and elevated, even by this transient intercourse with the people of another rank, and another place in the scale of society—and at length retiring from the spectacle, with a heart more linked to the general system of the country; and that, because this country has attached him, by those very ties which bind him to his own offspring, and to the sacred cause of their moral and religious cultivation.

There cannot be a fitter occasion than the present, for vindicating the wealthier, and for soothing and reconciling the poorer classes of society. The latter very generally think of the former, that they bear a haughty indifference to all their concerns. In this they are mistaken. The rich are not only willing, but many of them are earnestly and enthusiastically so, to forward the interests of the poor, if they but knew how to do it; and we trust, that, in a cause so undeniable as the present, they will nobly redeem, by the generosity of their contributions, all the discredit which has been so plentifully cast upon them. On the other hand, the rich often think of the poor, that kindness corrupts them into a habit of art and ingratitude. But in this they, too, are mistaken. Such a kindness as we are now pleading for, carries not one single element of corruption along with it. It helps the poor, without degrading them. The charity which humbles a man, never makes him grateful. But this is not such a charity. The erection of schools, where education is so cheap, that the poor will count it no hardship to pay, and where education is so good, that the rich will find it of no hurt to their children to send, does not bear upon it any of the signals of charity. The benefit of such an institution, is felt for ages after its origin is forgotten; and it will be the feeling of the people, not that they are brought nearer by it to a condition of pauperism—but simply, that, by being translated into the same facilities, in respect of education, with our country parishes, they have been admitted to the share which belongs to them, in the common privileges of our nation.

ON THE

TECHNICAL NOMENCLATURE OF THEOLOGY;

BEING THE

SUBSTANCE OF AN ARGUMENT

CONTRIBUTED TO

"THE CHRISTIAN INSTRUCTOR"

IN 1813.

Though faith be the main and radical principle of our religion, yet there are many of those Christians in whose speculations it bears a most prominent part, who incidentally betray a very glaring deficiency in the feeling and practice of faith. What we have in our eye, is that mingled sentiment of fear and aversion, with which they listen, even to the opinions that are evangelical, and substantially their own, when they come to them couched in a phraseology different from what their ears have been accustomed to. They must have something more than the bare and essential attributes of orthodoxy. Even orthodoxy is not welcome, unless she presents herself in that dress in which she is familiar to them; and if there be the slightest innovation in the form of that vehicle which brings her to their doors, she is refused admittance, or at the best treated as a very suspicious visitor. Now, in all this, we think we can perceive a want of those two very things, which they often insist upon, and with great justice, as the leading attributes of a true and decided Christian;—there is a want of faith, and a want of spirituality. We do not see how any variation in the external sign should painfully affect that mind, which has taken a firm hold of the thing signified. We do not see how the mechanical circumstances of phrase and expression should discompose that spirit, which maintains a direct intercourse with the Son of God, by confidence in Him as a real and living personage. We do not see how a reflecting Christian, with the realities of faith in immediate contemplation before him, can shrink in suspicion or disgust from these realities, when presented to him in language equally expressive and significant, but different from that which the usage of favorite authors has rendered familiar to him. It fills us with the painful suspicion, that there is little of the vitality of right sentiment in his mind, when he refuses it, though offered to him through the medium of language, as clear, as appropriate, and if he would only exercise his attention, as intelligible as that to which he has been habituated. We begin to fear, that all the charm of orthodoxy to him, is a voice falling upon his ear like a pleasant song; that the inner man has no share in it; that the Saviour, who, if present to the heart, can support it against the substantial terrors of death and of judgment, is surely not present, when this heart, instead of being filled with the spirit of power and of a sound mind, resigns itself to the most fearful and squeamish anxieties about words and phrases, and other unessentials, which form no real or necessary part of the kingdom of God.

This timidity operates upon writers, as well as upon readers; and it has had an undoubted effect in keeping back the style of theological authors. This is one reason why the theological style is so stationary. There can be no doubt as to the fact, that, with very few exceptions, the phraseology of our divines, and in particular of those termed evangelical, is below the elegant and cultivated phraseology of writers upon other subjects. The effect of this is undeniable. Men of tasteful and cultivated literature, are repelled from theology at the very outset, by the unseemly garb in which she is presented to them. Now, if there be nothing in the subject itself which necessarily leads to any uncouth or slovenly exhibition of it, why should such an exhibition of it be persisted in? If there be room for the display of eloquence in urgent and pathetic exhortation, in masterly discussion, in elevating greatness of conception; does not theology embrace all these? and will not the language that is clearly and appropriately expressive of them, possess many of the constituents and varieties of good writing? If theology, then, can command such an advantage, on what principle should it be kept back from her? Why must she be debarred from the use of an instrument, by which she can bring a whole class of men to a hearing, and compel their respectful attention? Is not the principle of *all things to all men* abandoned, when the partialities of men of taste are not adverted to? Is it not right that the fishers of men should accommodate their bait to the prize that they are aiming at? Is it not right that every man should be addressed in his own language? It was for this very purpose, that, in the first age of the church, God interposed with a miracle, and that the first teachers of the Gospel were endowed with the gift of tongues. It is true, that the style of theologians is not absolutely unintelligible to the men I am alluding to. In reference to the tasteful and literary classes of society, the theological style can scarcely be called a different tongue. It may, however, be called a different dialect; and if that dialect were translated into their own, it would, at least, be more clearly understood, and more patiently attended to. Is not the principle upon which a miraculous endowment was granted to the first Christians, of speaking to every man in his own tongue the wonderful works of God, the very same with the principle upon which the lessons of theology should be translated into all languages? Is it not just following out this principle, to translate the lessons of theology into the various modifications of the same language? Would it not be preposterous, to bring in the dialect of Yorkshire upon the parish churches of Fife or of Caithness? Then it is equally so to address men habituated to the language of general literature, in a style tainted with all the obsolete peculiarities of a former age, and disfigured by all the uncouthness of a professional dialect.

It will be seen therefore, that we are far, and very far from contending for a general abandonment of the present style. The principle of *all things to all men*, will provide for its continuance, so long as there is a public in existence, to relish, and be improved by it. We are convinced, that for many years to come, the great majority of theological books will and ought to be written in it. And as our Saviour said, "the poor ye have always with you;" so His Gospel will ever retain this distinctive attribute, that, "to the poor, it is preached." The average style of theology will accommodate itself to the general demand; and we shall be as loud as any of our readers, in protesting against the injustice of starving the majority, for the sake of the fastidious or the cultivated few. It does not follow, because we wish one translation more to be made into the dialect of general literature; that all the previous translations of theology, into the dialects of plain sense, of homely reflection, of forcible and impressive declamation, (even though it should be vulgar, and untasteful, and fitted only to impress people in the lower circles of society,) should therefore be destroyed. We do not want to debar the majority of the species from the province of religious instruction. All that we contend for, is an act of justice to the minority; that their peculiar taste should come in for its share of attention; that books should be written for them also; that proselytes to the good cause should be attempted from every quarter of society; that no department of human life should be left untried; that if a single human soul can be reclaimed by the translation which we are now demanding, the translation ought to be made; and that the fearfulness which prevents an author from giving it, or disposes a reader to receive it with resentment or dislike, is a sentiment which bears unfavorably upon the interests of the Christian religion.

But where lies the precise efficacy of such a translation? Will it accomplish a victory over the natual enmity of the mind to the things of the Spirit of God? Or, will the enticing words of man's wisdom be able to effect that, which we are taught to believe can only be accomplished by the demonstration of the Spirit and of power?

We believe, that repugnance to the peculiar doctrines of Christianity lies a great deal deeper than disgust at the common phraseology in which they are rendered; and we therefore do not think, that the translation of them into the tasteful and cultivated phraseology of literary men, will operate as a specific for carrying these men out of darkness into the marvellous light of the Gospel. We must distinguish here, betwixt the agent and the instrument. The translation of the Bible into a new language is only an instrument. The Spirit of God may, and actually does, refuse His agency to this instrument in a variety of individual cases; but this is no reason for keeping the instrument back. It does not hinder us from counting every translation into a new language to be a service to the cause. It does not, of itself, carry a saving influence into the minds of all who read it; but it is an established instrument by which the Spirit worketh; and as, in point of fact, it is the mean of saving some, it is most desirable that such a translation should be made. Now, what is true of a new language, is true of a new dialect. We do not detract from the agency of the Spirit by a translation into either of them; and the merits of the translation proposed by us, stand precisely on the same ground with the merits of the Bible Society, and can be vindicated on the same principles with the beneficent operations of that noble institution. Let theology, therefore, accomplish the translation of its reasonings and its exhortations into the dialect of taste. She may not reclaim to the truth all who make use of this dialect, but she does a great deal if, by means of this translation, she reclaims any of them; and we contend, that the worth of a single human soul demands the experiment to be made.

The case may be farther illustrated in this way: We do not say, that going to church is an infallible specific for conversion; but we say, that it adds to the chance of it; and if the rich people of the parish are kept back from church by the badness of the road, or the scantiness of the accommodation, then it were desirable that these should be amended, and that more souls should be brought within the reach of an established instrument for turning them to the truth. We do believe, that the alienation of these people from vital Christianity, lies a great deal deeper than their dislike at a miry road or a clay floor. It is not the removal of these that can remove the alienation,—but they lie in the way of an established instrument; they prevent the application of the word and of hearing. Bring them fairly within the reach of this application, and that word of God, which is quick and powerful, and sharper than a two-edged sword, *may* reach the disease, deep as it is, and may eradicate it.

The main obstacle to the reception of Christian truth, does not lie in the repugnance we feel to the phraseology in which she is conveyed to us. It is seated far deeper, and lies in an attribute of our fallen nature which is diffused universally among all the individuals of the species, the tasteful as well as the untasteful: It lies in the *enmity of the carnal mind against God;* and to subdue that enmity, a mightier element must be brought to bear upon the human soul than all the powers of eloquence or poetry. The mere removal of the present phraseology cannot do it; neither can repairing the road to church, or filling it with decorations, convert the soul of a single parishioner. Neither expedient would effect what is the exclusive office of the Spirit of God; but, by putting both expedients into practice, you secure a larger attendance upon the word,—you give it the benefit of a hearing,—and you bring into operation the instruments by which the Spirit worketh; Rom. x. 17. By pleading, then, for the translation of theology into a style as cultivated, and as much accommodated to men of general literature, as that which is employed on other subjects, we only extend the operation of the instruments. The agency of the Spirit of God, and the great steps of the process by which a human soul is called out of darkness into the marvellous light of the Gospel, are left on precisely the same scriptural footing as before; and we must do the profound and eloquent author of the work before us the justice to say, that no Christian writer whom we have yet met with, appears to stand more decidedly on the ground of Christianity in its most peculiar and evangelical form.*

But it is high time to introduce him to the notice of our readers. We confine our attention to his fourth Essay, entitled, "On the *Conversion* of Men of Taste to Evangelical Religion." But the term "evangelical" requires explanation, and we give it in the author's own words.

> "Christianity, taken in this view, contains a humiliating estimate of the moral condition of man, as a being radically corrupt: the doctrine of redemption from that condition by the merit and sufferings of Christ: the doctrine of a divine influence being necessary to transform the character of the mind, in order to prepare it for a higher station in the universe: and a grand moral peculiarity, by which it insists on humility, penitence, and a separation from the spirit and habits of the world. I do not see any necessity for a more formal and amplified description of that mode of understanding Christianity, which has assumed the distinctive epithet Evangelical, and which is not, to say the least, more discriminately designated among the scoffing part of the wits, critics, and theologians of the day, by the terms Fanatical, Calvinistical, and Methodistical."

A discussion may be so far condensed as to admit of no farther condensation; and it is this which constitutes the difficulty of reviewing the Essay before us. It is too rich in profound, and judi-

* The work reviewed was Foster's Essays.

cious, and original reflection, for us to attempt a complete outline of it. Under this impression, we pass over a great number of Mr. Foster's remarks, as to the vulgarity or barbarism of the prevailing theological style, and the causes which may be assigned for it. One of these causes is obvious to all. While other subjects in science and literature are exclusively taken up by the accomplished, and dignified by all their powers of conception and phraseology, it forms the distinction of Christianity, that it is most expressly sent to the class which philosophers have despised. The effect is undeniable, whether you conceive the writers to belong to that class, or to write for it. There will, in either case, be an accommodation to their taste; and the prevailing style of theological books will sink down to a humble and illiterate standard. There is another cause scarcely noticed by the author, which has the effect of perpetuating this style, even in spite of the accessions which evangelical religion may receive from the polished classes of society. When a man of high literary accomplishment is called out of darkness, he becomes the subject of an influence too strong to be counteracted by the antipathies of taste; and, in the mighty energy which gives birth to his conversion, all the lesser disgusts of his mind are overborne. It is the truth, and it alone, which rivets him; and the forms of the existing style in which it is conveyed to him, so far from repelling, may only be endeared to him, by being associated in his mind with what he esteems so valuable. We have reason to believe, that many capable of rendering the truth into a richer and finer dialect, abstain from the enterprise, because they find the truth itself to be enough for them, and count themselves occupied with better things, than the care of embellishing the vehicle in which it is carried. Many are thus lost to that cause, which our author, for the sake of those who stand without, is so wisely contending for. Even though they do not give their positive suffrages to the existing style, they may acquiesce in it; and, in spite of the proselytes which we hope vital Christianity is gaining every year from the ranks of philosophy and elegant literature, the phraseology into which she is rendered may not be the better of them.

We observe, with sincere pleasure, that the author gives his most unqualified reprobation, to those who turn in dislike from the truth, from the mere circumstances of meanness and contempt with which she is associated. These circumstances would not make any impression on a mind already devoted to the religion of Jesus Christ.

"No passion that has become predominant, is ever cooled by anything which can be associated with its object, while that object continues unaltered. The passion is willing even to verify its power, and the merit of that which interests it, by sometimes letting the unpleasing associations surround and touch the object for an instant, and then chasing them away, and it welcomes with augmented attachment that object, coming forth from them unstained; as happy spirits, at the last day, will receive with joy their bodies recovered from the dust, in a state of purity that will leave everything belonging to the dust behind. A zealous Christian exults to feel, in contempt of how many counteracting circumstances, he can still love his religion; and that this counteraction, by exciting his understanding to make a more defined estimate of its excellence, has but made him love it the more. It has now preoccupied even those avenues of taste and imagination, by which alone the ungracious effect of associations could have been admitted. The thing itself is close to his mind, and therefore the causes which would have misrepresented it, by coming between, have lost their power. As he hears the sentiments of sincere Christianity from the weak and illiterate, he says to himself, All this is indeed little, but I am happy to feel that the subject itself is great, and that this humble display of it cannot make it appear to me different from what I absolutely know it to be, any more than a clouded atmosphere can diminish my impression of the grandeur of the heavens, after I have so often beheld the pure azure and the host of stars. I am glad that it has, in this man, all the consolatory, and all the purifying efficacy, which I wish that my more elevated views of it may not fail to have in me. This is the chief end for which a divine communication can have been granted to the world. If this religion had been of a nature to seek to acquire lustre to itself from the mental dignity of its disciples, rather than to make them pure and happy amidst their littleness, it would have been sent to none of us; at least not to me: for though I would be grateful for an order of ideas somewhat superior to those of my uncultivated fellow Christians, I am conscious that the noblest forms of thought in which I apprehend, or could represent the subject, do but contract its amplitude, do but depress its sublimity. Those superior spirits, who are said to rejoice over the first proof of the efficacy of divine truth, have rejoiced over its introduction, even in so humble a form, into the mind of this man, and probably see, in fact, but little difference in point of speculative greatness, between his manner of viewing and illustrating it and mine. If Jesus Christ could be on earth, as before, he would receive this disciple, and benignantly approve, for its operation on the heart, that faith in his doctrines which men of taste might be tempted to despise for its want of intellectual refinement. And since all his true disciples are destined to attain greatness at length, the time is coming when each pious, though now contracted mind, will do justice to this high subject. Meanwhile, such as this subject will appear to the intelligence of immortals, and such as it will be expressed in their eloquence, such it really is now; and I should deplore the perversity of my mind, if I felt more disposed to like the character of the religion from that style of its exhibition in which it appears humiliated, than from that in which I am assured it will be sublime. If, while we are all advancing to meet the revelations of eternity, I have a more vivid and comprehensive idea, than these less privileged Christians, of the glory of our religion, as displayed in the New Testament, and if I can much more delightfully participate the sentiments which devout genius has uttered in the contemplation of it, I am therefore called upon to excel them as much in devotedness to this religion, as I have a more luminous view of its excellence. Let the spirit of the evangelical system once gain the ascendency, and it may thus defy the impressions tending to associate disagreeable ideas with its principles." Page 260.

"I am aware, that no species of irreligion can be much more detestable, than to sacrifice to the idol of taste anything which essentially belongs to Christianity. If any part of evangelical religion, separately from all injurious associations, were of a nature to displease a finished taste, the duty would evidently be, to repress its claims and murmurs. We should dread the presumption which would require of the Deity, that his spiritual economy should be both in fact, and in a manner obvious to our view, subjected or correspondent in all parts to those laws of order and beauty, which we have learnt, partly from the relations of the material world, and partly from the arbitrary institutions and habits of society. But, at the same time, it is a most unwise policy for religion that the sacrifice of taste, which ought, if required, to be submissively made to any part of either its essence or its form, as really displayed from heaven, should be exacted to anything unnecessarily and ungracefully superinduced by men." Page 306.

We cannot propose to follow our author, through all his observations upon the requisite changes that must be made in the theological style before it can be accommodated to men of taste and general literature. We fulfil our object, if we awaken the curiosity of our readers; nor shall we regret leaving them with an unquenched appetite, if it shall have the effect of carrying them direct to this masterly composition. We feel it our duty, however, to advert to one circumstance, which, if not attended to, may lead to the sacrifice of substantial sentiments. He allows, that theology, like every other science, must have its technicals; but, while he is for sparing these, he thinks that much may be done by substituting one set of words for another. Thus, for walk and conversation, substitute conduct, actions, and deportment; for flesh substitute sometimes body and sometimes natural inclination; and, in addition to these instances, we present our readers with the following extract:

"Though there are few words in strict truth synonymous, yet there are very many which are so in *effect*, even by the allowance and sanction of the most rigid laws to which the best writers have conformed their composition. Perhaps this is a defect in human thinking: perhaps every conception ought to be so exquisitely discriminative and precise, that no two words, which have the most refined shade of difference in their meaning, should be equally and indifferently eligible to express that conception: But what writer or speaker will ever exemplify, or even aspire to such perfection? If a divine felt that he had this extreme discrimination of thought, and that he meant something clearly different by the words—carnal, godly, edifying, and so of many others, from what he would express by the words sensual, pious, instructive, he would certainly do right to adhere to the more peculiar words: but if he does not, he may perhaps improve the vehicle without hurting the material of his religious communications, by adopting the general and classical mode of expression." Page 298.

Now, we assert, that even in some of these very changes, we can see a reason why, at the *outset* of the proposed reformation, the material of the religious communication may be hurt by adopting the general and classical mode of expression. The meaning of any word is collected from the general sense in which it is understood by the authors who make use of it. Now, we apprehend that the word *godly*, as it occurs in the works of evangelical authors, means a great deal more than the word *pious*, as it occurs in the lucubrations of our tasteful and academical moralists. It is true, that if you were to bring each party to their definitions, there may be no perceivable difference in the account which each gave of the signification of the two words. But it is not the formally announced meaning that we are concerned with. It is what the author himself calls the *meaning in effect;* and we contend, that this meaning is only to be sought from the general tone and sentiment of those who make use of the word in question. We assert, then, that, in point of fact, the word *godly*, in the mind of an evangelical author, denotes a sentiment, far more deeply seated in its principle, and far wider in its operation, than the word *pious* in the great bulk of classical and literary authors: that the one carries along with it the idea of a far more entire devotedness to God than the other; that the one brings you up to the high requisition of the New Testament, which calls upon you to do all things to God's glory; while the other is satisfied with less thorough and less painful renunciations, and may consist with many acts of accommodation to the world, which a Christian, in the full extent and significancy of the term, would shrink from. We therefore assert, that the effective meaning of the one word is different from the effective meaning of the other; that the translation would not be a fair one; that it would give us a meaning which came short of the original in energy and extent; and that, though you improve the vehicle of the religious communication, by patching upon it the livery of a classical author, you hazard the material of the communication itself, by bringing it down to the standard of his slender and inefficient conceptions.

We are quite aware, that with some this may not appear an apposite example. But it is for this very reason that we select it; because the cause why it does not appear apposite to them, is a strong confirmation of the truth which we are aiming to illustrate. Let it be recollected, that it is only at the outset of the proposed change, that we conceive danger to exist; and accordingly, however inapposite the above example may appear to some, we think that it will appear apposite enough to those whose reading has been confined to the Bible, and the older theologians. We are almost quite sure, that to their minds piety is a more meagre and unsubstantial word than godliness, and that in the substitution therefore of the one for the other, the sentiment appears enfeebled, and duty seems to sink downward from the high standard of its old requisitions. Before there is felt to be a perfect equivalency betwixt the two terms, the word piety must be used for some time by authors whose sentiments are as evangelical, and as deeply infused with the vitality of Christian sentiment, as the excellent compositions of the puritanical age. Now we know, that for some time, there have been such authors, and accordingly there are already some readers who feel the equivalency, and may therefore conceive the above example to be ill selected. We have no doubt, that in the progress of time, the great majority of readers will come to feel the perfect equivalency of the two terms; that when such writers as Foster, and Hall, and Gregory, and Hannah More multiply amongst us, the word piety will be raised above that humble pitch of sentiment to which it has been sunk by our slender divines, and unchristian moralists; that as it gets into better hands, all the associations of feebleness and inadequacy, which it derived from the tone of its old patrons, will be chased away from it; and after a temporary inconvenience, the religious communication will not only come out in an improved vehicle, but the material will pass to us in all its force, and in all its entireness.

While we are upon the influence of new words, it may not be foreign to our subject, but rather give additional illustration to it, if we apply the above remark to an amended translation of Dr. Campbell's. It is true, that μετανοια and μεταμελομαι, are words of different signification, and should be rendered by different words in the English translation. We fear, however, that the *meaning in effect* of Dr. Campbell's "reformation" is not equivalent to the μετανοια of the New Testament. It is true, that if for the meaning of the word reformation, you were to connect it with its derivatives, it may be made to express that full change, which we so often read of in the New Testament; and to be formed again conveys as strong an idea of regeneration, as to be "born again," and to be "transformed by the renewing of the mind." But no man knows better than Dr. Campbell did, that in the choice of words we must be regulated by the actual, and not by the etymological sense. Now were the actual sense of the word reformation to be taken from the average use of those who employ it, it would convey, I am afraid, an idea far short of "repentance unto salvation." We conceive that the term is currently employed to denote a change of external habit, without any reference to the operation of the inner principle which gave rise to it; and that the man who prunes his conduct of its notorious and visible deficiencies from propriety, is termed a reformed man. To make use of a phrase which we fear may be provincial, and therefore not understood by all our readers, the reformed man is equivalent to the man who has *turned over a new leaf;* and as this may be done, and has been done without the operation of a true Christian principle, the term reformation does not in effect come up to that total change of soul, and spirit, and body, which is implied in the μετανοια of the Evangelists. In a word, reformation, so far from being μετανοια, is only a fruit worthy of it. It is a stream flowing out of that well of water, which springeth up into everlasting life. Other streams may bear a deceitful semblance to it, and may wear its name; and we regret that a word should have been here employed which, in its effective meaning, stops short at the outward conduct, and carries us not up to that "renewal in the spirit of our minds," by which we "die unto sin, and live unto righteousness."

But to return to the author before us. If two churches lay at an equal distance from our dwelling-house, the one furnished with a good road, and the other with a bad one, the inducement to attend, in as far as this circumstance had weight, would lie on the side of the former. But if in point of fact, a lax and feeble Christianity was taught in the former, while in the latter, Christianity was taught in a pure and evangelical form; the repair of the last road would, on that very account, become an object more dear than ever to benevolence and true piety. In the same manner, if general literature be rendered attractive by the embellishments of taste, and of good expression, while the evangelical doctrines of the Gospel are set forward in that slovenly and vulgar style, which is calculated to repel attention at the very outset, it becomes of importance to inquire, what is the kind of lessons which general literature affords, and in how far they are congenial with the lessons of our Saviour. If we find that there is a total want of congeniality, the reformation proposed by the enlightened author before us, becomes on that very account, an object of higher necessity and importance. Now we think, that Mr. Foster has completely established this want of congeniality, and that in contrasting the spirit both of ancient and modern literature, with the spirit of the New Testament, he has proved the influence of the one to be in direct hostility to the influence of the other. On this very account, it becomes our bounden duty to give the one every attraction which the other is in possession of, provided that the material of the communication shall not be hurt or impaired by it. Let us, if possible, equalize the inducements, and give that which is salutary an air as inviting, as that which we think our author proves incontestably to be most poisonous and destructive. Hear him upon the tendency of Homer's poetry, the most powerful in the world for seducing a young and ardent imagination, and for imparting an unchristian tone of sentiment to its devoted admirers.

"I therefore ask again, how it would be possible for a man, whose mind was first completely assimilated to the spirit of Jesus Christ, to read such a work without a most vivid antipathy to what he perceived to be the moral spirit of the poet? And if it were not too strange a supposition, that the most characteristic parts of the Iliad had been read in the presence and hearing of our Lord, and by a person animated by a fervent sympathy with the work, do you not instantly imagine him expressing the most emphatic indignation? Would not the reader have been made to know, that in the spirit of that book, he could never become a disciple and a friend of the Messiah? But then, if he believed this declaration, and were serious enough to care about being the disciple and friend of the Messiah, would he not have deemed himself extremely unfortunate to have been seduced, through the pleasures of taste and imagination, into habits of feeling, which rendered it impossible, till they could be destroyed, for him to receive the only true religion, and the only Redeemer of the world? To show *how* impossible, I wish I may be pardoned for making another strange, and, indeed, a most monstrous supposition, namely, that Achilles, Diomede, Ajax, and Ulysses had been real persons, living in the time of our Lord, and had become his disciples, and yet, (excepting the mere exchange of the notions of mythology for Christian opinions,) had retained entire the state of mind with which their poet has exhibited them. It is instantly perceived that Satan, Beelzebub, and Moloch might as consistently have been retained in heaven. But here the question comes to a point; if these great examples of glorious character, pretending to coalesce with the transcendent sovereign of virtue, would have been probably the most enormous incongruity existing, or that ever had existed, in the whole universe, what harmony can there be between a man who has acquired a considerable degree of congeniality with the spirit of these heroes, and that paramount teacher, and pattern of excellence? And who will assure me, that the enthusiast for heroic poetry does not acquire a degree of this congeniality? But unless I can be so assured, I persist in asserting the noxiousness of such poetry.

"Yet the work of Homer is notwithstanding the book which Christian poets have translated, which Christian divines have edited and commented on with pride, at which Christian ladies have been delighted to see their sons kindle into rapture, and which forms an essential part of the course of a liberal education, over all those countries on which the Gospel shines. And who can tell how much that passion for war, which from the universality of its prevalence, might seem inseparable from the nature of man, may, in the civilized world, have been reinforced by the enthusiastic admiration, with which young men have read Homer and similar poets, whose genius has transformed what is, and ought always to appear purely horrid, into an aspect of grandeur." Page 346.

We cannot follow him through the masterly exposition of the modern writers, nor can we offer more than a passing tribute to those fine discriminating powers which Mr. Foster has exhibited in his observations on the Christianity of Samuel Johnson. We concur with him in his general condemnation of the British Classics; for both in their speculations upon the basis of duty, upon the prospects of man, upon the place which he occupies, and upon the relation which he stands in to his God, and in the consolations which they address to suffering and dying humanity, we recognize the features of a school at entire antipodes with the school of Christ. But we cannot do better on this part of the subject, than offer extracts from the author himself.

"One thing extremely obvious to remark is, that the *good man*, the man of virtue, who is necessarily presented to view ten thousand times in the volumes of these writers, *is not a Christian*. His character could have been formed, though the Christian revelation had never been opened on the earth; or though all the copies of the New Testament had perished ages since; and it might have appeared admirable, but not peculiar. There are no foreign unaccountable marks upon it, that could in such a preclusion of the Christian truth, have excited wonder; what could be the relations, or the object of such a strange, but systematical singularity, and in what school or company it had acquired its principles and its feelings? Let it only be said, that this man of virtue had conversed whole years with the instructors of Plato and Cicero, and all would be explained. Nothing would lead to ask, 'But with whom then has he conversed since, to lose so completely the appropriate character of his schools, under the broad impression of some other mightier influence?'

"The good man of our polite literature, never talks with affectionate devotion of Christ, as the great High Priest of his profession, as the exalted Friend, whose injunctions are the laws of his virtues, whose work and sacrifice are the basis of his hope, whose doctrines guide and awe his reasonings, and whose example is the pattern which he is earnestly aspiring to resemble. The last intellectual and moral designation in the world, by which it would occur to you to describe him, would be those by which the apostles so much exulted to be recognized, a disciple, and a servant of Jesus Christ; nor would he (I am supposing this character to become a real person) be at all gratified by being so described. You do not hear him avowing that he deems the habitual remembrance of Christ essential to the nature of that excellence which he is cultivating. He rather seems, with the utmost coolness of choice, adopting virtue as according with the dignity of a rational agent, than to be in the last degree impelled to it by any relations with the Saviour of the world.

"On the supposition of a person realizing this character, having fallen into the company of St. Paul, you can easily imagine the total want of congeniality. Though both avowedly devoted to truth, to virtue, and perhaps to religion, the difference in the cast of their sentiments would have been as great, as that between the physical constitution and habitudes of a native of the country at the equator, and those of one from the arctic regions. Would not the apostle's feeling of the continual intervention of ideas concerning one object, in all subjects, places, and times, have appeared to this man of virtue and wisdom, inconceivably mystical? In what manner would he have listened to the emphatical expressions respecting the love of Christ constraining us; living not to ourselves, but to him that died for us and rose again; counting all things but loss for the knowledge of Christ; being ardent to win Christ, and be found in him; and trusting that Christ should be magnified in our body, whether by life or by death? Perhaps St. Paul's energy, and the appearance of its being accompanied by the firmest intellect, might have awed him into silence. But amidst that silence, he must, in order to defend his self-complacency, have decided, that the apostle's mind had fallen, notwithstanding its strength, under the dominion of an irritable association; for he would have been conscious, that no such ideas had ever kindled his affections, and that no such affections had ever animated his actions; and yet *he* was indubitably a good man, and could, in another style, be as eloquent for goodness as St. Paul himself. He would therefore have concluded, either that it was not necessary to be a Christian, or that this order of feelings was not necessary to that character. But if the apostle's sagacity had detected the cause of this reserve, and the nature of his associate's reflections, he would most certainly have declared to him with great solemnity, that both these things were necessary, or that he had been deceived by inspiration, and he would have parted from this self-complacent man with admonition and compassion. Now, would St. Paul have been wrong? But if he would have been right, what becomes of those authors, whose works, whether from neglect or design, tend to satisfy their readers of the perfection of a form of character, which he would have pronounced fatally defective?

"Again, moral writings are instructions on the subject of happiness. Now, the doctrine of this subject is declared in the evangelical testimony: it had been strange, indeed, if it had not, when the happiness of man was the precise object of the communication. And what, according to this communication, are the essential requisites to that condition of mind, without which no man ought to be called happy; without which ignorance or insensibility alone can be content, and folly alone can be cheerful? A simple reader of the Christian Scriptures will reply, that they are a change of heart, called conversion,—the assurance of the pardon of sin through Jesus Christ,—a habit of devotion, approaching so near to intercourse with the Supreme Object of devotion, that revelation has called it communion with God,—a process of improvement called sanctification, —a confidence in the divine Providence, that all things shall work together for good,—and a conscious preparation for another life, including a firm hope of eternal felicity. And what else can he reply? What else can you reply? Did the lamp of heaven ever shine more clearly since Omnipotence lighted it, than these ideas display themselves through the New Testament? Is this, then, absolutely the true, and the only true account of happiness? It is not that which our accomplished writers in general have chosen to sanction. Your recollection will tell you, that they have most certainly presumed to avow, or to insinuate, a doctrine of happiness, which implies much of the Christian doctrine to be a needless intruder on our speculations, or an imposition on our belief; and I am astonished, that this serious fact should so little have alarmed the Christian students of elegant literature. The wide difference between the dictates of the two authorities is too evident to be overlooked; for the writers in question have very rarely, amidst an immense assemblage of sentiments concerning happiness, made any reference to what the New Testament so obviously declares to be its constituent and vital principles. How many times you might read the sun or the moon to repose, before you would find an assertion or a recognition, for instance, of a change of the mind being requisite to happiness, in any terms commensurate with the significance which this article seems to bear, in all the various forms in which it is expressed and repeated in the New Testament. Some of these writers appear hardly to have admitted, or to have recollected even the proposition, that happiness must essentially consist in something so fixed in the mind itself, as to be substantially independent of external circumstances; for their most animated representations of it, are merely descriptions of fortunate combinations of these circumstances, and of the feelings immediately caused by them, which will expire the moment that these combinations are broken up. The greater number have, however, fully admitted the proposition, and have given their illustration of the doctrine of happiness accordingly. And what appears in these illustrations as the highest form of happiness? It is probably that of a man feeling an elevated complacency in his own excellence, a proud consciousness of rectitude; possessing extended views, cleared from the mists of ignorance, prejudice, and superstition; unfolding the generosity of his nature in the exercise of beneficence, without feeling, however, any grateful incitement from remembrance of the transcendent generosity of the Son of man; maintaining, in respect of the events and bustle of the surrounding scene, a dignified indifference, which can let the world go its own way, and can enjoy its tranquillity the while; and living in a cool resignation to fate, without any strong expressions of a specific hope, or even solicitude, with regard to the termination of life, and to all futurity. Now, whatever degree of resemblance some of these distinctions may bear to the Christian theory of happiness, it is evident, that, on the whole, the two modes are so different, that the same man cannot realize them both. The result is obvious; the natural effect of incompetent and fallacious schemes, prepossessing the mind by every grace of genius, will be an aversion to the Christian views of happiness, which will appear at the least very strange, and probably very irrational." Pp. 382—388.

There is one point in which we are happy not to concur with the estimable author of the performance before us. He speaks as if the author, whose unchristian tendencies he has so successfully exposed, had such decided possession of the public taste, that it is impossible to dislodge them.

"Under what restrictions," says he in his concluding paragraph, "ought the study of polite literature to be conducted? I cannot but have foreseen, that this question must return at the end of these observations, and I can only answer, as I have answered before, Polite literature will necessarily continue to be the grand school of intellectual and moral cultivation. The evils, therefore, which it may contain, will as certainly affect, in some degree, the minds of the successive students, as the hurtful influence of the climate, or of the seasons, will affect their bodies. To be thus affected, is a part of the destiny under which they are born in a civilized country. It is indispensable to acquire the advantage; it is inevitable to incur the evil. The means of counteraction will amount, it is to be feared, to no more than palliatives. Nor can these be proposed in any specific method. All that I can do, is to urge on the reader of taste, the very serious duty of continually calling to his mind—and if he is a parent or preceptor, of cogently representing to his pupils—the real character of the religion of the New Testament, and the reasons which command an inviolable adherence to it."

In another place he says " he really does not see what a serious observer of the character of mankind can offer." When a man contemplates a mischief in all its inveteracy and extent, he is not to sink into hopeless despondency, because he finds he cannot sweep it away by the power of his own individual arm. What no single individual can effect, may be done by the operation of time, and the strength of numbers. We know of no single writer who has contributed more to the good cause than Mr. Foster himself. He has alarmed many a Christian for the safety of his principles. He has thrown a new element into our estimation of the classics. The element is a disquieting one, and it will unsettle that complacency with which we were wont to read and admire them. He has himself given some very fine and powerful specimens of the reformed dialect that he contends for; and, in the Essays before us, we meet with passages which can bear comparison with the happiest paragraphs of Johnson. He cordially allows, that in the subject itself there is a grandeur, which it were vain to look for in any of the ordinary themes of eloquence or poetry. Let writers arise, then, to do it justice. Let them be all things to all men, that they may gain some; and if a single proselyte can be thereby drawn from the ranks of literature, let all the embellishments of genius and fancy be thrown around the subject. One man has already done much. Others are rising around; and, with the advantage of a higher subject, they will in time rival the unchristian moralists of the day, and overmatch them. We look upon taste as too frail and fluctuating an element in the human character, to found any despair upon. It is not in this quarter where the stubbornness of the resistance lies. It is in the natural enmity of the human heart to divine things; and we rejoice to think, that this is a principle which is destined to receive its death-blow from a higher hand. The experience of a few years may well convince us, that there is nothing irreversible in human affairs; and that even minds and opinions are subject to as great and sudden revolutions as the fortunes or politics of the species. Let us not be appalled, then, by the existence of error, however deeply rooted, or widely spread among mankind. Let us not acquiesce in it as some hopeless calamity, which no resistance can overpower, and which can only be qualified by half measures and paltry mitigations. Let us lift an intrepid voice for the entire removal of all that offendeth.

ON THE EFFICACY OF MISSIONS,

AS CONDUCTED BY

THE MORAVIANS;

BEING THE

SUBSTANCE OF AN ARGUMENT

CONTRIBUTED TO

"THE ECLECTIC REVIEW"

IN 1815.

THE natural enmity of the human heart to the things of God, is a principle, which though it find no place in the systems of our intellectual philosophers, has as wide an operation as any which they have put down in their list of categories. How is it then that Moravians, who, of all classes of Christians, have evinced the most earnest and persevering devotedness to these things, have of late become, with men of taste, the objects of tender admiration? That they should be loved and admired by the decided Christian, is not to be wondered at: but that they should be idols of a fashionable admiration; that they should be sought after and visited by secular men; that travellers of all kinds should give way to the ecstasy of sentiment, as they pass through their villages, and take a survey of their establishments and their doings; that the very sound of Moravian music, and the very sight of a Moravian burial-place, should so fill the hearts of these men with images of delight and peacefulness, as to inspire them with something like the kindlings of piety;—all this is surely something new and strange, and might dispose the unthinking to suspect the truth of these unquestionable positions, that "the carnal mind is enmity against God," and that "the natural man receiveth not the things of the Spirit of God, for they are foolishness unto him, neither can he know them, because they are spiritually discerned."

But we do not imagine it difficult to give the explanation. It is surely conceivable that the actuating principle of a Moravian enterprise, may carry no sympathy whatever along with it, while many things may be done in the prosecution of this enterprise, most congenial to the taste, and the wishes, and the natural feelings of worldly men. They may not be able to enter into the ardent anxiety of the Moravians for the *salvation of human souls;* and when the principle is stripped of every accompaniment, and laid in naked and solitary exhibition before them, they may laugh at its folly, or be disgusted by its fanaticism. This, however, is the very principle on which are founded all their missionary undertakings; and it is not till after a lengthened course of operations, that it gathers those accompaniments around it, which have drawn upon the United Brethren the homage of men who shrink in repugnance and disgust from the principle itself. With the heart's desire that men should be saved, they cannot sympathize; but when these men, the objects of his earnest solicitude, live at a distance, the missionary, to carry his desire into effect, must get near them, and traversing a lengthened line on the surface of the globe, he will supply his additions or his corrections to the science of geography. When they speak in an unknown tongue, the missionary must be understood by them; and giving his patient labor to the acquirement of a new language, he furnishes another document to the student of philology. When they are signalized by habits or observances of their own, the missionary records them for the information and benefit of his successors; and our knowledge of human nature, with all its various and wonderful peculiarities, is extended. When they live in a country, the scenery and productions of which have been yet unrecorded by the pen of travellers, the missionary, not unmindful of the sanction given by our Saviour himself to an admiration of the appearances of nature, will describe them, and give a wider range to the science of natural history. If they are in the infancy of civilization, the mighty power of Christian truth will soften and reclaim them. And surely, it is not difficult to conceive, how these and similar achievements may draw forth an acknowledgment from many, who attach no value to the principles of the Gospel, and take no interest in its progress; how the philosopher will give his testimony to the merits of these men who have made greater progress in the work of humanizing savages, than could have been done by the ordinary methods in the course of centuries; and how the interesting spectacle of Esquimaux villages and Indian schools, may, without the aid of any Gospel principle whatever, bring out strains of tenderest admiration from tuneful poets and weeping sentimentalists.

All this is very conceivable, and it is what Moravians, at this moment, actually experience. They have been much longer in the field of missionary enterprise, than the most active and conspicuous of their fellow laborers belonging to other societies. They have had time for the production of more gratifying results; and the finished spectacle of their orderly and peaceful establishments, strikes at once upon the eye of many an admirer, who knows not how to relish or to appreciate the principle which gives life and perpetuity to the whole exhibition.

These observations may serve to account for the mistaken principle upon which many admirers of the United Brethren give them the preference over all other missionaries. We are ready to concur in the preference, but not in the principle upon which they found it. They conceive that the Moravians make no attempt towards christianizing the heathen, till they have gone through the long preparatory work of training them up in the arts of life, and in the various moralities and decencies of social intercourse. This is a very natural supposition; but nothing can be more untrue. It is doing just what every superficial man is apt to do in other departments of observation—mistaking the effect for the cause. They go to a missionary establishment of United Brethren among the heathen. They pay a visit to one of their villages, whether in Greenland, in S. Africa, or on the coast of Labrador. It is evident that the cleanly houses, cultivated gardens, and neat specimens of manufacture, will strike the eye much sooner—than the unseen principle of this wonderful revolution in the habits of savages will unfold itself to the discernment of the mind. And thus it is, that in their description of all this, they reverse the actual process. They tell us that these most rational of all missionaries, begin their attempts on the heathen by the work of civilizing them; that they teach them to weave, to till, and to store up winter provisions, and to observe justice in their dealings with one another; and then, and not till then, do they, somehow or other, implant upon this preliminary dressing, the mysteries and peculiarities of the Christian Faith. Thus it is that these men of mere spectacle begin to philosophize on the subject, and set up the case of the Moravians as a reproach and an example to all other missionaries.

Now we venture to say that the Moravians, at the *outset* of their conference with savages, keep at as great a distance from any instruction about the arts of weaving, and sewing, and tilling land, as the Apostle Paul did, when he went about among Greeks and barbarians, charged with the message of salvation to all who would listen and believe. He preached nothing but "Jesus Christ and him crucified," and neither do they; and the faith which attends the word of their testimony, how foolish and fanatical soever it may appear in the eyes of worldly men, proves it to be the power of God and the wisdom of God unto salvation. It is another evidence of the foolishness of God being wiser than men, and the weakness of God being stronger than men. However wonderful it may be, yet such is the fact, that a savage, when spoken to on the subject of his soul, of sin, and of the Saviour, has his attention more easily compelled, and his resistance more effectually subdued, than when he is addressed upon any other subject whether of moral or economical instruction. And this is precisely the way in which Moravians have gone to work. They preached the peculiar tenets of the New Testament at the very outset. They gained converts through that Faith which cometh by hearing. These converts multiplied, and, in many instances, they have settled around them. It is true that they have had unexampled success in the business of civilizing their disciples; but it has arisen from their having stood longer on the vantage ground of the previous knowledge of Christianity with which they had furnished them, than any other missionaries; and the peace, and order, and industry, which are represented by rash and superficial observers, as the antecedents of the business, are, in fact, so many consequents flowing out of the mighty influence which attends the word of their testimony.

It is well that the Moravians have risen into popular admiration. This will surely give weight to their own testimony about their own matters. And when one of their members publishes an account of the manner in which the United Brethren preach the Gospel, and carry on their missions among the heathen, information from such a quarter will surely be looked upon as of higher authority than the rapid description of a traveller. Now such a treatise has been published by Spangenberg; and it does not appear that any preparatory civilization is now attempted by their missionaries, who have been engaged in the business for many years, and have been eminent above all others, both for their experience and their success. We shall subjoin a few extracts as being completely decisive upon this point.

"The method of the brethren to bring the heathen to Christ was, in the beginning of their attempts, particularly in Greenland, nearly as follows:—

"They proved to the heathen that there is a God, and spoke to them of His attributes and perfections. In the next place, they spoke upon the creation;—how God had made man after His own image, which, however, was soon lost by the fall. They then made the heathen acquainted with the laws which God gave by His servant Moses. Hence they proved to them that they were sinners, and had deserved temporal and eternal punishment. And from this they drew the consequence, that there must be one who reconciled them to God, &c.

"This method of teaching they continued for a long time, but without any success, for the heathen became tired of such discourses. If it be asked, how happened it that the brethren fell upon the said method, I must confess that I am apprehensive I was myself the cause of it. The first brethren who were destined for Greenland, went to Copenhagen by way of Halle, where I at that time lived. They tarried a few days with me, and conversed with me relative to their intentions. Upon this, I gave them a book to read, (for I knew no better at that time,) in which a certain divine treated, among the rest, of the method to convince and to bring the heathen to Christ. The good man had probably never seen a heathen in all his life, much less converted any; but yet he imagined he could give directions how to set about it. The brethren followed them, but without success.

"Meanwhile, it pleased the Lord our Saviour to give the congregation at Herrnhut more insight into the word of atonement through the offering of Jesus.

Nor were the heathen wanting in declaring to those in Greenland, that they must preach Jesus Christ, if they meant to produce any blessing among the heathen. Upon this, the brethren began to translate some parts of the Gospel, especially what relates to the sufferings and death of Jesus, and read that to the heathen. This gave an opportunity to speak with them farther on that head. Then God opened their hearts that they attended to the word, and it proved to them also the power of God. They became desirous of hearing more about it, and the fire which had been kindled in them by the Holy Ghost, spread farther and farther. And thus many were converted to God: since which time the brethren were frequently asked by the heathen, why they did not preach sooner to them of Jesus; that they had been quite tired of hearing the discourses about God, and the two first parents, &c.

"About thirty years ago, when I lived in North America, I sometimes got the brethren that were used occasionally in the service of our Lord to come together, in order that I might converse with them about their labors. Johannes, an Indian of the Mahikander nation, who had formerly been a very wicked man, but was now thoroughly converted, and was our fellow-laborer in the congregation gathered from among the heathens at that time dwelling in Chekome kah, happened to be just then on a visit with us, and also came to our little meeting. He was a man that had excellent gifts, was a bold confessor of what he knew to be true, and understood the German language so as to express himself with sufficient clearness. As we were speaking with one another about the heathen, he said, among other things,—'Brethren, I have been a heathen and am grown old among them; I know, therefore, very well how it is with the heathen. A preacher came once to us, desiring to instruct us, and began by proving to us that there was a God. On which we said to him, "Well, and dost thou think we are ignorant of that? now go again whence thou camest." Another preacher came another time, and would instruct us, saying, Ye must not steal, nor drink too much, nor lie, &c.—We answered him, "Fool, that thou art! dost thou think that we do not know that? go and learn it first thyself, and teach the people thou belongest to not to do these things. For who are greater drunkards, or thieves, or liars, than thine own people?" Thus we sent him away also. Some time after this Christian Henry, one of the brethren, came to me into my hut, and sat down by me. The contents of his discourse to me were nearly these:—I come to thee in the name of the Lord of heaven and earth. He acquaints thee that he would gladly save thee, and rescue thee from the miserable state in which thou liest. To this end he became a man, hath given his life for mankind, and shed his blood for them, &c. Upon this he lay down upon a board in my hut and fell a-sleep, being fatigued with his journey. I thought within myself,—what manner of man is this? there he lies and sleeps so sweetly; I might kill him immediately, and throw him out into the forest, who would care for it? but he is unconcerned. However, I could not get rid of his words: they continually recurred to me; and though I went to sleep, yet I dreamed of the blood which Christ had shed for us. I thought—this is very strange, and went to interpret to the other Indians the words which Christian Henry spake farther to us. Thus, through the grace of God, the awakening among us took place. I tell you, therefore, brethren, preach to the heathen Christ and his blood, and his death, if ye would wish to produce a blessing among them. Such was the exhortation of Johannes, the Mahikander, to us.

"But the brethren were already, before that time, convinced that Jesus Christ must be the marrow and substance of the preaching of the Gospel among the heathen, even as He is in general called, with justice, the marrow and substance of the whole Bible. The ground of this position is contained in Sect. 9, and following, where we treated of the Apostles' labors among the Gentiles. Nor shall we do amiss if we follow the method of the Apostles, who, in their office, were under the peculiar leadings of the Holy Spirit, as far as it is applicable to us. Hence what Paul writes to the Corinthians—'I determined not to know anything among you save Jesus Christ and him crucified,'—is a firmly established rule for us in preaching to the heathen." (Spangenberg's Account of the Manner in which the United Brethren carry on their Missions among the Heathen. Sections 44—46.)

Before we give any more extracts from Spangenberg, we cannot help remarking on the efficacy of the simple word upon minds totally unfurnished by any previous discipline whatever. This is something more than matter of faith; it is matter of experience: it is the result of many an actual experiment upon human nature. And how comes it, therefore, that philosophers of the day are so often found to flinch from their favorite evidence on every question connected with the truth and the progress of Christianity? The efficacy of the Bible alone, upon simple and unfurnished minds, is a fact; and the finest examples of it are to be found in almost every page of the annals of Moravianism. The worthy men of this denomination have long labored in the field of missionary exertion, and Greenland was one scene of their earliest enterprises. In their progress thither, they were furnished with a cloistered speculation on the likeliest method of obtaining access to the mind of a savage for the truths of Christianity. These men had gone out of Germany without any other instruments for their work than the Word of God in their hands, and a believing prayer in their hearts. But the author of this speculation had thought, and thought profoundly on the subject; and the humble brethren bowed for once to the wisdom of this world, when his synthetic process for the conversion of savages was put into their hands, and they took it along with them. Thus furnished, they entered upon the field of exertion; and never was human nature subjected to experiment under circumstances more favorable. Never did it come in a more simple and elementary state under the treatment of a foreign application. There was no disturbing cause to affect the result of this interesting trial; no bias of education to embarrass our conclusions; no mixture of any previous ingredient to warp and to darken the phenomena, or to throw a disguise over that clear and decisive principle which was on the eve of emerging from them. The rationalizing process of the divine was first put into operation and it failed. Year after year did they take their departure from the simplicity of his first principles, and try to conduct the Greenlanders with them along the pathway which he had constructed for leading them to Christ. The Greenlanders refused to move a single step, and with as great obstinacy as the world of matter refuses to conform her processess to the fanciful theories of men. The brethren, disheartened at the result of an operation so fatiguing and so fruitless, resolved to vary the experiment, and throwing aside all their preparatory instructions, they brought the word of the testimony directly to bear upon them. The effect was instantaneous. God, who knoweth what is in man, knoweth also the kind of application that should be made to man. He glorified the word of His grace, and gave it efficacy. That word which He Himself commanded to be preached to all nations, to the barbarians as well as the Greeks, is surely the mighty instrument for the pulling down of strong holds; and the Moravians have found it so. The Greenland experiment has furnished them with a principle which they carry along with them in all their enterprises. It has seldom failed them in any quarter of the globe; and they can now appeal to thousands and thousands of their converts, as so many distinct testimonies of the efficacy of the Bible.

We like to urge the case of the Moravians, for we think that much may be made of it in the way of reclaiming that unhallowed contempt which some of the ablest, and most accomplished men of this country have expressed for a righteous cause. The truth is, that these Moravians have of late become the objects of a sentimental admiration, and that too to men whom the power of Divine grace has not yet delivered from their natural enmity to the truth as it is in Jesus. Their numerous establishments; and the many interesting pictures of peace, and order, and industry, which they have reared among the wilds of heathenism, have at length compelled the testimony of travellers. It is delightful to be told of the neat attire and cultivated gardens of savages; and we can easily conceive how a sprig of honeysuckle, at the cottage door of a Hottentot, may extort some admiring and poetical prettiness from a charmed spectator, who would shrink offended from the peculiarities of the Gospel. Now they are right as to the fact. It is all very true about the garden and the honeysuckle; but they are most egregiously wrong as to the principle: And when they talk of these Moravians as the most rational of missionaries, because they furnish their converts with the arts and the comforts of life, before they ever think of pressing upon them the mysteries of their faith, they make a most glaring departure from the truth, and that too in the face of information and testimony afforded by the very men whom they profess to admire. It is not true that Moravians are distinguished from other missionaries by training their disciples to justice, and morality, and labor, in the first instance; and by refraining to exhort to faith and self-abasement. It is not true nor does it consist with the practice of the Moravians, that, in regard to savages, some advance towards civilization is necessary, preparatory to any attempt to christianize them. This attempt is made at the very outset; and should they meet with a fellow-creature in the lowest state of uncultivation, it is enough for them that he is a man; nor do they wait the issue of any preparation whatever previously to laying before him the will of God for the salvation of mankind. The degree of cultivation, it would appear, is a thing merely accidental. It has too slender an influence upon the result to be admitted into their calculations; nor does it affect the operation of those great principles which are concerned in the transition of a human soul out of darkness into the marvellous light of the Gospel. Why lavish all your admiration upon the sensible effect, while ye shrink in disgust from the explanation of the principle? Why, ye votaries of science, whose glory it is to connect phenomena with their causes, why do you act so superficially in this instance, and leave with the fanatics whom you despise, all the credit of a manly and unshrinking philosophy? They can tell you all about it, for they were present at every step of the process; and the most striking development of the natural enmity ever witnessed, is to be seen in that mixture of contempt and incredulity, and wonder, with which you listen to them. One might be amused at observing so much of the pride of philosophy combined with so glaring a dereliction of all its principles; but a feeling more serious is awakened when we think of that which is spoken of in the prophecies of Habakkuk: "I work a work in your days, a work which ye shall in no wise believe, though a man declare it unto you."—"Behold, ye despisers, and wonder, and perish!"

Although it is at the hazard of extending this article to a disproportionate length, yet we feel strongly tempted to present another extract from Spangenberg. It tends to prove that the work of civilization is altogether subsequent to the work of conversion; and the attempts of the United Brethren in this way, are among men whom they had previously reclaimed from heathenism, by that peculiar method of evangelizing which has been already insisted on. We shall make no other change in the extract than to throw into Italics those parts of it which bear most decisively upon the argument in question.

"It is likewise a concern of the brethren, that have the care of the heathen, to bring those *that are converted to our Saviour* into good order outwardly. We have found in most places where brethren dwell among the heathen, that the latter go on without much care or thinking. Were they with suitable consideration to regulate their matters duly, to take care and manage what Providence gives to them, they would not so often be driven to the utmost distress. But instead of that, they are idle when they should labor, and when they have anything to eat they will squander it in an extravagant manner; and afterward they are miserably distressed for want of food, and tormented by the cares of this life.

"But *when they are baptized*, the brethren advise them to a regular labor, *e. g.* to plant in due season, to hunt, to fish, and to do everything needful: they also learn of the brethren how to keep and preserve what they may get for the winter. And being incapable of making a proper calculation, (for they have no almanacs,) and to regulate themselves according to the seasons, the brethren also assist them in this respect. I will illustrate this by an instance or two. Dried herrings are of great use to the Greenlanders in winter for their subsistence; but when they grow wet they are spoiled. To obviate this the brethren not only encourage the Greenlanders to be diligent in catching herrings at the proper season, but also to dry them well, and assist them in preserving them dry. If the brethren are among the Indians, they endeavor to get them to clear their fields at the right time, to surround them with hedges, plant them with Indian wheat, and to cut it down in a proper manner; thus a difference is very perceptible between *their people and other* Indians, for if those Indians who have neglected planting suffer hunger, the others have always so much as to be able to spare a part of it to them.

"Various things occasionally occur which must be brought into order among the heathen that are converted to Christ. If (*e. g.*) a provider dies in Greenland, (thus they call the head of the family,) the widow and her orphans are worse off than any one can imagine. Or if a husband loses his wife, and she has left a small child that still wants the mother's breast, he is as badly off, for it is very difficult to get a Greenland woman to suckle any child but her own. Hence it is that those Greenlanders that are yet heathen, and live among heathen, find themselves obliged at times to bury such a motherless infant alive. Now if the case occurs that the wife of a husband dies, leaving a sucking child behind, the brethren do not rest till they find a person that will take care of the little orphan, and give it suck with her own child. If the husband dies they divide the orphans, and take care to have them properly educated, and likewise that the widow may be supplied with the necessaries of life. In sickness, likewise, which happens among the heathen, the brethren are obliged frequently to take care of their people.

"There are indeed some people among the heathen that know good remedies for various disorders, and for this reason they are made use of by others. Among the Indians in North America, there are (*e. g.*) people who successfully cure the bite of serpents, and to whom the neighboring Europeans have recourse in such cases. Also among the negroes in the West Indies are skilful and experienced persons, to whom others apply in their diseases. But these heathenish doctors are jugglers, and generally affect to show they cure the sick by magic. Therefore believers from among the heathen, when sick, consult their teachers, and often apply with success such remedies as they have for their own use.

"Moreover, divers misfortunes that occur in the congregations among the heathen, reduce the brethren to the necessity of taking care of them also, in respect to their outward concerns. There was (*e. g.*) a congregation of Indians at Chekameka in the district of New York, which had formerly, in a fit of intoxication, and while they were still heathen, sold the right to their land for a trifle, and when, afterward, they became converted, occasion was taken from this to drive them out of their country. Most of these people took refuge with the brethren at Bethlehem in Pennsylvania, and were, with the consent of the governor of Pennsylvania, received and treated in a brotherly and hospitable manner. A piece of land was purchased for them on the Mahoni, which answered the purpose of hunting as well as for the cultivation of their corn, and they were assisted by the brethren in building, and in the management of their outward matters.

"The same thing happened with other Indians, who were obliged to quit the land they had sold at Wechquatnach.

"The Indian congregation at Meniolagomekah experienced the same fate, and the brethren could not forbear lending them a helping hand in such circumstances, and caring for their support.

"In the year 1755, the brethren who lived with the Indian congregation at the Mahoni, were surprised at the beginning of the night, by those Indians who had taken up the hatchet against the English (that is, according to their language, had begun the war). They killed eleven of the brethren, dispersed the whole congregation, and laid the whole place in ashes. But the brethren sought again for the scattered sheep, took them to Bethlehem, where they provided for them, and took the same care of their souls as they had done before." (Spangenberg, § 69—71.)

We have one remark more to offer on this part of the subject. Had the missionary system of the United Brethren attracted, fifty years ago, the attention of the same men of general literature, who are now so eloquent in its praises, it is evident that it could not have achieved their homage, nor excited their sympathy. At that early period of their labors, they had not the same commanding spectacle to offer as the result of their missionary labors. Sufficient time had not elapsed for the full effect and development of their principles; but they were busy at work with the principles themselves. They were preaching, and praying, and putting into action, the weapons of their spiritual ministry; and had the fastidious admirer of neat and interesting villages, taken a look at them during the earlier years of their missionary enterprise, he would have nauseated the whole precedure as the effect of mean revolting fanaticism. Now let it not be forgotten that what the Moravians were then, some of the later class of missionaries are at this moment. They have positively not had time for the production of the same striking and numerous results; but they are very busy and very promising in that line of operation which leads to them. To be an admirer of the result is a very different thing from being an admirer of the operation. To be the one, all that is necessary is a taste for what is wonderful, or what is pleasing; and what can be more wonderful, and, at the same time, more pleasing, than a group of Hottentot families reclaimed from the barbarism of their race, and living under obedient control to the charities and decencies of the Gospel? But that a person may become an admirer of the operation, he must approve the faith; he must be influenced by a love of the Lord Jesus Christ; he must have a belief in the efficacy of prayer; he must have a relish for that which a majority, we fear, of professing Christians would stamp with the brand of enthusiasm; in a word, his natural enmity to the things of God must be beginning to give way, and he be an admirer of the truth in all its unction and in all its simplicity. Let not, therefore, the later missionaries be mortified at the way in which they have been contrasted with the Moravians. They are just passing through the very ordeal through which these worthy men passed before them. It is a trial of their faith, and of their patience; and if they keep the same steadfastness, to the simplicity that is in Christ; if they maintain the same enduring dependence upon God; if they resist the infection of a worldly spirit, with the same purity of heart which has ever marked the United Brethren, and preserve themselves through all the varieties of disappointment and success as free from the temptations of vain glory, or bitterness, or emulation; then may they look forward to the day when they shall compel the silence of gainsayers by exhibitions equally wonderful and promising.

The United Brethren failed in their first attempt to settle on the coast of Labrador, in 1752; nor did they renew their attempt till an offer was made by Jens Haven, in 1764, to go out as a missionary to that country. He had been for some years a missionary in Greenland; and from the strong affinity between the two languages, he was able to make himself understood by the Esquimaux. This secured him a degree of acceptance among that barbarous people, which was never before experienced by any European; a circumstance highly agreeable to Sir Hugh Palliser, at that time Governor of Newfoundland, and which obtained for the missionary, the countenance of the Board of Trade and Plantations.

It was found necessary, however, to defer the missionary work for some years, till Mikak, an Esquimaux woman, was brought to London, and attracted the same kind of notice among people of rank and influence in the metropolis, that was afterwards excited by the appearance of the well-known Otaheitean in this country. She here met with Jens Haven, and earnestly solicited his protection for her poor countrymen, many of whom had been slaughtered in a late affray with the English. She was of great use in advancing the business of the mission; and a grant was at length obtained from the Privy Council, by which the Brethren's Society for the furtherance of the Gospel, obtained permission from the King and his Ministers, to make settlements on the coast of Labrador, and to preach the Gospel to the Esquimaux.

Under cover of this permission, Haven, accompanied with others, sailed for the coast of Labrador, purchased land from the Esquimaux, and in 1771, was busied in the erection of various conveniences for a settlement at Nain, where they were suffered to reside without disturbance from the natives who visited them. In 1776, they formed another settlement at Okkak, an island, about 150 miles to the northward; and one year after a third settlement at Hopedale, to the south of Okkak, completed the present list of the Moravian establishments in that country.

In reading their own account of these and similar enterprises, we cannot avoid being struck with the activity and perseverance of the missionaries; and the mere philosopher of second causes, would look upon these, aided as they frequently are by the most fortunate and unlooked-for conjuncture of circumstances, as sufficient to explain the whole secret of their unexampled success. But the Moravians are men of prayer. They wrestle with God, and never let go the engine, of which it has been said, that it moves Him who moves the universe. Were we to confine ourselves to a mere record of the visible events, we doubt not that many would receive it as a complete history of their missionary undertakings. But let us do no such injustice to their own narratives, and to the uniform spirit of piety and dependence which pervades them. Previously to the grant by the Privy Council, Jens Haven tells us, that the mission in Labrador was the constant subject of his prayers and meditations, and that with prayer and supplication he committed himself, and the cause he was to serve, unto the Lord. In the progress of the business we read much of his self-examinations and confessions, and of his crying out unto the Lord for help, and for faith to commit himself and his cause to Divine protection. This is a fair specimem of a Moravian missionary; and these are the deep and holy exercises with which the world cannot sympathize, and which the men of the world cannot banish altogether from the history of human affairs. They form the turning point of the machinery, without which nothing would be accomplished; and they who smile at the occult influence which lies in a believer's prayer, should be informed, that to this principle alone do the Moravian preachers attribute the whole of that sensible effect on which they lavish all their admiration.

Such has been the success of the Moravians in these three settlements, that, in 1788, the whole number of the baptized, from the commencement, amounted to one hundred and four, of which sixty-three were then alive; and the actual number of baptized, and of candidates for baptism, in 1812, was two hundred and ninety-two. They have translated the Gospels into the Esquimaux language, and are proceeding with the other books of the New Testament. They have taught many of the natives to read and to write. These poor barbarians can now carry on an epistolary correspondence with the Moravians in this country, and in point of scholarship, and of civil accomplishment, are farther advanced than the great mass of the peasantry in England.

The following extracts from their periodical accounts, will give a more correct exhibition of the spirit and proceedings of the missionaries, than can be done by any description.

"Your kind letter conveys strong proof of your participation in the work of God among the Esquimaux here, and of your joy at all the good which the Lord has done for us. You also mention that you join in our prayers that new life from God would visit our young people. We hope and trust with you that the Lord will, in his own time, so powerfully awaken them by his grace that they can no longer resist. With respect to the adults, we have again abundant cause for thankfulness in reporting what the Lord has done for them in the year past. The greater part are advancing to a more perfect knowledge of themselves and the power of His grace, and afford thereby a proof to others of the necessity of conversion. The schools have been attended, during the past winter, not without blessing, to which the books printed in the Esquimaux language, and sent to us by you, have contributed much. Since the departure of the ship last year, three persons have been admitted to the Holy Communion, one adult and three children baptized, and six admitted as candidates for baptism. Of the Esquimaux belonging to our congregation here, twenty-five are communicants, one of whom is excluded; fourteen baptized adults, of whom two are excluded; twenty-nine baptized children, and twenty candidates for baptism; in all eighty-eight persons. We cannot precisely state the number of Esquimaux who dwell on our land, as some of them purpose removing to Okkak, and one family from the heathen has come to us. The whole number may be about one hundred and fifty. As the highly respected British and Foreign Bible Society has again intimated their willingness to print part of the Holy Scriptures in the Esquimaux language, we accept their offer with much gratitude, and shall send, by the return of the ship, the Gospels according to St. Matthew, St.

Mark, and St. Luke, which our late brother Burghardt was still able to revise, requesting you, at the same time, to salute the society most cordially on our behalf, and to assure them of our great esteem and veneration. They have our best wishes and prayers, that their exertions may be crowned by the Lord with abundant success, in the salvation of many thousand human creatures in all parts of the globe.

"The outward wants of our Esquimaux have been but scantily supplied during the last winter, as the seal fishing in nets did not succeed, only sixty-six being taken, and they were able to get but little when they went out on kajaks, or on the thin ice. It was very providential that the supply of provisions sent for the Esquimaux by the ship last year, enabled us to relieve their most pressing necessities. The want was severely felt in spring, owing to the long continuance of the cold, with much snow, which prevented the seals from coming hither till late in the season. The Esquimaux had, consequently, to be supported for a considerable time out of the store, which occasioned us no small uneasiness, on account of the debts which they unavoidably contracted. Nor were these circumstances, as may be supposed, without a degree of influence upon the state of their minds, though we cannot say that they were productive of abiding detriment. They felt grateful, that by the Lord's mercy they were preserved from perishing through famine." Per. Acc. United Brethren, No. lxiv. p. 254

The above is from Nain ; the following is from Hopedale.

"Your kind expressions concerning us and our labors filled our hearts with gratitude. We can assure you, dear Brethren, that the daily mercies of our Saviour still attend us, both in our external and internal concerns. Poor and defective as we feel ourselves to be, he has not taken his grace and spirit from us, but forgiven us all sin, daily and richly supported and helped us in our labors, comforted us in all distress, preserved us in peace and brotherly love, and excited in us all an ardent desire to live unto and serve Him with all our hearts.

"Several of us have been ailing, but he approved himself our kind physician, and nothing essential has been neglected in the performance of our daily duties through illness. Constant communion with Him is the source of all spiritual life and strength, and we pray him to lead us more and more into that blessed track.

"With thanks to Him we are able to say, that the walk of most of our Esquimaux has been such as to give us heartfelt joy. Our Saviour has led them as the good shepherd in the way of life everlasting, and by his Spirit taught them to know that without him they can do nothing good. They set a value upon the word of God, and desire in all respects to live more in conformity to it. The love of our Saviour towards them excites their wonder, and they sometimes complain with tears, that they do not love him, and give joy unto him as they ought for his great mercy vouchsafed unto them. The word of his cross, sufferings, and death, melts their hearts, and causes them truly to repent of, and abhor sin, which nailed him to the cross, and to mourn and cry for pardon. Instances of this blessed effect of the doctrine of a crucified Saviour we have seen in our public meetings, in our private converse with them, and in the schools. The latter have been kept up with all possible punctuality and diligence.

"We can declare with truth, that Jesus Christ, our Saviour, has been the heart's desire of us all, towards whom we wish to press forward, that we may live to Him and enjoy more of His sweet communion. Notwithstanding all weakness and deficiency still observable in our small congregation, we have great reason to rejoice over most of them, especially over the communicants. The celebration of the Lord's Supper is to them a most important and blessed transaction. We have re-admitted to it those, whom you may remember last year to have fallen into foolish and superstitious practices during a time of sickness and frequent deaths, but who truly repented of their error.

"We pray for more spiritual life among our youth, in whom we have discovered too many traces of levity.

"Two adults and two children have been baptized, two girls, baptized as children, were received into the congregation, three were made partakers of the Lord's Supper, three became candidates for it, and one a candidate for baptism. One child died during the year past. At the conclusion of the year our congregation consists of eighty-eight Esquimaux brethren and sisters, of whom thirty-one are communicants. One hundred and twenty-two persons lived on our land. We have had no addition from among the heathen, none having resided in our neighborhood.

"To the worthy British and Foreign Bible Society we beg you to present our most cordial thanks, for the Gospel of St. John in the Esquimaux language, printed and bound up in the best manner. Our hearts are filled with gratitude towards them for this most valuable donation, and we pray the Lord richly to reward them for it, and to cause all their labors of love to succeed, for His glory and the welfare of mankind. Our people take this little book with them to the islands when they go out to seek provisions, and in their tents, or snow-houses, spend their evenings in reading it with great edification and blessing. They often beg us to thank the Society in their name when we write to England.

"We feel very sensibly the loss of private letters, and of the diaries and accounts of our congregations and missions by, the stoppage of communication between England and the Continent. O that the Lord would hold His hand over our settlements in Germany, since it appears as if they were threatened by a new war.

"As you approve of the building of a store-house for our Esquimaux, we shall now take steps to complete that work."—Per. Ac. lxiv. p. 260.

* Let it be observed, that Okkak, the most northerly of the three settlements, lies in a latitude little short of 58° N. and 2½° to the south of Cape Chudleigh; that on doubling this Cape, the coast trends S. S. W. as far as to 58½° of N. lat.; that it then takes a sweep to the northward, and thus forms a bay named, in the accounts of these missionaries, Ungava bay. The line of the voyage extends then from Okkak, along the coast of Labrador, to the Cape Chudleigh Islands, from whence it takes a south and westerly direction to the bottom of Ungava Bay. They were induced to undertake it by a statement of the Esquimaux visitors, who occasionally repaired to the establishments already formed, and reported that the main body of this nation lived near and beyond Cape Chudleigh. In addition to these accounts they received the most earnest applications to form a new settlement to the northward, applications to which they felt themselves the more inclined to listen, as the country around their present establishments was very thinly inhabited, and it appeared that the aim of the mission, to convert the Esquimaux to Christianity, would be much better obtained, if access could be had to the main body of the Indians, from which the roving inhabitants appeared to be mere stragglers.

Having obtained the consent of their superiors in Europe, a company was formed for the voyage, under the superintendence of

* The work reviewed in my paper was the "Journal of a Voyage from Okkak."

Brother Kohlmeister, who was eminently qualified for the charge, by a residence of seventeen years in Labrador, during which time he had acquired an accurate knowledge of the Esquimaux language, and was deservedly respected and beloved both by Christians and heathens. Brother Kmock accompanied him in the voyage, and their crew consisted of four Esquimaux families belonging to Hopedale. Having commended themselves in prayer to the grace and protecting care of God, their Saviour, and to the kind remembrance of their dear fellow missionaries, they set sail from Okkak, in a large decked boat, on the 24th of June, 1811.

In their progress they met with many interruptions from large fields of ice, which often presented a threatening appearance. They kept in general close to the shore, and had to work their way through numerous straits, formed by the small islands which lie scattered along the coast in great numbers, sometimes sleeping on board, and at others, pitching their tent on shore. They often met with very wild and singular exhibitions of scenery; and the Moravians, ever observant of all that is interesting in the appearances of nature, do not fail to gratify the reader by their description of them. The following is a specimen of the notice they take of these things, and the way in which they record them.

"June 25th.—We rose soon after two o'clock, and rowed out of the Ikkerasak with a fair wind. The sea was perfectly calm and smooth. Brother Kmock rowed in the small boat along the foot of the mountains of Kammayok, sometimes going on shore while the large boat was making but little way, keeping out at some distance to avoid the rocks. The outline of this chain of mountains exhibits the most fanciful figures. At various points the rocks descend abruptly into the sea, presenting horrid precipices. The strand is covered with a black sand. At the height of about fifty feet from the sea, the rocks have veins of red, yellow, and green stone, running horrizontally and parallel, and sometimes in an undulated form. Above these they present the appearance of a magnificent colonnade, or rather of buttresses, supporting a gothic building varying in height and thickness, and here and there intersected by wide and deep chasms and glens running far inland between the mountains. Loose stones above have in some places the appearance of statues, and the superior region exhibits various kinds of grotesque shapes. It is by far the most singular and picturesque chain of mountains on this coast. To the highest part of it we gave the name of St. Paul's, as it is not unlike that cathedral when viewed at a distance, with its dome and two towers."—p. 14.

On the day following they met with some of the believing Esquimaux, who were on their summer excursion, at which time they have many opportunities of mingling with the unconverted of their own nation. It refreshes our hearts to hear, that the wilds of a savage country exhibit a scene so soothing as that which these worthy men realized upon this occasion.

"The number of the congregation, including our boat's company, amounted to about fifty. Brother Kohlmeister first addressed them by greeting them from their brethren at Okkak, and expressing our joy at finding them well in health, and our hopes that they were all walking worthy of their christian profession, as a good example to their heathen neighbors. Then the Litany was read, and a spirit of true devotion pervaded the whole assembly.

"Our very hearts rejoiced in this place, which had but lately been a den of murderers, dedicated, as it were, by the angekoks, or sorcerers, to the service of the devil, to hear the cheerful voices of converted heathen most melodiously sounding forth the praises of God, and giving glory to the name of Jesus, their Redeemer. Peace and cheerful countenances dwelt in the tents of the believing Esquimaux."—p. 16.

What else is it than the spreading of this moral cultivation over the vast and dreary extent of that pagan wilderness, which is everywhere around us, that can lead to the accomplishment of the following prophecies? "Israel shall blossom and bud and fill the face of the world with fruit." "The wilderness and solitary place shall be glad for them, and the desert shall rejoice and blossom as the rose." "In the wilderness shall waters break out, and streams in the desert, and the parched ground shall become a pool, and the thirsty land springs of water. In the habitation of dragons where each lay, shall be grass with reeds and rushes."

They were detained from the 3d to the 15th of July, in Nullatartok bay, by the quantity of drift ice which set in upon the coast. This gave them time for exploring the neighborhood; and these observant men neglect nothing in their power that can be turned to useful information for future travellers. They make minutes of the bays, points, and islands, with which they are made acquainted by the natives. They record the face of the country, and the appearance of its mineralogical productions. They take great interest in relating the manners and peculiar practices of the people. They make collections of plants, and are amused with the examination of them. In a word, they notice all and record all, which can give interest to the narrative of an accomplished traveller; and the only additions which they graft upon all this, are a constant recognition of God, and an eye steadily fixed on his glory. Can it be this which has so long repelled the attention of worldly men from their labors and enterprises? which made their good be evil spoken of? and which, till within these few years, restrained them from offering to the public a mass of solid information that has now perished from the memory, and cannot be recalled?

The following is a specimen of the manner in which they mingle the business of piety, with the business of ordinary travellers.

"Perceiving that our abode in this place might be of some duration, we for the first time pitched our tents on shore. Our morning and evening devotion was attended by the whole party, and on Sundays we read the Litany and conducted the service in the usual way, which proved to us and our Esquimaux, of great comfort and encouragement in all difficulties. We were detained here by the ice from the 3d to the 15th, and our faith and patience were frequently put to the trial. Meanwhile we found much pleasure in walking up the acclivities of the hills and into the fine green and flowery valleys around us." —p. 22.

"6th.—In the evening we met in Jonathan's tent. Brother Kohlmeister addressed the company, and reminded them that to-day the holy communion would be celebrated in our congregations, which we could not do in this place under present circumstances. Then, kneeling down, he offered up a fervent prayer, entreating the Lord not to forget us in this wilderness, but to give us to feel His all-reviving presence, and to feed our hungry and thirsty souls out of the fulness of his grace. A comfortable sense of His love and peace, filled all our hearts on this occasion.'"

On the 16th, they advanced to Nachvak, and the scene of magnificence which opened upon them here, is well described by our travellers.

"16th.—The view we had of the magnificent mountains of Nachvak, especially about sunrise, afforded us and our Esquimaux great gratification. Their south-east extremity much resembles Saddle island, near Okkak, being high, steep, and of singular shape. These mountains in general are not unlike those of Kanmayok for picturesque outline. In one place tremendous precipices form a vast amphitheatre, surmounted by a ledge of green sod, which seemed to be the resort of an immense number of sea-gulls and other fowls never interrupted by the intrusion of man. They flew with loud screams backwards and forwards over our heads, as if to warn off such unwelcome visitors. In another place a narrow chasm opens into the mountain widening into a lagoon, the surrounding rocks resembling the ruins of a large gothic building, with the green ocean for its pavement, and the sky for its dome. The weather being fine, and the sun cheering us with his bright rays, after a cold and sleepless night, we seemed to acquire new vigor by the contemplation of the grand features of nature around us. We now perceived some Esquimaux with a woman's boat in a small bay, preparing to steer for Nachvak. They fired their pieces, and called to us to join them, as they had discovered a stranded whale. Going on shore to survey the remains of this huge animal, we found it by no means a pleasant sight. It lay upon the rocks, occupying a space thirty feet in diameter, but was much shattered, and in a decaying state. Our people, however cut off a quantity of blubber from its lips. The greater part of the blubber of, this fish was lost, as the Esquimaux had no means of conveying it to Okkak." —p. 26.

The following description of the manner in which the Esquimaux catch salmon-trout, is, we believe, a novelty.

"The Esquimaux about Okkak and Saeglek, catch them in winter under the ice by spearing. For this purpose they make two holes in the ice about eight inches in diameter, and six feet asunder in a direction from north to south. The northern hole they screen from the sun by a bank of snow about four feet in height, raised in a semi-circle round its southern edge, and form another similar bank on the north side of the southern hole, sloped in such a manner as to reflect the rays of the sun into it. The Esquimaux then lies down with his face close to the northern aperture, beneath which the water is strongly illuminated by the sunbeams entering at the southern. In his left hand he holds a red string, with which he plays in the water, to allure the fish, and in his right a spear, ready to strike them as they approach. In this manner they soon take as many as they want."—p. 28.

At Nachvak they had frequent opportunities of converse with the natives, and we know of no question more interesting than that which proposes the consideration of the best method of addressing Christianity to the minds of men totally unfurnished with any preparatory conceptions upon the subject. On other subjects of inquiry, the rashness of the theorizing spirit is exploded, and all speculation is made to vanish before the evidence of experiment. To the evidence on this question the Moravians are making daily additions: And the whole history of their proceedings bears testimony to the fact, that the Gospel is never preached in power but when it is preached in simplicity; that the refinements of men do but enfeeble the impression of it; and that the word of truth, as it came pure from the mouth of Christ, and of His apostles, may be addressed to savages at the very lowest degree in the scale of civilization. When taken in connection with this principle, we look upon the first meeting of a Christian missionary with savages, as a circumstance possessing a higher interest than any other thing that can be recorded of the intercourse of man with man; and the interest is considerably heightened, when, instead of the accomplished missionary, it is the Christianized heathen, who has himself lately experienced the love of the truth, and is become subject to its power, that addresses the words of salvation to the unawakened among his own countrymen. The following is a specimen.

"They (the natives) received the discourses and exhortations of the missionary with reverential attention, but those of their own countrymen with still greater eagerness, and we hope not without benefit. Jonas once addressed them thus:—'We were but lately as ignorant as you are now: we were long unable to understand the comfortable words of the Gospel: we had neither ears to hear, nor hearts to receive them, till Jesus by His power opened our hearts and ears. Now we know what Jesus has done for us, and how great the happiness of those souls is, who come unto Him, who love Him as their Saviour, and know that they shall not be lost when this life is past. Without this we live in constant fear of death. You will enjoy the same happiness if you turn to and believe in Jesus. We are not surprised that you do not yet understand us. We were once like you, but now thank Jesus our Redeemer, with tears of joy, that He has revealed Himself unto us.' Thus, with cheerful countenances and great energy, did these Christian Esquimaux praise and glorify the name of Christ our Saviour, and declare what He had done for their souls, exhorting the heathen likewise to believe.

"The above address seemed to make a deep impression on the minds of all present. One of their leaders or captains exclaimed with great eagerness in presence of them all,—'I am determined to be converted to Jesus.' His name is Onalik. He afterwards called upon Brother Kohlmeister, and inquired whether it was the same to which of the three settlements he removed, as it was his firm determination to become a true believer. Brother Kohlmeister answered, that it was indifferent where he lived, if he were only converted, and became a child of God, and an heir of life eternal. Another named Fullugaksoak made the same declaration, and added that he would no longer live among the heathen.

"Though the very fickle disposition of the heathen Esquimaux might cause some doubts to arise in our minds as to their putting these good resolutions into practice, yet we hope that the seed of the word of God, sown in this place, may not have altogether fallen upon barren ground."—p. 30.

In their progress northward to Cape Chudleigh, they fall in with other parties of the natives; and on the 22d of July we have the following description of an Esquimaux feast, at which the missionary himself addressed the heathen.

"22d.—The contrary wind forbidding our departure, Brother Kohlmeister, accompanied by Jonathan Jonas, and Kukekina, walked across the country to the N. W. bay, to return their visit. When they saw them coming at a distance, they fired their pieces to direct them to the tents, and came joyfully to meet the missionary and his party. Nothing could exceed the cordiality with which they received them. A kettle was immediately put on the fire to cook salmon-trout, and all were invited to partake, which was the more readily accepted, as the length of the walk had created an appetite, the keenness of which overcame all squeamishness. To do these good people justice, their kettle was rather cleaner than usual, the dogs having licked it well, and the fish was fresh and well dressed. To honor the missionary, a box was placed for him to sit upon, and the fish were served up to each upon a flat stone instead of a plate. After dinner, Brother Kohlmeister, in acknowledgment for their civility, gave to each of the women two needles, and a small portion of tobacco to each man, with which they were highly delighted.

"All of them being seated, a very lively and unreserved conversation took place, concerning the only way of salvation through Jesus Christ, and the necessity of conversion. With John and his mother Mary, Brother Kohlmeister spoke very seriously, and represented to them the danger of their state as apostates from the faith, but they seem blinded by Satan, and determined to persist in their heathenish life. The Esquimaux now offered to convey the party across the bay in their skin-boat, which was accepted. Almost all of them accompanied the boat, and met with a very friendly reception from our boat's company. In the evening, after some hymns had been sung by our people, Jonas addressed them and the heathen Esquimaux, in a short nervous discourse on the blessedness of being reconciled unto God.

"Kummaktorvik bay runs N. E. and S. W., and is defended by some islands from the sea. It is about four or five miles long, and surrounded by high mountains, with some pleasant plains at their foot covered with verdure. Its distance from Nachvak is about twelve miles. This chain of mountains, as will be hereafter mentioned, may be seen from Kangertlualuksoak, in Ungava bay, which is a collateral proof that the neck of land terminated to the N. by Cape Chudleigh, is of no great width. Both the Nain and Okkak Esquimaux frequently penetrate far enough inland to find the rivers taking a westerly direction, consequently towards the Ungava country. They even now and then have reached the woods skirting the estuaries of George and South rivers."—p. 35.

On the 2d of August, they passed a strait among the islands of Cape Chudleigh, when the coast takes a S. S. W. direction. At this place the tides rise to an uncommon height. The coast is low, with gently sloping hills, and the country looks pleasant, with many berry-bearing plants and bushes. It is from this point of the voyage, that they seem to enter upon new ground, for at a very great distance to the N. W. they descried a large island named Akpatok, which, according to the statement of the Esquimaux, incloses the whole gulf or bay towards the sea, consists of high land, and is connected to the western continent at low water by an isthmus. Now it is the North coast of this island which appears to be the line laid down in maps and charts as the coast of America to the south of Hudson's Straits. So that a large inland bay, separating the district of Ungava, from the island of Akpatok, and which, from the map accompanying this account, is made to extend from W. longitude 65° 45′ to 70°, and from N. latitude 60° 15′ to about 58°, appears to be an expanse of water wholly unnoticed by former navigators. At the bottom of this bay lies the Ungava country, and our party, in their progress towards it, had intercourse with the natives on the coast. Our missionary took an early occasion to make known his object in visiting them.

"Brother Kohlmeister visited the people in their tents. They were about fifty in number, men women, and children. He informed them that nothing could induce the missionaries to come into this country but love to the poor heathen, and an ardent desire to make them acquainted with their Creator and Redeemer, that through Him they might attain to happiness in time and eternity. Some seemed to listen with attention, but the greater part understood nothing of what was said. This of course did not surprise us, as most of them were quite ignorant heathen, who had never before seen a European. They, however, raised a shout of joy, when we informed them that we would come and visit them in their own country. Many were not satisfied with viewing us on every side with marks of great astonishment, but came close up to us and pawed us all over. At taking leave we presented them with a few trifles, which excited among them the greatest pleasure and thankfulness."—p. 47.

A few days afterwards we have the following specimen of the tides in this bay.

"7th.—On rising, to our great surprise, we found ourselves left by the tide in a shallow pool of water surrounded by rocky hills, nor could we at all discover the situation of our skin-boat, till after the water had begun to rise, and raised us above the banks of our watery dungeon, when with great astonishment, not having been able to find it on the surface of the sea, and accidentally directing our eyes upwards, we saw it perched upon the top of a considerable eminence, and apparently on shore. We then landed, and ascending a rising ground, beheld with some terror, the wonderful changes occasioned by the tides. Our course was visible to the extent of two or three English miles, but the sea had left it, and we were obliged to remain in this dismal place till about noon before the water had risen sufficiently to carry us out. We now began to entertain fears lest we might not always be able to find proper harbors so as to avoid being left high and dry at low water, for having anchored in nine fathoms last night, we were left in one and a half this morning. Uttakiyok and Kukekina were with us on shore. The eminence on which we stood was overgrown with vaccinia and other plants, and we saw among them marks of its being visited by hares. Near the summit was a spot covered by red sand which stained one's fingers, and among it were fragments of a substance resembling cast iron. We seemed here to stand ou a peninsula connected by an isthmus with another island, or with the continent, but probably at high water it may be a separate island."—p. 51.

In a few days they reached Kangertlualuksoak Bay, to which they gave the name of George river, after having formally taken possession of the country in the name of George III., whom they designate the Great Monarch of all those territories, in their explanation to the natives of a tablet solemnly raised in commemoration of this voyage. We do not see the necessity of this transaction, and confess that our feelings of justice somewhat revolted at it. How George III. should be the rightful monarch of a territory whose inhabitants never saw a European before, is something more than we can understand. We trust that the marauding policy of other times, is now gone by; and that the transaction in question is nothing more than an idle ceremony. At all events we do think that our worthy missionaries have, in this instance, made an unwitting departure from the character which belongs to them; and we implore them, as they value the approbation of all right-minded Christians, to keep by the simplicity of their one object, and never to venture one single footstep on the dubious ground of this world's politics. The following simple adventure is infinitely more in accordance with our minds.

"After dining on part of the venison, we returned to the great boat. On the passage we thought we perceived, at a considerable distance, a black bear, and Uttakiyok, elated with his recent success, hoped to gain new laurels. He entered his kayak, and proceeded as cautiously as possible along the shore towards the spot, landed, climbed the hill so as not to be observed, but when he had just got within gun-shot, perceived that his bear was a black stone. This adventure furnished the company with merriment for the remainder of the voyage to the boat."—p. 57.

They determined upon the mouth of George river as a suitable place for a settlement.

"12th.—Having finished reconnoitring the neighborhood, and gathered all the information concerning it which our means would admit, and likewise fixed upon the green slope or terrace above described as the most suitable place for a settlement, on account of the abundance of wood in its neighborhood, we made preparations to proceed. Uttakiyok, who had spent more than one winter in the Ungava country, assured us that there was here an ample supply of provisions both in summer and winter, which Jonathan also credited from his own observation. The former likewise expressed himself convinced that if we would form a settlement here, many Esquimaux would come to us from all parts. We ourselves were satisfied that Europeans might find the means of existence in this place, as it was accessible for ships, and had wood and water in plenty. As for Esquimaux, there appeared no want of those things upon which they live, the sea abounding with white fish, seals, sea-fowl, &c., and the land with reindeer, hares, bears, and other animals. The people from Killinek declared their intention of removing hither, if we would come and dwell among them, and are even now in the habit of visiting this place every summer. Our own company even expressed a wish to spend the winter here."—p. 57.

The season was now far advanced, and the danger of being overtaken by winter before they completed their return to Okkak, began to press upon them. But they had not yet got to the bottom of the bay which they had fixed upon as the final object of their voyage. The courage of their party was beginning to fail, and the missionaries themselves were in no small degree of perplexity. In this situation of difficulty, ordinary travellers would sit down to the work of calculation, and so did they; they would weigh reasons and probabilities, and so did they; they would gather information from the natives, and exercise their judgment upon it, and advise earnestly with one another, and so too did these humble missionaries. But there was still one other expedient which they resorted to, and in the instance before us, it helped them out of their difficulties. This expedient was prayer. They laid the matter before God, and He answered them. This, we imagine, is what ordinary travellers seldom think of doing; what the men of an infidel world would call fanaticism; but if there be any truth in the word of God, it is the likeliest method of obtaining counsel and direction under all our embarrassments. "If any of you lack wisdom, let him ask of God, that giveth to all men liberally, and upbraideth not; and it shall be given him. But let him ask in faith, nothing wavering." Their account of this matter is too interesting to be omitted.

"19th.—In the morning we met in our tent, where we were safe from the intrusion of the Esquimaux, to confer together upon this most important subject. We weighed all the circumstances connected with it maturely and impartially as in the presence of God, and not being able to come to any decision, where reasons for and against the question seemed to hold such an even balance, we determined to commit our case to Him who hath promised that "if two of His people shall agree on earth as touching anything that they shall ask, it shall be done for them;" (Matt. xviii. 19;) and kneeling down, entreated Him to hear our prayers and supplications, in this our distressed and embarrassing situation, and to make known to us His will concerning our future proceedings, whether we should persevere in fulfilling the whole aim of our voyage, or, prevented by circumstances, give up a part and return home from this place.

"The peace of God which filled our hearts on this memorable occasion, and the strong conviction wrought in us, both that we should persevere in His name to fulfil the whole of our commission, relying without fear on his help and preservation, no words can describe; but those who believe in the fulfilment of the gracious promises of Jesus, given to his poor followers and disciples, will understand us when we declare that we were assured that it was the will of God our Saviour that we should not now return and leave our work unfinished, but proceed to the end of our proposed voyage. Each of us communicated to his brother the conviction of his heart, all fears and doubts vanished, and we were filled anew with courage and willingness to act in obedience to it in the strength of the Lord. O, that all men knew the comfort and happiness of a mind devoted unto, and firmly trusting in God in all things."—p. 64.

On the 25th of August, they reached the termination of their voyage, and sailed up the river Koksoak, which discharges its waters into the bottom of Ungava bay. The estuary of Koksoak or South river, lies in N. latitude 58° 36′. It is as broad as the Thames at Gravesend, and bears a great resemblance to that river in its windings for twenty-four miles upwards. It is distant by sea from Okkak between 600 and 700 miles, and Cape Chudleigh is about half way. They were soon descried by the natives, who shouted them a rapturous welcome. Upon hoisting their colors. they were incessantly hailed by the inhabitants. There was a general cry of Europeans! Europeans! from the men in the kayaks, who, by all manner of gesticulations, expressed their pleasure, brandishing their oars, and shouting continually as they rowed alongside the boat. The women on shore answered with loud acclamations.

They were not long in acquainting the natives with the cause of their voyage, and it is delightful to observe the advantage they possessed in the zeal of their coadjutors among the converted Esquimaux, whom they brought along with them. Jonathan and Jonas conversed with them about the concerns of their immortal souls, declaring to them the love of God our Saviour towards them; and Sybilla, Jonathan's wife, was met with seated among a company of women, and exhorting them with great simplicity and fervor, to hear and believe the Gospel. On this subject we shall present only one extract more from the work before us.

"30th.—Our people, and with them the strange Esquimaux, met for public worship. Brother Kohlmeister once more explained to them our intention in coming thus far to visit them. He addressed them to the following effect:—'That already, many years ago, many excellent people, in the country beyond the great ocean, had thought of them with much love, and felt desirous that the inhabitants of the Ungava country also might hear the comfortable word of God, and be instructed in it, for they had heard that the Esquimaux here were heathen, who through ignorance served the Torngak, or evil spirit, and were led by him into the commission of all manner of sin; that they might hereafter be lost, and go to the place of eternal darkness and misery. Out of love therefore,' continued the missionary, 'they have sent us to you, and out of love we have come to you to tell you how you may be saved, and become happy, peaceful children of God, being delivered from the fear of death which is now upon you all, and have the prospect of everlasting peace and joy hereafter, even by receiving the Gospel, and turning to Jesus who is the only Creator and Saviour of all men. He died for *your* sins, for *our* sins, and for the sins of all mankind, as our surety, suffering the punishment we deserved, that *you*, by receiving Him, and believing on Him, might be saved, and not go to the place of eternal darkness and pain, but to the place of bliss and eternal rest. You cannot yet understand these comfortable words of the Gospel; but if it is your sincere wish to know the truth of them, Jesus will open your ears and hearts, to hear and understand them. These my companions were as ignorant as you, but they now thank God that they know Jesus as their Saviour, and are assured that through His death they shall inherit everlasting life.'

"During this address all were silent and very attentive. Some exclaimed, 'O! we desire to hear more about it.' Old Netsiak from Eivektok said 'I am indeed old, but if you come to live here, I will certainly remove hither also, and live with you and be converted.'

"When we put the question to them, whether they were willing that we should come and dwell with them and instruct them, they all answered, with a loud and cheerful voice, '*Kaititse tok! Kaititse tok!* O! do come soon and live with us, we will all gladly be converted, and live with you.' Jonathan and Jonas also bore ample testimony to the truth of what we had spoken, and their words seemed to make a deep impression on all their countrymen. Uttakiyok was above others eager to express his wish that we might soon make a settlement in the Ungava country. Five of the fourteen families who mean to reside here next winter are from Eivektok."—p. 75.

On the first of September, they took their leave of South river, not without every expression of regret and attachment from the natives, who, with a generous benevolence not to be surpassed in the refined countries of Europe, called after them, 'Come soon again, we shall always be wishing for you.' Their homeward voyage was more quick and prosperous: and on the 4th of October, they reached Okkak, after having performed a distance of from 1200 to 1300 miles.

The Moravian style, throughout the whole of their narrations, is lucid and perspicuous; replete with the phraseology of Scripture. It has a certain air of sweetness and gentleness about it, which harmonizes with all our other associations which regard this interesting people. With all their piety they mingle a very lively interest in the topics of ordinary travellers; and as the single aim of all their descriptions is to be faithful, they often succeed in a clear and impressive definition of the object which they wish to impress upon the imagination of the reader. This applies in particular to their sketches of scenery described in language unclouded by ostentation, and singularly appropriate to the subject of which they are treating. There is not the most distant attempt at fine writing. But if the public attention were more strongly directed to the productions of the United Brethren, and if the effect which lies in the simplicity of their faithful and accurate descriptions were to become the subject of more frequent observation, we should not think it strange that their manner should become fashionable, and that something like a classical homage should at length be rendered to the purity of the Moravian style.

However this be, it is high time that the curiosity of the public were more powerfully directed to the solid realities with which these wonderful men have been so long conversant. It is now a century since they have had intercourse with men in the infancy of civilization. During that time, they have been laboring in all the different quarters of the world, and have succeeded in reclaiming many a wild region to Christianity. One of their principles in carrying on the business of missions, is, not to interfere with other men's labors; and thus it is that one so often meets with them among the outskirts of the species, making glad some solitary place, and raising a sweet vineyard in some remote and unfrequented wilderness. It may give some idea of the extent of their operations, to state that, by the last accounts,* there are 27,400 human beings converts to the Christian faith, and under Moravian discipline, who but for them would at this moment have been still living in all the darkness of Paganism! Surely when the Christian public are made to know that these men are at this moment struggling with embarrassments, they will turn the stream of their benevolence to an object so worthy of it, nor suffer missionaries of such tried proficiency and success, to abandon a single establishment for want of funds to support it.

* In 1815.

But apart from the missionary cause altogether, is not the solid information they are accumulating every year, respecting unknown countries, and the people who live in them, of a kind highly interesting to the taste and the pursuits of merely secular men? Now much of this information has been kept back for want of encouragement. The public did not take that interest in their proceedings, which could warrant the expectation of a sale for a printed narrative of many facts and occurrences, which have now vanished from all earthly remembrance. It is true, we have Crantz's History of Greenland; and we appeal to this book as an evidence of what we have lost by so many of their missionary journals being suffered to lie in manuscript, among the few of their own brotherhood who had access to them. We guess that much may yet be gathered out of their archives, and much from the recollection of the older missionaries. Had it not been for the inquiries of that respected individual, Mr. Wilberforce, we should have lost many of these very interesting particulars, which are now preserved in the published letters on the Nicobar Islands, and these written by the only surviving missionary, after an interval of twenty-five years from the period of the actual observations. Surely it is not for the credit of public intelligence among us, that such men and such doings should have been so long unnoticed; and it must excite regret not unmingled with shame, to think that a complete set of their periodical accounts is not to be found, because there was no demand for their earlier numbers, and they had no encouragement to multiply or preserve them.

ON THE

STYLE AND SUBJECTS OF THE PULPIT;

BEING THE

SUBSTANCE OF AN ARGUMENT

CONTRIBUTED TO

"THE CHRISTIAN INSTRUCTOR"

IN 1811.

The public taste has of late years undergone a considerable change in works of imagination. The fictitious characters have become more natural; the story is a nearer imitation of real life; and the moral far more applicable than ever to the existing state of manners, and the actual business of society. Whatever may be the cause, the fact is undeniable. We are less disposed to sympathize with those high-flown sensibilities, which, however beautiful in fiction, are seldom exemplified in the every-day scenes of human experience. The popular taste is more a business taste than before. It runs less upon finery, and more upon plain and familiar usefulness. The men and women of our most popular novels bear a closer resemblance to those characters which we meet every week at our markets, and converse with at our tea-parties; and the poetry of a late fashionable school, derived its chief currency from the growing taste of the public for the truth and simplicity of nature.

In the volume before us,* we perceive something like the application of the same principle to a composition of piety. The chief aim of the writer is truth and perspicuity; and in the prosecution of this aim, he gives up everything that is calculated only to signalize and display himself. There is no superfluous expression, no ambitious oratory; he is always sure to take the line of shortest distance to the point he is going to. He expends all his strength on the idea; after which he has no other care, than to express it with clearness and effect in the fewest possible words.

* The work reviewed in this paper was Dr. Charters' Sermons.

He never aspires after mere gracefulness of composition; and, in his exclusive attention to what is useful, appears quite indifferent to the flow of his periods, and the musical construction of his sentences. We cannot look for anything like harmony in this aphoristic style of writing, where correctness takes at all times the precedency of ornament, and the elegant is sacrificed without remorse, whenever it would pervert or enfeeble the rigorous accuracy of the meaning.

It is not merely in point of expression, but in the choice of his subject, and the manner of treating it, that this author strikes out a path for himself, and stands distinguished from all popular and prevailing example. His great aim is to bring forward Christianity to the walks of ordinary business, and to send home its moral principles to the understanding and experience of ordinary men. Some would say, that he *brings down* Christianity to ordinary business; as if Christianity were degraded by such an application, and as if human life, in all its minuteness and variety, were not the proper theatre for the display and exercise of Christian principles. The author before us seems to have caught the true practical spirit of the New Testament, and to have aimed at the revival of that substantial style, which, however often exemplified in the discourses of our Saviour, has been suffered to run too much into idle speculation and controversy on the one hand, and into cold uninteresting generality on the other. He carries out religion from the house of prayer into the shop, the market, and the family. This imparts a secular tone to his performances, which is certainly not very usual in a composition of piety; but the true and the useful seem to be the favorite, if not the only, objects of this respectable writer. In the prosecution of these objects, there is, at times, a minuteness of application, which some will deem low and familiar; a plainness of expression, which some will term vulgar and slovenly; and even a simplicity, which, to some tastes, may appear to border upon childishness, and be somewhat allied to that overwrought simplicity which runs through the phrase and sentiment of Mr. Wordsworth, and which for a time disgusted the public even with his more meritorious poetry.

But there is still another point of resemblance betwixt these two writers, in their very different departments of literary exertion. In neither of them is the simplicity which we are now talking of,—the simplicity of weak and incapable minds. Both make a voluntary descent from the natural level of their powers and attainments. In the volume of Dr. Charters we meet with frequent displays of an understanding of the higher order; where there is often great depth of observation, and great vigor and brilliancy of eloquence, the occasional glimpses of a mind enriched with various literature, and which can appeal to the profoundest principles of political science, when they give effect or illustration to the lessons of the Christian morality. In a word, his is not the simplicity of impotence It is a simplicity assumed upon taste, and upon principle; and founded upon the maxim, that ornament is at all times to be sacrificed to truth, and perspicuity of observation. This is an object he never loses sight of, though it should land him at times in the trite, the inelegant, or the untasteful. He adheres to it with all the vigor of a true practical philosopher; and, in his exclusive preference for what is useful, suffers no example to restrain him from bringing forward truth however homely, and experience however minute, and however familiar.

Dr. Charters has taken occasion, in the first sermon in the volume before us, to announce his peculiar ideas upon this subject.

"To be plain, and memorable, and earnest," says he, "are the chief requisites in the style of a practical treatise.

"Labor is well bestowed in making the principles of religion plain; and they only who have tried to instruct the ignorant, know how much labor it requires, and how often the man of taste must deny himself; blunting the edge of his wit, dropping the graces of composition, breaking his large round period in pieces, making vulgar similes, and using words which shock the critic. When the labor of explanation is accomplished, the merit of the laborer does not appear, and credit is seldom given him for his condescension and self-denial.

"Works of taste are composed to please; but the object of religious instruction is more serious and severe; it is to undeceive, to reclaim, to conduct in a steep and thorny path. Taste and imagination revolt, leaving reason and the heart to ponder. 'The orator (says D'Alembert) sacrifices harmony, when he would strike by things: justness, when he would attract by expression.' This may be a good rule for the academy; but the sacred orator will never make the last of these sacrifices, and the first he will not account a sacrifice.

"Earnestness supersedes the use of ornaments, and declines them. In entering a cottage to give counsel and comfort, your fine clothes and fine language would disconcert rather than ingratiate. A familiar, serious, earnest manner is enough. Richard Baxter often introduces in his writings such objections, and doubts, and temptations, and fears, as had been proposed to him in private, and answers them as he did to the proposer. This gives to his style a character of truth and life. The language of conference about incumbent duties and trials, though proscribed by the critics as *colloquial*, is well adapted to religious instruction. It is opposed to an erroneous fastidious conceit about the dignity of pulpit composition. It is doing for the Gospel what Socrates did for philosophy, bringing it from the clouds to the earth; from the region of fancy to the abode of conscience; from hidden mysteries to the affairs of men; transforming it from a theatre of eloquence into a rule of life."

But a sermon, written on the above principle, does not appear to us to be exclusively addressed to the poor and the ignorant. It must be observed, that there is a very wide distinction betwixt a truth in practical morality, and a truth that is exclusively addressed to the understanding. In the latter case, the object, in announcing the truth, is gained, if it be understood. In the former case, that the object be fulfilled, the truth must not merely be understood, but acted upon. We could forgive the contempt of a profound mathematician, when he turns aside from some humble performance of the school-boy elements of his science; but that can by no means justify the indifference of the most exalted genius upon earth, when he turns aside from a performance that gives him a clear and simple exposition of his duty, merely because there is nothing in it to stimulate and exercise the powers of his understanding. Our sole object in reading a sermon, is not to rectify or inform our judgment: it is also to fill our minds with an habitual sense of duty, by the frequent recurrence of its attention to principles, which, in themselves, are clear and undeniable, but which, if not always present to the mind, leave it a prey to the inroads of vice, and licentiousness, and folly. When one man tells another his duty, it is not to protect his understanding from the sophistry of a false argument,—it is to protect his conduct from the still more bewildering sophistry of passion and interest. It is not to teach him what he did not know, and did not understand. The principle may be acquiesced in the moment that it is proposed; and has, in all likelihood, been acquiesced in a thousand times before. Still this does not supersede the usefulness of telling it over again. A moral principle, to exert any efficacy upon the conduct, must be present to the mind at the moment of deliberation. It is not enough, that in some former exercise of our understanding, this principle was attended to, and considered, and acquiesced in, and added to the list of our intellectual acquirements. It must be something more than understood. It must be attended to. It must be at all times in readiness for actual service, and ever prone to offer itself as a powerful and controlling element in the contest, which so often arises betwixt the opposite principles of our constitution. When we read a sermon, we sit down to it as an exercise of piety. We may meet with nothing which we did not know, and be told of nothing which we did not understand. It may add nothing to our speculation, but it will fulfil its chief aim, if it adds to our practical wisdom; if it gives our mind a steadier and more habitual direction to the principles of good conduct; if it adds to the promptitude with which we can summon up the suggestions of duty, to restrain and regulate our footsteps in the path of life, and arrest the rapidity of those erring and irregular movements, into which the turbulence of this world's passions is so ready to transport us.

We can conceive a philosopher to have made the study of human nature the business of his life, and to have even enlightened the world by his profound and accurate speculations on the different principles of our constitution. It is well known, that this does not prevent these principles, as they exist in his own mind, from being actually in a high state of disorder, and that the speculative wisdom which can trace the law of their operation, is totally different from that practical wisdom which can control their violence, and maintain them in an entire subordination to his sense of propriety. It is perfectly conceivable that, accomplished as his mind is in the science of its own character and phenomena, it may lose the direction of itself in the collisions of actual business, and exhibit the humiliating spectacle of weakness, and wickedness, and folly. Suppose him to be engaged in the management of some important affair, which is in danger of miscarrying from the misguided violence of his temper. Is there anything misplaced or superfluous, we would ask, in a friend taking him aside and entreating him to be calm? It is vain to say, that he has attended profoundly to the nature and effects of anger, and that he knows this part of our constitution better than any of his advisers. In spite of this circumstance, it would be looked upon as quite natural, quite in place, for an esteemed or confidential acquaintance to enter at large into the necessity of maintaining the discipline of his temper, and the mischief that would proceed from indulging it, even though in the whole course of his explanation, he was not to appeal to a single principle which had not been better explained, and more eloquently expatiated upon by our profound and philosophical moralist. It is not that he does not know his duty, but that, in the rapidity of his feelings, he is apt to forget, and needs to be reminded of it. It is, that his sense of duty is apt to be overpowered by the violence of his passions, and that to prepare him for the contest, we must strengthen his sense of duty, both by recalling his attention to it, and by applying that kind of authority which an earnest and sincere friendship usually carries along with it.

The sermon, which lays before us a simple exposition of our duty, stands precisely in the situation of such a friend. It is not that we are ignorant of our duty, but we find, that a frequent recalment of our mind to its simple and undeniable maxims, has the actual effect of imparting a greater steadiness to our conduct, and forms a useful part of moral and religious discipline. There is a difference between mistaking our duty and losing sight of it. The object of a sermon is to heal not the former, but the latter infirmity of our constitution,—not so much to enlighten us in the knowledge of our duty, as to enable us to keep it more constantly in view, that it may be ever present to the mind, and exert an habitual authority over the unruly passions and principles of our nature. We find, in point of fact, that the frequent direction of our mind to the duties and principles of conduct, is an improving exercise; and that a volume of sermons is a very effectual instrument for giving it this direction. It may neither regale the imagination, nor add a single truth to the list of our intellectual attainments; but it accomplishes its chief purpose, if we rise from it with a heart more penetrated with a sense of its religious obligations, and disposed to yield a readier submission to the authority of conscience and of scripture.

Upon these considerations, a plain volume of sermons is a useful manual, not merely for the peasant, but for the philosopher. We do not say, that it will help him in the business of philosophy, any more than that it will help an artificer in the processes of workmanship. But it will help him in an object which should be as dear to him as to any brother of his species; it will keep alive the vigilance of his moral principles; nor can we conceive a more interesting picture, than a man of science, rich in all the liberal endowments of a university, giving a holy hour to the culture of his heart, and to the truest of all wisdom, the wisdom of piety.

But it would not be altogether accurate, to characterize the volume before us as a plain volume of sermons. There is a great deal of very plain observation to be met with; for what is or what ought to be, more familiar to the understandings of all than the practical lessons of morality? It seems to be the maxim of Dr. Charters, to tell all the truth, and nothing but the truth; and in steady obedience to this maxim, he neither shrinks from what is trite and familiar, nor does he ever abandon the useful, in pursuit of the profound, the ingenious, or the elaborate. But in telling *all the truth*, there is an occasional call for a higher kind of effort, and it is an effort to which this respectable author proves himself fully equal. The great principles of duty are obvious and accessible to all; but it sometimes happens, that the judicious application of these principles requires all the effort and ingenuity of a mind, that is much cultivated in the experience of human affairs. Dr. Charters, in a former publication, observes: "Children of the poor often unite to inter a parent decently: it is a becoming and commendable testimony of respect; but it is still more commendable to minister to them in age and sickness; a few bottles of wine are of great use in the decay of life, and are better bestowed as a cordial, than as a mark of honor." We have heard this called low, but we confess that we see nothing in it, but the same homeliness and vigor of practical wisdom, which made Franklin so illustrious, and that we like the man, who, in his exclusive preference for the useful, will tell the truth as it stands, and lay aside ornament and superfluity, as fit only for the amusement of children. This same author can discuss the poor rates, upon the most liberal principles of political economy. He can shape his argument to the spirit and philosophy of the times; and, in the great object of illustrating the morality of the New Testament, he exhibits all the compass and cultivation of a mind, that is awake both to the events of public history, and to the very latest discoveries which have been made in the progress of philosophical speculation.

But it is high time that Dr. Charters should speak for himself. The volume before us consists of four sermons. It is a new edition, and different from a former work consisting of two volumes, and which has been in possession of the public a good many years. We confine our extracts to the volume before us, as exhibiting a very fair specimen of the characteristic manner of the author. His first sermon is upon *alms-giving;* and in the substantial maxims which he advances upon the direction of our charity, affords us a most refreshing contrast to that sentimental and high-wrought extravagance which sparkles in the poetry and eloquence of our fine writers. The author never forgets, that it lies within the province of virtue not merely to feel, but to do,—not merely to conceive a purpose, but to carry that purpose into execution,—not merely to be overpowered by the impression of a sentiment, but to practise what it loves, and to imitate what it admires.

"Compassion, improperly cultivated," says he, "springs into a fruitless sensibility. If a brother or sister be naked, and destitute of daily food, and if you say unto them, depart in peace, be ye warmed and filled, notwithstanding ye give them not those things which are needful for the body; what doth it profit? To enter the abodes of the wretched; to examine wants, and debts, and diseases; to endure loathsome sights and smells within the sphere of infection; to give time, and thought, and hands, and money: this is the substance, not the shadow of virtue. The pleasures of sensibility may be less, but so is the danger of self-deceit which attends it. Death-beds, in the page of an eloquent writer, delight the imagination; but they who are most delighted, are not the first to visit a dying neighbor, and sit up all night, and wipe off the cold sweat, and moisten the parched lip, and give easy postures, and bear with peevishness, and suggest a pious thought, and console the parting spirit. They often encompass the altar of virtue, but not to sacrifice.

"Extreme sensibility is a diseased state of the mind. It unfits us to relieve the miserable, and tempts us to turn away. The sight of pain is shunned, and the thought of it suppressed; the ear is stopped against the cry of indigence; the house of mourning is passed by; even near friends are abandoned, when sick, to the nurse and physician, and when dead to those who mourn for a hire; and all this under pretence of fine feeling and sentimental delicacy. The apples of Sodom are mistaken for the fruit of Paradise.

"Compassion may fall on wrong objects, and yet be justified and applauded. One living in borrowed affluence becomes bankrupt. His sudden fall strikes the imagination; pity is felt, and generous exertions are made in his behalf. There is indeed a call for pity; but upon whom? Upon servants, who have received no wages; upon traders and artificers, whose economy he has deranged; upon the widow, whom he has caused to weep over destitute children."

There is something in all the performances of Dr. Charters, that forcibly reminds us of the moral essays of Lord Bacon. If the reader is not repelled at the outset by the abruptness of his sentences, and the occasional homeliness of his phraseology, he will find in the sermons before us a rich vein of originality and just observation. His taste is perhaps too exclusively formed upon the older writers; and in his well-founded admiration of what may be called the *sturdiness* of good sense, and judicious reflections, he seems to look upon the mere embellishment of language as finical and superfluous, and calculated only to amuse a puny and degenerate age. We regret this the more, that it creates a prejudice against him at the outset. Not but that we have all faith to repose in the maxim of *magna est veritas, et prevalebit;* but we lament that even a temporary barrier should have been raised betwixt the public mind, and that excellent sense which is so well calculated to purify and enlighten it. Dr. Charters is entitled to a distinguished reception in the best company, but he has neglected the means of obtaining for himself a ready introduction. There is nothing in his air or first appearance that is at all calculated to announce his pretensions. It will take a time before these pretensions are thoroughly appreciated, though we have no doubt that the time is coming; and even after it arrives, he will be somewhat like certain philosophers of our acquaintance, who, without the air or the habiliments of gentlemen, have at length extorted an acknowledgment of their importance, and are, upon the reputation of their more substantial accomplishments, admitted into the society of elegant and well-dressed fashionables.

But this is all a question of taste, and it must never be forgotten, that of every species of composition, the popularity of a sermon should be the least dependent upon its fluctuations. The aim of poetry is to please. The aim of a sermon is to instruct; and its chief excellence consists in the soundness of these instructions, and in the clear and familiar manner with which it sends them home to the conscience and experience of its readers. We can conceive that the exploded phraseology of the older writers may again become fashionable, and that the public, in a fit of disgust at the flippancy of a superficial age, may recur for a time to that homeliness of language, with which it associates the manliness of a Bacon, a Barrow, a Butler, and an Atterbury. We think little of the strength of that man's philosophy, who would suffer the uncouth exterior of the above compositions to repel him from the sense and judicious observation which abound in them. And we fear that little can be said for the strength of that man's piety, who would turn in disgust from such a volume as that before us, merely because it failed to regale his fancy by the brilliancy of its images, or to lull his ear by the smoothness and harmony of its clauses. So long as principle and philosophy exist, the impressiveness of truth must prevail over the graces and embellishments of fine language. The latter is perpetually varying, but the former is immutable as the laws of our constitution, and lasting as the existence of the species.

We give the following specimen as an example of the practical and familiar manner of Dr. Charters.

"Every passion justifies itself, and arguments are opposed to alms-giving.

"*I may do what I will with mine own, and no one has a right to dictate.* But you can examine yourself, and think of the account which must hereafter be given of what is your own.

"*I have children to provide for.* Inquire, if there be bounds in providing for a family; if alms be a kind of riches which lay a good foundation for the time to come; and whether your children are like to profit most by the savings of avarice, or by the odor of a good name, and the blessing entailed by Providence on the posterity of the merciful.

"*I have a rank to keep, and the money expended does good to laborers, though not precisely in the form of alms.* The rich man in the parable, who was clothed with purple and fine linen, and fared sumptuously every day, could plead, that the furnishing his fine cloth and sumptuous fare did good to laborers; for it does not appear that he was an oppressor, or unjust.

"*The poor get enough from those who are better able to give.* You will find upon inquiry, that the poor still have wants, some of which you may be able to supply. The alms-giving of others will not justify your neglect. Every man must prove his own work, that he may have rejoicing in himself alone. If you give no alms of such things as you have, none of these things are clean to you.

"*When I grow rich I will be charitable.* If you are charitable in such ways as are now in your power, there is hope; but riches do not cure a worldly mind. The sin of covetousness, and the spirit of alms, are found in a low estate. Affections may fix on a cottage, or a little field: the heart may cling to a small sum; for a mess of pottage, the birthright that is despised will be sold. There may be a *willing mind* in the widow, whose possession is two mites; in the laborer, who spares part of his wages for those who cannot labor; in one who reaches a cup of cold water to the thirsty. *She has done what she could,* was the praise of Mary of Bethany. 'You have one maid,' said William Law to a devout lady, 'she is under your care, teach her the Catechism, hear her read, exhort her to pray, take her with you to church, persuade her to love the divine service as you love it, edify her with your conversation, fill her with your own notions of piety, and spare no pains to make her as holy and devout as yourself.'"

Now, all this is true; it is important, and must be appreciated by every heart that is anxious to be reminded of its duties. Some would call it insipid, though we cannot conceive how this should be the feeling of those who are rightly impressed with the magnitude of the subject, and who sit down to a sermon, with the fair and honest anxiety of giving new vigilance and direction to their moral and religious principles. In the language of Paul, it is right that we should become all things to all men, that we may gain some; and if a single proselyte can be gained to the cause of righteousness, by the embellishments of elegant literature, let every attraction be given to the subject, which taste and elegance can throw around it. But let it be remembered, that these attractions have no influence over the vast majority of the species, and that the only impression of which they are susceptible, is that wholesome and direct impression which a clear and simple exposition of duty makes upon the conscience. Let it further be remembered, that even among the cultivated orders of society, the appetite for mere gracefulness of expression is sure, in time, to give way to the more substantial accomplishments of good sense and judicious observation; and that, in every rightly constituted mind, the importance of what is true, must carry it over the allurement of what is pretty, and elegant, and fashionable.

The following extract, on the precautions which are necessary in the prosecution of a good work, affords a specimen of the manner in which Dr. Charters applies the lessons of a sound and experimental wisdom to the elucidation of his subject.

"Do not omit, or slur over, professional labors, for a labor of love. You may be censured for not listening to a tale of woe: and let the censurer, who has time, investigate the truth and falsehood of woful tales, and begging letters, and the use or abuse of subscription papers; but if your time be occupied with incumbent duties and real beneficence, you are above the region of sentimental clouds and vapors.

"Be discreet in soliciting for your favorite charity. Others may have objects equally useful, to which their alms are devoted. They may not be in circumstances to give, and yet too facile to resist importunity; they may come to mark and avoid you as impertinent and obtrusive. It is the safe and desirable course, at least for a quiet man, to interest himself in some charity which he can accomplish, without troubling other people.

"Consult your own temper; if it be extremely modest, you are not qualified to scramble for the power of patronage, or solicit for friends, or pry into secret wants, or to be officious. Inquire what good work may fall in with your constitutional temper, and not *force the course of the river*. Father Paul, when pressed on the subject of the reformation, said, God had not given him the spirit of Luther. They who have bold unembarrassed confidence in their own powers, are fittest for public usefulness.

"Take care, that meekness be not lost in the ardent pursuit of charity. One is apt to overrate the good object upon which he has set his heart, and to resent the opposition it may meet with from the ill-natured and selfish, or from those who have not the same conviction of its importance and utility. Keep your temper. From opposition and final disappointment, you may reap patience, and meekness, and humility; and these, as well as alms, are treasures in heaven.

"Guard against everything like unfairness; against concealing or disguising facts, and taking sensibility by surprise; against forwarding a good work by any indirection. It is of more importance, that integrity and uprightness be maintained, than that good works be multiplied."

There is a most unfortunate distinction kept up in the country betwixt moral and evangelical preaching. It has the effect of instituting an opposition where no opposition should be supposed to exist; and a preference for the one is, in this way, made to carry along with it an hostility, or an indifference to the other. The mischief of this is incalculable. It has the effect of banishing Christianity altogether from the system of human life; and the familiar business of society, which takes up such a vast majority of our time and attention, is kept in a state of entire separation from those religious principles, which are so well calculated to guide and to enlighten it. The effect is undeniable. If the main business of religion is performed not in the world, but away from it; if the labor of the week days is not supposed to bear as intimate a connection with religion as the exercises of the Sabbath; if the conduct of man in society does not come as immediately under the cognizance and direction of religious principles as the devout preparations of solitude; then by far the greater part of human life is lost to religion; and that noble principle which should exert an undivided sway over every hour and minute of our existence, is restricted in its operation to those paltry fragments of time which we can hardly extort from the urgency of our secular occupations.

There is a party of Christians who have the name of zeal, and who have even its sincerity, and yet, in point of fact, have done much to detract from the importance of religion, by keeping it at a distance from the familiar and every-day scenes of human society. They have offered it precisely the same kind of injury which the dignity of a monarch sustains by the dismemberment of his territories. They have narrowed that domain over which the authority of religious principle ought to have extended. Instead of vesting in religion a right of dominion over the whole man, they have restricted it to a mere fraction of his time, and his employment, and his principles. With the appearance of maintaining the elevation of religion, they have, in fact, degraded it from its high and undivided empire. They have confined its operations to a little corner in the life of man, instead of allowing it a wide and unexcepted authority over the whole system of human affairs.

On the other hand, there is a party of Christians who expatiate, in high terms, upon the morality of the Gospel, while they disown the power, and humility, and unction, of its peculiar doctrines. But to disown, or even to admit with a cold and unfeeling negligence, a single doctrine of the New Testament, is to forget its authority as a revelation from heaven. It is an approach to Deism. It is to take away from morality all that power and influence which it derives from religion. It is to expel from it the sanction of God; for where do we learn that the morality of the Gospel has the sanction of heaven, but from the Gospel itself? and how can we respect its lessons, if we withhold the cheerful and unqualified submission of our understandings from the authority of any of its doctrines?

Now, it is the happy combination of evangelical piety, with the familiar, wholesome, and experimental morality of human life, which, to our taste, constitutes the peculiar charm and excellence of the sermons before us.* Dr. Charters, in spite of the secular complexion that his continued reference to the business of life imparts to his performance, sustains through the whole of it the true unction of the apostolical spirit. The morality of the sermons before us never degenerates into a mere system of prudence, or into virtue reposing upon its own charms, or its own obligations: It is virtue resting upon revealed truth, and animated by the life and inspiration of the Gospel. The author of these sermons looks upon human life, not merely with the eye of a wise and philosophical

* We certainly could have wished, that the peculiar doctrines of the Gospel had been more explicitly noticed; that we had not merely been able to recognize their influence throughout the practical discussions of the volume, but that they had been more openly announced, and more emphatically stated. In our author's pages, indeed, we observe such a spirit pervading them, as nothing could have infused but a strong and decided impression of Christian truth. But, to give a prominency to that truth, to bring it particularly, and broadly, and frequently into view, is attended with great advantages, independently of its immediate effect on the instructions in which it is exhibited. And though we entirely disapprove of that ostentatious way in which some bring forward the characteristic truths of Christianity, we are persuaded that the other extreme of keeping them very much out of sight, is not justifiable on any good ground.

moralist; he looks upon it with the eye of a Christian, and transfuses the sanctity of the evangelical spirit into the most minute and familiar occurrences. As we move along, we feel ourselves not merely in the hand of an instructor, whose sense and experimental wisdom will guide us with safety and propriety through the world. We feel as if we were in the hands of a father or evangelist, whose venerable piety gives an air of sacredness to the subject, who consecrates the ground on which we are treading, and makes it holy. This, combined with the simplicity of his language, and his frequent allusions to scripture, has the effect of imparting a very decided feature of *Quakerism* to the whole of his compositions. In saying this, we do not conceive that we annex ridicule or discredit to the performance. All that we intend is aptly to characterize; and, in an age like the present, when piety is so prone to run into fanatical extravagance, and morality is ready to disown all that is peculiar or authoritative in the Christian revelation, we think it no small praise to be assimilated to a set of men, who, with all the apostolical simplicity of the first Christians, have, notwithstanding several erroneous tenets in their religious system, exemplified, in so striking a degree, by their mild and respectable virtues, the power and the practice of the Gospel.

The following extract from his second sermon, on the duty of making a testament, may serve to illustrate the above observation.

> "A solemn deed, which transfers our momentary interest in the things of time, reminds us that they are not our chief good. Perhaps there are few moments of your life when you are more loosened from the world, than the moment of subscribing a testament. The soul, amidst strong attachments to the world, needs such loosening. The young acorn inclosed in a husk, and adhering to the stem, resists the scorching of the sun and the shaking of the wind, but it is gradually ripened by the sun and loosened by the wind, till it be ready to drop into the earth, that it may rise again an oak of the future forest. Things inanimate and passive, in their progress, are only figures of the destiny of man; it is man's prerogative to co-operate in his progress, and predispose himself for his future high destination. A deed of conveyance disengages and elevates the heart. I have determined whose all these things shall be; but what is my portion? My heart and flesh shall faint and fail, but God is the strength of my heart and my portion forever.
>
> "The last transaction of life would be but little interesting, were our prospect bounded by the darkness, and solitude, and forgetfulness of the grave; far from anticipating the evil day, we would consign to oblivion the past and the future. It is immortality brought to light by the Gospel, which gives an importance, an interest, and a dignity, to the concluding scenes of life. These are not only observed and remembered by men who survive, and who are soon to follow; they are also recorded in the book out of which the dead will be judged. We act as on a theatre, where God and angels are spectators, and a crown of life is the prize. We feel a powerful and permanent motive, throughout life and at death, to be faithful in the few things now committed to our charge, *to live unto the Lord and to die unto the Lord*."

We regret that our limits do not allow us to indulge in any further extracts from this interesting performance. At the close of the volume, we have an Appendix, in which the author gives us a short exposition of different texts of Scripture, in pursuance of an idea of Lord Bacon's.

"We find," says his Lordship, "among theological writings, too many books of controversy, a vast mass of what we call positive theology, and numerous prolix comments upon the several books of Scripture; but the thing we want and propose is, a short, sound, and judicious collection of notes and observations upon particular texts of Scripture, without running into commonplace, pursuing controversies, or reducing these notes to artificial method, but leaving them quite loose and native."

ON THE

DIFFERENCE

BETWEEN

SPOKEN AND WRITTEN LANGUAGE;

BEING THE

SUBSTANCE OF AN ARGUMENT

CONTRIBUTED TO

"THE ECLECTIC REVIEW"

IN 1816.

There are many of the constituents of spoken eloquence that cannot be imbodied into a volume, or offered to the notice of the public eye through the medium of authorship. There are the tone of earnestness which may be heard, and the manner of sincerity which may be witnessed, and the eye of intelligent sensibility which may be seen, and the vehemence of an impassioned delivery which may be made to stimulate and to warn the spectators, and all that significancy of gesture and of action, which carries in it a real conveyance both of meaning into the understanding, and of affection into the hearts, of those who are listening to some exhibition of oratory,—every one of which may tell most eloquently and most powerfully upon an audience, and yet neither of which can be introduced by any artifice of human skill within the limits of a written composition. We can insert nothing into a book, but bare words; and though it be true that even words without any accompaniment whatever, may express all the fire, and all the earnestness, and all the glow and intensity of feeling, and all the tone of intelligence to which we have just now adverted; yet it is also true that there are many who possess all these attributes of the judgment and of the fancy, and who do not possess the faculty of putting forth the expression of them by the vehicle of a written communication. There are many who carry in their minds all the conceptions of genius, but who seem to want the one faculty of rendering them faithfully and impressively in written language—who can speak all their conceptions with adequate effect, and that too not merely because they have all the natural signs of communication at their command, but because such is the habit of their minds, that in the present extemporaneous workings of thought and of imagination, they experience a flow, and a facility, and an appropriateness of utterance, the distinct words of which, could they have been substantiated at the time in the indelibility of written characters, would have offered a lively impress of the talent which gave them birth; but which, in the cool and deliberate efforts of composition, they find, from a single defect either of practice or of original constitution, they are not able to create anew or to recall.

Written language is an expedient framed to meet the infirmities of our present state; and in a more perfect condition of being, it is conceivable that there may be no use and no demand for it. It is the immortality of our nature which makes it necessary for the purpose of stamping upon durable records the wisdom of one generation and transmitting it to another; and it is through a defect in the faculties of memory and imitation, that we are not able to send to a distance the products of a powerful and original mind, by the living conveyance of oral testimony. Just conceive these distempers of the species to be done away, and the faculty of writing would no longer be necessary to establish either a distant or a posthumous reputation. And this may lead us to perceive upon how slender a distinction it is that such a reputation is earned by some, and is utterly placed without the reach and the attainment of others; and how for the few names that have come down to posterity, as marking out the most able, or the most profound, or the most eloquent of our race, there may be thousands who possessed every one of these attributes as richly and as substantially as they, but who, now personally withdrawn from us, have no place whatever either in the praise or in the remembrance of the world.

There is one circumstance additional to all we have enumerated, which serves to widen the distinction between the effects of his spoken and of his written eloquence, when a preacher of sermons becomes an author of sermons. There is generally a strong disposition on the part of a people, to cherish a cordiality and a kindliness of good-will towards their minister. Conceive then a minister not merely to have done nothing to forfeit the attachment of his hearers, but everything to enthrone himself in their hearts, and so to have cultivated the duties of the pastoral relation, as to have become an object of devoted and enthusiastic regard to all his congregation. Here is a peculiar source of impression with which the public at large cannot possibly sympathize. They cannot be made to feel like his own people the personal worth of him who is addressing them, nor to kindle at the warmth of his known

22

and affectionate anxiety for their best interests, nor to be grateful for his unwearied kindness to themselves and their families, nor to read with indulgence what they are sure has flowed from the inspiration of fervent piety, nor to associate with the composition all that weight of authority which lies in the character of him who gave it birth, nor to hear the voice and perceive the expression of an unquestionable friendship throughout all its pages. In these circumstances a congregation is not to wonder, if the suffrage of the public voice shall not altogether harmonize with the acclamations of their loud and sincere popularity; or if they who are in full possession of all those accompaniments which give an aid and an energy to every sentence of the volume that has been presented to them, shall both feel its merits and sound its eulogies far beyond the pitch of its distant and general estimation.

This circumstance may serve to explain the cause of the multiplicity of those volumes of sermons which are annually presented to the world. But it will do more than explain, it will also justify this multiplicity. However little the community at large may be attracted by the nakedness of the written composition, it comes to the people who heard it with the force of all those associations which gave their peculiar effect to the spoken addresses of their minister. They read the volume differently from others; for they read it with the recollection upon them of the tone, and the manner, and the earnestness, and the impassionate vehemency of its author. They read it with the whole impression of his personal influence and character upon their minds; and this renders the volume a more useful and a more affecting memorial to them, than it ever can be to the public at large. And this is a reason that, apart from general advantage altogether, volumes of sermons should be frequently published for the good of the congregation in whose hearing they were delivered. It is true that the tameness of many sermons, and the exceeding frequency of their appearance before the eyes of the world, have served to vulgarize and to degrade them in the common estimation; but the benefit they confer on those to whom their author is endeared by the ties of long and affectionate intercourse, much more than compensates for that humble rank on the field of general literature, to which this class of compositions has now fallen.

These remarks by no means apply in their full extent to the volume that is now before us.* It possesses undoubted claims on the general attention of the public; but the deductions to which we have now adverted, must in a greater or less degree be made from every book of sermons. And accordingly we cannot but remark of the present volume, that however high and however well founded its claims may be, it does not in our judgment present to the world at large an adequate impress of that power of conception, that richness of fancy, that versatility of illustration, that de-

* The work reviewed in this paper was Dr. Jones' Sermons.

cisive boldness of announcement, that warmth of pastoral tenderness, and even that capability of impressive and significant language, which we know the author to possess, and by the weekly display of which he so often transports and overpowers the sensibilities of his own congregation. We trust that the work before us will stand high in general estimation; but we think that on the strength of the above remarks we may say with certainty of the sermons, that they will not occupy the same rank in general authorship, which they do in the esteem of those who sit under the ministrations of Dr. Jones, and bear witness to those rapid energies both of thought and of expression, which in the moment of delivery he brings so successfully into action.

This author is, in the whole style and substance of his sentiments, evangelical. It is quite clear from these sermons, that were he formally questioned as to his faith in the leading peculiarities of the Gospel, there is not one of them which he would not most firmly and most zealously recognize. And this may be ascertained in two ways;—either directly—by the precise and positive announcements which the author makes upon the subject, or indirectly—by the obviously prevailing tone which his belief in the truths of the New Testament gives to all his remarks. Now, there is a numerous class both of readers and of hearers, who will not be satisfied, except on the first evidence, of the orthodoxy of him who addresses them. There is what we would call a morbid jealousy upon this subject; and the preacher, if conscious of its existence, will go out of his direct and natural way for the purpose of meeting and appeasing it. Nay, such is the power of sympathy, that this jealousy on the part of others will often excite his own apprehensions; and, to insure his own orthodoxy, he will constantly make the most obtrusive and ostentatious displays of it—fearful lest every sentiment should not be in express and visible subordination to the strictest principles of Calvinism. He will not venture to urge a single duty, without guarding the exhortation by an interposed remark about the doctrine of merit, or of spiritual influence; and thus laboring under the burden of the whole system, he will prosecute his tardy way through the fields of practical Christianity—encumbering himself with the task of bringing out into manifest and undeniable display, the consistency of all that proceeds from him, with the articles of the evangelical creed.

Now it would seem that a mature and established faith in these articles, would give rise to a freer and more spontaneous and untrammelled style of observation, both on the duties and on the truths of the Christian religion. They will come at length rather to be proceeded on, than to be made the subjects of distinct and repeated avowal. They will not be so frequently nor so systematically asserted as at first; because, altogether free from any conscious disposition on his own part to question the truth of them, a Christian author will take them up as unquestionable, and turn them to their immediate and their practical application. He at length loses sight of them as topics of controversy; and resting in them with a kind of axiomatic confidence, he will consider it as quite unnecessary to vindicate or to avow them, or expatiate upon them, at every step in the train of his observations. In this way the train will get on more quickly, and the observations will be greatly more multiplied; a wider range will be taken by him, who, emancipated from all his fears and from all his scrupulosities, will feel himself at liberty to make a bold and immediate entrance upon every question of duty which presents itself, and to draw his illustrations from every quarter of human experience; and hence it is, that he will not be ever at the work of laying the foundation; but with a mind already made up on all the essential elements of the Christian faith, he will for that very reason be at large for a more extended scope, and be able to lay before his readers a richer and more abundant variety.

But we have dwelt sufficiently long on the preliminaries of the subject, and must now proceed to lay before the reader a few extracts from the book itself. Its author appears to possess that mature and established faith, to which we have just alluded. All his perceptions are evidently those of an evangelical mind, but of a mind so habitually and so thoroughly imbued with the essential peculiarities of the New Testament, that they have long ceased to offer themselves in that questionable light, which tends to excite so much vehement asseveration about them, from less confident and less experienced theologians. And accordingly, one great charm of his sermons is, that they are altogether free from that rigidity of complexion, which the intolerance and the jealousy of system too often impart to the performances of many Christian writers. He compromises no truth. He betrays no dereliction of the principles of that faith which was once delivered to the saints. Nay, when they form the direct topic of his expositions, he most fully and most earnestly contends for them. But instead of constantly laboring after the defence and establishment of these principles, he appears to give a far more effective testimony to their reality and importance, by assuming them, and adopting them, and conducting us at once to that subject which is more nearly and immediately allied to the text of Scripture he has fixed upon.

In the second sermon, on the Reward of receiving a Prophet, preached upon the introduction* of a minister among his people, we have the following sound and judicious advice to the people on the subject of their week-day intercourse with their clergyman.

* It is customary in Scotland, that on the first sabbath of a minister's connection with his people, the forenoon service should be conducted by a clerical friend of his own, who on preaching an appropriate sermon on the duties of ministers and people is said to introduce the minister to his new congregation.

"The object of his ministry, remember, is spiritual; and you receive him with the avowed intention of being assisted by him in forming your spiritual character. Take heed that you do not secularize him; for, if you do, the grand object of his settlement among you will be lost. Receive him to the hospitality of your families; but let not your table become to him a snare. Treat him as your companion and your friend; but never reduce him to the painful alternative of leaving your company, or compromising his character."—pp. 65, 66.

Dr. Jones has long been considered as a master in the art of arrangement,—of constructing such a skilful and comprehensive frame-work of a discourse, as enables him, by the filling up of its separate compartments, to exhaust the text, and the subject embraced by it. And we are persuaded from the examples of this in the sermons before us, that he would offer an acceptable service to the public, by presenting to them his compendiary views of the many texts he has elucidated in the course of his lengthened and laborious ministry.

We have already prepared the reader for the freedom and the frequency of this author's descents into all the minute and actual varieties of human experience. In his sermon on the Benefits of Religious Worship to a man's own household, we are much pleased at the readiness with which he enters into all the relations of a family. He is we think very usefully employed, when he steps into these every-day scenes, and prosecutes his remarks on such familiar exhibitions of human life as the following.

"Men of an irreligious character generally rush into the married state, either from unjustifiable motives, or with too high ideas of the felicity which it ought to confer. The natural consequence is, that they soon meet with disappointment. But, instead of imputing this, as they ought, to their own folly and rashness, they either unfairly lay the blame on the state itself, or ungenerously attach it to the person with whom they have entered into it. Hence, to the most idolatrous professions of attachment, succeed the most marked neglect, the most frigid coolness, the most brutish severity of temper, language, and conduct; the wife becomes the most miserable of mortals; and of all her misery her husband is the author. The religious man, on the contrary, instructed by the doctrines of the Gospel, will choose his companion for life from among those who fear the Lord; and towards her the predilection of judgment, and the affection of nature, are strengthened and improved by the principle of grace. His ideas of human felicity being corrected by the declarations of religion, and a sense of personal depravity, instead of disappointment, he experiences more real happiness in that state than his most sanguine hopes had anticipated. Well he knows, that in human beings perfect wisdom and goodness do not reside. Should he, therefore, discover in his wife a portion of that imperfection which enters into the character of every mortal creature, instead of alienating his affections, it will lead him to redouble his expressions of attachment and tenderness towards her. To love her person, to provide for her wants, to anticipate her wishes, to alleviate her pains, to prevent her fears, to raise her thoughts to Heaven, to assist her in placing her confidence in the Rock of ages, to promote her happiness and joy, are the subjects of his unremitted attention and prayers. A man himself, of like passions with others, he will not escape his share of provocation and offence; but conscience before God and towards his wife, will lead him sternly and successfully to repel their influence,"—pp. 109, 110.

"Although the head of a family, when religious, is its greatest blessing, yet if religion reign in its other branches he will not be its *only* blessing. Another will appear, the next in order, and very little inferior in point of importance, in the wife, the mother, and the mistress. In her, if the meekness of Christ be added to the softness of her sex—if the wisdom which is from above be added to natural sagacity and prudence,—if the love of God be combined with that to her husband, she will, by Divine grace, be an inestimable blessing to her family. She will soothe the cares of her husband, she will increase his substance, she will be a most effectual assistant in carrying on the instruction and government of the family, in which she will promote affection, regularity, and happiness; she will almost entirely bear its cares, and prepare its joys; she will encourage the faith and hope of every individual within it, and will walk with them as an heir of the grace of life."—p. 117.

"Nor must the importance of servants in the estimate of family happiness, be at all overlooked, for when they are of such as fear the Lord, they are a signal blessing to the family. In vain are the most magnificent palaces erected at the most enormous expense: in vain are they stored with all the profusion which the possession of wealth can suggest, and adorned with all the grandeur which the pride of rank can justify; in vain are they surrounded with all the pomp of greatness, and distinguished as the resort of the fashionable and the gay; with all these advantages, small, very small indeed, will be the comfort of their lords, if all the while the servants are perverse, vexatious, and dishonest."—pp. 118, 119.

But this author does not confine himself to any one range of topics. In some of his sermons he has selected a leading doctrine of Christianity, and in his illustration of it he gives his reader the full advantage of that bold and extensive style of thinking by which he places familiar truths in a new attitude and throws over them the light of novel and original illustration. He has escaped from that monotony of observation, into which the training of a scholastic orthodoxy has drawn so many of our theologians. He is uniformly scriptural; and it does not appear that he has uttered a single sentiment of which the most jealous and inquisitorial Calvinism can disapprove. But he betrays none of that fearfulness, none of that cautious keeping within the limits of a defined representation, which we suspect to have had a cramping and frigorific influence on much of our modern preaching. He expatiates with all the freeness of a mind at ease on the subject of orthodoxy; not because he disdains or refines any one of its articles, but because, incorporated as they are with his general habit of thinking, he feels about them all the repose of a most secure and inviolable attachment. There is accordingly, even when employed upon some peculiarity of the Christian faith, little of the tone of controversy, and no anxious setting off of his own doctrinal accuracy, to be met with; but with a mind evidently cast in the mould of evangelical truth, he oversteps all the abridged and compendiary systems of theology, and feels himself free to expatiate on a rich and variegated field of observation.

The above remark was forcibly suggested to us by the perusal of that sermon in which Dr. J. treats of the power of Christ to forgive sins. It has been denominated one of the greatest secrets of practical godliness, to combine a reigning sense of security in the forgiveness of sin with an earnest and an operative sentiment of abhorrence at sin itself. The believing contemplation of Christ, according to the real character which belongs to Him, resolves this mystery; and we felt as if a new flood of light was bursting in upon our mind on this subject by that power and liveliness of exhibition which characterize the sketches of our original and adventurous author. In the compass of a single paragraph, he has, to our satisfaction, given a convincing and impressive view of the link, by which justification and sanctification are riveted in the person of the same individual into one close and indissoluble alliance. He inquires into the kind of power that is requisite for the forgiveness of sins. It cannot be a power to dispense with the authority of the law. It cannot be a power to make the law bend to the criminal. It cannot be a power to frustrate the object of the law. And none therefore can have power to remit the sentence of the law upon the offender, but he who can magnify it and make it honorable; he who can uphold it in the immutability of all its sanctions; and, at the same time, he who can so turn and so subdue the personal character of the offender, that in virtue of the change of heart and of inclination which has taken place upon him, there might be a real security established for his future respect and obedience to all the commandments. It serves to magnify every idea of the exquisite wisdom which presided over the plan of our redemption, when we think how all this power meets in Christ; in Him who took upon His own person the punishment that we should have borne; in Him who, descending from His place of glory, has exalted the law by putting Himself under the weight of its indispensable sanctions; in Him who has at the same time had such a power committed to Him, that He can revolutionize by the Spirit which is at his giving, the whole desires and principles of those who believe in Him, so that they shall love the law of God, and delight in rendering to it all honor and all obedience. Contemplating this last as essential to the power of awarding forgiveness, it will dispose us cordially to go along with the whole process of sanctification, to perceive that the great Mediator must renew those for whom he has secured acceptance with God before He has completed His undertaking upon them; and that in fact we are not the subjects of His mediation unless we are prosecuting diligently the renewal of heart and of mind, and submitting ourselves faithfully to all the requirements of holiness. But on this subject let our author speak for himself.

"From what we have now seen of the nature of forgiveness of sins, it will be evident, that the person who undertakes to exercise this power should first of all be inflexibly just. The law of God is a charter of rights. With the preservation of that charter, everything dear to God and valuable to man is eternally connected. To permit the law to bend to the criminal *here*, would be attended with consequences of injustice, fatal beyond all calculation. Further, with inflexible justice, the person who undertakes to dispense forgiveness should be possessed of wisdom sufficient to determine whether, if sin should be forgiven, the object of the law could be secured, and supreme love to God, and disinterested love to man be maintained. He must moreover possess a power over the law, to suspend, alter, and reverse its sentence, which supposes a power superior to law, even to the law of God. He must also have such power with God as to prevail with Him to lay aside His anger, and to receive the criminal, when forgiven, into His favor. The human heart must be in his hand, and under his control, so as he may be able to expel one train of thoughts and opinions, and to induce another; to take away one set of passions, and dispositions, and to impart others; and, in fact, to alter the whole nature, character, and conduct of man. He must have so complete a dominion over Satan, as to be able to bind and dispose of him at his will. All human events must be under his absolute direction, so as not only to create prosperity and adversity, but to produce from them such impressions as he may require. He must have power over conscience itself, to make it speak, and speak with effect, when he pleases and how he pleases. To death he must be able to say come, and it shall come, go, and it shall go, and to make its valley dark or light, the portal of Heaven, or the gate of hell, as he shall appoint. Such must be the power of his command, that in obedience to it, the grave must surrender the prey which it has retained for ages. To him it must belong to open and shut when he pleases the bottomless pit, and effectually to command the waves of the lake that burneth with fire and brimstone, to recede or advance as he may appoint. Under his control must be the gates of the New Jerusalem, to open and none be able to shut, to shut and none be able to open, with the cherubim and the seraphim, and all the host which is within them; at his disposal must be thrones and dominions, principalities and powers, and all the happiness, and all the grandeur of the world of glory. In short, however great the power of any Being may be, unless it is infinitely just and wise, and placed with a controlling energy over the law of God, and has prevaling influence with God Himself,—unless it is equal to the government of the world, and death, and the grave, and heaven and hell,—in one word, unless it be the power of God, it is not a power adequate to the remission of the punishment of sin: for nothing less than this is the power requisite to forgive sins on earth."—pp. 143—5.

It may be said of Dr. Jones, that he is not an every-day writer of sermons. There is a certain intrepidity about him, both in his selection of topics, and in the free and original way in which he handles them. He possesses a mind stored with a variety of imagery and of information; and this circumstance enables him delightfully to blend with his illustrations of scriptural doctrine both the truths of science, and all that is most pleasing and attractive in the contemplations of poetry. We are quite sensible however, that in the exhibition he is now making before the public, he feels himself to be upon ceremony, and accordingly he has put the exuberance of his fancy under evident chastisement and restraint. There does not appear to be that power and vivacity of illustration, nor that copiousness of allusion, nor that fearless application of the lessons of philosophy and experience, nor that excursive boldness and variety of remark, which are well known to signalize his extemporaneous oratory, and by which he makes himself highly interesting and impressive to his hearers. Still, however, though in print he falls beneath his own habitual excellence in the pulpit, he retains so much of his peculiarity and of his power, as places him far above the tame, insipid, servile monotony of ordinary sermon-writers. And from the volume before us, were we to multiply extracts, we might present our readers with many specimens of a mind that can soar above the region of commonplace, and expatiate in the field of its own unborrowed light, and originate its own spontaneous ingenuities, and without disguising or even so much as throwing a shade over any of the substantial prominences of the Gospel, adorning the whole of its doctrine by such sallies of illustration, as any powerful mind which draws from its own resources, and disowns the authority of models, is able to throw into any track of contemplation over which it may happen to pass.

There are some people possessed with such notions about the simplicity of the truth as it is in Jesus, that the very appearance of originality alarms them. But it by no means necessarily follows that a writer on practical Christianity is, every time that he stretches his ingenuity, working out a laborious deviation from what is useful and applicable to the familiarities of human conduct and human sentiment. Every attempt to be wise above that which is written, should be discouraged, as being opposed to the spirit both of piety and of true philosophy. But still there is room for the exercise of our best and our highest faculties in the attempt to be wise up to that which is written; nor do we think that any fair conclusions drawn from such premises as are supplied by the written record, can be unprofitable for our instruction in righteousness. In his sermon on the "Doctrine of Salvation the Study of Angels," Dr. Jones has given us a happy example of the use to which a subject apparently remote from the powers of human contemplation, may be turned. In his reflections on the utility of the truth contained in his text, he has said, and said powerfully and irresistibly, as much as should rescue the doctrine of Salvation from unworthy treatment, and give it a dignity in the eyes of men. And we consider this as one out of several examples in which the author before us has even in his boldest and loftiest flights gathered a something to strengthen our more ordinary impressions, and to enforce and illuminate the duties of our more ordinary practice; and without that slenderness of effect which the refinement of our over-wrought contemplation sometimes leaves behind it, he often succeeds by a novelty which marks his every tract of sentiment and observation in augmenting and perpetuating the influence of what is most palpable in the lessons of the New Testament.

"Many deem the doctrine of Salvation low, mean, vulgar, and worthless; and they attempt to vindicate their conduct by saying with the unbelieving Jews, which of the scribes or rulers, which of the highly esteemed or dignitaries of our church, make it the theme of their beautiful addresses or fine harangues? Which of our celebrated men of science, discrimination, and taste, even amongst ecclesiastics, make it the object of their study, or the subject of their discourse? Does not the preaching of this salvation provoke contempt and scorn, and expose it to the resistless, overwhelming, degrading imputation of methodism and fanaticism? And yet angels, fascinated by its charms, suspending their studies of nature and their lofty pursuits in Heaven, descend from the celestial world to look into the salvation of Jesus; and whilst they look, they discover new beauties and new wonders incessantly arise, which continually kindle a desire again to look and continue the research. They bend and again they bend their lofty minds, and cannot quit the object; and by their conduct they seem to unite in sentiment with St. Paul, when he said, 'Yea, doubtless, and I count all things but loss for the excellency of the knowledge of Christ Jesus my Lord.' Yes! angels are captivated by the doctrines of salvation, which men presume to neglect; and archangels admire with rapture what men affect to despise. Surely this should convince them of their folly, discover to them the evils of their ways, and rescue the doctrine of salvation from such unworthy treatment."—pp. 288—9.

We trust that the following extracts will both vindicate and exemplify all that we have said in our attempts to sketch the characteristic merits and peculiarities of this author.

"While Christ ascended, His heart overflowed with love; His countenance beamed benignity; His lips uttered blessings; His hands dispensed grace. Whilst He ascended, His sacred person was clothed with the robes of light and immortality. He made the clouds His chariot, and He rode on the wings of the wind. A scene in every respect so sublime and so grand, was never before, nor never since exhibited to men or to angels. He shall so come in like manner, visibly, majestically, in the sight of the general assembly and church of the first born, with shouts, with the voice of the archangel, and the trump of God, attended by the cherubim and the seraphim, and all the heavenly host; His heart overflowing with love; His countenance beaming benignity; His lips uttering blessing; His hands dispensing glory; His sacred person clothed with the robes of light and immortality, making the clouds His chariot, and riding on the wings of the wind. When He had overcome the enemies which in the days of His humiliation opposed Him, He ascended to dispense judgment. When He shall have overcome all His enemies, He shall so come in like manner to judge the quick and the dead: to erect His awful tribunal; and to summon before it the whole human race; and to render eternal life or everlasting death to each man, according as his work shall be. There are two laws of nature which, like all its operations, are very simple in themselves, but mighty and wonderful in their effects. The one is that of attraction, by which one particle unites or coheres to another. The other is that of gravitation, by which things have a tendency to fall to the centre of the earth. By these two principles, God preserves in their appointed situation and order, animals, and vegetables, and minerals, and the sea, and the dry land, and rivers, and mountains; by these he firmly binds together all the atoms which compose the world, and girds the solid globe. By the same laws He both directs the motions, and preserves the order of the sun, and the moon, and the planetary orbs. But when our Lord ascended, He evinced His authority and power over these laws; He burst their mighty chains, and in opposition to their most powerful restraints, He rose from earth and soared above the ethereal heavens. In like manner, He shall so come. He shall dissolve the bonds of gravitation, and the sun, and the moon, and the stars, shall fall; the mountains shall remove: and the rivers shall fail; and the sea shall be dried up; and the solid globe shall be rent asunder in every direction. He shall untie the cords of attraction, and particle shall separate from particle, and atom from atom, and the whole world shall fall to pieces, and shall be no more. Thus the same Jesus who was taken up into Heaven, shall so come *in like manner* as he was seen to go into Heaven." —pp. 235—7.

"We ought not to waste our time in idle speculations. When Elisha was favored with witnessing the ascension of Elijah, the chariots of fire and the horses of fire having conveyed him out of his sight, he gathered up the mantle which had fallen from that great prophet, and hastening to the banks of Jordan, he smote the waters and passed between the divided parts of the stream, stopped not till he arrived at Jericho, and instantly began to discharge the duties of his office. But when the disciples of our Lord were permitted to witness His ascension, and to behold the cloud receive Him out of their sight, they lingered on the spot; they stood still; they steadfastly looked up; they gazed; thoughts arose in their breasts, and questions started in their minds, which they seemed inclined to indulge. Whither is He gone? What change has taken place upon Him? What is He now doing? They were on the verge of a thousand idle speculations, fraught with ten thousand dangerous errors. There is a point to which speculation may advance with safety, when it tends to enlighten the mind with truth, to season the heart with grace, and to rouse the active powers to holy conduct. But beyond this, it is vain, it is forbidden, it is fatal to proceed. At this point, the disciples of our lord had at this moment arrived. To prevent their going beyond it, angels interposed: 'Ye men of Galilee,' said they. 'why stand ye gazing?' The moments of speculation are over, and the time for action is come."—pp. 240—1.

We now take leave of Dr. Jones, with remarking that his volume bears the evidence of one who has not accustomed himself much to the practice of correct or elegant composition. He has evidently read much, but what he has excogitated for himself forms a far more abundant portion of his intellectual wealth, than what he has appropriated from others. It would appear as if the power and facility of his unwritten language had made him so independent of the ordinary means of conveyance by which a minister transfers the product of his own mind to the minds of his people, that his views, and his thoughts, and his modes of illustration, are no sooner conceived, than he is able to transfer them at once upon his hearers through the channel of contemporaneous communication. We have no doubt that in this way much powerful eloquence, and much solid instruction, and many felicities of thought and of expression, which were worthy of being preserved, are destined to be forgotten in the course of a few years, and so to perish forever from the remembrance of the world. We are glad, however, that the public have been presented with such a memorial of the author, as that which he has now furnished; and if we think it is not an adequate representation of all the talents and accomplishments of him who has produced it, yet we feel confident that it is calculated to extend the usefulness of Dr. Jones, as well as to advance his reputation beyond the narrow circle of his own auditory.

REMARKS

ON

CUVIER'S THEORY OF THE EARTH;

IN EXTRACTS FROM

A REVIEW OF THAT THEORY

WHICH WAS CONTRIBUTED TO

"THE CHRISTIAN INSTRUCTOR"

IN 1814.

"It is not our object to come forward with a full analysis of the theory of Cuvier. The appearance of the work has afforded matter of triumph and satisfaction to the friends of revelation, though, in these feelings, we cannot altogether sympathize with them. It is true that his theory approximates to the information of the book of Genesis more nearly than those of many of his predecessors; and the occasional exhibitions which appear in the course of his pages, have the effect at least of stamping the character of a disinterested testimony upon his opinions. This leads us to anticipate the period when there will be a still closer coincidence between the theories of geologists and the Mosaical history of the creation. It is well that there is now a progress to this object; that the chronology at least of Moses begins to be more respected; that a date so recent is ascribed to the last great catastrophe of the globe, as to make it fall more closely upon the deluge of the book of Genesis; and when we recollect the eloquence, and the plausibility, and the imposing confidence with which a theorist of the day has magnified the antiquity of the present system, we shall henceforth be less alarmed at anything in the speculations, either of Cuvier or of others, which may appear to bear hard upon the credit of the sacred historian."

"He assigns no distinct cause for the earth's revolutions, and leaves us utterly at a loss about the nature of that impelling principle, which gives rise to the sweeping and terrible movements that are thought to take place in the waters of the ocean. We expected something from him upon this subject under the article of Astronomical Causes of the Revolutions on the Earth's Surface: nor has he chosen to advert to the theory of Laplace, though in our apprehension, it would have imparted a great addition of plausibility to the whole speculation.

"It is to the diurnal revolution of the earth round its axis, that we owe the deviation of its figure from a perfect sphere. The earth is so much flattened at the poles, and so much elevated at the equator, that, by the mean calculations upon this subject, the former are nearer to the centre of the earth than the latter by thirty-five English miles. What would be the effect then, if the axis of revolution were suddenly shifted? If the polar and equinoctial regions were to change places, there would be a tendecy towards an elevation of so many miles in the one, and of as great a depression in the other, and the more transferable parts of the earth's surface would be the first to obey this tendency."

"But it is not necessary to assume so entire a change in the position of the earth's axis, as to produce a difference of thirty-five miles in any of the existing levels, nor would any single impetus, indeed, suffice to accomplish such a change. The transference of the poles from their present situation by a few degrees, would give rise to a revolution sudden enough, and mighty enough for all the purposes of a geological theory; and a change of level by a single quarter of a mile, would destroy the vast majority of living animals, and create such a harvest of fossil remains, as would give abundant employment to a whole host of future speculators."

"Now, we have two observations to offer on the said theory; one in the way of a humble addition, and the other in the way of an apology for it.

"First, from the planets moving all nearly in circular orbits, it is more likely that they have done so from the very commencement of their revolutions, than that they started at first with very unequal eccentricities, and have been reduced to orbits of almost similar form by the shocks which each of them individually sustained from comets. Assuming then, that originally the orbits were nearly circular, how comes it that they remain so, in spite of those numerous impulses, which the theory of Laplace, combined with the allegation of Cuvier that the catastrophes on the earth have been frequent, necessarily implies? Whether the impulse be in the line of the earth's motion, which it may very nearly be with a few of the comets. or whether it cross that line at a considerable angle, which would be the direction of the impulse with the great majority of them, still we cannot conceive from the great velocity of the impelling body, how the planet can avoid receiving from the shock, and far more from the repetition of it, such a change in its eccentricity, as would have given us at this moment a planetary system made up of bodies moving in very variously elongated ellipses. The way of evading this objection, is to reduce the momentum of the comet, by assigning to it as small a density as will suit the purpose ; but small as it may be, there is momentum enough, according to the hypothesis of Laplace, to change the position of the earth's axis. A repetition of such impulses upon the different planets in every conceivable variety of direction, would, in time, give rise to a very wide dissimilarity in their orbits ; and the fact, that such a dissimilarity does not exist, militates against that indefinite antiquity, which the deifiers of matter ascribe to the present system.

"But again, it does not appear to us, that the theory of Laplace is insufficient to account for the highly inclined position of strata, which may have been deposited horizontally. By the conceived impulse of a comet, the earth receives a tendency to a change of figure. This can only be produced by the motion of its parts, and a force acting on these parts is put into operation. Who will compute the strength of the impediment which this force may not overcome, or say in how far the cohesion of the solid materials on the surface of the globe will be an effectual resistance to it? May not this force act in the very way in which Cuvier expresses the operation of his catastrophe? May it not *break* and *overturn* the strata? And will it not help our conceptions to suppose, that masses of water, struggling in the bowels of the earth for a more elevated position, may have force enough to burst their way through the solid exterior, and tainting and mingling with the old ocean, may annihilate all the marine animals of the former era? Of the flood of the book of Genesis, we read that the *fountains of the great deep* were broken* up, as well as that the windows of heaven were opened.

"We feel vastly little either of confidence or satisfaction, in any of these theories. It is a mere contest of probabilities ; and an actual and well established testimony should be paramount to them all. We hold the testimony of Moses to supersede all this work of conjecture ; and we shall presently take up the subject of that testimony, and inquire in how far it goes to confirm, or to falsify the speculations of this volume.

"The qualifications of M. Cuvier as a comparative anatomist, give a high authority to his opinion on the nature of the fossil remains, and the kind of animals of which they form a part. His inquiries in this volume are confined to the remains of quadrupeds ; and the most amusing, and perhaps the soundest argument in the whole book, is that by which he unfolds his method of constructing the entire animal from some small and solitary fragment of its skeleton. We were highly gratified with his discussion upon this sub-

* It is remarkable that the original word for the *deep* corresponds, according to Dr. Campbell, in one of its significations, with the New Testament *hades*, conceived to be situated in the interior of the earth.

ject, nor can we resist the desire of imparting the same gratification to our readers, by the following extract:

"Fortunately, comparative anatomy, when thoroughly understood, enables us to surmount all these difficulties, as a careful application of its principles instructs us in the correspondence and dissimilarity of the forms of organized bodies of different kinds, by which each may be rigorously ascertained from almost every fragment of its various parts and organs.

"Every organized individual forms an entire system of its own, all the parts of which mutually correspond, and concur to produce a certain definite purpose, by reciprocal reaction, or by combining towards the same end. Hence none of these separate parts can change their forms without a corresponding change on the other parts of the same animal, and consequently each of these parts taken separately, indicates all the other parts to which it has belonged. Thus, as I have elsewhere shown, if the viscera of an animal are so organized as only to be fitted for the digestion of recent flesh, it is also requisite that the jaws should be so constructed as to fit them for devouring prey; the claws must be constructed for seizing and tearing it to pieces; the teeth for cutting and dividing its flesh; the entire system of the limbs, or organs of motion, for pursuing and overtaking it; and the organs of sense, for discovering it at a distance. Nature also must have endowed the brain of the animal with instincts sufficient for concealing itself, and for laying plans to catch its necessary victims.

"Such are the universal conditions that are indispensable in the structure of carnivorous animals; and every individual of that description must necessarily possess them combined together, as the species could not otherwise subsist. Under this general rule, however, there are several particular modifications, depending upon the size, the manners, and the haunts of the prey for which each species of carnivorous animal is destined or fitted by nature; and, from each of these particular modifications, there result certain differences in the more minute conformations of particular parts; all, however, conformable to the general principles of structure already mentioned. Hence it follows, that in every one of their parts we discover distinct indications, not only of the classes and orders of animals, but also of their genera, and even of their species.

"In fact, in order that the jaw may be well adapted for laying hold of objects, it is necessary that its condyle should have a certain form; that the resistance, the moving power, and the fulcrum, should have a certain relative position with respect to each other; and that the temporal muscles should be of a certain size. The hollow or depression, too, in which these muscles are lodged, must have a certain depth; and the zygomatic arch under which they pass, must not only have a certain degree of convexity, but it must be sufficiently strong to support the action of the masseter.

"To enable the animal to carry off its prey when seized, a correspondent force is requisite in the muscles which elevate the head; and this necessarily gives rise to a determinate form of the vertebræ to which these muscles are attached, and of the occiput into which they are inserted.

"In order that the teeth of a carnivorous animal may be able to cut the flesh, they require to be sharp, more or less so in proportion to the greater or less quantity of flesh that they have to cut. It is requisite that their roots should be solid and strong, in proportion to the quantity and the size of the bones which they have to break in pieces. The whole of these cicumstances must necessarily influence the development and form of all the parts which contribute to move the jaws.

"To enable the claws of a carnivorous animal to seize its prey, a considerable degree of mobility is necessary in their paws and toes, and a considerable strength in the claws themselves. From these circumstances, there necessarily result certain determinate forms in all the bones of their paws, and in the distribution of the muscles and tendons by which they are moved. The fore-arm must possess a certain facility of moving in various directions, and consequently requires certain determinate forms in the bones of which it is composed. As the bones of the fore-arm are articulated with the arm bone or humerus, no change can take place in the form and structure of the former, without occasioning correspondent changes in the form of the latter. The shoulder-blade also, or scapula, requires a correspondent degree of strength in all animals destined for catching prey, by which it likewise must necessarily have an appropriate form. The play and action of all these parts require certain proportions in the muscles which set them in motion, and the impressions formed by these muscles must still farther determine the forms of all these bones.

"After these observations, it will be easily seen that similar conclusions may be drawn with respect to the hinder limbs of carnivorous animals, which require particular conformations to fit them for rapidity of motion in general; and that similar considerations must influence the forms and connections of the vertebræ and other bones constituting the trunk of the body, to fit them for flexibility and readiness of motion in all directions. The bones also of the nose, of the orbit, and of the ears, require certain forms and structures to fit them for giving perfection to the senses of smell, sight and hearing, so necessary to animals of prey. In short, the shape and structure of the teeth regulate the forms of the condyle, of the shoulder-blade, and of the claws, in the same manner as the equation of a curve, regulates all its other properties; and as in regard to any particular course, all its properties may be ascertained by assuming each separate property as the foundation of a particular equation; in the same manner a claw, a shoulder-blade, a condyle, a leg or arm bone, or any other bone, separately considered, enables us to discover the description of teeth to which they have belonged; and so also reciprocally we may determine the forms of the other bones from the teeth. Thus, commencing our investigation by a careful survey of any one bone by itself, a person who is sufficiently master of the laws of organic structure, may, as it were, reconstruct the whole animal to which that bone belonged.

"This principle is sufficiently evident, in its general acceptation, not to require any more minute demonstration; but when it comes to be applied in practice, there is a great number of cases in which our theoretical knowledge of these relations of forms is not sufficient to guide us, unless assisted by observation and experience.

"For example, we are well aware that all hoofed animals must necessarily be herbivorous, because they are possessed of no means of seizing upon prey. It is also evident, having no other use for their fore-legs than to support their bodies, that they have no occasion for a shoulder so vigorously organized as that of carnivorous animals; owing to which they have no clavicles or acromion processes, and their shoulder-blades are proportionally narrow. Having also no occasion to turn their fore-arms their radius is joined by ossification to the ulna, or is at least articulated by the gynglymus with the humerus. Their food being entirely herbaceous, requires teeth with flat surfaces, on purpose to bruise the seeds and plants on which they feed. For this purpose also, these surfaces require to be unequal, and are consequently composed of alternate perpendicular layers of hard enamel and softer bone. Teeth of this structure necessarily require horizontal motions, to enable them to triturate or grind down the herbaceous food; and, accordingly, the condyles of the jaw could not be formed into such confined joints as in the carnivorous animals, but must have a flattened form, correspondent to sockets in the temporal bones, which also are more or less flat for their reception. The hollows likewise of the temporal bones, having smaller muscles to contain, are narrower, and not so deep, &c. All these circumstances are deducible from each other, according to their greater or less generality, and in such manner that some are essentially and exclusively appropriated to hoofed quadrupeds, while other circumstances, though equally necessary to that description of animals, are not exclusively so, but may be found in animals of other descriptions, where other conditions permit or require their existence.

"When we proceed to consider the different orders or subdivisions of the class of hoofed animals, and examine the modifications to which the general conditions are liable, or rather the particular conditions which are conjoined, according to the respective characters of the several subdivisions, the reasons upon which these particular conditions or rules of conformation are founded become less evident. We can easily conceive, in general, the necessity of a more complicated system of digestive organs in those species which have less perfect masticatory systems; and hence we may presume that these latter animals require especially to be ruminant. which are in want of such or such kinds of teeth; and may also deduce, from the same considerations, the necessity of a certain conformation of the æsophagus, and of corresponding forms in the vertebræ of the neck, &c. But I doubt whether it would have been discovered, independently of actual observation, that ruminant animals should all have cloven hoofs, and that they should be the only animals having that particular conformation; that the ruminant animals only should be provided with horns on their foreheads; that those among them which have sharp tusks, or canine teeth, should want horns, &c.

"As all these relative conformations are constant and regular, we may be assured that they depend upon some sufficient cause; and since we are not acquainted with that cause, we must here supply the defect of theory by observation, and in this way lay down empirical rules on the subject, which are almost as certain as those deduced from rational principies, especially if established upon careful and repeated observation. Hence, any one who observes merely the print of a cloven hoof, may conclude that it has been left by a ruminant amimal, and regard the conclusion as equally certain with any other in physics or in morals. Consequently, this single foot-mark clearly indicates to the observer the forms of the teeth, of the jaws, of the vertebræ, of all the leg-bones, thighs, shoulders, and of the trunk of the body of the animal which left the mark. It is much surer than all the marks of Zadig. Observation alone, independent entirely of general principles of philosophy, is sufficient to show that there certainly are secret reasons for all these relations of which I have been speaking.

"When we have established a general system of these relative conformations of animals, we not only discover specific constancy, if the expression may be allowed, between certain forms of certain organs, and certain other forms of different organs; we can also perceive a classified constancy of conformation, and a correspondent gradation between these two sets of organs, which demonstrate their mutual influence upon each other, almost as certainly as the most perfect deduction of reason. For example, the masticatory system is generally more perfect in the non-ruminant hoofed quadrupeds than it is in the cloven-hoofed or ruminant quadrupeds; as the former possess incisive teeth, or tusks, or almost always both of these, in both jaws. The structure also of their feet is in general more complicated, having a greater number of toes, or their phalanges less enveloped in the hoof, or a greater number of distinct metacarpal and metatarsal bones, or more numerous tarsal bones, or the fibula more completely distinct from the tibia; or, finally, that all these enumerated circumstances are often united in the same species of animal.

"It is quite impossible to assign reasons for these relations; but we are certain that they are not produced by mere chance, because, whenever a cloven-hoofed animal has any resemblance in the arrangement of its teeth to the animals we now speak of, it has the resemblance to them also in the arrangement of its feet. Thus camels, which have tusks, and also two or four incisive teeth in the upper-jaw, have one additional bone in the tarsus, their scaphoid and cuboid bones not being united into one; and have also very small hoofs with corresponding phalanges, or toe-bones. The musk animals, whose tusks are remarkably conspicuous, have a distinct fibula as long as the tibia; while the other cloven-footed animals have only a small bone articulated at the lower end of the tibia in place of a fibula. We have thus a constant mutual relation between the organs of conformations, which appear to have no kind of connection with each other; and the gradations of their forms invariably correspond, even in those cases in which we cannot give the rationale of their relations.

"By thus employing the method of observation, where theory is no longer able to direct our views, we procure astonishing results. The smallest fragment of bone, even the most apparently insignificant apophysis, possesses a fixed and determinate character, relative to the class, order, genus and species of the animal to which it belonged; insomuch, that when we find merely the extremity of a well-preserved bone, we are able, by careful examination, assisted by analogy and exact comparison, to determine the species to which it once belonged, as certainly as if we had the entire animal before us. Before venturing to put entire confidence in this method of investigation, in regard to fossil bones, I have very frequently tried it with portions of bones belonging to well-known animals, and always with such complete success that I now entertain no doubt with regard to the results which it affords. I must acknowledge that I enjoy every kind of advantage for such investigations that could possibly be of use, by my fortunate situation in the Museum of Natural History; and, by assiduous researches for nearly fifteen years, I have collected skeletons of all the genera and sub-genera of quadrupeds, with those of many species in some of the genera, and even of several varieties of some species. With these aids, I have found it easy to multiply comparisons, and to verify, in every point of view, the application of the foregoing rules."—pp. 90—102.

"Now, this is a most interesting specimen of M. Cuvier. It bespeaks the tone and the habit of a philosopher, and is well calculated to gain a favorable hearing, if not an authority, to all his other speculations. But it is quite true that a man may excel in one department of investigation, and fall short in another; and none more ready than the antemosaical philosophers, who oppose him, to exclaim, that, though M. Cuvier be a good anatomist, it does not follow that he is a geologist. Now we profess to be neither the one nor the other. The science of our professional department is different from both, and all that we ask of the geological infidels of the day is, that they will do us the same justice in reference to their speculations, that they take to themselves in reference to M. Cuvier. A man may be a good geologist, and be able to construct as good a system as the mineralogical appearances around him enable him to do. But this system is neither more nor less than the announcement of past facts, and geology forms only one of the channels by which we may reach them. But there are other channels, and the most direct and obvious of them all to the knowledge of the past is the channel of history. The recorded testimony of those who were present or nearer than ourselves to the facts in question, we hold to be a likelier path to the information we are in quest of, than the inferences of a distant posterity upon the geological phenomena around them, just as an actual history of the legislation of old governments, is a trustier document than an ingenious speculation on the progress and the principles of human society. You protest against the knife and demonstrations of the anatomist as instruments of no authority in your department. We protest against the hammer of the mineralogist and the reveries of the geologian, as instruments of no authority in ours. You think that Cuvier is very slender in geology, and that he has been most unphilosophically rash in leaving his own province, and carrying his confident imaginations into a totally different field of inquiry. We cannot say, that you are very slender in the philosophy of history and historical evidence, for it is a ground you scarcely ever deign to touch upon. But surely it is a distinct subject of inquiry. It has its own principles, and its own probabilities. You must pronounce upon the testimony of Moses on appropriate evidence. It is a testimony of a witness nearer than yourselves to the events in question; and if it be a sound testimony, it carries along with it the testimony of a Being who was something more than an actual spectator of the creation. He was both spectator and agent. And yet all that mighty train of evidence which goes to sustain the revealed history of God's administrations in the world, is by you overlooked and forgotten; and while you so readily lift the cry against the unphilosophical encroachment of foreign principles into your department, you make no conscience of elbowing your own principles into a field which does not belong to them.

"But it is high time to confront the theory of our geologist with the sacred history—with a view both to lay down the points of accordancy, and to show in how far we are compelled to modify the speculation, or to disown it altogether.

"First, then, it is so far well that Cuvier admits the very last catastrophe to have been so recent, and accomplished too like all his former catastrophes, by the agency of water. The only modification we have to offer here is, that whereas Cuvier represents it to be an operation of so violent a nature as to agitate and displace everything that was movable—we guess, from the history, that an olive tree was still standing, and not lying loosely on the ground, with part of its foliage. If we are correct in our assumption as to the specific gravity of the olive tree, it would, if separated from the soil, have been borne up on the surface of the water—and in that case the circumstance of a leaf being recently plucked or torn from the tree, would have been no indication whatever of the waters being abated from off the earth.

"Again, the researches of M. Cuvier present us with no fact militating against the recent creation of the human species. It has been said to be the subject of a recent discovery—but at the time of writing this volume, M. Cuvier could assert that no human remains had been hitherto discovered among the extraneous fossils. This he holds to be a decisive proof, that man did not exist in those countries where the fossil bones of other animals are to be found. This is no proof, however, that he did not exist in some other quarters of the globe antecedent to the last or any given number of catastrophes. He may have been confined to some narrow regions which escaped the operation of the catastrophe, from which he issued out to repeople the new formed land; or, the fossil remains of the human species, may exist in the bottom of the present ocean, and remain concealed from observation till some new catastrophe lay them open to the inquirers of a future era. But this is all gratuitous, and must give way to the positive information of authentic history.

"There is one very precious fruit to be gathered out of those investigations, an argument for the exercise of a creative power, more convincing perhaps than any that can be drawn from the slender resources of natural theism. If it be true, that in the oldest of the strata, no animal remains are to be met with, marking out an epoch anterior to the existence of living beings in the field of observation—if it be true that all the genera which are found in the first of the peopled strata are destroyed—if it be true that no traces of our present genera are to be met with in the early epochs of the globe,—how came the present races of animated nature into being? It is not enough to say, that like man they may have been confined to narrower regions, and escaped the operation of the former catastrophes, or that their remains may be buried under the present ocean. Enough for our purpose, that they could not have existed from all eternity. Enough for us the fact, that each catastrophe has the chance of destroying, or does in fact destroy a certain number of genera. If this annihilating process went on from eternity, the work of annihilation would long ago have been accomplished, and there is not a single species of living creatures that could have survived the multiplicity of chances for its extinction afforded by an indefinite number of catastrophes. If then there were no replacement of new genera, the face of the world would at this moment have been one dreary and unpeopled solitude; and the question recurs, how did this replacement come to be effected? The doctrine of spontaneous generation we believe to be generally exploded; and there is not a known instance of an animal being brought into existence, but by means of a previous animal of the same species. The transition of the genera into one another is most ably and conclusively contended against by the author before us, who proves them to be separated by permanent and invincible barriers. Between the one principle and the other the commencement of a new genera is totally inexplicable on any of the known powers and combinations of matter, and we are carried upwards to the primary link which connects the existence of a created being with the fiat of the Creator.

"But, generally speaking, geologists are not guilty of disowning the act of creation. It is in theorizing on the manner of the act, (and that too in the face of testimony which they do not attempt to dispose of,) that they make the most glaring deviation from the spirit and principles of the inductive philosophy. We have no experience in the formation of worlds. Set aside revelation, and we cannot say whether the act of creation is an instantaneous act, or a succession of acts ; and no man can tell whether God made this earth and these heavens in a moment of time, or in a week, or in a thousand years, more than he can tell whether the men of Jupiter, if there be any such, live ten years or ten centuries. Both questions lie out of the field of observation ; and it is delightful to think, that the very principle which constitutes the main strength of the atheistical argument, goes to demolish all those presumptuous speculations, in which the enemies of the Bible attempt to do away the authority of the sacred historian. 'The universe,' says Hume, 'is a *singular* effect ;' and we therefore can never know if it proceeded from the hand of an intelligent Creator. But if the Creator takes another method of making us know, the very singularity of the effect is the reason why we should be silent when he speaks to us ; and why we, in all the humility of conscious ignorance, should yield our entire submission to the information he lays before us. Surely, if without a revelation, the singularity of the effect leaves us ignorant of the nature of the cause, it leaves us equally ignorant of the *modus operandi* of this cause. If experience furnish nothing to enlighten us upon this question, 'Did the universe come from the hand of an intelligent God ?' it furnishes as little to enlighten us upon the question, 'Did God create the universe in an instant, or did he do it in seven days, or did he do it in any other number of days that may be specified ?' These are points which natural reason, exercising itself upon natural appearances, does not qualify us to know ; and it were well if a maxim, equally applicable to philosophers and to children, were to come in here for our future direction, 'that what we do not know we should be content to learn ;' and if a revelation, bearing every evidence of authenticity, undertakes the office of informing us, it is our part cheerfully to acquiesce, and obediently to go along with it.

"On this principle we refuse to concede the literal history of Moses, or to abandon it to the fanciful and ever-varying interpretations of philosophers. We have to thank the respectable editor of this work, Mr. Jameson, for his becoming deference to the authority of the Jewish legislator, and his no less becoming and manly expression of it. But we cannot consent to the stretching out of the days, spoken of in the first chapter of Genesis, into indefinite periods of time. We fear that the slower revolution of the earth round her axis, is too gratuitous to make the admission of it at all consistent with the just rules of philosophizing ; and there is, therefore, no other alternative left to us, but to take the history just as it stands. We leave it to geologists to judge, whether our concluding observations allow them room enough for bringing about a consistency between the first chapter of Genesis and their theories. In the meantime, we assert that the history in this chapter, maintains throughout an entire consistency with itself; a consistency which would be utterly violated, if we offered to allegorize the days, or to take them up in any other sense than that in which they obviously and literally present themselves. What shall we make of the institution of the Sabbath, if we surrender the Mosaic history of the creation? Is it to be conceived, that the Jews would understand the description of Moses in any other sense than in the plain and obvious one? Is it to be admitted, that God would incorporate a falsehold in one of His commandments, or at least prefer a reason for the observance of it which was calculated to deceive, and had all the effect of a falsehood? We cannot but resist this laxity of interpretation, which if suffered in one chapter of the Bible, may be carried to all of them, may unsettle the dearest articles of our faith, and throw a baleful uncertainty over the condition and the prospects of the species.

" We have heard it preferred as an impeachment against the consistency of the Mosaic account, that the day and night were made to succeed each other antecedently to the formation of the sun. This is very true; but it was not antecedent to the formation of light; it was not antecedent to the division of the light from the darkness; it may not have been antecedent to the formation of luminous matter: and though all this matter was not assembled into one body till the fourth day, it may have been separated and made to reside in so much greater abundance in one quarter of the heavens than in the other, as to have given rise to a region of light and a region of darkness. Such an arrangement would, with the revolution of the earth's axis, give rise to a day and a night. Enough for the purpose of making out this succession, if the light formed on the first day was *unequally* dispersed over the surrounding expanse, though it was not till this light was fixed and concentrated in one mass, that the sun could be said to rule the day.

" And here let it be observed, that it does not fall upon the defenders of Moses to bring forward positive or specific proofs for the truth of any system reconcilable with his history, beyond the historical evidence of the history itself. A thousand systems may be devised, one of which only can be true, but each of which may be consistent with all the details of the book of Genesis. We cannot, and we do not offer any one of these systems as that which is to be positively received, but we offer them all as so many ways of disposing of the objections; and while upon us lies the bare task of proposing them, upon our antagonists lies the heavy work of overthrowing them all before they can set aside the direct testimony of the sacred historian, or assert that his account of the creation is contradicted by known appearances.

" We crave the attention of our readers to the above remark; and, satisfied that the more they think of it, the more will they be impressed with its justness, we spare ourselves the task of bestowing upon it any further elucidation.

"We conclude with adverting to the unanimity of geologists in one point,—the far superior antiquity of this globe to the commonly received date of it, as taken from the writings of Moses. What shall we make of this? We may feel a security as to those points in which they differ, and, confronting them with one another, may remain safe and untouched between them. But when they agree, this security fails. There is no neutralization of authority among them as to the age of the world; and Cuvier, with his catastrophes and his epochs, leaves the popular opinion nearly as far behind him, as they who trace our present continent upward through an indefinite series of ancestors, and assign many millions of years to the existence of each generation.

"Should the phenomena compel us to assign a greater antiquity to the globe than to that work of days detailed in the book of Genesis, there is still one way of saving the credit of the literal history. The first creation of the earth and the heavens may have formed no part of that work. This took place at the *beginning*, and is described in the first verse of Genesis. It is not said when this *beginning* was. We know the general impression to be, that it was on the earlier part of the first day, and that the first act of creation formed part of the same day's work with the formation of light. We ask our readers to turn to that chapter, and to read the first five verses of it. Is there any forcing in the supposition, that the first verse describes the primary act of creation, and leaves us at liberty to place it as far back as we may; that the first half of the second verse describes the state of the earth (which may already have existed for ages, and been the theatre of geological revolutions) at the point of time anterior to the detailed operations of this chapter; and that the motion of the Spirit of God, described in the second clause of the second verse, was the commencement of these operations? In this case the creation of the light may have been the great and leading event of the first day; and Moses may be supposed to give us not a history of the first formation of things, but of the formation of the present system; and as we have already proved the necessity of direct exercises of creative power to keep up the generations of living creatures; so Moses may, for anything we know, be giving us the full history of the last great interposition, and be describing the successive steps by which the mischiefs of the last catastrophe were repaired.

"I take a friend to see a field which belongs to me, and I give him a history of the way in which I managed it. In the beginning I inclosed that field. It was then in a completely wild and unbroken state. I pared it. This took up one week. I removed the great stones out of it. This took up another week. On the third week, I entered the plough into it: and thus, by describing the operations of each week, I may lay before him the successive steps by which I brought my field into cultivation. It does not strike me that there is any violence done to the above narrative, by the supposition that the inclosure of the field was a distinct and anterior thing to the first week's operation. The very description of its state after it was inclosed, is an interruption to the narrative of the operations, and leaves me at liberty to consider the work done after this description of the state of the field as the whole work of the first week. The inclosure of the field may have taken place one year, or even twenty years before the more detailed improvements were entered upon.

"The first clause of the second verse is just such another interruption; and it is remarkable, that there is no similar example of it in describing the work of any of the following days, so as to divide one part of the day's work from the other. It is true, that, in some cases, it is said that God saw it to be good; but there is no imperfection ascribed to anything, as it resulted immediately from the creating power. It is always said to be good in that state in which it came directly out of his hand; and if in the second verse, it is said of the earth, not that it was good, but that it was without form and void; this may look not like a description of its state immediately after it came out of the hand of God, but of its state after one of those catastrophes which geologists assign to it. It is further remarkable, that there is a unity in the work of each of the five days. The work of the second day relates only to the firmament; of the third day, to the separation of sea and land; of the fourth day, to the formation of the celestial bodies; of the fifth, to the creation of the sea; and of the sixth, to that of land animals. This unity of work would be violated on the first day, if the primary act of creation were to form part of it; and the uniformity is better kept up by separating the primary act from all the succeeding operations, and making the formation and division of light, the great and only work of the first day.

"The same observation may apply to all the celestial bodies that are visible to this world. The creation of the heavens may have taken place as far antecedently to the details of the first chapter of Genesis, as the creation of the earth. It is evident, however, that if the earth had been at some former period the fair residence of life, she had now become void and formless; and if the sun and moon and stars at some former period had given light, that light had been extinguished. It is not our part to assign the cause of a catastrophe which carried so extensive a destruction along with it; but he were a bold theorist indeed, who could assert, that, in the wide chambers of immensity, no such cause is to be found. A thousand possibilities may be devised, each of which is consistent with the literal history of Moses; and though it is not incumbent on the one party to bring forward any one of these possibilities in the shape of a positive announcement, each of them must be overthrown by the other before that history can be abandoned; and it will be found, that while the friends of the Bible are under no necessity to depart from the sober humility of the inductive spirit, the charge of unphilosophical temerity lies upon its opponents."

SPEECH

DELIVERED

IN THE GENERAL ASSEMBLY OF 1833,

ON A

PROPOSED MODIFICATION OF THE LAW OF PATRONAGE.

I do not participate in the confidence of those who seem quite assured that the abolition of patronage, or a change in its law, is to usher in for us some great and speedy regeneration, or to be the stepping-stone, as it were, to a blissful millennium in the country and in the Church. I must confess myself to be not so sanguine; nor have I any great faith in the efficacy of a renovated constitution for bringing onward a renovated spirit, a renovated character, either among our ministers or among our people. It seems to me like the problem of the best construction for a house, with the misfortune, at the same time, of having nothing but frail materials to build it with; in which case, the study of the fittest proportions for durability and strength will be of little avail to us. I am not denying that there is an optimism of form in ordinary architecture, and that there is also an optimism of form in the architecture of an ecclesiastico-political fabric, if we knew but how to find it—an absolutely best and most perfect framework, to be obtained by somehow altering the present relation of its parts, and fixing on other adjustments of proportion and power, between the men of the congregation, and the men of the session, and the men of the presbytery, and, last of all, the man whom it is now proposed to remove altogether from the place which he at present occupies on the apex of the structure, and who has so long held the initial, and a great deal too much of an absolute, voice in the appointment of churches. By these changes, power will be differently partitioned, and the constitution forced into a different sort of body-politic from before; but it ought ever to be kept in mind, that we have nothing after all but poor human nature to piece and to build it with, and that with such materials we in vain expect to make good our escape from corruption, merely by passing from one form to another. It is for this reason that, however much I may sympathize with many of my friends in my wishes for a pure and efficient Church, I do not sympathize with them in the extravagance of their hopes. I will not be party to the delusion that our Church is necessarily to become more Christian, by the constitution of it becoming more popular; or by the transference of its authority from the hands of the few to the hands of the multitude. I do not see how the one is an unfailing corollary to the other; or how you are to get quit of the evils incidental, I fear, to all sorts of human patronage, merely by multiplying the number of human patrons. Multiplication, I ever understood, told only on the amount of the things to which it was applied, and not upon the character or kind of them. It results in a greater number of apples, but has no power to change them into apricots. Now, my fear is, that if utterly powerless for the transmutation of fruit, it is just as powerless for the transmutation of humanity. Our arithmetical reformers, who look to this mere arithmetic of theirs for the revival of our Church, are looking, I fear, to the wrong quarter for our coming regeneration. They but exchange one human confidence for another, placing it on a broader and more extended basis than before, but still on a basis of earthliness. It is a confidence which I cannot share in; nor do I comprehend how it is that, with minds so firmly, so undoubtedly made up, they count on a mere enlargement of the ecclesiastical franchise, as the high-road to the spiritual enlargement of the Church, to the increase and mighty resurrection of its vital godliness. They are forgetting all history and all observation. They are not looking even to the present state of those numerous dissenting bodies which, under a system of popular election, though retaining the form of sound words, have become spiritually dead; or, if they still own any fire and fervor at all, it is but the fervor of earthly passions, the fire of fierce and unhallowed politics. Neither are they recollecting those numerous Presbyterian churches in England, which, under the same system, have even cast the form of sound words away from them, and lapsed into Scocinianism; or the Presbyterian church in the north of Ireland, where, with that very constitution of the patronage which is held up as a specific against all sorts of evil, a large proportion both of the ministers and congregations lapsed into Arianism. But I hold it a far more serious inadvertency than this, that so many of my best friends should be looking, and with an anticipation quite unwavering and unclouded, to a sort of latter-day glory, and that on the stepping-stone of a mere constitutional reform,—a transference of power from the patrons to the people, or from one portion of our depraved human nature to another. Let them have a care, in all this unquailing confidence of theirs, lest they should become unmindful of the rock whence both patrons and people are hewn, lest they should be forgetting their orthodoxy, and forgetting their Bibles.

This does not supersede the question of the best constitution for the appointment of ministers to parishes, while it may help, I do think, to remove an obscuration which rests upon it. The truth is, that a prevalent error, on all the sides of the controversy respecting the better and the worse systems of patronage, is, that we are perpetually imagining a corrupt exercise of the power in the party with whom our antagonists are for vesting it; while we overlook the equal possibility of a corrupt exercise in the party with whom we are for vesting it ourselves. The enemies of the present system have constantly present to their minds the idea of a reckless and unprincipled patron, a case which has been too often verified. When in mitigation of the evil, it is alleged that the church have the power—the unlimited power, as I think—of rejecting the presentee, this is met by the conception of a Presbytery or a General Assembly, actuated by a haughty contempt for the popular taste, even when that taste is in unison with all that is most characteristic and peculiar in the Gospel of Jesus Christ: and this certainly is a case which may also be verified. Well, then, to make good our escape from these polluted quarters, let us suppose this power, both in the patron and in the church, to be done away, and an authority paramount to either vested in the suffrages of the people,—is it now, I would ask from every man of Christian integrity, or even of common observation,—is it now that we shall have found a secure asylum for the cause of truth and piety, in a region of ethereal purity of incorrupt and heaven-born principle? I speak not of popular ignorance; but I speak of the wrong and the wayward influences which might, so easily, be brought to bear on the popular will. I speak of their extreme facility to the solicitations of interested applicants, or urgent and interested advisers; and of the wild-fire rapidity wherewith a petition borne from house to house, and prosecuted with address and activity through a parish, might obtain a majority of signatures. It is very true there might be, and often is, a graceless patron, and it is just as true that there might be a graceless presbytery; but I would ask the advocates of universal suffrage, if there be no chance or possibility whatever, when their panacea comes to be applied, that the appointment of a minister may fall into the hands of a graceles population? But, apart from their want of grace, and with a much higher respect for the popular understanding than I believe is generally entertained, I do apprehend them exceedingly liable to be precipitated or betrayed into an unfortunate appointment through downright gullibility—insomuch that the so-called popular election might just resolve itself into the oligarchy of a few, or perhaps into the sovereign and directing will of but one individual. A people occupied with labor; not in circumstances for a leisurely, and comprehensive, and complete view of all parts of a subject; withal open to sudden impulses, and to be overborne by the influence of candidates, and the friends of candidates, are exceedingly apt to make a wrong outset, and irrecoverably commit themselves to an unfortunate choice. I should not anticipate a good series of appointments by laying the first step in the choice of ministers upon the congregation—the way, I do think, to begin with anarchy, and to end in virtual patronage. I think there is good reason why, in every instance, there should, whether express or implied, be a gregarious consent; but in no instance, I apprehend, is it good that the initial movement should be a gregarious one.

The question then is, On whom should the burden of this initial movement be laid? or, in other words, Who is to originate the specific proposition of a minister for filling up the vacancy? Had we to begin *de novo*, there might have been room for the agitation of various plans and various expedients. But I must confess that, whenever it can be done consistently with substantial justice to the people, or the substantial good of the Church, my inclination is to the existing state of things, or to avail ourselves as much as possible of the existing machinery. And certain it is, that, between the two kinds of patronage—the ostensible patronage of the present system, and that disguised patronage which operates with a force as resistless, though unseen, under the forms of a popular election—I would never once think of comparing the likelihood of a good result, in as far as that shall depend on the sense which each possessor of the power has of his own responsibility, before the eyes of a vigilant and interested public, who are anxiously looking on. A presentation by any existing patron is a distinct and noticeable act, clearly referable to the quarter whence it has come, and laying upon him who has issued it the whole burden of the disgrace or dissatisfaction which ensues, on the event of an appointment, either obnoxious at the time, or which shall turn out ill afterwards. The patron, again, who lurks unseen amid the recesses of a parochial community, and who, through the countless ramifications of his influence there, is really and in effect the master of the nomination, is shielded from the reproach of a worthless appointment, under the semblance of that free constituency by whose voice it has been declared; which constituency, in fact, take the reproach upon themselves, and feel it to be light when thus divided among all, with many countenances to face and many shoulders to bear it. It is thus, I believe, that the weight of the public mind could be brought to bear more wholesomely, and with a greater force of concentration, on the patron as at present constituted, than, under the system of popular election, it could be brought to bear either on the oligarchy or head-man of a parish; and this is not altogether a matter of reasoning; for, in so far, it has become of late, and that most palpably, a matter of experience. Patrons never acted more under the control of opinion than they do at this moment; and it is to be hoped that, along with this, there may be also the operation of a higher principle. But the question now respects the admission of the people to a larger influence than before; and it is an important aspect of the question, that, even anterior to any constitutional changes, this influence, we venture to say, has been prodigiously increased; for never, for a century back, has the known disposition of the parish told more powerfully than at the present moment on the determination of the patron. The public will has of late arisen to the might and the mastery of a giant force amongst us; and it were well if a wisdom, powerful to direct, should appear to guide that uplifted hand which is so powerful to destoy. The misfortune, and often the fatal mischief, is, that, in the waywardness of these new-found energies, the favorite exercise is to demolish, rather than to animate or control—not to try, in the first instance, what is best to be done with our institutions as they are, with the things standing in their places, but to begin with the work of remodelling society by an instant and universal displacement. In this disposition to attack the machinery itself, rather than attempt to regulate and rectify its movements, we arenot to wonder if the cry should be to abolish patronage, rather than impress a wholesome direction on it. This has manifested itself in other and greater questions than that of patronage, as by those who, instead of seeking but the amelioration of our establishment, are now meditating their deadly aim at its existence—thereby exemplifying the general tendency, on every sudden enlargement to the force and freedom of the popular will, the tendency to lay hands on all the ready-made instruments of usefulness, not for the purpose of wielding them to a greater public good or service than before, but for the purpose, with the wanton destructiveness of children loosened from restraint, of breaking them in pieces. Better a public astir and awake to every great interest, than in a dead calm or state of lethargy, did it but amount to such an impulse on the vessel as might bear it safely and prosperously onward. I should rejoice in the breeze; but I stand in dread of the hurricane.

Let me here remark, that though the First Book of Discipline vests the initiative in the people, this never seems to have been regularly acted on, or at least for a very brief period in the history of the Scottish Church. The truth is, that it had only the vacancies of eighteen years in which it could be exemplified; for by this time the First Book of Discipline, which never was ratified by Parliament, was matured into the Second Book of Discipline, when, in 1578, the initiative was differently ordered. Never, I believe, in modern Christendom, did a church effectuate a greater transformation on the character and state of any people, than did the Church of Scotland, in two distinct periods, which might well be termed the two golden ages of our Church, on the people of Scotland; and that, on each occasion, in the space of about half a generation—I mean from 1638 and 1690, during which periods, it is to be observed, although the power of consenting or objecting lay with the people, the initiative was vested in another and a distinct quarter, first in the session, and secondly, in the session and heritors. Could it be clearly made out, or did I confidently anticipate, that any Christian good would be effected by the transference of this initiative from its present into other hands, I should the more readily give into it; but having no such anticipation, I should prefer the improvement that was brought about in such a way as to yield the greatest amount of vital and substantial benefit, with the least amount of disturbance from external or constitutional changes. I am aware of the theoretical partiality which many of my friends have for the whole system of our ministerial appointments being out and out ecclesiastical, which it would be if, as by the act of Assembly 1649, the nomination were vested in the session, and the power of objecting in the people, and the final judgment, where these two parties were at variance, in the Presbytery. Even the act of Parliament, 1690, by which the nomination is vested, not in the elders alone, but in the elders and heritors, might be accommodated to this theory by the single qualification of heritors being communicants. Whether the same qualification applied to our existing patrons, that they should be in communion with the church, and so within our own ecclesiastical pale, and under our own ecclesiastical control,—whether this would reconcile them more to the present system of patronage, I do not know. But however much we may differ respecting the initiative, I not only feel inclined to go as far, but would even go farther than the advocates, either for the act of Parliament 1690, or for the act of Assembly 1649, respecting the safeguard or the check. The great complaint of our more ancient Assemblies, the great burden of Scottish indignation, the practical grievance which, of all others, has hitherto been felt most intolerable and galling to the hearts of a free and religious people, is the violent intrusion of ministers upon parishes. An effectual provision against this enormity, this unfeeling outrage, which in the exercise of a reckless and unprincipled patronage has so often been perpetrated in our beloved land, an outrage, by the appointment of an ungodly pastor, on the rights of conscience and the religious sensibilities of a sorely aggrieved people,—a provision against so deep and so wide a moral injury as this to the families of a parish, I should feel the most valuable of all the legislative expedients or devices which could be proposed on the present occasion, and would welcome it all the more cordially if we had not to go in quest of it without the limits of our actual occlesiastical constitution; or, in other words, if, instead of enacting a new law, we had but to declare our interpretation of an old one. Now the law of calls places such a facility in our hands; and as I feel I must not take up the time of the Assembly, let me state at once, and without farther preamble, my own preference as to the best way of restoring significancy and effect to this now antiquated, but still venerable form,—and this is by holding the call a solid one which lies, not in the expressed consent of the few, and these often the mere driblet of a parish : but larger than this, which lies in the virtual or implied consent of the majority, and to be gathered from their non-resistance or their silence. In other words, I would have it that the majority of dissentient voices should lay a veto on every presentation.

In this power of a negative on the part of the people there is nothing new in the constitution or practice of the Church of Scotland. It is the great barrier, in fact, set up by the wisdom of our forefathers against the intrusion of ministers into parishes. It could make no appearance in the First Book of Discipline, 1560, where it was provided that the people should have the initiative, or that the ministers should be appointed, not with their consent, but by their election. But after the probation of eighteen years, we have the Second Book of Discipline 1578, where the election is made to proceed by the judgment of the eldership and with the consent of the congregation, and care is expressed that "no person be intrusit contrar to the will of the congregation, or without the voice of the eldership." This interdict by the people is farther recognized and ratified in the act of Assembly 1649, and of Parliament 1690. It is, in fact, the appropriate, the counterpart remedy against the evil of intrusion. If we hear little of the application or actual exercise of this remedy during the times it was in force, it was because of a great excellence, even that pacific property which belongs to it of acting by a preventive operation. The initial step was so taken by the one party as to anticipate the gainsayers in the other. The goodness of the first appointment was, in the vast majority of instances, so unquestionable as to pass unquestioned ; and so this provision, by its reflex influence, did then what it would do still,—it put an end to the trade of agitation. Those village demagogues, the spokesmen and oracles of a parish, whose voice is fain for war, that in the heat and hubbub of a parochial effervescence, they might stir up the element they love to breathe in, disappointed of their favorite game by a nomination which compelled the general homage, had to sheathe their swords for lack of argument. It was like the beautiful operation of those balancing and antagonist forces in nature which act by pressure and not by collision, and, by means of an energy that is mighty, but noiseless, maintain the quiescence and stability of our physical system. And it is well when the action and reaction of these moral forces can be brought to bear with the same conservative effect on each other in the world of mind, whether it be in the great world of the state or in the little world of a parish. And the truth, the historical truth, in spite of all the disturbance and distemper which are associated with the movements of the populace, is, that turbulence and disorder were then only let loose upon the land, when this check of the popular will was removed from the place it had in our ecclesiastical constitution, and where it was inserted so skilfully by the wisdom of our fathers; that, instead of acting by conflict, or as a conflicting element, it served as an equipoise. It was when a high-handed patronage reigned uncontrolled and without a rival, that discord and dissent multiplied in our parishes. The seasons immediately succeeding to 1649, and 1690, when the power of negation was lodged with the people, not, however, as a force in exercise, but as a force in reserve,—these were the days of our church's greatest prosperity and glory, the seasons both of peace and of righteousness. Persecution put an end to the one period, and unrestricted patronage put an end to the other.

But the last element in the composition of this affair, and to which I have scarcely yet adverted, is the power of the church. For let the ancient privilege of a negation be again given to the people, and there will come to be a tripartite operation ere a minister shall be fully admitted into a parish—not a business, however, unmanageably complex on that account, else whence the rapid, and smooth, and practicable working of the British legislature? And here the question at once occurs, whether shall the objection taken to the presentee by the majority of the people be submitted for review to the Presbytery, as by the acts of 1649 and 1690, or shall it be held conclusive so as without judgment by us to set aside the presentation? My preference is for the latter, and I think that I can allege this valid reason for it. The people may not be able to state their objection save in a very general way, and far less be able to plead and to vindicate it at the bar of a Presbytery, and yet the objection be a most substantial one notwithstanding, and such as ought, both in all Christian reason and Christian expediency, to set aside the presentation. I will not speak of the moral barrier that is created to the usefulness of a minister by the mere general dislike of a people—for this, though strong at the outset, may, literally a prejudice or a groundless judgment beforehand, give way to the experience of his worth and the kindness of his intercourse amongst them. But there is another dislike than to the person of a minister,—a dislike to his preaching, which may not be groundless, even though the people be wholly incapable of themselves arguing or justifying the grounds of it—just as one may have a perfectly good understanding of words, and yet, when put to his definitions, not be at all able to explain the meaning of them. This holds pre-eminently of the Gospel of Jesus Christ, manifesting its own truth to the consciences of men, who yet would be utterly nonplussed and at fault, did you ask them to give an account or reason for their convictions. Such is the adaptation of Scripture to the state of humanity—an adaptation which thousands might feel, though not one in the whole multitude should be able to analyze it. When under the visitations of moral earnestness, when once brought to entertain the question of his interest with God, and conscience tells of his yet uncancelled guilt, and his yet unprovided eternity—even the most illiterate of a parish might, when thus awakened, not only feel most strongly, but perceive most intelligently and soundly, the adjustment which obtains between the overtures of the New Testament and the necessities of his own nature. And yet, with a conviction thus based on the doctrines of Scripture and the depositions of his own consciousness, he, while fully competent to discern the truth, may be as incompetent as a child to dispute or to argument it, and when required to give the reasons of his objection to a minister at the bar of his Presbytery, all the poor man can say for himself might be, that he does not preach the Gospel, or that in his sermon there is no food for his soul. It were denying the adaptation of Christianity to human nature, to deny that this is a case which may be often and legitimately realized. With a perfect independence on the conceits and the follies, and the wayward extravagance or humors of the populace, I have, nevertheless, the profoundest respect for all those manifestations of the popular feeling which are founded on an accordancy between the felt state of human nature and the subject matter of the Gospel; and more especially, when their demand is for those truths which are of chief prominency in the Bible, and let us add, in the Confessions and Catechisms of our Church—and their complaint, their sense of destitution, is from the want of a like prominency in sermons. But in very proportion to my sympathy and my depth of veneration for the Christian appetency of such cottage patriots, would be the painfulness I should feel when the cross-questionings of a court of review were brought to bear upon them; and the men, bamboozled and bereft of utterance by the reasonings which they could not redargue, or, perhaps, the ridicule which they could not withstand, were left to the untold agony of their own hearts—because within the Establishment which they loved, they could not find, in its Sabbath ministrations or week-day services, the doctrine which was dear to them. To overbear such men is the highway to put an extinguisher on the Christianity of our land,—the Christianity of our ploughmen, our artisans, our men of handicraft and of hard labor; yet not the Christianity theirs of deceitful imagination, or of implicit deference to authority, but the Christianity of deep, I will add, of rational belief, firmly and profoundly seated in the principles of our moral nature, and nobly accredited by the virtues of our well-conditioned peasantry. In the olden time of Presbytery—that time of scriptural Christianity in our pulpits, and of psalmody in all our cottages—these men grew and multiplied in the land; and though derided in the heartless literature, and discountenanced or disowned in the heartless politics of other days, it is their remnant which acts as a preserving salt among our people, and which constitutes the real strength and glory of the Scottish nation.

I beg to apologize for having occupied so much of the time of the Assembly, and would only now say, in conclusion, that, while on the whole I am inclined to prefer to any other change or abolition I have heard of, the continuance of the existing patronage, with a veto by the majority of the people, I would desire to be understood, that in all I have expressed, I have done it with the feeling of much diffidence; and if there be a firm certainty in my mind at all, on any single point connected with this argument, it is only of one thing,—that no good result will come, even from the likeliest of our mere outward and constitutional arrangements, apart from the personal Christianity, be they patrons, or ministers, or people, of those among whose hands the working of this new-formed mechanism is to be shared. The frame-work of our Church may be better moulded, and its parts put into goodlier adjustment than before; but, like the dry bones in the vision of Ezekiel, even when reassembled into the perfect skeleton, and invested, by a covering of flesh and skin, with the perfect semblance and beauty of a man—so our Church, even when moulded into legal and external perfection by human hands, may have all the inertness of a statue, and with the monumental coldness of death upon it, till the Spirit of God shall blow into it that it may live. I confess that, on the one hand, I sit more loose to the constitutional question, when I think that, from the hands of Christianized patrons, heaven can make the rich blessing of an efficient ministry to descend upon us; and that, on the other, I cannot partake in the vaulting confidence of many of my brethren, when I think that, in the hands of an unchristian people, a church may wither into spiritual destitution, bereft of all her graces and all her godliness. We occupy a singular position between the nobles and the population of the land; and I will not say but that the Christian independence of the Church is in just as great danger from the one quarter as from the other. I have the satisfaction of thinking that, even in the days of most arbitrary and unrestricted patronage, I ever contended for the Church's independence; and that, however unquestionable the right of the legal patron who signed the presentation, it was our unscathed prerogative to sit in judgment on the qualifications of the presentee—not in the limited sense either of moral or literary qualifications, but on all qualifications, in the most general meaning that could be affixed to the category, on the *qualis* in counterpart to the *talis*, on the *qualis minister* for the *talis populus*, or if such was the minister who ought to be appointed to such a parish, for the Christian good of its families. The due administration of such a power might have disarmed almost any system of patronage of its mischiefs; and, on the other hand, there is no system, whether of patronage or of popular election, that will ever work prosperously without the pure and the righteous exercise of it. And, therefore, whatever changes the system of our patronage is to undergo, I trust the Church will never let down the function which belongs to her; and as on questions of principle she has often withstood the presentations that were signed by the patron, so, on the same questions, that she will continue to withstand presentations, however signed by the patron, and however countersigned by the people—great in her virtuous opposition to the princes and the potentates of the earth; and greater still, if ever called to such a combat—greater still in her virtuous independence, whether of the frowns or the hosannas of the multitude.—I conclude with proposing the following motion: —"That the General Assembly having maturely weighed and considered the various overtures now before them, do find and declare, that it is, and has been ever since the Reformation, a fixed principle in the law of this Church, that no minister shall be intruded into any pastoral charge, contrary to the will of the congregation; and considering that doubts and misapprehensions have existed on this important subject, whereby the just and salutary operation of the said principle has been impeded, and in many cases defeated, The General Assembly further declare it to be their opinion, that the dissent of a majority of the male heads of families resident within the parish, being members of the congregation, and in communion with the Church, at least two years previous to the day of moderation, whether such dissent shall be expressed with or without the assignment of reasons, ought to be of conclusive effect in setting aside the presentee (under the patron's nomination), save and except where it is clearly established, by the patron, presentee, or any of the minority, that the said dissent is founded in corrupt and malicious combination, or not truly founded on any objection personal to the presentee in regard to his ministerial gifts or qualifications, either in general, or with reference to that particular parish; and in order that this declaration may be carried into full effect, that a committee shall be appointed to prepare the best measure for carrying it into effect accordingly, and to report to the next General Assembly"

A

FEW THOUGHTS

ON THE

ABOLITION OF COLONIAL SLAVERY.*

It must be still fresh in the remembrance of many, that the efforts of the British public, for the abolition of the Slave Trade, created the liveliest alarm in the minds of those who were connected, either by trade or by property, with the West Indies. And now that the measure has been carried into effect, and the trial has been made for years, of finding the requisite labor without the importation of negroes from abroad, it is palpable to all, that the forebodings which were then awakened have not been realized. That the West Indian interest has had to sustain reverses and difficulties under the new system of things, is undoubted, but these were not at all connected with the abolition of the Slave Trade. It is even the opinion of many proprietors, that an impulse of prosperity was given to our whole collonial system in the west, by a measure which was regarded beforehand with all the terror of an approaching death-blow; and that it in fact warded off the very extermination of which it was proclaimed to be the harbinger. At all events, the dread imagination has turned out to be a bugbear. Both Liverpool and Glasgow have survived an event which, in the belief of many, was to annihilate them; and both are alike the living evidences of a native and inherent vigor in commerce, that places it far above the need of such wretched auxiliaries as either fraud or violence to sustain it.

* The following paper was prepared upwards of fourteen years ago, as a preface to one of Mr. Clarkson's pamphlets, which was to have been put in circulation around the neighborhood of Glasgow, by the Abolition Society that is instituted there. But the process which I have ventured to recommend, does not altogether meet the views of many Abolitionists; and neither have I found that it meets, at every point, the views of the West India planters. Nevertheless, there is at least a theoretical beauty in the process, which might, perhaps, gain for it some degree of attention; and as to the experimental soundness of it, we have the testimony of Humboldt, who, in the course of his travels through the Spanish part of South America, saw whole villages of emancipated negroes, who had achieved their liberation in the way that is here delineated.
It should be understood, that our numerical details are given only for the purpose of illustration.

Another abolition is now in contemplation,—an abolition not of the Slave Trade, but of slavery itself; and the perfect safety of the first, seems to have had no effect in softening the dread or the disquietude that is felt because of the second. There is a recent pamphlet by Mr. Clarkson, that is well fitted to meet, and perhaps, to remove the apprehensions of the West India proprietors. It is entitled, "Thoughts on the Necessity of Improving the condition of the Slaves in the British Colonies, with a view to their ultimate Emancipation; and on the practicability, the safety, and the advantage of the latter measure." He first addresses himself to the question of right, and occupies sixteen pages with what might be called the juridical part of his argument; which, perhaps, is neither so useful nor so convincing as are the statements that follow, and throughout which he addresses himself to the interest of the slave-owners. By these statements he seems clearly to prove the success wherewith large and even sudden emancipations have been already accomplished, besides the happy result of certain partial experiments which have been made within the limits of the British colonies. The comparison, in point of cheapness, between free and forced labor, is particularly important; and, on the whole, it is fondly hoped, that the perusal of this little work, by the most eminent laborer in the cause, will serve both to enlighten its friends, and to disarm the antipathy of its adversaries. It is worthy of especial notice, that he who is best fitted to expound the views of the abolitionists, nowhere supposes that the emancipation is to be immediate, or that the work is to be done with a rash and rapid hand, but that in every step of the preparation for this great event, regard should be had to the interest of the proprietor, as well as to the comfort and principles of the slaves.

It is much to be regretted, that the abolitionists and the planters have hitherto stood at such an impracticable distance from each other; and more especially that a whole class of men, comprising in it many humane and accomplished individuals, should have had such an indiscriminate stigma affixed to them, by the more intemperate advocates of a good cause. There is a sacredness in property, which a British Legislature, in that calm and equitable spirit by which it is so honorably characterized, will ever hold in reverence; and everything ought to be done consistently with the great object of a full and final emancipation, to tranquillize the natural fears of the slave-holders, and, it may be added, to meet and to satisfy their natural appetite for justice. On the part of the abolitionists, there is a frequent appeal to the abstract and original principles of the question. But, on the part of the proprietors, it may be asked, who ought to be at the expense of reforming the mischief that has arisen from the violation of these principles?—whether the traders who have hitherto acted under the sanction and the shelter of existing laws, or the Government that framed these laws?—whether the party that have been lured into a commerce which they found to be tolerated and protected by the state, or the party that, by this very toleration, may be said to have given their promise and their authority in its favor?—whether the children who have been misled, or the parent who has misled them?—whether, in a word, the men who have been singled out for the execration of the public, or that same public, under whose observation, and by whose connivance, the property that they would now seize upon has been legalized, and its present possessors have made their sacrifices of time, and labor, and money, to obtain it. It were a noble achievement, this conversion of slaves into freemen; and therefore the more important for its ultimate success, that, in every step of its prosecution, there should be an even-handed justice to all the parties concerned. More especially, would it serve to accredit the philanthropy that is now so widely and so warmly embarked upon this undertaking, did they who advocate its designs also bear their part in the expenses of them; and it would do much to allay the fermentation that now is among the West India planters, could they have any satisfying demonstration from Parliament, that, however intent on the emancipation of their slaves, it should be so devised and carried into effect as not to infringe on the present worth of their patrimony.

The following suggestion is the more valuable that it hath come from a gentleman, who is himself a very extensive West India proprietor; and that while it holds out a complete remuneration to the owners of slaves, promises the conveyance of them into a state of freedom with a speed and a safety that ought to satisfy the most sanguine abolitionist.

The scheme may be expressed generally thus:—Let Government purchase from the West India proprietors, at a fair valuation, one day's labor in the week of all the slaves in their possession. This can be done by paying one-sixth of their whole price; after which, each slave hath at least one day in every week, in which he is a free laborer, and might earn for himself. He of course becomes the absolute owner of what he thus earns; and let it be competent for him, when it has accumulated to a sufficient sum, therewith to purchase, at a certain regulated price, another free day in the week. Having thus two days to himself, he is able to accelerate his future purchases of freedom; and thus, as the fruit of his own industry and care, might he, in a very few years, work out his complete emancipation.

Or the scheme may be made still more intelligible, when illustrated by numbers. Let the whole slave population of the British colonies be 800,000. At £50 each, which is a high estimate when thus made to include all ages, the sixth part of their whole value to the owners is short of seven millions. By funding this sum to the credit of the proprietors, one day's free labor to each slave might become the universal law of the British West Indies. The registry of slaves gives every facility for assigning the shares of this stock to the respective proprietors, whether they be principals or mortgagees upon the estates. And when once this arrangement is made, a patent and a practicable way is opened for the full deliverance of the negroes from a state of slavery. Whole gangs are not unfrequently hired out at 3s. 4d. currency a-head per day, and their maintenance: and there can be no doubt, from the difference between free and forced labor, that an ordinary working slave could earn for himself, on the day that is his own, at least 3s. 4d. sterling.* This sum weekly is more than £8 a year, or about a sixteenth part, perhaps, of his whole value; and for which last sum, therefore, he could, in less than three years purchase another free day each week. With the earnings of two free days, he could, in another three years, purchase two more, and then, in a year and a half, could work out the freedom of his whole week, or his entire emancipation. At all events, in seven or eight years, each individual, if in health and full strength, could work out his own deliverance from slavery; after which he might proceed to do the same for others of his family, if he has one. The freedom of a woman, when once accomplished in this way, would, by the existing law, secure the freedom of all the children that are afterwards born by her; and this would be of prime importance in extending the work of emancipation. The process is easily apprehended; and seems to meet all the formidable difficulties, and to combine all the most desirable advantages both to the slave and to his proprietor.

For, first, in reference to the slave, his emancipation cannot take effect till after he has been fully prepared for it, by the habits acquired during a long course of industry. These habits form the best guarantee of his fitness for the new state of freedom on which he is to enter. And there is nothing sudden or desultory in this transition. He at first is made to taste of liberty by having one day of it in the week; and this liberty can only be enlarged by the good use that he makes of that which he has gotten. He at length reaches the condition of entire freedom, by a process, the very description of which is, in itself, the best proof of his being a right subject for freedom, as well as the best preparation for it. No artificial education that can possibly be devised, would answer so well as this wholesome stimulus to exertion and good management.

But, secondly, the slave who idled his free time, whether in sleep or in amusement, would of course make no further progress towards a state of freedom. He would live and die a slave because he chose to do so. They from whose liberty most danger is apprehended, because of their idle or disorderly habits, would,

* It must be remarked, however, that free negroes are hired at rates which are exceedingly various in the different colonies.

by the very tenure on which it was held out to them, be debarred forever from the possession of it. And yet there can be little doubt, that slavery would rapidly decay and ultimately disappear under such an economy. There would be a piece-meal emancipation going forward—a gradual substitution of free for forced labor—an increase of regular and family habits—the growth of a better constituted population—an experience, on the part of planters, of the superior advantage of free labor, that would at length incline them to forward the cause of emancipation, and establish such a common interest between the two extreme classes in the colonies, as might ward off that threatened explosion which has so long hung over them.

And, thirdly, were such a process established, there would be an effectual protection to the colonies from the disquiet and the disturbance of any other proposals for emancipation. For were this object once set a-going in this one way, no other way could or ought to be entertained for a moment. The slaves must, under the system that is now recommended, be made conclusively to understand, that it is by their own persevering labor and frugality, and by this alone, that they are to make sure and speedy progress towards the consummation to which they are so fondly looking forward. Otherwise, the method is paralyzed. The industrious slave, who might otherwise embark with ardor upon this attempt, and persevere in it with unwearied constancy, and be cheered onwards by the brightening of his hopes, as he advanced nearer, every week, to the fulfilment of them,—he would be quite distracted and disheartened did he know of other methods in agitation, by which the idlest of the gang might come to emancipation as well as he, and all his labors have been rendered useless. It were a sore provocation to him, that he had wrought so fatigueingly, and paid so faithfully for a deliverance, which at length others had come at without any such expense, either of money or of enjoyment. So that if this particular method shall be adopted, it seems quite indispensable that all other methods, but those of purchase, shall be finally closed. And it does seem no small recommendation of the plan in question, that while compensation is thereby rendered to the planter for each of his slaves who is liberated, it is done by a process which at once trains them for a state of freedom, and confines them to the only safe and slow way by which they become prepared for the full enjoyment of it.

And again, in reference to the planters, it is thought by many, of such a proposal, that it is peculiarly accommodated to their interest. For, not to speak of the instantaneous satisfaction and calm which it is fitted to impart to the now restless and ruffled mind of the slave population—not to speak of its efficacy to rivet the most energetic and intelligent amongst them to a pacific career of diligence and good conduct, instead of unsettling and throwing them into dangerous excitement—not to speak of the union of interest and policy that is thus established between the master and the more influential part of his laborers, who will now feel their interest to be at one with the peace and good order of the colony, and to be separate from that of those who seek, by violence and insurrection, the object which they are pursuing by a steady course of industry and accumulation,—over and above these advantages, it is thought that, in this method, there is a peculiar adaptation to the present exigencies of the trade. For, by it the planter can disengage immediately one sixth of his capital in slaves, and have the full command of it. Should he choose to limit his West India business, he might transfer this capital to other uses. Should he choose to keep it up to its present amount, or even to extend it, he can have the free labor that will be thrown by this measure upon the market. As the process advances, and the slaves begin to purchase additional days of freedom for themselves, there will be the successive withdrawment of more capital—thereby enabling him to come gradually out of the business altogether, or to perpetuate, and even enlarge it, according to circumstances. In this way, the market for colonial produce may be lightened; or if there be encouragement, it may be more abundantly supplied. A very likely diversion for a great part of this free labor, would be to ordinary agriculture, for raising the means of subsistence: and this, of itself, might prove a wholesome diversion, to relieve and disembarrass an overdone trade. It is seldom that a merchant can extricate himself from the difficulties of such a trade, by withdrawing from it part of his capital, and obtaining an equivalent for the part thus withdrawn. There is generally a sinking, a surrender, a positive annihilation, and loss of capital, on these occasions. It is hoped that the public who are intent on the abolition of slavery, will not, through Parliament, which is the great constitutional organ for the utterance of their voice,—it is hoped that they will not refuse this advantage to the West India proprietors. And, on the other hand, it were equally desirable, that the other party, the proprietors, should cease their opposition to a measure thus accompanied with what appears, on every view that is taken of it, to be a very fair and beneficial compensation.

But lastly, in reference to the abolitionists, what a field would be opened, by this measure, for the enterprises of their philanthropy! What a coincidence would be brought about between the interests of the planters, and their own benevolent designs for the amelioration of the negroes! With what a mighty argument might they go forth among these neglected outcasts, when urging them to peace and contentment, and the calm prosecution of their ulterior objects, the fulfilment of which will at once enrich their masters, and emancipate themselves! Upon such a footing, the Missionaries of the good cause might be admitted, without suspicion, and with perfect safety, among all the plantations; and there is not one of them who could possibly inflict such an outrage on all right and humane policy, as to encourage the expectations of freedom in any other way than the one which the Legislature had provided, and for which it had granted so liberal and advantageous an outset. Every lesson which they urged, would be on the side of thrift, and sobriety, and regular labor; and, enforced, as they could not fail to be, by the rational hope of a great earthly reward, there would be a delightful harmony between these and the higher lessons of Christianity. We should soon see the charm of a Moravian transformation on the habits of many; and it may be confidently predicted, of those who labored most sedulously on their own day for the sum that was to purchase an immunity to themselves, that they would be the most faithful, through the remaining days, in the service of their proprietors. European friends would not be wanting, to aid and to foster their generous aspirings after liberty; and never was a safer and a quieter path opened for the attainment of this great blessing, than the one that is here recommended—not by a series of exasperations, and struggles, and horrid barbarities, but by those slow and pacific exertions which should bring them onward to liberty in successive footsteps, and thoroughly prepare them for the use and enjoyment of it, by the time that they had been conducted to its verge. It were indeed a mild, yet noble triumph of legislation, if such an experiment, on such a theatre, could, without the infringement either of peace or of justice, be guided onward to its successful termination—if it so re-united all interests, as to cement and to satisfy all parties; and it was at length found, that the security of the higher classes was best consulted by the gradual extension of light and liberty, and the benefit of equal laws, to the very lowest in the scale of society.

There are subordinate details which cannot be entered upon, and which yet, if unexplained, might leave a doubt or difficulty in the mind. It is thought, however, that, in practice, there is no insuperable, even no formidable barrier against the accomplishment of this scheme. The interest of mortgagees could be as effectually guarded as it is now, under the proposed arrangement. And as to the alleged danger of holiday riot and disturbance among the negroes, on their free day, it is not necessary that it should be on the same day of the week to all, either on a whole island, or even throughout a whole plantation. At the first, there need be no more liberty than one sixth of the negro population at a time, upon any estate; many of whom would most certainly be at hard, though voluntary work, and all of whom would be under the restraint of those laws which enforce decency and good conduct among all classes.

The Essays which follow were contributed in the form of Prefaces to so many of the works of old Christian authors, republished by Mr. Collins of Glasgow. They would not have appeared in the present publication, had it not been, that, besides being recommendatory of the Treatises in question, each is taken up with a distinct theological topic, on which we have attempted to bestow an independent treatment of our own.

We esteem it the happy symptom of a wholesome revival in the taste and spirit of the age, that of late there should have been such an increased demand, for the best of those practical writings on Christianity, which made their apperance in the last half of the 17th and first half of the 18th century. We have heard that MR. COLLINS's Series of "Select Christian Authors," which commenced about fifteen years ago, gave a powerful impulse to this revival. Certain it is, that his enterprise has been successfully followed up by numerous imitations; and it is our delightful confidence, that, both throughout Britain and America, the effect has been, to leaven the public mind anew, with the substantial doctrine, and no less substantial Christian ethics, that flourished at that period—when so many men of profoundest piety, were also men of profoundest acquaintance, both with the lessons of the divine word and with the experimental lessons of human nature.

We cannot look back to that time, which, in spite of all the ridicule that has been awakened by its occasional excesses, was in truth the Augustan age of Christianity in England, without being reminded of the saying that "they were giants in these days"—a character which they have rightfully earned, not more by their prodigious industry than by their colossal powers, on the strength of both which together, they achieved such an amount of active work, along with such a magnitude and number of massive publications. We know not which to admire most—the labor of their incessant ministrations, both in the pulpit and among families; or the labor of their prolific and profound authorship. It is the combination of the two which raises our admiration into wonder; and the feeling is greatly enhanced, when we contemplate the solid worth and quality of the compositions which they have given to the world.

To estimate them intellectually, account should be taken, both of their great discernment into the meaning of Scripture, and their deep insight into the mysteries of the heart. It was the conjunction of these two which so peculiarly qualified them "to give a word in season"—to point out the marvellous correspondence which obtains, between the sayings of the Bible and the countless varieties of life and character in the world; or between the characters graven by the fingers of the Almighty on the tablet of an outward revelation, and the characters graven by the same finger on the inward tablet of our own felt and familiar nature. In the language of the schools, they were skilful to adapt the objective to the subjective; or in the more simple and emphatic language of inspiration, to "manifest the truth of God to the consciences of men."

But it is in estimating them spiritually, that we come best to understand, wherein it was that their great strength lay. What forms the true secret of their effectiveness is the unction, or moral earnestness, by which their writings are so manifestly pervaded. The good things which proceeded from them, came from the good treasure of hearts quickened and renewed by the Holy Spirit. Besides that often they were men of first-rate talent, they generally were men of prayer; and this brought down an inspiring vigor on the exercises of the closet, as well as on the duties of their public and daily walk. It is thus that a devoted personal Christianity appears in almost every paragraph of the volumes which they have left behind them—those weighty products of great power and great piety—having in them a fragrancy and a force which now are seldom exemplified; and in virtue of which, they have not only been instrumental for the conversion of thousands in the days that are past, but still continue to shed a blessing of the highest order on the churches and families of our present generation.

INTRODUCTORY ESSAY

TO

THE IMITATION OF CHRIST;

IN THREE BOOKS.

BY THOMAS A KEMPIS.

We have sometimes heard the strenuous argumentation of the author of the following Treatise in behalf of holiness, excepted against, on the ground that it did not recognize sufficiently the doctrine of justification by faith. There is, in many instances, an over-sensitive alarm on this topic, which makes the writer fearful of recommending virtue, and the private disciple as fearful of embarking on the career of it—a sort of jealousy lest the honors and importance of Christ's righteousness should be invaded, by any importance being given to the personal righteousness of the believer: as if the one could not be maintained as the alone valid plea on which the sinner could lay claim to an inheritance in heaven, and at the same time the other be urged as his indispensable preparation for its exercises and its joys.

It is the partiality with which the mind fastens upon one article of truth, and will scarcely admit the others to so much as a hearing—it is the intentness of its almost exclusive regards on some separate portion of the divine testimony, and its shrinking avoidance of all the distinct and additional portions—it is, in particular, its fondness for the orthodoxy of what relates to a sinner's acceptance, carried to such a degree of favoritism, as to withdraw its attention altogether from what relates to a sinner's sanctification,—it is this which, on the pretence of magnifying a most essential doctrine, has, in fact, diffused a mist over the whole field of revelation; and which, like a mist in nature, not only shrouds the general landscape from all observation, but also bedims, while it adds to the apparent size of the few objects that continue visible. It is the same light which reveals the whole, that will render these last more brightly discernible than before; and whether they be the prominences of spiritual truth, or of visible materialism, they are sure to be seen most distinctly in that element of purity and clearness, through the medium of which the spectator is able to recognize even the smaller features and the fainter lineaments that lie on the ground of contemplation.

It is true, that the same darkening process which buries what is remote in utter concealment, will, at least, sully and somewhat distort the nearer perspective that is before us. But how much more certain is it, that if such be the grossness of the atmosphere as to make impalpable the trees, and the houses, and the hillocks of our immediate vicinity—then will the distant spires, and mountains, and villages, lie buried in still deeper and more hopeless obscurity. And so it is with revealed truth; the light of which is spread over a wide and capacious arena, reaching afar from the character of man upon earth to the counsels of God in heaven. When Christ told Nicodemus what change must take place upon the earthly subject, ere it could be prepared for the glories and felicities of the upper sanctuary, he was resisted in this announcement by the incredulity of his auditor. Upon this he came forth with the remonstrance: "If I have told you earthly things, and ye believe not, how shall ye believe, if I tell you of heavenly things?" And then he proceeds to tell of heavenly things,—of the transactions that had taken place in the celestial judicatory above, and which behooved to take place ere the sinner could obtain a rightful entrance into the territory of the blessed and the unfallen; of the love that God bare to the world; of the mission thereto on which He delegated His only and well-beloved Son; of the design of this embassy, and the way in which it subserved the great object of recovering sinners from their state of condemnation. These are proceedings which may properly be referred to the seat of the divine government, and to the principles which operate and have ascendency there. The doctrine of regeneration is fulfilled or verified upon the human spirit, that is intimately and consciously present with us. The doctrine of the atonement, or the manner in which the reconciliation of the guilty is brought into adjustment with the holiness of God, and with what He requires for maintaining the character and the dignity of His jurisprudence, is fulfilled or verified upon the divine Spirit, whose thoughts and whose ways are inscrutable to man—He not having ascended up into heaven. And the expostulation amounts to this:—If a man believe not in the doctrine of regeneration, how can he believe in the doctrine of the atonement? If he consent not to the one he gives no real credit to the other. He may fancy it, or feign it out to his imagination, but he has no faith in it.

The Bible makes known to us both man's depravity, and God's displeasure against him: and if with the eye of our mind we see not the one truth, which lies immediately at hand, neither with the eye of our mind can we see the other truth, which lies in fathomless obscurity, away from us, among the recesses of that mysterious Spirit, who is eternal and unsearchable. But the Bible also makes known to us, both the renewing process by which man's depravity is done away, and the reconciling process, by which God's displeasure against him is averted. If we believe not the former, neither do we believe the latter. If to our intellectual view, there be a darkness over the terrestrial operation, then is there an equal, or a more aggravated darkness, over that movement which took place in heaven, when the incense of a sweet-smelling savor ascended to the throne, and the wrath of the Lawgiver, who sitteth thereon, was turned away. And what is true of each of these doctrines, regarded abstractly, or in the general, is also true of their personal application. If we *find* not that a renewing process is taking effect upon us, neither ought we to *figure* that we have any part in the reconciling process. It is possible to conceive the latter, even while the old nature still domineers over the whole man, and its desires are indulged without remorse, or, at least, without any effective resistance. But this conception is not the faith of the mind. It is rather what the old writers would call a figment of the mind. The apostle adverts to unfeigned faith. But surely, if a man shall overlook the near, and dwell in thought, on the unseen distance that is beyond it; if, unmindful of any transition in his own breast from sin to sacredness, he nevertheless shall persist in the confidence of a transition from anger to complacency in the mind of the Divinity towards him; if, without looking for a present holiness on earth, he pictures for himself a future beatitude in heaven—he resembles the man who, across that haze of nature's atmosphere, which wraps all things in obscurity, thinks to descry the realities of the ulterior space, when he has only peopled it with gratuitous imagery of his own. The faith of such a one is feigned. He believes not the earthly things which are enunciated in Scripture; and, therefore, though he should take up with the heavenly things that are enunciated there, they are taken up by the wrong faculty. To him they are not the substantial objects of perception, but the allusions of fancy.

The traveller who publishes of distant countries, that we have never seen, may also have included our own familiar neighborhood in his tour, and given a place in his description to its customs, and its people, and its scenery. But if his narrative of the vicinity that is known were full of misrepresentations and errors, we could have no belief in his account of the foreign domains over which he had expatiated. When we believe not what he tells us of our native shire, how can we believe when he tells us of shires or provinces abroad? And by this we may try the soundness of our faith in the divine testimony. It is a testimony which embraces the things of earth and the things of heaven ; which teaches us the nature of man as originally corrupt, and requiring a power from above, that may transform it, as well as on the nature of God, as essentially averse to sin, and requiring an atonement that may reconcile and pacify it. If we believe not what is said of the nature of man, and of the doctrine of regeneration that is connected therewith, then we believe not what is said of the nature of God, and of the doctrine of redemption that is connected therewith. We may choose to overlook the former revelation, and stretch our attention onward to the latter, as that with which our fancy is most regaled, or our fears are most effectually quieted into pleasing oblivion. In this way, we may seize on the topic of imputed righteousness, by an effort of desire, or an effort of imagination; but if the man who does so have an unseeing eye towards the topic of his own personal sanctification, he has just as little of faith towards the former article as towards the latter, whatever preference of liking or fancy he may entertain regarding it. It may play around his mind as one of its most agreeable day-dreams, but it has not laid hold of his conviction. The light that maketh the doctrine which affirms the change of God's mind towards the sinner believingly visible, would also make the doctrine which affirms the change of the sinner's mind towards God believingly visible. If the one be veiled from the eye of faith, the other is at least equally so. It may be imagined by the mind, but it is not perceived. It may be conceived, but it is not credited.

There is a well-known publication, called the Traveller's Guide, which you may take as your companion to some distant land, but the accuracy of which you try upon the earlier stages of your journey. If wholly incorrect in the description which it gives of the first scenes through which you pass, you withdraw all your confidence from its representation of the future scenes; and it may even be so wide of the truth, in respect of the things that are present and visible, as should lead you to infer that you are altogether off the road that conducts to the place after which you are aiming. The Bible is a traveller's guide—and it portrays the characters of humility, and self-denial, and virtuous discipline, and aspiring godliness, which mark the outset of the pilgrimage,—and it also portrays the characters of brightness, and bliss, and glory, which mark its termination. If you do not believe that it delineates truly the path of transition in time, neither do you believe, however much you may desiderate and dwell upon the prospect, that it sketches truly, the place of joyful habitation in eternity. Or, at least, you may well conclude, if you are not now on the path of holiness, that you are not on the path to heaven. And if you believe not the Scripture, when it announces a new spirit as your indispensable preparation here, there may be a dazzling and deceitful imagination, but there is no real belief of what it announces, or of what it promises, about paradise hereafter.

It is thus that we would try the faith of Antinomians. Fancy is not faith. A wilful and determined adherence of the mind to some beatific vision, in which it loves to indulge, is not a believing assent of the mind to what a professed Teacher from heaven has revealed to us of the coming immortality. How can we believe, upon His authority, that we are to enter this region of purity and peace, if we believe not, on the same authority, that the road which leads to it, is a road of mortification, and of new obedience, and of strenuous conflict with the desires and urgencies of nature? If the eye of faith, or of the understanding, be opened on some field of truth that is laid before it, it will not overlook the propinquities of this contemplation, while it only admits the objects which lie on the remoter part of the territory. It is evidence which opens this eye; and that evidence which has failed to open it to what is near, will equally fail to open it to what is distant. But though the eye of the understanding be shut, the eye of the imagination may be open. This requires no evidence, and the man who is without faith in the realities which lie on the other side of death, may nevertheless be all awake in his fancy to those images of bliss with which he has embellished it, and may even possess his own heart with the pleasing anticipation of it as his destined inheritance. It is not upon his fancy, however, but upon his faith, that the fulfilment of this anticipation will turn,—a faith which, had it been real, would have had respect unto the prescribed road, as well as unto the revealed inheritance,—a faith which would have found him in holiness here, as well as in heaven hereafter. That semblance of it which the Antinomian has is a mere vagary, that may amuse or may harden him in the midst of his present worldliness, but which will be dissipated into nought at the judgment-seat, when, for the treacherous phantom which deceived him in time, a tremendous reality will be awarded to him for eternity.

We like not that writer to be violently alleged against, who expounds, and expounds truly, the amount of Christian holiness, because he says not enough, it is thought, of the warrants and securities that are provided in the Gospel for Christian hope. We think, that to shed a luminousness over one portion of the divine testimony, is to reflect, at least, if not immediately to shed, a light on all the other portions of it. The doctrine of our acceptance, by faith in the merits and propitiation of Christ, is worthy of many a treatise, and many are the precious treatises upon it which have been offered to the world. But the doctrine of regeneration, by the Spirit of Christ, equally demands the homage of a separate lucubration—which may proceed on the truth of the former, and, by the incidental recognition of it, when it comes naturally in the way of the authors's attention, marks the soundness and the settlement of his mind thereupon, more decisively than by the dogmatic, and ostentatious, and often misplaced asseverations of an ultra orthodoxy. And the clearer revelation to the eye of faith of one article, will never darken or diminish, but will, in fact, throw back the light of an augmented evidence on every other article. Like any object that is made up of parts, which we have frequently looked to in their connection, and as making up a whole—the more distinctly one part of it is made manifest, the more forcibly will all the other parts of it be suggested to the mind. And thus it is, that when pressing home the necessity of one's own holiness, as his indispensable preparation for heaven, we do not dissever his mind from the atonement of Christ, but in reality do we fasten it more closely than ever on the necessity of another's righteousness, as his indispensable plea for heaven.

Such we apprehend to be the genuine influence of a Treatise that is now submitted anew to the Christian public. It certainly does not abound in formal and direct avowals of the righteousness which is by faith, and on this account we have heard it excepted against. But we know of no reading that is more powerfully calculated to shut us up unto the faith—none more fitted to deepen and to strengthen the basis of a sinner's humility, and so reconcile him to the doctrine of salvation in all its parts, by grace alone—none that, by exhibiting the height and perfection of Christian attainments, can better serve the end of prostrating the inquirer into the veriest depths of self-abasement, when, on the humbling comparison of what he is, with what he ought to be, he is touched and penetrated by a sense of his manifold deficiencies. It is on this account that the author of such a work may, instrumentally speaking, do the office of a schoolmaster to bring us unto Christ: nor do we know at what other time it is, than when eyeing from afar the lofty track of spiritual and seraphic piety which is here delineated, that we more feel our need of the great High Priest, or that His peace-speaking blood and His perfect righteousness are more prized by us.

But it is not enough that we idly gaze on the heavenly course. We must personally enter it; and it is most utterly and experimentally untrue, that, in the prosecution of this walk, we meet with anything to darken the principles on which are made to hinge a sinner's justification in the sight of God. He who looks most frequently to Christ, for the purpose of imitation, will also gather most from him on which to prop his confidence, and that to on the right and evangelical basis. There is a sure link of concatenation in the processes of divine grace, by which a growing spiritual discernment is made to emerge out of a growing conformity to the will and the image of the Saviour. These two elements act, and re-act, the one upon the other. "He that keepeth my commandments to him will I manifest myself." "He whose eye is single shall have his whole body full of light."* "The Holy Ghost," who acts as a revealer, "is given to those who obey Him." "To him who hath, more shall be given." All proving that there is a procedure in the administration of divine

* By singleness of eye here, is meant not a single intentness of the mind upon one truth, but, as is evident from the context, that singleness of aim after an interest in heaven, which is not perverted or seduced from its object by the love of a present evil world.

grace, by which he who giveth himself up unto all righteousness is guided unto all truth.

And, it is to be hoped, that while the doctrine of justification is not argued, but rather enhanced and recommended by the perusal of such a work, its own distinct object will be still more directly subserved, of leading some to a more strict and separate devotedness of life, than is often to be met with in this professing age. The severities of Christian practice, which are here urged upon the reader, are in no way allied with the penances and the self-inflictions of a monastic ritual, but are the essentials of spiritual discipline in all ages, and must be undergone by every man who is transformed by the Holy Ghost from one of the children of this world to one of the children of light. The utter renunciation of self—the surrender of all vanity—the patient endurance of evils and wrongs—the crucifixion of natural and worldly desires—the absorption of all our interests and passions in the enjoyment of God—and the subordination of all we do, and of all we feel, to His glory,—these form the leading virtues of our pilgrimage, and in the very proportion of their rarity, and their painfulness, are they the more effectual tests of our regeneration. And one of the main uses of this book is, that while it enforces these spiritual graces in all their extent, it lays open the spiritual enjoyment that springs from the cultivation of them—revealing the hidden charm which lies in godliness, and demonstrating the sure though secret alliance which obtains between the peace of heaven in the soul, and patience under all the adversities of the path which leads to it. It exposes alike the sufferings and the delights which attach to a life of sacredness: and its wholesome tendency is to reconcile the aspirant after eternal life, to the whole burden of that cross on earth which he must learn to bear with submission and cheerfulness, until he exchanges it in heaven for a crown of glory. Such a work may be of service in these days of soft and silken professorship,—to arouse those who are at ease in Zion; to remind them of the terms of the Christian discipleship, as involving a life of conflict, and watchfulness, and much labor; to make them jealous of themselves, and jealous of that evil nature, the power of which must be resisted, but from the besetting presence of which we shall not be conclusively delivered, until death shall rid us of a frame-work, the moral virus of which may be kept in check while we live, but cannot be eradicated by any process short of dissolution.

INTRODUCTORY ESSAY

TO

TREATISES

ON THE

LIFE, WALK, AND TRIUMPH OF FAITH.

BY

THE REV. W. ROMAINE, A.M.

There is nothing of which some readers of religious books complain more grievously, than that they should be exposed to a constant and wearisome reiteration of the same truths; than that the appetite of the mind for variety should be left to the pain of its own unsated cravings, through the never-failing presentation of some one idea, wherewith, perhaps, it has long ago been palled and nauseated; than that, what they already know should yet again and again be told them—so as to subject their attention to topics that have become tasteless and threadbare, and their minds to a monotony of ideas, that may, at length, be felt to be quite insupportable. This objection has sometimes been urged against Mr. Romaine's excellent Treatises on Faith; and that, precious and important as they acknowledge the truths to be on which he unceasingly delights to expatiate, yet they consider the frequency of their recurrence has a tendency to produce in the mind a feeling, if not of weariness, at least of unnecessary repetition.

Now, Paul himself admitted that to write the same things was not grievous to himself, however grievous it may have been felt by those whom he was in the habit of addressing. And, lest they should have felt his repetitions to be matter of offence or of annoyance, he tries to reconcile them to these repetitions, by affirming, that whether they were agreeable or not, at least they were safe. "To write the same things to you, to me indeed is not grievous, but for you it is safe."

A process of reasoning gives a most agreeable play and exercise to the faculties. Yet how soon would such a process, if often repeated, feel stale to the intellectual taste. Even the pleasure we had at the first, from the important, and perhaps, unexpected result to which it had conducted us, would speedily wear off. It would, of course, instantly cease to be unexpected: and as to its importance, we know that this is a property of such truths as are most familiar and most generally recognized: and these, of all others, are least fitted to stimulate the mere understanding. Like the element of water, they may be the most valuable, yet least prized truths by us: and certain it is, that by the unvarying announcement of them, they would, at length, fall in downright bluntness and insipidity on the ear of the inner man. It is thus that a train of argument, the mere object of which is to gain the conviction of the understanding, does not admit of being repeated indefinitely. After having once carried the conviction, it ceases to be any longer needful—and as to the recreation which is thereby afforded to the intellectual powers, nothing is more certain, than that the enjoyment would speedily decay, should the very same reasoning, and the very same truths be often presented to the notice of the mind, so as at length to flatten into a thing of such utter listlessness, that no one pleasure could be given, and no one power could be awakened by it.

And what is true of a train of argument addressed to the reason, is also true of those images and illustrations which are addressed to the fancy. Whatever delight may have been felt at the original presentation of them, would rapidly subside were they ever and anon to be obtruded on the view. We know of nothing more exquisite than the sensation that is felt when the light of some unexpected analogy, or of some apt and beautiful similitude makes its first entry into the mind. And yet there is a limit to the enjoyment—nor would the attempt to ply the imagination at frequent intervals with one and the same picture be long endured. The welcome which it found from its own intrinsic loveliness, was enhanced by the charm of novelty; but when that charm is dissipated, then is it possible, that, by the mere force of repetition, the taste may decline into languor or even into loathing. Both the reason and the fancy of man must have variety to feed upon; and, wanting this, the constant reiteration of the same principles, and the constant recital of the same poetry, would indeed be grievous.

Yet are there certain appetites of the mind which have no such demand for variety. It is not with the affections, or the moral feelings, as it is with other principles of our nature. The desire of companionship, for example, may find its abundant and full gratification in the society of a very few friends. And often may it happen of an individual, that his presence never tires—that his smile is the sunshine of a perpetual gladness to the heart—that in his looks and accents of kindness, there is a charm that is perennial and unfading—that the utterance of his name is at all times pleasing to the ear; and the thought of his worth or friendship is felt as a cordial, by the hourly and habitual ministration of which the soul is upheld. The man who expatiates on his virtues, or who demonstrates to you the sincerity of his regards, or who refreshes your memory with such instances of his fidelity as indeed you had not forgotten, but which still you love to be retold—it is but one theme or one topic in which he indulges; and often will he retail in your hearing what substantially are the same things, —yet are they not grievous.

And the tale of another's friendly and favorable inclination to you will not merely bear to be often repeated, because in the conscious possession of friendship there is a perpetual enjoyment, but also because there is in it a constant preservative, and a charm against the discomfort to which a mind, when left to other influences, or to itself, might else be liable. When the heart is desolated by affliction, or harassed with care, or aggrieved by injustice and calumny, or even burdened under the weight of a solitude which it feels to be a weariness, who would ever think of apprehending lest the daily visit of your best friend should be grievous, because it was the daily application of the same thing? Would not you, in these circumstances, fondly cling to his person, or, if at a distance, would not your heart as fondly cling to the remembrance of him? Would not you be glad to bear up the downward and the desponding tendencies of the heart, by the thought of that unalterable affection, which survived the wreck of your other earthly hopes, and earthly interests? Would not you feel it a service, if any acquaintance of yours were to conduct him in person to your chamber; and there to bring upon you the very smiles that a thousand times before had gladdened your bosom, and the very accents of tenderness that had often, in days which are past, soothed and tranquillized you? Or, if he cannot make him present to you in person, is not a service still rendered, if he make him present to your thoughts? You have no doubt of the alleged friendship, but nature is forgetful, and, for the time being, it may not be adverting to that truth which, of all others, is most fitted to pacify and to console it. The memory needs to be awakened to it. The belief of it may never have been extinguished; but the conception of it may be absent from the mind, and for the purpose of recalling it, the voice of a remembrancer may be necessary. It is thus that the opportune suggestion of a truth, which has long been known, and often repeated, may still the tumults of an agitated spirit, and cause light to arise out of darkness. And who can object to sameness, and to reiteration, in such a case as this? The same position brought forward again and again, for the mere didactic purpose to convince or to inform, might, however important, soon cease to interest the understanding; and the same image, however beautiful, might, if often presented, soon cease to interest or to affect the fancy—but the affir mation of a friendship that is dear to your heart, may be repeated as often as is necessary to raise and to prolong the sense of it within you—and, although the theme of every day, still, instead of being grievous on that account, may it be felt like the renewed application of balsam to the soul, with as lively a sense of enjoyment as before, and with a delight that is utterly inexhaustible.

The same holds true of a moral principle. The announcement of it needs not to be repeated with a view to inform; but it may be repeated with a view to influence, and that on every occurrence of temptation or necessity. Were it our only business with virtue to learn what it is, it were superfluous to be told oftener than once, that anger degrades and discomposes him who is carried away by it, and ought to be resisted as alike a violation of duty and of dignity. But as our main business with virtue is to practise it, the very same thing of which by one utterance we have been sufficiently informed, might be often uttered, with propriety and effect, in order that we should be reminded of it. And, accordingly in some hour of great and sudden provocation, when another's fraud or another's ingratitude would take full possession of the feelings, and shut out from the mind's regard every element that had influence to still or to arrest the coming storm, were it not well, if some friendly monitor were standing by, and bidding him be calm? There might not, in the whole of the remonstrance, be one consideration employed, which has not often been recognized, nor one principle urged, which has not been admitted, long ago, into his ethical system, and is perfectly familiar to his understanding, as a sound principle of human conduct. Yet it is not superfluous again to urge it upon him. A practical object is gained by this timely suggestion—and it is the highest function of practical wisdom, not to devise what is new, but seasonably to recall what is old. When in the heat and the hurry of some brooding fermentation, there is one intense feeling that has taken exclusive occupation of the soul, it is well that some counteractive influence might be poured in, which shall assuage its violence. And this influence, generally, lies not with new truths which are then for the first time apprehended, but with old truths which are then brought to the remembrance. So that, while for the author to repeat the same things is not grievous, for the reader it may be safe.

The doctrine of Jesus Christ and Him crucified, which forms the principal and pervading theme in the following Treatises, possesses a prominent claim to a place in our habitual recollections. And, for this purpose, ought it to be the topic of frequent reiteration by every Christian author; and it may well form the staple of many a Christian treatise, and be the leading and oft-repeated argument of many a religious conversation. It is this which ushers into the mind of a sinner the sense of God as his Friend and his reconciled Father. That mind, which is so apt to be overborne by this world's engrossments—or to lapse into the dread and distrust of a conscious offender—or to go back again to nature's lethargy, and nature's alienation—or to lose itself in quest of a righteousness of its own, by which it might challenge the reward of a blissful eternity,—stands in need of a daily visitor who, by his presence, might dissipate the gloom, or clear away the perplexity, in which these strong and practical tendencies of the human constitution are so ready to involve it. There is with man an obstinate forgetfulness of God; so that the Being who made him is habitually away from his thoughts. That he may again be brought nigh, there must be an open door of entry by which the mind of man can welcome the idea of God, and willingly entertain it; by which the imagination of Deity might become supportable, and even pleasing to the soul: so that, when present to our remembrance, there should be the felt presence of one who loves and is at peace with us. Now, it is only by the doctrine of the cross that man can thus delight himself in God, and, at the same time, be free from delusion. This is the way of access for man entering into friendship with God, and for the thought of God, as a Friend, entering into the heart of man. And thus it is, that the sound of his Saviour's love carries with it such a fresh and unfailing charm to a believer's ear. It is the precursor to an act of mental fellowship with God, and is hailed as the sound of the approaching footsteps of Him whom you know to be your Friend.

When the mind, abandoned to itself, takes its own spontaneous and undirected way, it is sure to wander from God; and hence, if without effort, and without watchfulness, will it lapse into a state of insensibility in regard to Him. While in the corrupt and earthly frame of our present tabernacle, there is a constant gravitation of the heart towards ungodliness; and, against this tendency, there needs to be applied the counterpoise of such a force as shall either act without intermission, or by frequent and repeated impulses. The belief that God is your Friend in Christ Jesus, is just the restorative, by which the soul is brought back again from the lethargy into which it had fallen; and the great preservative by which it is upheld from sinking anew into the depths of its natural alienation. It is by cherishing this belief, and by a constant recurrence of the mind to that great truth which is the object of it, that a sense of reconciliation, or the felt nearness of God as your Friend, is kept up in the bosom. And if the mind will not, by its own energies, constantly recur to the truth, it is good that the truth should be frequently obtruded on the notice of the mind. "Rejoice in the Lord always, and again I say, rejoice." If there be an aptitude in man, which undoubtedly there is, to let slip the things that belong to his peace, it is good to be ever and anon presenting these things to his view, and bidding him give earnest heed unto them. It is not that his judgment would be thereby informed, nor that his imagination would be thereby regaled, but that his memory would be awakened, and his practical tendency to forget or fall asleep unto these things would be thereby made head against. And thus there are certain things, the constant repetition of which, by Christian writers, ought not to be thought grievous, and at all events is safe.

And there is a perpetual tendency in nature not only to forget God, but also to misconceive Him. There is nothing more firmly interwoven with the moral constitution of man than a legal spirit towards God, with its aspirings, and its jealousies, and its fears. Let the conscience be at all enlightened, and a sense of manifold deficiencies from the rule of perfect obedience is altogether unavoidable; and so there is ever lurking in the recesses of our heart a dread and a misgiving about God—the secret apprehension of Him as our enemy—a certain distrust of Him, or feeling of precariousness; so that we have little comfort and little satisfaction while we entertain the thought of Him. Were that a mere intellectual error by which we hold the favor of God to be a purchase with the righteousness of man, and so failing in the establishment of such a righteousness, we remained without hope in the world; or were that a mere intellectual error by which we continued blind to the offered righteousness of Christ, and so, declining the offer, kept our distance from the only ground on which God and man can walk in amity together; then, like any other error of the understanding, it might be done conclusively away by one statement or one demonstration. But when, instead of a fault in the judgment, which might thus be satisfied by a single announcement, it is a perverse constitutional bias that needs to be at all times plied against, by the operation of a contrary influence—then it might not be on the strength of one deliverance only, but by dint of its strenuous and repeated asseveration, that the sense of God as both a just God and a Saviour is upheld in the soul. This might just be the aliment by which the soul is kept from pining under a sense of its own poverty and nakedness—the bread of life which it receives by faith, and delights at all times to feed upon: and just as hunger does not refuse the same viands by which, a thousand times before, it has been met and satisfied, so may the doctrine of Christ crucified be that spiritual food which is ever welcomed by the hungry and heavy-laden soul, and is ever felt to be precious.

The Bible supposes a tendency in man to let slip its truths from his recollection, and, in opposition to this, it bids him keep them in memory, else he might have believed them in vain. It is not enough that they may, at one time, have been received. They must be at all times remembered. "And therefore," says Peter, "I will not be negligent to put you always in remembrance of these things, though ye know them and be established in the present truth." To know and to be assured is not enough, it would appear. They may at one time have consented to the words which were spoken, but the apostle presented them anew, in order that they might be mindful of the words which were spoken. Those doctrines of religion which speak comfort, or have an attendant moral influence upon the soul, must at first be learned; but not, like many of the doctrines of science, consigned to a place of dormancy among the old and forgotten acquisitions of the understanding. They stand in place of a kind and valuable friend, of whom it is not enough that he has once been introduced to your acquaintance, but with whom you hold it precious to have daily fellowship, and to be in your habitual remembrance. And this is eminently true of that doctrine which is so frequently reiterated in these Treatises, "that Christ died for our sins, according to the Scriptures." It is the portal through which the light of God's reconciled countenance is let in upon the soul. It is the visitor that ushers there the peace and glory of heaven, and, forcing its way through all those cold and heavy obstructions by which the legal spirit has beset the heart of proud yet impotent man—it is the alone truth that can at once hush the fears of guilt, and command a reverence for the offended Sovereign. No wonder, then, that its presence should be so much courted by all who have been touched with the reality and the magnitude of eternal things—by all who have ever made the question of their acceptance with God a matter of earnest and home-felt application; and who, urged on the one hand, by the authority of a law that must be vindicated, and on the other, by the sense of a condemnation that, to the eye of nature, appears inextricable, must give supreme welcome to the message that can assure them of a way by which both God may be glorified and the sinner may be safe. It is the blood of Christ which resolves this mystery, and it is by the daily application of this blood to the conscience that peace is daily upheld there. When the propitiation by Christ is out of the mind, then, on the strength of its old propensities, does it lapse either into the forgetfulness of God, or into a fearful distrust of Him. And therefore it is, that every aspiring Christian prizes every intimation, and every token of remembrance, by which to recall to his mind the thought of a crucified Saviour. And he no more quarrels with a perpetual sense of Him who poured out His soul unto death, than he would with the perpetual sunshine of a brilliant and exhilarating day: and just as a joy and a thankfulness are felt at every time when the sun breaks out from the clouds which lie scattered over the firmament—so is that beam of gladness which enters with the very name of Christ, when it finds its way through that dark and disturbed atmosphere which is ever apt to gather around the soul. The light of beauty is not more constantly pleasant to the eye—the ointment that is poured forth not more constantly agreeable in its odor—the relished and wholesome food not more constantly palatable to the ever-recurring appetite of hunger—the benignant smile of tried and approved friendship not more constantly delicious to the heart of man, than is the sense of a Saviour's sufficiency to him of spiritual and new-born desires, who now hungers and thirsts after righteousness.

This may explain the untried and unexpended delight wherewith the Christian hangs upon a theme which sounds monotonously, and is felt to be wearisome by other men: and this is one test by which he may ascertain his spiritual condition. There is much associated with religion that is fitted to regale even a mind that is unrenewed, if open to the charms of a tasteful, or pathetic, or eloquent representation. And thus it is, that crowds may be drawn around a pulpit by the same lure of attraction which fills a theatre with raptured and applauding multitudes. To uphold the loveliness of the song, might the preacher draw on all the beauties of nature, while he propounds the argument of nature's God: nor need the deep, the solemn interest of tragedy be wanting, with such topics at command as the sinner's restless bed, and the dark imagery of guilt and vengeance wherewith it is surrounded: and again, may the fairest tints of heaven be employed to deck the perspective of a good man's anticipations; or the touching associations of home be pressed into the service of engaging all our sympathies, with the feelings, and the struggles, and the hopes of his pious family. It is thus that the theological page may be richly strewed with the graces of poetry, and even the feast of intellect be spread before us by the able champions of theological truth. Yet all this delight would require novelty to sustain it, and be in full congeniality with minds on which the unction of living water from above had never yet descended. It is altogether diverse from that spiritual taste, by which the simple application of the cross to the sinner's conscience is felt and appreciated—by which the utterance of the Saviour's name is at all times welcomed like the sound of sweetest music—by which a sensation of relief enters, with all the power and freshness of a new feeling, so often as the conception of His atoning blood, and of His perfect righteousness, is made to visit us—by which the reiteration of His sacrifice upon the ear, has a like effect to disperse the habitual distrust or lethargy of nature, that the ever-recurring presence of a friend has to disperse the gloom of a constitutional melancholy. It is no evidence of his vital Christianity, that a man can enjoy a kindred recreation in those embellishments of genius or literature of which the theme is susceptible. But if its simple affirmations be sweet unto him—if the page be never lovelier in his eye than when gemmed with Bible quotations that are both weighty and pertinent—if when pervaded throughout by a reference to Christ, and to Him crucified, it be felt and rejoiced in like the incense of a perpetual savor, and he, withal a son of learning and generous accomplishment, can love, even in its homeliest garb the oft-repeated truth; and that, purely because the balm of Gilead is there,—this we should hold the evidence of one who, so far at least, has been enlightened, and has tasted of the heavenly gift, and has been made a partaker of the Holy Ghost, and has tasted of the good word of God, and the powers of the world to come.

We know of no Treatises where this evangelical infusion so pervades the whole substance of them as those of ROMAINE. Though there is no train of consecutive argument—though there is no great power or variety of illustration—though we cannot allege in their behalf much richness of imagery, or even much depth of Christian experience. And, besides, though we were to take up any of his paragraphs at random, we should find that, with some little variation in the workmanship of each, there was mainly one ground or substratum for them all—yet the precious and consoling truths, which he ever and anon presents, must endear them to those who are anxious to maintain in their minds a rejoicing sense of God as their reconciled Father. He never ceases to make mention of Christ and of His righteousness—and it is by the constant droppings of this elixir that the whole charm and interest of his writings are upheld. With a man whose ambition and delight it was to master the difficulties of an argument; or with a man whose chief enjoyment it was to range at will over the domains of poetry, we can conceive nothing more tasteless or tame than these Treatises that are now offered to the public. Yet, in despite of that literary nakedness which they may exhibit to the eye of the natural man, who possesses no spiritual taste, and no spiritual discernment, let such a man have his eye opened to the hidden glories of that theme, which, of all others, was dear to the bosom of their author, and, whether from the press or from the pulpit, was the one theme on which he ever loved to expatiate—let the sense of guilt but fasten upon his conscience, and the sure but simple remedy of faith in the blood of Christ recommend itself as that power of God which alone is able to dissolve it—let him be made to feel the suitableness that there is between this precious application, and that inward disease of which the malignity and the soreness have now been revealed to him—then, like as it is at all times pleasing, when there is laid over a bodily wound the emollient that relieves it, so is it at all times pleasing, whenever the spiritual malady is felt, to have recourse upon that unction by the sprinkling of which it is washed away. A feeling of joy in the Redeemer will be ever prompting to the same contemplations, and to the utterance of the same things. To a regenerated spirit, that never can be a weariness in time, which is to form the song of eternity.

But it is of importance to remark, that the theme on which Mr. Romaine so much loves to expatiate, is a purifying as well as a pleasing theme. It is not only not grievous to indulge in it, but, most assuredly, to every true-hearted Christian, it is safe. We are aware of the alleged danger which some entertain of the tendency of such a full and free exhibition of the grace of the Gospel, to produce Antinomianism. But the way to avert this, is not by casting any part of Gospel truth into the shade. It is to spread open the whole of it, and give to every one part the relief and the prominency that it has in Scripture. We are not to mitigate the doctrines of a justifying faith, and an all-perfect righteousness, because of the abuse that has been made of them by hypocrites—but. leaving to these doctrines all their prominency, we are to place by their side the no less important and undeniable truths, that heaven is the abode of holy creatures, and that, ere we are qualified for admittance there, we must become holy and heavenly ourselves. Nor is there a likelier way of speeding this practical transformation upon our souls, than by keeping up there, through the blood of Christ, a peace in the conscience, which is never truly done, without a love in the heart being kept up along with it. Those who are justified by faith in the righteousness of Christ, and, in consequence of which, have that peace with God which this author labors so earnestly to maintain in the mind, walk not after the flesh, but after the Spirit: and that man's faith in the offered Saviour is not real, nor has he given a cordial acceptance to that grace which is so freely revealed in the Gospel, if he do not demonstrate the existence of this faith in his heart, by its operation in his character. A hypocrite may pervert the grace of the Gospel, as he will seek a shelter for his iniquities, wherever it can be found. But because he receives it deceitfully, this is no reason why it should be withheld from those who receive it in truth. The truths which he abuses to his own destruction, are, nevertheless, the very truths which serve to aliment the gratitude and the new obedience of every honest believer, who gives welcome acceptance to all things whatsoever that are written in the book of God's counsel, and finds room enough in his moral system for both of the positions—that he is justified by faith, and that he is judged by works.

INTRODUCTORY ESSAY

TO

THE CHRISTIAN REMEMBRANCER.

BY

AMBROSE SERLE, Esq.

It is quite possible that a doctrine may at one time have been present to our minds, to the evidence of which we then attended, and the truth of which we did in consequence believe; and yet, in the whole course of our future thoughts, may it never again have occurred to our remembrance. This is quite possible of a doctrine in science; and it may also be conceived of a doctrine in theology, that on one day it may have been the object of faith, and never on any succeeding day be the object of memory. In this case, the doctrine, however important, and though appertaining to the very essence of the Gospel, is of no use. It is not enough that we have received the Gospel, we must stand in it. And it is not enough that we barely believe it, for we are told, on the highest authority, that unless we keep it in memory we have believed in vain.

This may lead us to perceive that there is an error in the imaginations of those who think, that after having understood and acquiesced in Christian truth, there is an end of all they have to do with it. There is, with many, a most mischievous repose of mind upon this subject. They know that by faith they are saved, and they look to the attainment of this faith as a terminating good, with the possession of which, could they only arrive at it, they would be satisfied; and they regard the articles of a creed in much the same light that they do the articles of a title-deed, which may lie in their repository for years, without once being referred to: and they have the lurking impression, that if this creed were once fairly lodged among the receptacles of the inner man, and only produced in the great day of the examination of passports, it would secure their entry into heaven—just as the title-deed in possession, though never once looked to, guarantees to them a right to all that is conveyed by it. The mental tablet on which are inscribed their articles of belief, is consigned, as it were, to some place of concealment within them, where it lies in a kind of forgotten custody, instead of hanging out to the eye of the mind, and there made the subject of busy and perpetual observation. It is not like a paper filled with the principles and standing rules of a court, and to which there must be a daily reference for the purpose of daily procedure and regulation. It is more, to make use of a law term, like a paper in *retentis*—perhaps making good to them certain privileges which never will be questioned, or ready to be produced on any remote and distant occasion, when such a measure may be called for. Now this is a very great misconception; and whenever we see orthodoxy contentedly slumbering over its fancied acquisitions, and resting securely upon the imagination that all its business is now settled and set by, we may be very sure that it is something like this which lies at the bottom of it.

To rectify this wrong imagination, let it never be forgotten, that everywhere in the Bible, those truths by the belief of which we are saved, have this efficacy ascribed to them, not from the mere circumstance of their having once been believed, but after they are believed, from the circumstance of their being constantly adverted to. The belief of them on the one hand is indispensable; for let this be withheld, and the habitual recurrence of the mind to them is of no more use, than would be its constant tendency to dwell on such fancies as it knew to be chimerical. But this habitual recurrence is just as indispensable; for let this be withheld, and the belief of them were of no more use, than would be that of any other salutary truth, forgotten as to the matter of it, and therefore utterly neglected as to its application. The child who is told of his father's displeasure, should he spend that hour in amusement which is required to be spent in scholarship, may believe this at the time of the announcement. But when the hour comes, should the intimation slip from his memory, he has believed in vain. And from the apostle's declaration, who assures us, that unless we keep the truth in memory we have believed in vain, may we gather what that is which forms the true function and design of the faith that is unto salvation. It is not that by the bare possession of the doctrines which it appropriates as so many materials, salvation may be purchased: it is that by the use to which these materials are put, we may come into a state of salvation. It is not that truths lying in a state of dormancy within us, form so many titles in our behalf to the purchased inheritance: it is that truths ever present to the waking faculties of our mind, (and they never can be so without being remembered,) have an influence and a power to make us meet for the inheritance.

On this important truth, so indispensable to secure the saving and salutary influence of the other truths of Christianity, when known and believed, we shall make three observations. The first regards the kind of effort that should be made, either by an inquirer or a Christian, in the business of prosecuting his salvation. The second regards the nature of that salvation. And the third regards the power of the truth, when summoned into the mind's presence by an act of recollection, to keep it in that right train both of purpose and desire which prepares and carries it forward to the enjoyment of heaven.

I. With regard to the kind of effort that should be made by an inquirer, he does not, we will venture to say, set earnestly out in quest of salvation without its coming primarily and prominently into his notice, that he is saved by faith. And hence very often a straining of the mind after this acquirement—an anxious endeavor to believe—a repeated attempt to grasp that truth, by the possession of which it is, that we obtain a right to life everlasting; and as the accompaniment of all this, a frequent work of inward search and contemplation, to try if that principle be there, on which there hinges so important a consummation as the favor of God, and the forgiveness of all trespasses. Now it is worth the remarking, on this subject, that there is no such thing as forcing the belief of the mind beyond what it sees of proof and evidence. We may force the mind to attend to a matter; or we may force it to conceive that matter; or we may force it to persevere in thinking and in dwelling upon it. But beyond the light of evidence you cannot force it to any kind of belief about it. Faith is not to be arrived at in this way; and we can no more command the mind to see that to be truth on which the light of evidence does not shine, than we can command the eye to behold the sun through a dark impalpable cloud, that mantles it from human observation. Should a mountain intervene between our eye and some enchanting scene that lies on the other side of it, it is not by any piercing or penetrative effort on the part of the eye, through this solid opaque mass, that we will obtain the sight after which we are aspiring. And yet there is a way of obtaining it. A mere effort of the eye will not do; but the effort of ascending the mountain will do. And, in like manner, a mere straining of the mind after any doctrine, with a view to apprehend it, will never, without the light of evidence, bring that doctrine into the discernment of the mind's eye. But such is the proclaimed importance of belief, as carrying in it an escape from ruin everlasting, and a translation into all the security of acceptance with God, that to the acquisition of it the effort of an inquirer is most naturally bent: and he is apt to carry this effort beyond the evidence; and the effort to behold beyond evidence is of a nature so fruitless and fatiguing, that it harasses the mind, just as any overstretch does toward that which, after all, is an impossibility. And yet there is a line of effort that is productive. There is a path along which the light of evidence will dawn, and that which is impossible to be seen without it, will be seen by it; and that, too, without distortion or unnatural violence upon the faculties. We are bidden seek the pearl of great price, and there must be a way of it. It is quite obvious, and not at all impracticable, to read the Bible with attention, and to wait upon ordinances, and to give vent to the desirousness of our hearts in prayer, and to follow conscience in the discharge of all known duties—and the truth which is unto salvation, and by the knowing and believing of which we acquire everlasting life, a truth that never can be seen while an opaque and impenetrable shroud is upon it, will at length break out into open manifestation. It does not do to be so urged by a sense of the necessity of faith, as to try the impracticability of making faith outrun the evidence. But it does well to be at the post, and along the path of inquiry and exertion, where it is promised that the light of this evidence will be made to shine upon us. If we keep by our duties and our Bibles, like the apostles who kept by Jerusalem till the Holy Ghost was poured upon them, there is not one honest seeker who will not, in time, be a sure and triumphant finder. And we ought to commit ourselves in confidence to this course, assured of the prosperous result that must come out of it. We ought not to be discomposed by our anxieties about the final attainment. Though the alternative of our heaven or hell hang upon the issues of our seeking to be justified by faith, still we ought not to try and toil to make our faith outrun the light of conviction. It should be our great encouragement, that it is not merely he who has found the Lord that is called upon to rejoice, but that it is said by the Psalmist, "Let the heart of them rejoice that seek the Lord." "Ask and ye shall receive: seek and ye shall find: knock and it shall be opened unto you."

Let us now conceive that the truth is gotten—that faith, which has been called, and aptly enough too, the hand of the mind, has appropriated and brought it within the grasp and possession of a believer, the question comes to be, How is this new acquisition to be disposed of? We may be sensible how often truths come to be known and believed by us, and how some of them perhaps have died away from our memory, and never been recalled: and yet we may be said to be in possession of them, for upon their bare mention we will instantly recognize them as doctrines we have already learned, and with the truth of which, at the time that we attended to their evidence, we were abundantly satisfied. Now, is it by such a possession of Christian truth that we will secure a part in the Christian salvation? It is not. It is not by first importing it into our conviction, and then consigning it to some by-corner of the mind, where it lies in a state of oblivion and dormancy—it is not thus, that our knowledge of God and of Jesus Christ becomes life everlasting. The truths which be unto salvation are not laid past like the forgotten acquisitions of science or scholarship. And we are wrong if we think, that just as the title-deeds of an earthly house in possession may be locked up in security, and never looked to but when the right of property is questioned—so our creed, with all its articles, may be laid up in the depository of our mind, and there lie in deep and undisturbed repose, till our right of entry into the house that is not made with hands, and is eternal in the heavens, comes under examination, among the other topics of the great day of inquiry. We do not think it possible that the essential truths of the Gospel can be actually believed, without being afterwards the topic of daily, and unceasing, and practical recurrence. But even though they could, they would, upon such an event, be of no influence towards the salvation of the believer. The apostle tells us expressly, if they are not kept in memory they are believed in vain. By the Gospel we are saved, not if we merely believe it, but if we keep it in memory. It is not enough that it have been once acquiesced in: it must ever, and through the whole futurity of our earthly existence, be habitually adverted to. It is not enough that it be sleeping in the mind's hidden repository: it must be in the mind's eye. It must be kept in remembrance; and that, too, for the purpose of being called to remembrance. It is not enough that it be in the mind's latent custody: it must be in constant waiting, as it were, for being summoned into the mind's presence—and its efficacy unto salvation, it would appear, consists not in the mind knowing it, but in the mind thinking of it.

This will be better illustrated by a particular truth. One of those truths to which the apostle alludes, as being indispensable to be kept in memory, in order to be of any efficacy, is, that Christ died for our sins. It is not enough then, it would appear, simply to have believed that Christ died for our sins. This fact must ever and anon be recalled to our memory. It is by no means enough, that we, at one time, were sure of this truth. It is a truth that must be dwelt upon. It is not to be thrown aside as a forgotten thing, which at one time gave entertainment to our thoughts. It must live in our daily recollections. It is not enough that we have taken hold of this dependence. We must keep hold of it: nor does faith even in this save us, unless that which is believed be the topic of ever-recurring contemplation.

For this purpose, the habit of a great and continuous effort on the part of the human mind is indispensable. We know how all the truths of Christianity, and this one among the number, are apt to slip from the attention; and what a combat with the tendencies of nature it takes to retain our hold of them. It is setting us to a work of great difficulty and great strenuousness, simply to bid us keep in memory the truths of that Gospel by which we are saved. They may have entered our mind with the force of all-powerful evidence—and they may have filled it with a sense of their supreme importance—and they may have ministered in the hour of silence and devotion, an influence to relieve, and to comfort and to elevate—and yet after all, will we find it a mighty struggle with the infirmities of our constitution, to keep these truths in memory all the day long. We will find, that among the urgencies of this world's business, the one and simple truth, that Christ died for our sins, will take its flight for hours together, and never once be presented to the mind, even in the form of a slight and momentary visitation. To be ever recurring to this truth—to give it an hourly place, along with the multitude of other thoughts that are within us—to turn it into a matter of habitual occupation for that mind, the property of which, throughout all the moments of its waking existence, is to be ever thinking—this is an enterprise in every way as arduous as to work against the current of nature. It is not laying upon us a task that is either easy or insignificant, when we are told to keep the essentials of the Gospel in our frequent remembrance. It is the experience of all who have honestly tried it, that it is exceedingly difficult—and yet, so far from a matter of insignificance, it is the averment of the apostle, that if we keep not the Gospel in memory, we will not be saved.

We know it to be a work of difficulty, for a man overcome with drowsiness, to keep his eyes open. Suppose that by so doing, he is only made to look on a set of of objects which offend and disturb him, we may readily conceive how gladly, in these circumstances, he will make his escape from the hateful imagery which surrounds him, by repairing to the sweet oblivion of nature. But, on the other hand, should his eyes, when open, have a scene of loveliness before them, by which the soul is regaled, and brightened into sensations that are every way agreeable, then, though an effort be necessary to keep himself awake, yet there is a better chance of the effort being actually made. There will be a reward and an enjoyment to go along with it; and the man, in these new circumstances, would both be in a state of pleasurable feeling, and, at the same time, in a constant struggle to maintain his wakefulness. However delightful the prospect that is before him, this will not supersede the necessity of a strenuous endeavor to keep himself in the posture of observation. And so of the mind's eye, in the mental scenery that is before it. Under all the stir, and activity, and delight of nature's movements, may the soul be profoundly immersed in the slumbers of nature's carnality. It may be spiritually asleep, even when busily engaged with the passing insignificant dreams of our present world. It is indeed a great transition on every son and daughter of our species when he becomes awake to the realities of faith, and is made to perceive the existence and the weight of things invisible. But if all he is made thus to perceive, be the dark and menacing imagery of terror—if he see nothing but God's holiness on the one hand, and his own sinfulness on the other—if on looking to the sanctuary above, he see nothing but the fire of a devouring jealousy in readiness to go forth over the whole region of disloyalty to heaven's law; and, on looking to himself, he see that he is within the limits of the territory of guilt, and liable to the doom that is in reserve for it, we may perceive the readiness with which many a half-awakened sinner will try to make his escape from the pain and the agitation of such frightful contemplations as these; and how gladly he will cradle his soul back again into its old insensibility, and find a refuge from the whole alarm of faithful sermons, and arousing providences, and constantly recurring deaths in the circle of his much-loved acquaintanceship, in the forgetfulness of a nature, which, by its own drowsiness, may be so easily lulled into a state of unconcern about these things. The man will not, if he can help it, make an effort to keep himself awake, if all he get by it is a spectacle of pain: if he get a spectacle of pleasure by it, he may be prevailed upon. Still, even in this latter case, an effort would be necessary: even after the dread representation of the law is succeeded by the bright and cheering representation of the Gospel, it will still be like the offering of a beauteous and inviting spectacle to the eyes of a man who is like to be overcome with drowsiness. There must be a sustained endeavor on his part to keep himself awake. He will ever and anon be relapsing into the slumbers of worldly and alienated nature, if he do not put forth a strenuousness on the object of keeping the truths of the Gospel in his memory. So long as he is encompassed with a vile body of sin and of infirmity, which will at length be pulverized by death, and transformed at the resurrection, there will be a struggle with the sleeping propensities that will still be about him towards the things that are unseen and spiritual. Great will be his pleasure, even here, in the objects of his believing contemplation; but great also must be the effort of painful and unceasing diligence to support the contemplation itself. He will just be like a drowsy spectator, with a fine and fascinating landscape before him, the charm of which he would like to prolong to the uttermost. And however engaging the prospect which the Gospel sets before him, however cheering the promises, however effectually the truth that Christ died for our sins, chases away all the fears of the law, when it proclaims, that for every sin that the creature has dared to perpetrate, a holy and an avenging God must be satisfied; still we mistake it, if we think that no effort on the part of the mind is necessary to detain within the reach of its vision this bright and beautiful representation. Though called to rejoice in the Lord alway, yet there must be a putting forth of strength and of vigilance in the work of looking unto Jesus, and of considering Him who is the Apostle and High Priest of our profession.

II. The nature of that salvation which the Gospel reveals, has been so fully exhibited by Mr. Serle, in the First Part of this excellent Treatise, as to render any lengthened exposition of it in this place unnecessary. But it is worthy of remark, that, perhaps, there is not a passage in the Bible more fitted to instruct us in what the salvation of Christianity really is, than the expression of the apostle, to which we have so frequently adverted, that unless we keep the truths of the Gospel in memory, we have believed in vain. The ordinary conception upon the subject is, that it is a rescue from hell, with a right of entry and admittance into heaven. And our faith is supposed to be our title-deed ; a passport of conveyance, upon the examination of which we are carried in the train of our Saviour and our Judge to paradise ; a thing we fear, apprehended by many to be of no other use than merely to be retained in a sort of secure keeping; that, when found in our possession on the last day, it may then be sustained as our claim to the promised inheritance of glory. Now the apostle tells us, that were it possible to believe the truth without being mindful of the truth, the belief is in vain: in other words, its main use to salvation does not lie in the possession of it then, but in the influence and operation of it now. When placed before the judgment-seat of Christ, it will be known whether we are of the faith; and there is no doubt that this faith will open the door of heaven's kingdom to all who possess it. But, let it well be understood, that this is not the alone, nor even the most important function of faith. It does not lie in useless reserve on this side of time, till the occasion comes round, when on the other side of time, it will vest us with a right of admittance into heaven. Its main operation is our good here, by the thing which has been believed being also the thing that is remembered. Were its only use to confer a title upon us, it might lie in store like an old charter, forgotten for years, but securing its purpose whenever there is a call for its production. But it has another use besides conferring a title : it confers a character. It does something more than cause the place to be made ready for us: it causes us to be made ready for the place. We believe in vain unless we remember: but it is the habitual advertency of the mind to the great truths of the Gospel—it is the unceasing recurrence of its thoughts to them —it is the practice of ever and anon calling them to consideration, and dwelling upon them from one day, and from one hour to another—it is this which appears to stamp upon faith its main efficacy towards salvation. And why? Because salvation lies in deliverance from sin, as well as from punishment—because salvation consists in being introduced to the character of heaven, as well as into heaven itself—because by salvation there is not merely the prospect of another habitation, but there is the working of another principle ; and the way in which the memory must be added to faith, else we have believed in vain, is, that the memory, by calling the truths of the Gospel into the mind's presence, reiterates upon the mind a moral and a sanctifying influence, which would be altogether unfelt if these truths were forgotten. It is because the memory perpetuates the flame which was first lighted by the faith of Christianity—it is because if faith work by love, then the memory is necessary to the alimenting of this holy affection; and if it be one use of faith to justify the sinner in the sight of God, a no less important use of faith is, that through a habitual remembrance of the truths that are the objects of it, the sinner is brought under the constant operation of a moral influence, by which he is sanctified and made meet for the inheritance.

III. The truths to which the apostle adverts, when he assures us, that unless we keep them in memory we have believed in vain, are, that Christ died for our sins, according to the Scriptures; and that, after He was buried, He rose again. Let the first truth be habitually present to the mind, and the mind will feel itself habitually lightened of the whole terror and bondage of legality. That weight of overhanging despair, which, in fact, represses every attempt at obedience, by making it altogether hopeless, will be taken off from the wearied spirit, and it will break forth with the full play of its emancipated powers on the free and open space of reconciliation. There is nothing that so chains the inactivity of a human being as hopelessness. There is nothing that so paralyzes him, as the undefined, but haunting insecurity and terror, which he cannot shake away. We must be sensible of the new spring that is given to the energies of him who is overwhelmed with debt, when he obtains his discharge. So long as he felt that all was irrecoverable he did nothing; but when he gets his enlargement, he runs with the alacrity of a new-acquired freedom in the path of industry. Now, in the spiritual life, it is this very enlargement which gives rise to this very activity. It is the glad tidings of a release, by Him who hath paid the ransom of our iniquities, that sets our feet in a sure place—that opens up to us a career of new obedience—that levels the barrier which keeps us without hope, and therefore without God in the world—that places us, as it were, in a free and unobstructed avenue, in which, by every step that we advance upon it, we draw nearer to that Jerusalem above, the gates of which are now thrown open to receive us. The real effect of the doctrine of Jesus Christ and Him crucified, upon the believer, is utterly the reverse of this world's imagination upon the subject. It does not beget the delusion in his mind of an impunity for sinning; but it chases away that heavy soporific from his moral faculties, which the sense of a broken law, when unaccompanied by the faith of an offered Gospel, will ever minister to the heart; that let him struggle as he may, and keep as strenuously from sinning as he may, it will be of no use to him. The truth that Christ died for our sins, so far from a soporific, is a stimulus to our obedience; and it is when this truth enters with power into the heart, that the believer can take up the language of the Psalmist and say, "Thou hast enlarged my heart, and I will now run in the way of thy testimonies."

But if such be the influence of this truth when present to the mind, it must, in order to have a habitual influence, be habitually present. In order to work upon the habit and character of the soul, it must ever be offering itself to the notice, and ever reiterating the impulse it is fitted to give to all the feelings, and to all the faculties. We know not a single doctrine, which by its perpetual recurrence to the thoughts, is more fitted to keep the mind in a right state for obedience. Now, in order that the great work of sanctification go forward, the mind should be constantly in this state. Let this truth be expunged, and for all the purposes of spiritual conformity to the will of God, the whole man will go into unhingement. But let this truth be lighted up in the soul—let it be kept shining at all times within its receptacles—let the trust never cease to lean upon it, and the memory never cease to recall it, and the hope never cease to dwell upon it—let it only show itself among the crowd of this world's turmoils and anxieties—and whatever the urgencies be, which harass and beset a man on the path of his daily history, let such be the habit of his mind, that in obedience to this truth, the thought is present with him of his main chance being secured; the animating sense of this will bear him on in triumph through manifold agitations: and when like to sink and give way under the pressure of this world's weariness, and this world's distraction, this will come in aid of his faltering spirit, and carry him in sacredness, and in safety to his final landing-place.

We have not room to expatiate on the influence of the other truth, that Christ rose again—that He eyes every disciple from that summit of observation to which He has been exalted—that the sin for which He died He holds in irreconcilable hatred—and that the purpose of His mediatorship was not merely to atone for its guilt, but utterly to root out its existence and its power from the hearts of all who believe in Him. The Christian who is haunted at all hours of the day by this sentiment, will feel that to sin is to thwart the purpose upon which his Saviour's heart is set, and to crucify Him afresh. This, however, to be kept in power, must be kept in memory. And as with the former truth, if we carry it about with us at all times, we will walk before God without fear, so with it and the latter truth put together, if both are carried about with us, will we also walk before him in righteousness, and in holiness, all the days of our lives.

But it ought to be remembered, that if we are not mindful of these truths, we positively do not believe them. If we have not the memory, it is a clear evidence that we have not the faith. It is impossible but the mind must be always recurring to matters in which it has a great personal interest, if it only have a sense of their reality. We should try ourselves by this test, and be assured, that if we are not going on unto perfection through the constant and practical influence of the great doctrines of Christianity upon our heart, we need yet to learn what be the first principles of the oracles of God.

It is from these considerations that we estimate so highly the following valuable Treatise of Mr. SERLE, "THE CHRISTIAN REMEMRRANCER," in which the great and essential truths of Christianity are exhibited in a luminous and practical manner. But, it is not merely those more essential truths of the Gospel which form the foundation of a sinner's hope, that he brings to our remembrance; the operative nature of these truths, as inwardly experienced by the believer, in the formation of the spiritual life—the sanctifying influence of Christian truth over the affections and character of the believer—the whole preceptive code of social and relative duties to which, as members of society, Christianity requires our obedience—in fine, the whole Christian system of doctrines and duties is presented in a plain and practical manner, well fitted to assist the understanding in attaining a correct and intimate acquaintance with the truths of Christianity; while the brief, but distinct and impressive form in which they are presented, is no less fitted to assist the memory in its recollection of them. The Treatise, as the Author remarks, is rather intended for hints to carry on the mind to farther meditations, than for full and exact meditations themselves; and it is brought into narrow compass, that the serious Christian may find it a little *Remembrancer*, with many short errands to his heart. And as the reader, from our previous observations, will not fail to remark, that it is not the mere knowledge or possession of any truth, but the constant remembrance of it, which can give it an operative influence over the mind, and make it issue in those practical results which such a truth is fitted to produce—so, however important those precious truths are which are so clearly and impressively presented in the following Treatise, yet they can have no saving or salutary influence, without being kept in constant remembrance.

If it have not been our habit hitherto to call to mind the essential truths of the Gospel, we ought to begin now, and by reason of use we will be sure to make progress in it. Whether it be the work of an artisan, or the work of a merchant, there is room for this thought in short and frequent intervals, that Christ died for our sins; and we are confident that, if we are believers, the thought will leave a pacifying and a holy influence behind it. God has proclaimed a connection between the presence of Gospel truth to the understanding, and the power of Gospel affections over that heart. He has told us that faith worketh by love; and we, by constantly recurring to the great objects of faith, are putting that very instrument into operation by which God sanctifies all those who have received his testimony in behalf of Jesus Christ his Son.

If we receive the truths of Christianity, we are not merely put in possession of them as title-deeds to a blessed inheritance above, to be presented after death for our entrance into heaven: they are also instruments to be made use of before death, for graving upon us, as it were, the character of heaven. And when the day of judgment comes, it is not by a direct inspection of the title-deeds that our right to heaven will be ascertained; it is by the inspection of that which has been engraven by the truths of Christianity, operating as so many instruments upon our character. Christ will look to the inscription that has been made upon our hearts and lives: so, while nothing can be more true, than that it is by faith we are justified, it is in fullest harmony with this truth, that it is by works we are judged.

INTRODUCTORY ESSAY

TO THE

CHRISTIAN'S GREAT INTEREST.

IN TWO PARTS.

BY THE REV. WILLIAM GUTHRIE.

THERE are few subjects or exercises more deeply important to professing Christians, than that which forms the principal topic in the following admirable Treatise—the work of self-examination. But self-examination is a work of great difficulty, and is accordingly shrunk from, or altogether declined by the great body of professing Christians. It is more the habitual style of the mind's contemplations to look at that which is without, than at that which is within—and it is far easier to read the epistles of the written Record, than to read the tablet of one's own heart, and so to ascertain whether it be indeed a living epistle of Christ Jesus our Lord. There is something so shadowy and evanescent in the phases of the human spirit—such a want of the distinct and of the tangible, in its various characteristics—such a turmoil, and confusion, and apparent incoherence in the rapid succession of those thoughts, and impulses, and emotions, which find their way through the avenues of the inner man—that men, as if lost in the mazes of a labyrinth, deem the world which is within to be the most hopeless and impracticable of all mysteries—nor in the whole range of their varied speculations, do they meet with that which more baffles their endeavors to seize upon, than the busy principle that is lodged within them, and has taken up its residence in the familiar intimacies of their own bosom.

The difficulty of knowing our own heart is much enhanced, if we are in quest of some character or some lineament which is but faintly engraven thereupon. When the thing that we are seeking for is so very dim, or so very minute, as to be almost indiscernible, this makes it a far more fatiguing exercise—and, it may be, an altogether fruitless one. Should then the features of our personal Christianity be yet slightly or obscurely formed, it will need a more intense and laborious scrutiny ere we can possibly recognize them. Should there be a languor in our love to God—should there be a frailty in our purposes of obedience—should there be a trembling indecision of principle, and the weakness or the wavering of a mind that is scarcely made up on the question of a preference for time or for eternity, let us not marvel, though all disguised as these seeds and elements of regeneration within us may be, amid the vigorous struggles of the old man, and the remaining urgencies of a nature which will not receive its death-blow but with the same stroke that brings our bodies to the dust—let us not marvel, if in these circumstances the hardships of the search should deter many from undertaking it—and though after months, or even years of earnestness in religion, the disciple may still be in ignorance of himself, as if blindfolded from the view of his own character; or, if arrested at the threshold by a sense of its many difficulties, the work of self-examination has not yet been entered on.

It is thus that the dark and unsearchable nature of the subject operates insensibly but powerfully as a restraint on self-examination—and certainly there would be encouragement felt to begin this exercise, were it made to appear in the light of a more practicable exercise, that could really and successfully be gone through. It is just as if set upon the task of searching for some minute article on the floor of an apartment, of which the windows had been partially closed—a weary and a hopeless undertaking, till the sun has fully risen, and the shutters have been altogether unfolded, and the greatest possible supply of light has been admitted into the room. Then the search might be entered upon with vigor, and just because now it could be entered upon with the alacrity of a comfortable expectation. The work is less repulsive, because easier—and now might the whole surface of this trial for a discovery be patiently explored, just because now a greater visibility had been poured over it.

This leads to a remark, which though a mere preliminary to the subject of self-examination, we nevertheless deem to be one of great practical importance. We think that however inscrutable at this moment our mind may be, and however faintly the marks and the characteristics of our Christianity are delineated thereupon, yet that even now the inward survey ought to be commenced, and renewed at frequent intervals, and daily persevered in. But, meanwhile, and to facilitate the search, we should do the very thing that is done in the case of a dark apartment. There should be as much light as possible thrown upon the subject from without. If the lineaments of grace within us be faint, that ought instantly to be done which might have the effect of brightening them into a more lucid distinctness, and so making the work of discovery easier than before. If the love, and the joy, and the grateful devotedness to his Saviour's will, wherewith the heart of a believer is animated, be hardly discernible in his efforts to ascertain them, this is the very reason why all those direct expedients should forthwith be resorted to for stirring up the love, and for exciting the joy, and for fixing in the bosom that grateful devotedness which he is now going so fruitlessly in quest of, and which, if they exist at all, are so shrunken in magnitude, or so enveloped in their own dimness, that they have hitherto eluded all his endeavors to seek after them, if haply he may find them. Now it is not by continuing to pore inwardly that we will shed a greater lustre over the tablet of our own character, any more than we can enlighten the room in which we sit by the straining of our eyes towards the various articles which are therein distributed. In the one case, we take help from the window, and through it from the sun of nature—and this not to supersede the proposed investigation on our part, but altogether to aid and encourage us in that investigation. And in the other case, that the eye of the mind may look with advantage upon itself inwardly, should it often look outwardly to those luminaries which are suspended from the canopy of that revelation which is from above—we should throw widely open the portal of faith, and this is the way by which light is admitted into the chambers of experience—in defect of a manifest love, and a manifest loyalty, and a manifest sacredness of heart, which we have been seeking for in vain amongst the ambiguities of the inner man, we should expose the whole of this mysterious territory to the influences of the Sun of righteousness, and this is done by gazing upon him with a believer's eye. It is by regarding the love wherewith God in Christ hath loved us, that the before cold and sluggish heart is roused into the respondency of love back again. That the work of reading be made more easy, the character must be made more legible. That Christianity be clearly reflected from our own bosom, all must be laid open to the Christianity of the Record. If we derive no good from the work of self-examination, because we find that all is confusion and mistiness within, then let us go forth upon the truths which are without, and these will pour a flood of light into all the mazes and intricacies of the soul, and, at length, render that work easy, which before was impracticable. No doubt, it is by looking inwardly that we discover what is in the mind—but it is by looking outwardly that we so brighten and bring out its characteristics, as to make these discernible. The gratitude that was before unfelt, because it lay dormant, let us awaken it by the sight of Him who was lifted upon the cross for our offences, and then will it meet the observation. The filial affection for our Father in heaven, which before was dead, let us quicken it into a felt and gracious sensibility, by looking unto Him in His revealed attitude of graciousness, and at our next exercise of self-inspection, we will be sure to find it. To revive the power of a life that is to come, which the despair of guilt had utterly extinguished in the soul, let us cast our believing regard on the promises of the Gospel—and this will set it up again, and then will we more readily ascertain, that our happiness in time is less dear to us than our hopes for eternity. It is thus that by the contemplation of that which is without, we brighten the consciousness of that which is within—and the more manifest the things of revelation are to the eye of faith, the more manifest will the things of experience be to the eye of conscience —and the more distinctly we can view the epistles of Christ in the written Record, the more discernible will its counterpart be in that epistle which is written not with pen and ink, but by the Spirit of God, on the fleshly tablets of our own heart. And so the work of faith, instead of being proposed by us as a substitute, we should propose as the readiest help, and far the best preparative for the work of self-examination.

It were well, if thus we could compose the jealousy of those who deem it legal to go in quest of evidence—but better still, if we could guide the practice of those with whom the business of salvation forms a practical and not a merely theoretical or speculative question.

And *first*, we would say to them, that so far from setting faith aside by the work of self-examination, we hold that it is the former which supplies the latter with all its materials, and sheds that light over them which makes them visible to the eye of consciousness. Were there no faith, there would be no fruits to inquire after—and it were utterly in vain to go a seeking where there was absolutely nothing to find. To a sinner in distress, we unfold the pardon of the Gospel; and we bid him look unto Jesus that he may rejoice. We surely could not say less than this to an inquirer in darkness, even though it be a darkness that has gathered and rests over the tablet of his own character, and hides from his own view all that is good and gracious thereupon. Should the eye fail of its discernment when turned inwardly upon the evidences, we should bid it turn outwardly upon the promises, and this is the way to bring down a clear and satisfying light upon the soul. Just as in some minute and difficult search over the floor of an apartment, we throw open all its windows to the sun of nature, so we ought, by faith, to throw open all the chambers of the inner man to the light of the Sun of Righteousness. They are the truths that be without, which give rise to the traces of a spiritual workmanship within—and the indistinctness of the latter is just the reason why the soul should be ever aiming by attention and belief at a communication with the former. When self-examination is at a loss to read the characters which are written upon the heart, it is faith alone which can make the inscription more legible—and never will man get acquainted with the home of his own bosom, but by constant supplies of light and influence from abroad. If we feel, then, an outset of difficulty, in the work of self-examination, let us go anew to the fountain-head of revelation, and there warm, into a sensibility that may be felt, the cold and the faded lineaments of that image which it is the genuine tendency of the truth as it is in Jesus to impress upon the soul. That we may prosper when we examine ourselves, whether we are in the faith, we should have the faith. We should keep it in daily and habitual exercise, and this will strengthen it. If we be familiar with the truths that are without, less will be our difficulty in recognizing the traces that are within. The more we gaze upon the radiance, the brighter will we glow with the reflection—and so far from opposition in the exercises of self-examination and of faith, there is the most necessary concert, the most important and beautiful harmony.

But, *secondly*—whatever difficulties there be in self-examination, we should even now make a beginning of the work. We should at least try it—and if we do not succeed, repeat it again and again. We should set ourselves formally down to it, as we would to a prescribed task—and it were well too if we had a prescribed time every day for the doing of it, and let a whole month of honest and sustained perseverance pass over our heads, ere we say of the work that it is impracticable. The more we live a life of faith through the day, the more distinct and legible will be that other page in the record of our personal history, which we shall have to peruse on the evening—and however little we may have sped at this trial of self-examination, we will either be encouraged or rebuked by it, into a life of greater effort and watchfulness on the morrow. In the business of each day, there will be a reference to the account and settlement that we make at the end of it —and the conclusion of each night will serve either to rectify the errors of our preceding history, or to animate us the more in that path by which we are moving sensibly onward to the heights of moral and spiritual excellence. Thus indeed will we make a business of our sanctification—and, instead of that vague, and shadowy, and altogether chimerical affair which we apprehend to be the religion of many a professor in our day, will it become a matter of solid and practical acquisitions, each of which shall have a visible reality in time, and each of which, by adding to the treasure in heaven, will have its distinct bearing on the interests of eternity.

Now when we set about any new exercise whatever, we first begin with that which is easy, and afterwards proceed therefrom to that which is more arduous. In the work of self-examination, there is a scale of difficulty—and it were well, perhaps, that we should make our first entrance upon the work at some of its lower gradations, lest we begin our attempt at too high a place, and be repelled altogether, by finding that it is utterly inaccessible.

To guide us aright, then, in this matter, we might observe, that the overt acts of our visible history, are far more noticeable by the eye of self-examination than those affections of the heart by which they have been prompted—and, therefore, if not yet able to read the devices of the inner man, let our first attempt be to read the doings of the outer man: "Hereby know we that we know Him, if we keep his commandments." This is a palpable test, in as far, at least, as the hand, or the mouth, or the footsteps, or any of the bodily organs, are concerned—and a series of questions regarding these were a good elementary introduction to the work of self-examination.—Have we, throughout the whole course of this day, uttered the language of profaneness, or contempt, or calumny? Or have we said any of those foolish things which might be ranked among the idle words of which men shall give account on the day of judgment? Or have we expressed ourselves to any of our fellows in the tone of fretfulness and irritation? Or have we on Sabbath refrained our attendance on the public ministrations, and instead of the readings and the contemplations, and the devout exercises of sacredness, have we given any time to the business and society of the world? Or have we been guilty of disrespect and negligence towards parents, and masters, and superiors of any kind? Or have we done any acts of mischief and revenge to the man whom we hate? Or have we wilfully directed our eye to that which was fitted to kindle the affections, or lead to the purposes of licentiousness? Or have we put forth a hand of violence on the property of our neighbor; and, what is an offence of the same species, have we taken an undue advantage of him in the petty contests and negotiations of the exchange, or of the market-place? Or have we spoken, if not a direct falsehood, at least a cunningly devised utterance, which, by the tone, and manner, and apparent artlessness of it, was calculated to deceive? Or have we gone to any of the excesses of intemperance, whether of that drunkenness which inflames the faculties, or of that surfeiting which damps and overweighs them. And what this day have been our deeds of beneficence—what our attentions of kindness and charity—what our efforts or our sacrifices in the walk of Christian usefulness—what our almsgiving to the poor—what our labors of piety, either among the habitations of ignorance, or with the members of our own family? These are all matters that stand broadly and discernibly out to the eye of consciousness. They form what may be called the large and legible types on the tablet of self-examination. They form, as it were, the primer, or the alphabet of this most important branch of scholarship. It is as easy for us to frame a catalogue of these questions, and sit regularly down every evening to the task of applying them in succession to our recent history, and meet them with as prompt and clear a reply, as it is for us to tell at the end of each day, what were the visits that we performed, or the people whom we have conversed with, or the walks that we have taken, or the bargains that we have concluded. There 's nothing of reconditeness or mystery whatever in this process, at least, of self-examination; and by entering immediately upon it, may we at length be qualified for those more profound exercises by which the intimacies of the heart are probed; and be able to arrive at a finding, and a familiarity with the now hidden depths of a spiritual experience.

There is much to be gathered even from this more rude and elementary process of self-examination. "By their fruits shall ye know them," says our Saviour; and, after all, much may be learned of the real character of our affections, from the acts in which they terminate. In natural husbandry, one may judge of the vegetation from the crop. It is not indispensable that we dive into the secrets of physiology, or that we be skilled in the anatomy and organization of plants, or that, with the eye of direct observation, we can satisfy ourselves as to the soundness of the root, or the healthful circulation of the juices which ascend from it. There is no doubt, that a good internal economy forms the very essence of vegetable health; and yet how many an agriculturalist, from whom this essence lies hid in deepest mystery, can pronounce upon that which is spread visibly before him, that there has indeed been a grateful and prosperous return for his labors. He knows that there has been a good and abundant growth, though, in the language of a Gospel parable, whose design is to illustrate this very thing, "he knoweth not how." And so, to a great extent, of spiritual husbandry. One may be profoundly ignorant of moral science. He may not be able to grope his way among the arcana of the inner man. There might not be a more inscrutable thing to him in nature, than the mystery of his own spirit; and not a darker or more impenetrable chaos, than that heart which ever teemeth with the abundance of its own thoughts and its own counsels. Yet from the abundance of that heart the mouth speaketh; and words are audible things—and out of that heart are the issues of life; and the deeds of our life or history are visible things—and as the heart prompteth so the hand performeth—and thus a legible expression is sent forth, even from the depths of an else unsearchable cavern, which we at least have never entered, either to sound its recesses, or to read the characters that are graven within its secret chambers of imagery. If we cannot go profoundly to work, let us go to it plainly. If the fountain be hid let us take cognizance of the stream that issueth from the outlets. If we cannot guage the designs, let us at least institute a questionary process upon the doings; and if we have wearied ourselves in vain at searching for the marks of grace upon the soul, let us remember that the body is its instrument and its vehicle, and we may at least examine ourselves as to all its movements of accordancy with the ten commandments.

Let us therefore be in earnest in this work of self-examination, which is reputed to be of so much difficulty, and immediately do that which we can; and thus will we at length be qualified for doing that which we at present cannot. Let it be the task of every evening to review the palpable history of every day; and if we cannot dive into the heart, we may at least take cognizance of the handywork. We may not yet be able to analyze the feelings which enter into the hidden life of obedience; but we can take account of the literalities of obedience. The hasty utterance by which we wounded another's sensibilities—the pleasantries by which we enlivened a festive circle, at the expense of some absent character—the tone of offence or imperiousness into which some domestic annoyance hath provoked us—the excess into which we have been betrayed amid the glee of merry companionship—the neglect of prayer and of the Bible, into which we have once more been led by distaste, or indolence, or the urgency of this world's business—these, and many more, are surely noticeable things, which can be recalled by the memory, and rebuked by the moral sense, of the most ordinary Christian; and which, if so dealt with at the close of any day, might give to the morrow's walk a greater care and a greater conscientiousness.

What we ought to do is to begin now the work of self examination—we should now make a practical outset, and do forthwith all that our attainment and ability will let us—we should not despise the day of small things, nor idly postpone the work of self-examination till a sense, and a spirit, and a subtlety, which we at present have not, shall come upon us, as if by inspiration. If the inward motions be too faint and fugitive for us to apprehend, let us lay hold at least of the outward movements, and by a faithful retrospect and reformation of these, will our senses at length be exercised to discern both the good and the evil. What we ought to chase away from the habit of the soul is a certain quietism of inert and inactive speculation, when lulled by the jingle of an unmeaning orthodoxy, it goeth not forth with its loins girded, as well as its lamp burning, and only dreams of a coming glory, and immortality, and honor, instead of seeking for them by a patient continuance in well-doing. We ought earnestly to make a business of our Christianity, and be diligent in doing that which our hand findeth to do; and if at present the mysteries of a deeper experience look so remote and inaccessible that we cannot apprehend them, let us at least question ourselves most strictly as to the doings of our ordinary path; and under the guidance of that Spirit whose office it is to reveal all truth, will we, at length, be disciplined for greater things than these.

In prosecuting the business of self-inspection, it is of importance that we be guided aright in our inquiries into our spiritual state; and we know of few works better fitted to assist the honest inquirer in his search, than MR. GUTHRIE'S "CHRISTIAN'S GREAT INTEREST." It is divided into Two Parts, "The Trial of a Saving Interest in Christ," and "How to attain to a Saving Interest in Christ;" and we think it impossible to peruse this valuable Treatise, with the candor and sincerity of an honest mind, without arriving at a solid conclusion as to our spiritual condition. His experimental acquaintance with the operations and genuine fruits of the Spirit, and his intimate knowledge of the workings of the human heart, fitted him for applying the tests of infallible truth to aid us in ascertaining what spirit we are of—for exposing and dissipating the false hopes of the hypocrite—for leading the careless Christian to investigate the causes of his declension in godliness, and to examine anew whether he be in the faith—and for detecting and laying open the fallacies and delusions which men practise on themselves, in regard to the state of their souls. He faithfully exposes the insidious nature of that deceitfulness of the human heart, which lulls men into a false security, while their Christianity is nothing more than a heartless and hollow profession, and they are standing exposed to the fearful condemnation denounced against those who have "a name to live, but are dead."

Nor is his clear and scriptural exhibition of the dispensation of grace less fitted to guide the humble inquirer into the way of salvation. As a faithful ambassador of Christ, he is free and unreserved in his offers of pardon and reconciliation, through the death and obedience of Christ, to the acceptance of sinners; but he is no less faithful in stating and asserting the claims of the Gospel, to an unshrinking and universal obedience, and to an undisputed supremacy over the heart and affections. And to aid the sincere Christian in the cultivation of the spiritual life, he urgently enjoins an implicit acquiescence in the guidance and intimations of the Holy Spirit, through whose operation it is that a cordial and affectionate faith in the whole of God's testimony can be wrought in the soul; by whose spiritual illumination it is that the truth becomes the instrument of sanctifying and saving us; while by the inward experience of the Spirit's light, and comfort, and renewing power, combined with the outward and visible growth of the fruits of righteousness, in the character, we acquire the best and surest evidence that we have obtained a saving interest in Christ.

The intimate acquaintance which he manifests with the spiritual life, and his clear, affectionate, and earnest expositions of the peculiar doctrines of the Gospel, render this Treatise a precious companion to the sincere Christian; while his powerful and urgent appeals to the conscience are peculiarly fitted to awaken men to a concern about those matters to which the Scriptures attach such an infinite importance; to lead them in earnest to avoid the possibility of continuing in deception; and to constrain them to seek after a full assurance on that subject on which, above all others, it becomes men to be well assured.

INTRODUCTORY ESSAY

TO THE

GRACE AND DUTY OF BEING SPIRITUALLY MINDED,

DECLARED, AND PRACTICALLY IMPROVED.

BY JOHN OWEN, D.D.

We formerly observed, in our Essay to "Guthrie's Christian's Great Interest," that such is the great difficulty of self-examination, that it were well, if, instead of attempting at first the more arduous, the Christian disciple should begin with the more elementary of its exercises. And for this purpose, at his entrance upon this most useful work, he might commence with a daily review, if not of the affections of his heart, at least of the actions of his visible history. These are far more palpable than the others, and have somewhat of that superior facility for the observation of them, which the properties of matter have over those of the hidden and unseen spirit. The great thing wanted is, that he should be encouraged to make the attempt in any way—and therefore do we repeat our admonition, that on each evening, ere sleep has closed his eyes, he should summon to his remembrance those deeds of the day that have passed over him, which else might have vanished from the mind forever, or at least till that eventful occasion when the book of their imperishable record shall be opened. And it is good also that he should sit in judgment as well as in memory over them. Let him thus judge himself, and he shall not be judged. The daily remembrance of the one great Sacrifice will wash away the guilt of those daily aberrations that are faithfully recalled and truly repented of; and if there be a reality in that sanctifying influence which faith is said to bring along with it, then will the very act by which he confesses the remembered sins of the day, both bring peace to his conscience, and purity to his conduct.

And this mere cognizance, not of the heart, but of the handywork, brings us to the faith and spirituality of the Gospel by a shorter path than may be apprehended. It is true, that the mind is the proper seat of religion; and however right our actions may be in the matter of them, they are of no account in Christianity, unless they have proceeded from a central and spontaneous impulse which originates there. They may be moulded into a visible propriety by an influence from without, or have arisen from secondary motives, which are of no account whatever in the estimation of the upper sanctuary; and hence it is a possible thing that we may delude ourselves into a treacherous complacency, because of the many deeds of integrity, and courteousness, and beneficence in which we abound. Still, however, it will speedily be found, that in the midst of all our amiable and constitutional virtues, there are the outbreakings of evil upon our conduct, and such as nothing but a spiritual principle can effectually restrain. In taking cognizance of these, then, which we do in the first stage of self-examination, we are brought to feel the need of something higher than any of those powers or properties wherewith nature has endowed us—we are taught the nakedness of our moral condition—we are convinced of sin, and thrown upon those resources out of which pardon is administered, and help is made to descend upon us. We are not therefore to underrate the examination of our doings, or think that when thus employed, we are only wasting our thoughts on the bare and barren literalities of that bodily exercise which profiteth little. Even on this lower walk we shall meet with many deficiencies and many deviations: and be often rebuked into a sense of our own worthlessness; and shall have to lament, in the many offences of the outer man, how dependent we are both on a sanctifying grace and an atoning sacrifice. Or, in other words, by a regular habit of self-examination, even in the rudest and most elementary branch of it, may we be schooled into the doctrines of sin and of the Saviour, and from what is most observable in the outer path, may gather such intimations of what we are, and of what we need, as will conduct us to the very essence of vital Christianity.

Now, after this, there is what we would call the second stage in the work of self-examination. Our reason for advising a Christian to begin first with a survey of the handy-work, ere he proceeds to a search and scrutiny of the heart, is, that the one is greatly more manifest than the other. Now it is said in Scripture, "that the works of the flesh are manifest;" and what we would have him to remark is, that, in the enumeration of these works, the apostle takes account of wrong affections as well as of wrong actions. Wrath, for example, and hatred, and envy—these, in the estimation of the apostles, are alike manifest with drunkenness, and open quarrelling, and murder. It would appear that there are certain strong and urgent feelings of the inner man, which may be as distinctly taken cognizance of, as certain glaring and palpable misdeeds of the outward history. And therefore, while, for the first stage of self-examination, we proposed, as the topics of it, the doings of the visible conduct, we would suggest, for the second stage, the evil desires of the heart, which, whether they break forth or not into open effervescence, at least announce, and that most vividly, their existence and their power, to the eye, or rather to the sense of conscience, simply by the felt emotion which they stir up within, by the fierceness wherewith they rage and tumultuate among the secrecies of the bosom.

It is certainly worth adverting to, that while it is said of the works of the flesh, that they are manifest, the same is not said of the fruits of the spirit. And this, we are persuaded, will meet the experience even of the most spiritual and advanced Christian. Is there any such, who can say of his love to God, that it is a far more intense and sensible affection within him, than the anger which he often feels at the provocations of insult or dishonesty? Or will he say, that his joy in spiritual things has in it the power of a more noticeable sensation, than his joy in the fame or good fortune of this world? Or is the gentleness of his renewed heart a thing that can so readily meet the eye of observation, as the occasional violence, or even as those slighter touches of resentful and uncharitable feeling wherewith he at times is visited? Has he not often to complain, that in searching for the evidences of a work of grace, they are scarcely, if at all, discernible; whereas, nothing is more manifest than the constant risings of a sinful affection, and that weight of a carnal and corrupt nature, wherewith the inner man is well nigh overborne? Is it not distinctly his experience, that while the works of his flesh are most abundantly manifest, the fruits of the Spirit are of such slender or questionable growth, as well nigh to escape his observation? And does not this furnish a ground for the distinction, that whereas the former might well constitute the topics for the second stage of self-examination, the latter has their more befitting place as a higher and more advanced stage of it.

And here will we make another appeal to the experience of a Christian. Does he not feel of his evil affections, that not only are they more manifest to his own conscience, than his gracious and good ones; but is it not further true, that they are more manifest even now than they were formerly—that he has a more distinct feeling both of their existence and their malignity at this moment, than he had years ago—that he is greatly more burdened with a sense of their besetting urgency, and is hence apt to infer, that of themselves, they are surely more aggravated in their character—and that he is getting worse, perhaps, instead of advancing, as he heartily and honestly wishes to do, in the course of his sanctification? The inference is not a sound one; for both to the eye of the world, and to the eye of witnesses in heaven, he is growing both in humility and in holiness. But if his growth in humility should outstrip his growth in holiness, then to his own eye may there be a fuller and more affecting manifestation of his worthlessness than before. While the sin of his nature is upon the decay, there may, at the very time, be a progress in his sensibility to the evil of it. Just in proportion to the force of his resistance against the carnality of the old man, does he come more pressingly into contact with all its affections and its tendencies; and so, these being more deeply felt, are also more distinctly recognized by him. It was thus with Paul, when he found the law in his members, that warred against the law of his mind; and when he complained of his vile body; and when he affirmed of the struggle between the opposite principles of his now compound nature, that it not only harassed, but hindered him from doing the things which he would. He did not grow in corruption, but he grew in a more touching impression, and a clearer insight of it; and so of the Christian still, that more in heaviness though he be, under the felt and conscious movements of an accursed nature, which is not yet extinct, though under a sure and effectual process of decay, it is not because he is declining in religious growth, but because he is advancing in religious tenderness; striking his roots more profoundly into the depths of self-abasement, and therefore upwardly shooting more aloft than ever, among the heights of angelic sacredness.

We say this, partly for comfort, and to remind the Christian that it is good for him, in every stage of his career, to keep himself weaned from his own righteousness, and wedded to the righteousness of Christ. But he will also perceive how it is, that just as he grows in positive excellence, so does he become more feelingly alive, and more intelligently wakeful to the soil and the sinfulness wherewith it is still tarnished; and thus will every new accession to his Christianity facilitate the work which we have prescribed for him, on the second stage of self-examination.

It is thus, then, that we would introduce him to the business of making search and entry into the recesses of the inner man. Let him begin with the evil affections of his nature, for these are at first far more more discernible than the others; and even though under the power of grace they are withering into decay, still from the growth of his moral and spiritual delicacy, may they remain more discernible to the very end of his history in the world. They are therefore more easily recognized, than are the features of the new character, and should, of consequence, have an earlier place in the course of self-examination, that important branch of Christian scholarship. As the habit of reviewing the handy-work, prepared him for entering on the review of the heart, so the habit of reading those more palpable lineaments which are graven thereupon, may prepare him for scrutinizing that more hidden workmanship, which under the processes of the economy of grace, is carried forward in the soul of every believer. And agreeably to this, we would have him to take account, on each successive evening, of every uncharitable feeling that hath arisen through the day, of every angry emotion wherewith he has been visited, of every impure thought that he either loved to cherish, or did not rebuke with a prompt and sensitive alarm away from him, of every brooding anxiety that seemed to mark how much the crosses of time preponderate with him over the cares and concerns of eternity—withal, of that constant and cleaving ungodliness which compasses us about with all the tenacity and fulness of a natural element, and makes it so plain to the enlightened conscience, that though the heart were exempted from all the agitations of malice or licentiousness, yet still that Atheism, practical Atheism, is its kindly and congenial atmosphere. In taking such a nightly retrospect as this, how often may he be reminded of his preference for self in the negotiations of merchandise—of the little temptations to deceit, to which he had given a somewhat agreeable entertainment—of the dominant love of this world's treasure, and how it tends to overbear his appetite for the meat that endureth, his earnestness for being rich towards God!—These, and many like propensities as these, will obtrude themselves as the mementoes of nature's remaining frailty; they will be to him the indications of a work that is still to be done, the materials for his repentance every night, the motives and the impulses for his renewed vigilance on the morrow.

We now enter on the third and last stage of self-examination, at which it is that we take cognizance of a past work of grace that is going on in the soul; and read the lineaments of our new nature; and from the fruits of the Spirit having now become distinct and discernible within us, can assuredly infer, that now we are possessed of the earnest of our inheritance, and have the witness within ourselves, that we are indeed the children of God. And we think, that the humbler exercises which we have now insisted on, may prepare the way for this more subtle and recondite part of the work of self-examination. Certain it is, that it might subserve the object of bringing the Spirit of God into closer and more effectual fellowship with the soul. Only, let the notice which one takes of his evil affections, be the signal to him for entering, and that immediately, into a war of resistance, if not of extermination, against them. Having learned the strength and number of his enemies, let him forthwith be more determined in his guardianship; and, in proportion as he succeeds, in that very proportion does he invite the approach of the Spirit of all grace, and will have the benefit of his power and workmanship upon the soul. "Grieve not the Spirit," says the apostle, and quench not his influences. Just as the disciple mortifies the pride, or the peevishness, or any of those evil propensities which are the works of the flesh, does he take away those topics of offence and discouragement which keep the Holy Ghost at a distance—does he remove the obstacles that lie in the way of his operation—does he begin, in fact, that good work which the Spirit will carry on—does he cease to do evil, and learn from the Spirit, and is enabled by the

Spirit, to do well. Thus it is, that he is made to advance from one degree of grace to another; and, instead of mystically waiting for an illumination and a power which he has no reason to believe will ever come upon him, idly looking forward to it in the shape of a sudden and auspicious visitation, let him enter, even now, on that course of new obedience, along which a disciple is conducted from the first elements of his spiritual education, to those brightest accomplishments which a saint on earth has ever realized.

There is one very immediate result that comes out even of this earlier part in the work of self-examination. If one be led, from the discovery of what is evil, to combat it, then is he led to be diligent, that he may be found without spot, and blameless in the great day of reckoning. He is working out his salvation from sin. He embarks on the toils of the Christian warfare. He fights the good fight, and forthwith makes a busy work a strenuous conflict of his sanctification. And he should not linger another day, ere he commence in good earnest this purification for eternity. He should remember that the terms which the Bible employs, are all expressive of rapidity:—To *flee* from the coming wrath; and flee from those evil affections which war against the soul; and *make haste* to keep the commandments; and tarry not in turning to Christ, and turning from all his iniquities.

There is nothing of which the earnest and aspiring disciple is more ready to complain, than that, while all alive to the sense of his corruptions, he is scarcely sensible of the work of grace that should be going on. The motions of the flesh are most distinct and most discernible, while, on the question of the Spirit's operation upon his heart, he is in a state of utter blindnes and bewilderment. He feels weighed down by the remaining carnality of his nature, while he feels not within him any growing positive conformity to the character of one of heaven's children. There is a more galling sensation than before of all about him that is evil, but often without anything to alleviate the oppressive thought, by the consciousness of much that is truly and unequivocally good. And thus a discomfort in the mind of many an incipient Christian —an apprehension that he has not yet tasted of the Spirit of God, nor has any part in that which is called the seal of his redemption, the earnest of his inheritance.

Now it may comfort him to know, that this very dejection of his heart may, of itself, be a fruit and an evidence of the Holy Ghost having been at work with him. This painful sensibility to what is wrong, may evince him to be now at the place of breaking forth, now at the very turning point of his regeneration. The very heaviness under which he labors, is perhaps as decisive a symptom as can be given, that he is now bending his upward way along the career of an arduous, but still advancing sanctification. When the Psalmist complained of himself that his heart clave unto the dust, and therefore prayed that God would quicken him, he perhaps did not know that the quickening process had begun with him already, and that even now he was actuated by the spirit of grace and of supplication—that ere the lineaments of an affirmative excellence could come visibly forth upon his character, it was for him to supplicate the new heart and the right spirit, because for all these things God must be inquired after, and that he now had come the length of this inquiry—that so far from this despondency being a proof of the destitution of the Spirit, one of the first fruits of the Spirit, in the apostle and his converts, was that they groaned inwardly, being burdened, being now touched as they never were before with a feeling of their infirmities. To the now renovated eye, the soil that is upon the character is more painfully offensive than before; and to the now softened heart, there is the grief of a moral tenderness because of sin, that was before unfelt, but now is nearly overwhelming. The dead know not that they are dead, and not till the first moments of their returning life, can they be appalled by the feeling of the death-like paralysis that is upon them. And let us not then refuse that, even under the burden of a heavy-laden consciousness, the reviving Spirit may be there—that like as with the chaos of matter, when he moved upon the face of the waters he troubled and bedimmed them, so his first footsteps on the face of the moral chaos may thicken that turbulence which he is at length to harmonize—that the sense of darkness which now oppresses the soul, is in fact the first gleaming of that light by which the darkness is made visible —and the horror by which it is seized upon, when made to feel itself in a sepulchre of corruption, is its first awakening from the death of trespasses and sins, the incipient step of its spiritual resurrection.

But, while we allege this as a word in season to the weary, yet should we like a higher class of evidences, than this for the workmanship of God upon our souls—we desire a substantive proof of our regeneration, a legible impress of some one feature that only belongs to the new man in Christ Jesus, and might be an encouraging token to ourselves, that on the groundwork of our old nature the true spiritual portrait is begun, and is now actually in progress towards that last finish, by which it is prepared for a place among the courts or palaces of the upper sanctuary. It is at this point in the series of our self-examinations, that we are met with its most formidable difficulties. It is easy to take account of the visible doings. It is easy to take account also of the evil or corrupt affections. But to find a positive encouragement in the sense that we have of the now gracious affections of a renovated heart—to descry in embryo the rudiments of a moral excellence that is yet unformed—to catch the lineaments of that heavenly image, which is but faintly noticeable under that aspect of vigor and entireness which still belongs to the old and the ordinary man —this is found by many an anxious inquirer to be indeed a baffling enterprise; and though he believe in Christ, he has been known to wander in darkness, and even in distress, because short in all his weary endeavors after the full assurance of hope unto the end.

Now, ere we suggest anything for the guidance of his inquiries, let us remind him of the difference which there is between the assurance of hope and the assurance of faith. The one is a certainty, founded on the observation that he has taken of himself—and because he perceives, from the real work of grace which has been performed on him, that he is indeed one of the children of God. The other is a certainty, founded on the cognizance that he has taken of God's promises—and because he perceives, both from their perfect honesty, and from the ample unrestricted scope of their address to all and to every of our species, that he may venture a full reliance for himself on the propitiation that has been made for the world, on the righteousness that is unto all and upon all who believe. Now the assurance of a hope is far, and may be very far posterior to the assurance of faith. One cannot too soon or too firmly put his confidence in the word of God. The truth of his sayings is a matter altogether distinct from the truth of our own sanctification. Even now, upon the warrant of God's testimony, may the sinner come into acceptance, and take up his resting-place under the canopy of Christ's mediatorship, and rejoice in this, that the blood which he has shed cleanseth from all sin; and, with a full appropriation of this universal specific to his own guilt, may he stand with a free and disburdened conscience before the God whom he has offended. He may do all this even now, and still it is but the assurance of faith, the confidence of one who is looking outwardly on the truth and the meaning of God's declarations. The assurance of hope is the confidence that one feels in looking inwardly to the graces of his own character, and should only grow with his spiritual growth, and strengthen with his spiritual strength. But we may be certain of this, that the best way by which we attain to the latter assurance, is to cherish the former assurance even to the uttermost. Let us send forth our believing regards on the Sun of Righteousness, and thus shall we admit into our bosom both a heat that will kindle its gracious affections, and a light that will make them manifest. In other words, let us be ever employed in the work of faith, and this will not only shed a brightness over the tablet of the inner man, but it is the direct method by which to crowd and to enrich it with the best materials for the work of self-examination.

Let us now, then, specify a few of these materials, some of the fruits of that Spirit which is given to those who believe, and on the production and growth of which within them, they may attain the comfortable assurance in themselves, that they are indeed the workmanship and the husbandry of God. Some, perhaps, may be led to recognize their own likeness in one or other of the features that we delineate, and so to rejoice. Others may be left in uncertainty, or even be made certain that, as yet, they have no part nor lot in the matter of personal Christianity. But whatever their conclusions may be, we would commit all of them alike back again to the exercise of that faith, out of which alone it is that the spiritual life can be made to germinate, or that it can at all be upheld.

The experience of one man varies exceedingly from that of another; but we would say, in the first place, that one very general mark of the Spirit's work upon the soul, is the new taste and the new intelligence wherewith a man now looks upon the Bible Let that which before was dark and mystical now appear light unto him—let a power and a preciousness be felt in its clauses, which he wont altogether to miss in his old mechanical style of perusing it—let there be a sense and a weight of significancy in those passages which at one time escaped his discernment—let there now be a conscious adaptation between its truths and the desires or the necessities of his own heart—and, above all, let there be a willing consent and coalescence with such doctrines as before revolted him into antipathy, or at least were regarded with listless unconcern—in particular, let there be a responding testimony from within to all which that book affirms of the sin of our nature—and, instead of the Saviour being lightly esteemed, let his name and his righteousness have all the power of a restorative upon the soul. Should these things meet in the experience of any one, then it needs not that there should either be a voice or a vision to convince us, that upon him the Holy Spirit of God has had its sure, though its silent operation—that he has been plying him with his own instrument, which is the word of God—that it is he, and not nature, who has evolved from the pages of Scripture this new light on the mind of the inquirer—that, apart altogether from the visitation of a trance, or a glory, or the inspiration of a whisper at midnight, there has been a wisdom from above, which, through the medium of the written testimony, has addressed itself to the man's understanding; and the perception which he now has of the things of faith, is not the fruit of his own spontaneous and unaided faculties—that the things which he has gotten from Scripture, he in fact has gotten from the Spirit, who holds no other communication with the human mind than through the avenues of God's unalterable record,—they may be the very things which the natural man cannot receive, and neither can he know them, because they are spiritually discerned.

But, while we hope that this may fall on some with an impression of comfort, it is right that it should be accompanied with a caution. Though true that there may be a desire for the sincere milk of the word, which evinces one to be a new-born babe; yet it is alse true, that one may have tasted of the good word of God, and finally apostatize. And lest any who have been so far enlightened by the Holy Ghost should be of this hopeless and ill-fated class, let us warn them to take heed lest they fall—lest they fall more particularly from the evidence on which we have now been expatiating—lest they lose their relish, and so give up their reading of the Bible—lest the first love wherewith they at one time regarded it should again be dissipated, and that spiritual appetite which they felt for the essential simplicities of the Gospel, should at length decline into a liking for heartless controversy or for barren speculation. Let such strive, by prayer and by a constant habit of perusal, to retain, yea, to augment their interest in the Bible. Let them be assured, that a kindredness in their heart with its flavor and its phraseology, is a kindredness with heaven—nor do we know a better evidence of preparation for the sanctuary, than when the very truths and very words of the sanctuary are precious.

But again, another fruit of the Spirit, another sign, as it were, of his workmanship upon the soul, is that we love the brethren, or, in other words, that we feel a savor which perhaps we had not formerly in the converse, and society, and whole tone and habit of spiritual men. The advantage of this test is, that it is so very palpable—that with all the obscurity which rests on the other evidences, this may remain a most distinct and discernible one, and be often the solitary vestige, as it were, of our translation into a new moral existence, when some dark cloud hath overshadowed all the other lineaments of that epistle which the Spirit hath graven upon our hearts. "Hereby know we," says the apostle, "that we have passed from death unto life, even that we love the brethren." One may remember when he had no such love—when he nauseated the very air and aspect of sacredness—when the world was his kindred atmosphere, and worldly men the only companionship in which he could breathe with native comfort or satisfaction—when the very look and language of the peculiar people were an offence to him, and he gladly escaped from a clime so ungenial with his spirits, to the glee of earthly fellowship, to the bustle of earthly employments. Was it so with him at one time, and is it different now? Has he a taste for association with the pious? Does he relish the unction that is upon their feelings, and has he now a tact of congeniality with that certain breath and spirit of holiness, the sensation of which, at one time, disgusted him? Then verily we have good hopes of a good, and, we trust a decisive transformation—that this taste for converse with the saints on earth, is a foretaste to his full enjoyment of their converse in heaven—that there is a gradual attemperment going on of his character here to the condition which awaits him there—that he has really been translated from the kingdom of this world to the kingdom of light—and if it be true, that to consummate our preparation for hell, we must not only do those things which are worthy of death, but have pleasure in those that do them, we cannot understand why a growing affection on his part for the servants of God should not be sustained, as the comfortable token that he is indeed under a process of ripening for the delights and the services of the upper sanctuary.

But there is room here too for a caution. There may be a sentimental homage rendered even by a mere child of nature to Christianity. There may be a taste for certain aspects of sacredness, without any kindred delight in sacredness itself. There may be a predilection of the fancy for some of the Spirit's graces, which yet may augur no more one's own vital participation in that Spirit, than would his relish for the simplicity of Quaker attire, or his admiration of that Moravian village, where his eye rested on so many peaceful tenements, and his ear was ravished at intervals with the voice of melting psalmody. And more recently, there is the excitement of all that modern philanthropy which requires combination, and eloquence, and adventure, and busy management; and thus an enjoyment in religious societies, without enjoyment in religion. There may go on animating bustle in the outer courts, to interest and engage the man who had no sympathy whatever with those chosen few that now were admitted among the glories of the inner temple. And, therefore, let us try if, apart from the impulse of all these externals, we indeed breathe in a kindred atmosphere, when we sit down in close and intimate fellowship with a man of prayer—if we can listen with eager and heart-felt satisfaction to the experience of an humble Christian—if, when sitting by the bed of the dying believer, we can sympathize with the hope that beams in his eye, and the peace that flows through his heart like a mighty river—or if, when the Bible is upon his lips, and he tries to quote those simple sayings by which the departing spirit is sustained, we can read and rejoice along with him.

But, without attempting anything like a full enumeration of the Spirit's fruits, we shall advert to the one that perhaps of all others is most indispensable—a growing tenderness because of sin—a quicker moral alarm at its most distant approaches, at its slightest violations of purity or rectitude—a susceptibility of conscience, which exposes one to distress from what was before unheeded, and left no infliction of remorse behind it—an utter loathing at that which was, perhaps, at one time liked or laughed at, even the song, and the oath, and the gross indelicacy of profane or licentious companionship—a sensitive and high-minded recoil from the lying artifices of trade—and withal, the pain of a violated principle at those Sabbath desecrations in which we wont to rejoice. This growing hostility to sin, and growing taste of its bitterness, are truly satisfying evidences of the Spirit's operation; and more particularly, when they stand associated with a just estimation of the Gospel. Did the candidate for heaven still think that heaven was won by obedience, then we might conceive him urged on to the warfare of all his energies against the power of moral evil, by the terrors of the law. But, thinking as he does, that heaven is a gift, and not a recompense, it delivers, from all taint of mercenary legalism, both his love of what is good, and his hatred of what is evil. It stamps a far purer and more generous character on his resistance to sin. It likens his abhorrence of it more to the kindred feature in the character of God, who cannot do that which is wrong, not because he feareth punishment, but because he hateth iniquity. To hate the thing for which vengeance would pursue us, is not so disinterested as to hate the thing of which forgiveness hath been offered; and so, if two men were exhibited to notice, one of them under the economy of works, and the other under the economy of grace, and both equally assiduous in the conflict with sin, we should say of the latter, that he gave far more satisfying proof than the former, of a pure and God-like antipathy to evil; and that he, of the two, was more clearly the subject of that regenerating process under which man is renewed, after the image of his Creator, in righteousness and in true holiness.

We might have given a larger exemplification of the Spirit's fruits, and of those topics of self-examination, by which the Christian might rightly estimate the true state of his spiritual character; but instead of multiplying our illustrations, would we refer our readers to the following profound and searching Treatise of Dr. Owen, "On the Grace and Duty of being Spiritually Minded." Dr. Owen's is indeed a venerated name, which stands in the first rank of those noble worthies who adorned a former period of our country and of our church. He was a star of the first magnitude in that bright constellation of luminaries, who shed a light and a glory over the age in which they lived; and whose genius, and whose writings, continue to shed their radiance over succeeding generations. The following Treatise of Dr. Owen holds a distinguished rank among the voluminous writings of this celebrated author; and it is characterized by a forcible application of truth to the conscience—by a depth of experimental feeling—an accuracy of spiritual discernment into the intimacies and operations of the human mind—and a skill in exploring the secrecies of the heart, and the varieties of affection, and the ever-shifting phases of character,—which render this admirable Treatise not less a test, than a valuable guide to the honest inquirer, in his scrutiny into the real state of his heart and affections. Amidst the difficulties and perplexities which beset the path of the sincere inquirer, in the work of self-examination, he will be greatly aided in this important search by the attentive and serious perusal of this Treatise. In it he will find, in minute delineation, the varied tastes and emotions, of affection and of feeling, which belong to either class of the carnal or spiritually minded; and in the faithful mirror which it holds up to the view, he cannot fail to discern, most vividly reflected, the true portraiture of his own character.

But it is not merely as a test of character, that the value of this precious Treatise is to be estimated. By his powerful expositions of the deceitfulness of the human heart, he endeavors to disturb that delusive repose into which men are betrayed in regard to futurity, under the guise of a regular outward observance of the duties of religion, and a fair external conformity to the decencies of life, while the principle of ungodliness pervades the whole heart and affections. And here his faithful monitions may be profitable to those who, insensible to the spirituality and extent of the divine law, are also insensible of their fearful deficiency from its lofty requirements—who have never been visited with a conviction that the principle of love to God, which has its seat in the affections of the heart, is an essential and indispensable requisite to all acceptable obedience—and that, destitute of a relish and delight in spiritual things, and with a heart that nauseates the sacredness of holy and retired communings with God, whatever be their external decencies, or outward conformities to the divine law, they still are exposed to the charge and the doom of being carnally minded.

But this Treatise contains a no less important delineation of the state of heart, in those who have become the humble and earnest aspirants after heaven, and are honestly cultivating those affections of the renewed heart, and those graces of the Christian character, which form the indispensable preparation for the delights and the employments of the upper sanctuary. He marks with graphic accuracy the tastes and the tendencies of the new creature; and most instructive to the Christian disciple is it to learn, from one so experimentally acquainted with the hidden operations of the inner man, what are the characteristic graces of the Spirit, and resemblances of the divine nature, that are engraven on his soul, by which, amidst all the short-comings and infirmities of his nature, not yet fully delivered from the bondage of corruption, he may, nevertheless. have the comfort and the evidence that he is spiritually minded.

And one principal excellence of this useful Treatise is, to guard the believer against the insidiousness and power of those spiritual enemies with which he has to contend—with the deceitfulness of the heart, the natural and unresisted current of whose imaginations is only vanity and evil continually—with the ensnaring and besetting urgencies of worldly things, into whose presence his duties and avocations will unavoidably introduce him—with the ever busy temptations of the adversary of souls, to retain or to recover the spirit which is striving to enter in at the strait gate. And, sheathed in the Christian panoply, he reminds him of the struggle he must hold, of the watchfulness he must exercise, and of the constant and persevering warfare he must maintain with them in his earthly journey, ere he can reach the Jerusalem above. In these spiritual tactics, Dr. Owen was most profoundly skilled;

and it is profitable to be instructed in the guardianship of the heart against its own treacheries, and against those evil influences which war against the soul—which hinder the outset, or are adverse to the growth, of the spiritual life—and which so often grieve the Spirit, and lead him to withdraw his gracious operations, so indispensable for giving the truth a sanctifying influence over his mind. And no less important is it to be instructed in the means for the successful cultivation of the Christian life; and, by an entire renunciation of self-righteousness, and even of dependence on grace already received—by casting himself, in the confidence of faith and of prayer, on Him who is all his strength and all his sufficiency—by being strong in the grace of the Lord Jesus—and by abounding in the exercises of faith and of love, of watchfulness and of prayer, of obedience and of dependence on the Spirit of truth, to maintain an evergrowing conformity to the divine image, and to press onwards in his earnest aspirings to reach those higher altitudes in the divine life, which will fit him for a high place among the companies of the celestial.

On the means for the attainment of these higher graces of the spiritual life we might have expatiated; but we must close our remarks, without almost one glance on the heights of Christian experience; or those loftier attainments after which we are ever doomed to aspire, but with hardly ever the satisfaction, in this world, of having realized them; or those high and heavenly communions, which fall to the lot of men of such a sublime sacredness as Dr. Owen; but for which it would almost appear indispensable, that the spiritual life should be nourished in solitude, and that, afar from the din, and the broil, and the tumult of ordinary life, the candidate for heaven should give himself up to the discipline of prayer and of constant watchfulness. It is, indeed, most humbling to reflect on the paltry ascent that we have yet made along that hidden walk, by which it is that the pilgrim travels towards Zion; and how short we are, after years of something like earnestness, from those untouched and untrodden eminences which are so far above us. Where, may most of us ask, is our delight in God? Where is the triumph of our serene confidence in him, over all the anxieties of this world? Where that love to Christ, and that rejoicing in him, which, in the days of primitive Christianity, were so oft exemplified by the believer, and formed, in truth, the hourly and familiar habits of his soul? Do we count it enough, in the absence of this world's smiles, and when the whole sunshine of them is withdrawn from the bosom, that we still live amid the bright anticipations of Faith, with the protection of heaven above us, and the full radiance of eternity before us? These are the achievements to which we must yet press onward; and perhaps the sensation of a pressure that has yet been ineffectual, is the only evidence, in regard to them, which we can allege of a gracious tendency at least, if not of a gracious acquirement. It is the proof, not of what we have reached, but of the direction in which we are moving. And, at the very time that we are burdened under a feeling of our deficiencies, may we, from our constant inclination to surmount them, and our many unsatisfied longings after the standard that is higher than ourselves, gather some perhaps of our most precious and legitimate encouragements in the work of self-examination.

INTRODUCTORY ESSAY

TO

CALL TO THE UNCONVERTED;

NOW OR NEVER; AND FIFTY REASONS.

BY RICHARD BAXTER.

Having already introduced to the notice of our readers one of Richard Baxter's most valuable Treatises,* in the Essay to which we adverted to the character and writings of this venerable author, we count it unnecessary at present to make any allusion to them, but shall confine our remarks to the subject of the three Treatises which compose the present volume, namely, "A Call to the Unconverted to turn and live;" "Now or Never;" and "Fifty Reasons why a Sinner ought to turn to God this Day without delay."

These Treatises are characterized by all that solemn earnestness, and urgency of appeal, for which the writings of this much admired author are so peculiarly distinguished. He seems to look upon mankind solely with the eyes of the Spirit, and exclusively to recognize them in their spiritual relations, and in the great and essential elements of their immortal being. Their future destiny is the all-important concern which fills and engrosses his mind, and he regards nothing of any magnitude but what has a distinct bearing on their spiritual and eternal condition. His business, therefore, is always with the conscience, to which, in these Treatises, he makes the most forcible appeals, and which he plies with all those arguments which are fitted to awaken the sinner to a deep sense of the necessity and importance of immediate repentance. In his "Call to the Unconverted," he endeavors to move them by the most touching of all representations, the tenderness of a beseeching God waiting to be gracious, and not willing that any should perish; and while he employs every form of entreaty, which tenderness and compassion can suggest, to allure the sinner to "turn and live," he does not shrink from

* The Saints' Everlasting Rest, with an Essay by Mr. Erskine.

forcing on his convictions those considerations which are fitted to alarm his fears, the terrors of the Lord, and the wrath, not merely of an offended Lawgiver, but of a God of love, whose threatenings he disregards, whose grace he despises, and whose mercy he rejects. And aware of the deceitfulness of sin in hardening the heart, and betraying the sinner into a neglect of his spiritual interests, he divests him of every refuge, and strips him of every plea for postponing his preparation for eternity. He forcibly exposes the delusion of convenient seasons, and the awful infatuation and hazard of delay; and knowing the magnitude of the stake at issue, he urges the sinner to immediate repentance, as if the fearful and almost absolute alternative were "Now or Never." And to secure the commencement of such an important work against all the dangers to which procrastination might expose it, he endeavors to arrest the sinner in his career of guilt and unconcern, and resolutely to fix his determination on "turning to God this day without delay."

There are two very prevalent delusions on this subject, which we should like to expose; the one regards the *nature*, and the other the *season* of repentance; both of which are pregnant with mischief to the minds of men. With regard to the first, much mischief has arisen from mistakes respecting the meaning of the term *repentance*. The word repentance occurs with two different meanings in the New Testament; and it is to be regretted, that two different words could not have been devised to express these. This is chargeable upon the poverty of our language; for it is to be observed, that in the original Greek the distinction in the meanings is pointed out by a distinction in the words. The employment of one term to denote two different things has the effect of confounding and misleading the understanding; and it is much to be wished, that every ambiguity of this kind were cleared away from that most interesting point in the process of a human soul, at which it turns from sin unto righteousness, and from the power of Satan unto God.

When, in common language, a man says, "I repent of such an action," he is understood to say, "I am sorry for having done it." The feeling is familiar to all of us. How often does the man of dissipation prove this sense of the word repentance, when he awakes in the morning, and, oppressed by the languor of his exhausted faculties, looks back with remorse on the follies and profligacies of the night that is past? How often does the man of unguarded conversation prove it, when he thinks of the friend whose feelings he has wounded by some hasty utterance which he cannot recall? How often is it proved by the man of business, when he reflects on the rash engagement which ties him down to a losing speculation? All these people would be perfectly understood when they say, "We repent of these doings." The word repentance so applied is about equivalent to the word regret.

There are several passages in the New Testament where this is the undoubted sense of the word repentance. In Matt. xxvii. 3, the wretched Judas repented himself of his treachery; and surely, when we think of the awful denunciation uttered by our Saviour against the man who should betray him, that it were better for him if he had not been born, we will never confound the repentance which Judas experienced with that repentance which is unto salvation.

Now here lies the danger to practical Christianity. In the above-cited passage, to repent is just to regret, or to be sorry for; and this we conceive to be by far the most prevailing sense of the term in the English language. But there are other places where the same term is employed to denote that which is urged upon us as a duty—that which is preached for the remission of sins—that which is so indispensable to sinners, as to call forth the declaration from our Saviour, that unless we have it, we shall all likewise perish. Now, though repentance, in all these cases, is expressed by the same term in our translation as the repentance of mere regret, it is expressed by a different term in the original record of our faith. This surely might lead us to suspect a difference of meaning, and should caution us against taking up with that, as sufficient for the business of our salvation, which is short of saving and scriptural repentance. There may be an alternation of wilful sin, and of deeply-felt sorrow, up to the very end of our history—there may be a presumptuous sin committed every day, and a sorrow regularly succeeding it. Sorrow may imbitter every act of sin—sorrow may darken every interval of sinful indulgence—and sorrow may give an unutterable anguish to the pains and the prospects of a death-bed. Couple all this with the circumstance that sorrow passes, in the common currency of our language, for repentance, and that repentance is made, by our Bible, to lie at the turning point from a state of condemnation to a state of acceptance with God, and it is difficult not to conceive that much danger may have arisen from this, leading to indistinct views of the nature of repentance, and to slender and superficial conceptions of the mighty change which is implied in it.

We are far from saying that the eye of Christians is not open to this danger—and that the vigilant care of Christian authors has not been employed in averting it. Where will we get a better definition of repentance unto life than in our Shorter Catechism? by which the sinner is represented not merely as grieving, but, along with his grief and hatred of sin, as turning from it unto God with full purpose, and endeavor after new obedience. But the mischief is, that the word repent has a common meaning different from the theological; that wherever it is used, this common meaning is apt to intrude itself, and exert a kind of habitual imposition upon the understanding; that the influence of the single word carries it over the influence of the lengthened explanation—and thus it is that, for a steady progress in the obedience of the Gospel, many persevere, to the end of their days, in a wretched course of sinning and of sorrowing, without fruit and without amendment.

To save the practically mischievous effect arising from the application of one term to two different things, one distinct and appropriate term has been suggested for the saving repentance of the New Testament. The term repentance itself has been restricted to the repentance of mere sorrow, and is made equivalent to regret; and, for the other, able translators have adopted the word reformation. The one is expressive of sorrow for our past conduct; the other is expressive of our renouncing it. It denotes an actual turning from the habits of life that we are sorry for. Give us, say they, a change from bad deeds to good deeds, from bad habits to good habits, from a life of wickedness to a life of conformity to the requirements of heaven, and you give us reformation.

Now there is often nothing more unprofitable than a dispute about words: but if a word has got into common use, a common and generally understood meaning is attached to it; and if this meaning does not just come up to the thing which we want to express by it, the application of that word to that thing has the same misleading effects as in the case already alluded to. Now, we have much the same kind of exception to allege against the term reformation, that we have alleged against the term repentance. The term repentance is inadequate—and why? because, in the common use of it, it is equivalent to regret, and regret is short of the saving change that is spoken of in the New Testament. On the very same principle, we count the term reformation to be inadequate. We think that, in common language, a man would receive the appellation of a reformed man upon the mere change of his outward habits, without any reference to the change of mind and of principle which gave rise to it. Let the drunkard give up his excesses—let the backbiter give up his evil speakings—let the extortioner give up his unfair charges—and we would apply to one and to all of them, upon the mere change of their external doings, the character of reformed men. Now, it is evident that the drunkard may give up his drunkenness, because checked by a serious impression of the injury he has been doing to his health and his circumstances. The backbiter may give up his evil speaking, on being made to perceive that the hateful practice has brought upon him the contempt and alienation of his neighbors. The extortioner may give up his unfair charges, upon taking it into calculation that his business is likely to suffer by the desertion of his customers. Now, it is evident, that though in each of these cases there has been what the world would call reformation, there has not been scriptural repentance. The deficiency of this term consists in its having been employed to denote a mere change in the deeds or in the habits of the outward man; and if employed as equivalent to repentance, it may delude us into the idea that the change by which we are made meet for a happy eternity is a far more slender and superficial thing than it really is. It is of little importance to be told that the translator means it only in the sense of a reformed conduct, proceeding from the influence of a new and a right principle within. The common meaning of the word will, as in the former instance, be ever and anon intruding itself, and get the better of all the formal cautions, and all the qualifying clauses of our Bible commentators.

But, will not the original word itself throw some light upon this important question? The repentance which is enjoined as a duty—the repentance which is unto salvation—the repentance which sinners undergo when they pass to a state of acceptance with God from a state of enmity against him—these are all one and the same thing, and are expressed by one and the same word in the original language of the New Testament. It is different from the word which expresses the repentance of sorrow; and if translated according to the parts of which it is composed, it signifies neither more nor less than *a change of mind.* This of itself is sufficient to prove the inadequacy of the term reformation—a term which is often applied to a man upon the mere change of his conduct, without ever adverting to the state of his mind, or to the kind of change in motive and in principle which it has undergone. It is true that there can be no change in the conduct without some change in the inward principle. A reformed drunkard, before careless about health or fortune, may be so far changed as to become impressed with these considerations; but this change is evidently short of that which the Bible calls repentance towards God. It is a change that may, and has taken place in many a mind, when there was no effectual sense of the God who is above us, and of the eternity which is before us. It is a change, brought about by the prospect and the calculation of many advantages; and, in the enjoyment of these advantages, it hath its sole reward. But it is not done unto God, and God will not accept of it as done unto him. Reformation may signify nothing more than the mere surface-dressing of those decencies, and proprieties, and accomplishments, and civil and prudential duties, which, however fitted to secure a man's acceptance in society, may, one and all of them, consist with a heart alienated from God, and having every principle and affection of the inner man away from him. True, it is such a change as the man will reap benefit from, as his friends will rejoice in, as the world will call reformation; but it is not such a change as will make him meet for heaven, and is deficient in its import from what our Saviour speaks of when he says, "I tell you nay, except ye repent, ye shall all likewise perish."

There is no single word in the English language which occurs to us as fully equal to the faithful rendering of the term in the original. Renewedness of mind, however awkward a phrase this may be, is perhaps the most nearly expressive of it. Certain it is, that it harmonizes with those other passages of the Bible where the process is described by which saving repentance is brought about. We read of being transformed by the renewing of our minds, of the renewing of the Holy Ghost, of being renewed in the spirit of our minds. Scriptural repentance, therefore, is that deep and radical change whereby a soul turns from the idols of sin and of self unto God, and devotes every movement of the inner and the outer man, to the captivity of his obedience. This is the changè which, whether it be expressed by one word or not in the English language, we would have you well to understand; and reformation or change in the outward conduct, instead of being saving and scriptural repentance, is what, in the language of John the Baptist, we would call a fruit meet for it. But if mischief is likely to arise, from the want of an adequate word in our language, to that repentance which is unto salvation, there is one effectual preservative against it—a firm and consistent exhibition of the whole counsel and revelation of God. A man who is well read in his New Testament, and reads it with docility, will dismiss all his meagre conceptions of repentance, when he comes to the following statements:—"Except a man be born again, he cannot see the kingdom of God." "Except ye be converted, and become as little children, ye shall not enter into the kingdom of heaven." "If any man have not the Spirit of Christ, he is none of his." "The carnal mind is enmity against God; and if ye live after the flesh, ye shall die: but if ye, through the Spirit, do mortify the deeds of the body, ye shall live." "By the washing of regeneration ye are saved." "Be not then conformed to this world, but be ye transformed by the renewing of your minds." Such are the terms employed to describe the process by which the soul of man is renewed unto repentance; and, with your hearts familiarized to the mighty import of these terms, you will carry with you an effectual guarantee against those false and flimsy impressions, which are so current in the world, about the preparation of a sinner for eternity.

Another delusion which we shall endeavor to expose, is a very mischievous application of the parable of the laborers in the vineyard, contained in the twentieth chapter of the Gospel by Matthew. The interpretation of this parable, the mischief and delusion of which we shall endeavor to lay open, is, that it relates to the call of individuals, and to the different periods in the age of each individual at which this call is accepted by them. We almost know nothing more familiar to us, both in the works of authors, and in the conversation of private Christians, than when the repentance of an aged man is the topic, it is represented as a case of repentance at the eleventh hour of the day. We are far from disputing the possibility of such a repentance, nor should those who address the message of the Gospel ever be restrained from the utterance of the free call of the Gospel, in the hearing of the oldest and most inveterate sinner whom they may meet with. But what we contend for, is, that this is not the drift of the parable. The parable relates to the call of nations, and to the different periods in the age of the world at which this call was addressed to each of them, and not, as we have already observed, to the call of individuals, and to the different periods in the age of each individual, at which this call is accepted by them.* It is not true that the laborers who began to work in the vineyard on the first hour of the day, denote those Christians who began to remember their Creator, and to render the obedience of the faith unto his Gospel with their first and earliest education. It is not true, that they who entered into this service on the third hour of the day, denote those Christians, who after a boyhood of thoughtless unconcern about the things of eternity, are arrested in the season of youth, by a visitation of seriousness, and betake themselves to the faith and the following of the Saviour who died for them. It

* To render our argument more intelligible, we shall briefly state what we conceive to be the true explanation of the parable. In the verses preceding the parable, Peter had stated the whole amount of the surrender that he and his fellow disciples had made by the act of following after Jesus; and it is evident, that they all looked forward to some great temporal remuneration—some share in the glories of the Israelitish monarchy—some place of splendor or distiction under the new government, which they imagined was to be set up in the world; and they never conceived anything else, than that in this altered state of things, the people of their own country were to be raised to high pre-eminence among the nations which had oppressed and degraded them. It was in the face of this expectation, that our Saviour uttered a sentence, which we meet oftener than once among His recorded sayings in the New Testament, "Many that are first shall be last, and the last shall be first." The Israelites, whom God distinguished at an early period of the world, by a revelation of Himself, were first invited in the doing of His will (which is fitly enough represented by working in His vineyard) to the possession of His favor, and the enjoyment of His rewards. This offer to work in that peculiar vineyard, where God assigned to them a performance, and bestowed on them a recompense, was made to Abraham and to his descendants at a very early period in history; and a succession of prophets and righteous men were sent to renew the offer, and the communications from God to the world, followed the stream of ages, down to the time of the utterence of this parable. And a few years afterwards, the same offers, and the same invitations, were addressed to another people; and at this late period, at this eleventh hour, the men of those countries which had never before been visited by any authoritative call from heaven, had this call lifted up in their hearing, and many Gentiles accepted that everlasting life, of which the Jews counted themselves unworthy. And as to the people of Israel, who valued themselves so much on their privileges—who had turned all the revelations, by which their ancestors had been honored, into a matter of distinction and of vain security—who had ever been in the habit of eyeing the profane Gentiles with all that contempt which is laid upon outcasts, this parable received its fulfilment at the time when these Gentiles, by their acceptance of the Saviour, were exalted to an equal place among the chiefest favorites of God; and these Jews, by their refusal of Him, had their name rooted out from among the nations—and those first and foremost in all the privileges of religion, are now become the last. Now this we conceive to be the real design of the parable. It was designed to reconcile the minds of the disciples to that part of the economy of God, which was most offensive to their hopes and to their prejudices. It asserted the sovereignty of the Supreme Being in the work of dispensing His calls and His favors among the people whom He had formed. It furnished a most decisive and silencing reproof to the Jews, who were filled with envy against the Gentiles; and who, even those of them that embraced the Christian profession, made an obstinate struggle against the admission of those Gentiles into the church on equal terms with themselves.

is not true, that they who were hired on the sixth and ninth hours, denote those Christians, who, after having spent the prime of their youthful vigor in alienation from God, and perhaps run out some mad career of guilt and profligacy, put on the Christianity along with the decencies of their sober and established manhood. Neither is it true, that the laborers of the eleventh hour, the men who had stood all day idle, represent those aged converts who have put off their repentance to the last—those men who have renounced the world when they could not help it—those men who have put on Christianity, but not till they had put on their wrinkles—those men who have run the varied stages of depravity, from the frivolous unconcern of a boy, and the appalling enormities of misled and misguided youth, and the deep and determined worldliness of middle age, and the clinging avarice of him, who, while with slow and tottering footsteps he descends the hill of life, has a heart more obstinately set than ever on all its interests, and all its sordid accumulations, but who, when death taps at the door, awakens from his dream, and thinks it now time to shake away his idolatrous affections from the mammon of unrighteousness.

Such are the men who, after having taken their full swing of all that the world could offer, and of all that they could enjoy of it, defer the whole work of preparation for eternity to old age, and for the hire of the laborers of the eleventh hour, do all that they can in the way of sighs, and sorrows, and expiations of penitential acknowledgment. What! will we offer to liken such men to those who sought the Lord early, and who found him? Will we say that he who repents when old, is at all to be compared to him, who bore the whole heat and burden of a life, devoted throughout all its stages to the glory and the remembrance of the Creator? Who, from a child, trembled at the word of the Lord, and aspired after a conformity to all his ways? Who, when a young man, fulfilled that most appropriate injunction of the apostle, "Be thou strong?" Who fought it with manly determination against all the enemies of principle by which he was surrounded, and spurned the enticements of vicious acquaintances away from him; and nobly stood it out, even though unsupported and alone, against the unhallowed contempt of a whole multitude of scorners; and with intrepid defiance to all the assaults of ridicule, maintained a firmness, which no wile could seduce from the posts of vigilance; and cleared his unfaltering way through all the allurements of a perverse and crooked generation. Who, even in the midst of a most withering atmosphere on every side of him, kept all his purposes unbroken, and all his delicacies untainted. Who, with the rigor of self-command, combined the softening lustre which a pure and amiable modesty sheds over the moral complexion of him who abhors that which is evil, and cleaves to that which is good, with all the energy of a holy determination. Can that be a true interpretation, which levels this youth of promise and of accomplishment, with his equal in years, who is now prosecuting every guilty indulgence, and crowns the audacity of his rebellion by the mad presumption, that ere he dies, he shall be able to propitiate that God, on the authority of all whose calls, and all whose remonstrances, he is now trampling? Or follow each of them to the evening of their earthly pilgrimage—will you say that the penitent of the eleventh hour, is at all to be likened to him who has given the whole of his existence to the work and the labor of Christianity? to him who, after a morning of life adorned with all the gracefulness we have attempted to describe, sustains through the whole of his subsequent history such a high and ever brightening example, that his path is like the shining light, which shineth more and more unto the perfect day; and every year he lives, the graces of an advancing sanctification form into a richer assemblage of all that is pure, and lovely, and honorable, and of good report; and when old age comes, it brings none of the turbulence or alarm of an unfinished preparation along with it—but he meets death with the quiet assurance of a man who is in readiness, and hails his message as a friendly intimation; and as he lived in the splendor of ever-increasing acquirements, so he dies in all the radiance of anticipated glory.

This interpretation of the parable cannot be sustained; and we think, that, out of its own mouth, a condemnation may be stamped upon it. Mark this peculiarity. The laborers of the eleventh hour are not men who got the offer before, but men who for the first time received a call to work in the vineyard; and they may therefore well represent the people of a country, who, for the first time, received the overtures of the Gospel. The answer they gave to the question, Why stand you so long idle? was, that no man had hired them. We do not read of any of the laborers of the third, or sixth, or ninth hours, refusing the call at these times, and afterwards rendering a compliance with the evening call, and getting the penny for which they declined the offer of working several hours, but afterwards agreed when the proposal was made, that they should work one hour only. They had a very good answer to give, in excuse for their idleness. They never had been called before. And the oldest men of a Pagan country have the very same answer to give, on the first arrival of Christian missionaries amongst them. But we have no part nor lot in this parable. We have it not in our power to offer any such apology. There is not one of us who can excuse the impenitency of the past, on the plea that no man had called us. This is a call that has been sounded in our ears, from our very infancy. Every time we have seen a Bible on our shelves, we have had a call. Every time we have heard a minister in the pulpit, we have had a call. Every time we have heard the generous invitation, "Ho, every one that thirsteth, come ye unto the waters," we have had a solemn, and what ought to have been a most impressive, call. Every time that a parent has plied us with a good advice, or a neighbor come forward with a friendly persuasion, we have had a call. Every time that the Sabbath bell has rung for us to the house of God, we have had a call. These are all so many distinct and repeated calls. These are past events in our life, which rise in judgment against us, and remind us, with a justice of argument that there is no evading, that we have no right whatever to the privileges of the eleventh hour.

This, then, is the train to which we feel ourselves directed by this parable. The mischievous interpretation which has been put upon it, has wakened up our alarms, and set us to look at the delusion which it fosters, and, if possible, to drag out to the light of day, the fallacy which lies in it. We should like to reduce every man to the feeling of the alternative of repentance now, or repentance never. We should like to flash it upon your convictions, that, by putting the call away from you now, you put your eternity away from you. We should like to expose the whole amount of that accursed infatuation which lies in delay. We should like to arouse every soul out of its lethargies, and giving no quarter to the plea of a little more sleep, and a little more slumber, we should like you to feel as if the whole of your future destiny hinged on the very first movement to which you turned yourselves.

The work of repentance must have a beginning; and we should like you to know, that, if not begun to-day, the chance will be less of its being begun to-morrow. And if the greater chance has failed, what hope can we build upon the smaller?—and a chance too that is always getting smaller. Each day, as it revolves over the sinner's head, finds him a harder, and a more obstinate, and a more helplessly enslaved sinner, than before. It was this consideration which gave Richard Baxter such earnestness and such urgency in his "Call." He knew that the barrier in the way of the sinner's return, was strengthened by every act of resistance to the call which urges it. That the refusal of this moment hardened the man against the next attack of a Gospel argument that is brought to bear upon him. That if he attempted you now, and he failed, when he came back upon you, he would find himself working on a more obstinate and uncomplying subject than ever. And therefore it is, that he ever feels as if the present were his only opportunity. That he is now upon his vantage ground, and he gives every energy of his soul to the great point of making the most of it. He will put up with none of your evasions. He will consent to none of your postponements. He will pay respect to none of your more convenient seasons. He tells you, that the matter with which he is charged, has all the urgency of a matter in hand. He speaks to you with as much earnestness as if he knew that you were going to step into eternity in half an hour. He delivers his message with as much solemnity as if he knew that this was your last meeting on earth, and that you were never to see each other till you stood together at the judgment-seat. He knew that some mighty change must take place in you, ere you be fit for entering into the presence of God; and that the time in which, on every plea of duty and of interest, you should bestir yourselves to secure this, is the present time. This is the distinct point he assigns to himself; and the whole drift of his argument, is to urge an instantaneous choice of the better part, by telling you how you multiply every day the obstacles to your future repentance, if you begin not the work of repentance now.

Before bringing our Essay to a close, we shall make some observations on the mistakes concerning repentance which we have endeavored to expose, and adduce some arguments for urging on the consciences of our readers the necessity and importance of immediate repentance.

1. The work of repentance is a work which must be done ere we die; for, unless we repent, we shall all likewise perish. Now, the easier this work is in our conception, we will think it the less necessary to enter upon it immediately. We will look upon it as a work that may be done at any time, and let us, therefore, put it off a little longer, and a little longer. We will perhaps look forward to that retirement from the world and its temptations which we figure old age to bring along with it, and falling in with the too common idea, that the evening of life is the appropriate season of preparation for another world, we will think that the author is bearing too closely and too urgently upon us, when, in the language of the Bible, he speaks of "*to-day*," while it is called to-day, and will let us off with no other repentance than repentance "*now*,"—seeing that now only is the accepted time, and now only the day of salvation, which he has a warrant to proclaim to us. This dilatory way of it is very much favored by the mistaken and very defective view of repentance which we have attempted to expose. We have somehow or other got into the delusion, that repentance is sorrow, and little else; and were we called to fix upon the scene where this sorrow is likely to be felt in the degree that is deepest and most overwhelming, we would point to the chamber of the dying man. It is awful to think that, generally speaking, this repentance of mere sorrow is the only repentance of a death-bed. Yes! we will meet with sensibility deep enough and painful enough there—with regret in all its bitterness—with terror mustering up its images of despair, and dwelling upon them in all the gloom of an affrighted imagination; and this is mistaken, not merely for the drapery of repentance, but for the very substance of it. We look forward, and we count upon this—that the sins of a life are to be expunged by the sighing and the sorrowing of the last days of it. We should give up this wretchedly superficial notion of repentance, and cease, from this

moment, to be led astray by it. The mind may sorrow over its corruptions at the very time that it is under the power of them. To grieve because we are under the captivity of sin is one thing—to be released from that captivity is another. A man may weep most bitterly over the perversities of his moral constitution; but to change that constitution is a different affair. Now, this is the mighty work of repentance. He who has undergone it is no longer the servant of sin. He dies unto sin, he lives unto God. A sense of the authority of God is ever present with him, to wield the ascendency of a great master-principle over all his movements—to call forth every purpose, and to carry it forward through all the opposition of sin and of Satan, into accomplishment. This is the grand revolution in the state of the mind which repentance brings along with it. To grieve because this work is not done, is a very different thing from the doing of it. A death-bed is the very best scene for acting the first; but it is the very worst for acting the second. The repentance of Judas has often been acted there. We ought to think of the work in all its magnitude, and not to put it off to that awful period when the soul is crowded with other things, and has to maintain its weary struggle with the pains, and the distresses, and the shiverings, and the breathless agonies of a death-bed.

2. There are two views that may be taken of the way in which repentance is brought about, and whichever of them is adopted, delay carries along with it the saddest infatuation. It may be looked upon as a step taken by man as a voluntary agent, and we would ask you, upon your experience of the powers and the performances of humanity, if a death-bed is the time for taking such a step? Is this a time for a voluntary being exercising a vigorous control over his own movements? When racked with pain, and borne down by the pressure of a sore and overwhelming calamity? Surely the greater the work of repentance is, the more ease, the more time, the more freedom from suffering, is necessary for carrying it on; and, therefore, addressing you as voluntary beings, as beings who will and who do, we call upon you to seek God early that you may find him—to haste, and make no delay in keeping his commandments. The other view is, that repentance is not a self-originating work in man, but the work of the Holy Spirit in him as the subject of its influences. This view is not opposite to the former. It is true that man wills and does at every step in the business of his salvation: and it is as true that God works in him so to will and to do. Take this last view of it then. Look on repentance as the work of God's Spirit in the soul of man, and we are furnished with a more impressive argument than ever, and set on higher vantage for urging you to stir yourselves, and set about it immmediately. What is it that you propose? To keep by your present habits, and your present indulgencies—and build yourselves up all the while in the confi-

dence that the Spirit will interpose with His mighty power of conversion upon you, at the very point of time that you have fixed upon as convenient and agreeable? And how do you conciliate the Spirit's answer to your call then? Why, by doing all you can to grieve, and to quench, and to provoke Him to abandon you now. Do you feel a motion towards repentance at this moment? If you keep it alive, and act upon it, good and well. But if you smother and suppress this motion, you resist the Spirit—you stifle His movements within you: it is what the impenitent do day after day, and year after year—and is this the way for securing the influences of the Spirit, at the time that you would like them best? When you are done with the world, and are looking forward to eternity because you cannot help it? God says, "My Spirit will not always strive with the children of men." A good and a free Spirit He undoubtedly is, and as a proof of it, He is now saying, "Let whosoever will, come and drink of the water of life freely." He says so now, but we do not promise that He will say so with effect upon your death-beds, if you refuse Him now. You look forward then for a powerful work of conversion being done upon you, and yet you employ yourselves all your life long in raising and multiplying obstacles against it. You count upon a miracle of grace before you die, and the way you take to make yourselves sure of it, is to grieve and offend Him while you live, who alone can perform the miracle. O what cruel deceits will sin land us in! and how artfully it pleads for a "little more sleep, and a little more slumber; a little more folding of the hands to sleep." We should hold out no longer, nor make not such an abuse of the forbearance of God: we will treasure up wrath against the day of wrath if we do so. The genuine effect of his goodness is to lead to repentance; let not its effect upon us be to harden and encourage ourselves in the ways of sin. We should cry now for the clean heart and the right spirit; and such is the exceeding freeness of the Spirit of God, that we will be listened to. If we put off the cry till then, the same God may laugh at our calamity, and mock when our fear cometh.

3. Our next argument for immediate repentance is, that we cannot bring forward, at any future period of your history, any considerations of a more prevailing or more powerfully moving influence than those we *may* bring forward at this moment. We can tell you now of the terrors of the Lord. We can tell you now of the solemn mandates which have issued from his throne—and the authority of which is upon one and all of you. We can tell you now, that though, in this dead and darkened world, sin appears but a very trivial affair—for everybody sins, and it is shielded from execration by the universal countenance of an entire species lying in wickedness—yet it holds true of God, what is so emphatically said of him, that he cannot be mocked, nor will he endure it that you should riot in the impunity of your wilful

resistance to him and to his warnings. We can tell you now, that he is a God of vengeance; and though, for a season, he is keeping back all the thunders of it from a world that he would like to reclaim unto himself, yet, if you put all his expostulations away from you, and will not be reclaimed, these thunders will be let loose upon you, and they will fall on your guilty heads, armed with tenfold energy, because you have not only defied his threats, but turned your back on his offers of reconciliation. These are the arguments by which we would try to open our way to your consciences, and to awaken up your fears, and to put the inspiring activity of hope into your bosoms, by laying before you those invitations which are addressed to the sinner, through the peace-speaking blood of Jesus, and in the name of a beseeching God, to win your acceptance of them. At no future period can we address arguments more powerful and more affecting than these. If these arguments do not prevail upon you, we know of none others by which a victory over the stubborn and uncomplying will can be accomplished, or by which we can ever hope to beat in that sullen front of resistance wherewith you now so impregnably withstand us. We feel that, if any stout-hearted sinner shall rise from the persual of these Treatises with an unawakened conscience, and give himself to an act of wilful disobedience, we feel as if, in reference to him, we had made our last discharge, and it fell powerless as water spilt on the ground, that cannot be gathered up again. We would not cease to ply him with our arguments, and tell him, to the hour of death, of the Lord God, merciful and gracious, who is not willing that any should perish, but that all should turn to him, and live. And if in future life we should meet him at the eleventh hour of his dark and deceitful day—a hoary sinner, sinking under the decrepitude of age, and bending on the side of the grave that is open to receive him—even then we would testify the exceeding freeness of the grace of God, and implore his acceptance of it. But how could it be away from our minds that he is not one of the evening laborers of the parable? We had met with him at former periods of his existence, and the offer we make him now we made him then, and he did what the laborers of the third, and sixth, and ninth hours of the parable did not do—he rejected our call to hire him into the vineyard; and this heartless recollection, if it did not take all our energy away from us, would leave us little else than the energy of despair. And therefore it is, that we speak to you now as if this was our last hold of you. We feel as if on your present purpose hung all the preparations of your future life, and all the rewards or all the horrors of your coming eternity. We will not let you off with any other repentance than repentance now; and if this be refused now, we cannot, with our eyes open to the consideration we have now urged, that the instrument we make to bear upon you afterwards is not more powerful than we are wielding now, coupled with another consideration which we shall insist upon, that the subject on which the instrument worketh, even the heart of man, gathers, by every act of resistance, a more uncomplying obstinacy than before; we cannot, with these two thoughts in our mind, look forward to your future history, without seeing spread over the whole path of it the iron of a harder impenitency—the sullen gloom of a deeper and more determined alienation.

4. Another argument, therefore, for immediate repentance is, that the mind which resists a present call or a present reproof undergoes a progressive hardening towards all those considerations which arm the call of repentance with all its energy. It is not enough to say, that the instrument by which repentance is brought about, is not more powerful to-morrow than it is to-day; it lends a most tremendous weight to the argument, to say further, that the subject on which this instrument is putting forth its efficiency, will oppose a firmer resistance to-morrow than it does to-day. It is this which gives a significancy so powerful to the call of "To-day while it is to-day, harden not your hearts;" and to the admonition of "Knowest thou not, O man, that the goodness of God leadeth thee to repentance; but after, thy hardness and impenitent heart treasurest up wrath against the day of wrath and revelation of the righteous judgments of God?" It is not said, either in the one or in the other of these passages, that, by the present refusal, you cut yourself off from a future invitation. The invitation may be sounded in your hearing to the last half hour of your earthly existence, engraved in all those characters of free and gratuitous kindness which mark the beneficent religion of the New Testament. But the present refusal hardens you against the power and tenderness of the future invitation. This is the fact in human nature to which these passages seem to point, and it is the fact through which the argument for immediate repentance receives such powerful aid from the wisdom of experience. It is this which forms the most impressive proof of the necessity of plying the young with all the weight and all the tenderness of earnest admonition, that the now susceptible mind might not turn into a substance harder and more uncomplying than the rock which is broken in pieces by the powerful application of the hammer of the word of God.

The metal of the human soul, so to speak, is like some material substances. If the force you lay upon it do not break it, or dissolve it, it will beat it into hardness. If the moral argument by which it is plied now, do not so soften the mind as to carry and to overpower its purposes, then, on another day, the argument may be put forth in terms as impressive—but it falls on a harder mind, and, therefore, with a more slender efficiency. If the threat, that ye who persist in sin shall have to dwell with the devouring fire, and to lie down amid everlasting burnings, do not alarm you out of your iniquities from this very moment, then the same threat may be again cast out, and the same appalling circumstances of terror be thrown around it, but it is all discharged on a soul hardened by its inurement to the thunder of denunciations already uttered, and the urgency of menacing threatenings already poured forth without fruit and without efficacy. If the voice of a beseeching God do not win upon you now, and charm you out of your rebellion against him, by the persuasive energy of kindness, then let that voice be lifted in your hearing on some future day, and though armed with all the power of tenderness it ever had, how shall it find its entrance into a heart sheathed by the operation of habit, that universal law, in more impenetrable obstinacy? If, with the earliest dawn of your understanding, you have been offered the hire of the morning laborer and have refused it, then the parable does not say that you are the person who at the third, or sixth, or ninth, or eleventh hour, will get the offer repeated to you. It is true, that the offer is unto all and upon all who are within reach of the hearing of it. But there is all the difference in the world between the impression of a new offer, and of an offer that has already been often heard and as often rejected—an offer which comes upon you with all the familiarity of a well-known sound that you have already learned how to dispose of, and how to shut your every feeling against the power of its gracious invitations—an offer which, if discarded from your hearts at the present moment, may come back upon you, but which will have to maintain a more unequal contest than before, with an impenitency ever strengthening, and ever gathering new hardness from each successive act of resistance. And thus it is that the point for which we are contending is not to carry you at some future period of your lives, but to carry you at this moment. It is to work in you the instantaneous purpose of a firm and a vigorously sustained repentance; it is to put into you all the freshness of an immediate resolution, and to stir you up to all the readiness of an immediate accomplishment—it is to give direction to the very first footstep you are now to take, and lead you to take it as the commencement of that holy career, in which all old things are done away, and all things become new—it is to press it upon you, that the state of the alternative, at this moment, is "now or never"—it is to prove how fearful the odds are against you, if now you suffer the call of repentance to light upon your consciences, and still keep by your determined posture of careless, and thoughtless, and thankless unconcern about God. You have resisted to-day, and by that resistance you have acquired a firmer metal of resistance against the power of every future warning that may be brought to bear upon you. You have stood your ground against the urgency of the most earnest admonitions, and against the dreadfulness of the most terrifying menaces. On that ground you have fixed yourself more immovably than before; and though on some future day the same spiritual thunder be made to play around you, it will not shake you out of the obstinacy of your determined rebellion.

It is the universal law of habit, that the feelings are always getting more faintly and feebly impressed by every repetition of the cause which excited them, and that the mind is always getting stronger in its active resistance to the impulse of these feelings, by every new deed of resistance which it performs; and thus it is, that if you refuse us now, we have no other prospect before us than that your cause is every day getting more desperate and more irrecoverable, your souls are getting more hardened, the Spirit is getting more provoked to abandon those who have so long persisted in their opposition to his movements. God, who says that his Spirit will not always strive with the children of men, is getting more offended. The tyranny of habit is getting every day a firmer ascendency over you; Satan is getting you more helplessly involved among his wiles and his entanglements; the world, with all the inveteracy of those desires which are opposite to the will of the Father, is more and more lording it over your every affection.

And what, we would ask, what is the scene in which you are now purposing to contest it, with all this mighty force of opposition you are now so busy in raising up against you? What is the field of combat to which you are now looking forward, as the place where you are to accomplish a victory over all those formidable enemies whom you are at present arming with such a weight of hostility, as, we say, within a single hairbreadth of certainty, you will find to be irresistible? O the bigness of such a misleading infatuation! The proposed scene in which this battle for eternity is to be fought, and this victory for the crown of glory is to be won, is a death-bed. It is when the last messenger stands by the couch of the dying man, and shakes at him the terrors of his grizly countenance, that the poor child of infatuation thinks he is to struggle and prevail against all his enemies; against the unrelenting tyranny of habit—against the obstinacy of his own heart, which he is now doing so much to harden—against the Spirit of God who perhaps long ere now has pronounced the doom upon him, "He will take his own way, and walk in his own counsel; I shall cease from striving, and let him alone"—against Satan, to whom every day of his life he has given some fresh advantage over him, and who will not be willing to lose the victim on whom he has practised so many wiles, and plied with success so many delusions. And such are the enemies whom you, who wretchedly calculate on the repentance of the eleventh hour, are every day mustering up in greater force and formidableness against you; and how can we think of letting you go, with any other repentance than the repentance of the precious moment that is now passing over you, when we look forward to the horrors of that impressive scene, on which you propose to win the prize of immortality, and to contest it single-handed and alone, with all the weight of opposition which you have accumulated against yourselves—a death-bed—a languid, breathless, tossing, and agitated death-bed; that scene of feebleness, when the poor man cannot help himself to a single mouthful—when he must have attendants to sit around him, and watch his every wish, and interpret his every signal, and turn him to every posture where he may find a moment's ease, and wipe away the cold sweat that is running over him—and ply him with cordials for thirst, and sickness, and insufferable languor. And this is the time, when occupied with such feelings, and beset with such agonies as these, you propose to crowd within the compass of a few wretched days, the work of winding up the concerns of a neglected eternity!

5. But it may be said, if repentance be what you represent it, a thing of such mighty import, and such impracticable performance, as a *change of mind*, in what rational way can it be made the subject of a precept or an injunction? you would not call upon the Ethiopian to change his skin—you would not call upon the leopard to change his spots; and yet you call upon us to change our minds. You say, "Repent;" and that too in the face of the undeniable doctrine, that man is without strength for the achievement of so mighty an enterprise. Can you tell us any plain and practicable thing that you would have us to perform, and that we may perform to help on this business? This is the very question with which the hearers of John the Baptist came back upon him, after he had told them in general terms to repent, and to bring forth fruits meet for repentance. He may not have resolved the difficulty, but he pointed the expectations of his countrymen to a greater than he for the solution of it. Now that Teacher has already come, and we live under the full and the finished splendor of His revelation. O that the greatness and difficulty of the work of repentance, had the effect of shutting you up into the faith of Christ! Repentance is not a paltry, superficial reformation. It reaches deep into the inner man, but not too deep for the searching influences of that Spirit which is at His giving, and which worketh mightily in the hearts of believers. You should go then under a sense of your difficulty to Him. Seek to be rooted in the Saviour, that you may be nourished out of His fulness, and strengthened by His might. The simple cry for a clean heart, and a right spirit, which is raised from the mouth of a believer, brings down an answer from on high, which explains all the difficulty and overcomes it. And if what we have said of the extent and magnitude of repentance, should have the effect to give a deeper feeling than before of the wants under which you labor; and shall dispose you to seek after a closer and more habitual union with Him who alone can supply them, then will our call to repent have indeed fulfilled upon you the appointed end of a

preparation for the Saviour. But recollect now is your time, and now is your opportunity, for entering on the road of preparation that leads to heaven. We charge you to enter this road at this moment, as you value your deliverance from hell, and your possession of that blissful place where you shall be forever with the Lord—we charge you not to parry and to delay this matter, no, not for a single hour—we call on you by all that is great in eternity—by all that is terrifying in its horrors—by all that is alluring in its rewards—by all that is binding in the authority of God—by all that is condemning in the severity of His violated law, and by all that can aggravate this condemnation in the insulting contempt of His rejected Gospel;—we call on you by one and all of these considerations, not to hesitate but to flee—not to purpose a return for to-morrow, but to make an actual return *this very day*—to put a decisive end to every plan of wickedness on which you may have entered—to cease your hands from all that is forbidden—to turn them to all that is required—to betake yourselves to the appointed Mediator, and receive through Him, by the prayer of faith, such constant supplies of the washing of regeneration and renewing of the Holy Ghost, that, from this moment, you may be carried forward from one degree of grace unto another, and from a life devoted to God here, to the elevation of a triumphant, and the joys of a blissful eternity, hereafter.

INTRODUCTORY ESSAY

TO THE

CHRISTIAN'S DAILY WALK

IN HOLY SECURITY AND PEACE.

BY THE REV. HENRY SCUDDER.

It is well known, that though Christianity was persecuted by the Jews from the very outset of its promulgation, it was some time before this religion provoked the wrath or the intolerance of the Romans. The truth is, that on the part of the government at Rome, there was a very general connivance at religion in all its numerous varieties. And the reason of this was, that under the system of Paganism no one variety, or modification, was thought to exclude another. Each country was conceived to have its local deity—and each element of Nature to have its own pervading spirit—and each new god of the provinces over which they extended their power, offered no disturbance to the habits of their previous theology, but was easily disposed of by the bare addition of another name to the catalogue. At this rate there was no conflict and no interference. By learning the religion of another country, they simply extended their acquaintance with the world of supernatural beings; just as by the conquest of that country, they extended their acquaintance with the visible and the peopled world around them. In such a capacious and elastic creed as that of Paganism, there was room enough for all the superstitions of all people. The sincerest possible homage for the gods of one territory, admitted of an homage equally sincere for the gods of another territory. Nay, by the same solemn act of worship, they may, each and all of them, have been included, at one time, in one general expression of faith and reverence. And this is the whole amount of the boasted tolerance of antiquity.

We may easily perceive, how, in exception to this general spirit, Christianity, from being the object of lenity, and even of occasional protection by the Roman power, soon became the victim of its fiercest persecutions. For a few years, its character and pretensions were not distinctly understood. It seems in truth to have been regarded as a mere speciality of Judaism, and even though it had partaken of all the narrowness of the parent religion from which it sprung, yet would it have continued to share in the same immunities, had it maintained the same indolent contempt for the idolatry of the surrounding nations. But when it made a farther development of its spirit; when it began to be felt in the force of its active proselytism; when it was seen, that it not only admitted of no compromise with the articles of another faith, but that it aimed at the overthrow of every religion then in the world; when men at last perceived, that instead of quietly taking its place among their much-loved superstitions, it threatened the destruction of them all,—then, though truth and argument were its only weapons, did the success with which they were wielded as much offend and terrify the world as if they hadbeen the weapons of ordinary warfare; and though Jesus Christ would have been welcomed to a share of divine honors along with other deities, were his followers resisted even unto blood, when they advanced his claim, not to be added to the list of those deities, but utterly to discard and dethrone them.

Now it may be thought that there can be nothing analogous to this process in the present day, and within the limits of Christendom. But the truth is, that what obtained among the literal idolaters of a former age, is still more strikingly exemplified by those of the present, who, in the spiritual and substantial sense of the word, are chargeable with the whole guilt of idolatry. There may be among us the most complacent toleration for a mitigated and misconceived Christianity, while there is no toleration whatever for the real Christianity of the New Testament. So long as it only claims an assigned place in the history of man, while it leaves the heart of man in the undisturbed possession of all its native and inborn propensities—so long as it confines itself to the demand of a little room for its Sabbaths and its decencies, while it leaves the general system of human life to move as before, at the impulse of those old principles which have characterized the mind of man throughout all the generations of the world—so long as it exacts no more than an occasional act of devotion, while it suffers the objects of wealth and fame, and temporal enjoyments, to be prosecuted with as intense and habitual a devotion as ever—above all, so long as the services which it imposes are not other than the services which would have been rendered at all events to the idol of interest, or the idol of reputation,—then Christianity, so far from being the object of any painful recoil on the part of man, is looked upon, by very many in society, as a seemly and most desirable appendage to the whole mass of their other concerns. It is admitted to fill up what would be felt as a disagreeable vacuity. The man would positively be out of comfort, and out of adjustment, without it. Meagre as his Christianity may be, the omission of certain of its rites, and certain of its practices, would give him uneasiness. It has its own place in the round of his affairs, and though what remains of the round is described very much in the way it would have been, had there been no Christianity in the matter, yet would the entire and absolute want of it make him feel as if the habit of his life had undergone a mutilation, as if the completeness of his practical system had suffered violence.

And thus it is, that Christianity, in a moderate and superficial form, may be gladly acquiesced in, while Christianity after it comes to be understood in the magnitude of its pretensions may be utterly nauseated. When it offers to disturb the deep habit and repose of nature—when instead of taking its place among the other concerns and affections of a disciple, it proceeds to subordinate them all—when instead of laying claim to a share of human life, it lays claim to the sovereignty over it—when not satisfied with the occasional homage of its worshippers, it casts a superintending eye over their hearts, and their business, and their lives, and pronounces of every desire which is separate from the will and the glory of God, that it is tainted with the sin of idolatry,—when it thus proposes to search and to spiritualize, with the view of doing away all that is old, and of making everything new, ancient Rome was never more in arms for her gods, than modern humanity is in arms for her obstinate habits, and her longing propensities. And yet if Christianity would tolerate nature, nature would in return tolerate Christianity. She would even offer to her the compromise of many hours and many services. She would build temples to her honor, and be present at all her sacraments. We behold an exhibition of this sort every day among the decent and orderly professors of our faith; and it is not till this antipathy be provoked by a full disclosure of the spirit and exactions of the Gospel, that the whole extent of that antipathy is known.

We may expatiate on the social or civil virtues, such as justice, for example, without coming into collision with the antipathies of nature. Even worldliness herself may listen with an approving ear to the most rigid demonstration of this virtue. For though justice be a required offering at the shrine of the Gospel of Jesus Christ, it may also be, and it often is, both a required and a rendered offering at the shrine of honor and interest. The truth is, that a man may have his heart fully set upon the world; and a portion on this side of time may be the object in which he rests, and upon which all his desires do terminate; and yet he may not feel himself painfully thwarted at all by the demand of an honesty the most strict and inviolable. A compliance with this demand may not break up his other idolatries in the least. In the practice of a truth and an integrity as unlimited as any law of God can impose, may he be borne rejoicingly along on the full tide of prosperity; and by every new accession to his wealth, be multiplying the ties which fasten him to the world. There is many an intense votary of gain, who will bear to be told that he should be perfectly fair and upright in the prosecution of it, and who will not bear to be told, that the very intensity of this prosecution marks him out as a child of earthliness—makes it manifest, that he is striking all his roots into a perishable foundation—proves him to be the victim of a disease, the symptoms of which lie much deeper than in his external conduct—proves him, in short, to be unsound at heart, and that, with a principle of life, which will survive the dissolution of all that is visible, he, in strenuously laboring after its fancied interest, is fast heaping upon it the wretchedness of eternity. That morality which barely ventures to regulate the path that he is now walking towards the objects of this world's ambition, he will tolerate and applaud. But the morality which denounces the ambition, the morality which would root out the very feelings that hurry him onwards in the path; which bids him mortify his affections for all that this world has to offer; which tells him not to set his mind on any created thing, but to set his mind on the Creator, and to have nothing farther to do with the world, than as a place of passage and preparation for an abode of blessedness in heaven,—the morality which tells him to cease his attachment from those things with which he has linked the ruling desires, and all the practical energies of his existence,—such morality as this, he will resist with as much strenuousness as he would do a process of annihilation. The murderer who offers to destroy his life will not be shrunk from in greater horror, or withstood in a firmer spirit of determination, than the moralist who would force from him the surrender of affections which seem to be interwoven with his very being, and the indulgence of which has conferred upon it all the felicities of which he has yet experienced it to be capable. A revolution so violent looks as repulsive as death to the natural man; and it is also represented under the image of death in the Scripture. To cease from the desire of the eye, is to him a change as revolting as to have the light of the eye extinguished. To cease from the desire of the flesh, is to crucify the flesh. To cease from the pride of life, is to renounce the life of nature altogether. In a word, to cease from the desire of the old man, is not to turn, but to destroy him. It is to have him buried with Christ in baptism. It is to have him planted together with Christ in the likeness of his death. It is not to impress a movement, but to inflict a mortification.

But there is another very general misapprehension of peculiar Christianity, as if it dispensed with service on the part of its disciples; as if it had set aside the old law of works, and thus superseded the necessity of working altogether; as if, in some way or other, it substituted a kind of lofty mysticism in the place of that plain obedience which is laid down for us by the ten commandments—sweeping away from its new dispensation the moralities and observances of the old one, and leaving nothing in their place but a kind of cabalistic orthodoxy known only to the initiated few, and with the formal profession of which they look mightily safe and mightily satisfied.

Now we cannot become acquainted with Christianity without perceiving, that after the transition has been made from the old economy to the new, there is a service. This transition is signified by images expressive of the total change that is made in our relations and circumstances, when we pass from Nature to the Gospel—as the dissolution of a first marriage, and the entrance upon a second—a dying and a coming alive again—a release from one master, even the law, who formerly had the dominion over us, and an engagement with another Master, even God, under whom we are to bring forth the fruit that is lovely and acceptable in his sight—all marking the very wide dissimilarity that there is between the two states, and that when we have crossed the line of separation between them, we have indeed got into another region, and breathe another atmosphere altogether from what we did formerly—and yet there continues to subsist a service, performed, no doubt, in a different spirit and in a different manner from what it was before, but still a service. And indeed it is quite manifest, from the apostolical writings, that the life of a Christian is expected to be all in a glow with labor and exertion, and manifold activity—not spent in the indolence of mystic contemplation, but abounding in work, and work too persevered in with immovable steadfastness, and emanating from a zeal that ever actuates and ever urges on to the performance of it. This is the habit of a disciple upon earth, and it would appear to be his habit even after he is transported into heaven: "There thy servants serve thee." So that whether we look to those years which are preparatory to our entering upon the inheritance of glory, or to the eternity in which the inheritance itself is enjoyed, still we find that under the economy of grace there is a busy, strenuous and ever-doing service. It is not in fact by exemption from service, but by the new spirit and principle wherewith the service is actuated, that the economy of grace stands distinguished from the economy of the law. We are delivered from the law, not that we should be delivered from the service of obedience, but that we should serve in newness of spirit, and not in the oldness of the letter.

The *first* remark that we offer, in the way of illustrating this distinction between the new and the old economy, is, that there is indeed a very different spirit between two men, one of whom works, and that most incessantly, from the love that he bears to the wages, and the other of whom works, and that just as incessantly, from the unconquerable taste and affection which he has for the work itself. It is conceivable that the servant of some lordly proprietor, is remunerated according to the quantity of game which he fetches from the woods and the wastes of that ample domain over which he expatiates—and that, under the dominion of a thirst for lucre, from morning to night he gives himself up to the occupation of a hunter. But it is conceivable of another, that the romance, and adventure, and spirit-stirring hazard and variety of such a life, are enough to fasten him, and that most intently, throughout all the hours of the day, on the very same enterprise: and thus, with a perfect likeness in the outward habit, may there be in the habit and desire of the heart a total and entire dissimilarity. The service is the same, but the spirit of the service is widely dissimilar. And this may just hold as true of the commandments of a heavenly, as of an earthly master. The children of Israel looked to the decalogue that was graven upon tablets of stone, and they knew that on their observation of it depended their possession of the land of Canaan, the prosperity of their seasons, and the peace of their habitations from the inroad of desolating enemies. The love they bore to their inheritance, is love quite distinguishable from the love they bore to that task which formed the tenor upon which they held it—and it may just be as distinguishable in him who seeks to purchase, by his obedience, the heavenly Canaan set forth to us in the Gospel, and who thinks of this Canaan as a place of splendor, and music, and physical gratifications; who looks onward in fancy to its groves and its palaces, or who, as it stands revealed in perspective before him, on the other side of death, figures it at large as a place of general and boundless enjoyment, where pleasure ever circulates in tides of ecstacy, and at least there is a secure and everlasting escape from the horrors of the place of condemnation. A love for the work, and a love for the wages, are here two different affections altogether; and to reduce them to one, you must present heaven in its true character, as a place of constant and unwearied obedience. The Israelite toiling in drudgery at the work of his ordinances, and that for the purpose of retaining his pleasant home on this side of death—or the formal Christian walking the routine of his ordinances, and that for the purpose of reaching a pleasant home on the other side of death—either of them breathes a totally different spirit from the man who finds the work of obedience itself to be indeed a way of pleasantness and a path of delight to him—who, without the bidding of his master at all, would, at the bidding of his own heart, just move his hand as his master would have him to do—who is in his element when engaged in the work of the commandments, and to whose renovated taste and faculties of moral sensation, the atmosphere of righteousness is in itself the atmosphere of peace and joy.

The services of two men may thus externally be the same, and yet, the spirit that animates the one and the other may just be as different, as sordidness and sacredness are wide of one another. And a difference of spirit is everything to Him with whom we have to do. He sits at the head of a moral empire; and affection, and motive, and design are mainly the things of which he takes cognizance; and discerner of hearts as he is, it is the desire of the heart upon which he fastens his chief attention; and in his judgment it is indeed a question most decisive of character whether this actuating desire be love to the work of righteousness, or only love to wages distinct from the work. To serve in the first of these ways, is to serve in the newness of the spirit. To serve in the second of them, is to serve in the oldness of the letter; and the substitution of the one for the other, is that great achievement which the Gospel personally and substantially makes on every man who truly embraces it. It forms as essential a part of that covenant which God makes with the believer as does the forgiveness of sin. "This is the covenant, that I will put my law in his heart." When it only stood graven upon a table of stone, obedience was an affair of labor. But when the law is graven on the fleshly tablet of the heart, obedience is an affair of love. It is everything to God whether his service be felt by us as the drudgery of a task, or as the delight of a congenial employment —whether we painfully toil while it is doing, and are glad when it is over—or are pleasantly carried along, through all the steps of it, as of a work that we rejoice in—whether it be our hope, that after the keeping of the commandments there will be a great reward, or it be our happy and present sensation, that in the keeping of the commandments there is a great reward. It is this which distinguishes the service of our heavenly from that of our earthly master. With the latter, after the work cometh the payment, and the doing of the one is a distinct and separate thing from the enjoyment of the other. With the former, after the work done now, cometh more work; after the business of using aright a few talents, cometh the business of ruling and of managing aright many things; after the praises and the services of the church below, come the higher services, and more ecstatic praises, of the sanctuary above; after the uprightness and the piety of our present lives, cometh the busy obedience of that everlasting land, which is called the land of uprightness: and how totally different then must the newness of the spirit be from the oldness of the letter; when, as with the one, the work is gone through from the mere impulse of a subsequent reward, which selfishness may seize upon and appropriate to its own indulgence, so with the other, the work is gone through from the impulse of its own native charm on the heart and taste of the delighted laborer, who is happy in the service of God here, and whose brightest anticipation is, that he shall be translated into the capacity of serving him more constantly and perfectly hereafter!

But, *secondly*, to do the work, because of the love that we bear to the wages which our master gives us, is doing service in a spirit altogether different from that of doing the work because of the love that we bear to the master himself. The set and tendency of the heart are altogether distinct in the one case from what they are in the other. In the first way of it, the heart is set altogether upon its own gratification, and is under the entire dominion of selfishness. In the second way of it, it is set upon the gratification of another. The two are as distinct, as is the spirit of him who labors with the reluctancy of a slave, from the spirit of him who labors with the devotedness of a generous and disinterested friend. Now this is a change in the style and spirit of our obedience, which it is the object of Christianity to accomplish. To serve God in the oldness of the letter is to eke out by tale and by measure a certain quantity of work which we offer as an incense to his selfishness—and in return for which he deals forth upon us a certain amount of wages as a regale to our selfishness back again—with as little of heart all the while in such an exchange, as there is in the trafficking of mutual interest and mutual jealousy which takes place at a market. There is no love between the parties—no generous delight in ministering the one to the satisfaction of the other—no pleasure in pleasing—no play of a reciprocal affection—no happiness felt from the single circumstance that happiness has been bestowed. If this be the character of our service under the law, there is surely room for a mighty amendment, or rather for a total revolution, of its spirit and principle under the Gospel. Even had the law been rigidly kept on the side of man, and its stipulations been rigidly fulfilled on the part of God, there would still have been a coldness, and a distance, and a tone of demand, on the one side, and a certain fearfulness of diffidence and distrust on the other, under such an economy. But the fact is, that the law has not been kept; and the consciousness of this perpetually overhung the wretched aspirant after a righteousness which he never could fulfil; and he felt himself haunted at every footstep of his exertions by the fear of a reckoning; still floundering however, while failing at every turn, and burdened in spirit by a heavy and enfeebling sense of despair. And that Being can never be regarded with joy, who is regarded with jealousy. It is impossible that terror and love can both exist in the same bosom towards the same God. It is not in sentient nature to feel affection towards one of whom we are afraid—and so long as the controversy of tasks undone, and accounts unpaid, remained unsettled, there was no getting at affection towards God. In these circumstances, the history of man might be covered all over with deeds of religiousness, but the heart of man is bound as to its desires and likings, with a spell that is utterly indissoluble. It is frozen out of all love, by the chilling influences of distrust, and terror, and guilty consciousness. He would fain propitiate God for the sake of his own security, but he is too much engrossed with himself to care about pleasing God for the mere sake of pleasing Him. Obedience on such a principle as this, appears to lie at an immeasurable distance from him; and if he does persevere in a sort of religious drudgery, done in bondage, and done in slavish apprehension, it is the obedience of one who serves in the oldness of the letter, but not in the newness of the spirit.

Now to effect a transformation in the spirit of our services was one great design of the Gospel of Jesus Christ—not to abolish service, we should remark, but to animate it with a new principle—not to set aside work, but to strike out a pure and copious fountain in the heart, from which it might emanate—to strike off those fetters by which the moral and sentient nature of man was linked, as to all affection for the Godhead, in a kind of dull and heavy imprisonment—and bid those feelings which had long been pent and stifled in imprisonment there, go freely forth, both with trust and with tenderness, to the Father from whom we had been so sadly alienated. For this purpose a Mediator was appointed, and the account now taken up and discharged by him, is no longer against us—and for our sins, we are told, if we would only give credit to the saying, we shall no more be reckoned with—and the Deity reveals Himself in a new aspect of invitation to His creatures, and just that he may awaken the new affections of confidence and love in their before fearful and suspicious bosoms. We cannot love God in the face of a debt uncancelled and of a sentence unrecalled, and of a threatening that is still in force against us, and of mighty and majestic attributes all leagued for their own vindication to the object of destroying us. But we can love God when we are told, and we believe what is told of the ransom that is paid, and of the sentence and the threatening being all already spent on the agonies of another's endurance, and of His attributes aroused to vengeance because of sin, now pacified because of a sacrifice—so that mercy is free to send forth her beseeching calls, and, emancipated from the claims of truth and justice, can now abundantly rejoice over all the works and perfections of the Godhead. The cross of Jesus Christ is not merely the place of breaking forth into peace and reconciliation, but it is also the place of breaking forth into the love and new obedience of a regenerated nature. He who hath blotted out the handwriting of ordinances that was against us, which was contrary to us, and took it out of the way, nailing it to His cross—it is He who hath slain in our hearts their enmity against God—and now that we can love God because He first loved us, and sent His Son into the world to be the propitiation for our sins—now, and now only, can we serve Him in the newness of the spirit, and not in the oldness of the letter.

It should be our aim then to keep our hearts in the love of God—and this can only be done by keeping in memory the love that He hath borne unto us. With this affection all alive in our bosoms, and seeking how most to please and to gratify the Being whom it regards—let us never forget that this is His will, even our sanctification: that like as He rejoiced at the birth of nature, when, on the work being accomplished, He looked upon everything that He had made, and saw in the beauty, and luxuriance, and variety, which had just emerged from His hands, that all was very good—in like manner, and much more, does He rejoice in that new creation, by which moral loveliness, and harmony, and order, are made to emerge out of the chaos of our present degeneracy. The righteous Lord loveth righteousness, and the spectacle of our worth and excellence is to Him a pleasing spectacle—and what He wants is, to form and to multiply, by the regenerative power of His Spirit, the specimens of a beauty far higher in kind than all that can be exhibited on the face of visible nature: and our truth and our charity, and our deep repentance for sin, and our ceaseless aspirations after loftier degrees of purity and godliness—these imprint so many additional features of gracefulness on that spiritual creation over which the holiness of His character most inclines Him to rejoice; and we knowing that this is the mind of the Deity, and loving to gratify the Being whom we love, are furnished with a principle of obedience, more generous, and far more productive of the fruits of righteousness, than the legal principle, which only seeks to be square with the Lawgiver, and safe from the thunders of His violated authority. There is no limitation to such an obedience. The ever-urging principle of love to God is sure at all times to stimulate and to extend it: and what with a sense of delight to the work itself, and with the sense that God whom we love delights in the work also and rejoices over it, is there a newness of spirit given to obedience under the economy of the Gospel, altogether diverse from the oldness of the letter, which obtained under the economy of nature and of the law.

But, *thirdly*, there is nothing perhaps that will better illustrate the distinction between service rendered in the newness of the spirit, and service rendered in the oldness of the letter, than one simple reflection upon what that is which is the great object of the dispensation we sit under—to be made like unto God, like unto Him in righteousness, and like unto Him in true holiness. Now just think what the righteousness of God is like. Is it righteousness in submission to the authority of a law? Is it righteousness painfully and laboriously wrought out, with a view to reward? Is it righteousness in pursuit of any one pleasure or gratification that is at all distinct from the pleasure which the Divinity has in the very righteousness itself? Does not He desire righteousness simply because He loves it? Is not He holy, just because holiness is the native and kindred element of His Being? Do not all the worth and all the moral excellence of the Godhead, come direct from the original tendencies of His own moral nature? And would either the dread of punishment or the hope of remuneration be necessary to attach Him more than He already is, by the spontaneous and unbidden propensities of His own character, to that virtue which has been His glory from everlasting, and to that ethereal purity in which He most delights to expatiate? It is not at the beck of a governor—it is not with a view to prepare Himself for an appearance at some bar of jurisprudence—it is nothing else in fact but the preference He bears for what is right, and the hatred He holds for what is wrong—it is this, and this alone, which determines to absolute and unerring rectitude all the purposes and all the proceedings of the Deity. And to be like unto Him, that which is a task when done under the oldness of the letter, must be done in newness of spirit, and then will it be the very transport of our nature to be engaged in the doing of it. What is now felt, we fear, by many as a bondage, would, were we formed anew in the image of him who created us, become a blessedness. The burden of our existence would turn into its beatitude—and we, exempted from all those feelings of drudgery and dislike which ever accompany a mere literal obedience, would prosecute holiness with a sort of constitutional delight, and so evince that God was assimilating us to Himself, that He was dwelling in us, and that He was walking in us.

And the Christian disciple who is thus aspiring after that obedience, which while it fulfils the demands of the law in the letter, is also rendered in newness of spirit, will find in the following Treatise, "SCUDDER'S CHRISTIAN'S DAILY WALK IN HOLY SECURITY AND PEACE," a valuable companion and counsellor to guide him in every condition of life, and under all the vicissitudes to which life is subject—to instruct him how to prosecute his daily walk so as to secure his peace, and to possess his soul in patience, in his journey through life, and to render the circumstances of his lot, whether prosperous or adverse, subservient to the still higher purpose of promoting his holiness and his growth in the divine life, to fit him for the heavenly rest which awaits him at the close of his earthly pilgrimage. In this Treatise, the Christian disciple will learn to combine a service the most rigid in the letter, with those principles of the renewed heart which render it at the same time a delightful and an acceptable service. He will learn how to walk with God, while engaged in the service of man. It is the production of a man who had reached to great attainments in the spiritual life, and whose wise and experimental counsels are well fitted to guide him amidst the doubts and difficulties which may beset his path in the Christian warfare. It has received the approving testimony of two of the most eminent Divines of a former age, Dr. Owen and Richard Baxter, and we know of no work which better merits the high commendation which these competent judges have bestowed on it.

But without expatiating on the excellencies of a work, the value of which can only be estimated by those who have devoted themselves to a serious perusal of its pages, we shall conclude with two inferences from the prefatory observations with which we have introduced this Treatise to the notice of our readers. The first is, that virtue, so far from being superseded by the Gospel, is exalted thereby into a far nobler, and purer, and more disinterested attribute of the character than before. It becomes virtue, refined from that taint of sordidness which formerly adhered to it; prosecuted not from an impulse of selfishness, but from an impulse of generosity—followed after for its own sake, and because of the loveliness of its native and essential charms, instead of being followed after for the sake of that lucre wherewith it may be conceived to bribe and to enrich its votaries. Legal virtue is rendered in the spirit of a mercenary, who attaches himself to the work of obedience for hire. Evangelical virtue is rendered in the spirit of an amateur, who, in attaching himself to the work of obedience, finds that he is already in the midst of those very delights, than which he cares for none other in time, and will care for none other through eternity. The man who slaves at the employment to escape the penalty or to secure the pay, is diametrically the reverse of that man who is still more intensely devoted to the employment than the other, but because he has devoted to it the taste and the affections of his renovated nature. There is a well of water struck out in his heart, which springeth up unto spiritual life here, and unto everlasting life hereafter. There is an angelic spirit which has descended upon him from above; and which likens him to those beings of celestial nature, who serve God, not from the authority of any law that is without, but from the impulse of a love that is within; whose whole heart is in the work of obedience, and whose happiness is without alloy, just because their holiness is without a failing and without a flaw. The Gospel does not expunge virtue; it only elevates its character, and raises the virtue of earth on the same platform with the virtue of heaven. It causes it to be its own reward; and prefers the disciples of Jesus Christ from the condition of hirelings who serve in the spirit of bondage to the condition of heirs who serve their reconciled Father in the spirit of adoption; who love what He loves, and with a spirit kindred to His own, breathe in the atmosphere which best suits them, when they breathe in the atmosphere of holiness.

Our second inference is, that while the life of a Christian is a life of progressive virtue, and of virtue, too, purified from the jealousies and the sordidness of the legal spirit, still to be set on such a career, we see how indispensable it is that we enter by Christ, as by the alone gate of admission through which we can reach the way of such a sanctification. How else can we get rid of the oldness of the letter, we would ask? How be delivered from the fears and disquietudes of legality? How were it possible to regard God in any other light than one whose very sacredness made him the enemy of sinners, and so made him hateful to them? We are bound over to distrust, and alienation, and impracticable distance from God, till the tidings of the Gospel set us free. There is a leaden and oppressive weight upon our spirits, under which there can be no play of free, or grateful, or generous emotion towards the Father of them, till we hear with effect of the peace-speaking blood, and of the charm and the power of the great propitiation. Faith in Christ is not merely the starting-post of our reconciliation with God; it is also the starting-post of that new obedience which, unchilled by jealousy, and untainted by dread or by selfishness, is the alone obedience that is at all acceptable. The heart cannot go freely out to God, while beset with terror, while combined with the thoughts of a yet unsettled controversy, while in full view of its own sinfulness, and still in the dark about the way in which a Being of unspotted purity and inflexible justice, can find out a right channel of conveyance for the dispensation of His mercy—how he can be just, while the Justifier of the ungodly. It is the cross of Christ that resolves all these painful ambiguities. It is this which dissipates all these apprehensions. It is this which maintains, in sanctity unviolated, the whole aspect and character of the Godhead; while there beameth forth from it the kindest expression of welcome even on the chief of sinners. Let that expression be but seen and understood, and then will that be to us a matter of experience which we have tried, and tried so feebly, to set forth as a matter of demonstration. Our bonds will be loosed. A thing of hopeless drudgery, will be turned into a thing of heart-felt delight. The breath of a new spirit will animate our doings; and we will personally, and by actual feeling, ascertain the difference that there is between the service of a Lawgiver pursuing us with exactions that we cannot reach, and the service of a Friend, who has already charmed us both into confidence and gratitude, and is cheering us on through the manifold infirmities of our nature, to the resemblance of himself in all that is kind, and upright, and heavenly, and holy. It is only, we repeat it, through the knowledge of Christ and of him crucified, that we can effect this transition from the one style of obedience to the other style of obedience. It is only thus that we become dead unto the law, and alive unto God. It is only thus that we can serve him with all the energies of an emancipated heart, now set at large from that despondency and deadness which formerly congealed it. "I will run the way of thy commandments," says the Psalmist, "when thou hast enlarged my heart." Make room in it for the doctrine of the cross, and this will enlarge it. And, therefore, to sinners do we declare, that Christ is set forth as a propitiation, and all who believe in him shall have the benefit; and to believers do we declare, that God hath called them not to uncleanness, but to holiness; that, naming the name of Christ, their distinct business is to depart from all iniquity, and to do the commandments, not because they can purchase admission to heaven by the doing of them, but because heaven is purchased for them already: and to be educated for heaven, they must learn to do what is right—not that they can earn a title upon God, but because God has been graciously pleased to confer this title upon them; and now it is their part to do what is "well-pleasing in his sight—walking worthy of the Lord unto all pleasing—being fruitful in every good work—and giving thanks unto the Father, who hath made them meet to be partakers of the inheritance of the saints in light."

INTRODUCTORY ESSAY

TO

TRACTS

BY THE REV. THOMAS SCOTT,

RECTOR OF ASTON SANDFORD.

THERE is no delusion more prevalent, or more difficult to dissipate from the minds of men, than the imagined power which this world possesses, to confer solid good or substantial enjoyment on its votaries. Their life is one unceasing struggle for some object which lies at a distance from them. Their path upon earth is an attempted progress towards some attainment, which they conceive to be placed at an onward point in the line of their futurity. They are fighting their way to an arduous eminence of wealth or of distinction, or running with eager desire after some station of fancied delight, or fancied repose, on this side of death. And it is the part of religious wisdom, to mark the contrast which obtains between the activity of the pursuit in the ways of human business, or human ambition, and the utter vanity of the termination—to compute the many chances of disappointment—and, even when the success has been most triumphant, to compare the vehemence of the longing expectation with the heartlessness of the dull and empty acquirement—to observe how, in the career of restless and aspiring man, he is ever experiencing that to be tasteless, on which, while beyond his reach, he had lavished his fondest and most devoted energies. When we thus see that the life of man in the world is spent in vanity, and goes out in darkness, we may say of all the wayward children of humanity, that they run as uncertainly, and fight as one who beateth the air; or, to quote another Bible declaration, "Surely man walketh in a vain show, surely he vexeth himself in vain."

But these animadversions on that waste of strength and of exertion, which is incurred by the mere votaries of this world, are not applicable merely to the pursuits of general humanity, they are frequently no less applicable to our pursuits as Christians; and even with eternity as an object, there is a way of so running, and of so contending for it, as to make no advances towards it. A man may be walking actively with this view, and yet not be walking surely. A man may have entered into a strenuous combat for the rewards of immortality, and yet not obtain either the triumphs or the fruits of victory. There may be a great expense of movement, and of effort, and of diligence, and all for the good of his soul; and yet the expense be utterly unproductive of that for which his soul is anxiously putting forth the energies which belong to it. He may be walking on a way of toilsome exertion, and yet not be going on in his way rejoicing. A haunting sense of the vanity of all his labor, may darken and paralyze every footstep of his attempted progress towards heaven, and make him utterly the reverse of that Christian who is steadfast, and immovable, and always abounding. The man can never be satisfied with his own movements, who is not making sensible progress towards some assigned object of desire; and should that be a blissful eternity, there will adhere to him all the discomfort of running uncertainly, so long as he is not getting perceptibly nearer to the fulfilment of his wishes. It were lifting off the weight of a mountain from the heart of many a laboring inquirer, could he be set on a sure place, and a clear and ever brightening object be placed before him in the march of his practical Christianity—could such a distinct aim and bearing be assigned to him, as, with a full knowledge of the purpose of all his doings, and a hope of the purpose being accomplished, he might, in whatever he did, do it with cheerfulness and vigor—could he be made to understand whither his labors are tending, and for this end something precise, and definite, and intelligible, were at length to evolve itself out of the mists and the mazes of human controversy—could all the wranglings of disputation be hushed, and, amid the din of conflicting opinions about faith, and works, and the agency of man, and the sovereignty of God, an authoritative voice were heard to lift the overbearing utterance of "This is the way, walk ye in it"—could he be rescued from the indecisions of those who are ever learning, and never able to arrive at the knowledge of the truth,—then, like Paul, might he both be strong in orthodoxy, and strong in the confidence and consistency of his practical determinations. He would not be, what we fear many professing Christians are, at a loss how to turn themselves, and in the dire perplexity of those who labor without an object and without an end.

There are three different states of activity in the prosecution of our religious interests, to which we shall advert, all of which are exemplified in human experience; and we shall attempt to point out what is right and what is wrong in each of them.

The first state of activity is exemplified by those who seek to establish a righteousness of their own; the second by those who seek to be justified by faith; and the third by those who seek under Christ, as the accepted Mediator, to attain that holiness without which no man can see God—to reach that character, without which there is no congeniality with the joys or the exercises of heaven.

I. In the New Testament, the Jews are charged with a prevailing disposition to establish a righteousness of their own, but this formed no local or national peculiarity on the part of the Jewish people. It is the universal disposition of nature, and is as plainly and prominently exemplified among professing Christians of the day, as it ever was by the most zealous adherents of the Mosaic ritual. It is true, that out of the multitude of its ceremonial observations, a goodly frame-work could be reared of outward and apparent conformities to the will of God; and nothing more natural than for man to enter into that which is the work of his own hands, and then to feel himself as if placed in a tabernacle of security. But there are other materials besides those of Judaism, which men can employ for raising a fabric of self-righteousness. Some of them as formal in their character as the Sabbaths and the Sacraments of Christianity—others of them with the claim of being more substantial in their character, as the relative duties and proprieties of life,—but all of them proceeding on the same presumption, that man can, by his own powers, work out a meritorious title to acceptance with God, and that he can so equalize his doings with the demands of the law, as to make it incumbent on the Lawgiver to confer on him the rewards and the favor which are due to obedience.

Now it is worthy of remark, that though few are prepared to assert this principle in all its extent, and though it even be disowned by them in profession, yet in practice and in feeling it adheres to them. To the question, What shall I do to be saved? it is the silent answer of many a heart, That there is something which I can do, and by the doing of which I can achieve my salvation. A sense of his own sufficiency lurks in the bosom of man, long after, by his lips, he has denied it; and it is a very possible thing to be most steadfast in the arguments, and most strenuous in the asseverations of orthodoxy, and yet practically to be so undisciplined by its lessons, as that the habit of the whole man shall be in a state of real and effective resistance to them.

And thus it is, that, among the men of all creeds, and of all professions in Christianity, do we meet with the attempt of establishing a righteousness of their own. The question of our interest with God is no sooner entertained by the human mind, than it appears to be one of the readiest and most natural of its movements to do something for the object of working out such a righteousness. The question of, How shall I, from being personally a condemned sinner, become personally an approved and accepted servant of God? no sooner enters the mind, than it is followed up by the suggestion of such a personal change in habit or in character, as it is competent for man, by his own turning and his own striving, to accomplish. The power of which I am conscious—the command with which I feel myself invested over both my thoughts and my doings—the authoritative voice which the mind can issue from the place of fancied sovereignty where it sits, and from which it exacts both of the outer and the inner man an obedience to all its inclinations,—these are what I constantly and familiarly press into my service; and I find that, in point of fact, they are able to conduct me to many a practical attainment. Nor is it to be wondered at, that when the attainment in question is such a righteousness before God as may empower me to lift a plea of desert in his hearing, the presumption should still adhere to me, that this also I can achieve by my own strength—this also I shall win, as the fruit of my own energies, and my own aspirations.

Now, what stamps an utter hopelessness upon such an enterprise as this, is both the actual deficiency of every man's conduct from the requirements of God's law, throughout that part of his history which is past, and the deficiency, no less obvious, of every man's powers from a full and equal obedience to the same requirements, during that part of his history which is to come. Without entering into the abstract question of justice, whether the rigor of a man's future conformities should make up for the offence of his bygone disobedience, and deciding this question by the light of nature or of conscience, certain it is, that no man, under the revelation of the Gospel, can feel himself, even though he were on a most prosperous career of advancing virtue, to be in a state of ease in the sense of the guilt that has already been incurred, and of the transgressions which have already been committed by him. On this subject, there are certain texts of the Bible which look hard upon him—certain solemn announcements about the immutability of the law, which cannot fail to disturb, and, it may be, to paralyze him—certain damnatory clauses about the very least act of iniquity, on which he, conscious of great and repeated acts of iniquity, may well conclude himself to be a lost and irrecoverable sinner—certain mighty asseverations, on the part of God's own Son, about the difficulty of annulling the sanctions of his Father's government, and that it were easier for heaven and earth to pass away than for these to pass away, which may well fill the heart of every conscious offender with the assurance, that his condemnation is as unfailing as the truth of God, and greatly more unfailing than are the present ordinances of creation. These both tell the enlightened sinner that his case is beyond the remedy even of his most powerful exertions; and they also make exertions which, in the spirit of hope and of confidence, might have been powerful, weak as childhood, by the overwhelming influence of despair. The man feels that the sentence which is already past, lays the weight of an immovable interdict upon all his energies. His interest with God looks to be irrecoverable, and any attempt to recover it is like the frantic exertions of a captive raving in despair around the unpracticable walls of the dungeon which holds him. While the handwriting of ordinances is still against him, and not taken out of the way, it looks to him like the flaming sword at the gate of Paradise, forbidding his every attempt to force the barrier of that blissful habitation. The man is in a state of spiritual imprisonment, and he feels himself to be so. The menacing urgencies of the law may put him into a kind of convulsive activity, while the unrelenting severity of the law leaves him not one particle of hope to gladden or to inspire it. Thus he runs without an object, and struggles without even the anticipation of success.

The thing which makes the remembrance of the past shed a blight so withering and so destructive over the attempted obedience of the future, is, that we cannot admit the truth of the matter into our understanding, without admitting, at the same time, into our hearts, an apprehension which instantly stifles, or puts to flight the alone principle of all acceptable obedience. The truth of the matter is, that the promulgations of the law cannot be surrendered, without a surrender of the attributes of God, and thus it is, that with every man who thinks truly, the consciousness of being a sinner, brings along with it the fear of God as an avenger. And it is impossible for sentient nature to love the Being whom it so fears. It is impossible, at one and the same time, to have a dread of God, and a delight in God. There may be love up to the height of seraphic ecstasy, where there is the fear of reverence, but there is no love in any one of its modifications, where there is the fear of terror. Let God appear before the eye of our imagination, in the light of a strong man, armed to destroy us, and if the only obedience which our heart can render be love, then is our heart put, by such an exhibition of the Deity, into a state of rebellion. There may be physical, but there is no moral obedience. The feet may be made to run, and the hands to move, and the tongue to speak, or to be silent, and the whole organization of the body may be squared into a rigorous adjustment, with a set of outward and literal conformities, and yet the soul which animates that organization, be all in a fester with its known delinquencies against the law, and its dark suspicious antipathies against the Lawgiver. And thus it is, that let the present moment be the point of our purposed reformation, not only may God charge us with the unexpiated guilt of all that goes before it, but, if we have a just and enlightened retrospect of what we were, and an equally just and enlightened conception of Him with whom we have to do, there will be a taint of substantial worthlessness in all that comes after it. That which stands so strong a bar in the way of reconciliation, will just stand equally strong as a bar in the way of repentance. The sense of God's hostility to us, will so provoke our fear and our hostility towards Him, as to haunt, and utterly to vitiate the whole character of our proposed and attempted obedience. When the body, worn out by the drudgery of its painful and reluctant observations, shall resign its ascending spirit to Him who sitteth on the throne, he will not recognize upon it one lineament of that generous and confiding affection, which gives all its worth to the love and the loyalty of paradise. He will not discern one mark of preparation for an inheritance in heaven, upon him who on earth made many a weary struggle to attain it.

There are, it must be admitted, many who do not think truly of the law; and who, not aware of its lofty demands, think they do enough, when they maintain a complacent round of seemly, but at the same time most inadequate observations—among whom all is formality without, and all is repose and settledness within—who pace, with unwearied step, the circle of ordinances, and are just as regular in their attendance, as is the bell which summons them to the house of prayer—who would feel discomfort out of their routine, but have the most placid and immovable security within it—and who, amid the engrossment of their many punctualities, have never thought of admitting into their bosoms one fear, or one feeling, that can at all disturb them. These are running uncertainly; but they are not harassed by any sense or suspicion of it. They are only beating the air; but they are not fatigued by the consciousness of its being a fruitless operation. They are in a state of repose; but it is the repose of death. They have accommodated their conduct to the established decencies of the world; but the spirit of the world has never quitted its hold of them. Their portion is on this side of the grave—their delights are on this side of the grave—their all is on this side of the grave. They go to church, and they sit down to the sacrament, and they maintain within their houses a style of Sabbath observation; but these are merely habits appended to the mechanical, and not to the moral or spiritual part of their constitution. They may do all this, and be strangers to the life of faith, to the exercise of devout affection, to the habit of communion with God, as the living God; to all those processes, in short, which mark and carry forward the transformation of the soul, from its congeniality with the elements of nature and of sense, to its congeniality with the elements of spirit and of eternity. There may be a work of drudgery with the hands, and with the doing of which, too, they are pleased and satisfied, while there is no work of grace upon the heart. The outer man may be in a state of incessant bodily exercise. The inner man may be in a state of entire stagnancy. They do, in fact, run uncertainly. They do, in fact, fight as he who beateth the air. But they have no fear of coming short—no feeling to imbitter the course of their religious activity; and without the wakefulness of any alarm upon the subject, do they so contend as to lose the mastery, do they so run as that they shall not obtain.

Now this is not the class that we have chiefly had in our eye. The men to whom we principally allude, are those who run, but without hope, and without satisfaction—men who fight, but without any cheering anticipations of victory. They are seeking a righteousness by works; and are, at the same time, disheartened at every step, by the consciousness of no sensible advancement towards it. Unlike the latter, they think more truly and more adequately of the law. The one class see it only in the light of a carnal commandment. The others see it according to the character of its spiritual requirements. The one, without an enlightened sense of the law, are what the apostle represents himself to have been when without the law, alive; even like all those religious formalists, who look forward to eternal life on the strength of their manifold and religious observations. The others, with this enlightened sense, are what the apostle represents himself to have been after the law came, dead; or they feel all the helplessness of death and of despair, even as he did, when, amid his strenuous but unavailing struggles, he was forced to exclaim, "O wretched man that I am, who shall deliver me?" And thus it is, we believe, with many whose hearts have at length been struck by a sense of the importance of eternal things—who have begun to feel the weight of their everlasting interests—who are sensible that all is not right about them, and are seeking about for that movement of transition, by which they may be carried forward from a state of wrath to a state of acceptance—who, in obedience to the first natural impulse, strive to amend what is wrong in conduct, and to adopt what is right in conduct, but find, that after all their toil, and all their carefulness, that relief is as far from them as ever—who set up a new order in their lives, and propose to find their way to peace on the stepping-stones of many and successive reformations, but find, that as they pile their offerings of obedience the one upon the other, the law rises in its exactions; and what with a claim of satisfaction for the past, and of spiritual obedience for the future, it exhibits itself to their appalled imaginations, in the dimensions of such a length, and a breadth, and a height, and a depth, as they never can encircle—who, in the very proportion, it may be, of their pains and their earnestness, are ever acquiring more tremendous conceptions, both of the extent of its requisitions, and the terrors of its authority—who thus feel, that by every trial of obedience, they are just multiplying their failures, and swelling the account of guilt and of deficiency that is against them—who feel themselves in the hopeless condition of men, whose every attempt at extrication, just thickens the entanglements that are around them, and whose every effort of activity fastens them the deeper in an abyss of helplessness. This is the real process, we will not say of all, but of many a convert to the light and power of the Gospel. This is the sure result with every man who seeks to establish a righteousness of his own, if, along with this attempt, he combines an adequate conception of the law in the spirituality of its demands, of the law in the certainty of its exactions. He feels urged, on the one hand, by its menacing and authoritative voice, to do. He feels convicted, on the other, by a sense of the guilt or inadequacy which attaches to all his doing. He feels himself in the hand of a master issuing an impracticable mandate, and lifting at the same time an arm of powerful displeasure, for all his past and all his present violations. He cannot sit still under the power and frequency of the applications which are now making to his awakened conscience. He flies for deliverance, but it is like the flight of a desperado from his sure and unrelenting pursuers.

In the olden books of Scotland, and in that traditional history which is handed down from the pious of one generation to another, we meet with this very process not unaptly described under the term of law-work. It is well delineated in the lives of Brainerd and Halyburton. There is an intermediate period of darkness, and despondency, and distress, in many an individual history, between the repose of nature's indifference, and the repose of Gospel peace and Gospel anticipations. The mind, in these circumstances, is generally alive to two distinct things: first, to the truth and immutable obligation of God's law; and, secondly, to the magnitude and irrecoverable evil of its own actual deficiencies. It is at one time urged on by an impulse of natural conscience, to a set of active measures for the recovery of its lost condition. It is at another time mortified into a despairing sense, that all these measures are utterly fruitless and unavailing. And thus amid the agitations of doubt, and terror, and remorse; and sinking under the weight of an oppressive gloom, which is ever deepening, and ever aggravating around it, is it at length practically and experimentally convinced, by many a weary but unsuccessful struggle, that in itself there is no strength; that the man who runs upon his own energies, runs uncertainly; and that he who fights with his own weapons, fights as one that beateth the air.

II. Having tried to seek a righteousness by works, and having failed, the next trial of many an inquirer after peace, is, to seek a righteousness by faith. And here we cannot but advert to the prejudice of the general world against the doctrine of acceptance through faith, as if it were a doctrine most loved, and most resorted to, by those who felt no value for the worth of moral accomplishments, and bestowed no labor on the cultivation of them. We beg the attention of our readers to the contrast which obtains between a very prevailing fancy upon this subject, and the fact, as it stands experimentally before us. The fancy is, that those who disclaim a justification by works, are those who take the least pains in the doing of them. The fact is, that it was by their very pains to be perfect and complete in the doing of them, that they found this foundation to be impracticable; and, now that they are upon another foundation, it is unto them, and not unto others, that we look for works in their greatest abundance, for works in their greatest purity. The fancy is, that, by linking their whole security, not with the rewards of obedience, but with the grace of the Gospel, these people have given up all business with the law. The fact is, that, ever since they thought of religion at all, they have been by far the busiest of all their fellows about the requisitions of the law. It was their schoolmaster, to bring them unto Christ; and now that they are so brought, the keeping of the law forms their daily and delightful occupation. It may well rank as one of the curiosities of our nature, that they who are most hostile to the doctrine of the efficacy of faith, because they think that works of themselves are sufficient for salvation, are, in the real and practical habit of their lives, most negligent in the performance of them; and, on the other hand, that they who are most hostile to the doctrine of the efficacy of works, because they think that it is by the power of faith that we are kept unto salvation, are the men who have most to show of those very works on which they seem to stamp so slight an estimation. And, to complete this apparent mystery, they who impute nothing but licentiousness to orthodoxy, tolerate licentiousness only in those who are the enemies, and never in those who are the professors of it—look upon the alliance between vice and evangelical sentiment to be a far more monstrous and unlikely alliance than that which often obtains between vice and an irreligious contempt for all the peculiarities of our faith—reproach the doctrine of the Gospel for its immoral tendencies, and yet, for every flaw in the morality of its disciples, will they lift the reproachful cry of their lives and their opinions being in a state of disgraceful and hypocritical variance with each other: proving, after all, that the men who build their security most upon faith, are the men to whom even the world looks for most in the way of practical righteousness; are the men whose delinquencies are ever sure to raise the loudest murmurs of wrath or of astonishment from by-standers; are the men over whom satire feels herself to have the greatest advantage, when by any peccadillo of conduct, they furnish her with a topic, either of merriment or severity. And what else can we make of all these inconsistencies, than that there is a deep and prevailing misconception about the real character of the evangelical system? and that, while there has been imputed to it a cold and repulsive aspect towards virtue, their lies veiled under this a powerful and a working principle, from which even the public at large expect a more abundant return than they do from any other quarter of human society, of all the graces and all the accomplishments of virtue?

There is a change in the direction of our mind, when, from the object of being justified by works, it turns itself to the new object of being justified by faith. It is then only that it puts itself in quest of the only justification which is possible; and yet, when thus employed, there is still a way of running uncertainly. For, first, as virtue is a thing which attaches personally to him who performs it, so is faith a thing which attaches personally to him who possesses it. The one has just as local a residence within the mind, as the other. To have kind affection, and to have it not, argues a difference in the state of one's heart; and to have faith, or to have it not, argues just as effectually a difference in the state of one's understanding. To believe is to do that which we ought. To disbelieve, is to do that which we ought not. And further, we are expressly told in the Gospel, that, with the right thing about us, there is linked our inheritance in heaven; and with the wrong thing about us, there is linked our everlasting consignment to hell. Here then is faith, like virtue, a personal acquirement; the possession of which is a right thing, and the want of which is a wrong thing. With such a statement before us, there is nothing more natural, than that we should look upon faith as standing in the same place, under the dispensation of the Gospel, that obedience did, under the dispensation of the Law; that we should set about the acquirement of the one very much in the way in which we set about the acquirement of the other; that we should put ourselves to work with the terms of the new covenant, just as we had been in the habit of working with the terms of the old covenant; strive to render our half of the bargain, which is faith, and then look to God for His half of the bargain, which is our final and everlasting salvation.

Under the economy of "Do this and live," the great point of anxiety with him who is laboring for the good of his soul, is, "O that I had obedience!" Under the economy of "Believe, and ye shall be saved," the great point of anxiety with him who is laboring for the good of his soul, is, "O that I had faith!" There is, in both cases, an earnestness, and perhaps a striving after the acquirement of a certain property of character. The only difference between the two cases, lies in the kind of property. But, just as the mind may put forth a strenuousness in its attempt to realize the grace of temperance, or in its attempt to realize the grace of patience; so may the mind put forth a strenuousness in its attempt to realize the grace of faith; and, with the success of this endeavor, may it connect the prize of a happy eternity, and be virtually in the same attitude of laboring to substantiate a claim under the Gospel, as it formerly was under the law. So that, in fact, the old legal spirit may be as fully at work with the new requirements, as ever it was with the old ones. The prospect of bliss may still be made to turn as much as before upon a performance. The only change is in the terms of the performance. But, in point of fact, men may make a work of faith. They may offer it to heaven, as their part of a new contract into which God has entered with the guilty. Faith and reward may stand related to each other, as the corresponding terms of a stipulation, in the same way that obedience and reward did. The favor of God, instead of being seen as a gift held out for our acceptance, may still be seen as a thing to be gained by a mental work, done with the putting forth of mental energies. In the doing of this work, there may be felt all the darkness, and all the anxiety, and all the spirit of bondage, which attached to the work of the old covenant. And thus it is that there are many, with the doctrine of the Gospel in their minds, and the phraseology of the Gospel on their lips, upon whom the grace of the Gospel is utterly thrown away, and who, as if still goaded on by the threats and exactions of the law, continue to run as uncertainly, and to fight even as one who beateth the air.

Now, it is evident, that in this way the Gospel may be so misconceived, as to have no right or appropriate influence whatever on the mind of an inquirer. If salvation, instead of being looked to, as by grace through faith, be looked to, as by faith, in the light of a rendered condition on the part of man, upon which he may challenge a certain stipulated fulfilment on the part of God,—then, all the distance, and suspicion, and unsatisfied longings, by which he felt himself to be harassed and enfeebled, when attempting to work and to win under the old economy, may still attend him, as he tries to work and to win, under the new. With his mind thus unfortunately set, he may still regard God in the light of a jealous exactor, and himself in the light of a lacking tributary. He may still be looking to the condition of his faith, and trembling at the defects of it; just as, before he attended to the Gospel, he looked to the condition of his obedience, and trembled at the defects of it. It may still, in his eye, retain the whole spirit and character of a negotiation between two parties; and all the uncertainty of whether with him, as one of these parties, there has been a failure or a fulfilment, may still adhere, to agitate and to disturb him. At this rate, the Gospel ceases, in fact, to be Gospel. It loses its character in his eye, as a dispensation of mercy. The exhibition it offers, is not that of God holding out a benefit, in the shape of a gift, for our acceptance; but of God holding out a benefit, in the shape of a return for our faith. So that, ere we can look with a sentiment of hopeful confidence towards him, we must first look with a feeling of satisfaction to ourselves. Now, this is not the way in other cases of a gift. Should a friend come into my presence with some dispensation of kindness, it is enough to put the whole joy of it into my heart, that I hear his assurances of good-will, that I behold his countenance of benignity, and that I see the offered boon held out to me for acceptance. It is true, that I would neither feel the charm of all this liberality, nor attempt to lay hold of what it offers, unless I gave credit to the offerer. But then, I am not thinking of this credit. I am not perplexing myself with any question about its reality. I am not first looking to myself, that I may see whether the belief is there—and then looking to the giver, that I may stretch forth a receiving hand to the fruit of his generosity. I am looking all the while to that which is without me; and it is from that which is without me, that all the influences of hope and of gratitude, and the pleasure of a felt deliverance from poverty, descend upon my soul. It is very true, that, unless I gave credit to my visitor, nothing of all this would be felt; and I may even carry my unbelief so far as to think that the offer was intended, not to relieve, but to affront me; and that, were I extending my hand to receive it, it would instantly be drawn back again in derision, by my insulting acquaintance. So that, without faith, I cannot obtain the benefit in question. But it is not to faith as an article in the agreement—it is not to faith as a meritorious service—it is not to faith as the term of a bargain, that the benefit is rendered. Faith acts no other part in this matter, than the mere opening of the hand does in the matter of putting into it a sum of money. It does not affect the character of the Gospel, as being a pure matter of giving on the one side, and of receiving on the other. And it is when we look to God in the light of a Giver—it is when we look to Him holding out a present, and beseeching our acceptance—it is when we look to Him setting forth Christ to the world as a propitiation for sin, and setting Him forth as effectually to us, as if there were no other sinner in the world but ourselves—it is when the outgoings of the mind's regard are thus turned towards the God who is above us, and the promises and declarations which are without us—and not when the mind is looking anxiously inward upon the operations of its own principles—it is then, and only then, that the sinner is in the attitude of a likely subject for the Gospel, and for the reception of all its influences.

It has been well observed, that the mind is often put into disquietude, by looking to the act of faith, when it might derive to itself peace, and comfort, and joy, by looking to the object of faith. In the latter case, one turns to the mercy of God in Christ freely held out to him; in the former case, he turns his eye towards one of his own mental operations. While doing the one, a pure and unclouded hilarity might emanate upon the heart, from the countenance of the all-perfect Creator;—while doing the other, this light is but reflected back again in dimness and deficiency, from the work of a sinful and imperfect creature. The one is like taking in from the sun in the firmament a flood of direct and unmitigated splendor; the other is like taking in a sullied and confused image of him, thrown back on the spectator from the surface of a foul and troubled water. Let him see God just in the way in which God is soliciting the notice of the guilty towards Him—let him look unto Christ, even as Christ is actually set forth to the view of the world—let him direct his upward gaze to that spiritual canopy of light and of truth which is above him—and, from these, through the medium of faith, there will descend upon his soul, that which can clear, and elevate, and transform it. But instead of so looking, and so sending forth the eye of his contemplation, let him turn it with minute and microscopic search towards this medium—let his attention be pointed inwardly, towards the nature and quality of his faith, and the danger is, that he loses sight of the very things which furnish faith with the only materials for its exercise. He may seek in vain for the operation of faith, and that, just because the objects of faith are withdrawn from it. He may seek with much labor and anxiety for what he cannot find, because, when the things to be looked for have taken their departure from the mind's eye, the exercise of looking has ceased. Instead of the outgoings of his belief being towards the beseeching God, and the dying Saviour, and all the evidences and expressions of good-will to men, with which the doctrine of man's redemption is associated, he has bent an anxious examination towards the state of that condition in which he conceives the offered mercy of the Gospel to turn; and amid his doubts of its existence, or his doubts of its entireness, does he remain without comfort and without satisfaction about his eternity.

It is true, that without faith the mind is in darkness. But faith enlightens a dark mind, only in the sense in which an open window enlightens a before darkened chamber. It is not the window which enlightens the room. It is the sun which enlightens it. And should we, sitting in our chamber, be given to understand that a sight of the sun carries some delight or privilege along with it, it is not to the window that we look, but to the sun and through the window that we look. And the same of looking to Jesus. While so doing, our direct employment is to consider Him—to think of the truth and the grace that are stamped upon His character—to hear His promises, and to witness the honesty and the good-will which accompany the utterance of them—to dwell on the power of his death, and on the unquestionable pledge which it affords, that upon the business of our redemption He is in good earnest—to cast our regard on His unchangeable priesthood, and see, that by standing between God and the guilty, He has opened a way by which the approach of the most worthless of us all have been consecrated and rendered acceptable. It is by the direct beaming of light upon the soul, from such truths and such objects as these, that the soul passes out from its old state into a new state that is marvellous. Anything that can arrest or avert the eye of contemplation away from them, is like the passing of a cloud over the great luminary of all our comfort, and our spiritual manifestation. If, instead of looking to the object that is without us, from which the light proceedeth, we look only to the organ within us, through which the light passeth; we, while so employed, are as little looking unto Jesus, as he is looking to the sun in the firmament, all whose powers are absorbed in examining the composition of the glass of his window, or the anatomical construction of his eye. The songs, and the offers of deliverance, are altogether unheeded by him who is profoundly intent, at the time, on the phenomena of hearing. The beauties of the surrounding landscape may scarcely be perceived, or, at least, not be relished and admired by the observer, so long as all his faculties are busily engaged with an optical demonstration. And the proclamations of Gospel mercy are equally unheard, and its aspect of glad and generous invitation is equally disregarded by him, who, ruminating on the mysteries of his own heart, perplexes himself among the depths and the difficulties of faith.

It is known to anatomists, that to have a view of the objects of surrounding nature, the image of all that is visible must be drawn out on the retina of the eye. But the peasant, who knows not that he has a retina, has just as vivid a perception of these objects, as the philosopher had who first discovered the existence of it. And, in like manner, a babe in Christ might have a lively manifestation of the Saviour, who knows nothing of the metaphysics of faith—who is in utter darkness about all the controversies to which it has given birth—who sees with his mental eye, while in the profoundest ignorance about the construction of his mental eye—who cannot dive into the recesses of his own intellectual constitution, but, by the working of that constitution, has caught a spiritual discernment of Him, whom to see and to know is life everlasting.—"Father, I thank thee, that whilst thou hast hid these things from the wise and the prudent, thou hast revealed them unto babes."

There is not a readier way of running uncertainly, than strenuously to put forth effort in a matter over which the will has no control: and this is often done by those, who, in their anxious desire to get that faith on which salvation is made to turn, try, with all their might and all their diligence, to believe. Now this is what we never can do separately from evidence. To carry the conviction of the understanding, without proof addressed to the understanding, is impossible. If we are out of the way of meeting with the evidence of the truth, we never will attain a belief of the truth. It is no doubt possible, by the mere dint of mental exertion, to conceive what a doctrine is, and to retain that doctrine in our mind, and to recall it when it happens to be away from us: but it is not possible, without a satisfying evidence of the doctrine, actually to believe in it. Here then is a way in which we may incur the expense of effort, and the effort be altogether unavailing. We may be trying to believe, while we are looking the wrong way for it. It is not merely by poring over the lineaments of our own heart—it is not by witnessing the deficiencies of our faith, and still looking, and continuing to look to the place of these deficiencies—it is not by the reflection of evidences from within, while every avenue is closed of communication from without, that light first arises in the midst of darkness. To obtain any such reflection, a beam of manifestation must be admitted from without, making it the entrance of the word of God which gives light unto us and the Spirit of God shining upon His testimony, which causes the demonstration of it to come with power, and with assurance, upon him who is giving earnest heed to the word of that testimony. So that, on the other hand, there is a way in which the will may be rightly and profitably employed in the matters of believing. There is a way in which the advice, of try to believe, is applicable, and may be successfully carried into effect. It is by our will that we open the pages of the Bible. It is by our will that we stir up our minds to lay hold of Him who speaketh there. It is by our will that we fulfil His own precept of hearkening diligently. It is by our will that we keep ourselves at the assigned post of meeting between us and the Holy Ghost; and as the apostles did before us, wait for His coming with supplication and prayer. But it is in the act of attending to the word which is without us, that light finds access to our heart. If ever it fall upon us at all, this is the way in which it will come; and, if we are not widely mistaken, we utter an advice which is applicable to the case of at least some dark and disconsolate inquirers, when we say, that instead of fetching their peace and their joy in believing primarily from themselves, they should fetch it from the truths which are without them, and from the great Fountain of Truth and of Grace that is above them. Acquaint thyself with thy Creator, and be at peace, and go unto Christ, all ye who labor and are heavy laden, and He will give you rest.

Thus will we find the righteousness that we are in quest of. Thus will we meet a plea of acceptance already made out for us, and be given to perceive that the only obedience in which God can consistently with the honors of His government admit us into His favor, is an obedience which has been already rendered. If we commit ourselves to this with a perfect feeling of security, as the ground of our dependence, it will never, never give way under us. He who trusteth in Christ shall never be confounded or put to shame. The righteousness which we vainly strive to make out in our own person, is worthless as pollution itself, when put by the side of that righteousness which has been already made out in the person of another; a righteousness, all the claims of which, and all the rewards of which, are offered to us; a righteousness, which, if we will only humble ourselves to put on, shall translate us into instant reconciliation with God, and, at length, exalt us to a place of unfading glory. Look then unto Jesus. Consider Him who is the Apostle and the High Priest of our profession. We should cast our open and immediate regard upon Him who is evidently set forth crucified before us. And as it was in the act not of looking to their wounds, but in the act of looking to the brazen serpent, that the children of Israel were healed, even so is the Son of man lifted up, "that whosoever believeth in Him should not perish but have everlasting life."

III. We have already attempted to prove, that the man who seeketh a righteousness by works, seeks it in a way which must land him in vanity and disappointment, and that he alone has attained the position with which he may take up and be satisfied, who has found the righteousness that is by faith. He alone who has accepted of the Gospel offer, and puts his trust in its faithfulness, knows what it is to set himself down under a secure and unfailing canopy; and to delight himself greatly with the abundance of peace which he there enjoys. It cannot be adequately conceived by those who have never felt it; and therefore it is, that when a man looks to the offer of that righteousness which is unto all, and upon all who believe, as addressed to himself,—and when, treating it accordingly, he makes it the subject of his actual acceptance, along with the faith which has taken possession of him,—then enters the peace of God in Christ Jesus, which passes all understanding. When, weaned from every other dependence, he has at length learned to leave the whole weight both of his plea and of his expectation upon the Saviour, it is not easy to form an adequate thought of the change which then takes place upon his condition; how, by so doing, the whole deadness and heaviness of his soul are cleared away; how, as if loosed from a confinement in which it hath lain past from infancy, it breaks out into free and fearless intercourse with that God before whom it trembled; or away from whom all its thoughts and all its desires lay hid in carnal insensibility. They who never felt of faith in any other way than as a mere unmeaning or cabalistic utterance, and are strangers to the term as fixed and substantiated in experimental reality, on a positive operation of the soul, perceive not the magnitude nor the glory of that transition which it causeth the soul to undergo. They know not the import of being made alive thereby unto God. But there are some who, though destitute in fact of this faith, may have some obscure fancy of what the effect must be, when the Being, with whom all power and all immensity stand associated, enters into a new relation with one of his own creatures, altogether opposite to that in which he stood before; and, instead of an enemy whom one fears, or a master whom one dislikes, or a dark and distant personage, from whom one has lived all his days in utter estrangement, he draws near to the eye of the inner man in the living character of a friend, and admits us into the number of his children, through the faith that is in Christ Jesus, and pours the spirit of adoption upon us. So that, unburdened of guilt and of suspicion, we may come unto God with full assurance of heart, as we would do to a reconciled father. When such terms as these, from being felt as sounds of mystery, come to be imbodied in actual fulfilment, and to be invested with the meaning of felt and present realities; then does the inquirer find within himself, that to become a partaker of the faith of the New Testament, is indeed to pass out of darkness into a light that is marvellous. The one and simple circumstance of being now able to go out and in with confidence unto God, opens the door of his prison-house, and sets him at liberty. And let us not wonder, that, with the new hope which is thus made to dawn upon his heart, a new feeling enters along with it, and a new affection now comes to inspire it. Who can say, in short, that the entrance of the faith of the Gospel is not the turning point of a new character, that that is not the moment of all old things being done away, from which the man began to breathe in another moral atmosphere, and to conceive purposes, and to adopt practices, suited to another field of contemplation now placed before him? And thus, by the single act of believing—by giving credit to the word of God's testimony, when he holds himself forth to us as God in Christ, reconciling the world unto himself, and not imputing unto them their trespasses,—by conceiving of Christ, that He gives an honest account of the errand on which He came, when He says, that He "came not to condemn the world, but to save it,"—by conceding the honor of truth to Him who is the Author of the Bible, and so believing just as it is there spoken,—a course is set into operation, competent to the effect of an entire revolution, both in the prospect and in the moral state of him who is influenced by it,—translating him from a state of darkness, or a state of dismay, to peace, and joy, and spiritual life, impressing a new character upon his heart, and turning into a new course of joy the whole of his habits and of his history.

Now, it is in the prosecution of this course—a course not of legal, but of evangelical obedience—a course in which, instead of winning the favor of God as the result of it, we are upheld by the favor of God freely conferred upon us in Christ Jesus, from the commencement and through the whole process of it,—a course, in which we walk with God as two walk together who are agreed, instead of walking with Him as if dragged reluctantly along by a force which it were even death to bring down in wrath and in hostility against us,—a course which we prosecute with the will, now gained over by gratitude, and touched by the love of moral and spiritual excellence, and enlightened in the great and final object of salvation, which is to prepare us for the kingdom of God in heaven, by setting up the kingdom of God in our hearts, even righteousness, and peace, and joy in the Holy Ghost,—a course, the distinct object of which is to transform the character of man from its selfishness and its ungodliness, and not so much to surround him with celestial glories, as to give to him the worth, and the feelings, and the principles of a celestial mind.

Now, it often happens, that long after a formal admission has been given to the doctrines of the Gospel, the mind may practically be far from being in a state of adjustment with a course of obedience, prosecuted in such a spirit, and with such an object as we have now been describing. There may be a course of very strenuous performance; but the old legal spirit may be yet unquelled, and the mind of the inquirer be still weighed down under a sense of hopeless and inextricable bondage. There may, at the same time, be a speculative conviction of the vanity of good works; and many a weary attempt be made to raise up faith with a set of qualifications, which are destitute, in themselves, of all power and of all sufficiency to propitiate the favor of God. It, however, cannot be disguised, that works, in some shape or other, are as strenuously called for under the latter, as under the former dispensation; and we speak of an actual state of ambiguity on this subject, in which many have been involved, and where many have lingered for years in great helplessness and distress, when we say, that, unable to attain a clear and satisfactory perception of the way in which faith and works stand related to salvation, they have toiled without an object, and labored to get onwards without coming sensibly nearer to any landing-place. There is a want of drift in their manifold doings. They are at one time fearful of being in the wrong, when they attempt to multiply their conformities to the divine law; learning so much from one class of theologians of the vanity of works, and the danger of self-righteousness. They are, at another time, impelled to action by a vague and general sense of the importance of works; learning from the Bible, and even from these very theologians, that works, brought down to utter insignificance at one part of the doctrinal argument, reappear at a future part of it, vested with a real importance in the matter of salvation. And thus do they vacillate in darkness, between a kind of general urgency to do upon the one hand; and, on the other, a kind of indistinct impression that, as a Christian, his business is not to do, but to believe. And so there is either a halting of the mind, or an unceasing vibration of the mind, between two opinions; neither of which, at the same time, is very distinctly apprehended. The Christian who is steadfast and immovable, and always abounding in the work of the Lord, knows that his labor in the Lord is not in vain. Now he does not know this. He has been schooled, by an ill-conceived orthodoxy, into a suspicion of the worth and efficacy of all labor, and so is haunted and harassed by the imagination, that all his labor is in vain. The perplexity thickens around him, among the uncertain sounds of a trumpet coming to his ear, with what to him are dark and contradictory intimations; and we are not drawing a fanciful representation, but offering a faithful copy of what is often realized in human experience, when we say, that there are many inquirers, who, thus lost and bewildered in the midst of difficulties, embark in a race that is at once fatiguing and fruitless, and engage in a painful service, which they afterwards experience to be utterly unproductive.

The life and experience of the Rev. Thomas Scott, the Author of the excellent Tracts which compose the present volume, afford a striking exemplification of the different states of activity in the prosecution of a religious life, which we have endeavored to illustrate. He was long perplexed and bewildered amidst the errors which we have been exposing, and made many vain and fruitless attempts to attain to peace, by endeavoring to establish a righteousness of his own, and it was not till humbled under a sense of the vanity and fruitlessness of all such attempts, that he took refuge in the all-sufficient righteousness of Christ, and found that peace he was so earnestly in quest of. In his "Force of Truth," he gives an honest and faithful delineation of the severe and protracted conflict he sustained, ere he found himself established on the sure foundation of the righteousness which is by faith. He experimentally found, that such an obedience as man can render, must be an obedience without hope, and without affection, and without one element which can liken it to the obedience of heaven—that the mere animal drudgery, to which a man feels himself impelled, by the impulse of force, or of fear, upon his corporeal powers, bears not only a different, but an essentially opposite, character, to that of an acceptable loyalty. He found that it is no religion at all, unless the heart consent to it, and the taste be engaged on its side, and the love which terror scares away, be the urging and inspiring principle; and the Lawgiver, instead of laying a reluctant constraint upon His creatures, sits enthroned in far more glorious supremacy over their will, thus exalting the service of God, from what it must be under the law, to what it may be under the Gospel. But when the Gospel came to him, in all the power and beneficence of conversion and grace, transforming the service of God from the oldness of the letter to the newness of the spirit, by listing, on the side of godliness, all the faculties and affections of his moral nature, he became the humble, devoted, and self-denying Christian; and admirably illustrated the sure operation of genuine faith, in producing practical righteousness, and in forming those who are under its influence, in all the virtues and accomplishments of Christianity. Mr. Scott was an eminently useful minister of the Gospel. His sound, judicious, and practical writings, form a most valuable accession to the theology of our country. The lessons of such a life, and such an experience as he has honestly delineated, are highly instructive to every class of Christians, but, to the sincere inquirer after truth, we would especially recommend them; and, under such convictions as the "Force of Truth" may produce, he will find in the subsequent Tracts, which compose the present volume, an excellent and practical exposition of those more peculiar doctrines of the Gospel, the right understanding of which is so necessary to the attainment of peace and of holiness; and these expositions will derive a peculiar weight and importance, as coming from such a sound and experimental Christian.

INTRODUCTORY ESSAY

TO

PRIVATE THOUGHTS ON RELIGION

AND

A CHRISTIAN LIFE.

BY WILLIAM BEVERIDGE, D.D.

THERE is a passage in the New Testament, where the law is made to stand to the sinner in the relation of a first husband; and on this relation being dissolved, which it is at the moment when the sinner becomes a believer, then Christ stands to him in the relation of a second husband; under which new relation, he brings forth fruit unto God, or, to use the expression of the apostle, "lives unto God." There is another passage from which we can gather, what indeed is abundantly manifest from the whole of Scripture, that to live unto God is in every way tantamount to living unto Christ—it being there represented as the general habit of believers, "to live no longer unto themselves, but unto Him who died for them and rose again." So that though there be no single quotation, where the two phrases are brought together, still it is a sound, because truly a scriptural representation of the state of a believer, that he is dead unto the law, and alive unto Christ.

Now we are sensible, that these, and similar phrases, have been understood in two meanings, which, though not opposite, are at least wholly distinct from each other; that is, either as expressive of the judicial state, or the personal character of a believer. By one's judicial state, we mean that state into which he is put by the judgment or sentence of a law. If the law, for example, condemn us, we are judicially, by that law, in a state of condemnation. This may be viewed distinctly from our personal character. Now the first meaning of the phrases, or that by which they are expressive of a judicial state, would be more accurately rendered, by slightly changing each of the phrases, into "dead by the law," and "alive by Christ." Whereas the "being dead unto the law," and "alive unto Christ," serve, without any change, accurately to express the second meaning, or that which is descriptive of the personal character of those to whom it is applied. There is no liberty used with the Bible, when we affirm, that whether the one or other of these meanings be indeed the meaning in any particular case, the doctrine involved in each is true and scriptural doctrine —that, in the first instance, every believer is dead by the law, and alive by Christ; and that, in the second instance, he is dead unto the law, and alive unto Christ,—or, in other words, that in whomsoever the former truth has been realized, the latter truth shall be realized also.

Every believer, and indeed every man is dead by the law. This is naturally the judicial state of all. The law issued its commandments, and made death the penalty of their violation. We have all incurred that penalty. It demanded not any given fraction of obedience, but a whole obedience—and this we have all come short of. We have at least incurred the sentence; and if the execution of it has not yet been fully inflicted, it is at least in sure reserve for those on whom it is to fall. They are like malefactors in custody. Their doom is awaiting them. They are not yet dead in reality, but they are dead in law. They have the dread prospect of the reality before them; and if they have nought but the law to deal with, they may well tremble or be in despair, as the prisoners of a hopeless condemnation.

The greater part of men are at ease, even amid the urgencies of a state so alarming. That they have broken the law of God gives them no concern; and their life passes as carelessly along, as if the future reckoning, and future vengeance, were all a fable. So cheap do they hold the high jurisprudence of Heaven, that they are scarcely conscious of having offended against it; or if ever visited with the suspicion that their obedience is not up to the lofty standard of God's commandments, they compound the matter in another way, and bring down the commandments of God to the lowly standard of their own obedience. God hath revealed Himself to the world, under the impressive character of a God who is not to be mocked—yet would they inflict upon Him most degrading mockery, by robbing every proclamation of His against the transgressors of the law of all effect and all significancy. If there be any dignity in Heaven's throne, or any truth, and power, and force of character in Him who sitteth thereon, His ordinations must stand fast, and His penalties, by which their authority is guarded, must have fulfilment. The government of the Supreme would be despoiled of all its majesty, if mercy were ever at hand to obliterate the guilt of our rebellion against it. The carnal heart of man may be proof against these demonstrations of guilt and of danger; yet, notwithstanding, it is true that we have incurred the debt, and come under the denunciations of a law, whereof it has been said, that heaven and earth must pass away ere one jot or one tittle of it shall fail.

This is the appalling condition of humanity, however seldom it may be adverted to, and however slightly it may be felt, in the listlessness of nature. To the great majority of men, all secure and unconscious as they are, it gives no disturbance. They are so much hurried with the manifold relations in which they stand to the things and the interests that are around them, that they overlook their great relation to God the Lawgiver, and to that law, all whose mandates have a force and a sanction that cannot be recalled. They are asleep to the awful realities of their state. They have trampled upon an authority which must be vindicated. They have incurred a threatening which must be discharged. They have insulted a throne whose dignity must be asserted—and cast contempt on a government, which shall rise in its might and its majesty from the degradation which they have tried to inflict upon it. The high attributes of the Divinity are against them. His Justice demands a satisfaction. His Holiness cannot but manifest the force of its recoil from moral evil. His word stands committed to the death and the destruction of sinners—and a nature so immutable as His, never can recede from those great principles which mark the character of His administration. The greater part of men escape from all this terror, while they live in mere insensibility; and some there are, who, because less enormous transgressors than their fellows, can lull their every apprehension, and be at ease. But the law will admit of no compromise. It will treat with no degree or modification of evil. They have broken some of the things contained in the book of God's law, and by the law they are dead.

The most exempt, perhaps, from all disquietude on the score of that death to which the law has condemned them, are they who, decorous in all the proprieties, and honorable in all the equities, and alive, by the tenderness of a softened, sympathetic nature, to all the kindnesses of life, stand the freest from all those visible delinquencies by which the law is most notoriously and most disgracefully violated. They lie not—they steal not—they defraud not. They are ever prompt in humanity, and most punctual in justice. They acquit themselves of every relative duty to the satisfaction of those who are the objects of it; and exemplary in all the moralities of our social state, they sustain upon earth a high and honorable reputation. Nevertheless it is possible, nay it is frequent, that a man may be signalized by all these graces of character, and yet be devoid of godliness. The first and greatest commandment, which is the love of God, may be the object, not of his occasional, but of his constant and habitual disobedience. In reference to this part of the law, he may have not merely fallen into many sinful acts, but more desperate still, he may be in a continual state of sinfulness. Instead of offending God at some times by the deeds of his hand, he may be offending him at all times, by that settled and invariable bent which there is in the desires of his heart. That bent may be wholly towards the world, and wholly away from him who made the world. He may have a thousand constitutional virtues: to use a familiar expression, he may have many good points or properties of character, and yet God not be in all his thoughts. His Father in heaven may have as little reason to be pleased with him, as an earthly father with that child, in whose history there may be a number of conformities with his own will, but in whose heart there is an obvious sullenness, or at least an utter disregard and indifference towards him. "Give me thy heart," says God, and "Love Him with all thy heart," says the law of God. It is by viewing the law, in all its height, that we are made to feel how deep the condemnation is into which the law has placed us. Our actions may look fair in the eye of society, while it is manifest, to the eye of our own conscience, that our affections are altogether set on time, and on the creature, and altogether turned from the Creator. Those virtues, which give us a flourishing name upon earth, are not enough to transplant us into heaven. The law which said, "Do these things and live," finds its very first doing, or demand, unsatisfied, and bars our entrance into heaven. It convicts us, not perhaps of many specific sins; but, most awfully decisive of our fortune through eternity, it convicts us of an unremitting course or current of sinfulness; and so, dead by the law, the gate of life is shut against us.

The counterpart to this awful truth, that by the law the sinner is dead, is that by Christ the believer is made alive. We may understand, in word and in letter, how this can be, even though we ourselves have had no part in the process. We may have the knowledge, though perhaps not the faith in it; and just as a spectator might look intelligently to a process in which he does not personally share, so might we have the literal apprehension of that way by which the sinner, who by the law is judicially dead, might by Christ become judicially alive. But aware of it though we be, it cannot be too often reiterated; and may the Spirit give a power and a demonstration to this important truth, when we say again how it is that the transgressor is made free. The sentence then is not annulled, it is only transferred. It is lifted up from his head, because laid on the head of another, who rather than that man should die, did Himself bear the burden of it. For this purpose did he bow Himself down unto the sacrifice, and submitted to that deep, that mysterious endurance, under which He had to sustain the weight of a world's atonement. The vials of the Lawgiver's wrath were exhausted upon Him. The law was magnified and made honorable in Him. In Him the work of vengeance was completed, and every attribute of the Godhead that man had insulted by his disobedience, did, on the cross of Christ, obtain its ample reparation. There, and under a weight of suffering which nought but the strength of the Divinity could uphold, the sacredness of the Divinity was awfully manifested; when, like a rainbow after the storm, the mercy of heaven arose out of the dark and warring elements, and has ever since shone upon our world, like a beauteous halo that now circles and irradiates all the other perfections of the Godhead. And the sight of it is as free to all as is the sun in the firmament. The elements of light and of air, and the other common bounties of nature, are not more designed for the use of each and all of the human species, than is the widely sounding call of "Look unto me all ye ends of the earth, and be ye saved." And whosoever he be that looks, and looks believingly, shall live. He is lightened of the burden of his guilt so soon as he puts faith in the Saviour. That great peace-offering for the sins of the world, becomes a peace-offering unto him. He exchanges conditions with his surety. His guilt is put to Christ's account, and Christ's righteousness is put to his account. He obtains his full discharge from the sentence that was against him; and whereas by the law he was dead, he hath made his escape from this judgment, and now by Christ is alive.*

We wish that we could give the adequate impression of that perfect welcome and good-will, wherewith all men are invited to the mercy-seat. Under the economy of the law there was a curse pronounced upon every one who continued not in all the words that were written in its book to do them; and the question is, how can any who has transgressed so much as one of these precepts, make his escape from this felt denunciation? Many there are who, to bring this about, would still keep up the old economy of the law, though in such a reduced and mutilated way, as might permit of an outlet to all but the most enormous of criminals. But the Gospel provides this outlet in another way, more direct, and distinct, and consistent, by taking down the old economy and setting up a new economy altogether. Christ hath redeemed us from the curse of the law being made a curse for us; and while by this expedient the honors of the commandment have been fully vindicated—by this expedient, also, the mercy of God, as if released from the impediment which held it, now goes forth rejoicingly, and in all its amplitude, to the farthest limits of a guilty world. There is not one so sunk in iniquity, that God, in Christ, does not beseech to enter forthwith into reconciliation. There is not one man under sentence of death by the law, to whom eternal life is not offered, and offered freely, as the gift of God through Jesus Christ our Lord. The sceptre of forgiveness is held out even to the chief of sinners; and a way of access has been opened, by which one and all of them are invited to draw nigh. Heaven would have shrunk, so ethereal and so sensitive is its holiness—it would have shrunk, in quick and immediate recoil, from the approaches of the guilty; but the way by which they now come is a consecrated way, consecrated

* For a full and explicit statement of this doctrine, we refer the reader to the 6th, 7th, 8th, and 9th articles of Bishop Beveridge's belief, as drawn up by himself in the following Treatise.

by the blood of an everlasting covenant; and along which all of us are beckoned to move, by every call, and every signal of encouragement. We are dead by the law, but it is a death from which we are bidden, by the voice of the Gospel, to come forth. And he that believeth therein, "though he were dead, yet shall he live."

This is the truth implied in the expression, that a Christian is dead by the law, and alive by Christ. We shall now consider the truth implied in the other expression, that a Christian is dead unto the law, and alive unto Christ. The former expression is significant of the judicial state of a believer. The latter is significant of his personal character. We may perhaps better understand the phrase of being "dead unto the law," when we think of such analogous phrases, as, the being dead unto sin; or dead unto the world; or dead to the fascinations of pleasure; or dead to the sensibilities of the heart; or dead to the urgencies of temptation. It expresses character, for it expresses man's insensibility, or the property that he has of being unmoved by certain objects that are addressed to him, but which either pleasurably or painfully affect the feelings of other men. He who can look unsoftened and unimpressed on a scene of wretchedness, or of cruel suffering, is dead to compassion. He who pities, and is in tenderness, is alive to it. He who can look without delight on the glories of a landscape, is dead to the charms of nature's scenery. He who can be told, without emotion, of some noble deeds of generosity or honor, is dead to the higher beauties of the mind, to the charms of moral grace, or of moral greatness.

A man is dead unto that, which, when present to him as an object of thought, is nevertheless not an object of feeling; and more especially when that which is lovely is placed within his view, and no love is awakened by it. It will therefore require some explanation, that we might apprehend aright the phrase of the apostle—"dead to the law." He cannot mean to say of himself, that he is dead to the beauties of that holiness which it contains—that he is dead to the worth of those virtues which lie engraven either on the first or second division of its tablet of jurisprudence—that he sees nought to admire in the godliness that is set forth in the one, or the humanity that is set forth in the other—that he is utterly devoid of aught like a taste, or an inclination within him, which can at all respond to that picture of moral excellence which the law puts before him; and so yielding no homage of desire towards it, he may have as good as renounced it in his doings. This surely is not the interpretation which can be put upon it; for the apostle elsewhere says of himself that he delighted in the law; and he eulogizes it as holy, and just, and good. Holy men of old loved the law, and it was their meditation all the day long—and the lyre of the Psalmist is re-echoed by the longings of every Christian heart, when he says, "O how I love thy law;" and "blessed is the man that delighteth greatly in its commandments."

There must be something else then, in and about the law, to which a believer is dead, than either the rightness of its precepts, or the moral and spiritual beauty of its perfections, when these are realized upon the character. Every true believer is most thoroughly alive both to the one and the other—and the question remains, What is it of the law to which he has become dead? Perhaps this question is best answered by the apostle's own statement, that we are dead in Christ, or that we have been partakers in his death—not that we partake with him in its sufferings, for this he endured alone, but we partake with him in its immunities, now that the sufferings are over. The believer stands now in the same relation to the law, that the man does, who has already sustained the execution of its sentence upon his person. It has no further claim upon him. He needs to fear no more, for he has to suffer no more. Its threatenings have all been discharged—not upon himself, it is true, but upon another for his sake, and by whom they have forever been averted from his own soul. He may now fear as little, and feel as little, of the law's severity, as can the dead body of the executed criminal: and it is in this sense that the believer is dead unto the law—not dead to the worth and the loveliness of its commandments, but altogether dead to the terror of its condemnation—not unmoved by the grace and the rightness of its moralities, but wholly unmoved, because now wholly placed beyond the reach of its menaces—not dead to its voice, when it points to the way of peace and pleasantness, but now conclusively dead to its voice as a relentless judge, or its countenance as a fierce and determined avenger, so that the believer may at once walk before God without fear, and yet walk before Him in righteousness and in holiness.

The older authors, whose writings are so much more richly fraught than those of our own days with the produce of deep and well-exercised intellect, on the various questions of theology, tell us of the law being now set aside as a covenant, while it remains with us as a rule of life. This single change of economy teaches us, to what of the law it is that we are dead, and to what of it we are still alive. We are dead to all those jealousies which are apt to arise about the terms and the punctualities of a bargain. There is no longer the lifting up of a bond, upon the one side, and this reacted to by the spirit of bondage, upon the other. There are a dread and a distrust, and the feeling of a divided interest, between two parties, when it is the business of the one to look after the due performance of certain covenanted articles, and of the other, by his square and regular performance of these, just to do as much as that he may escape the denounced penalty, or as that he may earn the stipulated reward. "I call you no longer servants but sons," did our Saviour say to His disciples; and this, perhaps, goes most effectually to distinguish between the obedience which is under the old, and that which is under the new economy. We do the very same things under both, but in a wholly different spirit. As sons, we do them from the feeling of love. As servants, we do them by the force of law. It is the spontaneous taste of the one. It is the servile task of the other. The meat and drink of the servant lie in the hire which is given for the doing of his master's will. The meat and drink of the son lie in the very doing of that will. He does not feel it to be a service, but the very solace and satisfaction of his own renovated spirit. It is well to apprehend this distinction; for it, in truth, is that which marks, most precisely, the evangelical from the legal obedience. To all these feelings, which have been termed the feelings, or the fears of legality, the believer under the economy of the New Testament is altogether dead. He is not exempted from service, but it is service in the newness of the spirit, and not in the oldness of the letter—not gone about in the style of a hireling, who looks merely to his reward, and is satisfied if he can but fulfil the literalities of that contract by which the reward is secured to him. We see how at once, by this single change, a new character is given to his obedience—how, when dead to the law, which tells him to do this and live, he looks away from all those narrow suspicions, and all those besetting fears, wherewith a mercenary service is encompassed—and how when alive to the Gospel, which first gives him life, and then bids him do, he instantly ascends upon a higher walk of obedience, being now urged onward by a taste for the virtues of the law, and not by the terror of its violation—and instead of looking for some distinct reward after the keeping of the commandments, which in truth argues nothing spontaneously good in the character at all, feeling even now, that in the keeping of the commandments there is a very great reward.

With this explanation of what it is to be dead unto the law, we may fully understand what it is to live unto Christ. As to be dead unto any object, is to want that sensibility which the object is fitted to awaken—then to be alive unto any object, is just to have the sensibility. One of our poets designates the child of sensibility to be one who is feelingly alive to each fine impulse. It is thus that we are alive to the call of distress—alive to the charms of a landscape—alive to the obligations of honor—alive to the charms of gratitude or friendship. It marks an attribute of the personal character, because it marks its degree of sensibility to any such objects as are presented to it; and we may easily consider what the result will be when Christ is the object, and when he to whom this object is addressed is alive unto Christ. Let us only conceive him to cast an intelligent look upon the Saviour, to compute aright the mighty surrender which He had to make, when He had to surrender the glory of heaven, for a death equivalent in its soreness to the eternity of accursed millions in hell—

let us think of the tenderness to our world which urged Him forth upon the errand to seek and to save it, and the strength of that unquenchable love which so bore him up amid the pains and the perils of His great undertaking—let us but look on the fearful agonies, and listen to the cries, that, in the hour and power of darkness, were extorted from Him, who had the energy of the Godhead to sustain Him, and who, from the garden to the cross, had to travel through a mystery of suffering, that sinners might go free—let us but connect this terror, and these shrinkings, of the incarnate Godhead, with the peace of our own unburdened consciences, as we draw near unto the mercy-seat, and plead our full acquittal from that vengeance which has already been discharged, from that penalty which has been already borne—let us bring together in thought, even as they stand together in reality, the love of Christ and our own dear-bought liberty, and that to Him all the immunities of our present grace, and all the brightest visions of our future immortality are owing. To be awake unto all this with the eye of the understanding, and to be alive unto all this with the susceptibilities of the heart, is just to be in that practical state which we now endeavor to set forth—and under which it is, that every true Christian gives up the devotedness of his whole life, as an offering of gratitude to Him who hath redeemed it—and feeling that "he is not his own, but bought with a price, lives no longer to himself, but to the Saviour who died for him and who rose again."

But it is the unceasing aim of gratitude to gratify its object; and the question comes to be, What precise direction will this affection, now stirring and alive in our hearts towards Christ, impress upon our history. This will resolve itself into the other question, of how is it that Christ is most gratified? what is it that He chiefly wills of us, or that we can do, which His desires are most set upon? For the resolution of this inquiry, the Scriptures of truth give us abundance of testimonies. His will is our sanctification. The great and ultimate object for which He put forth His hand upon us was to make us holy. He gave Himself up for us, that we might give ourselves up unto the guidance of that word, and the gracious operation of that Spirit, whereby He purifies unto Himself a peculiar people, and makes them zealous of good works. He has now risen to the throne of His appointed Mediatorship; and the voice that He addressed to His first disciples, still issues therefrom to the disciples of all ages—"If ye love me, keep my commandments;" and, "Ye are my friends, if ye do whatsoever I command you." Now the commandments of Christ to whom we are alive, are just the individual commandments of that law to which we are dead. The things to which we were before driven by the terrors of authority, are the very things to which we are now drawn by the ties of gratitude. God in His love to righteousness framed all the virtues which compose it into the articles of a covenant that we had violated, but which now in Christ is settled and set by. And God in His still unabated love to righteousness, yet wills to impress all the virtues of it upon our person. What before He inscribed on the records of a written commandment, He would now infuse within the repositories of a believer's breast—and those precepts which, under the old economy, were the ground of a condemnation that is now taken away, compose, under the new economy, a rule of life, the obligation of which remaineth with us forever.

Though the law be now taken away from the eye of the believer, yet Christ stands in its place, and these very virtues which were exacted by the one, are still taught and exemplified by the other.* He is the image and representation of His Father, and long ere the moralities of absolute and everlasting rectitude were impressed on a tablet of jurisprudence, they had their place and their living delineation in the character of the Godhead. The laws and threatenings of the tablet are now expunged and taken away from the sight of the believer, but the character remains in full view, and now more impressively bodied forth than ever, because now a sensible representation has been given of it in the person of Jesus Christ. And to be alive unto Christ, is to be alive to the beauties of this representation. There is more implied by it than gratitude for His love. It further implies the admiration of His loveliness. With both together we superadd to the obedience of His precepts, the imitation of His example; and it is in the busy prosecution of them, that every true disciple abounds in the fruits of righteousness, and so lives unto God. The matter of the commandment is the same that it ever was. The motive only is changed. Then we wrought for the favor of God; or rather, under the despair of having fallen short, we wrought for the purpose of some possible escape, or to mitigate the vengeance that we found to be awaiting us. Now we work in the secure and conscious possession of this favor, and rejoice in the will and the ways of Him who rejoices over us to do us good. It has ceased to be the service of constraint. It has come to be the service of willingness. It is a thank-offering, and more than this, it is our now voluntary deference to that law whose precepts we love, and love the more, that we have now been placed beyond the reach of its penalties. It is to the latter only that we are dead, for to the former we are most thoroughly alive; and, instead of the servilities of a forced obedience, we now render unto God the spontaneous homage of a freeman, the love and loyalty of a friend.

It is thus that every true disciple, while dead unto the law, is living unto God. We can imagine the law to be written on a tablet, and suspended between us and God; Him pointing both to

* We again refer the reader to that Section, in the Second Part of this work, which treats of "The Imitation of Christ," for an admirable illustration of our preceding argument.

its precepts and its penalties, and we become conscious of our utter deficiency from the one, and tremblingly alive to a dread of the other. It is well that this be felt by the sinner, till he is prevailed upon to flee from the coming wrath which is thus denounced upon him by the law, and to flee for refuge to the hope set before him in the Gospel. Thus it is, in the language of Paul to the Colossians, that the hand-writing of ordinances that was against us, is blotted out, and taken out of the way; and the believer is now dead to the terror of all those penalties, to which aforetime he had been most powerfully alive. The penalties are now taken out of sight, but the precepts are not taken out of sight. It is true that the frightful inscription, which stood as a barrier or an interdict between him and God, is now removed; and the consequence is, that he is now brought nigh unto God, whose character has undergone no change, but who bears the same unaltered love to all the moralities of righteousness as before. And so those identical virtues which, under the law, are addressed unto men as the precepts of an authoritative code, and have been resisted by all, are still addressed unto men as the persuasions of a now reconciled friend, and which every believer in Jesus Christ finds to be irresistible. They stood then associated with the frown, and the compulsion, and the curse, and all the other accompaniments of a ministry of condemnation, to which by this time he is dead. They stand now associated with the kindness, and the affectionate urgency, and the sympathy of manifested example, and the native beauties of holiness, to all of which he is now most thoroughly, and most feelingly alive. The expression of a wish from God under the new dispensation, has a greater moral ascendency over the believer's heart, than even a commandment had under the old. In a word, the spirit of bondage has fled away, and in its place has come the spirit of adoption, in the power of which he lives unto God, and abounds in all the fruits, and all the performances of willing obedience.

We may now understand how it is that a change in the judicial state brings about a change in the private character; how it is, that he who is dead by the law, when he is made alive by Christ, becomes dead unto the law and alive unto Christ. When we receive the truth that is in Jesus, we are justified: for then we are justified by faith. And to understand the way in which this truth makes us holy; or, how it is that we are sanctified by faith, we have only to consider the believer as dead unto the law, in the sense wherein we have already explained it, simply because he now believes that Christ hath redeemed him from its condemnation and its curse. It is because of the connection between his faith and his peace. He is no longer alive to the terror of those threatenings which are by the law, now that he sees its threatenings to have been all of them discharged. He is no longer under the dread of its vengeance, now that the vengeance is absorbed.

He is no longer afraid of a reckoning for the debts and deficiencies that he had incurred, seeing that Christ has been reckoned with as his surety—bearing the penalties of his disobedience, and giving him in exchange, the reward of His own perfect righteousness. It is just because he has been made judicially alive by Christ, that he is now dead to all the alarm of that judicial condemnation under which he aforetime lay. The one comes simply and immediately out of faith in the other; and is the same sort of moral phenomenon with that of a man ceasing to have the apprehension of a danger that impended over him, on the moment of being made to perceive that the danger has passed away.

But, the believer is not only dead unto the law, but alive unto Christ. This is because of the connection between his faith and his gratitude. It is by Christ's work that we are released from the pains of a violated law; but yet, it is His will that we do the precepts of it; and in His person too there is the highest exemplification of its graces and virtues. When we believe in His work, we become alive to a sense of cordial and willing obligation; and when we understand what His will is, we become alive to the moralities of that very law, to whose menaces we are altogether dead. It is at that transition by which we are released from its penalties, that we become riveted to the admiration of its perfections, and the devoted followers of its truth and justice, and humanity and holiness. Every man who has been made alive by Christ, must be alive to Him; so as to live no longer to himself, but to live unto Christ who died for him, and who rose again. There is nought in the Gospel which exempts us from obedience, but everything in it and about it which excites to obedience—to obedience in a better spirit than we could possibly have under the law—to obedience, if we may so speak, in a higher style of it,—not the obedience that is extorted by terror or by power, but the obedience to which we are urged by taste and by gratitude. And amid all the darkness of human controversy and explanation, one thing is clear—even the apostolical test of our truly knowing Christ, that we keep his commandments.

But, while we insist on this as the true test of discipleship, we are no less strenuous in insisting on a sound faith, convinced as we are of the intimate connection which subsists between a sound faith and a sound practice. Without the former we have the highest authority for stating, that it is impossible to please God; though the latter we hold to be no less necessary as the indispensable preparation for heaven, since without holiness no man can see God; and therefore would we labor to make every inquirer acquainted with the foundation of a Christian's hope, as well as the rule of a Christian's practice. And, for this purpose, instead of offering any further exposition of our own on these two most important topics, we would recommend to his perusal the two following Treatises of Bishop Beveridge, "Thoughts on Religion," and "On a Christian Life," where he will find an admirable conjunction of the great doctrines of Christianity, with those graces and accomplishments of the Christian character, which form the necessary fruits and consequences of a genuine faith in these doctrines; and from which are derived the only motives of sufficient power and potency, for establishing the authority of Christian morality in the heart, and for securing obedience to it in the life.

In his first Treatise this learned and pious prelate gives an enumeration of the articles of his faith, with a clearness and precision which indicate that he had a distinct and scriptural view of the dispensation of grace, in all its relations and dependencies; while the "Resolutions" formed thereupon, deduced as they are from the articles of his faith, and deriving from them their whole force and urgency of motive, are admirably fitted for regulating the affections and conduct of the aspiring candidate for heaven. And we apprehend, that it is from the want of such distinct and well-defined rules for the government of their thoughts, and actions, and general intercourse in the world, which this pious bishop deemed so necessary for the regulation of his own heart and life, that many professing Christians, not otherwise defective in a sound orthodoxy, do nevertheless exhibit much that is defective and inconsistent in their Christian profession. In this so important a branch of Christian duty, and so conducive to the consistency and comfort of the Christian life, the example of this excellent prelate is highly worthy of imitation; and when entered into, in an humble dependence on the strength and sufficiency of Him in whose grace alone he can be strong, the Christian disciple will find it conducive to his personal sanctification and growth in the divine life.

The second Treatise contains a no less excellent and valuable exposition of several important topics, which are intimately connected with the formation and successful prosecution of the Christian life. His observations on the Christian education of children, are entitled to the serious regard of those parents who are in earnest to bring up their children in the nurture and admonition of the Lord; and in the subsequent topics, which form the concluding portion of his work, there is a close and forcible application of truth to the conscience, addressed with all the power and solemn earnestness of a man, who felt as well as understood the truths he was expounding. Bishop Beveridge was an eminent and successful minister of the Gospel of Christ, and was a distinguished ornament of that church of which he was a dignitary; and we cannot give a better portraiture of this truly good and pious man, both as a private Christian and as a public functionary, than by transcribing the following character of him, as drawn by his biographer.

"This great and good bishop had very early addicted himself to piety and a religious course of life, of which his Private

Thoughts upon Religion will be a lasting evidence. They were written in his younger years; and he must a considerable time before this, have devoted himself to such practices, otherwise he could never have drawn up so judicious and sound a declaration of his faith, nor have formed such excellent resolutions so agreeable to the Christian life in all its parts. These things show him to be acquainted with the life and power of religion long before, and that even from a child he knew the Holy Scriptures. And as his piety was early, so it was very eminent and conspicuous, in all the parts and stations of his life. As he had formed such good resolutions, he made suitable improvements upon them; and they, at length, grew up into such settled habits, that all his actions savored of nothing but piety and religion. His holy example was a very great ornament to our church; and he honored his profession and function by zealously discharging all the duties thereof. How remarkable was his piety towards God! What an awful sense of the divine Majesty did he always express! How did he delight in His worship and service, and frequent His house of prayer! How great was his charity to men; how earnestly was he concerned for their welfare, as his pathetic addresses to them in his discourses plainly discover! How did the Christian spirit run through all his actions, and what a wonderful pattern was he of primitive purity, holiness, and devotion! As he was remarkable for his great piety and zeal for religion, so he was highly to be esteemed for his learning, which he wholly applied to promote the interest of his great Master. He was one of extensive and almost universal reading; he was well skilled in the oriental languages, and the Jewish learning, as may appear from many of his sermons; and indeed he was furnished to a very eminent degree with all useful knowledge. He was very much to be admired for his readiness in the Scriptures: he had made it his business to acquaint himself thoroughly with those sacred oracles, whereby he was furnished unto all good works: he was able to produce suitable passages from them on all occasions, and was very happy in explaining them to others. Thus he improved his time and his abilities in serving God, and doing good, till he arrived at a good old age, when it pleased his great Master to give him rest from his labors, and to assign him a place in those mansions of bliss, where he had always laid up his treasure, and to which his heart had been all along devoted through the whole course of his life and actions. He was so highly esteemed among all learned and good men, that when he was dying, one of the chief of his order deservedly said of him, 'There goes one of the greatest, and one of the best men, that ever England bred.' "

INTRODUCTORY ESSAY

TO

THE REIGN OF GRACE,

FROM ITS RISE TO ITS CONSUMMATION.

BY ABRAHAM BOOTH.

There is no one term which is more frequently employed in the Bible, to denote our relationship to God, than the term *covenant*. But though the import of this term is sufficiently understood when it relates to the intercourse between man and man, we fear it is very indistinctly apprehended when it expresses our relation to God. A covenant is an agreement between at least two parties, and it is generally at first proposed by one of them, and then acceded to by the other. If the former be very distinct, and absolute, and peremptory in the terms that he lays down, the latter, in the act of giving his acquiescence, feels that he is coming under very distinct and certain obligations. The engagement is just felt to be as formal upon the one side, as it is upon the other —and when it is a contract between man and man, there is a strict and definite understanding, both with him who originated the articles, and him who complies with them.

It is thus, in any social or earthly covenant. We there see how anxiously the utmost explicitness is secured, by one clause and one stipulation after another, that each may know the distinct place he has to occupy, and the distinct part he has to perform. There is a certain relative position in which the one party stands to the other, so that when the one enters upon his place in the covenant, and then acts the part that is assigned to him, the other conforms to the covenant by entering upon his place, and acting the part that is assigned to him. Were there a loose or obscure understanding on the one side, then, on the other side, there might be freedom for a loose and obscure understanding also. But a well-framed covenant does away all looseness, and admits of nothing but what is strict and determinate; so that all who are concerned may have a clear and well-defined path to walk in. The formal and peremptory attitude of one party in the covenant, calls for a corresponding attitude from the other, and summons him to an observation just as pointed and as rigorous as the terms that are imposed. And the line of performance for each is so marked out, that each is fully aware when he keeps by it, and as fully aware when he steps aside into any track of deviation.

Now, if such be the real force and import of a covenant, what a lesson does it hold forth, when this is the very term that the Bible so often employs in expressing that transaction by which a man enters into a right relationship with God. What a power of rebuke is conveyed by this single term, on the loose, and indefinite, and floating imaginations of almost every man, as to the right federal position which he himself should occupy, and as to the question, whether he has actually and personally entered upon it. What a fell denunciation does this one vocable carry with it, not merely on the unsettledness of his accounts with God, but on the unsettledness even of his conceptions, as to the footing upon which, if we may use the expression, the account is opened with Him. How vague the apprehensions of the vast majority are, as to the terms in which an agreement is struck with God, and as to the way and method in which that agreement is kept up and maintained with Him. And this charge extends a great deal farther than to those who profess no care and no concern about the matter. How many may be specified of those who are versant in the whole orthodoxy of the new covenant, and yet with whom the question is altogether undetermined, whether it be a covenant that they have individually laid hold of. They love the evangelical language, and they like to breathe in the atmosphere of an evangelical society, and they feel that the decided preference of their taste is towards the tone and habit of evangelical professorship, and yet, with all this, they have not set themselves to the question, "What shall I do to be saved?" with that pointedness, and formality, and mature deliberation upon articles, which the very term of a covenant appears to demand of them. They breathe, perhaps, many good desires, and are in the way of many good impulses, and give their most cordial assent to the truth and importance of all the scriptural doctrine that is proposed to them; nay, can speak soundly and well about the new covenant, and yet have never distinctly, and solemnly, and individually, charged the obligation of its articles upon themselves—living very much adrift and at random after all—with no distinct place of relationship to God, personally and actually in occupation—with no urgent or practical sense of any clearly articled engagement between Him and them, viewed in the light of two parties linked together by the tie of mutual promises, and respectively bound to certain mutual performances, and habitually unconscious, all the day long, of having taken up any position in which they have certain appropriate duties to discharge, and every occupier of which has the right to look from the other party in the contract for the fulfilment of certain stipulations.

Meanwhile there is no want either of clearness or of precision with God. All is pointed and peremptory in the manifesto that He has given of Himself to the world. He wills us to enter into covenant with him, but lays down the terms of it in a way so distinct and so authoritative, as to preclude and lay an interdict upon all others. In framing the articles of this covenant, all the high and unchanging principles of heaven's jurisprudence were concerned—and we behold upon the face of it, the sure impress of that moral character which obtains in the sanctuary above. It is a document which announces the truth, and the justice, and the uncompromising dignity of the government by which it has been issued; and there is indeed a striking contrast between the disregard in which it is held by men on earth, and the intense earnestness of that gaze which it drew from the choirs and the companies of the celestial. "Which things the angels desire to look into." So that there is no lightness, and no looseness, in the terms of that proposal which came down to us from heaven. The question, of how an alliance between God and sinners could be struck, and how a right ceremonial of approach and meeting between the parties could be adjusted, and what sort of compact ought to be devised, so as to satisfy the claims, and suit itself to the character of each—these are questions which, however slighted in a world, where all that is above, is looked to through the dull medium of its gross and incumbent carnality—they are questions which have exercised the purest and mightiest intelligences in nature, and which belong to the very essence of the rectitude that is everlasting. They are questions, for the right determination of which, we see all heaven, as it were, in a busy movement of concern—and the public mind of God's unfallen universe, at least, directed in solemn contemplation towards them, and an overture made out with all the form and circumstance of a covenant that was to be unalterable; and this delivered into the hands of a Mediator, who, both by the dignity of His person, and the power of His high, though mysterious achievements, has added to the weight and sacredness of the whole transaction;—and thus has it been ushered in with a style of authority to the notice of our species, who are called to listen, that they may hear of the only way in which God will be approached, and of the only terms in which He will treat with them. And is not this a call upon us to look more strictly into the matter of our relationship with God, and a reproach to us for the vague indifference of our minds upon the subject, and an urgent application to our conscience, whether we have taken up our part in the account, and whether there has been such an event in our history, as a great federal transaction between us and the Lawgiver in heaven; whether we have struck with Him, or closed with Him, upon His own terms;

whether the fulfilment of our part of the covenant in time, is our habitual business, and the fulfilment of His part of it, both in time and in eternity, is our habitual expectation—in a word, whether we are living as we list, or living by the terms of a treaty actually concluded and entered upon between us and God. These are questions that need to be addressed, not merely to those on whom the terms and the obligations of religion have no hold, but to those who are longing after it, though in hitherto fruitless aspirations; to those who, yet wrapt in a kind of general mistiness, have never seen the certainty of that track which they have to pursue, and never felt the solidity of that ground which they have to walk upon—who sigh, and expatiate, and spend their earnestness among fruitless generalities—who still feel themselves bewildered in the haze of undefined speculation—and have neither the confident look, nor yet the confirmed footstep of him who knows his calling, and who has actually taken hold of a sure and a well-ordered covenant.

We apprehend that there is an actual, and a highly interesting class, who exemplify the very condition of mind which we now attempt to characterize. The truth is, it marks a sort of transitive state in the progress from nature to grace, which the great generality of inquirers have to undergo. There is such a thing as a longing desirousness to be right, but without any clear or steady perception of the avenue that leads to it—an honest, but yet an undirected inclination of the mind towards God—a heart under the visitation of strong concern, that its possessor should be what he ought, and do what he ought, but still laboring in the midst of many fears and many fluctuations, and that just because he looks with a still clouded eye, on the field of spiritual contemplation that lies before him. This is a state, which reminds us somewhat of the exercise of the Psalmist, when he says, "My soul breaketh for the longing that it hath unto thy judgments at all times," and that, shortly after he had said, in the perplexity of his felt darkness, "Open thou mine eyes, that I may behold wondrous things out of thy law." Now we would pronounce of him who is in this state, that his face is towards Zion. He is seeking the Lord, if haply he may feel after Him and find Him; and laboring to enter upon a rest which he hath not yet attained to—familiar with all the sounds and all the doctrines of orthodoxy, but without being conscious, as yet, of having taken up that position which orthodoxy would assign individually to him—rather trying to put himself into the attitude of readiness for the Lord, than actually waiting in that attitude for the coming of the Lord—thoroughly aware that there is a posture of preparation, but utterly in the dark, whether it is a posture that he has personally assumed—and in the face of a covenant offered from heaven for his acceptance, with all its articles penned under the dictates of clear and unerring wisdom, still "running as uncertainly, still fighting even as one that beateth the air."

This is a matter which ought not to be left in a state of unsettledness. If ever there was a business which it were desirable should be brought to a point, it is surely that which involves in it the state of a creature towards God. Of all the questions that lie within the compass of human speculation, this ought not to be abandoned to the caprices of a loose and floating imagination. "What shall I do to be saved?" and "wherewithal shall I come before God?" these are interrogatories precise in the object of them, nor should we rest satisfied with anything short of a precise and clearly intelligible solution. It is woful to think of the frivolity wherewith the mind can shift itself away from the urgency of these questions, and by an act of indefinite postponement, can commit them to a futurity that, in all likelihood, will ever be receding till that hour which separates its misspent time from its unprovided eternity. Were there anything slack or indeterminate in the articles of God's message to the world, this might well apologize for a corresponding remissness on the part of man. But when this message has come in pointed application to us, and armed with all the rigor and imperative force of an *ultimatum*, and has taken the shape of a covenant, in which God offers His terms, and both demands and entreats our compliance with them—there is no room left for parrying or evasion; nor do we meet aright this advancing movement on the part of God, but by our distinct response to His distinct and peremptory overtures.

It were well, if, under the impulse of such considerations, we were to take up the language of the Prophet, and say, "Come then, and let us join ourselves to the Lord." There is one way of setting forth upon this movement, to which nature feels a very strong and general inclination. Nothing can be more natural than the conclusion—that hitherto we have done wrong, and are therefore out of terms and out of friendship with God. Let us henceforth do right, and thus we shall recover the ground from which our own sins have disposted us. There is a universal propensity among men to feel in this manner. It is by our own doings that we have forfeited our claim upon God; and it is by our own doings that the claim is to be re-established. The truth is, that though the old covenant of—"Do this and live," is now an utter wreck, in virtue of man's disobedience, yet the feelings and tendencies of man's unrenewed nature still retain, as it were, the very mould and impress of such a covenant; and we are not aware of a more prevailing imagination, or of one that lurks more insidiously, and operates more powerfully in the human bosom, than that acceptance with God can somehow be carried by a certain character of meritoriousness, in the desire of our own hearts, and in the doing of our own hands. And this, our first attempt, is so to manage as that heaven shall be rightfully ours, in virtue of our rendered services, and that it shall come to us on the footing of a legal payment, by which value is given for the value that has been received. The secret, but certain aim, in the first instance, of every man who goes out in quest of immortality, is so to qualify himself, as that he may demand it as a right at the bar of justice, instead of suing for it as a boon at the bar of mercy. And this is what the Bible calls " going about to establish a righteousness of our own"—founding a plea on which we may challenge heaven as our well-earned remuneration, or as the fulfilment of a bargain between two parties—standing on the even ground of "work and win," upon the one side, and "accept of that work, and bestow an adequate reward for it," upon the other. The man who works with this for his object, is said to work in the spirit of legality; and this we hold to be the aspiring and universal spirit of nature, in its first attempts to reunite with the God from whom sin has so widely dissevered it.

This fond and clinging tendency on the part of man, to get into terms with God on the footing of the old covenant, after that covenant has been broken into shreds, or, if he persist in his tendency, will gather itself up against him into a body of overwhelming condemnation, has come down to us from our first parents, and is deeply incorporated with that nature which they have transmitted over the whole family of their descendants. It is not peculiar to Jews, who wanted to make a righteousness out of their Mosaic law. It extends to the men of all countries, and of all colors, who, out of the law of conscience, or the law of conventional propriety in their neighborhood, or the law to which tradition, and revelation, and custom, have made their respective contributions, still want to rear a righteousness of their own, which God, on the principles of justice, shall be bound to accept, and, on the same principles, shall be bound to reward. This spirit of legality, whatever may be its disguises, has a prompting and a presiding influence at the outset of all our returning movements unto God. And it is a spirit to which He has most broadly adverted in the new covenant, that he has framed for the purpose of bringing sinners again into fellowship with Himself, and there He peremptorily refuses to give it any countenance. He utterly refuses to enter into any degrading compromise with human sinfulness—and, setting up the authority of His law, as a thing that was unchangeable and irreducible, He holds that, by one act of disobedience, the foundation of merit, on the part of the creature, is utterly cut away. It is said of God, that He cannot lie, and therefore may it be said of Him, that He cannot accept the unfinished conformities of man to a rule that is inflexible; He cannot accept of these as the claims to which are to be adjudged the high rewards of heaven's jurisprudence. We are outcasts from the old covenant, if, in a single instance, we have made free with the authority of God, or trampled on any of His requirements. And on the face of the new covenant, there is nothing that stands out more strongly, than the decisive check which it has laid on the spirit of legality, than the wide and welcome way in which it throws open the gate of heaven to all, if willing to enter there on the footing of a divine grant, and the firm interdict which, at the same time, it throws across the path of all who offer to approach on the footing of their own merits. There is not one more obvious or prominent characteristic of the Gospel, than just the way in which it meets and encounters the spirit of legality at the very outset, and must either conquer it into entire submission, or decline to treat with it altogether. It holds forth an alternative, on the one side of which the access between God and man is hopelessly and everlastingly barred, and on the other side of which there is a patent way of approach, even to the place "where His honor dwelleth," and where His favor is as free as the elements of air and light, to all who will. All who propose to join themselves to the Lord in that covenant, to which He has actually put His consenting hand, ought to be aware of this—nor are they prepared for such a movement, till brought to acquiesce in the saying, "that not by works of righteousness which we have done, but according to His mercy He hath saved us."

But it is altogether worthy of remark, that the mercy by which we are saved, is mercy in conjunction with righteousness. On the work of our redemption, the sacredness of the Godhead stands as prominently out as does the tenderness of the Godhead. God did not so love the world, as, under the simple instigation of a compassionate feeling towards it, to send a message of forgiveness, and thus make known to sinners the mere clemency of His nature. He so loved the world, as to send His only begotten Son into it, who took upon Him the punishment of our guilt, and the whole burden of that obedience which we should have rendered; and thus made known the righteousness of His nature, as well as its clemency, in that He thereby approved Himself just, while the Justifier of those who believe in Jesus. This is the leading characteristic of the Gospel dispensation. It is a dispensation of mercy, but of mercy in alliance with truth; a mercy illustrative of all those high and unchangeable perfections which belong to the great moral Sovereign of the universe. He makes us all welcome to pardon, but it is to pardon sealed by the blood of a divine atonement. He beckons the guiltiest of men to draw nigh, but it is only by the path of an appointed and consecrated mediatorship. He holds out the remission of sins to one and to every; yet it is not a simple sentence of remission that He passes upon any, but a sentence of justification; or, in other words, a sentence given in consideration of a righteousness. To every sinner there is declared the offer of his remission, that in laying hold of it, he may do homage to the gentle and compassionate attributes of the Deity. But to every sinner there is declared at the same time, the righteousness on which this deed of remission is founded, that he may also do homage to the august and holy attributes of the

Deity. He who confides in the general mercy of God, would break up this association, which God will never consent to dissolve. His hatred of sin, and the high moral regard He bears to the worth and the rectitude of virtue, are stamped on every feature of that economy which He has instituted for the acceptance and recovery of the sinful. It is thus that the priesthood of Christ stands forward to observation, in characters of sanctity, as bright and legible as it does in the characters of benignity. And therefore it is not a proffer of bare mercy, but of propitiated mercy, that is held out for our acceptance. God does not set forth Himself with a general declaration of pardon to the sins of mankind; but He sets forth His Son a propitiation for the sins of mankind. And what we have to look to, is not the mercy of God unguarded and unqualified; but the mercy of God in Christ, and through Christ, reconciling the world.

There is no question that appears to have been more solemnly entertained, and more deliberately weighed in the counsels of the upper sanctuary, than how to determine the footing on which the guilty shall be taken back again, into acceptance with the God whom they had offended. And to provide a solid footing, Christ had both to serve and to suffer in our stead. Lest our sins should pass unreckoned, and so escape the punishment that was due to them, they were reckoned unto Christ; and lest the righteousness that He as Mediator has brought in, should pass unreckoned, and so miss of a reward, it is reckoned unto us. And thus, in the highest exhibition of generosity that ever was given to the world, we behold, at the same time, all the precision of a justice that could not deviate, and all the unchangeableness of a truth that could not fail. Had we fulfilled the law of God, heaven would have been ours, and it would have been given to us because of our righteousness. We have broken that law, and yet heaven may be ours, not because of our righteousness, but still because of a righteousness; and the honor of God is deeply involved in the question, What and whose righteousness this is? It is not the righteousness of man, but the righteousness of Christ reckoned unto man. The whole distinction between a covenant that is now exploded, and the covenant that is now in force, hinges upon this alternative. If we make a confidence of the former plea, we shall perish; and if of the latter, we shall have life everlasting.

God is merciful; and in virtue of this, it was His longing desire to frame a deed of reconciliation, and to convey it to our world. But God is also righteous; and in virtue of this, the very peculiar economy of a mediatorship, and an incarnation, and a sacrifice, had to be instituted, through which this deed of mercy was to pass; and in its way, it became tinged as it were, with the full expression of the entire and unbroken character of the Godhead. So, that when it reaches the sinner, it bears upon it the impress of the divine justice, as well as of the divine benignity. It is only by the acceptance of this deed on the part of the sinner, that God will consent on His part to take the sinner into acceptance. He will not enter into fellowship with the guilty, but in such a way as shall secure their complete recognition of all the attributes of His nature. Forgiveness by a mere demonstration of mercy is not that way. Reward from Him as a generous master, to man for his own righteousness, through an unworthy servant, is not that way. The way must be such as to manifest not a degraded, but a vindicated Sovereign; and so, that the mercy which He awards shall be that, not of fallen, but of exalted majesty. And hence the peremptory announcement, that no man cometh unto the Father but by the Son, and the no less peremptory rejection of every man who offers by any other approach, to draw nigh unto the sanctuary. The whole character of heaven's jurisprudence hangs upon the question, Whether man shall stand before God upon his own righteousness, or the righteousness of Christ? nor is there a more direct and pointed article in that covenant by which a sinner joins himself to God, than, that on the one ground he will never meet with acceptance, and on the other ground, he will never miss it.

It is painful to be told of the insecurity of all those refuges to which nature most fondly clings, and in which she most rejoices as her favorite hiding-place. Man is never more in his element, than when building a security before God, on some plea or palliation of his own; and it is not without a sigh, or without a struggle, that he can behold the foundation of all merit in himself utterly swept away. The only redress we can offer, is to assure him of the stability of that other, and that only foundation on which we invite him to build. It is to announce to him, in the language of Scripture, that as he has failed in making out a righteousness by his obedience to the law, "Christ is the end of the law for this righteousness, to every one that believeth." It is to make him perceive, that if he will only consent to stand on the righteousness of Christ, as the alone ground of his dependence, God will stand by the articles of His own covenant, for the fulfilment of which we have both His affirmation and His oath, as our immutable guarantees. He will never mock the confidence which His own word has inspired, and therefore one and all should encourage themselves on the strength of this assurance, and cast the cause of their acceptance on that unfailing plea, that is never lifted up by man without ascending in welcome to the throne of God. The merit of His well-beloved Son is to Him the incense of a sweet-smelling savor, so that the guiltiest creature who takes shelter there, has posted himself on the very avenue, along which there ever rolls the tide of divine complacency. We should invest ourselves then with this merit, and wrap ourselves firmly in it, as in a covering. We should put on Christ, who is offered to us without money and without price. We should present ourselves before

God, with His invitation as our alone warrant, and the truth of His promises, which are yea and amen in Christ Jesus, as our alone confidence. His place in the new covenant is to declare our forgiveness, through the blood of a satisfying atonement. Our place in the covenant, is to give credit to that declaration. If each of the parties take his own place, all the promises that have passed from the one to the other will have their fulfilment. If we have faith in God, according to our faith, so will be His faithfulness.

The act of laying hold of this covenant, is primarily and essentially an act of the mind. It is a business, at the doing of which, there may have been no visible or external movement at all; a transaction entered upon, and completed in no other character of agency, than the character of thought, and the fruit of a silent interview between the Spirit of God and the spirit of man, the former showing unto the latter the things of Christ, and the latter rendering the consent of his understanding and belief to this demonstration. These are the unseen but substantial steps, by which an act of reconciliation is struck between the two parties, and both the overtures on the one side, and the responses on the other, may be altogether mental. When God makes it known to the sinner, by His word and Spirit, that Christ hath wrought out a perfect righteousness, to the whole use and validity of which he is just as welcome as if the righteousness were personally his own; and when the sinner, persuaded of the truth of this, is simply translated into the same confidence before God that he would have had, had his own personal righteousness been perfect like that of Christ's; then the covenant of grace is in very deed entered upon, and without any other forth-putting on the part of God, than the exhibition of His word to man, and any other forth-putting on the part of man, than the acquiescence that he has rendered thereto. God's declaration of a righteousness unto all, and upon all who believe, constitutes His offer. The credit we give to this declaration constitutes our acceptance. To receive Christ, we have only to believe in His name. It is altogether a mental process. Our renunciation of the plea of our own righteousness, is a mental act. Our reliance on the plea of the righteousness of Christ, is a mental act. Our drawing upon God for forgiveness and justification in the name of this righteousness, is a mental act. And God hath graciously bound Himself to accept and to honor this method of drawing. He has so ordered the covenant between us and Him, that on our simply counting Him faithful who hath promised, He counts Himself pledged to the fulfilment on us of what is so promised. Could we state the thing more freely we would do it, for sure we are that the more freely it is stated, the more truly it is stated. We have failed in making out a title-deed to God's favor by our own obedience. Christ hath made one out for us by His obedience. If we believe it to be a good title-deed, it is ours, if we will. Should we be satisfied with it, God is. We are putting honor upon Christ, when we trust in the plea of His righteousness; and God is putting honor upon Christ, when He sustains the validity of this plea. Thus, there is a common place of meeting between God and the sinner, when the belief of the one, and the blessing of the other, come into close and rejoicing fellowship. Should any one who reads his Bible, and relying on God's testimony conceive this belief, then, on the strength of this mental inclination alone, he has laid hold of the covenant. He has become invested with a complete righteousness, the whole reward of which will be conferred on him, simply because of his reliance upon it. It is his by faith. A negotiation has been going on between God and his soul, and such is the force and obligation of the contract which has resulted from it, between the two parties—that while the one is bound to depend, the other is bound not to disappoint him.

We never shall obtain any secure or legitimate rest to our minds, till we have thus found it in Jesus Christ, as the Lord our righteousness—till we have come to trust wholly in His merit, and not at all in our own, as our alone plea of meritorious acceptance with the righteous Lawgiver—till the free offer of a title to eternal life, through the obedience of another, be met by our faithful acceptance of it; and on cleaving to it as our single but sufficient claim to reconciliation, have learned in this attitude to walk in quietness, and with confidence before God.

It is not in our power to reason any one into this confidence. It springs in the heart of man, on the simple statement of the truth, and by the manifestation of that truth, by the Spirit, unto the conscience. Argument and eloquence are alike unavailing towards the production of it. It is by the doctrine being presented to the mind, and the mind perceiving in the doctrine a counterpart to its own wants; it is thus that the faith comes which is unto salvation. We have endeavored to offer a faithful exhibition of the truth as it is in Jesus; and it is the part of the inquirer to ponder it attentively, and the Spirit may so convince of sin, and may so manifest the suitableness of the proffered Saviour, as to assure him, that this is indeed the wished-for remedy to the grievous and deep felt disease. And therefore would we state the averments of Scripture, on this most essential and interesting of all subjects, with the view of putting it to those who have sought for rest, and have not yet found it, whether these words bear not the evidence of a testimony from heaven, seeing it is only by a sure and simple reliance upon them, that they can reach the object they have so long and so vainly been in quest of.

"Christ was delivered for our offences." "Christ hath made an end of transgressions, and brought in an everlasting righteousness." "God hath set Him forth a propitiation for the sins of the world." "He died the just for the unjust, to bring us unto God.' "He has been made sin for us, though He knew no sin, that we might become the righteousness of God in Him." "Justified by faith, we have peace with God, through Jesus Christ our Lord." "And all who believe in Him, are justified from all things, from which they could not be justified by the law." Inasmuch that one shall say, "In the Lord have I righteousness;" and "this is the name whereby He shall be called, The Lord our righteousness." The labor of a whole life directed to the object of establishing a merit of our own, will only widen our distance from peace; and, we know of nothing that will send this visitant to our agitated bosoms, but a firm and simple reliance on these declarations. The unbelief of man is the only obstacle which the mercy of God in Christ has to struggle with; nor do we know of one other step that is necessary, but an act of faith on the part of the sinner, that this mercy may take its ample effect and fulfilment upon his person. It is simply by an act of believing, by a pure act of the mind, that he enters into reconciliation, and a covenant is established, as steadfast and immutable as it is in the power of solemn guarantees to make it—a covenant with only one tie, but that a most sufficient one, to bind it, even the tie which subsists between the faith of the creature, and the faithfulness of the Creator.

And it is for the purpose of presenting to our readers a full and very able exposition of the truths on which we have been insisting, that we have introduced into our Series of Christian Authors the following Treatise, on "*The Reign of Grace, from its rise to its consummation*," by ABRAHAM BOOTH, which we earnestly recommend to their attentive perusal, as one of the most powerful and luminous, and comprehensive expositions of the dispensation of grace with which we are acquainted. In this Treatise, they will find the Gospel of the Grace of God exhibited in all the fulness and freeness of its unrestricted offers of mercy, through the Saviour, to guilty man—in all the extent of its exuberant blessings, in its rich provisions for deliverance from condemnation and guilt, and restoration to the favor and friendship of God—in all the efficacy of its renovating and sanctifying influences in forming us to holiness, and in assimilating us to the spirit and character of God—and in all the benign and diversified operations, which a God of infinite wisdom and love has fitted it to produce, by causing it to reign unto eternal life through Jesus Christ, as made of God unto us wisdom, and righteousness, and sanctification, and complete redemption.

Originating, as those blessings and privileges do, in this grace, it is of mighty importance for us to ascertain, whether we have closed with God on the terms of His own covenant, and thus have been made partakers of this grace, and whether its reign has been established in our hearts. And we cannot refer the reader, who is in earnest about his salvation, to any Treatise better fitted than that of Abraham Booth, to give him sure and satisfying evidences for ascertaining the soundness and security of his hopes for eternity. He presents grace, as reigning through Jesus Christ unto eternal life, to sinners; and he invites the chief of sinners, by putting faith in the testimony of God, to lay hold of the offered grace, and thus appropriate to themselves the blessings of pardon, and peace, and justification, which God has provided through the atonement and righteousness of Christ; and which, in the proclamations of the Gospel, are freely and unreservedly offered to all who will. On this, the alone warrant of faith, he invites all to enter into peace and reconciliation with God, and by judging Him faithful who hath promised, to enjoy the blessedness of the man whose sins are covered, and to whom the Lord does not impute transgression.

But while faith in the free grace and offered pardon of the Gospel puts peace and joy into the heart of the believer, it is no less fitted to produce purity and holiness. This, indeed is the tendency, as well as the main and ultimate design of the Gospel, and it is on this account that we estimate so highly the Treatise we are now recommending, that it so nobly vindicates the doctrines of grace as doctrines according to godliness. And if there is any portion of this work to which, more than another, we would particularly direct the attention of our readers, it is to those chapters "On Grace as it reigns in our Sanctification," and "On the Necessity of Holiness and good Works." There is, in the minds of many, a fancied alliance between free grace and an immunity to sin; that, since pardon is the free gift of God, through the blood of the atonement, there is no restraint laid on men's inclinations to sin—that since we are justified wholly by the righteousness of another, the necessity of personal righteousness is as wholly superseded—and that since we cannot earn heaven by our own obedience, all the motives and securities for obedience are removed. We have not room to attempt an exposure of this oft-repeated, but unfounded, assertion—an assertion, to which the clearest averments of Scripture, and the experience of every true believer, give the most triumphant refutation. And we count it unnecessary to enter into any defence of the doctrines of grace from the charge of licentiousness, after the able and unanswerable vindication which the present volume furnishes. We do not indeed deny, that many professors of the Gospel give some color for such an impeachment, by profaning that holy name by which they are called, and by failing to adorn the doctrines of grace by lives and conversations becoming the Gospel; but such men have never felt the *reign of grace* in their hearts, otherwise it would not have failed to teach them "to deny ungodliness and worldly lusts, and to live soberly, righteously, and godly in the world;" and, while such men repose a fancied confidence in the death of Christ as their deliverance from condemnation, and as their passport to heaven, they have utterly mistaken one of the main designs of Christ's death, which was "to deliver us from all iniquity, and to purify us unto Himself a peculiar people zealous of good works." If heaven consists in God's manifesting the spiritual glories of His holy and perfect character, then must our spirit and character be kindred to His own, before we can delight in the love and contemplation of such glory. To love and enjoy God, we must be like God. And they utterly mistake the design of the Gospel, who conceive of it as a mere act of indemnity; and the Gospel has not been believed by them at all, if it has not come to them in the power and beneficence of holiness and grace, to change their hearts and their affections into the love of what is holy, and righteous, and excellent; nor can they entertain any well-founded hopes of heaven hereafter, in whom there is no process of restoration going at present to the lost image of the Godhead, and in whose hearts grace is not exerting its reigning power, to assimilate them to the spirit and character of God.

Whatever there may be now, in the days of Paul, at least, there were men who turned the grace of God into licentiousness, and who ranked among the privileges of the Gospel an immunity for sin. And it is striking to observe the effect of this corruption on the mind of the apostle;—that he who braved all the terrors of persecuting violence, that he who stood undismayed before kings and governors, and could lift his intrepid testimony in the hearing of an enraged multitude—that he who, when bound by a chain between two soldiers, still sustained an invincible constancy of spirit, and could live in fearlessness, and triumph, with the dark imagery of an approaching execution in his eye—that he who counted not his life dear unto him, and whose manly breast bore him up amidst all the threats of human tyranny, and the grim apparatus of martyrdom—that this man so firm and so undaunted, wept like a child when he heard of those disciples that turned the pardon of the cross into an encouragement for doing evil. The fiercest hostilities of the Gospel's open enemies he could brave, but when he heard of the foul dishonor done to the name of his Master, by the moral worthlessness of those who were the Gospel's professing friends, this he could not bear—all that firmness, which so upheld him unfaltering and unappalled in the battles of the faith, forsook him then; and this noblest of champions on the field of conflict and of controversy, when he heard of the profligacy of his own converts, was fairly overcome by the tidings, and gave way to all the softness of womanhood. When every other argument fails, for keeping us on the path of integrity and holiness, we should think of the argument of Paul in tears. It may be truly termed a picturesque argument, nor are we aware of a more impressive testimony in the whole compass of Scripture, to the indispensable need of virtue and moral goodness in a believer, than is to be found in that passage where Paul says of these unworthy professors of the faith, "For many walk, of whom I have told you often, and now tell you even weeping, that they are the enemies of the cross of Christ; whose end is destruction, whose god is their belly, and whose glory is in their shame, who mind earthly things."

INTRODUCTORY ESSAY

TO

SERIOUS REFLECTIONS ON TIME AND ETERNITY.

BY JOHN SHOWER.

AND

ON THE CONSIDERATION OF OUR LATTER END,

AND OTHER CONTEMPLATIONS.

BY SIR MATTHEW HALE, Knt.

There are certain truths, which lie remote from all direct and immediate observation—and which require more than one step on the part of the human mind, ere they are arrived at—which can only, in fact, be reached by a reasoning process, that consists of many steps; and for the describing of which, the habit of sustained attention, and the talent of sound and legitimate inference, and the power of combining principles which are known, and thence eliciting a truth or a doctrine that was unknown, must all be summoned to the work, and be put into strenuous and continued exercise for days, or often for months together, ere the toils of the devoted inquirer be rewarded by the discovery that he is in quest of. There is much, for example, both of mathematical and political science, which is incontrovertibly true, but which, instead of being taken up at one act by the understanding, as if it lay on the very surface of contemplation, can only be grasped into the possession of the mind, by being travelled to through a long intermedium of many transitions and many arguments—and they are only a gifted few who can bear the fatigues of such a journey, and to whom the labors of the midnight oil afford a congenial and much-loved employment, and who have had their intellectual powers disciplined to the march of a logical or lengthened investigation. The Smith of the one science, and the Newton of the other, afford very striking illustrations of this kind of mental superiority over the rest of the species—and in virtue of which they were enabled to discover what before to the whole of mankind was utterly unknown; and in virtue of which their followers are enabled to see what the majority of mankind do not see. It is only seen in fact from a summit of demonstration—and this is only attained by a series of ascending movements—and the few who have made their way to the temple which stands upon such an eminence as this, find inscribed upon it "the temple of philosophy." Now, what we maintain is, that this is altogether distinct from "the temple of wisdom." Its successful worshippers are men of reach, men of acquirement, and men who, from the elevation they have won, and on which they have posted themselves, can command a farther prospect over some walk, or some domain of the great intellectual territory, than their fellows around them. And yet they are not on this account men of wisdom, nor have we arrived at the true meaning and application of this epithet, if we either think that to be wise we must be philosophers, or that, if philosophers, we are therefore wise.

There are certain other truths, difficult of access, which are distinct, and distinguishable we think from those that we have just now adverted to—not such as are gained by a continuous effort along a line of investigation—not such as come in view upon the eye of the beholder, after he has scaled one of the altitudes of science—not such as lie remote, by being placed at a distance, but such rather as lie hidden from common minds, because deeply enveloped under the surface of common observation. To come at these, is not to plod and to persevere from one acquisition to another, as in the former instances. It is done by a process perhaps, too, in which all the elements of ratiocination are concerned, but a process so rapid, as to be felt even by the owner of the mind through which it passes, like an act of momentary intuition. Such is the quickness of his penetrating eye, that what to others is a thick and impalpable veil, hides not from him the truth or the principle which lurks beneath it—and with one glance of perception, can he discern many of the secret things which lie under the broad and ostensible face of human affairs—and this faculty of his though certainly sharpened by cultivation, and cradled up to its present maturity among the varieties of experience and of life, is not of slow operation like the former, but is sudden in all its exercises, and quite immediate in all the information which it fetches to its owner. One of its main offices is to detect what is latent, and to ordinary minds, inaccessible in the character of man. This it does not by any tardy movement of the understanding, but by something like the tact of an instantaneous discernment, by the look of an instinctive sagacity, directed towards any exhibition either in the countenance or in the conduct of another. It is this faculty which gives the eye of a lynx to the satirist; and which endues, with all his readiness and address, the wily ambassador, who, himself unseen, can cast a piercing intelligence through all the windings and intrigues of a cabinet; and which dexterously guides its possessor's way among the politics of a city corporation; and which even achieves, as wondrous triumphs as any of subtlety and skill among the severest collisions, or the low jockeyship of a market. It is far more diffused than science and scholarship are through the various ranks of society. You will meet with it in the homeliest walks of life—nay, sometimes, in all its perfection, under the guise, and in the attitude, of a country simpleton. It is not confined to the chicanery of courts. For the play of as deep and as dexterous artifice may be set agoing in the negotiations of private interest, as has ever been recorded in the annals of diplomacy. And whether it be swindling without the law, or swindling within the law, may there be the same over-reach of one shrewder understanding over the blind and unsuspecting confidence of another, in the contests of ordinary trade, as in the contests of politics. The man who is thus gifted, sees deeper than his fellows. He can read the vanity, or the weakness, or the delicacy which are in another's heart, and he can practise accordingly. It is true, that he may be thus wise as a serpent, and yet harmless as a dove. But the mere wisdom of the serpent is not true wisdom, in the soundest acceptation of the term. The epithet wise, according to its largest and its soundest acceptation, is neither exemplified by him, who, by dint of meditation, sees farthest into the secrets of philosophy, or who, by dint of shrewd and oft-repeated observation, sees deepest into the mysteries of our nature—nor have we yet reached the conception of a truly wise man, if we think, that to be wise we must be political, or, that if political, we are therefore wise.

The consideration of our latter end, which forms the principal topic of the following volume, is that which the Scripture affirms to be true wisdom. "Oh that they were wise, that they understood this, that they considered their latter end." But the truth of our mortality, by the considering of which aright we are wise, belongs neither to the former, nor to the latter classification. We do not need to travel far in quest of its discovery. Neither do we need to dive among the recesses of a profound observation, that we may be able to fetch it up, and to appropriate it. It is a truth which, on the very highway of ordinary life, forces itself on the recognition of every man. That world, through which we are all journeying, abounds in the sign-posts of mortality; and many is the passing funeral which obtrudes this lesson upon our eyes; and many are the notes of that funeral bell which tolls it upon our hearing;—and well may the old, when they think of a former generation, levelled and taken off by the hand of death, learn how sure it is, that the living and busy society around them will at length be swept away;—and even to the young, and those the likeliest of us all, does death hang out its memorials, and gives them to know that it wields an indiscriminating arm;—and even from those whom it spares the longest, and comes to the last, may we learn how short a process of arithmetic it is which conducts every one of us to our latter end,—and thus, through all the possible avenues of sense, and experience, and feeling, do such intimations multiply upon us, and these so plain and so powerful, and ever and anon recurring with such pathos and in such frequency, that, but to those who are sunk in idiotism, is it a lesson read and recognized of all men. Nor is there a living man who does not know, that the march of our actual generation is but one vast progressive movement to the grave. It is not the acquirement of new truths, but the right use and consideration of old ones, which constitutes wisdom. It is not the discovery of what was before unknown, which signalizes the wise man above his fellows. It is the right and the rational application of what they know as well as he, but which they do not reflect upon, and do not proceed upon as he. It is not the man who outpeers his acquaintances in intellectual wealth, neither is it the man who outdoes them in homebred sagacity—it is neither the one nor the other, who, in the best, and most significant sense of the term, is the man of wisdom. It is he, who acts upon the sureness of that which is sure. It is he, who proceeds upon the reality of that which is real. It is he, who feels greatness of desire after that which is great, and smallness of desire after that which is small, and shapes his doings to the actual dimensions of every object which is presented to his understanding. And neither is it necessary that, in respect of understanding, he should have a capacity for more than truths which are familiar to all, and are acknowledged of all. He has not to go in quest of strange or distant novelties, but only to trace to its right purpose that which is near to him, and within reach of every man. In a word, he has not to learn that which is known only to a few, he has only to consider that which is known to all. "O that they were wise, that they understood this, that they would *consider* their latter end!" He has not to be taught the number of his days, but taught *so* to number them, as to apply his heart unto wisdom.

He is not in the soundest physical condition, who lives on the high-wrought delicacies of an artificial and expensive preparation; but he, the organs of whose bodily constitution are best suited to the bread and the water, and the universal aliments which nature has provided for the healthful sustenance of her children. And he is neither in the best spiritual, nor even in the best intellectual condition, the faculties of whose soul are ever on the stretch after lofty and recondite doctrine, or its appetite for knowledge pre-occupied with various and exquisite speculation—but he, who thrives on the daily nourishment of such truth as is familiar to all—he, whose clear and vigorous eye admits most copiously of that light, which is poured around the orbit—he, the food of whose understanding is that common food which is most abundant, and would also be most salutary, but for the common disease that overspreads the families of our species—he who, with no taste, and no capacity for what is remote or ingenious, rightly comprehends the truth that is at hand, and goes not beyond the simple elements of being in any of his mental exercises, but who, if right in these, has reached a wisdom which philosophy cannot reach, and who, if sound in his practical estimate of what is due to Time, and what is due to Eternity, is a man of nobler aims, and far more solid and exalted wisdom, than science can induce upon any of its votaries. He lives not upon the niceties, but upon the staple of spiritual fare, and his spiritual frame is thereby upheld in strength and in prosperity ; and in the plain certainties of the coming death, and the coming judgment, does he walk in a way more truly elevated, than that which is trodden by any son of literary ambition ; and hence the impress of dignity and wisdom which we have seen to sit on the aspect of him, who, the father of a cottage family, has no respite from toil but the Sabbath, and no reading but his much-read Bible, and that authorship, of old and humble piety, which lies in little room upon his shelves. To learn discriminatively and justly what wisdom is, you have just to place the most brilliant and accomplished philosopher by the side of this venerable sage of Christianity. The one knows much, but his is a knowledge which terminates in itself. The other knows little, but his is a knowledge which is turned to the purpose of his guidance here, and his provision for eternity hereafter. Wisdom is not bare knowledge. It is knowledge directed to its best and fittest, and most productive application. Thus it is, that there may be much knowledge without wisdom, and there may be much wisdom with little knowledge. It is not he who knows most, who is most wise, but he, who uses aright that which is known and familiar to all men. For, let it be observed, that it is with spiritual as with natural food. The most useful ingredients of it are the most abundant. Men may refuse to partake of them, and starve and die, and thus become, what the majority of our species actually are—dead in trespasses and sins. To bring a man alive again from the apparent death of nature, we never think of wooing back the departed senses by the offer of luxuries. But we admit a supply of air, and try if we can breathe in this universal element ; and make use of cold water, which is to be had in every dwelling-place ; and ply his taste with some simple preparation ; and could we restore him to the common enjoyment of these very commonest articles, we would be satisfied. And so it is in the case of spiritual torpor. To call it back to sensibility, we would never think of elaborate demonstration. But we would ring into our patient's ear the message of death, which everybody knows, but few know with application. We would try to awaken his inner man, by the tidings of its immortality, which all profess to have faith in, while scarcely any human being lives under the power of it. We would sound the trump of alarm, and loudly speak of an angry God and a coming vengeance, notes as familiar to his hearing as is that of the wind of heaven which blows over him, while, in their terror and in their urgency, they are as unfelt by the soul, as if its ears of communication with a human voice were altogether closed. We would deal forth upon him the simplicities of the Gospel—and tell of sin and of the Sacrifice—intimations which may be as readily taken up by the peasant as by the philosopher—but which, until roused from their carnal lethargy, are unlike unheeded by them both. To recall them from such a paralysis as this, we would not ply them with that which is severe and elaborate, but would, if possible, quicken and revive them by that which is elementary. And not he who is led on by argument to that which is remote, but he who receives the touch of a quickening influence from that, the certainty of which is obvious to all, while the sense of it is nearly unfelt by all—he it is who hath attained the only true understanding—he it is who is wise unto salvation.

We cannot but perceive, how, while the doctrines of our faith are plain, in opposition to what is recondite, not requiring, like the difficulties of science, a prolonged and strenuous investigation—yet still plain as they are, they need the influence of the Spirit for the true understanding of them, just as a dead body needs the touch of some miraculous personage, ere it can breathe the all-encompassing atmosphere, or use the universal elements, or be sustained by the common bounties of nature. And so of the soul. It is not by conducting it through any lengthened, or logical demonstration of the schools, that we restore it to that intelligence, the possession of which assures the possessor of life everlasting. It is by visiting it with the manifestation of certain great and impending, but withal simple realities. The wisdom which is thus gotten, is altogether distinct from the wisdom of philosophy—hidden in fact from many such wise, and many such prudent, and revealed unto babes.

Let us just look to the practical habit of nature, and see that, in the face of the clearest and plainest arithmetic, it gives a superiority to the present over the future world, and then may we acknowledge, that if it be needful to heal the diseased eyes of the blind, ere they can see of the common light, or to heal the diseased lungs of the consumptive, ere they can breathe aright of the common air, or to heal the diseased constitution of the sickly, ere they can turn into aliment the common food of all men,—so is it equally needful that a physician's hand be laid upon our diseased spirits, ere they be nourished by truths so palpable, as that eternity is greater than time, and the enjoyment of God in heaven, greater than that of all those earthly blessings which he causes to descend on our fleeting pilgrimage.

We know not on whom it is, that the burden of this sore disease still lies, in all its native aggravation, or from whom it has been taken away. We can only address our admonitions to the reader at a venture. It is like the shooting of an arrow among a multitude, when who knows what individual will be struck by it? It is under the declaration of the truth, that a child of darkness becomes a disciple of light. But even the same truth which awakens the former, is the very truth which needs to be repeated, again and again, in the hearing of the latter, to keep him awake. The pure mind must be stirred up in the way of remembrance. And it is not enough that truth be received at the first; in the language of the Bible, it must also be considered. The food which is taken in is of no use, unless, by a digestive process, it be turned into aliment. Truth is the food of the soul. We receive it by faith. But if we keep it not in memory, we, in the words of the apostle, have believed in vain. The shortness of life, and the certainty of its approaching extinction, may come upon the spirit in a powerful, but momentary visitation. This gleam of light must be brightened, and sustained, and perpetuated. It must be kept alive amid the shock of many rude and adverse elements. It must shine as a lamp upon all our paths. The converse of this world's companies should not darken it. The heat and the hurry of our daily business should not stifle it. That sorrow which worketh death, should not swallow it up into the oblivion of our immortality, nor should the still more dangerous gale of prosperity blow this pure and sacred flame into utter annihilation. It is not enough that we acknowledge the truth at stated times; we must give earnest heed to it, lest *at any time* we should let it slip. It is not enough that we should know our latter end—nor has our understanding of this been advanced into true wisdom, till it be our care and our habit to consider our latter end.

The practical habit of our souls ought to be a habit of anticipation, and of anticipation reaching even unto death, and to the immortality which lies beyond it. A realizing sense of what that is, which a coming futurity is to bring with speed, and perhaps with suddenness, to our doors, would change the habit and posture of the soul altogether. Could we only figure to our imaginations the ebbing, and the quivering, and the agony of death, and then charge ourselves with the certainty that death is coming,—could we be ever looking onwards to the day when the last trumpet shall call us from our graves to the judgment-seat, and give a settled home in our bosoms to the truth of this awful revelation, that judgment is coming,—could we carry our frequent and daily thoughts to the margin of eternity, and, after contrasting the delight and the dreariness of its two immeasurable rigions, with the interests of that short-lived day which separates the morning from the evening of our existence in the world, consider how surely, on the rapid wing of succession, eternity is coming,—and simple as these ponderings are, let them just enter with the power which they ought, and in the new complexion which they cast on all that is intermediate between us and eternity, and they will both give us other minds, and make other men of us. These truths are plain enough for the peasant—but there is in them a challenging authority, which reaches even unto the prince. They are fit for the homeliest understandings. Yet homely as they are, may they be offered to men of all ranks, and all classes in society, and they do *look hard upon the pursuits of our existing generation.* With so mighty an instrument of demonstration, as the calculus of those months that will soon pass away, and of those years that are so easily summed up, do we bring the lesson of our mortality to bear upon them. And be they the children of wealth, resting their security on that corruptible foundation, of which gold and silver are the materials,—or be they children of poverty, who think that they have lost their all, because, without a portion in time, they have cast eternity, as a thing of worthlessness, away from them, —or, in a word, be their condition what it may, let them be of that innumerable multitude who use the world not as a road, but as a residence,—we tell them that they are carnally-minded, and if not arrested on the way, they are fast posting to that death which is the doom of all who are so. Awaken, awaken, from these manifold delusions by which nature is encompassed!—and seek to be spiritually-minded, that you may have life and peace.

So closely allied is the consideration of our latter end with the very essence of wisdom, that we know not a likelier expedient for shutting us up, and that immediately, unto Christ—unto Him, who is called the wisdom of God as well as the power of God—unto Him, in comparison of the excellency of whose knowledge all was but loss, in the estimation of the apostle; insomuch that he determined to know nothing save Jesus Christ and Him crucified. What is it that makes us tarry in the great work of seeking a secure righteousness before God? It is because we feel secure enough in the meantime with the possession of health, and the enjoyment of a warm and well-sheltered home, and the engrossments of business, and the delights of a gay, and pleasing, and varied companionship. These, mixed up with a tolerable sense of our own deficiencies, and our own duties, serve altogether to make us easy in this evil world, and to keep off from our imaginations all that can give dread or disturbance in the thought of another world. The truth is, that in these circumstances, and with these feelings, the question, "Wherewithal shall I appear before God?" is never seriously entertained. It does not come upon the mind with the urgency of a matter in hand,—and, in reference to the undoubted fact, that the most earthly men are also the most inimical to that doctrine which affirms the ground of our evangelical acceptance before God, we believe the secret but substantial explanation of the whole matter to be, that the soul which keeps a firm hold upon time, is careless and thoughtless about the goodness of its foundation for eternity, He likes this world best, and if he make good a portion here, he will not trouble himself with any nice or scrupulous examination of what that is, which makes the best title-deed for an inheritance hereafter. And this will explain a fact which we think must be familiar to many—the very summary process upon which a man of the world comes to his easy and agreeable conclusion on the question of his eternity—the very comfortable balance which he strikes between his good points and his bad ones—so as to set aside all his sins from the final result of this computation, and bring into view nothing but his humanities and his virtues, on which to rear a confidence before God. It is not by fully tracing, but, in the language of parliament, by blinking the question, that he comes to a deliverance which is satisfying enough to his mind about the world at a distance, amid so much to satisfy him, in the visible and surrounding world with which he has presently to do. It makes all the difference, between the earnestness of our preparation to meet the creditor, who threatens instant diligence upon our person, and the creditor whose application for payment we can, by an act of the fancy, put off, and postpone to an indefinite distance away from us. And next time you see a thriving, prosperous, good-humored man of the world evince his hatred of the doctrine of faith, and of all that is said about acceptance in Christ, and a right basis of justification before the eye of the Lawgiver—before you admit the soundness of his notions about a safe and sufficient passport to eternity—consider well whether eternity be at all a matter of concern with him—and whether it is not the entertainment of sense which gives him all his delight, and the business of sense which gives him all his occupation.

Now, conceive the two elements of eternity and time to be so revealed to his soul, as to stand in their just and naked proportion before him. Conceive, that the one is seen advancing in nearness and magnitude towards him, and the other as fast flitting into evanescence away. Conceive the scales so to fall from his eyes, that, through all the delusions which the god of this world spreads over the surface of what is present and visible, he beholds the impressive mockery which death stamps upon every enjoyment that is on this side of it; and feels, that if he fall short of the enjoyment which is on the other side of it, he is undone. Let all this be only mixed up with a right sense of sin and of the Saviour—and not one moment will intervene, ere, under the curse and consciousness of the one, he seeks for deliverance from the other. Let him thus be made to hear the footsteps of the last messenger—and he will feel all the urgency of a present claim and of a present creditor at his door; and he will be driven to the necessity of a present settlement, and he will not be so easily set at rest about the footing upon which he stands. His search for securities, will be the search of a man in earnest; and a real practical earnestness is all that we require—assured, as we are, that the man who is truly seeking for a foundation, will not be satisfied till he finds a solid one; and that out of the frail materials of human virtue no such foundation can be formed; and that an obedience, rendered without heart, and mixed up with all the infirmities both of forgetfulness and pollution, will never quiet the conscience of him who has at all been visited by a realizing sense of these things. Thus it is, that to consider our latter end is to tread on one of the likeliest pathways to the Saviour. Nor do we know a more effectual way of being prompted forward to that place of refuge—where we shall find a blood to wash away our guilt, and a righteousness that can never fail us. So that, could we only demonstrate with power, how short-lived the period, and how tottering the basis of all earthly enjoyments, we should not despair of soon finding the alarmed sinner within his secure resting-place, on that foundation which God hath laid in Zion.

There is often, in the pencilled descriptions of the moralist, a kind of poetical and high-wrought imagery thrown around the chamber of death; and that, whether it be the terrors of guilt, or the triumphs of conscious virtue, which are conceived to mark this closing scene of our history in the world. It is well to know what the plain and experimental truth is, upon the subject. In the case of a worldly and alienated life, the remorse is not nearly so pungent, the apprehensions not nearly so vivid and terrifying, the impression of future and eternal realities not nearly so overpowering, as we are apt to fancy upon such an occasion. The truth is, that as it was throughout the whole of his living, so it is generally in dying. He is still engrossed with present and sensible things; and there is positively nothing in the mere approach of dissolution that can raise up the ascendency of faith, or render him less the slave of sight, and of the body, than he was before. There is the present pain, there is the present thirst, there is the present breathlessness; and if, amid the tumults of his earthly fabric giving way, and the last irregular movements of its deranged mechanism fast drawing to their cessation, he send for the minister to soothe him by his prayers, even he forms but one of the present varieties. There is no actual going forth of the patient's mind towards the things which are above. The faith which he has so long shut out, does not now force its entrance into a bosom, habituated to the reception of no other influences, than what the world, and the things of the world, have so long exercised over him. We may see torpor upon such an occasion, and call it serenity. We may witness an uncomplaining silence, and call it resignation. We may never hear one note of alarm to drop from the lips of the dying sufferer; and therefore say that he met with Christian fortitude his end. But all these may meet upon a death-bed; and yet, the positive confidence of looking forward to heaven as a home, a positive rejoicing in the hope of the glory of God, a believing, and a knowing, that "when the earthly house of this tabernacle is dissolved, they shall have a building of God, a house not made with hands, eternal in the heavens," may never enter his bosom. There may be the peacefulness of insensibility, even while the life of him who has been a stranger to the faith of the Gospel is waning to its extinction—but a peace mixed up with the elevation of such prospects as these, is never felt, apart from the thought of Christ as "the Lord our righteousness." It is altogether a romance to talk of such anticipations of triumph, to him who looks back upon his own obedience, and then looks forward to his rightful and his challenged reward. If we want our dying hour to have the radiance of heaven's gate thrown over it—if we want, amid the failure of expiring nature, to have some firm footing, on which we might strongly and securely rest; there is positively none other, but that to which the consideration of our latter end should *now* be urging us forward—and, therefore, should we call upon ourselves *now* to take up with Christ as our foundation, and to associate all our confidence in God, with the obedience which he has wrought, with the ransom which he has rendered.

We cannot better enforce these solemn considerations on the minds of our readers, with the view of shutting them up to the faith that is in Christ, than by referring them to SHOWER'S "Serious Reflections on Time and Eternity," and Sir MATTHEW HALE "On the consideration of our Latter End." In SHOWER'S excellent Treatise, they will find the serious reflections of a mind, which, by the habit of solemn consideration, and the exercise of a vigorous faith, habitually felt the power and the reality of those important truths, respecting which mankind in general maintain an obstinate, and almost incurable heedlessness. There is scarcely any form of words, or any mode of computation, or any point of contrast, which he has not employed, to give the reader a vivid and substantive impression of the littleness of Time, and the greatness of Eternity. The truths on which he insists, are truths of the plainest and most elementary kind; but thoroughly aware that the practical consideration of them constitutes the essence of true wisdom, he endeavors, by the most forcible arguments, and the most touching appeals, and the most persuasive earnestness, to arrest mankind in their career of thoughtlessness and unconcern, and to turn their resolute and sustained attention to the consideration of their latter end, and so to number their days, that they may apply their hearts to that highest of all wisdom—a preparation for the coming eternity; and with the real and tender solicitude of men in earnest, lay to heart those things which pertain to their everlasting peace, ere time be hid from their eyes.

The "Consideration of our Latter End," and the other kindred pieces of Sir MATTHEW HALE, are not only marked by the same solemn earnestness, but possess all that graphic power of thought, and depth of experimental feeling, which characterize the writings of this extraordinary man. The character and writings of this great and good man have already been adverted to in a former Essay in this series of "Select Christian Authors,"* which precludes the necessity of our entering into any farther exposition of them. But we cannot help observing, that if Sir MATTHEW HALE, whose genius and learning rendered him one of the most distinguished ornaments of his age, and whose character and wisdom still associate him in England's best remembrances, with the noblest of her worthies, counted it a wisdom superior to all human learning, to consider his latter end—and if, amidst the numerous and important avocations of that high official station which he occupied, rendered still more arduous and difficult, by the anarchy and confusion of that revolutionary period in which he lived, this good man was not unmindful to address those monitory lessons to his countrymen, which we now present anew, as salutary admonitions to the present generation,—then have we a testimony to the worth and surpassing excellence of this wisdom, above all the acquisitions of science and philosophy, which cannot be disregarded, without incurring the imputation of folly. Science and human learning we hold in high estimation, and let them be diffused throughout every corner of our land; but what we affirm is, that they do not meet the necessities of man's moral constitution. The man of science may be rich in all these acquisitions, and yet be destitute of that knowledge which forms a right preparation for the duties of time, or a sound preparation for the glories of eternity; while the humble peasant, whose mind has never been illuminated with science, may be illustrious in wisdom of a far higher order, and, by turning the consideration of his latter end to its right and practical use, may have attained to that knowledge in which the apostle determined alone to glory, "the knowledge of Jesus Christ and him crucified."

It is the great design of such a consideration, to lead us to that Gospel which is freely offered to all. But though the Gospel be offered freely, it only becomes ours by our receiving it freely; and seldom is it so received by him who, after being laid on the bed of his last sickness, has still a Saviour to seek, instead of a Saviour to enjoy. The evil heart of unbelief, which he has cherished through life, cleaves to him, and keeps its hold till the last hour of it: and, therefore, never does the mind entertain a delusion more ruinous, never is eternity placed on a more desperate stake, than by those who put away from them *now* the offers of salvation, and think that *then* they shall have it for the taking. It is the part, then, of all to look forthwith and earnestly to the Saviour—to contemplate him in his revealed offices—to make a real and intelligent work of closing with him—to receive him as their atonement—to render allegiance to him as their Lord and their Proprietor—and submit themselves unto Him, that he might rule

* Judge Hale on the Knowledge of Christ Crucified, and other Divine Contemplations, with an Introductory Essay, by the Rev. David Young.

in them by his Spirit, and over them by his Law. Whether they be the unconverted, who have yet to lay hold of Christ, or the already converted, whose business it is to keep that hold—we know not how the consideration of their latter end can be turned more substantially to the purposes of wisdom and of true understanding, than by leading them supremely to prize, and immediately to acquire, that knowledge of Jesus Christ our Lord, which is life everlasting

INTRODUCTORY ESSAY

TO THE

CHRISTIAN'S DEFENCE AGAINST INFIDELITY;

CONSISTING OF,

1. LESLIE'S SHORT AND EASY METHOD WITH THE DEISTS.
2. LYTTLETON'S OBSERVATIONS ON ST. PAUL.
3. DODDRIDGE'S EVIDENCES OF CHRISTIANITY.
4. BATES ON THE DIVINITY OF THE CHRISTIAN RELIGION.
5. OWEN ON THE SELF-EVIDENCING LIGHT OF SCRIPTURE.
6. BAXTER ON THE DANGER OF MAKING LIGHT OF CHRIST

There are several ways in which a man, who practises the art of divination, might try to make good his pretensions to this supernatural endowment. He might do so by attempting to pronounce on the kind and the quantity of money which I have about my person. He might pass a confident utterance on a matter that is hidden from every human eye but my own, even on the number and the character of those pieces of coin which I am carrying about with me,—and this description of his may be rigidly true, in all its varied particulars,—and at different times may he make distinct and repeated trials of the same kind, and succeed in every one of them. And surely it is conceivable, that these examples of an unfailing coincidence, between what he says, and what I myself know of the subject, may be so striking, and so multiplied, and so obviously free of all the symptoms and all the preparations of jugglery, as to leave upon my mind, not merely a firm, but also a most just and rational conviction, that the man is what he pretends to be; that there is a reach of discernment about him, beyond all that is known of the powers or the principles of nature; that in fact, he has established himself to be a miraculous personage, and by evidence, too, of such a kind, as, with a man of sober and enlightened judgment, might be altogether irresistible.

Now, it is to be remarked of such evidence, that, in the main strength of it, and in the proper and original impression of it, it is addressed exclusively to myself. I may make known to others the whole history of this wonderful transaction. I may report to them all the cases of successful divination which have been accomplished upon me. But still the evidence of these cases has to pass through the intervening medium of my testimony. Before that others can feel the same power of evidence with myself, they must be made to undergo the same treatment: or the same divination must be practised successively and individually upon each of them. They may choose to discredit my testimony. They may distrust my powers of memory and observation. They may suspect a collusion between me and an artful pretender. They may look upon me as a man either of dishonest purpose, or of diseased imagination. They may muster up a thousand possibilities, to ward away from them a conviction, which I know and am assured to be a just one. And thus it is that I may, on the one hand, be surrounded by the incredulity of all my fellows, and I may be assailed, in every direction, by the imputations of falsehood or fanaticism; and yet, with the personal access I have had to an evidence to which none of my acquaintances have been admitted, and with a proper confidence in the soundness of my own recollections, and with the sense of a single-minded integrity throughout the whole of this business, I may, on the other hand, though accosted at every turn by the ridicule and the reproaches of my acquaintances, be fully warranted to place my immovable confidence in him with whom I have held the intercourse of all these intimate and peculiar communications.

But let us now vary the supposition, and conceive that our extraordinary personage embarks his pretensions on another and a higher species of divination; that, instead of attempting to divine the money which is in my pocket, he attempts to divine the thoughts which are in my heart; that, laying claim to the wondrous prerogative of supernaturally knowing what is in man, he offers to scrutinize my mind, and to read to me the varied characters which, in the shape of opinion, and desire, and ruling passion, and prevailing infirmity of temper, stand engraven in its chamber of imagery; that he unfolds to me the workings of my own soul, and lays before me a picture of the inner man, that can be vividly recognized by the eye of my own conscience; that he proves to me, how this little world of self, with all its affections and its tendencies, which stand so hidden from general observation, by a thick and an impalpable veil, is altogether naked and open before him; that he makes me perceive, by his insight into the thoughts and intents of my heart, how he is indeed a most skilful and a most enlightened discerner; that, by his piercing inspection into the secrecies of my bosom, he can so divide asunder my soul and spirit, as to make every one of them manifest in his sight. Why, is it not conceivable, that in this way, too, there may be multiplied upon me the instances of a penetration far above the powers of humanity; that every new case of such a divination may serve to strengthen my confidence in him who performs it; and that, at length, I may be so overpowered by the evidence which he thus brings to bear upon me, as to give my full consent to all his pretensions, and to embark my every prospect, and my every determination, on his authority, as a messenger from God?

And yet, when I do so, I do it upon the strength of evidence, directed individually to myself. I cannot make another man the partaker of this evidence. I cannot possibly put him upon that station of advantage which I occupy. I cannot translate into his bosom my own direct and immediate consciousness of the movements which are going on in my bosom; nor can I furnish him with a window of observation, through which he may note the coincidence between those divinations which have been attempted on my mind, and my mind, which is the subject of these divinations. I am the only man living who can be made directly to perceive this coincidence, and to me exclusively and appropriately belongs the main strength of the evidence that is founded upon it. There lies an impassable barrier between me and my next-door neighbor, in virtue of which I find it impossible to make a full or an adequate communication of this evidence to him. There may be divinations conceived, where the subject of them is equally accessible to all men. But the peculiarity of the divination that I am now insisting on, is, that the subject of it is accessible only to the individual on whom it is practised. Ere my neighbor can possess the evidence which it affords, he must be made the subject of a distinct divination. Before this takes place, he has nothing to rest upon but my testimony, which he may reject as false, or which he may deride as fanciful, or which he may utterly despise, as symptomatic of folly and of superstitious weakness. Still, however, in the face of all this, I may obstinately adhere to my own conviction, and be right in doing so. My contemptuous neighbor has no access to the materials upon which my judgment is founded. He cannot bring himself into a state of contiguity with my mind, nor obtain such a view of its workings, as to see how good the evidence is that I have for my conviction; nor, until he has forced his way within the penetralia of the inner chamber, will I, with a right sense of my integrity, and a right confidence in my judgment, hold him entitled to pronounce it a bad evidence. I alone have access to the depositions of my own consciousness. And I have faith in their veracity. And I can judge of the accordancy between them, and the divinations of the man who calls himself a prophet. And I may see it to be an accordancy so close, and so minutely variegated, and so often exemplified, and so sustained throughout all the successions of my experience and my history, that, believing it to be miraculous, I may say, and say with justness, that surely God is in him of a truth. And thus may I exhibit, not merely an inflexible, but a sound and philosophically consistent faith, even in circumstances where, abandoned by the sympathy of all my fellows, I am traduced as a hypocrite, or reviled as an enthusiast.

There is something to confirm all this in Scripture history. Our Saviour, in the course of His conversation with the woman of Samaria, achieved upon her a work of divination. He read to her a passage out of her present and her by-gone history; and she was so far impressed with the circumstance, as to say, "Sir, I perceive that thou art a prophet." She repeated the circumstance to her countrymen; and it is recorded, that some of them bore such respect to her testimony, that they believed on Jesus, "for the saying of the woman, which testified, He told me all that ever I did." But though some, not all; for it is further said, that "many more believed because of his own word." True, it is not said that this word carried the same kind of evidence to them, that it did to the woman of Samaria. It is not said, that, disbelieving her testimony, they were at length made to believe, by means of a similar divination practised upon themselves. But we may, at least, gather from the passage, that the evidence on which their faith rested did not lie in any external miracle. This is not what they alleged as the ground of their faith. But they "said to the woman, Now we believe, not because of thy saying; for we have heard him ourselves, and know that this is indeed the Christ, the Saviour of the world."

But any deficiency of information in this passage, is amply made up in other passages. The miracle of tongues, for instance, held out to the notice of the world, by the first teachers of Christianity, should have compelled the attention of all whom they addressed, to the subject-matter of their testimony. A few moments of serious and candid examination, would have convinced them of such a reality in this exhibition, as entitled the first preachers of the Gospel to a further and a respectful hearing. But there were many in those days who wanted this seriousness and this candor; and they passed a rejection so summary upon the message that was proposed, that they would not even listen to the terms of it; and they put it away from them at the very threshold of its earliest intimations; and we are, accordingly, told by the apostle, that the gift of tongues, instead of exciting their inquiry, excited their ridicule, insomuch, that they pronounced those who exercised it to be mad; and we also read of certain despisers, who, upon the very same exhibition, said, mocking, that "these men are full of new wine;" and thus it is that they persisted in their unbelief, and wondered, and perished. Now, the way in which we understand the gift of tongues to have been a sign unto them, is, that it sealed their condemnation. It convicted them of a dishonest partiality on the side of falsehood. It made the Gospel the savor of death unto death unto them. The sign of tongues was a sign which they spake against; and this wilful, perverse, unfair, and, at all hazards, determined opposition, drew upon them the fulfilment of such sayings, as, that unless those works had been done among them which had never been done before, they had not had sin; and that it would be more tolerable for Sodom and Gomorrah in the day of judgment, than for those who witnessed such miracles, but who so loved the darkness rather than the light, as to resist the impression of them.

Thus much for those who believed not. And as to those who believed, it does not appear to us that it was the miracle of tongues, or indeed any external miracle whatever, which wrought in them the saving faith of the New Testament. A previous miracle might, in many cases, have been the instrument by which their attention was gained: but we think that the evidence upon which their conversion hinged, beamed upon their minds from the subject-matter of the testimony. It was in the act of listening to what is called the prophecy, or, (taking this term according to its undoubted sense in many passages of Scripture,) it was in the act of listening to the exposition of Christian doctrine, that they felt the impression of that evidence which we have already insisted on—even the evidence of such a divination as was beyond all that could be accomplished by the sagacity of man. The truth of what the apostles told them was made manifest to their consciences. What their Christian teachers said they were, they felt themselves to be; and they recognized the coincidence, and they were arrested by it. They gave them credit for a supernatural commission, when they discerned such a reach of penetration into the secrecy of their bosoms, as they judged to be supernatural. And the evidence they thus obtained, was not diluted by its transmission upon a vehicle of testimony, from the experience of one man to the hearing of another man. All who believed shared in the same experience. Each of them was made the subject of a separate divination. Each carried home the word spoken, and found it totally with all that he perceived of his own character. The evidence came with the whole force of its powerful and primitive impression upon every conscience. And we think that nothing more needs to be said, in order to understand the kind of influence by which, when the first teachers prophesied, or expounded their message and their doctrine, "and there came in one that believed not, or one unlearned, he was convinced of all, he was judged of all: and thus were the secrets of his heart made manifest; and so, falling down on his face, he worshipped God, and reported that God was in them of a truth."

But these gifted teachers of our faith not only spoke to the men of their own age, they also wrote for the men of other ages. They have left behind them an enduring memorial of their doctrine and their testimony. They have graven it on an imperishable record; and we know not a more deeply interesting question, within the whole compass of Theology, than—Whether, while the word of the apostles is thus transmitted by writing, the evidence which lay in that word at its first and its oral delivery, is transmitted along with it to succeeding generations? May we, in the reading of that word, gather the same evidence for its truth, which the unbelievers, and the unlearned in the apostolic age, did in the hearing of it? In one short sentence, Has this evidence descended? Has it been actually translated into the pages of the Bible? Does this book stand to us in the place of its human composers, who have long ere now been consigned to the silence of the grave? Can it do by itself now, what they personally, and of themselves, did then? Can it evince such a power of divination into the secrecies of the heart, as to bear, upon its own forehead, the attestation of God being in it of a truth? An unlettered man of the present day, knows nothing of its external evidence. He is an utter stranger to the erudition and the history of the eighteen hundred years which have elapsed, since the first promulgation of Christianity in the world. It is all a dark and an unknown interval to him. Nor can he fetch a single argument, for the establishment of his faith, from across an abyss which looks so obscure and so fathomless. Now the question is—May he fetch any such argument from the book itself? When, in the act of reading it, the word is brought nigh unto him, is there anything within it by which it can announce its own authority, and hold out, to a simple and untaught reader, the light of its own evidence? Does the word written inherit all the powers of the word spoken? Does there emanate from the doctrine, as recorded by the apostles, that virtue to arrest, and to carry the conviction, which actually did emanate from the same doctrine, as told by the apostles? Insomuch, that the Bible shall be not merely the messenger of its own contents, but shall also be the messenger of its own credentials: that wherever it goes, it shall bear abroad with it the legible and the satisfying inscription of its own truth; that by the light which beams from its pages, it shall make known the celestial character which it wears, and the celestial origin from which it sprung; that it shall emit, upon every side of it, the lesson of its rightful authority; and that, though it borrowed not one particle of aid from the skill and the scholarship of its controversial defenders, it shall be able to speak for itself, to find its way even among the humblest of our cottages, to reclaim, and to convince, and to enlighten their darkest population, and to put the stamp of a sound and a clear intelligence on all the discipleship which it earns among them.

We do not see how we could have abridged our observations at any former point of this argument; and, after all, have we only arrived on the margin of a vast and untrodden field, and feel ourselves placed on the mere threshold of a subject far too big and too unwieldly for the present Essay. We will not attempt the impossibility of entertaining the question we have just now started, in such a way as to meet the every doubt, and to pursue the every illustration, and at length to bestow upon our argument its complete and conclusive establishment. We firmly believe, that there is no one position in Theology, which can be more strongly and more philosophically sustained, than the self-evidencing power of the Bible. For a full and satisfactory exposition of this subject, we must refer our readers to Dr. Owen's Treatise, in the present volume, "On the Self-Evidencing Light and Power of the Scriptures," and all we shall do, at present, is just to bring forward as much, in the way of remark, as we have room for, on the important point which has been suggested.

When this evidence first dawns on the mind of an inquirer, there is one striking point of accordancy which generally offers itself to his contemplation; even that accordancy which subsists between the inward experience of his own heart, and the outward description of it that is laid before him in the Bible; and is, in fact, like the exact correspondence which obtains between the cipher and the thing to be deciphered. There is no one announcement which the Bible maintains more steadily, and which it keeps by more perseveringly, and which, in opposition to all the wisdom of this world, and to all the delusion and vanity of the people who live in it, is it ever holding forth more fearlessly, and more unrelentingly, than the utter alienation and worthlessness of man in reference to God. It makes the entire corruption of our species the basis of its system. It never either questions or qualifies this position; but takes it up, and proceeds upon it; and we recognize it at every turn as the great and the pervading element of Christianity. And when a man, unwarped from all the influences by which he has hitherto been blinded, looks inwardly upon himself, and perceives that it is really so,—when enabled to pierce his way through all those plausibilities of character which have hitherto lulled him into a deceitful security, he is made to see how utterly devoid he is of what may be called the main or the elemental principle of righteousness, even a principle of allegiance to God,—when it becomes evident to him, that at the very moment that the virtues of instinct or of natural endowment, throw a lustre of moral accomplishment around him, and draw upon his person the eye and the homage of society, he is neither thinking of the God who made him, nor making His will the standard of obedience; but, with the full bent of his affections to the creature rather than to the Creator, he is in fact making the world that divinity to which he renders the incense of a perpetual offering; and withholding his heart from Him who claims the ascendency over all its desires, and giving it up in unreserved devotedness to the idols of sense and of time. Why, when he thinks of this as the very turning point of the controversy between God and His creatures; that to do this is to trample on the authority of the first and the greatest commandment; that let him be kind or amiable, or generous or upright, there is that universal attribute of the carnal mind, even enmity against God, which spreads itself over the whole system of his feelings, and deeply infuses the very best of them with the guilt and the malignity of sin,—when he contrasts his forgetfulness of God, and his utter indifference to God, with the weight of those unnumbered obligations that he owes to Him who called him into being, and who enriched him with all his faculties, and who gives him every breath, and whose right hand upholds him continually,—when thus enabled to descry, through the mists of a pride that is now mortified, and the false brilliancies of an imagination that is now arrested, how, with a heart withheld from God, he in fact has been carrying about with him, from the first infancy of his recollection, the very seed and principle of rebellion against his Maker,—when he comes to see all this, and, furthermore, to see how the same lesson, which his now enlightened experience is reading to him, in characters so distinct and so vigorous in his own person, stands engraven as vigorously and as distinctly on the record of Scripture; how the very thing has all along been most firmly, and in the face of this world's resistance, stated in his Bible, which is now opening upon his conviction, from the clearer view that he now takes of the lineaments of his own heart. Is it, after all this, to be looked at as a mystery, that he should proffer his respect to a volume which tells him what no other volume ever told him, but which he now sees, by his own discernment, to be true; that he should feel constrained towards that book in which he has found such an exact image of himself, as is not to be found within the whole range of human literature; or when an utterance of the Bible thus meets with its counterpart in his own bosom, and it be an utterance which nature never could have prompted, because revolting to all the pride and to all the sagacity of nature, shall he be any longer suspended in doubt or in amazement, though so convinced and so judged, and with the secrets of his heart so made manifest, his belief should at length be overpowered by this and similar instances of such a wondrous divination?

There is no room for dilating on other instances, or for describing the whole compass of Scripture, with the view of pointing out the every passage from which there glances, on the reader whose eyes have been opened, this evidence of divination. We cannot show how the very offer of such a Saviour as can alone quell the apprehensions of sinful nature, and makes the conscience feel at peace with God, is virtually in itself an act of divination—or how the distaste of nature for the truths of the Gospel, a distaste asserted in the records of the Gospel itself, forms another striking example of divination—or how the way in which this distaste is made to give place to a spiritual relish, and a spiritual discernment of these things, tallies with other verses of the Bible, and goes to swell and to multiply the evidences of divination—or how the actual revolution, felt by every believer whose heart is now open to the charm and the significancy of that which he at one time recoiled from in nauseous antipathy, forms an argument here of a weightier character than that of divination. We cannot venture at present on so wide a field: the evidence is in fact too abundant for it. The number of verses is too great which exhibits a harmony between the doctrines of the Bible and the findings of experience. But it may at least be remarked, that it is an evidence out of which something may be gathered to meet the case of every inquirer. For first, if he be in a state previous to conversion, this evidence accumulates upon him by every statement he finds about the deadness and the darkness, and the dread of his alienated bosom in reference to God—and he feels it to agree with the testimony of his own conscience—and he sees in the Bible the reflection of his own most intimate experience, as it tells him that he is living without hope and without God in the world, and that a moral impotency has got hold of him, and that he cannot render, in his own strength, a spiritual obedience, and that there lies upon him the utter impossibility of conceiving love to God, whom, without the faith of the New Testament, he ever will look upon as a distant and inaccessible Lawgiver. And secondly, if he be on the eve of conversion, he finds out other points of accordancy. He looks at the Gospel, and sees there what he can see nowhere else—a something to tranquillize the fears of guilt, to meet its necessities, to bring the sinner, who by nature stands afar off, near unto God—and as he feels this wondrous virtue of the peace-speaking blood, he believes that an application so suitable *to* man, could only proceed from Him who knew what was *in* man. And, finally, if he be already converted, this evidence strengthens upon him every day; and pours a growing light upon his path; and when he looks at his Bible, he sees that it contains within its pages an exact transcript of his own feelings and his own exercises; and as he looks at his own heart he sees the intimations of the Bible realized upon all its movements; and the points of accordancy between the outward die and the inward mould, he perceives to be far too minute and manifold and inscrutable to have been divined by the sagacity of man—and the conviction meets upon him with every new step in the progress of his history—and just as the Christians of old believed that God was in the apostles of a truth, so does a Christian of this day believe that God is in the Bible, which the apostles have left behind them—and to the truth of this belief, all the thoughts, and all the transactions of his inner man, lend their testimony—as he feels within himself the conflict of two opposing principles, and the habitual prevalence of one of them; or as he feels within himself the faith which worketh by love, and the love which yieldeth obedience; or as he feels within himself the process of sanctification; or as he feels within himself the peace and the joy, and the spirit of adoption. which sounds to the world an unintelligible mystery; or, as he finds on his own person the fulfilment of prayer, and the fruits of the Spirit, and a growing conformity to the example of Christ, and a growing meetness for the inheritance of a blissful eternity.

But we will not oppress ourselves with the magnitude of this argument, by attempting to dispose of it, in all its parts, and in all its illustrations, within the compass of an Essay; and we shall close this part of our argument by the three following remarks:—

1. This argument, so far from precluding the testimony of the Spirit, is the very argument which the Spirit brings before us in the exercise of his legitimate functions. He tells us of nothing that is out of the field of revelation, or out of the field of human experience. The telescope does not add a single character to the distant landscape, but brings home to our discernment all the actual and antecedent characters which existed in it. In like manner, the Spirit of God adds nothing to the word of God. He makes use of the word as His instrument. He gives us a clear view of those characters which stand engraven upon the Bible, and of those lineaments which Nature hath drawn upon our own hearts; and therefore gives us a clear view of that accordancy of divination out of which the whole of this argument emerges.

2. The evidence which is thus furnished, is, no doubt, an internal evidence; but it is altogether dissimilar from that internal evidence, which some would most presumptuously and most unphilosophically rear, as an accordancy between what they see in the Bible, and what they imagine to be the plans and the processes of the Divinity. This evidence is nearer home, more within the compass of human experience, and in every way more consonant to the cautious and solid temper of the modern philosophy, and rests exclusively on the wondrous harmony that subsists between what is seen in the Bible, and what is felt within the familiar recesses of one's own heart, and the authoritative informations of one's own consciousness.

3. It is an evidence that might be felt, in all its strength, by an unlettered workman—and he may have well warranted convictions upon the subject—and yet, from the very nature of the evidence, he may be unable to pass an adequate communication of it into another's bosom—and he may be loaded with contempt for a set of impressions which to others are utterly inexplicable: and thus it is a very possible thing, that what is called madness, may be soberness and truth—and what is branded as Methodism, may be indeed the soundest and the most enlightened philosophy.

There is another very palpable argument for the reality of some such evidence as we have tried to illustrate, which it is impossible to overlook; and the question we have to put is, what is that evidence on which a man becomes a believer within the limits of Christendom, where the Bible is circulated? And we would appeal to the ministers of Christ, for they can speak experimentally upon this question,—tell us, amongst all the transitions you have witnessed from darkness to the marvellous light of the Gospel, what the effective consideration was which accomplished such a change! Tell us, ye men whose office it is to preside over this department of human nature, who have long been conversant with the phenomena which it offers, and have doubtless treasured up in your remembrance, some cases of conversion, where the after-life of the individual stood so nobly contrasted with his by-gone history, as to attest, in characters the most decisive and undeniable, the reality of his faith! Tell us, if you have ever detected the instrumental cause of that faith—or what that was which the convert was looking to, when this principle dawned into existence—or from what quarter of contemplation the light of truth beamed upon his understanding—or where, in the whole compass of that field upon which the thoughts of man can possibly expatiate, did he meet with the charm which cleared all his doubts and all his darknesses away from him; which established his feet on a way of rectitude that he had never before walked, and animated his bosom by that Spirit of power and of a sound mind, the workings of which he had never before experienced! O where lieth the mystery of these persuasive influences which must have gathered around him, at that point of his earthly career, when the doctrine of Christ first took an ascendency over his judgment, and the morality of Christ shed its rich and beauteous accomplishments over his practice and conversation! Did it lie, we ask, in anything external to the subject-matter of the testimony? or did it lie within the subject-matter of the testimony itself? Did the light lie in that history which the documents of antiquity enable you to give of the Book? or did it lie in that doctrine and information which stand engraven upon its pages? Did it lie in the exhibition you made of the proof for the communication? or did it lie in the exhibition you made of the substance of the communication? Tell us the argument of that awakening sermon under which you remember some secure hold of infidelity to have been stormed. Was it in the act of combating the hostility of literature, when, in all the pride of erudition, you did demonstrate the faithful conveyance of the Scriptures of truth from the first age of Christianity? Or was it in the act of combating the hostility of nature's blindness and nature's opposition, when you opened these Scriptures, and made the truth itself manifest to the consciences of men? This last we imagine to be the only way of converting the souls of men. It is not done by descending into the depths of the earth, and there fighting the battles of the faith against the dark and the visioned spectres of geology. It is not done by ascending up into the heavens, and fetching down from these wondrous regions some sublime and specious illustration. It is done, by bringing the word nigh unto them—by entering with it into the warm and the well-known chambers of their own consciousness—by making them feel the full force of its adjustments to all their wants and to all their experience—by telling them of that sin, under the conviction of which nature tries to forget God, or would fly affrighted from His presence—and of that Saviour who alone can hush the alarms of nature. These are the lessons which can do to this very hour what they did in the days of the apostles. They can make the unbeliever and the unlearned feel himself to be judged of all, and convinced of all—and thus can manifest the secrets of his heart, so as that he shall acknowledge God to be in them of a truth.

And here, by the way, we cannot but remark, what a powerful argument the subject we have been illustrating furnishes in behalf of Bible and Missionary Societies. Did we propose to make our next-door neighbor a believer unto life, we should feel that the most direct instrumentality we could bring to bear upon him, would be to ply his conscience with the word of the testimony. And, did we go to the neighbor beyond him, we would just do the same thing. And though, in passing from one man to another, we widen the distance from our own home, we would never think of making any change on the kind or on the method of application, by which we tried to subdue them all unto the faith of the Gospel. And in this way would we proceed till we got to the verge of Christendom—and if such be the right and the effective treatment for the last man we found within its limits, tell us, for in truth we cannot perceive it, why, on leaving him, it should not be a treatment equally right and equally effective for the very first man we meet with beyond it. How can the evidence lose its power in the transition which we make at this particular moment? What ingredient of strength has fallen away from it? What is it that the man on this side of the line has, which the man on the other side of the line has not? Neither of them is made to witness a miracle. Neither of them has heard a single word about the original vouchers for Christianity, or about the faithful transmission of its credentials along the line of many generations. Neither of them has been initiated into the scholarship of its argumentative evidence: and if you will just demand no more for the Christianization of the latter, than what you count to be enough for the Christianization of the former, it were easy to prove, that the man who is standing without has just as much to help on his discipleship as the man who is standing within. Both of them have the same mental constitution. Both are in the same state of darkness and alienation from God. Both labor under the same fears, and may have the same feeling of their moral and spiritual necessities. In a word, each of them possesses a bosom alike framed to meet, by its responding movements, the message and the information of the New Testament. The thoughts of the one heart are as effectually reached by the word of God, which discerns and divides them asunder, as the thoughts of the other heart. And if, on the strength of these principles, we may go, by a single inch, beyond the outskirts of Christendom, on the very same principles is the whole extent of the habitable world laid open to the enterprises of Bible Societies and Christian Missionaries. There is not a human being who does not carry within him a mould of correspondence to that die which was wrought by the wisdom of God; and which is fitted to meet the case and the circumstances of all His children; and which, in fact, makes the evidence of the Bible as portable, as Bibles and teachers are portable, and which may, and therefore ought, to be carried round the globe; and should be made to traverse in every direction the wide domains of humanity, and be carried to every island and every district where men are to be found, and to circulate in full throughout all the tribes of this world's population, and to leave not so much as one straggling remnant of the species unvisited, nor to stop short in this noble enterprise, till the word of the testimony has been proclaimed among all nations, and kindreds, and families.

And if it were not so—if there was no such evidence, as that for which we are contending, by what practical avenue could the faith of the Gospel be made to find an entrance and an establishment among the great mass of our *own* population? Take away from us the self-evidencing power of the Bible, and you lay an interdict on the Christianity of cottages, on the Christianity of workshops, on the Christianity of crowded and industrious establishments, on the Christianity of nearly all our cities, and all our parishes. That the hope which is in us may have the property of endurance, there must be a reason for the hope; and where, we ask, in the whole field of their habitual contemplations are the toil-worn children of poverty to find it? Are they to search for this reason among the archives of history? Are they to gather it out of the mouldering erudition of other days? Are they to fetch it up from the profound and the puzzling obscurities of argumentation? Are they to encounter the toils of scholarship, and ere the light of revelation can guide or can gladden them, think you that they must learn to number, and to balance, and to confront the testimonies of former generations? No! Refuse us the evidence we have been insisting on, and in doing so, you pass an obliterating sponge over nearly all the Christianity that is in our land. It might still continue to be talked of in the cloistered retirements of literary debate and speculation. But the mighty host of our people could take no more rational interest in its questions, than they could in any controversy of the schools. And if the truth of this volume be not legibly stamped upon its own pages—if all the evidence by which we have affirmed it to be most thoroughly and most visibly impregnated be a delusion—if all the varied points of accordancy, between the book of revelation and the book of human experience, be not sufficient to attest the divinity which framed it—or if this attestation be beyond the understanding of an ordinary peasant—then must Christianity be ever shut up from the vast majority of our species; nor do we see one possible way of causing it to circulate at large among the families of our land.

But let us not be understood, by these remarks, to undervalue the power and the importance of the external evidences of our faith. Though it is to the subject-matter of the testimony itself, that we would send the inquirer for the most satisfying conviction of the truth; yet we hold it of paramount importance to exhibit the strength of argument, and the irresistible force of evidence, which can be adduced for the authenticity and divine authority of Revelation, to silence the gainsayer, and to vindicate Christianity from the assaults of infidelity. And we know not a finer assemblage of evidence for the divine Record, to meet and to overthrow the sophistries and objections with which scepticism is ever assailing it, or to resolve the doubts and difficulties which may agitate the mind of the honest inquirer, than the able and interesting Treatises of which the present volume is composed. The writers display, in an uncommon degree, extensive knowledge and profound erudition; and they possess every talent and qualification which is essential to solid argument, legitimate reasoning, and sound induction. With a manly spirit, suited to the rectitude of their cause, and possessed of an *experimental* assurance of the truth which they advocate, their arguments are more characterized by heartfelt power than subtle ingenuity; and, with a feeling of confidence in the strength of their cause, they manifest that dignity which best comports with the sacredness and majesty of truth, by rearing the fabric of their own evidence, without descending to notice all the oft refuted, yet still re-echoed sophistries and cavils of infidelity. The evidences they present, however, are so extensive and varied, that every order of mind is addressed with suitable proofs for its conviction; and though it would be impossible to advert to every trivial objection which infidelity has invented, or every cavil which impiety has urged, yet without fear or evasion, they have fairly selected, and triumphantly met those difficulties and objections, which infidelity has represented as most formidable to Christianity. Aware that there are infatuated men who reason against Christianity, as if it were pregnant with every mischief—who seem to delight in the imagination, that such an overwhelming calamity as a belief in its doctrines shall never overtake them—and who resist its pretensions with such inflexible obstinacy, as if the abrogation of Christianity would introduce a new order of blessing into our world, —the writers in the present volume not only introduce Christianity as presenting her credentials, but as stating and expounding her *beneficent* message. While deducing the legitimate internal evidences, arising from the nature, character, and design of Christianity, and its peculiar adaptation to renovate the moral condition of man, they intermingle their evidences with a luminous exhibition of the dispensation of grace—a dispensation so holy, perfect, and beneficent in its character and operation, that while it is well fitted to bless the life that now is, it furnishes the only solid and comfortable hope for eternity.

In Leslie's "Short and Easy Method with the Deists," and "The Truth of Christianity Demonstrated," we have the historical evidence for the truth of Scripture exhibited in a form so convincing and satisfactory, that the mind which can reject such evidence must evince a total perversity of reason, as well as an abjuration of all such testimony as can substantiate the truth of any by-gone event in this world's history,—which would go to expose every authentic record to the charge of fabulousness, and reduce the best established facts into a state of doubt and uncertainty. The firm coherence of his argument, and the soundness of his marks for distinguishing between truth and falsehood, which he so legitimately applies for ascertaining the authenticity of the facts of Scripture history, render his statements so conclusive and irresistible, that no reply can be made to his demonstrations, which does not imply a dereliction of reason and principle which the bitterest enemy of Christianity would be ashamed to avow. His proofs possess that speciality of character, that, even by the confession of infidelity itself, they can belong only to genuine records, and can never be found but in connection with events which, in truth and reality, had a positive existence. It must, therefore, be a daring and hardy scepticism indeed, which can elude or resist the force of those unequivocal proofs, by which the author indubitably establishes the authenticity of the facts which are recorded in Scripture.

Not less conclusive, in another department of evidence, do we hold Lord Lyttleton's "Observations on the Conversion and Apostleship of St. Paul." The soundness of his reasonings, established on the well-known principles of human nature, and the no less sound and philosophical deductions which he makes from the whole sentiments and conduct of the apostle, render his arguments in favor of Christianity so clear and irresistible, that we think no honest mind can give his "Observations" an attentive and unprejudiced perusal, without arriving at a thorough and well-established conviction of the truth of Christianity. To reject such evidence, or to arrive at any other conclusion, would be to betray a most wilful perversity of mind, and to commit a most grievous outrage on the soundest principles and laws of human judgment. From the impossibility of accounting for such conduct by the ingenuity of imposture, it must be by a total inversion of all the motives and principles which are known to influence human conduct, that an opposite conclusion can be drawn to what our author has deduced from an examination of the life and labors of St. Paul—that he was indeed a divinely-commissioned agent of Heaven, and that the Christian dispensation, which he labored to establish, has indubitable claims to a divine original.

In Dr. Doddridge's Discourses on the "Evidences of Christianity," we have a full and comprehensive survey of all the variety of evidence which is generally adduced in support of the authenticity and divine authority of the New Testament. The Treatise is no less characterized by the clear and forcible argument which pervades it, than by the affectionate earnestness which it breathes, and the close and pathetic appeals which the excellent author makes to the minds of his readers, on the pre-eminent importance of the truths of the divine record, and of the no less unspeakable danger of neglecting or contemning the Gospel message.

The next Treatise, by Dr. Bates, on "The Divinity of the Christian Religion," contains a no less comprehensive, and still more powerful exhibition of the various evidences which can be adduced for establishing the truth of Christianity. The evidences from history, from prophecy, from miracles, from the testimony of credible witnesses, are all brought in distinct and convincing review before the mind; and our readers cannot peruse this admirable Treatise, without an increased feeling of confidence in the variety and fulness, and invincible character of that rich assemblage of evidence, on the immovable basis of which Christianity is established. And while he satisfactorily establishes the truth of Christianity, he does not leave his readers in ignorance of what Christianity is. He not only presents the testimony which accompanies truth, to carry conviction to the understanding, but he presents the truth itself, in such a form as is fitted to commend it to the conscience. And such is our feeling of confidence in the truth, for attesting its own divinity, that we hold the truth itself to possess a power of manifestation, which addresses the heart with a more prevailing and resistless energy, than either the power of demonstration can press, or the evidence of the most incontestable miracles can enforce.

Dr. Owen's Treatise "On the divine Original, Authority, and Self-Evidencing Light and Power of the Holy Scriptures," embraces a distinct, but most important species of evidence; and this article will be held in high estimation by those who desiderate a satisfactory conviction of the claims of the Bible to divine inspiration, of which he adduces the most solid and indubitable proofs; and he affords a no less clear and satisfactory explanation to those who possess no distinct apprehension of the manner in which the word came forth from God, and was again given out by those inspired men to whom it was communicated, as well as the security and infallible certainty that what they gave out as the mind and will of God was indeed of divine original, and a divine communication. On this firm and immovable basis he establishes the authority of the Scriptures, their claim to a supremacy over the mind and will of those to whom this revelation has come, and the fearful danger of a neglect or a rejection of the message. And the truths which are made to evolve, in the progress of his demonstration, bear a hard and humbling aspect to that proud philosophy which cherishes a feeling of sentimental adoration of the works of nature, which are but the subordinate reflectors of the glory of the Deity, while it turns with antipathy and disgust from that word which the Deity has magnified above all his works, as giving a fuller and more glorious manifestation of his mind and character—a manifestation of the Deity so surpassing and exalted above that which is exhibited in the visible creation, that, in comparison with the light, and power, and extent of that manifestation which is given out in the Bible, it may well be said to have no glory, by reason of the glory that excelleth. And while we award our meed of praise to the writers of the previous Treatises in this volume, who have reared such a collective body of evidence to meet and overthrow the no less impotent than impious assaults of infidelity, yet do we hold Dr. Owen to have rendered a more essential service to the cause of Divine Revelation, when, by his clear and irresistible demonstrations, he has proved that the written word itself possesses a self-evidencing light and power for manifesting its own divine original, superior to the testimony of eye-witnesses, or the evidence of miracles, or those supernatural gifts with which the first teachers of Christianity were endowed for accrediting their divine mission. And well may the profane or the infidel contemners of revealed truth tremble at their presumption, when they are told not only of the superiority of the word of God in its power of manifestation above all His works, but of the light and power which the written word possesses to attest its own divinity, above all that external evidence which infidel philosophers so much desiderate for establishing the truth of Divine Revelation.

The Treatise of Richard Baxter "On the Folly and Danger of making light of Christ" closes the volume; and though it does not partake of the character of direct evidence, yet we hold it to be of prime importance to the cause of Christian truth, as it detects and exposes the latent causes of infidelity in the worldliness, or love of pleasure, or the diversified pursuits which engross the mind, to the utter exclusion of the salvation which the Gospel reveals. And truly does he resolve the largest portion of the infidelity which exists, into the infidelity of the heart, and not of the understanding. From the irreconcilable characters of God and Mammon, of Christ and Belial, of the love of the Father, and the love of the world, those infatuated men who are determined to render their homage to the one, must necessarily entertain feelings of hostility to the other; and this hostility of the affections exerts a secret but blinding and delusive influence over the judgment, and in spite of the clearest and most incontrovertible evidence, betraying it into a disbelief of what the depraved heart must wish were not true. Aware as we are, of the extreme reluctance with which men whose minds have become poisoned with the pride of infidelity, or whose hearts have become depraved with the love of sin, admit any argument in favor of Christianity, we could not close our volume without bringing the forcible and pathetic appeals of Richard Baxter to bear upon their consciences. And if there be one piece in this volume, which, in preference to another, we would more urgently recommend to their serious regard, it would be this invaluable Treatise of Richard Baxter. Aware as he was of that deep and desperate infatuation by which so many are deceived to their eternal undoing, with the tenderness and pathos of a man whose heart glowed with angelic benevolence—and with the earnestness and urgency of a man who felt the importance of his message; does he endeavor to persuade men by all that is commanding in the authority of God—by all that is winning in the love of Christ—by all that is inviting in a blessed immortality—and by all that is tremendous in eternal perdition, to flee from the wrath to come, and to lay hold of the offered remedy. And if such men continue in their wilful and obstinate rejection of the Gospel, and heedlessly neglect, or perversely resist, the mercy which it offers, then it is not from want of clear and incontrovertible evidence, but from a desperately wicked and deceitful heart which is deceiving them to their ruin; and we know not by what power, or by what sophistry such infatuated men can turn away from them the force of this fearful declaration, that "if our Gospel be hid, it is hid to them that are lost: *in whom the god of this world hath blinded the minds of them which believe not*, lest the light of the glorious Gospel of Christ, who is the image of God, should shine unto them."

It is well that Christianity has such a firm basis of argumentation to rest upon. It is well that she can be triumphantly borne throughout the whole range of human literature, and can bear to be confronted with all that the fancy or the philosophy of man have ever devised against her reputation. We count every one illustration of her external evidence to be an accession to her cause, nor can we look at the defensive barrier which has been thrown around her, without wishing that the public eye might often be directed to the strength and the glory of her venerable outworks. But let it not be disguised. The surrender of the understanding to the external argument is one thing; the rational principle of Christianity is another. And, therefore, there must be something more than the bare evidence of Christianity, to work the faith which is unto salvation. Many are the accomplished philosophers who have rejected this evidence, and to them it will stand in place of the miracle of tongues to the unbelievers of old. It will be a sign to justify their condemnation. But many also have admitted the evidence, and still the opinion has been as unfruitful of all that is religious, as the conclusion they have come to on any literary question. And, men of genius and accomplishment as they are, they must, to obtain the faith of the Gospel, just put themselves on a level with the most untaught of our peasantry. They must submit to be tutored by the same evidence at last. They must labor after the same manifestation of the truth unto their consciences. They must open their Bibles, and give earnest heed unto the word of this prophecy. To the spirit of earnestness they must add the spirit of prayer. They must knock for light at the door which they cannot open, till the day dawns and the day-star arise in their hearts—and then will they find, that, by a way hidden from the wise and the prudent, but revealed unto babes, the word of prophecy may become more sure than any miracle can make it—more sure, than if a voice of attestation were to sound forth upon them from the canopy of heaven—and greatly more sure than by all that contradictory evidence, which links the present with the past, the period in which we now live with that wondrous period, when such a voice was heard by human ears on the mount of transfiguration.

It is true that the word of the testimony is often perused in vain—that in the reading of the Scriptures, the veil which is upon the heart of the natural man often remains untaken away—and that, after all that is done with him, he persists in blind and wilful obstinacy, and will neither see the doctrine of the Bible, nor the reflection of that doctrine upon his own character. To work this effect, the word must be accompanied by the demonstration of the Spirit, and who shall limit his operations? When we think of the influences of Him who is promised in answer to prayer, and when we farther think of the extent of warrant that we have for prayer, even that we should ask for all such things as are agreeable to the will of God, who willeth all men to be saved, and to come to the knowledge of the truth, and who is ever ready to put a blessing on His own word; then, to the diligent reading of the word, let him add the humble, earnest, and sincere prayer, that "God who commanded the light to shine out of darkness, may shine into his heart, to give him the light of the knowledge of the glory of God, as it is revealed in the face of Jesus Christ."

INTRODUCTORY ESSAY

TO

THE LIVING TEMPLE;

OR,

A GOOD MAN THE TEMPLE OF GOD.

BY THE REV. JOHN HOWE, A.M.

It is well remarked by the excellent John Howe, in the following Treatise, that the "Living Temple," or, as it is frequently styled in the New Testament the "Kingdom of Heaven," which God is setting up in the world, "is not established by might or by power, but by the Spirit of the Lord; who—as the structure is spiritual, and to be situated and raised up in the mind or spirit of man—works, in order to it, in a way suitable thereto; that is, very much by soft and gentle insinuations, to which are subservient the self-recommending amiableness and comely aspect of religion, the discernible gracefulness and uniform course of such in whom it bears rule, and is a settled, living law. It is a structure to which there is a concurrence of truth and holiness; the former letting in a vital, directive, formative light—the latter, a heavenly, calm, and god-like frame of spirit." To the same import is the declaration of our Saviour, when, in answer to the Pharisees, who demanded of Him when the kingdom of God should come, replied, "The kingdom of God cometh not with observation; neither shall they say, Lo, here! or, lo, there! for, behold, the kingdom of God is within you." We are thus given to understand, that the kingdom which God is establishing in the world, does not consist in external forms and observances—that it is not of a temporal, but of a spiritual character—and that, unlike the establishment of earthly kingdoms, it cometh with none of those visible accompaniments which meet the eye of public observation.

The establishment of a new kingdom in the world carries much in it to strike the eye of an observer. There is a deal of visible movement accompanying the progress of such an event—the march of armies, and the bustle of conspiracies, and the exclamations of victories, and the triumph of processions, and the splendor of coronations. All these doings are performed upon a conspicuous theatre; and there is not an individual in the country, who, if not an actor, may be at least an observer on the elevated stage of great and public revolutions. He can point his finger, and say, Lo, here! or, lo, there! to the symptoms of political change which are around him; and the clamorous discontent of one province, and the warlike turbulence of another, and the loud expressions of public sentiment at home, and the report of preparation abroad —all force themselves upon the notice of spectators; so that when a new kingdom is set up in the world, that kingdom cometh with observation.

The answer of our Saviour to the question of the Pharisees, may be looked upon as designed to correct their misconceptions respecting the nature of the kingdom which he was to establish. There is no doubt that they all looked for a deliverance from the yoke of Roman authority—that, in their eyes, the Captain of their Salvation was to be the leader of a mighty host, who, fighting under the special protection of God, would scatter dismay and overthrow among the oppressors of their country—that the din of war, and the pride of conquest, and the glories of a widely extended dominion, and all the visible parade of a supreme and triumphant monarchy, were to shed a lustre over their beloved land. And it must have been a sore mortification to them all, when they saw the pretensions of the Messiah associated with the poverty, and the meekness, and the humble, unambitious, and spiritual character of Jesus of Nazareth. We cannot justify the tone of His persecutors; but we must perceive, at the same time, the historical consistency of all their malice, and bitterness, and irritated pride, with the splendor of those expectations on which they had been feasting for years, and which gave a secret elevation to their souls under the endurance of their country's bondage, and their country's wrongs. It marks—and it marks most strikingly—how the thoughts of God are not as the thoughts of man; that the actual fulfilment of those prophecies which related to the history of Judea, turned out so differently from the anticipations of the men who lived in it; and that Jerusalem, which, in point of expectation, was to sit as mistress over a tributary world, was, in point of fact, torn up from its foundations, after the vial of God's wrath had been poured in a tide of unexampled misery over the heads of its wretched people. Now, what became all the while of those prophecies which respected the Messiah? What became of that kingdom of God which the Pharisees inquired about, and of which, however much they were in the wrong respecting its nature, they were certainly in the right respecting the time of its appearance? Did it actually appear? Is it possible that it could be working its way, at the very time that every hope which man conceived of it was turned into the cruellest mockery?

Is it possible that the truth of prophecy could be receiving its most splendid vindication, at the very time that every human interpreter was put to shame, and that all that happened was the reverse of all that was anticipated? Surely if any kingdom was formed at that time, when the besom of destruction passed through the land of Judea, and swept the whole fabric of its institutions away from it—surely if it was such a kingdom, as was to spread, through the seed of Abraham, the promised blessing among all the families of the earth, and that, too, when a cloud of ignominy was gathering upon the descendants of Abraham—surely if at the time when Pagans desolated the Land of Promise, and profaned the temple, and entered the holy place, and wantoned in barbarous levity among those sacred courts where the service of the true God had been kept for many generations—surely if at such a time and with such a burden of disgrace and misery on the people of Israel, a kingdom was forming that was to be the glory of that people—then it is not to be wondered at that no earthly eye should see it under the gloom of that disastrous period, or that the kingdom of God, coming as it did in the midst of wars and rumors of wars, when men's eyes were looking at other things, and their hearts were failing them, should have eluded their observation.

In common language, a kingdom carries our thoughts to the country over which it is established. The kingdom of Sweden directs the eye of our mind to that part of Europe; and in the various places of the Bible where the kingdom of God and the kingdom of heaven are mentioned, this is one of the significations. But it has also other significations. It sometimes means, not the place over which the royal authority extends, but the royal authority itself. In the first sense, the kingdom of heaven carries our attention to heaven; but with this as the meaning, we could not understand what John the Baptist pointed to, when he said "the kingdom of heaven is at hand." But, in the second sense, it is quite intelligible, and means that the authority which subordinates all the families of heaven to the one Monarch who reigns there, was on the eve of being established with efficacy on earth; or, in other words, that the prayer was now beginning its accomplishment—"Thy will be done on earth as it is in heaven." Hence it is that some translators, for the term *kingdom*, substitute the term *reign;* and make our Saviour say, that the reign of God cometh not with observation, for the reign of God is within you. The will of man is the proper seat of the authority of God. It is there where rebellion against Him exists in its principle; and where that rebellion is overthrown, it is there where the authority of God sits in triumph over all His enemies. Give Him the will of man, and invest that will with an efficient control over the doings of man, and you give Him all He wants. You render Him the one act of obedience which embraces every other. "Give me thy heart," is a precept, the performance of which involves in it the surrender of all the man to all the requirements. It brings the whole life under its authority; for it takes that into its keeping out of which are the issues of life. And could these hearts of ours be brought into subjection to the first and great commandment, obedience would cease to be a task; for we would delight to run in the way of it. To do it would be our meat and our drink. We would know, in the experience of our own lives, that the commandments of God are not grievous. It is only grievous to do that which is against the bent of the will. But to do that which is with the bent of the will, contains in it all the facility of a natural and spontaneous movement. It is doing what is a pleasure to ourselves. It is said to be one of the attributes of rebellion, that it walks in the counsel of its own heart, and in the sight of its own eyes. But this is only when the heart is alienated from the God of heaven, and the eyes are blinded by the god of this world. Give us a heart which the purifying grace of the Gospel hath made clean, and eyes to which Christ hath given light, and then it is no longer rebellion to walk in the counsel of such a heart, and in the sight of such eyes. Obedience against the desires and tendencies of the heart is painful as the drudgery of a slave; and, in fact, to the eye of God, who thinks that if He has not the heart He has nothing, it is no obedience at all—but obedience, with these desires and tendencies, is carried on with all the spring and energy of a pleasurable exercise. And, oh! precious privilege of him who is made by faith to partake in the heart-purifying influences of the Gospel! It is the very pleasure which we take in the doing of God's will, and which makes it so delightful to us, that gives to our performances all their value in the eye of God. We will be at no loss to understand the happiness of a well-founded Christian, when the doing of that which is in the highest degree delightful to himself, meets, and is at one, with all the security of God's friendship and God's approbation. We are now touching upon such an experience of the inner man as the world knoweth not, and are describing the mysteries of such a kingdom as the world discerneth not; but whether all our readers go along with us or not, it remains true, that if the love of God be made to reign within us, His will becomes our will. And this commandment proves itself to be the first of all; for when it is fulfilled, the fulfilment of all the rest follows in its train—and the greatest of all; for it, as it were, takes a wide enough sweep to inclose them all, and to form a guard and a security for their observance.

The reign of God on earth, then, is the reign of His will over the unseen movements of the inner man. This is the kingdom He wants to establish. It is the submission of that which is within us, that He claims as His due; and if it be withheld from Him, all the conformity of our outer doings is a vain and an empty sacrifice. Give us a right mind towards God, and you give us, in the individual who owns that mind, all the elements of loyalty. It is there where His authority is felt and acknowledged to be a rightful authority. It is there where its requirements are looked at by the understanding, and laid upon the conscience, and move the will with all the force of a resistless obligation, and form the purpose of obedience, and send forth that purpose, armed with the full power of a presiding influence, over every step and movement of his history. It is in the busy chamber of the mind where all that is great and essential in the work of obedience is carried on. The mighty struggle between the powers of heaven and of hell is for the possession of this little chamber. The subtle enemy of our race knows, that while he has this for his lodging-place, the empire is his own—and give him only the citadel of the heart, and he will revel in all the glories of his undivided monarchy. The strong man reigns in his house with the full authority of its master, till a stronger than he overcome him, and bind him, and take possession of that which he before occupied. And such is the spirit that worketh in the children of disobedience. It is in the heart of man that he worketh, and is ever plying it with his wiles and contrivances, and turning its affections to the creature, and blinding it to all that is glorious or lovely in the image of the Creator; and by his power over the fancy, causing it to imagine a greatness, and a stability, and a value, and an enjoyment in the things of the world which do not belong to them ; and whispering false promises to the ear of the inner man, and seducing him as he did the first of our race, so as to bring him into the snare of the devil, and to take him captive at his will. In the same manner, he who came to destroy the works of the devil, bends his main force to the quarter where these works are strongest, and their position is most advantageous to the enemy. The heart of man is the mighty subject of this spiritual contest, and the possession of the heart is the prize of victory. To those who have not yet learned to take their lesson from the Bible, all this sounds like a fabulous imagination, or the legendary tale of an artful priesthood to a drivelling and superstitious people. But it is all to be met with in God's revealed communication. You are ignorant of what you ought to know, if you know not that a contest is going on among the higher orders of being for the mastery of all that is within you. Let Christ then dwell in you by faith. He is knocking at the door of your heart, and if you will open it to receive Him, He will enter it. He will sweep it of all its corruptions. He will enable you to overcome, for then greater will be He that is in you than he that is in the world. The kingdom of God is righteousness and peace, and joy in the Holy Ghost ; and He making you, by the power of His Spirit, to abound in these fruits, will in you make another addition to that living temple—that spiritual kingdom which God is establishing in the world.

Man has revolted from God, and a fearful change has taken

place in his moral constitution; and thus the things of sight and of sense, instead of leading his thoughts to God, have become the idolatrous objects of his affections. In his original state of innocence, man not only held direct and intimate communion with God, but all that he saw, and all that he enjoyed, conducted his thoughts and his affections to that Being whose love and whose authority reigned in supremacy over his heart. The gratification of his desire for created things, was then in perfect harmony with the love of the Creator. And man would just now have been in this condition if he had not fallen. He would not have counted it his duty, to have violently counteracted his every taste, and every desire, for the things which are created. The practical habit of his life would not have been a constant and strenuous opposition to all that could minister delight to the sensitive part of his constitution. He would not have been ever and anon employed in thwarting the adaptations which God had ordained between the objects that are around him, and his organs of enjoyment. It is true, that when Eve put forth her hand to the forbidden fruit, it was after she had looked upon the tree, and seen that it was good for food, and pleasant to the eyes: but the very same thing is said of the other trees in the garden, "for out of the ground made the Lord to grow every tree that is pleasant to the sight, and good for food." Our first parents tasted of all these trees without offence,—and in that habitation of sweets many an avenue of enjoyment was open to them; and a thousand ways may well be conceived, in which the loveliness of surrounding nature would minister delight both to the eye and the feeling of our first parents,—and from every point of that external materialism which God had reared for his accommodation, would there beam a felicity upon the creature whom He had so organized, as to suit his capacities of pleasure to his outward circumstances. We are not to conceive, that during that short-lived period of the world's innocence, and of Heaven's favor, there was no gratification transmitted to the soul of man from the sensible and created things which were on every side of him. His taste was gratified,—and amid the pure luxury, and among the delicious repasts of paradise, might be perceived in him a principle of desire, corresponding to what in our days of depravity is termed the lust of the flesh. His eye was gratified,—and as he surveyed the beauties of his garden, and felt himself to be its vested and rightful proprietor, would he experience a principle of desire, which, in its transmission to a corrupt posterity, has now become the lust of the eye. His sense of superior dignity was gratified,—and as he stalked in benevolent majesty among the tribes of creation that had been placed beneath him, would he feel the kindlings of that very affection, which, tainted by the malignity of sin, has sunk down among his offspring into the pride of life. All these affections, which in a state of guilt have so virulent an operation on the heart, as to be opposite to the love of God,—there is not one of them but may have had a pure and a righteous counterpart in a state of innocence.

And the whole explanation of the matter appears simply to be this. Adam lived at that time in communion with God. In all that he enjoyed, he saw a Giver's hand, and a Giver's kindness. That link, by which the happiness he derived from the use of the creature was associated with the love of the Creator, was clearly and constantly present with him. There was not one thing which he either tasted or saw, that was not regarded by him as a token of the Divine beneficence; insomuch that the expression of a Father's care and a Father's tenderness, beamed upon his senses, from every one object with which his senses came into intercourse. Whatever he looked upon with the eye of his body, was but to him the material vehicle, through which the love of the great Author of all found its way to him, with some new accession of enjoyment; nor could there one pleasurable feeling then be made to arise which was not most exquisitely heightened, and most intimately pervaded, by the grateful remembrance of Him who had placed him in his present condition, and whose liberal hand had done so much to bless and to adorn it. In the case of a human benefactor, there is no difficulty in perceiving, that there is room in the heart, both for a sense of gratification from the gift, and for a sense of gratitude to the giver. In the case of the heavenly Benefactor, the union of these two things stood constant and inseparable, and was only dissolved by the fall. A sense of God mingled with every influence that came from the surrounding materialism upon our first parents. It impregnated all. It sanctified all. The things of sense did not detain them for a single moment from God; because, while busied with the work of enjoyment, they were equally busied with the work of gratitude. All that they tasted, or handled, or saw, were memorials of the Divinity; insomuch that His visible presence in the garden was never felt to be an interruption. It only made Him present to their senses, who was constantly present to their thoughts. It for a time withdrew them from some of the scenes on which his character was imprinted; but it summoned them to a direct contemplation of the character itself. While it suspended their enjoyment of a few of the tokens of his love, it gave them a nearer and more affecting enjoyment of its reality; and instead of reluctantly withdrawing from those objects which were merely dear to them as the reflections of His kindness, when He called them to an act of fellowship with the kindness itself, did they recognize His voice, and obeyed it with ecstasy.

Now, without adverting to the way in which the transition from the former to the present state of man's moral nature has taken place—such in fact has been the transition, that the two states are not only unlike, but in direct and diametric opposition to each other—there is no such change in his physical constitution, but that what tasted pleasurably to him in his state of innocence, tastes pleasurably to him still—and what looked fair to him in external nature then, looks fair to him now—and in many instances, what regaled his senses in the one state, is equally fitted to regale them in the other. The purity of Eden did not lie in the want or the weakness of all physical sensation; neither does the guilt of our accursed world lie in the existence, or even in the strength, of physical sensation. But in the former state, the gift stood at all times associated in the mind of man with the Giver. God rejoiced over his children to do them good; and they, while rejoicing in the good that they obtained, felt it all to be heightened and pervaded by a sense of his kindness. Every new accession to their enjoyment, instead of seducing them from their loyalty, only served to confirm it; and brought a new accession to that love, which made their duty to be their delight, and their highest privilege and pleasure to be the keeping of His commandments. The moral and spiritual change which our race has undergone, consisted in this—that the tie in their minds was broken, by which the enjoyment of the gift led to a sense and a recognition of the Giver. It is the breaking asunder of this link which simply and essentially forms the corruption of man. He drinks of the stream, without any recognition of the fountain from which it flows. God is banished from his gratitude and from his thoughts. With him the whole business of enjoyment is made up of an intercourse between his senses, and the objects that are suited to them. There is no intercourse between his mind and that Being, who is the Author both of his senses, and of all that is fitted to regale them. He makes use of created things, and has pleasure in the use of them. But in that pleasure he rests and terminates. Instead of vehicles leading him to God, they are in his eye stationary and ultimate objects; the possession of which, and the enjoyment of which, are all that he aspires after. Pleasure is prosecuted for itself. Wealth is prosecuted for itself. Distinction is prosecuted for itself. There is no wish on the part of natural men for a portion in anything beyond these. God is not the object of their desire, and he is just as little the object of their dependence. It is neither God whom they are seeking, nor is it to God that they look for the attainment of what they are seeking. They count upon fortune, and experience, and the constancy of the course of nature, and anything but the power, and the purposes, and the sovereignty of God. He, in fact, is deposed from his supremacy, both as an object of desire and an object of dependence. Men have deeply revolted from God; and they have raised the world, not into a rival, but into the sole and triumphant divinity of their adoration. The lust of the flesh, and the lust of the eye, and the pride of life, may have all had their counterpart in the constitution of Adam ere he fell; but instead of averting his eye from the

Father, they brought the Father more vividly into his remembrance—instead of intercepting God, they conducted both his thoughts and his affections to the Being who openeth his hand liberally, and satisfieth the desire of every living thing. But with the diseased posterity of Adam, these affections are only so many idolatrous desires towards the creature—so many acts of homage towards the world, regarded in the light of a satisfying and independent deity—and therefore is it said of them, that "they are not of the Father, but of the world."

Now, to bring this home to familiar experience—who is there, in looking forward with delight to some entertainment of luxury—or who is there, in prosecuting with intense devotion some enterprise of gain—or who is there, in adding to the pomp of his establishment, that ever thinks of God as having furnished the means, or as having created the materials of these respective gratifications? They look no farther than to the materials themselves. For the indulgence of these various affections, they draw not upon God, but upon this solid and visible world, to which they ascribe all the power and all the independency of God. They look not to any pleasure which they enjoy as emanating from the first cause. They see it emanating from secondary causes; and with these do they stop short, and are satisfied. It is this which stamps the guilt of atheism on the whole practical habit and system of human life. In the prosecution of its objects, not one civil obligation may have been violated—not one deed may have been committed to forfeit the respect of society—not one thing may ever have been charged upon this world's idolater to alienate the regard, but everything may have been done by him to conciliate the kindness, and draw down upon him the flattery of his fellow-men. But, alas! he has broken loose from God! He lives, from the cradle to the grave, without any practical recognition of Him in whom he lives, and moves, and has his being. A demonstration of social virtue, so far from offending, may minister to his complacency. But to bid him crucify his affections for the things of sense, is to bid him inflict a suicide upon his person. And thus, while beneficent in conduct, and fair in reputation among his fellows, may he in prospect be linked with the fate of a world that is soon to be burnt up, and in character be tainted with the spirit of a world that is lying in wickedness. And thus it is, that there may be spiritual guilt in the midst of social accomplishment—there may be wrath from heaven in the midst of applause and connivance from the world—there may be impending disaster in the midst of imagined safety—there may be abomination in the sight of God, in the midst of highest esteem and popularity among men.

There is nothing in the daily routine of this world's luxury, or this world's covetousness, or this world's ambition, which suggests to its carnal and earth-born children the conviction of sinfulness.

The round of pleasure is described, or the career of adventure is prosecuted, or the path of aggrandizement is entered upon; and it does not once meet the imagination of this world's votary, that, in every one of these pursuits, he is widening his departure from God. He is not aware of the deathly character of his habits; and, protect him only from the voice of human execration, he hears, or hears without alarm, that voice of truth which pronounces him wholly given over to idolatry. And yet can anything be more evident, even of the most harmless and reputable members of society, than that the gifts of a kind and liberal Father have stolen away from Him the affections of His own children—than that they have taken up with another portion, than with Him who originates and sustains them—than that they have built their foundation on the creature, and look on the Creator with the defiance at least of unconcern? They in reality have disjoined themselves from God. Instead of being conducted by the sight of the world to the thought of God, they look no further than the world, and it stands in their hearts contrasted with God. Instead of the one leading to the other, the one detains and withdraws from the other. They are so conversant with the world as to lose sight of God. For this we can appeal to the conscience of every natural man, and on this we ground the affirmation, that though in the keen pursuit of the money which purchaseth all things, he may have never deviated from the onward path of integrity, he has been receding by every footstep to a greater distance from heaven—and with an eye averted from God, has been looking towards those things, the love of which is opposite to the love of the Father.

And it is because men are thus engrossed with the visible objects of time, that they have lost sight of their own individual concern in that spiritual kingdom which God is setting up in the world. Because it does not rank among the visibilities of earth, it is looked at by them with the most heedless indifference, and they regard its existence as a fiction of the imagination. The subject of that kingdom is indeed invisible. It worketh its silent and unseen way through the world of souls, and it may be multiplying its subjects, and widening the extent of its dominion every day, without the eye of man being able to perceive it. There is a day of revelation coming; and the hidden things which are to be laid open on that day are the secrets of the heart. But, in the meantime, the heart is, in a great measure, shut up from observation; and many of its movements will remain unnoticed and unknown till that day shall discover them. And we are expressly told, that that greatest of all movements, by which it turns from Satan unto God, is a hidden operation. It is said of the Spirit, who worketh this movement, that no man knoweth whence it cometh, or whither it goeth. It makes its noiseless way through streets and families. The visible instrument which God employs may come equally to all who are within its reach; but the effect which the Spirit giveth to that instrument, is not a matter of direct perception, nor can we tell who the individual is whose heart it will ply with the word of God, so as to give all the weight and power of a hammer breaking the rock in pieces. O how much of the inner man remains impenetrably hidden under all that is visible in the general aspect of society! To man himself it is an unknown field, though the beings who are above man have all their eyes upon it. In looking to human affairs, it is the only field they deem worthy of contemplation. The frail and fleeting materials of common history, are as nothing in the eye of those who count nothing important but that which has stamped upon it the character of eternity. To recommend it to them, it must have the attribute of endurance; or, in other words, it must be related to souls, which are the only subjects in this world that God hath endued with the vigor of immortality. Now the soul of man is invisible to us, nor can we see, as through a window, its desires, and its movements, and its silent aspirations. There is a thick covering of sense thrown over it; and thus it is, that what, to the eye of angels, appears the only worthy object of attention in the history of the species, is, to the eye of man himself, an unknown mystery. His eye is engrossed with the glare of what is seen, and of what is sensible; and the secrecies of the soul lie on the background of his contemplation altogether. He knows as little about the busy doings which go on in the heart of his neighbor, as he knows of what goes on on the surface of some remote and undiscovered world. In the wideness of immensity, there are fields so distant as to be beyond the ken of eye or of telescope: but there is also a field immediately around us, which lies wrapt in unfathomable secrecy. O it is little dwelt upon by man, whose thoughts are so taken up with what the eye seeth, and the ear can listen to. But on this field there are doings of mightier import than the whole visible universe lays before us. It forms part of the world of spirits. It is the field of discipline for eternity. It is the field on which is decided the fate of conscious and never-ending existence. It is a province in the moral government of God, and in worth outweighs all the splendor and all the richness of that material magnificence which is around us. The earth is to be burned up, and the heavens are to pass away as a scroll; but on this near, though unnoticed field, there is a mighty interest now forming, which will survive the wreck of all that is visible: and it is there that God gains accessions to his kingdom which endureth forever.

But there are two remarks by which we would limit and define the extent of what is said by our Saviour, about the kingdom of God coming not with observation. It holds true of every man who becomes the subject of that kingdom, that by his fruits ye shall know him. There is a visible style of conduct which bespeaks him to be a different man from others, and a different man from what he himself was before he entered into the kingdom of God. Let the reign of God be established over the inner man, and it will tell, and tell observably, upon the doings of the outer man. But remark here, that though the kingdom of God may be the subject of observation where it exists, yet the bringing of that kingdom into existence, or, in other words, the coming of that kingdom may not be with observation. Now, what is true of an individual, is true of many. The formation of the kingdom of God, in the hearts of the majority of a neighborhood, would give rise to a spectacle fitted to strike the general eye; and there is something broadly visible in the complexion of a renovated and moralized people. There is a change of aspect in the doings of every man who is born again, that meets the observation of his neighbors; and a sufficient number of such men would give rise to such a general change as to solicit general observation. But though the change, after it is established, may excite their notice, yet the coming on of the change may not excite their notice. The steps by which it is accomplished may elude the notice of the generality altogether. The little stone may be too small to draw upon it the attention of a distant world; but it may compel their attention by its progress, and even long before it filleth the whole earth, the whole earth may be filled with inquiries after it. The work of the Spirit is visible, but the working of the Spirit is not visible. He bloweth where He listeth; and though the kingdom of God, that he is to establish in the world, shall swallow up all the rest, and by its magnitude force itself upon the general observation, yet, in the first stages of its progress, and in the act of coming, it may not be with observation.

Our other remark is, that though the kingdom of God cometh not with observation, yet by the prophecies of God, the origin and the sudden enlargement of that kingdom, have a place assigned to them in the march of visible history. The four great monarchies form conspicuous eras in the history of man. They come with observation, and they mark, in a general way, the infancy, and the growth, and the matured establishment of that kingdom which cometh not with observation. We lie at the feet of Nebuchadnezzar's image. This is the place in the descending scale of ages which we occupy; and the present political aspect of Europe was seen afar by the prophet Daniel through the vista of many generations. The ten kingdoms into which the Roman empire was divided, form the closing scene in his magnificent representation of futurity; and it is this distant period which, in the mighty range of his prophetic eye, he is employed in contemplating, when he tells us of a kingdom made without hands, and, from the size of a little stone, growing into a mountain which filled the whole earth. The coming of these ten kingdoms carried on it a broad aspect, which addressed itself to the senses of men. They were ushered in with all the notes and characters of preparation. Kings met, and kings combated on a conspicuous arena; the loud uproar of the battle was heard, and the rumor of it spread itself; and each of the predicted kingdoms made its entrance into the world, with the pomp, and the circumstance, and the visible insignia of war. It is in the time of these kingdoms that the kingdom of God is to break forth on every side; and the want of those visible accompaniments, which mark the progress and the establishment of other kingdoms, signalizes the kingdom of God, and stamps upon it the peculiar character of coming not with observation. There is a silence and a secrecy in the progress of this kingdom, which do not belong to the others. It has its signs too, but they are not such signs as the Pharisees were looking for, when they asked about the kingdom of God, and about the signs of its appearance. The interpreters of prophecy have been watching, for whole centuries, all the variations which take place in the restless politics of this world—they have been pursuing every fluctuation in the ever-changing history of the times,—but the ten toes of Nebuchadnezzar's image still represent the great outline of European society. It is not in the revolutions of political power that we are to look for the direct or immediate symptom of God's approaching kingdom. The effect of that kingdom is to revolutionize the hearts of men. The Alexander of a former day, filled with generous resentment at the wrongs of his outraged country, and gathering energy from despair, and marching at the head of a population rallying around the standard of revenge, out of all his provinces, and aided by the tempests of heaven, might have overwhelmed that power which had spread its desolating triumphs over half the monarchies of Europe. But all this might have been done, and the little stone have remained all the while stationary, and the flock of Christ received no addition to its numbers; and should the same rapacity of ambition exist among the rulers of the world, and the same profligacy among the people, and the same baleful infidelity among the learned, and the same lofty contempt for the holy spirit and doctrines of the Gospel among the upper classes of society, and the same devotedness to the good things of life spreading among all its classes a spiritual indifference to the law of God,—then the kingdom of God has made no progress, and all the characters of Antichrist stand as deeply engraved as ever upon the aspect of the existing generation. But should the heart of the present Nicholas receive a secret visit from that Spirit which bloweth where He listeth—should it be turned, with all its affections, to the Saviour who died for him—should the renewed soul of the monarch own in silent reverence the power of a higher monarchy, and, instead of his plans and his purposes of ambition and war, should his heart be filled with the holy ambition of dedicating all his means and all his energies to the spread of Christianity in the world; then, in the solitude of his inner chamber, an unseen preparation might be going on for helping forward the establishment of the kingdom of God; and when we think of the small place which these doings occupy in the columns of a gazette, or in the deliberations of a cabinet, or in the earnest contemplation of the general mind in Europe—above all, when we think that they are chiefly carried on by men who, through the great mass of society, are derided or unknown—then may we well understand how a kingdom, spreading its unseen influence through such private channels, and earning all its triumphs in the hearts and bosoms of individuals, is a kingdom which cometh not with observation.

We may easily understand, from what has been stated, how inefficient must be many of the methods which are actually resorted to for extending true religion, or the kingdom of God, in the world. It is not by crusading it against the power of infidel governments, that you will establish this kingdom. It is not by enacting it against the heresy of unscriptural opinions, that you will carry forward the establishment of this kingdom. It is not by the solemn deliberations of a legislature, sitting in judgment over questions that can only be carried into effect by the civil authority of the state, that you can at all help forward the establishment of this kingdom in the world. We will venture to say, that the mad enterprise of the middle ages did not add one subject to the kingdom of God. They may have stormed the holy city, so as to plant upon its battlements the standard of Christendom; but they did not storm a single human heart, so as to plant within it a principle of holiness. The citadel of the heart must be plied with another engine; and the strong man who reigns and who occupies there, may smile, and may sit in secure defiance to the warlike preparations of a whole continent. No external violence of any kind can force the will and the principle of man to its subserviency. Whatever effect it may have on the territory of earthly princes, it cannot add a single inch to the territory of the kingdom of God; and that whether the instrument of religious frenzy be an army or a parliament, after expending all its force, and doing nothing, it is at length, by the working of another instrument, and the silent but powerful efficacy of another expedient, that we make a way for the establishment of God's Living Temple in the world.

This brings us to the question, What is this instrument? The Spirit of God is the agent in every conversion of every human soul from Satan unto God. He is the alone effectual worker in this matter, but He worketh by instruments; and it is our part to put them in readiness, and to do those things to the doing of which He stands pledged to impart the efficacy of His all-subduing influences. It was the Spirit, and He alone, who gave the apostles all the enlargement they got on the day of Pentecost: but they put themselves in readiness, by obeying the prescribed direction to go to Jerusalem; and there they waited and they prayed for the promise of the Father. Had they not been at their prescribed post, they would have obtained no part whatever in the promised privilege; and in like manner we, with every sentiment of dependence on the power of the Spirit, should, both for ourselves and others, do those things, in the doing of which alone we have reason to expect that He will come down with all that energy of impression, and all that richness of gift and of endowment, which belong to Him. The apostles were the human instruments for the dispensation of the Spirit in those days; and we cannot do better than to take our lesson from them, and observe what they had to do, that the Spirit of God, working along with them, might turn the hearts of men, and extend the proper kingdom of God over the proper ground which that kingdom has to occupy. They laid before those to whom they addressed themselves the word of God, and they prayed for the Spirit of God, that He might take hold of His own instrument, and make it bear with effect upon the consciences and the understandings of men. The lesson is a short one, but it comprises all that we have to do in the work of extending Christianity through the world. Be it on our own behalf, and with a view to bring down upon our own souls the benefits of the Gospel, and the best thing we can turn ourselves to is to read diligently the Bible, and to pray diligently for that Spirit, who pours the brilliancy of a warm and affecting light over all its pages. Be it on behalf of others, and with a view to secure to them the benefits of the Gospel, then, if they are immediately around us, the best thing we can do is to ply them with the instructions of the Bible, and to pray for the coming down of that power which can alone give these instructions all their efficacy. Hence the stationary apparatus of a country where Christianity is established—consisting of schools, where the reading of the Bible is taught; and churches, where the meaning of the Bible is expounded; and official men, whose business it is to pray themselves, and to press the exercise of prayer on others, to that God who orders intercession in behalf of all, because He willeth all to be saved. But should it be in behalf of men who live in a distant country—and the precept of "Go and preach the Gospel to every creature," gives a legitimacy to the attempts of Christianizing them, which all the ridicule and all the wisdom of this world cannot overthrow—then the stationary apparatus becomes a movable one; and the word of God, translated into other languages, and human messengers to carry that word and to expound it—and Christians abroad to spread around them the message of salvation, and Christians who stay at home praying to the God of all influence, and giving Him no rest till He pour such a blessing on other lands that there shall be no room to receive it. This lays before us the godly apparatus, which we rejoice to observe is in growing operation among the men of the present day; and while Bible Societies, and Missionary Societies, and Praying

Societies, have the full cry of ridicule discharged upon them by the men of the world—while the disgrace of an obscure and contemptible fanaticism is made to lie upon all these operations—while the affairs of temporal kingdoms, and the fluctuations of their ever-veering politics, fill up the columns of every newspaper, and form the talk of every company—there are holy men now dealing with the hearts and the principles of the people in our own country, and of savages in distant lands; and amid all the noisy contempt and resistance they have gathered around them, with the sanction of apostolical example, and the persevering use of apostolical instruments, are they working their silent, but effectual way to the magnificent result, and the final establishment of the kingdom of God in the world.

And thus it is, that men become themselves living temples of God, and that God's living temple, his spiritual kingdom, is extended and established throughout the world. And we cannot better reply to the question, What is the best instrument for promoting and extending the kingdom of God in the world? than by referring our readers to the following Treatise of JOHN HOWE, "The Living Temple, or a Good Man the Temple of God." This Treatise, which we have introduced to the notice of our readers, is less known to the Christian public than some of the other productions of this celebrated author. It is not because that, either in itself or in its subject, it possesses less worth or less importance than those pieces of this author, which are better known and have acquired greater popularity—for, in respect to both, it holds a high rank among the numerous and valuable productions of this much-admired writer. But we apprehend the reason of its not obtaining such general circulation, arises from the circumstance of the main subject of the Treatise—the formation of God's Living Temple in the world—being intermingled with his lengthened and elaborate demonstrations of the existence of God—and from his profound and metaphysical controversies with Spinoza and the French infidels, respecting the uncreated Being, and the eternal self-existence of the Deity, extending through nearly half the original Treatise. And, though we hold this profound and erudite exposure of atheism, to contain the most perfect and unanswerable demonstration of the existence of a God with which we are acquainted—yet the deep and metaphysical character of his argumentation, renders it too occult and abstruse to be easily apprehended by ordinary readers; and thus is it fitted to repel them from entering on a piece of superlative excellence. It was under this conviction, and to render the Treatise more acceptable and useful to the Christian public, that we have divested the present edition of those elaborate disquisitions, into which he had been drawn by the French infidels, and which were extraneous to the specific design of the work, and have only presented our readers with what relates to the author's main subject—the method by which the reign of truth and holiness is established in the hearts of men, in order to their becoming temples of the Living God.

To those who desiderate a full and comprehensive exhibition of the Gospel scheme, for the restoration of our fallen and apostate race to the lost image and communion of the Godhead, we would recommend this invaluable Treatise to their perusal. He gives a deeply affecting, but justly descriptive representation of the apostasy, and consequent ruin and depravity of man, in his melancholy but magnificent delineation of the ruined, desolate, and forsaken condition of that noble Living Temple, where God once dwelt, and which was once blessed and beautified by the Divine Presence. And he gives a no less powerful and scriptural representation of the wisdom and glory, of the plans and purposes, of the Divine Mind, for the rebuilding of this fallen and deserted temple by Emmanuel, that God might, in perfect consistency with the holiness and righteousness of His august government, again tabernacle with man—and that the love, and the loyalty, and the obedience which were due to Heaven's great Monarch, might be re-established in the hearts of men, in order that they might again be restored to that blissful communion and intercourse with God which they had forfeited by their apostasy. And who can estimate the might and the magnitude of that great undertaking, by which Emmanuel achieved the restoration of this ruined temple? How the temple of His own body had to be destroyed, that by His sufferings and death He might expiate the guilt of an apostate world—and make reparation for the offence done to Heaven's righteous government—and effect a reconciliation between God and His alienated creatures—and obtain the communication of the Holy Spirit to renovate and adorn this desolated ruin, that the great Inhabitant might return and again occupy His long-deserted temple. It is because men are insensible to the extent of the ruin and the desolation which sin has effected, that they are so insensible to the greatness of that deliverance which the Saviour had to achieve for the restoration of man to the enjoyment of the Divine Presence.

To establish the reign of truth and holiness in the hearts of men, and thus to render them fit temples for the Divinity, is the grand and ultimate design of God in that wonderful dispensation which is revealed in the Gospel. O it is little thought of by men, in whose hearts the god of this world has established his reign, what a mighty change must be effected ere they become living temples of God! It is because they are so insensible to the nature and extent of the ruin, that they are so insensible to the magnitude of that change which they must undergo ere they become fit for the divine residence. It is not a repair, but a rebuilding. It is not a reform, but a thorough regeneration. It is fearful to think of the delusion which prevails in the great mass of society respecting this mighty change. It is not merely the infidel and the practical atheist, to whom HOWE so well addresses the language of terror and alarm, that require to be awakened. When we think of the spiritless indifference, and cold irreligion of many professors of Christianity —when we think of the lukewarm decencies, and heartless conformities, of many who profess their attachment to the Saviour— and compare them with that spirituality of mind, and renovation of heart, which this excellent author so well sets forth, as constituting the Living Temple, it may well alarm the consciences of many a decent and reputable professor of the Gospel. And it ought to reach conviction to the heart of many, whose complacency in their own state has never been disturbed, that, amidst the many earth-born qualities and endowments with their character in society is adorned—while their hearts are devoted to earthliness, and the world forms the object of their idolatrous affections—they are still unfit for the divine residence, and are living without God in the world.

Now, it is the scriptural view of the magnitude of the change that is implied in becoming a Christian, which makes Christianity, in the entire sense of the term, so revolting both to the pride and the sagacity of nature. It looks so wild and impossible an enterprise to draw away the affections from that which appears to give life and motion to the whole of human industry. The demand appears so extravagant, when asked to renounce our liking for what all men like—and we appear to be pushing the exactions of religion so unreasonably far, when we represent it as incompatible with the love of wealth, or grandeur, or animal gratification—that to the eye of many a cool and sober-minded citizen, it appears in the light of a very unlikely speculation. With the eye of a strong practical understanding, much and judiciously exercised in the realities of business, he regards the man of such lofty and spiritual lessons as a visionary altogether—but he shrewdly guesses that there is no danger of obtaining many real disciples to a system, so utterly at variance with the most urgent principles of the human constitution.

Now, to repel the contempt, and also the apparent common sense of all this resistance, we might easily demonstrate, that without any mitigation whatever of the spirit of Christianity, the service of God would still remain a reasonable service. But we shall content ourselves with urging upon you one argument which the Bible furnishes, which is, that the world passeth away, and the lust thereof. There is a result pointed to here, ye sage and calculating men, who are looking so intently forward to the result of your varied speculations. There is an event which is surely coming upon you all, and which will put to shame all the glory of secular wisdom, and hurry to a prostrate ruin all the might and magnificence of your grovelling enterprises. In a few little years, and time will arbitrate this question. It will tell us who is the visionary—he who is wise for this world, or he who is wise for eternity. A day is coming, when the busy ambition of your lives will all be broken up—when death will smile, in ghastly contempt, over the vanity of earthly affections—when, summoning you away from this warm and comfortable dwelling-place, he will call your body to its grave, and your spirit to its reckoning—and upon the falling down of that screen which separates the two worlds, will it appear that the man who has sought his portion among the schemes, and the pursuits, and the passing shadows of our present state, was indeed the visionary. With this element of computation do we neutralize all the contempt which nature feels and nature expresses against the abstractions of a spiritual Christianity—and pronounce of him who disowns it, that he is indeed the blind and pitiable maniac, wasting himself upon trifles, and lost and bewildered among the frivolities of an idiot's dream.

On entering some busy place of commercial intercourse, and perceiving what it is that forms the ruling desire of every heart, and the ruling topic of every conversation—and feeling the resistless evidence that is before him, of the world being the resting-place of every individual, and its perishable objects forming all that they long for, and all that they labor after—and, at the same time, observing what a face of respectable intelligence is thus lavished on the pursuits of earthliness—a Christian looker-on cannot but feel the strength of that discountenance which is thus laid on the views and the principles of spiritual men. The vast aggregate of mind and of example in the world appears to be against him ; and he feels as if left alone to his own visionary speculation, a gaze of universal contempt was directed against that peculiarity, in which he meets so few to share and to sympathize with him. But let him only look a little further on, and this will both revive his confidence, and retort on the whole opposing species the very charge by which he was well nigh overwhelmed. In a few years, and all that is visible of the mass of life, and thought, and ambition, that is before him, will be a mouldering mass of dust and rottenness in the churchyard. There is evermore a rapid transference of that living crowd, one by one, from the place of business to the place of burial. In a few years, and the transference will be completed, and every one of these intense, and eager, and speculative beings, shall have disappeared from this busy scene, and shall have gone to share in the still more awfully interesting and important scenes of eternity.

INTRODUCTORY ESSAY

TO

THE SELECT LETTERS

OF THE

REV. WILLIAM ROMAINE, A.M.

In our former Essay to Mr. Romaine's Treatises on the Life, Walk, and Triumph of Faith, we observed, that the great and unceasing topics on which he delighted to expatiate were, the atoning blood and perfect righteousness of Christ, as forming the great and only foundation of his hope and of his confidence towards God. These important doctrines of the Christian faith, form the no less favorite and oft-recurring theme which pervades, and is diffused through the whole texture of the excellent Letters of which the present volume is composed. And though they may not be fitted to stimulate the understanding, or to regale the fancy of the merely intellectual reader; yet, to the simple-hearted and spiritually-minded Christian, these precious and consoling truths, however frequently presented, will be felt in all the freshness and power of their peace-making, holy, and regenerating influence. In this respect, he imitated the example of the great apostle of the Gentiles, who expressed his determination to know nothing among his people "save Jesus Christ and Him crucified."

We have frequently insisted on one great claim that the doctrine of Christ crucified has upon our attention; namely, that, by the knowledge of it, we obtain deliverance from the greatest calamity which hangs over our species; and that is, the curse of God's violated law, with all the pains and penalties which are consequent thereupon. We shall, in our following observations, advert to another mighty claim which the same doctrine has upon our attention; namely, that, by the knowledge of it, we farther obtain the meritorious, or the rightful possession of God's favor; so that we do not simply enter upon the bliss of eternity as having become ours in fact, and by a mere deed of generosity, but we enter upon it as having become ours in equity, and by a deed of justice. Through Christ crucified we acquire a title to heaven as our reward, and that as much as if we ourselves had done that stipulated work, for which heaven was rendered to us as the stipulated wages: and this is a very different footing from that of the bare conveyance of a gift, for it is a conveyance that is secured and shielded by the guarantees of a covenant; so as to make it, not a mere act of mercy, but an act of righteousness for God to bestow; and we, in receiving, lay hold not merely of a donative, but also of our due.

Now, there are many who do not perceive that this second privilege, of being instated, through Christ crucified, in a righteousness before God, is essentially distinct from the former privilege, that of being delivered from guilt. They contemplate the whole of a sinner's reconciliation with God, as one general benefit coming out of the atonement that has been rendered for him on the cross, and which does not admit of being severed into parts, as has been done by the adepts of an artificial and scholastic theology. They are not disposed to look separately to our being freed from condemnation, and so rescued from hell; and to our being vested with a positive righteousness, and so made the rightful heirs and expectants of heaven. They would rather abide by their habit of viewing the gift that is by Jesus Christ as one and indivisible; and regard the attempt to decompose it into ingredients, more as a subtilty of human invention, than as the dictate of a mind that has been soundly and scripturally informed. And thus would they treat lightly the distinction that has been so much urged by some theologians, between the passive and the active obedience of Christ; or between the efficacy of the one to redeem from the incurred penalty, and the efficacy of the other to reinstate in the forfeited reward; between the tendency of His sufferings to avert all the wrath of the Divinity, and so to turn away from us the displeasure under which we lay, and the tendency of His services to restore to us the forfeited reward, and so transfer to us, for whom these services were undertaken, God's favor and kindness, as much as if they had been rendered in our own person and by our own performances. This attempt to mark off the mediatorship of Christ into two great departments, has been branded as an attempt to be wise above that which is written; and, when pursued into the still greater nicety of endeavoring to trace and to follow it throughout the line of demarcation that is betwixt them, then has the whole speculation been denounced as one that ministers questions of strife rather than of godly edifying, and to which we cannot turn aside, without being involved in perverse disputings, and the jangling of vain controversy.

Now, we fully participate in this dislike at all such metaphysics of theology, as minister nothing in the way of comfort, or of direction, or of salutary influence to the plain mind of a plain and practical inquirer. And therefore we shall attempt nothing at present that is not quite broad and palpable, and shall avoid everything that would require an eye of very minute or microscopic discrimination. It may be a matter of no great usefulness so to arrange and to classify the privileges of a believer, as accurately to refer each to the distinct services by which Christ hath insured it for those who put their trust in Him. But surely it is of importance to know what these privileges are, and for this purpose to make them the objects, if not of any acute or subtile exercise of the understanding, at least of simple enumeration. And we should feel as if much had been left untold, were we not made to know that Christ hath brought in an everlasting righteousness, as well as finished transgressions, and made an end of sins—that He hath won for us the reward of heaven, as well as averted from us the vengeance of hell—that He hath not only redeemed us from the sentence of death, but hath built up for us a title unto life everlasting—that, besides expunging our name from the book of condemnation, He hath graven it in the book of life—that, instead of standing before God simply as acquitted creatures, and therefore preserved from the place of condemnation, we stand before Him in the robe of another's righteousness, and therefore with the investiture of such an order of merit, as makes it fit that we should be translated to a high place of favor and of dignity. We want not to probe and to penetrate into the hidden intricacies of the question. But surely, if to be simply dismissed from the bar at which we stood as arraigned criminals be one thing, and it be another to be thence preferred to a title of renown, or to some station wherewith happiness and honor await us near the palace of our sovereign, then it concerns us to know that there is a justification as well as an atonement; that there is a righteousness as well as a redemption; that Christ hath done more than advance us to the negative or midway condition of mere innocence; that He hath wrought out for us a mightier transition than to a state of exemption from the torments of the accursed; that He hath not only retrieved our condition, but hath reversed it, utterly changing the character of our eternity, and turning it from an eternity of torment to an eternity of triumph—having both borne the full weight of our sufferings by taking on Himself the guilt of our sins, and having given us of His own righteousness, as our passport and title-deed to the glories of paradise.

And this view is not without warrant and authority from Scripture. The redemption which is through the blood of Christ is the forgiveness of sins. The righteousness of Christ, which is made to rest on all who believe, brings along with it a title to positive favor, which is something more than forgiveness. The creditor who cancels our debt, does us a distinct and additional good, when, furthermore, he puts the deeds or the documents into our hands by which we are constituted the rightful claimants of any given property. And so Christ, in one place, is represented as a surety for the sins of those who believe in Him ; and in another, as having purchased for them an inheritance, to which they, and they alone, have the right of entry and of possession. Moreover, we read of Christ being " delivered for our offences, and raised again for our justification ;" or, that by His death He made atonement for sin ; and by His resurrection He re-entered heaven, and is there employed in preparing those mansions by which are rewarded the righteousness of those who believe in Him. One fruit of the mediation of Christ is said to be peace with God. But not only so, writes the apostle ; in addition to having drawn back His hostility, He sends forth upon us His loving-kindness. And hence another fruit of the mediation is, that we have access to the grace wherein we stand. Yet it must be owned, that, notwithstanding the real distinction which there is between release from a penalty and admittance to a positive reward, and the corresponding distinction that has been made by theologians, between the passive obedience of Christ, by which it is held that the one has been averted, and the active obedience of Christ, by which it is held that the other has been rightfully earned for us,—it must be owned, we say, notwithstanding, that it is the obedience of Christ unto the death which seems to have formed the main price, not only of all the immunities, but of all the privileges that believers enjoy. It was from His death that the incense of a sweet-smelling savor arose unto God. It was because of His death that God highly exalted Him, and gave Him a name above every name. It was from the grave that He ascended, rich in the spoils of a superabundant merit, wherewith He decks and dignifies all His followers. And thus there is not only a remission, but a righteousness that has been wrought out by the expiation on the cross. It was there that He became sin for us, though He knew no sin ; and it was also in virtue of what has been done there, that we are made the righteousness of God in Him. The hope of our glory, as well as the price of our deliverance, stands connected with the knowledge of Jesus Christ and Him crucified.

We affirm it to be of the very essence of Gospel mercy, that, instead of a mere demonstration of Heaven's love, there went along with it a full demonstration of Heaven's righteousness—that it rendered glory to the law, and by the very act wherewith it rendered grace unto those who had trampled on the law. The forgiveness that is unto the sinner under this dispensation, bears upon it an awful character of sacredness and majesty—seeing that it never could have issued on a guilty world but through the channel of a consecrated priesthood, and with the blood of a divine expiation. There is pity on high to the children of men—but it is pity enshrined in holiness, and to which there is no other way of access than by the safeguards of a government that is unchangeable. We cannot come unto the throne of grace but through a mediatorship, where at once may be seen the manifested truth and vindicated justice of the Godhead—nor can we obtain the compassion of our offended Lawgiver, without knocking at the door of a sactuary, where dwell, in still unviolated purity and greatness, all the wondrous attributes that belong to Him.

Now, this is what we hold to be the leading and the characteristic peculiarity of the dispensation under which we live. All that we receive is, doubtless, in the way of a gift—and yet it is a gift for which a price has been rendered, so as to make it legally and rightfully ours. The penalty is remitted to us, but not till it was paid down, as it were, by another's sufferings. Heaven has been granted to us, but not till it was purchased by another's services. So that the believer has not merely privileges simply and gratuitously conferred upon him; but he is invested with a right to these privileges. He can lay claim to them as a thing of obligation—not in virtue of any equivalent that has been rendered by himself, but in virtue of a full equivalent that has been rendered by another. When eternal life is bestowed upon us, it is not in the shape of a bare donative, the fruit of a movement of generosity alone. It is a reward granted to us on consideration of a righteousness, although that righteousness is not properly and personally ours. Still, it is the fulfilment of a stipulation—the implementing of a contract or a covenant between parties; and when man enters upon his blissful eternity, he only takes possession of that which is his due, and which God hath bound Himself, as by the conditions of a treaty, to award unto him.

And here it is of importance to mark—how much more secure our hope of heaven is, when laid upon such a foundation. Had the sinner nothing else to build upon than the single attribute of mercy, well might he dread the outbreaking upon his person of the other attributes, and feel the perpetual disturbance of fears and of jealousies in his bosom, as he bethought him of the majesty of God, and the unchangeable recoil of a nature that could hold no fellowship with evil. Now, how it must overrule these terrors, when, with the righteousness of Christ as a plea put into his hand, he now finds even the most menacing attributes of the Divinity enlisted on the side of his salvation. Were his hopes suspended singly on the pity of God, while the question of all his other perfections was yet undisposed of, there would still be room in the sinner's heart for many doubts and many disquietudes. But how it must allay all these, and what firmness it must give to his anticipations of heaven, when, instead of vaguely trusting for it to the indulgence of God, he in Christ hath acquired a distinct and a well-defined right to it. He is like the man who at first eyed some beautiful estate with fond and foolish expectation, because of the reported generosity of him who owned it—but who afterwards had the title-deed put into his hand, on which he might challenge the property as his own, and step into the secure and undisputed possession of it. And thus may a Christian look forward to heaven. He can plead a right for it. He can argue in his behalf a purchase-money that is commensurate to the purchase. He can speak of a value that has been given, and which is adequate to the value that he expects. And he lives beneath his privileges—he is insensible to the whole worth and security of his condition, if his spirit do not rest and be at ease among the guarantees of a sure and a well-ordered covenant—and if, while he rejoices in the gift of his coming inheritance, he do not fortify his trust by thinking well of the soundness and the equity of his claim to it.

But while we like to say everything to a believer that should minister to the stability of his confidence, we would say nothing that could minister to his pride, or excite a sense of haughty independence in his bosom. It is not as if he defied God, and entered with Him on a field of litigation. It is not as if he challenged, and with a tone of resolute assertion, that which he felt to be rightfully his own, and demanded it accordingly. What might disarm him of this spirit altogether is, that though now possessed of a right to the citizenship of heaven, the right was not won by himself, but conferred upon him by a Mediator. It is not an inherent, but a derived privilege, and for which he stands indebted to another's bounty. What, we ask, are the suitable feelings with which he ought to prosecute his claim upon God, when, in fact, God was the Being who furnished him with this claim against himself? God so loved the world, as to send His Son into it, that He might legalize a place and a possession in heaven for all who believe on Him. Should the lorldly proprietor make over to a tenant at will the privilege of a perpetual occupation, and give him secure and rightful possession of all the requisite title-deeds, and furnish him out of his own hand with the materials of such a plea or legal argument as might insure him against all opposition: all this goes to vest him with the power of challenging for his own, that which has been conferred upon him by another. But this, so far from impairing the character of what he has gotten as a gift, only serves to complete and to enhance it, and should humble him the more into the gratitude and admiration of so noble a benefactor. And so of all that we obtain by the Gospel. It is a gift all over; and though it includes titles as well as benefits, let it ever be remembered, that they are not titles that we have earned, but titles that have been bestowed upon us. It is the thought of this that should rectify our carriage towards God. It is true, that by the economy of the New Testament, they who believe have a right to the honors of immortality. But the right has been given. It has generously and gratuitously descended from above; and they on whom it hath alighted, while they rejoice in the security thereof, still walk before God with the modesty of His gifted dependents. So far from being arrogant, because of the claim wherewith they have been invested, it only serves as another topic of humility and thankfulness. They appear before God in a robe of righteousness, but they know that it is a robe of His putting on. In His presence they wear an order of merit, but what they wear another hath won—the meed of another's services—the fruit of the travail of another's soul. They feel the whole security of an unquestionable right without its arrogance, and are at once high in the conscious possession of their great prerogative, and humble under the feeling that they are debtors for it all. The reward is a gift; for the righteousness which hath earned the reward is a gift also. Heaven may at first be thought of, not as a present but as a purchase; but it is the more emphatically a present, that by another's purchase it has become justly and legally theirs. It is this which gives its specific character to the economy of the Gospel. It is free in the distribution of its blessings; yet, ere the blessings are granted, there must be granted a right to the possession of them—and the sinner having no such right in his own person, must derive it from abroad, and owe that to another, which in himself it is impossible to acquire. Heaven becomes his, not merely in love, but in law: and in consideration of Him who hath fulfilled the law, the bliss of eternity is as much awarded to him by a God of judgment, as it is made over to him by a God of mercy. Yet the law does not obliterate the love, but only makes it more prominent. For it was in love that God sent His Son into the world, and in love for the guilty did the Son, in their stead, obey all the precepts, and suffer all the penalties; and though without a righteousness none shall enter into paradise, yet was it love that provided the righteousness, and now presses it on the acceptance of all. None shall be admitted into heaven but from the vantage ground of a finished obedience; but it was God Himself who reared the vantage ground, and who placed the believer thereupon. The whole security of a righteousness is His, the whole glory of it is another's. That he shall have a righteousness is indispensable. For this there seems to have been some deep and awful necessity in the divine jurisprudence; and it has been so provided for, that now the sinner can rightfully claim, and God, without the compromise of His character as a Judge, can rightfully bestow. But the very thing which has established the sinner's plea, has deepened the sinner's obligations; and, in very proportion to the triumph which he feels because of the validity of his right, are both the gratitude and the self-renunciation wherewith, in the language of the prophet, he makes the declaration—"In the Lord have I righteousness."

We shall close our remarks by adverting to a phrase that we often hear uttered, in the act of combating the resistance of man to the overtures of the Gospel; and that is, *the legal spirit.* Now, if by this be meant the demand that nature has for a righteousness wherein to appear before God—this is just as it should be. There is, and there ought to be, a secret misgiving of the heart when nothing but the general mercy of God is before us, on which to build our reliance. The thought of God's other attributes will intrude and mar the soul's attempt to tranquillize itself. The sense of a holy and unalterable law, whose demands must be met in one way or other, is ever present to the conscience; and, without some adjustment in which it can repose, will leave it unsatisfied. There is a longing for the bliss of eternity, but at the same time a certain unutterable sense upon the heart, that without a something whereby the justice of God might be propitiated, and a homage might be done to the principles of a government that is lofty and unchangeable, this bliss can never be arrived at. We feel, that ere we can enter upon life everlasting, every legal penalty must be done away, and a sufficient legal plea be established on which to found our right of admittance before the throne of God. The notions and the feelings of jurisprudence are mixed up with our every speculation on the road to heaven; and it is the inextinguishable sentiment of every bosom, that, in order to man being inducted there, a something must be done upon which God might hold him to be righteous, and deal with him accordingly. A sense of the need of such a righteousness is universal, and is historically marked both by the sacrifices of heathenism, and by the manifold labors and formalities of superstitions both in and out of Christendom. There is the unexcepted sense of a great moral jurisdiction on the part of God over his creatures, and of a law which they are bound to observe—and of the need that there is, if men shall obtain the rewards and preferments of eternity at all, that the law shall give the authority of its consent, so that they may be legally and rightfully conveyed to him. Hence, under all the disguises of all the superstitions upon earth, the universal cry of man for a righteousness in order to find acceptance with his God—a cry which the Bible does not resist, but to which it fully and explicitly responds, when it affirms of the sanctions of the law, that they are irreversible, and that heaven and earth must pass away rather than that one jot or one tittle of the law shall fail.

Now, it may serve to guide us out of all our perplexities, and to establish us on the right landing-place, did we see what is right, and accurately distinguish it from what is wrong in this legal spirit. In so far then, as the legal spirit prompts him by whom it is actuated, to seek for a legal right of admittance into heaven, we have nothing to say against it. It seems the general apprehension of nature, in all countries and in all ages, that there is no reaching a habitation of bliss and of divine favor through eternity, but by the stepping-stone of a righteousness—and this apprehension we hold to be a sound one. The error lies not in seeking such a sighteousness, but in seeking it from the wrong quarter. The capital delusion is in attempting to build up a righteousness out of our own doings, instead of fleeing for shelter under the offered righteousness that has already been built up out of the doings of another. This is all that we hold to be wrong in the legal spirit; for, in as far as the mere attempt to make up a title-deed is concerned—in as far as the wish is felt to have a right of entry to the inheritance that is above put into our hands, which may be examined at the court of Heaven's judicatory, and be there sustained as in every way valid and constitutional,—this, for which nature everywhere has so strong an appetite, so far from being denounced as wrong in Scripture, it is the great design of the Gospel to meet and to satisfy. The object in the general is not wrong—though it is very possible that we may go miserably astray, by looking for it in a wrong direction. It is by looking for it in ourselves that we err so grievously, when we should look unto Jesus Christ, and say, in the words of the prophet, "In the Lord have I righteousness." The errand upon which he came, was to bring a righteousness into the world, that each sinner who would, might lay hold of his sacred and available plea for admittance into heaven. This is the righteousness that God hath ordained as the channel of approach, by which even the worst of transgressors may draw nigh; of which they are all invited to make confident mention in their prayers for acceptance; and on account of which God stands pledged to accept and to reward them accordingly. In the New Testament it is called the righteousness of God. It is not because of our desire for a righteousness that we are on the wrong path to heaven; but, because instead of submitting to this righteousness of God, we seek to establish one of our own. In a word, it is self-righteousness that is the great stumbling-block in our way. It is the vain enterprise of working an adequate and a satisfying merit out of our own obedience. It is challenging the inspection of our almighty Lawgiver, on a heart that has deeply revolted against him, and on a history deformed by transgressions innumerable—and bidding him look thereupon with complacency. It is laboring to arrive at rest by means of a degraded law, brought down to the standard of our own weak and worthless compliances—and without homage to the purity and the unchangeableness of Heaven's government,—it is arrogating the rewards of Heaven for our own polluted righteousness, as being in itself good enough for God. Now this is the tendency of nature against which the Gospel hath set itself—not to thwart our demand for a righteousness, but to lay in the dust all confidence in a righteousness of our own,—and after having asserted the prerogatives of an outraged law, by laying the whole burden of its atonement and obedience on Him who hath suffered in our stead, and in our stead hath fulfilled all righteousness; to make open proclamation to our world, that all are welcome unto God—that now there is a way of access unto him, even for the most grievous of offenders,—but that this way is, and must be, under the cover of the great Mediatorship. You will breathe a new air, you will break forth on a scene of freedom and enlargement; all will be light, and love, and liberty, the moment that you can say, with the concurrence of your faith, "In the Lord have I righteousness:" and, feeling that nothing else will avail for Heaven's approbation, you can join the apostle in his sentiment, that, for the meritorious favor of God, I desire to count as nothing my own services: I desire and am determined "to know nothing else save Jesus Christ and Him crucified."

We know of no Treatise better fitted to banish the legal spirit, or to dispossess the mind of its natural tendencies to establish a righteousness of our own, than the excellent LETTERS of Mr. ROMAINE, which we have given in the present selection. The Letters were all addressed to friends, for whose spiritual welfare the author cherished a deep interest; and they were therefore designed to communicate comfort, or counsel, or direction, for resolving the doubts, or relieving the perplexities to which the Christian is exposed. To dissipate these doubts and perplexities, which he well knew originated most frequently in a self-righteous spirit, he continually directs their believing view to Jesus Christ. And well knowing that the manifestations of the love and grace of our heavenly Father, revealed to the soul by the blessed Saviour, could alone dispel the fears and the jealousies of nature, his constant aim was to point their eye, and direct their steps, to "the Lamb of God, who taketh away the sins of the world." And thus, by the simple reliance of faith on the all-sufficient atonement and perfect righteousness of Christ, he directed them to find that peace and hope which could alone sustain their souls in the serenity of their confidence towards God, and to obtain those spiritual communications of grace, which could alone nourish the divine life within them, and carry them forward in a progressive course of sanctification and holiness, to render them meet for heaven. Richly experiencing these consolations and hopes in his own soul, and knowing the alone source from whence they were derived, the doctrine of the cross became the subject of his constant meditation, and the name of Jesus the much-loved theme on which he delighted to expatiate. Amidst all his difficulties and perplexities, his confidence was stayed with the assurance that "the Lord reigneth;" and, by judging Him faithful who had promised, he maintained in his soul a rejoicing hope of eternal life, through his Lord and Saviour Jesus Christ. It was thus that he maintained a perennial and unfading communion with God—that he daily and habitually rejoiced in the light of his reconciled countenance—that his gratitude and love were sustained in a strong and invariable glow—and that his sanctification and holiness were promoted. And no one can peruse the following Letters, without perceiving that the doctrines of free grace are doctrines according to godliness—that they serve no less to aliment the love and the obedience, than the peace and the joy of the believer—and that justification by faith in the Saviour's righteousness alone, forms not only the surest ground of hope, but the best security for an humble and holy devotedness of life to God.

INTRODUCTORY ESSAY

TO A TREATISE

ON THE FAITH AND INFLUENCE OF THE GOSPEL.

BY THE REV. ARCHIBALD HALL.

It is remarkable, that our Saviour, after foretelling the destruction of Jerusalem, and giving the assurance that He will speedily come to avenge His elect, makes this solemn and awakening inquiry: "Nevertheless, when the Son of man cometh, shall He find faith on the earth?" We cannot so far dive into the unrevealed secrets of prophecy, as to affirm how much, or how little, of analogy there is between the destruction of Jerusalem and the final dissolution of our world. It is impossible, in reading the woes and denunciations of our Saviour upon this subject, to rid ourselves of the impression, that there is a general resemblance between these two events. Both of them are described under the figure of the coming of the Son of man. At both of them there is a work of vengeance to be done, and a fell manifestation given of God's wrath against the finally and obstinately impenitent. In both an old economy is entirely swept away, and a new order of things emerges from the ruins of it. But there is one point of the comparison, at which, instead of a likeness, we believe it to be the general apprehension of Christians, that there must be a strong dissimilarity. We are apt to look forward to a mighty spread and revival of the Gospel in the latter days. Ere the day of judgment shall arrive, we count on the restoration of Jews, and the flocking in of Heathens, and the consummation of a great moral triumph over the world's blindness and depravity; and, in short, a whole species visibly awakened from the lethargy of nature, and turned, intently turned, on the things of eternity. Now, we dispute not that in our book of prophecy there is a warrant for all these expectations. But the difficulty is, how to find an adjustment between these high millennial hopes on the one hand; and on the other, the sudden and overwhelming surprise wherewith the last day is to come on an unbelieving world. If it be as applicable to the breaking up of our globe as it was to the breaking up of Jerusalem, that its coming is to be as a thief in the night, and that it shall bear with it a sudden destruction, on men steeped in the delusion of all around them being peace and safety, and that, wholly given over to earthliness, they shall be caught at unawares, while " eating and drinking, marrying and giving in marriage,"—if it be really true, that it is in the midst of holiday enjoyments, and among the songs of mirth and revelry, that the sound of the last trumpet shall be heard, and the Judge is to descend with the authority of a sudden arrest on all the pursuits and frivolities of a then unthinking generation, may it not, after all, be true of this His latter visitation, as it was of His former one, that when the Son of man cometh He shall not find faith upon the earth?

Now we shall leave the difficulty where we found it—and instead of devising explanations for other men and other ages, let us try to ascertain in how far the rebuke of the Saviour is applicable to ourselves.

But ere we proceed, let us, in explanation of the term *faith*, advert to the wide distinction which obtains between the popular imagination of what it is, and the apostle's definition of what it is. The common conception about it is, that it consists in a correct apprehension of the truths of theology—or soundness of belief as opposed to error of belief. It appears to be a very prevalent impression, that faith lies in our judging rightly of the doctrines of the Bible—or that we have a proper understanding of them. And, in this way, the privileges annexed to faith in the New Testament, are very apt to be regarded as a sort of remuneration for the soundness of our orthodoxy. Heaven is viewed as a kind of reward, if not for the worth of our doings, at least for the worth and the justness of our dogmata. Under the old economy, eternal life was held out as a return to us for right practice. Under the new economy, is it conceived by many, that it is held out to us as a return for right thinking. Figure two theologians to be listed, the one against the other, in controversy. He who espouses error is estimated to be a heretic, and wanting in the faith. He who espouses truth, is estimated to be a sound believer, so that his faith resolves itself into the accuracy of his creed. It is not, Do this, and you shall live—but it is, Think thus, and you shall live,—and this seems to be the popular and prevailing imagination of being saved by faith, and being justified by faith.

Now look to the apostolical definition of faith, as being the " substance of things hoped for, and the evidence of things not seen" —or as being that, which substantiates or realizes the things that we hope for, and which makes plain to our conviction the things that we do not see. It is the assured expectation of that which we hope for, and the assured conviction of that which we do not see—and lest any obscurity should be left to hang over this his description of faith, he exemplifies it by the history of many prophets and eminent worthies who had gone before him. In the reading of this catalogue, we find, that with all the instances, there was such a living power and truth given to the things that are distant and unseen, as caused them to overbear the impression of things that are visible, and of things that were at hand. The faith of these excellent ones, gave that character of certainty to invisi ble things, as made them to have the like influence upon conduct, that they would have had, though they had been so many near and besetting realities which the eye of sense could apprehend. And thus it is, that one of the patriarchs was moved to obedience by "things not seen as yet," and that another went forth looking to a "city which hath foundations," and that a third cherished the hope of a most unlikely fulfilment, resting it alone on the faithfulness of a divine Promiser, and that all of them declared plainly, by their movements, how they sought a country. Abraham, by the offering up of Isaac, earning the triumph of hope over sense; and Isaac speaking with assurance of the things that were to come; and Moses having "respect unto the recompense of reward, and enduring as seeing Him who is invisible;" and many more who braved the most appalling cruelties, in the hope of a better resurrection. In each of the instances, the apostle's definition was bodied forth, as it were, on the believer's history. The leading character of their faith, was just the assured expectation of things hoped for, and the conviction of things not seen. There was no quarrelling about orthodoxy. There was no settlement of any controversial question. The faith did not lie in the mere rectitude of any speculative opinion. It lay in a simple and undoubting anticipation of what an invisible God told of certain invisible things that were to come. And thus the future had the same practical ascendency over them, that the present has over other men. They walked by faith, and not by sight. They looked beyond the things that were seen and temporal, to the things that were unseen and eternal.

Now let us take this view of faith—let us look to it, not as the mere acquiescence of the understanding in the dogmata of any sound or recognized creed, but as that which brings the future and the yet unseen of revelation so home to the mind, as that the mind is filled with a sense of their reality, and actually proceeds upon it. Conceive it to be that which places the unseen Creator by the side of what is visible and created, and so gives the predominancy to His will over all those countless diversities of influence, wherewith sense hath enslaved the vast majority of this world's generations. Or conceive it to be that which places eternity by the side of time, and so regards the one as a mere path or stepping-stone to the other; that the man whom it possesses actually moves through life in the spirit of a traveller, feels his home to be heaven, and all his dearest hopes and interests to be laid up there; walking, therefore, over the world with a more light and unencumbered footstep than other men, just because all its adversities to him are but the crosses of a rapid journey, and all its joys but the shifting scenery of the land through which he is travelling, and visions of passing loveliness. Keep by this definition of faith, and bear it round as a test among all the families of your acquaintance. Go with it to the haunts of every-day life, and see if it can guide you to so much as one individual, whose doings plainly declare that he is pressing onwards to an immortality, for the joys and exercises of which, he is all the while in busy preparation; and we fear, that even in this our professing age, faith is scarcely and rarely to be found; that nearly a universal species are carried through life in one tide of overbearing carnality; that the present world domineers over almost every creature that breathes in it; and were the Son of man now to descend in the midst of us, we know not how few they are who would meet and satisfy his inquiries after faith upon the earth.

For let there first pass under our review, that mighty host who live in palpable ungodliness, who, if you cannot say of them that they are against God, are at least without God in the world; who spend their days, not perhaps in positive hostility, but certainly in most torpid apathy and indifference towards the Father of their spirits; who, feelingly alive to all the concerns of time, are dead and insensible to all that is beyond it. These indisputably are children without faith. Eternity is a blank in their imagination. They are alike unmoved by its hopes and by its fears, and it offers as little of influence to move them, as does that dark and unpeopled nothingness which lies beyond the outskirts of creation. The thought of a distant planet that rolls afar in space, carries in it no practical operation on their business or their bosoms. And the thought of some distant misery or happiness that may cast up in eternity, has just as little of practical operation over the minds of the vast majority of this world. That which lies between, acts as an insuperable barrier between the things of faith and their principles, whether of feeling or of action; and so it is that they can fetch, from the region which lies on the other side of the grave, no moving force which might practically tell on their hearts or on their history upon this side of it.

It were certainly premature and presumptuous to make these affirmations of all; but we leave it to your own observation, whether it does not apply, and in its full extent, to many of your friends or familiars in society—to many, and very many, who daily throng our markets, and sit around our boards of festivity, and labor from morning to night among the cares of family management, and exchange the calls, and the salutations, and the inquiries of civil companionship; and whether in the pursuits of science, or merchandise, or amusement, are severally busy, each with a world of his own, from which God is shut out, and in which eternity is forgotten. Nothing can be more wide of apostolical faith than the spiritual frame and habit of these. They mind earthly things. They have no conversation in heaven. The world is their all, and it is within the compass of its visible horizon that their every wish and every interest lies. The terrors of another world do not agitate them. The hopes of another world do not enliven them. To both they are profoundly asleep, and that too at the very time when all within them is restless, and anxious, and astir about the matters of the short-lived day that is passing over them. This is the general description of all those who live without God and without hope. Does it apply to any of you? Then you may have honor, and decency, and kindness, and courtesy, and agreeable manners, and even exemplary morals, but you have no faith.

And it brings out this want of faith into more distinct exhibition, that they who exemplify it are so susceptible of a powerful impulse from futurity. It is not that we want the faculty of anticipation, for this, in fact, is the main-spring of all the activity that we see afloat in the world. Man lives on the prospect that is before him. It is in the pursuit of some distant advantage, or in the avoidance of some distant evil, that all his powers of thought and action are expended. Were the machinery of his moral system capable of no impulse from futurity, then it might alleviate the charge that we prefer against him, when we state his life to be an idiot's dream, on the brink of an eternity, that, ere a few little days, will absorb him, an unsheltered and unprovided creature, into a receptacle of despair. But it only marks the more striking his blindness to the futurities of an eternal world, that he is so vigilant, and so busily alive to all the futurities of the present world—that he proves himself so eminently a creature of foresight in all that regards the pursuits or the interests of time, while this high characteristic of his nobler and loftier nature, seems to abandon him in all that regards the great concerns of immortality —that the very same man who can sit up late, and rise up early, for the purpose of building an earthly fortune in behalf of his children, and of his children's children, should never bestow the carefulness of half an hour on the fate and fortune of his own imperishable soul—that he who can regale his imagination with the perspective of thriving descendants, whom the wealth that he now accumulates is to grace and to ennoble, should never turn his eye to that grave in which his own body will then be mouldering, or to that land of condemnation in which his own desolate spirit will then wander in the nakedness of its unatoned guilt, and of its unchanged and unrenewed earthliness—that he who, in bequeathing to posterity, can stretch his mind forward to the time when his own name shall be forgotten, and the tomb-stone that covers him shall have gathered upon it the mould of its distant antiquity,—that he who can thus devise and make disposition of his earthly treasure for centuries to come, should be so shut and fastened in all his sensibilities to a treasure in heaven, and an inheritance that fadeth not away. It is this busy excitement of his about the futurities of earth which brings out, by contrast, to more striking and surprising manifestation, the utter lethargy of his soul about those futurities of an everlasting condition that are so sure to overtake him. It is this which gives its most conclusive demonstration of Nature's apathy, and Nature's blindness, and prepares us for the announcement, that when the Son of man cometh he may not find faith upon the earth.

But let us pass onward to a class of somewhat different aspect from that of the palpably regardless; who have been so far mindful of religion as to put on its decencies, and at least its public devotions; who fill their Sabbath pew on every recurring occasion, with the members of a well-trained and well-mustered family, of whom we will grant that their presentation at church, is just a thing as regular and sure as the tolling of the bell that summons them; who are ever in their places at the periodic celebration of our great Christian festival; and who, even in addition to their Sabbath and their sacramental observances, have such a style of worship and of exercise at home as is in perfect keeping with their more ostensible proprieties. One would imagine of such quiet, and orderly, and church-going men, that truly they are walking with a pilgrim step to another and a happier land; that it was not the happiness of the present, but the hope of the future which concerned them; that instead of being taken up with the fleeting interests of sense, they were indeed taken up with those distant and unseen things, by the power of which it is that we estimate their condition as believers; that so many goodly symptoms, in the way of form, and ordinance, and manifold compliance with the established usages of Christianity, argued them to be indeed of the faith—and, at all events, that, in respect of moral and spiritual characteristics, they are of a species altogether distinct from those infidels who disown the Gospel, or those ungodly who despise it.

And yet it is most true, that all this seeming sanctity may consist with an entire and unbroken habit of worldliness; that all this clock-work religion may stand as little connected with the aspirings of a mind that is heavenly, as do the routine evolutions of any piece of mechanism; that the keeping of all the Sabbath punctualities, may argue no more a heart set on the things that are above, than would the putting on of our Sabbath vestments; and the church, and the sacrament, and the family exercises, taking their respective places in the round of many a sober citizen, along with his busy shop, and his comfortable meals, and his parties of agreeable fellowship, may, one and all of them, be only so many varieties of earthliness. It is really so very possible to have gotten, whether by inheritance or by accident, into a habit of unvaried regularity, and to have a kind of conscience about it too, and to feel a violence done to our religious sensibilities, whenever it is broken in upon, and to have persevered so long in a certain style of observation, that a positive discomfort is suffered, should any inroad be made upon it—it is so possible, that all this may meet, and be at one, with the downward tendencies of a heart which is altogether of the earth, and earthly. It does not follow, that because a man of forms, he is therefore a man of faith. There may be much without him that bears upon it the aspect of religiousness, while there is nought within him of "the substance of things hoped for, and the evidence of things not seen." He differs, it is true, from the Sabbath breaker, and the profane absentee from all our ordinances; but the difference may be altogether complexional. To superinduce the ordinances of the Gospel on a man's history, is one thing; that they should spring from a spontaneous affection for the Gospel in a man's heart, is another. The example of parents may have superinduced them; or the force of natural habit may have done it; or a taste for the decencies of family regulation may have done it,—and thus it often holds practically true, that the punctuality of his Sabbath worship may no more argue him a disciple or an expectant of immortality, than does the punctuality of his morning walk. And, accordingly, we fear it to be true of many such, that with all their external tribute at the altar of piety, there is nought of the living spirit of piety in their bosoms—that they stand as firmly riveted to the dust of our perishable world, as do the most profane and profligate of their fellows—that their hearts are just as much with the interests of a passing scene, and in every way as naked of all influence from the things of eternity. So that were you to follow many a pains-taking and assiduous formalist, throughout the line of his week-day movements, you would say of him, too, that the world was his home, and heaven but the vision or the entertainment of his fancy—that nought, either of substance or of evidence, stood associated with his thoughts of futurity on the other side of death—that, wanting this, he wanted all that could really signalize him from earthly men, as a traveller toward Zion—that all which could be alleged of his observations or his prayers, only proved him to wear the livery of the faithful, without their spirit or their character: for, look to him diligently, and you will find him to be just as intent on lucre, as keen in bargains, as busy and breathless in all the pursuits of merchandise, as agonized by the crosses of misadventure, as enraptured at the sight of profits and of snug accumulations; in a word, not only as laborious with his hand, but, more material still, as wholly given over, with his heart, to the pursuits and interests of a short-lived day, as are the great bulk, and commonplace, of our ordinary men.

But, again, if faith, in the apostle's sense of it, cannot be ascribed to the openly regardless, and cannot be ascribed to those seemingly religious, whose only homage to the cause is that of their personal attendance upon its decencies and its forms—ought it not, at least, to be ascribed to another and a higher class—even to those who are zealous for the faith? It might well be imagined, of him who thinks to purchase heaven by his works of devoteeship, that, all scrupulous as he is of Sabbath and sacramental proprieties, he may still be wanting in the faith. But, can this be alleged of him who has oft been heard to speak of faith and of works together—and who, after argumenting the utter worthlessness of the latter, has confined most rigidly to the former all of power and of efficacy that there is in the business of salvation? How is it, that the man who ever and anon pronounces on the vanity of his own righteousness, and professes the righteousness of Christ, as appropriated and laid hold of by faith, to be the alone plea on which a sinner can be justified—how is it that he can, at the same time, be destitute of faith? Surely, if faith is to be found at all upon our earth, it must be among those men of a jealous and stickling orthodoxy, who are ever on the alert, and on the alarm, when human morality lifts its pretensions against the supremacy of faith, and offers presumptuously to usurp, or to derogate, from its honors. Where is faith to be met with, if not among its own professed and earnest advocates?—and how can the credit of faith be denied to those, who say, they hold by it alone as their passport to heaven, and that to it alone they look for being justified?

To know, and to think, that a man is justified by faith, is one thing; actually to have that faith, is another. One may know, that he who possesses a certain title-deed, has the property of certain lands—but this is wholly different from his being himself the possessor of it. Your religious knowledge may qualify you for enumerating all the powers and privileges which belong to faith—but it does not therefore follow, that this faith actually belongs to you. It is but a distant connection to have with an earthly estate, that you know what sort of rights they are, by the holding of which it becomes the property of the owner. This you may know most thoroughly, and yet have no personal interest in the rights or in the property whatever. And distant, indeed, is your connection with heaven, if you but know, how it is by faith that man acquires a part and an inheritance therein. The question recurs, Have you that faith? It is not of your knowledge, or your opinion, that we at present inquire. You may know that faith justifies a man, and yet have no faith whatever of your own. It may be a favorite dogma, this article of justification; and you, having the dogma, yet wanting the faith, may have no justification. You may embrace, and with fond affection too, the sound doctines upon this subject, and yet not, by any faith of your own, have actually embraced the righteousness of Christ: and so this doctrine of theology may be of as little avail towards the peace and joy of your eternity, as any doctrine of politics, or of philosophy, or of agriculture.

Neither is it enough, that you assert with vehemence, and abide with most opinionative tenacity by, the right doctrines of justification. Who has not witnessed the very same vehemence, and the very same tenacity, on other fields of speculation? All that ardor, and earnestness, and intolerance of what is pronounced to be damnable error, which are so often exhibited in theological controversy, may often be resolved into the pride of argument, the impatience of defeat, the jealousy of other powers and other understandings. These are the principles which uphold the zeal and strenuousness of so many combatants on the arena of a merely secular debate, and make each so resolute in the affirmation and defence of his own dogma. And on no other principles may you have taken your side on the agitated question of our acceptance with God; and may have urged it with most intense affection and energy, that this acceptance hangs upon faith, and upon it alone. This you may do, and yet be personally without the faith yourself—a fierce and eager partisan, and on the right side too, of this evangelical warfare—though, within the receptacles of your moral system, there be nought of "the substance of things hoped for," and nought of "the evidence of things not seen."

We think that, on the first blush and aspect of it, the thing is quite palpable to the eye of general observation. It is surely an oft-exemplified phenomenon, that a man should be quite sturdy in his adherence to the orthodox creed, and yet be all the while a man of earthly pursuits and earthly affections. He may lay claim to the dogmata thereof, as all his own,—and yet the living realities of which they treat, may never have impressed one touch of their practical and persuasive ascendency over him. His mouth may be filled with the language, and his understanding be busied with the arguments, of orthodoxy, and yet the spiritual things, of which words are but the representatives and the symbols, may never once have come into living play, either with the purposes of his life, or with the affections of his still unregenerated bosom. He may stand up for all the articles, and yet be standing up for mere phraseology, and nothing more. It may be a mere germ of curiosity, or imagination, with the terms of theology; while the truths of it have never once stood before the eye of his conscience, clothed in all the urgent and impressive characters of their high bearing upon his everlasting welfare. They may have never, indeed, carried him forward to any one of those futurities, to which he will be so speedily conducted, by the flight of those successive years that roll over him. The coming death, and the coming judgment, and the coming eternity, may all be unheeded, and at the very moment, too, when he is agitating the terms on which death is plucked of its sting, and judgment is disarmed by mercy, and an avenue to the bliss of eternity is again opened for those sinners who had cast it away from them. The urgencies of the present world may enslave him, even while the concerns of the future world are to him the topics, both of busy thought and busy conversation. The matters of God's kingdom may be quite familiar to him in word, which never are felt by him in their power. They have had interest enough to attract his gaze, but not energy enough to move his practice. They play, in speculation, around his fancy or his head, but they have never yet stimulated him to action; and while his talk is of the mysteries of heaven, his path in life is that of a devoted worldling.

There may be something in the apostolical definition of faith that is fitted to expose, and perhaps to remedy this delusion. It is such a faith as, at least, carries hope in its train. It has for its object such things as are hoped for—that is, hoped for to the individual himself. One may believe of a thousand things in which he personally has no share and no interest—but hope implies a certain degree of appropriation. It may be easy to give a general consent to the truth—that, by Christ the Saviour, the gate of heaven has been opened for sinners—but, by the faith of our text, the sinner sees the gate of heaven to be open for himself; and so he rejoices in the bright anticipation, and betakes himself to all the required and preparatory movements for his entrance thereinto. One can imagine, that the report of a Saviour for the sinners of another country, would carry in it none of the personal excitement of hope, and none of the personal exertion correspondent thereunto, to the sinners of our own land. And yet it is conceivable, that this message of a distant salvation for others, and in which we ourselves had no individual concern, might busily engage our speculations, and be the topic amongst us of a very intent controversy; and might arrange us into parties, according to the interpretation that we gave of the terms, on which God took into acceptance the strayed children of this remote branch of his family. And thus, one class of our home theologians might think truly, and have the sound opinion, on this matter; and so have their minds imbued with the accurate belief. Yet, from the nature of the thing, it is a belief which carries no hope along with it—and just, we apprehend, such a belief as is to be met with among many of the actual zealots of orthodoxy in our present day. They treat the matter, it is to be feared, as a thing that lies remote from themselves—as a mere theme for the understanding; which they look to as they would to any other abstract contemplation, but which they do not look to as that which bears, specifically and distinctly, upon their own interest. Whatever faith they have, is a faith without hope—but this is not the faith of our text. This is not the assured expectation of things hoped for. This is not the case of a man, who hath closed with the overtures of the Gospel for himself; and is looking onward to heaven, not merely as a place that has been opened, by a Redeemer's hand, for a certain number of travellers, but a place that has been opened for him, as one of these travellers. This would change the character of his faith. This would turn him from a controversialist into a pilgrim. In the former view of it, there was nought addressed but his intellect. The latter view of it, offers that which is addressed to his affections and his hopes—which opens for himself a vista into heaven; and, revealing to him the holiness, both of the habitation, and of the highway that leads to it, instantly betakes him unto the way of holiness.

There are two questions which, could we answer in a way that might be readily apprehended, would go far to satisfy you, as to the process by which a real principle of faith in the mind, is followed by the life of faith in the history—so as to land every honest believer of the present day, in those very activities which signalized the patriarchs of the old dispensation, and separated them, by a holy and a heavenward walk, from the general habit of an unbelieving world.

The first of these questions is—By what stepping-stone is a believer conducted from his faith to his hope? What is there, in the Christian message, that warrants him to single out heaven as the distinct object of his own journeyings through the world, and his own preparations for it, as a place whither he might bend his footsteps, and to which he might look forward, as the home and the resting-place of his own special expectations? Had it been a message of salvation only to the people of another land, he might have put faith in it without drawing hope from it. And how is the message actually constructed, so as that the faith, which he places therein, should light up the animating sentiment of hope in his bosom?

Were the Gospel but a message of salvation to some foreign land, there would be no link by which faith might pass into hope. And neither would this transition follow, were it only a message to some of our own neighborhood, exclusive of ourselves. But this is not the bearing of the message. It carries a tender of salvation to all. It points the eye of each, and of every man, to an open heaven, and invites him to enter thereinto. By such terms as, *all*, and *any*, and *every*, and *whosoever*, it brings its offers of reconciliation most specifically to bear on each unit of the human population. Insomuch that, if the word of salvation hath come to him, the offer of salvation hath been made to him. Just as much as if not another individual but himself had stood in need of Christ's propitiation, is the whole benefit of that propitiation pressed upon his acceptance. Just as much as if he had been the solitary and the sinful occupier of the only world where rebellion against heaven was known, and as if the Bible had been constructed for the one purpose of reclaiming him to the friendship of his offended God, has that Bible come to his door, armed with the full force of its importunities and its calls. It is as legitimately his right to take to himself the call of reconciliation that is sounded there, as if put into his hand by an angel from the sanctuary, with a special bidding, from heaven's Lord, that he should read, and should rejoice in it. It is true, that this is not the way in which the message is actually brought home; and that, instead of this, the everlasting Gospel is preached unto them that dwell on the earth, and to every nation, and kindred, and tongue, and people. But, while thus it goeth forth diffusively over all, it sendeth out a voice which speaketh distinctly unto each; and, in virtue of the terms that we have now specified, does it happily combine, a wide expansion of itself over the face of the world, with a pointed application of itself to every heart, and to every habitation. That faith may become hope, nothing more is necessary, than to believe in the message, according to the sense of the message. It is to believe with understanding. It is to put the right interpretation on these simple words, *all*, and *any*, and *every*. It is to conceive of myself, that surely I am within the scope of a vocabulary, which is comprehensive of the whole species, and not exclusive of a single member belonging to it. I cannot believe in the announcement, that Christ "tasted death for every man," without rejoicing in this, that He hath tasted death for me. I cannot have faith in the invitation, "Let whosoever will, come and drink of the water of life freely," without feeling of myself, that I have been made the object of a marked and separate entreaty. It is thus that there is a hope of faith, as well as a hope of experience. There is a hope that hangs direct on the faithfulness of God. The man who argues on the side of orthodoxy, and feels not his personal interest therein, is blind to the important significancy of those very terms in which the doctrines of the Bible have been conveyed to him. He either knows them not, or attends to them not. All that we want for the lighting up of hope is faith, with understanding; and only grant it to be an intelligent faith, and then will it be the assured expectation of things hoped for.

But there is another question which must be answered, ere we can complete the analogy between the state of an expectant under the old, and of an expectant under the new dispensation. We can perceive how a hope—a hope of his own individual preferment to blessedness and glory, may arise in the bosom of each, from the terms in which both the Jewish and the Christian message was conveyed to all who stood within reach of the hearing of them. But it might be imagined of this hope, that it should simply find an entrance into the heart, and there minister of its own sweet and placid sensations to the inner man. What is there in it that should put into motion the intercourse, or connect the faith of a believer with that new and busy career of activity on which he forthwith embarks himself? We can understand how a Christian, like Abraham of old, might see his day of triumph afar off and be glad. But what is there in the mere belief of the things which have been told unto him, and in his assured expectation of those things that should liken his history to that of Abraham, who, at the bidding of a voice from heaven, submitted himself to the toils and the trials of a new obedience? We can see how the faith of the Gospel might germinate that specific anticipation of heaven, which might give to the mind of a Christian all the spiritual elevation of Abraham? But by what distinct impulse is it that this faith originates a personal movement on the part of its disciple, so as that he shall walk in the footsteps of his father Abraham? We now understand the pathway between faith and hope. We now want to understand the pathway between faith and service—and how it is that the hope which gladdens alike the patriarch of the old, and the believer of the new economy, should further stimulate them alike to the same exertions and the same sacrifices.

Now, it was by looking to the terms of the message, according to the meaning of these terms, that we attempted to trace the connection between faith and hope; so it is in this, and in no other way, that we would trace the connection between faith and obedience. The accompaniment of such a term as that of "whoever," with the invitation of the Gospel, gives me to understand of that invitation as directed specifically to myself, and my heart responds to it accordingly. And the accompaniment of such a sentence with the same invitation, as that "he who turneth to Christ must depart from his iniquities," gives me to understand, that while I look to heaven with the delightful sensation of hope in my bosom, I must also look to it with the diligence of an intent and busy traveller, who knows that in moving thitherward, he must move himself away from the habit and character and earthly desires of a world lying in wickedness. This is the way, and we know of no other, by which faith and obedience are so linked together, as that when the one enters the heart, the other forthwith comes out on the history. It is done by the power of a whole faith in a whole testimony. It is by keeping the ear of the mind open to the whole utterance of that voice which hath spoken to us from heaven. It is by treating God's communications as Abraham of old did. When he heard God say, "This is the land which I give unto thee," he rejoiced in hope; and when he heard him say, "Walk thou before me, and be thou perfect," he went forth in obedience. And so with the Christian, who can both look with glad anticipation to eternal life as the gift of God through Jesus Christ our Lord, and who can labor with assiduity for the same eternal life, as knowing that the unholy and the unheavenly shall never enter thereinto. It is the word which causes him to hope—and it is also the word which causes him to obey. It at one time is the word of promise, and at another the word of authority—and he, an honest believer, listens to both, and proceeds upon both. With the docility of a little child, he accommodates his responses to the lesson that is set before him—and, at one and the same time, is he the most joyful in hope and the most devoted in service.

To illustrate and enforce this latter and most important topic, forms the principal subject of the following excellent Treatise of the Rev. ARCHIBALD HALL, "*On the Faith and Influence of the Gospel.*" His great design is to elucidate the nature of true faith, and to show its practical influence on the heart and character of the believer. The attentive reader will not fail to perceive, that a real and appropriating faith of the truths of the Gospel is a very different thing from the mere mental perception of these truths, or the cold and intellectual abstractions about which the mind may be busied, but which minister neither peace nor hope to the mind, nor exert any sanctifying or subduing power over the heart and affections.

There are no two terms in the whole New Testament, which stand more frequently and familiarly associated with each other, than faith and obedience. Wherever the privileges and blessings of the Gospel are truly appropriated by faith, the precepts of the Gospel maintain their authority over the conduct of the believer. Whenever the peace of the Gospel takes up its residence in the heart, the practice of the Gospel comes out in living exemplification on the personal character and accomplishments of the believer. It is thus that faith demonstrates its existence in the heart, by its operation on the character. It forms, indeed, the principal excellence of the following Treatise, that it exhibits the intimate connection which subsists between faith and obedience. It shows, that though faith be a simple principle, yet the object of faith is the whole testimony of God. That faith has to do not merely with one set of truths, but that it has to do with all the truths which are contained in the whole of God's revelation. That while the truth, that "Christ died for our sins," exerts its appropriate influence on the mind of the believer, and he is thus made to feel the charm of the peace-speaking blood of Christ, the truth, that "without holiness no man can see the Lord," also exerts its appropriate influence on his mind; and he is thus urged on to "perfect holiness in the fear of the Lord." When the believer is made to know, that "there is no condemnation to them who are in Christ Jesus," he is also made to know, that "they walk not after the flesh, but after the Spirit." It is thus that his mind comes under the various influences, which the various truths of God's testimony are fitted to exercise over it; and while he is a trusting and rejoicing disciple, he is, at the same time, a watchful, praying, and obedient disciple.

But faith, by opening up a new region of manifestation to the mind of a believer, brings his heart into contact with those motives and influences which give rise to the new obedience of the Gospel. When contemplating Jesus Christ and him crucified, he builds on this all his hopes of acceptance before God, he finds not only peace, but a purifying influence descend on his heart. It removes the spirit of bondage and of fear, which weighed down the soul to the inactivity of despair, and introduces the spirit of love and adoption, which makes him run with alacrity in the way of all God's commandments. So long as the question of his guilt remained unsettled, instead of loving, he could only dread, the Being whom he had offended; but when a sense of forgiveness enters his heart, he enters, with hopeful and assured footsteps, on a course of cheerful obedience. When love to God, which the consciousness of guilt kept away, is introduced into his soul by faith in the atoning blood of Christ, the inspiration of a new and invigorating principle takes possession of the believer, and he becomes animated with the life and the love of real godliness. Faith in the doctrine of the atonement is as much the turning point of a new character, as of a new hope. It is here Gospel obedience takes its commencement, because it is here that filial love and confidence in God take their rise. Christ came not only to redeem us from all iniquity, but to "purify us unto himself a peculiar people, zealous of good works." The reception of Christ is always accompanied with the gift of the renewing Spirit, whose peculiar office it is to promote our growth in grace, and to perfect us in holiness; and the genuine believer will always experience the truth and the reality of the apostle's declaration—"If any man be in Christ, he is a new creature."

DISTINCTION,

BOTH IN PRINCIPLE AND EFFECT,

BETWEEN

A LEGAL CHARITY FOR THE RELIEF OF INDIGENCE,

AND

A LEGAL CHARITY FOR THE RELIEF OF DISEASE.

[*Read before the Royal Institute of France.*]

---

1. It had been good for the well-being of states, if legislation had at all times kept within its own proper boundaries—whereas, by stepping beyond these, it has often marred the interest which it meant to provide for, and inflicted a sore distemper on human society. This has nowhere been more strikingly exemplified, and in a way more instructive to the governments of other countries, than by the Poor-law of England.

2. We often hear of the wisdom of nature, as evinced in the laws and adaptations of the material world; but the same wisdom may be as visibly discerned in the frame and principles of our mental constitution—the spontaneous working of which often leads to a far better result, than all the skill and vigilance of statesmen can possibly effectuate. A commerce which results from the free enterprise of individuals, each devising and laboring for his own special advantage, is greatly more flourishing and more conducive to the real prosperity of a kingdom, than a commerce which is nourished by the bounties, and at the same time guided by the regulations of a Statute-book. The whole of political economy bears evidence to the perfection of what may be termed the natural system of human industry and human exchanges—in opposition to the artificial system, that, whether in the form of encouragements or restraints, acts with all the mischievous influence of a disturbing force on the operations of a previous and better mechanism.

3. One of the most interesting verifications of this remark may be seen in the history of pauperism. It is quite palpable that nature has at least made some provision in the very make and con-

stitution of humanity, for the alleviation, often prevention, of the ills of extreme want. It, in the first place, has endowed man with a strong and urgent principle of self-preservation, and has superadded the goading agonies of hunger to the fear of perishing—so as to afford the most powerful stimulus that can well be imagined, for the utmost possible exertion to secure an adequate and regular supply of food. In the second place, it has implanted a strong relative affection, as that of parents to children, of children back again to parents, even of more distant kindred for each other—so as to enlist the energies of all the effective members in a household, for the maintenance, not of themselves only, but of the most weak and helpless under their own roof; and, over and above this, so as often to prompt them to the large assistance of those, who, though beyond the limits of the home in which they live, are yet of the same blood and family. But there is a third principle, and from which it is obvious that nature meant the kindness of man for man to extend over a wider field of operation than within the circle of the same relationship—the principle of compassion, that powerful impellent to deeds of generosity; and in virtue of which, it is nearly as intolerable for one man to see another in the agonies of hunger, as to be the victim of these agonies himself. This opens up two resources for the relief of poverty—First the kindness of poor to poor, or rather of immediate neighbors for each other, living in the same vicinity and occupying nearly the same level on the ground-floor of society—Secondly the kindness of rich to poor, which we place last in the enumeration; because truly we regard it as the least powerful and the least prolific of the whole—believing as we do, that, in the principle of self-preservation whereby each man is led to care for himself, and the principle of relative affection whereby each man is led to care for those of his own kindred, and the principle of compassion whereby each man is led to care for those of his own acquaintance or neighborhood who have fallen into distress, we behold the most important of nature's ordinations—first for the prevention, and then for the relief, of extreme want and wretchedness in the world.

4. But, to make our reasoning still more distinct and conclusive, we shall attempt to demonstrate of each of these principles, separately and in order, that in respect of beneficial operation, each is so injured and enfeebled by the hurtful influence of a public charity for the relief of indigence—as altogether to have greatly deteriorated the condition of the poor and working classes, in every neighborhood where such a provision has been established.

5. And first then it is obvious, that a law by the state, of public and proclaimed charity for the relief of indigence, must slacken the operation of what has been termed the strongest law of nature—even the law of self-preservation. It tends to supersede the care and industry, which, but for its own mischievous and se-

ducing influence, a man might have otherwise put forth—in laboring to realize a sufficiency for himself and for his children. It is a law of exemption from toil, from prudence, from foresight and economy, from every restraint on the gratifications of present and powerful appetite; and from all those busy expedients wherewith a man, who is left to depend on himself, devises for the security or the advancement of his own condition in the world. A man feels discharged from all strenuousness or self-denial, when the care of his own subsistence is thus taken out of his hands; and the state undertakes to do for him that which, but for its interference, he would infallibly and in obedience to the calls of hunger and necessity have otherwise done for himself. A universal guarantee against starvation, operates towards a universal relaxation of industry and providential habits among the families of a land. A man will not accumulate of his savings against the evil day, if that day have already been provided for by the institutions of his country. He is thus tempted to idleness, nay tempted either to profligacy or premature marriage, by the expenses of which he is no longer deterred—when these expenses are shifted from himself to a public and compulsory fund, raised for all sorts of destitution, in whatever way that destitution may have been formed. It is thus that many a single parish in England holds forth in miniature the example of an over-peopled world. It labors and is in distress from the redundancy of its own numbers; and whether this excess proceeds from the number of illegitimate births, or from the regular family births of too early and too frequent marriages—certain it is, that there are thousands of parochial communities in England, where the overplus of laborers has effected an unnatural reduction of price in the labor market—so as to have inflicted a sore and general degradation on the circumstances of the working classes. It is thus that the Poor-law of England has created far more of want and wretchedness than it can by any possibility relieve; or, in other words, a law in the constitution of the country, by superseding a wiser and better law in the constitution of human nature, has depressed the condition of the lower orders in society, and aggravated tenfold the poverty which it had vainly proposed to do away.

6. But secondly, there is another law, inserted by the hand of Nature in the mechanism of our constitution; and which, when teft undisturbed to its own proper direction and force, goes far to alleviate the ills of poverty, we mean the law of relative or family affection—as of parents to children, of children back again to parents, of brothers and sisters to each other; and even of more distant members in the same circle of relationship. And, besides this, there is a certain sentiment of pride which comes in aid of the more intense kindness that operates within the limits of a common household, or, more extended still, of a common kindred, though parted into separate domestic establishments, and in virtue

of which many a sacrifice is made to support and to save each other from the degradations of charity, so long as charity is not legalized. But both affection and honor give way, before the temptations of a public and authorized provision for the relief of indigence; and accordingly in England, under its late and still under its present parochial economy, there do occur the most scandalous desertions of very near relatives, and which, by the force of habit and under the countenance of general example, have ceased to be scandalous there. Aged parents, instead of being taken into the houses of their children now advanced to manhood and in a state of sufficiency for supporting those to whom they owe their birth, are abandoned for life to the cheerless imprisonment of a Poors-house; and on the other hand, parents, in the full vigor of manhood and the natural protectors of their own families, have been tempted in hundreds perhaps in thousands every year to abscond from their dwellings, and leave all the inmates to the charity of the parish bound by law to provide for them. We have counted in one newspaper no less than forty advertisements of runaway husbands from the town of Manchester, who had left their families on the parish fund, and for the discovery and apprehension of whom a reward was offered by the managers. This unnatural desertion of their own kinsfolk is the epidemic vice of England—only, however, because a legal guarantee against the starvation of those who are thus deserted is its epidemic temptation. It is in striking contrast with the general habit of Scotland, in the great majority of whose parishes such a guarantee is practically unknown; and where, almost universally, such an abandonment, either of parents by their own children or of children by their own parents, would, as a thing of exceeding rare occurrence, be deemed a monstrous exception to the most binding duties, the most sacred proprieties of Christian and humanized life. We have already considered the effect of a law of pauperism, in releasing man from the duties which he owes to himself. Its effect in releasing him from the duties which he owes to those of his own relationship, is no less obvious. In both instances, it directly tends to multiply the number of paupers, and, great as this economic evil is, it is surpassed by the moral evil of a system, under which the sustenance of man is made independent of his own virtue and prudence; and the sustenance even of his nearest relatives is alike independent of those parental and filial affections, which are nature's strongest securities for the maintenance and uprearing of successive families in the world. Surely better than to have thus counteracted such urgent and universal principles as these, would it have been that the hand of power had not interfered with them; but leaving them to their own native and spontaneous operation, that legislation had kept within her own rightful province, and let the business of charity alone.

7. But thirdly, besides the strong feeling of relative affection

between men and men of the same kindred, Nature hath established another guarantee against the ills of extreme want; and another feeling strong too and of wider operation than the former, we mean the feeling of compassion—of which all might be the objects; but which acts with peculiar force and great practical effect, between men and men of the same neighborhood. And so it is not to be told how much is given and received throughout the families, even of the poorest localities, by the internal operation of charity amongst themselves. It is true that the contributions of each might be individually small, but this is made up for by their number and constancy. It is quite palpable, even on the most cursory observation, how mutually helpful, by personal service and attendance, they are to each other, in seasons of sickness; but it requires much intercourse, and a very intimate acquaintance with the habitudes of the poor who are congregated together in the same community, to be made sure of their great mutual generosity, in imparting, from their own scanty share of the necessaries of life, to the naked and the hungry, and the members, whether young or old, of those bereaved households whom the hand of death has deprived of their parents or natural protectors. Such, nevertheless, is the actual finding of all who have given themselves to the business of observation on this most interesting walk. The Reverend Mr. Carlyle of Dublin informs me, that he can depone, from his minute and statistical acquaintance with one of the poorest sections in the city of Dublin—that the amount given and received by the operation of a charity purely internal, or which reciprocates between the families of the district, exceeds all computation. This fully accords with my own experience, when minister in Glasgow, where I had a parish of ten thousand people, the poorest of the poor; and where, from instances too numerous to be mentioned, I learned the delightful lesson—that the spontaneous charity of neighbors for each other was a more certain as well as more abundant source of relief, in cases of extreme indigence, than that legal charity, by which, when in full operation, the other is well nigh superseded. Never did a case occur without the most timely forthgoings of aid and sympathy from the immediate neighbors—insomuch that I have often expressed it as my confidence, that, if surrounded by human eyes and human ears, I had no fear of human feelings being also awakened, so as to make it a moral impossibility that any man should starve in the sight of his fellows. Perhaps the most vivid illustration of this cheering truth in the history of our nature is to be gathered from Buxton's Tour through the Prisons of Great Britain. The legal allowance of bread to the prisoners varies at different places. In Bristol it was below the par of human subsistence. The allowance was too small for the criminals; and for the debtors there was no allowance at all. The prisoners of the latter class, therefore, are left, either to the assistance of their friends or to the charity of the public. But it occasionally happened, that both these resources failed them—when they would have inevitably perished of hunger but for the generosity of the criminals, who, rather than brook the spectacle of a fellow-creature suffering under one of the sorest agonies of nature, shared their own scanty pittance along with them. This I hold to be one of the finest examples which can be quoted of the strength of human compassion—proving that it survives the depraving process which conducts a criminal to his cell. We have only to carry back this experience from prisons to parishes, in order to be convinced of the safety, wherewith the evils of extreme want might generally be left to the workings of individual sympathy in every neighborhood where they occur. If a man in the agonies of hunger, and giving authentic tokens of this sore distress, be within sight and hearing of his fellows—then, by an urgent and irrepressible law of nature, do they feel the promptings of a desire to relieve him which they are unable to resist. But not if a law of the state have ordained its own prescribed and authoritative method of relieving. Such a law has practically the effect of absolving every man from the obligation of caring for his neighbors; and by laying its arrest on a thousand rills of beneficence, which would else have flowed in refreshing and kindly circulation throughout the mass of society, it has shut far more copious and effective sources of relief for human wretchedness than itself can open.

8. The arrest thus laid on the popular habit of mutual service and sympathy between poor and poor, will prove a far greater loss to the destitute than can be possibly made up to them by all the dispensations of legal charity. The spontaneous offerings of private benevolence will be sadly abridged—because men naturally feel themselves released from the care of all the want and suffering around them, when made to understand that the State has taken that care upon themselves. Those of the same rank with the dependent and the needy keep back from the work of relief, because of an imagined sufficiency in the law, which meanwhile is never realized. Those of a higher rank, the wealthy on whom the burden of the compulsory provision is laid, have an additional reason for their insensibility to the calls of distress. It is not merely that their forced contributions to the Poor-rate supersede, in their own minds, the obligation of any further, or free-will offering. But the truth is, that the whole effect of such an artificial system of charity is to banish from its ministrations all the better and kindlier feelings of our nature. What is given by the ordination of law is given without good-will; and what is received by the same ordination is received without gratitude. That, which ought at all times to have been a thing of love, is transformed into a thing of fierce and fiery litigation. The clear and right proceeding in the management of our nature—were to leave to justice the things of justice, and to humanity the things of humanity. But the first

has been made to usurp the province of the second; and in the confusion of these two moral elements, which should have ever been kept distinct from each other, the one party have been led to demand what they ought to have supplicated; and the other party, in the attitude of defensive jealousy, stoutly to withhold what in the exercise of an enforced compassion they would freely and willingly have given. This will account for the state of mutual exasperation which obtained, and which recent changes have for a time at least only inflamed the more, between the paupers and the proprietors of England; and the loss to a great extent of their spontaneous liberality must be added to the other and still larger privations, which, under the guise of kindness, the law of a compulsory provision for the poor has entailed on the victims of its folly.

9. Shortly then to recapitulate the four causes of deterioration in the comforts of the poor, which the allowances of no public charity can by any possibility countervail—we refer once more—First, to the augmenting improvidence and idleness which are generated by the system—Secondly, to the reduction which it effects on that mutual kindness, which, in a natural state of things, obtains between those of the same kindred—Thirdly, to a similar reduction made by it on those interchanges of sympathy and aid, which take place among the poor themselves of the same neighborhood, when the laws of their country do not contravene the laws and tendencies of their own moral nature—and Lastly, the alienation which it begets of the rich from the poor, whom it arrays into two hostile parties against each other—the one fiercely clamoring for those imagined rights, of which they never would have dreamed, had not this perverse and mischievous law of pauperism inspired the notion of them; and the other party as fiercely resisting the encroachments on their property of that popular demand, which they fear will be ever increasing and never satisfied. We are not to wonder, that, with such powerful counteractions, the number of poor is found greatly to outstrip the provision which is made for them; and that a law which carries in it an aspect of munificence to the lower orders of society, has in truth depressed their condition, and aggravated the evils which it meant to remedy or alleviate.

10. It would detain us too long from the main subject of this essay, did we say all that is important to be noticed or known, respecting the utter powerlessness of law—if it proceed in the way of a public and positive administration of relief, even to abridge, and far less to do away with the indigence of the land. But we cannot omit to assign a great master reason, why the consequence of such a law is the very opposite of this—so that, instead of abridging, it is sure not only to multiply the wants of the poor; but to effect a great and general deterioration in the circumstances of the working classes at large. We advert to the undoubted

stimulus, which a Poor-law gives to population—both adding to the frequency and the precipitation of marriages; and thereby causing, not only a great number of families, but of larger families than before. It is thus that the market for labor comes to be overstocked, and the sure effect of this over proportion of laborers is the under price of labor. The greater the number of workmen the smaller must be the wages; and it gives a fearful aggravation to this mischief, that a very small addition to the number of laborers, creates a very great reduction in the wages which are paid to them. Let there be but the excess of one twentieth in the quantity of labor; and we mistake the consequence, if we think that there will be only the fall of one twentieth in the remuneration which is made to it. Even so few as a twentieth part of the whole number, unemployed, and soliciting admission in the places already occupied and full by those who have gone before them, would create so intense a competition throughout the general body of workmen as might bring down wages one-fourth, one-third, or even one-half, of what they might be, were the number of human beings in no more than equal proportion to the demand for their industry. It is thus that the whole body of the common people suffer a general and severe depression even from a slight redundancy in their numbers; and legislation is sure to find itself embarked in a vain enterprise, when it attempts to overtake this constantly increasing destitution, by a larger dispensation of charity than before. In an economy of legalized pauperism, the necessities and the demands ever multiply beyond the supplies—as in England, where the gigantic expenditure of eight millions was lavished on the relief of that poverty which its own system may be said to have created; and where, in many of its parishes, the sum necessary for the maintenance of the poor had nearly overtaken the rent of the land. It was high time to review an administration so replete with evils; and which every year was rendering more burdensome and oppressive than before. It remains to be seen whether the great abridgments which have been effected, in consequence of the last reforms on the pauperism of England, are but temporary; and the effect of that more rigorous administration, which, however natural at the outset of a new process, may afterwards relax—when the native principle of the whole system may again develop its powers of mischievous expansion, and prove of the legal and compulsory provision for indigence, that no ingenuity of man can repress its overgrowth. It may require the experience of some years to determine this question.

11. The most important change which has taken place in their management of the poor, is the substitution of what is termed in-door relief, for those allowances which the paupers wont to receive at their own houses; and which are now in a great measure superseded, by the admission of those who apply for legal

charity to a general alms-house erected for the district—often comprising a good many parishes. In this way the relief is made greatly more unpalatable to the applicants. It is held out to them in the most repulsive form. If they consent to accept of it, it is at the expense of liberty and home, and all those old associations of place and neighborhood, which they are forced to renounce for the discipline and confinement of the great public asylum which has been provided for them. It is thus that the treatment of poverty is assimilated to the treatment of crime. The inmates of the institution receive a maintenance—but a perpetual imprisonment, though somewhat mitigated by certain relaxations, is the penalty which they have to pay for it.

12. The experiment is yet far from being completed, but the progress of it is highly instructive as far as it has gone. In some parishes, every pauper who under the former regime was in the habit of receiving out-door relief; but who in exchange for this, was required under the present system to become the inmate of an asylum—has refused the alternative and withdrawn his name from the lists and the allowances of pauperism altogether. It is thus that many thousands of these parochial pensioners all over England, have been driven by the severities or terrors of the new system from the domain of pauperism; and, after betaking themselves to their own resources, do in fact find a sufficiency in these for an independence and a comfort which they never formerly enjoyed. This history, repeated and exemplified in thousands of the parishes in England, is rich in principle, and fraught with the discovery of an important truth. It proves that there was no call, no natural necessity, for that part at least of the enormous expenditure of the former system from which they are now relieved—and that not by any skilfulness in the management of their new system; but by the mere repulsion of its discouragements, and of the dread which is inspired by it. Instead then of boasting of the wisdom of their new economy, they have far greater reason to acknowledge the egregious folly of their old one; and when in so many of their parishes, they witness the palpable fact, that the great majority of their former paupers, after being deprived of their old allowances, can contrive to live and in all appearance as comfortably as before—this might lead them to apprehend, that, to a great extent at least, the artificial charity of law is uncalled for, and even prepare them for the conclusion that it perhaps were better if the law could be dispensed with altogether.

13. But perhaps it is too much to expect, that a country shall so speedily retrace its way, and so as to make even in one generation, a total recovery of itself from the error of centuries. But other countries, at least, may learn a lesson from the experience of England. They should know how to make a right interpretation of the abridgment which is now being made on the ex-

penses of English pauperism. It demonstates that there is no necessity, either in nature or in the state of human society, for such a system at all; and it is therefore to be hoped, that other nations will avoid that great blunder in the domestic policy of England, which has been fraught with so many evils to all the classes of society, and to none more than to the poor themselves. Foreigners are far more likely to profit from the history of this great and memorable delusion than the country itself which has been the victim of it, and which at this moment makes striking display of the tenacity of inveterate and long-established error, in extending the same hurtful policy to Ireland—thereby to aggravate the distempers of that unhappy land.

14. And it is further instructive to observe the expedient by which it is attempted to correct this wrong legislation—not by abolishing the legislation, but by counteracting it with other legisgislation, wrong too, though in an opposite direction to the former. Thus, a compulsory provision for the poor wears an expression of kindness to the humbler classes of society. But when pauperism, fostered into being by this unwise ordination, made alarming progress, and threatened to annihilate the property of the higher classes—then to arrest and neutralize this mischief, they have devised another ordination, by which to make the pauperism as repulsive as possible to the feelings of those who claim a part in its ministrations. They still keep up the notion of their right to a maintenance in the hearts of the destitute; but, by the new law, it is a maintenance on terms the most hateful and humiliating, and that for the purpose of scaring away as many as possible, of those applicants, who, under the old system, did beset the parish vestries of England—the wretched victims of their own indolence and dissipation. We cannot imagine a state of the law, more fitted to engender the utmost acerbity of feeling among the poor; and indeed to alienate the general body of the common people from the government under which they live. Surely it were better that charity had been left to its own spontaneous operation, and so as to insure the kindly play of good will on the part of its dispensers, and gratitude on the part of its recipients; surely this must give rise to a better and a blander community, than when the one party are led to challenge a sustenance as their privilege and their due; and the other party, to defend themselves against the encroachment, labor to make the privilege as worthless as they may, by assimilating to the uttermost the treatment of paupers to the treatment of criminals. In such a condition of things, we behold the materials of a fierce and fiery fermentation in the hearts of the lower orders—most hurtful to their own spirits, and most hazardous to the peace of society. The first great blunder in this legislation, was to ordain a law of compulsory relief at all; and when, to save the ruinous consequences of this law, the relief was made as degrading as pos-

sible, this was attempting to correct one evil by another, or to bring about a right result by what mathematicians would call a compensation of errors. The first may be regarded as a disturbing force in one direction, and the second as a disturbing force in the opposite direction. Let both be removed, and the business of charity, when restored to its own proper character, would proceed in the right and natural course, without error and without deviation.

15. In every way then, it is better for a nation to keep itself clear of any legal enactment for the relief of indigence; and more especially for a government, not to take out of the hands of its people, the duties which they owe either to themselves or to their relatives, or to their neighbors. The great lesson to be learned from the example of England is, that the economic condition of the lower classes is not improved but deteriorated by the establishment of a compulsory provision for the destitute—which provision too, besides aggravating the miseries of their state, has, by introducing the heterogeneous element of an imagined right into the business of charity, turned what ought to have been altogether a matter of love into a matter of angry litigation, and greatly distempered the social condition of England, by the heart-burnings of a perpetual contest between the higher and humbler orders of the commonwealth.

16. But it must be admitted, that, though this be the wise and even benevolent part of a government, devising for the welfare of its subjects, it may not be the policy by which best to conciliate the affections of the multitude. There is in it a certain unmoved and cold-blooded aspect of insensibility to distress—the appearance of a heartless indifference to the sufferings and the sympathies of our common nature. It has been matter of boasting complacency to the writers of England, when expatiating on the perfection of their own government—that they could speak, not merely of the wisdom and the justice, but also of the humanity of their laws: and the law to which they make their most confident appeal in support of this assertion, is their own law of pauperism. It no doubt conduces mightily to the strength and popularity of any government, when it can stand forth in the guise of kindness to the most helpless of its people; but kindness in the expression, or even in the real and honest purpose, may often be cruelty in effect. And never was this more strikingly exemplified than by England's famous law—prompted we have no doubt, by feelings of the sincerest benevolence; but which, notwithstanding, has enhanced and multiplied tenfold the sufferings that were meant to be relieved by it. It has become therefore all the more desirable, that the occasions should be pointed out, on which a government might have the opportunity of coming forth *ostensibly* as the friend, and so at the same time as to relieve and *substantially* to be the benefactor of the afflicted—

with the same aspect of munificence and mercy to the destitute upon its forehead, which made the government of England so popular at the first enactment of its Poor-Law; but without those tremendous consequences on the character and comfort of the lower orders, which the experience of centuries has demonstrated to follow inevitably in its train.

17. It is the part of every well-principled government to discriminate between a seeming and a real good to the population; and never for the sake of popularity to provide the former, even if it only practise thereby a harmless deceit on the public imagination—and still more, if under the guise of an apparent blessing to the poor, there lurks an influence at once ruinous both to the moral and economic prosperity of the lower orders. But, on the other hand, should the good to be provided be free of any such alloy, and at the same time be as apparent as it is real, then, it is not only a well-principled but an eminently politic and wise proceeding in a government, to determine on the adoption of it—thereby earning the grateful affections of the people; and, at the same time, scattering amongst them those solid and unquestionable benefits, which may abide the test of experience, and prove to be of great and actual service to the interests of humanity. Now, a law of relief for general indigence does not realize both these conditions. It may carry upon its front an aspect of benignity to the poor; but fraught with innumerable evils, will at length turn out to be the mockery of an unreal blessing, or rather a deadly act of hostility to their best interests; and all the more grievous, that it is in the semblance and with the promises of truest friendship. In defect of such a law then, can any other law of relief be specified in which both the conditions will hold?—full of promise even at the outset, and not behind in performance afterward—a law which not only expresses some great purpose of obvious benevolence, but which executes that purpose to the full; and without inflicting, as the law of pauperism unquestionably does, deterioration or discomfort on the objects of its care.

18. A law of relief for general indigence does not fulfil these conditions; but a law of relief for disease may. There is no fund that can possibly be raised, which will overtake the former. But with a small fraction of the country's wealth, the latter can be overtaken. The distinction between these two objects—that is, between a public charity for the relief of indigence, and a public charity for the relief of disease—must not have occurred to the civilized governments of Europe, else it would have been more frequently acted on; and yet on the moment of its being stated, it is a distinction abundantly obvious in itself, and alike obvious in the reasons of it. An ostensible provision for the relief of poverty creates more poverty. An ostensible provision for the relief of disease does not create more disease. The human will is enlisted on the side of poverty by the provision which is

made for it. No such provision will ever enlist the human will on the side of disease. Let proclamation be made of a law which guarantees every man against starvation—and this were tantamount to the proclaiming a jubilee of exemption from the toils of industry, from the cares of providence, from the duties of family and the sympathies of social life; and by the check thus given to all the natural incentives, whether of private exertion for one's own interest or of private charity for the good of others, there might ensue a constantly increasing poverty that will ever keep ahead of the increasing fund, by which it is vainly hoped to quell the mischief that rises into greater dimensions with every new and larger attempt to overtake it. To think of providing for the wants of poverty by the ordination of an adequate supply, is every way as irrational, as to aim at the extinction of a fire by pouring oil upon it. It is not so with the attempt to provide, and that even in the most legal, and certain and open manner, for the wants of disease. And this is the reason of the difference. Though poverty in itself, be not pleasant, yet the path of indolence and dissipation which leads to it, is abundantly pleasant and alluring; and so thousands are prepared to rush upon this descending path, on the moment that the consequent poverty is disarmed of its terrors, by the protection and the promises of law. It is thus that under such a system men are tempted, and that in constantly increasing numbers, to become voluntarily poor; but no system, no multiplication of funds or of hospitals, will (with a few rare exceptions, far too rare to be practically of any weight in a general argument) tempt men to become voluntarily diseased. No man will break a limb for the sake of its skilful amputation in an infirmary; or put out his eyes for the benefit of admittance to a blind asylum; or become wilfully dumb, or deranged, or leprous, that he might lay claim to any treatment or guardianship, which may have been provided at the expense of the nation for these respective maladies. In the very constitution of our sentient nature, in its repugnance to pain and physical suffering, we have the strongest possible guarantee against men wilfully becoming patients, in order to their admission into an asylum for disease. We have no such guarantee, but the opposite, against men becoming paupers, in order to their admission into an asylum for indigence. An indefinite provision for want is ever sure to multiply its objects; and the evil recedes and enlarges, with every advance that is made upon it. A certain definite provision on the other hand for disease will be as sure to overtake its objects. By every new contribution we approach the nearer to a distinct and satisfactory fulfilment; nor does the benevolence whether of the government or of associated philanthropists, need to stay its hand, under the apprehension that one sufferer more will be added to the melancholy catalogue of disease, because of all the care and tenderness which can possibly be bestowed upon it. This forms the great distinction between the two cases. The open proclamation of a free entry into asylums of disease would make a clear abridgment of human misery, and bring no new or additional disease into existence. The like proclamation of a free entry into the asylums of indigence, would bring a world of new poverty into existence, and swell more every year the amount of pauperism. The final outgoing of such a system were at length to absorb all the resources of the country, and beggar its whole population.

19. The antipathy of all our most enlightened political economists to a public charity for the relief of indigence, has been ascribed to a cold and unfeeling hardihood of soul. And the imputation may be true sometimes; but is calumny in all those instances, numerous it is to be hoped, when the moving principle of their hostility is a real concern for the substantial interests of the lower orders—the desire to ward off a system which they honestly believe to have a withering influence both on the character and comfort of the general population. At all events, if it can be demonstrated of any public charity, that it is altogether free of this deleterious tendency, and works an unquestionable good to its objects, without any alloy to discourage or repel the attempts of the benevolent to support it—this holds out a noble opportunity for the enemies of a Poor-law, to redeem their character, and manifest the real spirit and design by which they are actuated. Now, a public charity for disease just presents this very opportunity. The halt, and the blind, and the maimed, and the impotent, and the dumb, and the lunatic—stand before us. with a special mark impressed upon them by the hand of Providence, and which at once announces both their necessity and their claim, for the unqualified sympathy of all their fellows. It would give rise to no ulterior demand on the benevolence of the country, though receptacles were opened wide enough and frequent enough to harbor them all. A certain definite amount of suffering and distress would be cleared away from the territory of human wretchedness, without any baleful operation on the territory beyond it. That mischief, which, like the spreading leprosy, is ever sure to follow a public and certain provision for indigence, is, on an obvious principle, never to be apprehended from a provision however public and however certain for the cure or alleviation of disease. If it was under the burden of such an apprehension, that these philanthropists stood aloof, and refused their countenance and their aid to the one species of charity—let them now, when relieved from the burden, come forth both with their testimony and their wealth in support of the other species of charity. If in the first place they kept feeling at abeyance, because philosophy forbade the indulgence of it—let them in the second place, when there is no cold obstruction in the way, demonstrate the power and promptitude of their humanity, by a

ready forthgoing of their sympathies, now emancipated from all restraint, on those involuntary distresses which nature and necessity have imposed. By their opposition to the institutes of pauperism, they have proved themselves to be before others in the soundness of their understandings—let them by their large and willing support for the institutes of disease, prove that they are not behind others in the sensibilities of the heart. If at the dictate of reason they withheld their liberalities from the one cause—when the other presents itself, and reason not only withdraws its disallowance but urges its unexceptionable claims, then let them show that they have an eye for pity and a hand open as day for melting charity.

20. That this lesson has yet to be learnt by the great majority of our philanthropists, is obvious from the review of those public charities, which have been founded by the munificence of individuals—whether in the form of bequests or of benevolent associations. It is not many years ago, since a Royal Commission was appointed in Britain, to inquire into the public charities of England and Wales; and it is striking to observe the large number of those which have the relief of indigence for their object, and the very small number which are instituted for the treatment of disease. In the account now before us of these charities abridged from the Commissioners' Reports, we reckoned from the commencement of their enumeration no less than a hundred and thirty-six various charities of London and Bristol, of which the great majority were for indigence alone; and a few for education, before we arrived at one for disease being a charity for blind persons. The erection of alms-houses, the distribution of bread, the supply of coals, loans or gifts of money to the indigent; and a countless variety of other distinctions, but all pointing to the general object of the relief of poverty—these outnumber the institutions for education at least in the proportion of six to one, and the institutions for disease in the proportion of fifty to one. We feel quite assured, whether we take a general survey of the whole country or limit our attention to one of its large towns, that, in the testamentary dispositions of the benevolent, there is a very great and general misdirection of wealth to the wrong object. A known and certain provision held out to indigence, will create the indigence—a provision, however certain or however ample made, for disease, will never create or multiply the disease. And yet, in spite of this obvious consideration, far the greatest proportion of the legacies which are left for benevolent purposes, are left for the relief of poverty which can never be overtaken; and so small a proportion left for disease which may be overtaken, as to come greatly short of the necessity. Within these few years, there have been two magnificent sums bequeathed in charity to the city of Edinburgh; and this will add two asylums to a number formerly in excess—because asy-

lums not for any specific maladies but for general want. Meanwhile the Infirmary is inadequately supported. The Deaf and Dumb Asylum is limited, with a very few exceptions, to those whose relatives can afford to pay for their maintenance. The Blind Asylum is on a very limited scale, and in great difficulties; and there is no institution at all in the capital of Scotland, for the gratuitous admission of lunatics. By a more judicious destination of their wealth on the part of those two individuals, a real and unquestionable blessing would have been conferred on society—families relieved of their blind, or fatuous, or other diseased members; and without any substitution of families alike helpless and unfortunate in their places. But the reverse of this takes place with the asylums for indigence. Hundreds of poor may be admitted within their thresholds; but these are sure to be replaced by an equal, we think by a greater number, and the general community labors under as great a burden of want and wretchedness as before.

21. It is instructive to observe the relative estimation in which these two objects are held by the charitable—we mean the relief of poverty, and the relief of disease. We thought it a good way of settling this question, to take the volume which presented an account of all the public charities that had been found in a certain number of the towns and parishes in England, abridged from the Reports of the Royal Commissioners on Charitable Foundations. These charities, in the great bulk of them originated in the spontaneous benevolence of individuals who very generally conveyed, not by gifts while they were living, but by bequests which took effect after their death, the whole or part of their wealth to certain philanthropic purposes. It is marvellous to contemplate the preference which these testators had for the relief of poverty, rather than for the relief of disease. The distinction which we have so much insisted on must not have been present to their minds. They must not have adverted to the utter failure of every attempt by public charity to overtake the indigence of the land, or even to diminish the amount of it—seeing that the relieving process, in virtue of which a certain number were fed and clothed, was followed up and accompanied by a creative process, in virtue of which at least an equal, we think a greater amount of poverty, or of hunger and nakedness, was created in general society. And neither along with this must they have adverted to the obvious impossibility of a similar effect in the treatment of disease—seeing that the relieving process in this department of charity never could be so followed up by a creative process, in virtue of which any more disease could be called into existence. We have reckoned the number of such destinations of which an account is given in the work now referred to—comprehending the Charities of London, along with those of ten other great towns, besides a number of parishes in England; and we find,

that, while there are only eleven distinct allotments of land or money for the relief of disease in all these places, there are among the same places no less than 712 for the relief of indigence. It must also be mentioned that the number of Educational Charities amounts to 202; but perhaps it will exhibit a fairer proportion of the two, if we look separately to each of the distinct localities; and, accordingly, the following are a few examples out of the many. In the borough of Stafford, we have an account of 19 charitable bequests for the indigent, seven for education, and none for disease. For the town of Northampton, we have an account of 31 charitable funds for indigence, and 9 for education, and none for disease. In the city of Gloucester, we have an account of 21 instituted funds for charity, 6 for education, and none for disease. In the town of Leeds, we have an account of 13 public benefactions for the poor, and 8 for education. In the city of York, we recognize 48 benefactions for poverty, and 23 for education. In the large and populous town of Manchester, we mark 31 distinct heads of charity for the poor, and 19 for education. It should be observed, however, that we count every object to be education, which goes any way to the instruction of the people, whether it be in religious doctrine or in ordinary scholarship—including therefore the sums allocated for the repairs of churches, and the preaching of sermons, as well as for the expenses of week-day seminaries. In the laborious enumeration that we drew out, we generally rated all the individual bequests as one, which were made over to one and the same institution. Of the 11 cases of provision for disease we state as specimens the conveyance by Robert Hudson, of eight acres on trust, to apply the rents in providing medicine and medical aid for the poor of the parish of Selby; and the munificent bequest of Mr. Thomas Henslow of £20,000 for a blind asylum at Manchester. It was altogether in keeping with this, that the same individual should bequeath £1,000 for the Manchester Infirmary, and £1,000 for a Lunatic Hospital.

22. We are aware that we have taken account of but a very small proportion of the charities in England, and have not even completed the list of the charities in all the places which we have now specified. We were necessarily limited to the examination of such charities as the royal commissioners were empowered to inquire into; but they were not excluded from taking cognizance of the institutions for disease, any more than of the institutions either for want or for learning; and the proportions we have now been enabled to exhibit, do, it is certain, evince most strikingly, a preference on the part of the benevolent founders for those charitable institutions, which have for their object the relief of that indigence into which men might voluntarily descend, and to which descent these bequests hold out a resistless temptation. It is melancholy to think, that, by a small fraction of the wealth thus thrown away, institutions for disease might have been pro-

vided all over the land, and so as to leave no involuntary sufferer under the inflictions of nature and necessity, in want of any likely appliance, by which to cure or to alleviate his distress.

23. It is not for us to enter into a full detail on the public charities of France. We rejoice to observe in the city of Paris so many institutions for disease, while the sums spent on the public relief of indigence, derived chiefly from the produce of public shows and public amusements, form but an insignificant fraction of what is expended on the same object in London. We, at the same time, were astonished at the immense proportion which the number who received charity at their own houses, bore to the population of the city—having in 1835 amounted to one in 12.32 of the whole community. It is our confident opinion, yet we desire to express it with all humility and respect, that the sure effect of such distributions is to augment the discomfort and moral deterioration of the lower classes. The sum given to each individual is small; but it should ever be recollected, that the mischief is not proportionally small. That relaxation of industrious and providential habits, and that relaxation also of the family and relative obligations, which are the sure consequences of pauperism, are not to be measured by the sum received, but by the sum expected; and each, in virtue of the natural confidence which every man has in his own good fortune, may look for a larger share of the public beneficence, than he shall ever succeed in realizing. It is thus, we apprehend, that every known charity for the relief of indigence multiplies its objects; and it is woful to think, that, while the amount of suffering is increased thereby, it is in virtue of a process which carries along with it the tenfold greater evil of an increase of depravity. The decay of character and the decay of comfort keep pace with each other—for who does not acknowledge, that, if the pride of honest independence, an affection for one's own kindred, and a sympathy for those of one's own neighborhood are all enfeebled under a system of pauperism—that system must have a withering influence, both on the worth and the well-being of society? The evil we imagine to be greatly aggravated by those places of reception (*Hospices*) —where applicants, with no other qualification than poverty, find a harbor and a maintenance provided for them. If the out-door relief be of small account—beyond this there is the ulterior prospect of an in-door admittance, to all the necessaries at least, if not the comforts of existence. The magical influence of hope will extend to a far greater multitude than to those actual receivers of charity, who are so far fortunate as to have their hopes at least in part realized. The indolence, the improvidence, the dissipation, the disregard to every claim of family or neighbor—these are the fertile causes of want, or of want unrelieved. And these are stimulated throughout the mass of the community by the promises of pauperism, to a far greater extent than the promises

are ever realized. We think, it may with all safety be affirmed, that neither Paris nor any town in Europe has at this moment a less, we think it has a much greater amount of unrelieved poverty, because of the public charities for general indigence which have been established in the midst of them—beguiling the people from a dependence on themselves; and from the duties of family and social life, which they owe to the helpless who are around them.

24. Yet however mischievous in their operation these public institutions for the relief of indigence may be, we do not plead for the *immediate* abolition of them. We think that even justice requires the continuance of their wonted allowances, to all whom the very existence of these proclaimed charities has allured from the habits of industry and self-dependence. Let them be seen therefore to their graves in the sufficiency of their present allowances, unless it be found on a scrutiny of their cases that they may be committed back again to their own resources. It is only by a gradual process that we desire the extinction of any of those institutions against which we have contended. We would steadily refuse the admission of any new applicants, while we would spare the old recipients; and would rather wait to be delivered from the burden of aiding them by the operation of death, than incur the violence of a movement *per saltum*, by the instant dismissal, either of the actual inmates from their asylums, or of the actual out-door pensioners from the periodical grants which they have been in the habit of receiving. We would not thus violate the law of continuity; but suffer every institute for the relief of poverty gradually to die a natural death, by the successive deaths of the individuals who now depend upon them. Only we would take on no new individuals; and feel assured, that, if these either were taught to draw upon their own resources, or were left to the sympathies whether of neighborhood or of relationship, we should find, as the result of this change of system—that the community would become economically more comfortable, and morally more virtuous than before.

25. It were well that the governments, both of states and of cities, were more alive to the distinction which we have endeavored to unfold, between the one species of charity and the other. The argument against a public charity for indigence, applies so little to the public charities for disease—that practically, while the former ought to be abolished, the latter, with a proper degree of regulation and watchfulness, might be encouraged to the uttermost. If a government endangered somewhat its popularity, by suffering the one class of institutions to fall into desuetude—this, it is to be hoped, would be greatly more than compensated, by the patent character of beneficence and mercy, which stood on their ordinance of an instant provision for all those maladies that come under the best and most effectual treatment in a public asylum. A door might be opened, not only with

safety, but with an unalloyed blessing to society—wide enough for the reception of all the maimed, and all the impotent, and all the bereft of their faculties, whether of sight, or reason, or speech or hearing. Infirmaries and fever-hospitals; and even dispensaries, though these last seem the most difficult to be guarded from abuse, might be multiplied to the extent of the necessity if not of the demand for them. We are aware of the complaints which have been made, and nowhere more than in Paris, of the undue advantage that even patients as well as paupers might take of the provision that is made for them. But surely disease admits of being more distinctly and decisively tested than poverty. Neither is the one so multiplied by institutions raised in its behalf, as the other is. No man can counterfeit the loss of a limb, or even the loss of his sight, and reason, and hearing, so as long to impose on the guardians of an asylum into which he may have found his way. But any man can counterfeit poverty; or, what is still more decisive, he not only can but he will create poverty —when the temptation of a public and a promised relief are held out to a little more indolence, or a little more dissipation. If there have been mutilations practised, or if there have been a voluntary contraction of real diseases, in order to qualify for the sustenance and the shelter held forth in a place of cure—these, it is demonstrable, compose but an insignificant fraction, compared with that host of unworthy applicants, who crowd the avenue which leads to a place of supply for the wants of indigence. The few and incidental evils which might at times be realized even in an infirmary (*hopital*), do not obscure the line of demarcation between such an institution and a poor's house (*hospice*)—the evils of which are sure to be multiplied tenfold, with every increase of its funds and its allowances. The fictitious disease which knocks at the door of an asylum, bears a very small proportion to the fictitious poverty. But the great distinction between the two charities lies in this—that the real disease (excepting that which is contracted by vicious indulgence) brought into existence by the provision made for it, bears the proportion of an infinitesimal to the real poverty, which comes into being under the malignant influence of a public charity—by the relaxation of industrious and economical habits, as well as of all those ties that bind the members whether of a household or of a neighborhood into a common sympathy with each other.

26. And there is one class of sufferers about whom there can be no mistake, and who possess an indisputable and pre-eminent claim upon human sympathy. We mean those—on whom all the resources of the medical art have been expended in vain; and who, after a season of full probation in an hospital of disease, are at length pronounced to be beyond hope and beyond recovery. The great desideratum is an asylum, or place of refuge for these poor incurables—who, instead of being devolved a heavy and

hopeless burden on the families to which they belong, should at least have it in their power to enter some such house of mercy open to receive them—where they might meet with every possible alleviation which human skill can devise, or human kindness can administer. For their sakes it were well, if even the title of the institution were softened from a House for Incurables to a House for Convalescents—through which all who leave the infirmary may pass on their transition to perfect health and strength, after the medical treatment is over; and only those be detained whom the hand of nature has stricken with irrecoverable disease, and whom the God of nature has thus signalized and marked out for the unqualified sympathy of all their fellows.

27. The whole of this argument receives a beautiful illustration, or I would even say, is strengthened and confirmed, by the example of our Saviour. He could have brought, nay, he actually on two occasions did bring down, food by miracle, to appease the hunger of a starving multitude: but refused to do so a third time, when, in the sordid expectation of a meal, they ran after him for the purpose of being again regaled by his bounty. "Verily you have come not to see the miracle but to eat of the loaves and be filled." What a contrast between this reserve in the supply of food, and the unexcepted freeness of his ministrations in the supply of health, which he brought down by miracle on every patient who applied to him for a cure. There is no recorded example of his ever having bid away from him the maimed, or the impotent, or the palsied, or the lunatic, or the vexed with sundry and sore diseases; but in every case of which we read, "He looked to them and had compassion on them, and healed them all." I have often thought of this history as a guide and an example to us, in our public charities. For in the notoriety which he attained, any charity of his was in fact a public charity; and it is obvious, that, had he brought down food indefinitely by miracle, it would have discharged the people from all their habits of industry and foresight, and disorganized the whole of Judea, by trooping multitudes running after this great prophet for the purpose of being fed by him. But no such consequence was to be apprehended when, instead of a miraculous almoner to all his countrymen, He became a miraculous Physician to those limited and comparatively few who sought the relief of their malady at His hand; and, accordingly, when, in the march of his wise and effective beneficence through the land of Judea, the dumb, and the blind, and the afflicted with various infirmities, came forth of the surrounding villages—he laid no prohibition on these children of blameless and helpless disease. We have much to learn from this proceeding of our Saviour's; but, whatever discouragements we may draw from his example in the erection of an asylum for indigence, we can draw none against the erection of an asylum for disease. And while the boding apprehension both of moral

and physical disaster hangs over the one institution—do we infer of the other that its door may be thrown open, and all its accommodations be widened and multiplied, till every imploring patient be taken in, and a harbor of sufficient amplitude be provided for all those sufferings which an uncontrollable necessity has laid upon the species.

AN HISTORICAL AND CRITICAL VIEW

OF THE

SPECULATIVE PHILOSOPHY OF EUROPE

IN THE NINETEENTH CENTURY.

BY J. D. MORELL, A.M.

[*From the North British Review for February. London:* 1847.]

THE Author of this important work began his studies on the Mental Philosophy in London; proceeded thence to Glasgow; after an attendance on the classes there, went to Germany, where he heard lectures, and read the works of its great masters; last of all, passed into France and became conversant with the writings of Cousin, and others of the Eclectic School now forming in Paris. Such a thorough work of preparation bids well for great results, a first specimen of which we have in the volumes before us: and truly, the force and clearness wherewith they are written, and this by one who has travelled so extensively over his own select and favorite department in the territory of human knowledge, fully warrants the expectation of still greater and more important services at his hand.

And it is long since any work has made its appearance before a public in a state of greater expectancy and readiness for its lessons. The subject of it is altogether adapted to the necessity of our times. We can imagine no two things more alien from each other than is the speculative philosophy of Britain from that of Germany; and, for the sake of that truth which is one and universal, a common understanding, an adjustment between them, is imperiously called for. The mental habitudes of the two countries are wide as the poles asunder; and did this divergency take effect only in some region far aloft, and where it could have no possible bearing upon human interests or human affairs, we might simply gaze upon it as a matter of philosophic curiosity. But touching, as it does, on the nearest and most affecting of all our concerns, the prospect of a collision now at hand between the two philosophies in question cannot but awaken a certain sense of fearfulness in the minds of those who both admit the supreme homage that is due to truth, and at the same time the homage that is due to religion; and, accordingly, it is not too much to say that such a fearfulness is now beginning to be felt. For we may now lay our account with a far more copious influx than heretofore of the German metaphysics into this country. Not only is the language more generally studied among the upper classes of British society; but there is in progress at this moment, a regular series of translations, and that, too, of those authors who have most signalized themselves by a certain daring recklessness of speculation, which, while it will repel the confidence of many, might captivate and engage many more by the spectacle, at all times interesting, of great mental intrepidity and mental power. The very strangeness and peculiarity, both of diction and thought, will set the curiosity of numbers upon edge; and, besides, with such heralds as Coleridge and Carlyle, whose writings have so powerful a hold on our literary public, to open the way for them, we may surely reckon on their welcome entertainment by thousands of the readers in our land. Now, all this is not only the anticipation, but the dread of many who feel as if the stability of our creeds were fast giving way; or as if all our creeds, and institutions, and existing usages, were now on the eve of some frightful overthrow. Nor do we hold these terrors to be altogether spectral and imaginary. But it is well to know the dimensions of the spectre; for, if seen in its own definite magnitudes and outlines, it might cease to be so formidable. A bugbear is always more terrific than the nucleus or the naked reality from which it hath expanded; and, at all events, it is right to be told what the precise force and armor is of the enemy we might be called to encounter. This service, and a most important one it is, has been ably executed by the author of the work under review. It is entitled, "An Historical and Critical Review of the Speculative Philosophy of Europe in the Nineteenth Century." As regards the historical part, we feel truly thankful for his informations; and as to the critical, in which, over and above his informations, we have also his judgments, we are thankful for this part too of his work, but will take leave to share it with him.

We confess, that our chief earnestness is to find, amid all these conflicting systems and speculations, that our theology is safe; nor do we altogether understand the obviously sensitive aversion of our author to the idea of coming into collision with it. We fully acquit him of all that mock homage rendered by Hume and other infidels to Christianity—as if its questions were unfit for the tribunal of reason, and should ever be carried thence to the only competent and higher tribunal of faith. We rejoice to observe of Mr. Morell, that he is altogether free of such contemptuousness; and that, when he does speak of Religion, it is in terms of uniform respect for it, even in its most serious and evangelistic form.

But if so, what then is he afraid of? Most assuredly Religion is worthy of his respect only in so far as it is true; and if true, why does he shrink back from it, as if it were a heterogeneous element, and not to be admitted into the field of his argument—even although the philosophy of which he is the historian makes free with the very essence and first elements of religion, and, if left all to its own way, would end in sweeping it from the face of the earth? And, besides, must not truth in every one department be in fullest harmony with truth in every other? and where, we ask,—we shall not say the impiety,—but where is the philosophy of refusing evidence, if it only be logical and legitimate evidence, from whatever quarter of human contemplation it may come? Most assuredly we shall not denounce any system or any speculation that is here recorded, however extravagant or profane it may chance to be—we shall not denounce it as impious; though surely we are at liberty to charge it as unphilosophical, yet only on such evidence and for such reasons as might rightfully challenge the belief of soundly philosophic men. We desire to wear no other shield for our defensive, and to wield no other armor for our offensive warfare, in fighting the battles of the faith.

And, now that we have done with these preliminaries, our first, and, as yet, very general remark, is, that our author seems to us in the natural spirit of one who magnifies his office, somewhat to have misstated its place among the sciences, and greatly to have exaggerated the pretensions and powers of the mental philosophy. Nor is he at all singular in this. Leibnitz, in one of his Logical and Metaphysical Tractates, entitled, "Reflections on Locke's Essay of the Human Understanding," tells us, that "of all inquiries, this is the most important, for that it is the key to every other. Dr. Brown, in his Second Lecture, entitled, "Relation of the Philosophy of the Mind to the Sciences in General," offers a number of like testimonials, which would need to be greatly qualified. He tells us "how essential a right view of the *science of mind* is to every other science, even to those sciences which superficial thinkers might conceive to have no connection with it." He further speaks of "a close acquaintance with the nature of that *intellectual medium* through which alone the phenomena of matter become visible to us, and of those *intellectual instruments* by which the objects of *every* science, and of every science alike, are measured, and divided, and arranged." And then he says of mind, that "it is an agent operating in the production of new results, and employing for this purpose the known laws of thought, in the same manner as, on other occasions, it employs the known laws of *matter*." And, lastly, without multiplying our quotations from him any further, he concludes, that "to the philosophy of *mind*, then, *every* speculation, in *every* science, may be said to have relation as to a common centre." Even the calmly sedate and sober-minded Dr. Reid tells, in his own person, "that a distinct knowledge of the powers of the mind would undoubtedly give great light to many other branches of science;" and quotes with approbation from Mr. Hume the following sentence, that "all the sciences have a relation to human nature; and, however wide any of them may seem to run from it, they still return back by one passage or another. This is the centre and capital of the sciences, which being once masters of, we may easily extend our conquests everywhere." Now, without citing innumerable depositions to the same effect from Locke and many others, there is one thing, on which we touch but slightly at present, as we may recur to it afterwards, yet which we should like even now the reader to bear in mind. It is one thing to say, with Mr. Hume, that *human nature* is the centre of the sciences, and altogether another thing to say that the *knowledge of human nature* is the centre of the sciences. We should greatly like that this distinction were clearly apprehended. We shall not dispute the temperate and well-weighed deliverance of Reid, that this knowledge would give light to other branches of science; while we cannot go the length to which the analogies of Dr. Brown would carry one, as if all other science hung upon the philosophy of mind in the same way that it hangs upon mind itself. It is most true, that, according to the powers of an instrument, so, when fully used, will be its performances; and, according to the mental faculties, so, when in like manner used, will be the mental acquisitions. But though the acquisitions depend, and wholly depend upon the faculties, they do not thus depend upon our knowledge of the faculties. There can be no question, that as is the psychology of mind, so is the state of its sensations and of its beliefs, nay, of all its sciences—insomuch, that a different or reverse psychology would give rise to different or reverse sciences. But it follows not, and it argues a subtle misunderstanding of the whole matter to think otherwise, it follows not that, therefore, the study of this psychology is a prerequisite to the study of the sciences. Without the visual faculty, there could be no vision; yet is there no antecedent necessity to become acquainted with the visual faculty ere we can see. Without the knowing faculty, there could be no knowledge; yet there is not, on that account, the antecedent necessity for our making acquaintance with the knowing faculties ere we can know. Ere we look out upon the external world, we do not look back upon the image of it, as graven on the retina—nay, though that image had never been observed, though the first touch of the dissecting instrument had so deranged the structure of the eye, as to make the exhibition of it impossible, yet, with the exception of this single phenomenon, might the beautiful science of optics have been as complete and comprehensive a science as it is at this moment. And, in like manner, we are not to wait for the perfecting of mental science, ere that hopeful progress can be made towards the perfecting of all the other sciences. It may be very long before those physiologists be at one, who speculate on the functions of the optic nerve which retires behind the organ of vision, till lost in obscurity among the convolutions of the brain—yet do all men see aright notwithstanding. And it might be just as long before that our mental physiologists. or psychologists, come to a full and final settlement on all their questions; yet, meanwhile, might all other men of science, save themselves, by philosophizing aright on all the other departments of human knowledge. It it quite a just representation to speak of the mind as the centre of all the sciences, even as the sun is the centre of our planetarium. But it was not the Copernican system, discovered only a few centuries ago, which set the planets rightly agoing. It did not give the law to their movements; it only discovered the law. And neither does the mental philosophy give the law to the mental processes; it but discovers their law. In estimating the real worth of this philosophy, and the relation in which it stands to the other sciences, there is often a strange confounding of the knowledge of things with the things themselves. Had sceptics never questioned the authority of first principles, and so thrown us back on the study of mind and of its laws, the science of psychology, most interesting in itself, yet, for the mere purpose of giving evidence or stability to any of the other sciences, might never have been called for.

We are not going to depreciate the mental philosophy; or, at least, we claim the justice of being read to the end, ere such a charge shall be fastened on us. Though we see much to admire in M. Comte, yet do we hold him utterly in the wrong, in his treatment of the mental and metaphysical sciences; nor upon this subject can we go along with our own Abraham Tucker—while it must be admitted, that there is much of substantial truth in his following deliverance: "The science of abstruse learning," he says, "I consider in the same light with the ingenious writer who compared it to Achilles' spear, that heals the wounds it had made before. It serves to repair the damage itself had occasioned, and this, perhaps, is all it is good for. It casts no additional light on the paths of life, but disperses the clouds with which it had overspread them before. It advances not the traveller one step on his journey, but conducts him back again to the spot from which he had wandered." The child sees an apple on the table, and affirms an apple to be there. A Berkleian philosopher labors to disprove the assertion. A second metaphysician arises and repels the sophistry of the first. But it is not he who gives the law to the child—he but recognizes and respects the law already planted in its constitution by the hand of nature. A sound metaphysics is not the fountain-head of all science. It is but the protector or guardian of the fountain-head, and stationed there to ward off the inroads of those who would vitiate or disturb it. The following sentences from Kant himself are altogether to our mind. "To deny its utility (of mental science) is to deny the utility of a police, because their only function is to prevent the outrages to which we should be otherwise exposed, and so as that everybody might in safety go about his own business." Had there been no perverse metaphysics to bewilder men, each of the sciences might have gone about its own business safely and prosperously; and, save for the interest which attaches to its own lessons, a counteractive metaphysics might never have been required.

But on this subject let us hear Mr. Morell himself, and the more that his arguments, or rather his illustrations, in favor of the mental philosophy, are somewhat peculiar. It is high time, indeed, that he should speak in his own person; and there is scarcely a paragraph that we could quote from these masterly volumes, for the purpose of introducing him to the notice of our readers, which would not introduce him favorably. His phraseology is not always marked by the most rigorous precision; but throughout there is a charm of good writing which never fails us—yet in a philosophic style, too, and that of singular transparency, and expressiveness, and power. We have seldom read an author who can make such lucid conveyance of his thoughts, and these never of light or slender quality, but substantial and deep as the philosophy with which he deals. Even when not convinced by his reasonings, it is difficult to resist the impulse by which we feel ourselves carried along in the flow of his commanding and well constructed sentences. Yet there is nowhere the semblance of an elaborate construction; but altogether in the manner of one who wields the pen of a ready writer *calamo currente*—yet of meaning so patent and palpable, that the reader might follow him *oculo currente.* Even the hieroglyphics of the Kantian philosophy brighten into illuminated characters, at the touch of its accomplished historian.

The following is his reply to the objection against the practical utility of speculative philosophy:—

"Such an objection, we reply, if insisted on, would prove fatal to the cause of almost every branch of human science. It is never expected, and indeed it is not possible, that the mass of mankind should be acquainted with the process, by which any kind of investigation whatever is carried on. The search after truth, even the truths of the phenomenal world, is a process to them completely enveloped in darkness; all they have to do is to reap the practical fruits of any discovery, when it is made, without casting one single thought upon the steps by which others have arrived at it. If we look for a moment at the law by which thought is propagated, we find that it always descends from the highest order of thinkers to those who are one degree below them; from these again it descends another degree, losing at each step of the descent something more of the scientific form, until it reaches the mass in the shape of some admitted fact of which they feel there is not a shadow of doubt, a fact which rests on the authority of what all the world above them says, and which, therefore, they receive totally regardless of the method of its elimination. Take, for example, any great fact or law of nature ascertained by means of physical science. Such a fact is first of all perchance wrung from the most close and laborious mathematical analysis; a few perhaps may take the trouble to follow every step of this process; but the mass even of natural philosophers themselves are content to see what is the method of investigation, to copy the formulas in which it results, and then put it down as so much further accession to their physical science. The mass of intelligent, educated minds, again, with a general idea only of mathematical analysis, accept the fact or law we are now supposing, as one of the many beautiful results of investigations, which they acknowledge to be far beyond the reach of their own powers;—and from them, lastly, it descends to the rest of the community as a *bare fact*, which they appropriate to their own use simply as being a universally acknowledged truth. The first school-boy you meet would very likely tell you with some accuracy what is the rapidity of light; but as to any observations on the occultations of Jupiter's satellites, or on the phenomena of aberration, or any other such method of computing it, on these he has never bestowed a thought. The commonest seaman that has learned the use of his sextant, applies to his own purposes all the necessary formulas of trigonometry; but as to the methods of investigating such formulas, such matters lie entirely out of his reach.

"This law of the descent of thought, however—this gravitation of ascertained truth from the higher order of mind to the lower, is not confined to the mathematical sciences, nor is it here alone that the results of investigation are transmitted by what may be termed *formulas*. There are such things as historical formulas, as formulas for the various theories of the fine arts, and so also are there philosophical or metaphysical formulas. The results of long and patient reflection, in this last case particularly, imbody themselves in some general principle, and this principle, after it has been tested, gradually spreads itself downwards from mind to mind, until thousands act upon it every day of their life, to whom all philosophical thinking is completely foreign. When, therefore, the objection is raised, that metaphysical inquiries lie beyond the reach of the mass, and cannot practically subserve the general interests of mankind, it is entirely forgotten or overlooked, that the *results* of such inquiries are intelligible to all; nay, that they are amongst the most practically efficient and influential of all truths which can possibly exist in the mind of man."—Vol. i., pp. 19-21.

Now between the mathematical formula as convertible into popular use, although the product it may be of the ratifications and discoveries of many successive ages—between this and the mental, or as perhaps our author would rather term it, the metaphysical formula, there might be one most important difference. The former supplies a new instrument of observation, which, but for the labors of the mathematician, could never have been formed or brought into operation. Whereas the service of the latter formula, and for which we are indebted to the labors of the mental analyst, might only be as follows—not to supply a new, but only to certify and authenticate an old instrument of observation, given ready-made to all men by the hand of nature; and which all men could have confidently and successfully made use of, without the necessity of being told so by a right metaphysics, had not a wrong metaphysics cast obscuration over the dictates, and disturbed the confidence of nature. And this view is in perfect keeping with the historical illustrations which are subjoined to the extract that we have now made from our author. What was it that displaced the formula of Aristotle? Was it not the formula of Lord

Bacon? And what is to displace the formula of Locke, as aggravated since into the worst formulas of Condillac and Cabanis? It will not, I fear, be the formula of Kant, which itself stands in need of correction, and has fallen short of the achievement by Dr. Reid, whose formula it was that displaced the formulas of Berkeley and Hume? But must we first study Berkeley and Hume upon the one hand, and then to rid us of their scepticism, make a study of Dr. Reid upon the other, ere that we make the confident use which nature bids us of our senses, and proceed on the reality of an external world? Or, to go further back, must we first learn the metaphysics of Aristotle, which tyrannized for nearly two thousand years over the understandings of men, and then unlearn them by the corrective metaphysics of the Novum Organum?—whose whole lesson it is, that ere we can ascertain the visible properties of anything, we must look at it—or the audible, we must listen—or the tangible properties, we must handle—or the dimensions, we must measure it—or the weight we must weigh it; or, in short, whatever other property falls within the range of observation, we must take the proper observational method for the determination of it. Now that we have been recalled from the wrong to the right direction, there seems no practical necessity for taking up our heads, either with the disturbing force which turned us away, or with the counteractive force which took us back again. Bacon was the vigorous policeman who drove away Aristotle; but now that the service is effected, is it aught more incumbent to study him ere we enter upon any of the experimental sciences, than to take lessons at the Scottish school of metaphysics ere we venture upon the every-day use of our eyes? Most assuredly we have no wish to depreciate the mental philosophy, or, still less, to banish it from the high place which it deserves to occupy in the encyclopedia of human knowledge. Yet might it not be true, that, but for its perversities, and so the needful correction of them, as men could have gone aright about their ordinary business, so philosophers could have gone aright about the business of all the other sciences, although both the right and the wrong metaphysics had banished forever from the remembrance of the world?

The use of our right mathematical formula is not to displace or set aside a wrong mathematical formula, by which men had been formerly misled in their computation of longitudes; but it is to point out a method wholly unknown till the period of its discovery, and without which no sound computation could possibly have been made. On the other hand, the main use of a right metaphysical formula is not to supply us with any new method of investigation; but to vindicate the old and natural methods from which we should never have been tempted, save for the wrong metaphysical formula which a better metaphysics have now superseded. The mathematical formula supplies a new lesson till then unheard of. The metaphysical but restores our confidence in the old lessons of common sense, old as human nature itself, and which we never had deserted, or in which we should never have lost our confidence, had not a perverse metaphysics arisen to disturb and darken it. Now that this service has been rendered, the sciences might be prosecuted with all vigor and effect, although the right and the wrong metaphysics were alike forgotten.

And, besides, it should not be forgotten that Bacon's Novum Organum is properly not a product of the mental philosophy after all. His main converse was with the outer world, with scarcely, if ever, a reflex look on the world that is within. A few pages, comparatively, says Mr. Morell, " would suffice to contain everything he wrote of a strictly metaphysical character."—(Vol. i., 79.) A pretty good evidence this of what can be achieved for science without the aid of that philosophy which claims to be the source of all and the regulator of all. It is worthy of all consideration, that, in contradistinction to those of Descartes, Bacon's views were chiefly of an objective character, and that upon them he constructed that method of philosophizing to which all the observational sciences are so indebted, not even excepting the science of mind itself. Surely if, at the commencement of that great epoch in the history of science, the mental philosophy had so little to do with it, we might well believe, that, after the stream of investigation had been turned and men were set on the right path, what had thus begun without the aid of metaphysics, could also without its aid be continued and carried forward.

But we must be done with these preliminary, and, as yet, very general observations, that we might address ourselves more closely to the work before us. We shall not attempt, however, even so much as an abstract of its multifarious contents ; nor will our space, though enlarged to the maximum allowance, permit of more, than, first, our account and estimate of the leading systems which are here made to pass before us, and, secondly, our estimate of Mr. Morell's own philosophy, as far as this can be gathered from his commentaries. In the execution of this twofold task, its distinct parts may not always stand separately out from each other, but be occasionally blended into one; and throughout there must be a strenuous effort for the utmost possible condensation, that some room might be left for our views of the present state and future prospects both of the philosophy and the faith in our own land—so far as these might be affected by the growing admiration and interest which are now felt in the teeming speculations of Germany.

And, surely, we might well presume, that for the intelligent British reader, it is not required that we should dilate on the sensational philosophy of Locke, or tell how it ripened into the scepticism of Berkeley, and afterwards into the more thorough and consistent scepticism of David Hume. Nor need we to dwell long on the "common sense" philosophy, distinctive of the Scottish school, and first constructed by Dr. Reid for the overthrow of that scepticism. Yet as our argument mainly turns on a comparison between his system and that of Kant, and this in order to a precise reckoning of the additions made by the latter to the former, as well as of the divergencies between them—we must bestow a few sentences at least upon our own countryman, ere we venture our account of him who might well be styled the great Coryphaeus of German transcendentalism.

The main principles of Dr. Reid's philosophy are shortly as follows:—The first to be singled out is his doctrine of *immediate perception*, in virtue of which we have the instant belief of an external reality, without the intervention of any image or any process between the percipient mind and the object that is perceived. This is a primary fact in the human constitution, of which we have the absolute assurance that so it is, although no account can be given of how it is. As being a first principle, he insists that no such account should be required of it; and that "it is not easy to say whether the authority of first principles is more hurt by the attempt to prove, or the attempt to overturn them: for such principles can stand secure only upon their own bottom; and to place them upon any other foundation than that of their intrinsic evidence, is in effect to overturn them." Or to take a sentence from Mr. Morell, "there is an absurdity in the very endeavor to prove a primary belief, which no reasoning on one side or the other can in any degree alter, much less overturn." There can be no doubt whatever that Dr. Reid's view of perception is just what we have stated,—though here and there in his writings there do occur expressions which are fitted to cast a certain obscuration over it. For example, we agree with our author in regretting that he should have called perception an act of the mind. It is no more an act of the mind than the sight of any visible thing before me is an act of the eye. Looking may be an act, but perceiving is not—for in the perception which comes by looking the mind is altogether passive—the result being an irresistible conviction of the existence of that which is perceived. Again, sensation is conjoined with perception; and as it was the confounding of these two which gave rise to all the scepticism that he labored to overthrow, the greatest and most strenuous effort of his philosophy is to discriminate between them. But then he should scarcely have said that sensation is the sign and perception of the thing signified—as if, in the business of perception, the mind had first to interpret the sign aright, and afterwards proceed to the thing signified. The mind does not look back upon itself ere it looks out on visible things; but instanter and at once it holds converse with these through the organs of sense; and what our author so well calls "the *immedi-*

atecy of our knowledge of the external world" is the unavoidable result of it.

Now, it is from our desire to keep this process clear and unencumbered, and because we would preserve for it all its own undoubted simplicity, that we demur to the proposed substitution of Mr. Morell, when, for Dr. Reid's account of perception, that it is altogether an act of the mind, he affirms that the very essence of perception consists in the felt relation between mind and matter. Now, there can be no relation felt between mind and matter at the time when the mind is not in thought. And what we affirm is, that matter might be perceived, and with the strongest sense and conviction in the mind of its reality, when the mind itself is altogether out of the reckoning, or when no reflex view is taken of mind at all. In childhood, when most assuredly there is the strongest possible conviction of the reality of external things, there is then a direct view taken of objects, *and nothing more.* The mind does not take cognizance, or any reflex view at all of itself. Even Fichte, or Morell for him, can tell us that "the mind, however, is at first unconcious of its real movements; it is entirely sunk in its own involuntary representations, as though they were external objects; its whole being is altogether of the spontaneous* kind; it is yet only potentially that, which it may afterwards by reflection become actually."—(*Morell*, ii., 81.) Such, then, is the state of perception and belief in childhood. It is perception alone, and without reflection, which has all to do with it. Our views, then, are wholly objective; and surely Mr. Morell will not affirm that the ground on which in childhood we believe the reality of external things is not the very ground on which we believe the same in manhood. Surely there is not one ground for this belief in childhood, and another ground for it in manhood. Now, it would clear off many perplexities from this argument were it once admitted, that in the business of perception the mind's regards are altogether objective. It is not more necessary to be conscious of the mind in the business of perceiving, than to be conscious of the eye in the business of seeing; or the consciousness of mind is as little an ingredient of perception as the consciousness of the eye is an ingredient of sight. Doubtless, the mind itself is indispensable to perception, just as it is to all its other functions; but it follows not that our knowledge of the mind, or any reflex view of it, is therefore indispensable. We can perceive without thinking of the mind, as we can see without thinking of the eye. There lies a subtle misunderstanding in that we confound the mind itself with our thought or our

* The reader is requested to bear in mind this admission of the German philosopher, that there is a period of our mental history anterior to reflection or to the cognizance which the mind takes of its own operations, when nevertheless it has the strongest possible faith in the objective reality of sensible things; as on this undoubted truth a most important conclusion will be found to depend.

knowledge of the mind ; and the consequence has been, that undue mixing up of the subjective with the objective in which chiefly it is that the erratic movements of the German philosophy have taken rise.

But notwithstanding this preliminary difference between our author and ourselves, we feel quite sure he will agree with us, in that whatever be the inaccuracies of language into which Dr. Reid may have fallen, we have not overstated his real principle and meaning in regard to the perfect simplicity and immediateness of that one step, *and only one*, by which, through our organs of sense, we come at our belief in the reality of external things. But this is only one part of his "common sense" philosophy. It recognizes other original principles in the constitution of the mind besides the one now specified, and by which we believe in the reality of things sensible. There are other things besides these, for example things necessary and immutable, of which he says that "although not immediate objects of perception, they may be immediate objects of other powers of the mind." He further says, "that it were impossible to derive some of our most important ideas from sensation and reflection, as Mr. Locke has defined them;" and that by our understanding, that is by our judging and reasoning powers, we are furnished with many simple and original notions. Again, that we have other ideas than those of sensation or reflection, in the confined sense which Mr. Locke ascribes to it, which other ideas are present to the mind when it defines, when it distinguishes, when it judges, when it reasons, *whether about things material or intellectual;* and that by these powers our minds are furnished, not only with many simple and original notions, but with all our notions which are accurate and well defined, and which alone are the proper materials of reasoning—none of these being notions of the objects of sense, or notions of the operations of our own minds; in other words, they are furnished to the mind in another way than by faculties of external or internal observation. He did not share in the error of Dr. Ferguson, that human knowledge is confined entirely to the observation of facts, and to the deduction from these of general rules; but denied that experience or observation is the only source from which truth can be derived, and pointed out the existence of certain intellectual and necessary judgments beyond the bounds of all experience. We might here state some of the ideas which do not come to us through the medium of sensation—as the ideas of space, of time, of casualty, of personal identity, of substance, of good and evil—to which last or moral ideas, we should add those ideas of quantity and number which form the materials of all abstract mathematical reasoning. These ideas do not take their origin in the observational faculties, neither are our notions or beliefs regarding them derived from experience

Now, for comparing the Scottish and German philosophies whether as it respects their similarities or their differences, it is of importance to mark how far these primary beliefs of Dr. Reid are at one with the primitive judgments of Kant, or with his forms of the understanding. They may have been better named by the latter of these two philosophers—he may have probed more deeply into their foundations, or rather, perhaps, into their methods of development—he may have constructed a fuller and more accurate list of them; and without pronouncing on his scheme for their application, or by which he would bring his categories to bear on the objects of the external world, it might be fully conceded, that altogether he has enlarged, and in some respects amended, the philosophy of Dr. Reid. Yet let us not, because of the altered nomenclature or the new garb that has been thrown over them, let us not overlook the substantial identity, and that in the most important respect of all, between the principles of the Scottish school, and those from which Kant has earned his chief reputation. The great step, in fact, for our deliverance from the sensationalism of Locke, and the consequent scepticism of Berkeley and Hume, was first taken in this country—and this by the establishment of the doctrine, that the senses were not the only inlets of our knowledge; but that there were other and higher principles of belief bound up with the interior conditions and structure of the mind itself, and existing apart from or anterior to all experience, although it may have been experience which at first evolved them. It forms a main peculiarity of Dr. Reid's system, that the intellect has notions and beliefs from within itself and not derived from converse with the outer world; although in coming forth to hold such converse, it may, in virtue of these its inherent principles and powers, be enabled to arrange and systemize, and to apprehend many relations not cognizable by the senses, and yet between objects which are presented by the senses to its contemplation. On this subject we can perceive no originality in Kant, and this notwithstanding the distinction which he makes between the *matter* of our knowledge and the *form* of it—the one supplied to us by the sensitive faculty, and the other by the understanding. It is true that he did make a wide and most important deviation, but such a deviation as led the speculative world back again to that abyss of scepticism from which Reid had delivered the previous generation. Had Kant kept closer by the Scottish philosophy, or made a further extension of its principles, it would have prevented all that is sceptical or pyrrhonic in those numerous systems of Germany, to which his own philosophy has given birth.

And here we must be permitted to make use of Dr. Reid's own homely, though it may be not very academic phraseology, and scarcely recognized nowadays as the language of men of science. It did the required service, notwithstanding; and what was of avail then against the pyrrhonism of Britain, should, in our humble estimation, be of like avail now against the pyrrhonism of Germany.

In the impression made by external objects upon the mind, he distinguished two things—the sensation and the perception, by which latter faculty it is that we have an immediate and irresistible conviction of the reality of these objects. And, in proceeding to the other fundamental laws of human belief, which are tantamount to the primitive judgments of Kant, he also distinguished between two things, the notion and the belief. Had these judgments been but notions, and nothing else, then would he have dealt with them just as he did with the mere sensations, viewed them but as mental phenomena, and looked no further. But if, besides being notions, they are also beliefs, then, though when regarded only as acts of belief, they are but mental phenomena, and nothing more, yet, as every belief implies an object, a something that is believed—he carried forward his contemplation to these objects, and under that law of belief which he himself promulgated, he could not do otherwise than treat them as realities. And most assuredly, in thus treating them, he did no more than what all men from the beginning of the world had done before him. Dr. Reid may have been the first to proclaim the law; but most assuredly he did not make it, nor did his proclamation of it tend at all to its enforcement, or add in the least to its practical authority—for this law of man's primary beliefs is as old as the species, and has been most faithfully and implicitly acted upon throughout all its generations. Kant, on the other hand, though he calls them judgments, yet treats them but as notions—for, judgments though they be, the things judged of are no things at all, or but mere nothings in his estimation. As mere noumena, the mind is their only domicile; and certainly if they were but notions or conceptions, we should, in studying or holding converse with them, keep within the mind as their proper and only home. But as they are beliefs, we must be permitted to go in quest of the things that are believed; and then with some of them, at least, we shall find ourselves carried forth from the subjective region of the noumena within to the objective region of the phenomena around us. The beliefs have their occupancy in the former; but the things believed have their occupancy, their *locum standi*, their verification and their being in the latter of these two regions.

It is difficult in few words to make the leading principle of Kant intelligible to the reader who may not yet have studied him. But let us attempt this as briefly as we may. He assigns two fundamental sources for our knowledge—the senses and the understanding. By the former, we receive impressions from the phenomena of the outer world, such, perhaps, as an inferior animal receives who may have no higher faculty than the senses alone.

By the latter we are enabled to think of these phenomena, and so to view them in certain lights, or according to certain relations, and hence to invest them with certain properties of which the inferior animals have no idea. In the performance of this office, it proceeds according to certain laws termed by Kant *forms of the understanding*, whence issue its own *primitive judgments* of the crude material that has been furnished by the senses; which judgments are not derived from the experience, but are given forth by the understanding itself in virtue of the constitution which inherently and originally belongs to it. It is by the senses that we receive our *intuitions* of outward objects. It is by the understanding that we receive our *conceptions* regarding them.

But perhaps we cannot do better than present the reader with the following extract from Kant himself:—

"Of these two faculties, the one is not to be preferred to the other. Without the sensational faculty (*la sensibilité*) no object would be given to us; without the understanding, none would be thought. The thoughts without material (without matter) are void. Intuitions without conceptions are blind. Therefore, it is altogether as necessary to make our conceptions sensible (that is, to apply them to the objects which intuition furnishes), as it is to make our intuitions intelligible (that is, to bring them under our conceptions). These two powers or capacities cannot exchange their functions. The understanding cannot seize intuitively on anything, and the senses cannot think anything. It is only from their union that cognition arises. But we must not confound their respective places, but ought, if we would abide in the truth, to distinguish them carefully."—*Critic of Pure Reason.*

Now, we are quite willing to acquiesce in this distinction. Let our senses be held as the organs by which we admit from without those phenomena that constitute the rude and unshaped material of our notions; and let the understanding be held as the seat of the notions, or primitive judgments, as they are termed by Kant, and which he draws out into so many categories. But we are not willing to admit that these judgments or categories are altogether subjective, so as to have no counterpart realities in the outer world—or that they "never can be allowed to make good any kind of objective knowledge whatever" (*Morell*, i., 215)—or, as Cousin expresses it in his account of the Kantian philosophy, that the intuitions of sense represent objects, but that the conceptions of the understanding represent nothing. Now, it is here where the pyrrhoism of Kant begins, and it is here that we would take our stand against him. Without the understanding, we might not have been able to form a notion of unity, the first of his categories. But present me with a single object, as with the sole tree in a field, and I am just as sure of there being one tree there, and only one, as of there being a tree at all. Or let there be four trees, so as to exhibit a plurality—the second of his categories—and I am just as sure of the objects being really four, though without the understanding I never could have counted them, as the senses have made me sure of the objects themselves. Or let my attention be directed to a stone of enormous size and weight, and in which I am led by my understanding to conceive both an accident and a substance—the seventh of his categories—I do more than conceive of these; I believe that outside of me there lies a body having the objective reality of great heaviness, and of a substratum withal or a matter that sustains this property and all the others which belong to it. Or, lastly, and to make use of his own example, let me fall in with the body of a murdered man, then, by his eighth category of cause and effect, the murder will instantly suggest the *notion* of a murderer. But it will do more than this. It will as instantly and powerfully suggest the *conviction* of a murderer; and this causality, which he would represent as having no other *locale* than in the mind, or as being merely a law of human thought, we, and every man else on the face of the earth, believe as firmly as in our own existence, to have had its *locale* in the outer world,—or, in other words, that the relation of cause and effect between these two objects, the murderer and the murdered, have had as sure place and fulfilment, not within us but without us, on the spot where the deed was perpetrated, as the objects themselves have.

We are told by Cousin that the great reform of mental science in the eighteenth century, which began in Scotland, was afterwards taken up in Germany, and in the hands of Kant was mightily extended. But the truth is, that if Kant had made a fuller surrender of himself to our Scottish philosophy, it would have saved him from his worst and greatest error. It is true that, in partial concurrence with Dr. Reid, he did make surrender of that pyrrhonism which Hume and Berkeley had before planted in our organs of sense, these outworks, as it were, of the mental constitution. But it was only to carry with him this pyrrhonism entire to the citadel of the intellect, for its expulsion from whence a new battle must be fought—a battle to which both Morell, and even Cousin himself, give a somewhat uncertain sound. It is our confident persuasion that the full and conclusive victory can be effected in no other way than by calling in the aid of our common sense philosophy, when all it will have to do is just to fight its old battle over again. It was the assertion of the fundamental laws of human belief which cleared away idealism from the region of the senses, and it is only the reassertion of these that can clear it away from the higher region of the understanding. Meanwhile, a certain crude material of things which, though only termed phenomena, are admitted to be real, with a curious investiture of properties and forms affirmed to be unreal—this is all which, at the hands of the Kantian philosophy, we have for a universe.

But there is another distinction made between these two. The sensational faculty (*la sensibilité*) is viewed as altogether passive: and this passiveness is termed its receptivity. It receives its impressions from phenomena without; and the representations given of these, called also intuitions, are held to be pure results of the manner in which it has been affected by the phenomena. Whereas the understanding is said to be a faculty of which the development is spontaneous. The one is deemed to be a capacity, the other a power. If the former be a receiver, the latter is spoken of as a giver—"as giving form and figure to the material furnished by sensation." (*Morell*, i., 208.) Now we are quite willing to admit, that, while it is only by the *intuitions* of sense we come into converse with phenomena at all, we could not without the *conceptions* of the understanding apprehend the relations of the phenomena to each other, or the various forms and categories which we attach to them. But we insist that when looking outward on any scene of contemplation, the relations and forms suggested by things within our view are something more than objects of conception. They are objects of belief—a belief, the acts of which have their standing-places in the mind, but the objects of which have their standing-place in the scene that is before us. The understanding is said to be a formal and regulative faculty. But we do not go forth to form and to regulate. The forms and regularities are previously there; and the understanding so constituted as to have the power of recognizing them, regards them as so many objective realities. This "truth-organ within the human soul" (*Morell*, ii., 508) is just as little creative and as much receptive as are the organs of sense. It is true, that we can direct the understanding by our power of attention, just as we can direct the eye by our power of looking. But the view taken by the one is as much a result from the state of things without as is the view impressed upon the other, and the beliefs to which it leads stand as little in need of being verified by any logical or philosophical deduction whatever. It is of importance to guard and limit the expressions which the disciples and admirers of Kant are so apt to fall into. For example, the understanding is spoken of as being, in contradistinction to the senses, an active and *constructive* faculty; and the *constructions* that have been attempted under this idea of it are among the worst extravagances of German speculation. The will, too, has been vested with such a command over this constructive intellect, that in framing their schemes of universe, it might well be said of Schelling and others—that they construct *at pleasure*. And even those of them who are not disposed to take any flight beyond the actual stable objective universe in which they find themselves, will still speak of it, not as being a goodly and well-ordered system in itself, but rather as a chaos of shapeless and crude phenomena, without form and void, which the senses, these organs of the outer man, have gathered from this rude and primitive outfield and got within their hold—thence to be taken up as raw material into the manufactory of the intellect, by whose powers and primitive judgments it is that they are put in order and elaborated into a sort of painting or panorama, or phantasmagoria of their own making.

But returning to Kant, as being a disciple at first of the Leibnitzian-Wolfian school of philosophy, it is to be expected of his own philosophy that we might there discern the traces of his descent from his old and illustrious master. Every one knows the celebrated aphorism cited by Locke in a letter to Leibnitz,—"Nihil est in intellectu quod non prius in sensu:" and of the no less celebrated addition which Leibnitz made to it, when, in his reply to the English philosopher, he returned it in this extended form,—"Nihil est in intellectu quod non prius in sensu, *nisi intellectus ipse*." There is much truth in the saying of Madame de Staël—"From this principle is derived all that new philosophy which exercises so much influence over the mind of Germany." But the question is, have they made a legitimate derivation from it?

What is true of the intellect being in the intellect, must be also true of all its contents. Let us grant that the primitive judgments of Kant form part of these contents; and our former question recurs, whether are these judgments but conceptions, or are they beliefs? It were a false psychology which should give a wrong deliverance upon this question. If they are really beliefs, and yet are proceeded with as if they were only conceptions, this were a misunderstanding of the actual state of our mental phenomena. If but conceptions, then are they wholly subjective, nor can we find any valid outlet from these to things objective, or to an objective world. But if they are beliefs, then when viewed only as acts of belief are they subjective also. But the question remains—if beliefs, what are the objects of belief, what are the things believed? And should these things be external to the mind, or apart from the mind—then is there thus and at once opened up a ready channel from the subjective to the objective; and on this consideration alone should we contend for the objective reality of unity, and plurality, and causation, and substance, nay, even of space and time—all of which things Kant has doomed to perpetual imprisonment within the chambers of the human intellect. The consideration now stated may be repudiated as too plain, and all the more so, that it is couched in the homely and common-sense phraseology of Dr. Reid. Nevertheless, it is the very consideration on which the scepticism of his day was put to flight, and the reality of an external world was again admitted into the creed of philosophers; and as it was of avail then in making valid the testimony of the senses, it should be of equal avail now in making valid the testimony of the intellect. There seems no alternative between the admission of both and the rejection of both; and if space, and time, and causation, and substance, and number, and the relations of quantity, merely because taken cognizance of by the mind in another way, are to be deprived of all objective reality, then we see not how the outward phenomena should be permitted to retain theirs; or how a greater deference should be rendered to the voice of the senses than to the voice of the higher faculties. It does seem a marvellous inconsistency on the part of Kant, that he should thus have admitted a counterpart reality over against the impressions made upon the senses, and allowed of no such counterpart to the conceptions of the understanding. Had these been conceptions alone, we could have understood and have agreed with him; but ranking, as they do, among our original and indestructible beliefs, we cannot but charge him with a scepticism in every way as inveterate as has ever been exemplified in the history of human speculation. We might as well have the old and entire scepticism of David Hume back again—for certain it is that by some such grievous mismanagement in his demonstration as Cuvier has charged him with, has Kant both sanctioned and given rise to the worst excesses of those who followed in his train.

But even Fichte himself, among the first and most distinguished of these followers, will bear us out, in the principle at least of what we are contending for, even that there can be no belief without an object. In the transition which he made from his first to his second philosophy, the following is stated to have been the process of thought by which he arrived at it:

> "Allow that our free activity represents certain notions to itself, there must be, thought Fichte, something which is represented. Mere knowing can be nothing, unless there is something which is known; mere thinking can be nothing, unless there is something which is thought; and mere perception can be nothing, unless there is something which is perceived. To make our subjective activity in the act of knowing, perceiving, &c., *the absolute*, is to suppose that the only reality in the universe is a perceiving which perceives nothing, a thinking which thinks nothing, a knowing which knows nothing."—Vol. ii., p. 93.

After this we might well admit the principle of Leibnitz, that the intellect itself, with all its contents of course, is in the intellect. But if there are beliefs there, and the objects of these beliefs be things out of the intellect, it is surely competent for us to entertain these things; and, in obedience to our own mental constitution, whose prompt and powerful biddings should be heard, nay, and will be heard above all the voices of all the philosophers, it is alike competent for us to believe them. Let us then go forth of the intellect, and hold our believing converse with the things outside, which Nature thus tells us to be so many realities. The transition from the subjective to the objective, is by a way open to all men, notwithstanding the manifold attempts of speculators to obstruct and to darken it.

But on this subject we have met with nothing more satisfactory than the following pregnant sentences from M. Cousin, when defending himself against the attacks of Schelling, who is disdainful of psychology, and affirms that it cannot conduct to the knowledge of real objects or to existences, for that this were stepping beyond its only province, the province of consciousness, and all which is in the consciousness is purely subjective. Cousin, on the other hand, holds that there is a faculty within us, by which we take direct knowledge of truth, and not only of necessary and universal principles, but of real objects and existences; and, like other continental writers, he denominated this the faculty of *reason*. Let us acquiesce for the time being in this phraseology, and we shall understand the force of the questions which he puts to Schelling in the introduction to his History of Moral Philosophy: "Is this faculty of reason less legitimate because it falls under the eye of consciousness? And who has demonstrated that consciousness not only looks upon that which it sees, but has the astonishing property of metamorphosing it by this its magical look, and so as to impose upon it its own nature?" Again, "Reason is not struck with impotency because it acts under the eye of consciousness. It does not for that change its nature. It does not lose the divine force which is in it, and the wings which have been given to it to attain to [the knowledge of] beings, and so rise even to Him from whom it emanates. Consciousness attests this magnificent development of reason—it does not, however, make the development, nor does it belong to it to alter the character thereof." We do hope that our reader enters into these replies. Consciousness might depone to the fact, that there are certain knowing faculties in the mind; but it does not, therefore, usurp the office of these faculties, which surely, on the other hand, do not lose the power of doing their own work merely because consciousness is looking on, or has set his eyes upon them. Or, turning back to the plain language of Dr. Reid, consciousness tells us of certain beliefs in the mind. But if we will only distinguish, like our own common-sense philosopher, between the acts of belief, and the objects of belief, we should be at no loss to understand what it is that consciousness does in this matter, and what it is that is done by our other faculties. The act of belief is a subjective thing; and it is for the consciousness to take cognizance thereof, as this is the faculty which has to do with things subjective. The object of belief or thing believed may be out of the mind, and therefore an objective thing—and so taken cognizance of not directly by the consciousness, but left to be taken cognizance of by its own distinct and proper faculty. Consciousness is itself a knowing faculty, and its office is to tell us what is in the mind; and therefore what the other knowing faculties of the mind are. But it deals not with the objects of these faculties—for then would the censure of M. Schelling hold good, that it was stepping beyond its province. It therefore deals not with the object of these other faculties, but leaves the charge and cognizance of them respectively to the faculties themselves. We humbly think that had

Morell, and even Cousin himself, at all times kept this distinction in view, it would have saved certain misapprehensions or misstatements into which both of them have fallen. The above extracts, however, from Cousin, give the clearest possible view of the distinct provinces of consciousness and reason; or, speaking more generally, of the distinction that obtains between the reflex view which consciousness takes of the faculties, and the direct working of the faculties themselves.

After this we do not see where the difficulty lies of a transition from the subjective to the objective, or how it is that either Cousin or Morell should make such a work about it. If consciousness depone to a certain primary and original belief, what more have we to do than to give ourselves up to it, and follow its guidance over that outer domain or department of truth which belongs to it? Or if consciousness depone to the existence and the workings of a certain faculty—call it reason or perception—what more have we to do than just to learn of that faculty the informations which it gives?—authoritative informations they of course will be, and such as should carry the belief of the whole human race along with them, seeing that they are dictated by the resistless and fundamental laws of the human understanding. Once that the way is opened up between a sound psychology and a sound ontology, or rather between psychology and all the objective sciences, let us walk on that way with confident footstep, and not still be groping for it—not still be lying at the foundation, instead of going on unto perfection. But one or two extracts from Morell must be presented to the reader ere the conclusion can be fully made out that we want to impress upon him.

In his Critique on James Mill, one of the ablest in the work, we have the following important passage:—

"Now we believe that a thorough analysis of the case shows, that *reason* has as much right to assure us of the nature and existence of being or substance, as perception has to assure us of the phenomena that we term qualities; that just in the same manner as we have an inward intuition of the one by the senses, so we have an inward intuition of the other by the reason. The cognizance of attributes by perception is as much a *subjective process*, as much a part of my inward consciousness, as is the cognizance of matter or substance by the reason; and if we deny the validity of the latter, there is no superior evidence why we should accept that of the former. As well may we, in fact, reject the quality itself as an objective phenomenon, as the substratum in which it adheres. We know the *properties* of the external world, says our author, because we have sensations which convey them. But what are sensations except states of mind? If a state of mind termed *sensation* can give us the knowledge of properties, why may not a state of mind termed intuition or reason give us the knowledge of substance? *Reason has as much right to take us out of ourselves as perception, and if the one cannot assert objective validity, neither can the other.* There is no valid medium, therefore, as it seems to us, between complete subjective idealism, like that of Fichte, on the one side, and the admission of ontology as a proper branch of scientific investigation on the other."—Vol. i., p. 328.

The sentence marked by ourselves in italics forms with us an all-sufficient, and indeed the only refutation against the scepticism of Kant and his followers. It is identical with the refutation of Dr. Reid against the scepticism of David Hume, and by which he vindicated, not the objective reality alone of sensible things, taken cognizance of by the faculty of perception, but of things intellectual, which are taken cognizance of by other and higher faculties. It is true that Reid had not learned to refer these latter judgments to the one faculty of reason, as Kant and Cousin do. But practically there is a full agreement between him and the latter of these two philosophers—although the former of them, in differing from Reid, and because misled by his own exclusive tendencies to the subjective, fell into a sad aberration, to the grievous and irreparable damage both of his own philosophy and that of those who succeeded him. The reader will not fail to observe, that while, in the above extract from Morell, he assigns to perception, as distinct from reason, the office of assuring us of the reality of phenomena, it would appear, from our brief extracts of Cousin, that with him it is the office of reason to assure us of all reality whatever. This, to the vast majority of British readers, is an unwonted application of the term, nor would they at once understand by "reason" any other than the faculty of reasoning. But reason, by the new classification or new nomenclature, is now understood to be the faculty of a direct and immediate apperception of existences, whether it be of our own existence, or that of things apart from ourselves. Reason, therefore, differs from reasoning or "*la raison*" from "*le raisonnement.*"

But ere we proceed further, we must present another extract from Dr. Morell, taken from his estimate of Dr. Reid:—

"We cannot but regard it, however, as unfortunate, that Reid should have framed his idea of mental philosophy so completely upon the model of the natural sciences, that he should have determined to confine it within the narrow limits of psychology, and attempt nothing beyond the mere classification of phenomena. The psychological *method*, which he followed, we regard as excellent, nay, as the only true one, since it is absolutely necessary to determine the power and validity of the instrument by which all our knowledge is acquired, before we define what that knowledge is, and to what extent it can reach. But is it necessary to pause, when we have classified the various mental phenomena which every day's experience gives us, and altogether interdict any further advancement? True it is, that we are able to *perceive* nothing beyond phenomena, but are we on that account to neglect the deductions of reason, the loftiest of our faculties, when it would lead into the region of existence itself? Whether we will or not, we *must* allow some ontological conclusions, inasmuch as we cannot conceive of the attributes either of matter or mind, without the notion of a substance in which they adhere. As far as experience goes, it would be quite sufficient to call a material object a cluster of qualities, or to denominate mind a combination of powers, but reason does not allow us to stop until we have added a substratum to which both qualities and powers belong. If all the pure and legitimate deductions of our reason are included in the idea of psychology, we are content to confine philosophy within its limits; but if not, then we contend for a science of ontology, that has for its matter all that belongs to the essence of man, of the universe, and of God, viewing them as objective realities, whose existence we never could assume from the mere observation of phenomena, could never deduce by logical processes, but which we draw as the necessary conclusions of our higher reason. In this way we should be led into a loftier region of thought, to a kind of *prima philosophia*, where the sciences of mind, of matter, and of Deity, all unite in one."—Vol. i., pp. 239, 240.

The charge which he here prefers against the Scottish school, and which both Kant and Cousin had made before him, is repeated in various other passages, as, when speaking of those who follow the psychological method, he says that "they give us, for the most part, a valid philosophy, but too often a shallow one." Again—"Scotland, true to its principles of 'common sense,' has insisted on the validity of those ideas which appear to be the natural product of the human reason, and resisted every attempt to resolve them into sensational elements ; and Germany, boldly grappling with the deepest questions of ontology, has drawn a broad distinction between the phenomenal world, as viewed by the senses, and the real world, as comprehended by the intellect." Lastly—"The English and Scottish writers generally interdict the ontological branch of philosophy, as lying beyond the reach of our faculties. Intellectual science with them is confined, for the most part, to psychology, that is, to the analysis and classification of our mental phenomena." We beg that our readers will re-peruse both the paragraphs and the sentences that we have now taken from Morell, that they might better understand wherein it is that we agree, and wherein we differ with him, and not with him only, but with the continental philosophy in general, as contrasted with our own.

First, then, we most cordially unite with Mr. Morell in affirming the as great objective reality of those things which the reason takes cognizance of, as of those which are taken cognizance of by the senses. Let us take but one instance—the moon and the high water, both of which we do see. We believe in the objective reality of both these phenomena ; but we believe, also, in the objective reality of that vinculum which we do not see, and which binds them together in the relation of cause and effect. We have read nothing more masterly or decisive than the utter overthrow by Cousin of the sceptical metaphysics of Kant.

But, *secondly*, we do not agree with Mr. Morell in the censure which he passes on the Scottish philosophers of mind, because that, after having demonstrated the objective reality of certain things that came under its judgment, they did not go out upon these things, in order to philosophize on their nature and properties. Would he have had them, for example, after having vindicated the reality of a sensible and external world, would he have had them to enter on the respective walks of investigation whereof it is the theatre—on chemistry, or natural history, or natural philosophy? Their own proper science makes no such requisitions as these, and as little does it call for a science of ontology at their hands. The study of the knowing faculties is altogether distinct from the study of the things to be known by them; and to complain of the mental philosopher because he has not gone forth beyond the limits of his own domain, is just as irrational as to complain of him who has constructed a telescope, that he has not also constructed a treatise on astronomy. Our complaint of the Scottish savans and professors is exactly the reverse of that which our author has preferred against them—even that they mix up too much of psychology with the treatment of their respective sciences. We will not even exempt the chairs of logic and ethics, as generally conducted, from this condemnation; for however cognate these sciences might be reckoned to the science of mind, it is one thing to tell what be its phenomena and laws, and another to tell what be the principles and methods, whether of good reasoning or good morals. It is not that we undervalue mental sience. So far from this, we would assign for it a separate chair, where might be expounded the principles and processes of the human mind, and, amongst these, the fundamental laws of human belief—to which laws the other professors might refer when thrown back upon them at such times as scepticism might choose to question the first principles of any of their sciences. When the informations of the telescope are questioned, we are necessitated to explain the properties and vindicate the power of the instrument—after which we look not *to* the teloscope, but *through* it and *from* it to the planets; and then we should never think of mixing up any demonstration of the eye and object glasses of the telescope with our demonstration of the satellites and rings of Saturn. We, to this extent, keep the two subjects, or the two sciences of optics and astronomy, clear of each other; and it had been well if, to the same extent, the mental psychology had been kept clear of all those studies which, as directed to objects distinct from the mind, might be classed under the general appellation of the objective sciences. We as little think of the mind when engaged in the prosecution of any of these sciences, as the astronomer thinks of his telescope when looking through it on the phenomena of the heavens. The Scottish philosophers did well in confining themselves to their own proper and self-prescribed task, the description or demonstration of the human mind; and in stopping where they did, they evince a more enlightened discernment than our author, of the limits and landmarks which separate the various provinces in the territory of human thought.

But Mr. Morell has no quarrel with them because they did not go forth upon any of the domains of physical science. His charge against them is that they did not go forth on the science of ontology. Now if they were right in refraining from the former, we hold them pre-eminently right in not venturing one footstep upon the latter. We feel equally sure as our author of the *existence* of a substratum for both mind and matter, and by which their respective phenomena are sustained; but when he tells us of his as great certainty as to the *nature* of it, then we must frankly avow, that we have no more faith in an ontology grounded upon such a basis, than we have in the ontology, altogether monstrous though it be, of Schelling, whose intellectual intuition into the mysteries of being is just as worthy of our confidence, as is the reason of Kant, when coupled with the illegitimate extension to which it has been carried hy his followers.

But this review is lengthening on our hands. We are not getting fast enough on in this fragmental way of it. Our prescribed limits make it imperative that we should dwell no longer on the separate portions of the work before us. We must therefore proceed instanter to the summing up—to the judgment, leaving the grounds of the judgment to be gathered by the readers of these volumes. At this rate we must omit for the present most of what we at first contemplated, in the hope, however, of other opportunities. Meanwhile let us limit ourselves to such generalizations as shall best enable us, in briefest space, to pronounce between our own home philosophy and that of the continent.

In what remains then, and before our final reckoning with Mr. Morell himself, we shall have chiefly to deal with the French philosopher Cousin, whom indeed Mr. Morell may be said to have constituted the arbiter amongst the various systems and speculations which are made to pass before us in his historical review. He could not have fixed on an abler or more accomplished critic of all bygone philosophy in modern times. Warm from our admiration of that masterly analysis by which, in his sixth lesson on the philosophy of Kant, he lays bare the turning-point on which this great thinker descends into the abyss of scepticism, and also of his eloquent advocacy for the prerogatives of common sense, even as interpreted and acted on by the humblest of our species*—we feel it difficult to speak with all that freedom which still his own errors, as they appear to us, would require and justify. But to this we are encouraged by his noble declaration, when to vindicate his treatment of Kant, he tells us that he shall ever prefer common sense to genius, and the general mind, or mind of the whole world, to that of any man whatever.

Cousin, then, founder of the eclectic school in France, fully admits—nay, in his strictures on Kant, argues with the utmost ability and address, the distinction between what he terms the spontaneous and the reflex exercises of the human understanding.

* See his "Leçons sur la Philosophie de Kant, 1844."—P. 150. This work is the fittest bridgeway of communication that we happen to know, for an ordinary British reader, to all which might heretofore have seemed obscure and inaccessible to his eyes in the transcendentalism of Germany—clearing up in it all that is unintelligible, and thereby disarming it of all that is formidable—for even in the walks of high Philosophy, as well as of superstition, will it often be found that ignorance is the mother of devotion.

We have long been in the habit of recognizing these under the title of the mind's direct and reflect processes, and we shall continue so to name them. Now as Fichte affirms in a previous extract, and as Cousin repeatedly affirms in the best and ablest of his passages, the direct is anterior to the reflex. In other words, the mind's first and earliest converse is not with itself, but with things exterior to and apart from itself. Such is the order of nature, that invariably, in nature's education of all spirits, the objective precedes the subjective. During the first years of its tuition in the school of nature, the life of the mind may be said to be a life of objectivity all over. It is wholly taken up with outward things; and it is when thus engaged, that almost all its primary beliefs are formed—its belief in the reality of space and time—its belief in the reality of sensible objects, and not only of material phenomena, but of the material substratum which upholds them—its belief in those likenesses, whether among objects or events, by which it is afterwards enabled to generalize them either into the classes of natural history or the laws of natural philosophy; and, to add no more, its belief in that pervading causality which binds together every event in nature with something prior that went before, with something posterior which comes after it. These beliefs are felt and familiar beliefs—are the universal inmates of every bosom; and took up their firm occupancy there, while the mind was exclusively employed in looking forth of itself among outward things, and long before it cast any inward regard on its own contents or its own processes.

Let it not be imagined, from our representation of the matter, or from the view that we are now giving of the state of the case, let it not be imagined that we are lapsing into the sensationalism of Locke, or setting aside the primitive judgments of Kant. The child who has struck the table with its spoon, and elicited a noise, and then strikes again with a firm expectation of the same noise, is the subject alike of the sensation spoken of by the one philosopher, and of the judgment spoken of by the other. It has the experience of both; and in connection with the first, or with the sensation, it believes in the reality of the spoon and of the table, and also of the noise; while, in virtue of the second, or of the judgment, it as firmly believes, that when it makes the like stroke as before, a like noise will ensue from it. In other words, it assigns the same outward and objective reality to the causation that it does to the visible objects, whether of sight or of hearing, wherewith it is occupied. And why is it that Kant should assign these things differently? How comes he to believe in the reality of those phenomena which his senses tell him of, and not also to believe in the objective reality of that causation which binds them together, and which his judgment tells him of? Is it because the one is further in than the other—the organs of these primitive judgments of his, than the organs of sight or hearing—is it because of this, that he takes the report of the senses on things without while he rejects all the informations of the understanding or the reason, save only on things subjective and ideal, and wholly within the mind. This is too ridiculous. Both are alike receptive of truth from without. Nature strongly teaches the same confident reliance on the testimony of the sentinels at the gate, and on that of the informants who fill the station of waiters in the inner chambers of the mind. And this appeal to the original and imprescriptible beliefs of humanity forms our great, indeed our only, defence against the scepticism of Berkeley, or Hume, or Kant, or in whatever form, at the hands of other philosophers, or other fashions of philosophy, it may afterwards assume.

Now, it is on the strength of these very considerations, or the authority of our direct and primary judgments, *and these given forth anterior to any reflex view that we take of them*, that Cousin argues, with the most consummate ability and address, against the scepticism of Kant, when he denies the objective reality of space and time, and of his various categories of the understanding. But there is still another consideration which, with all deference to his fine intelligence, we should like him to ponder well and to apply, and for which we crave a close attention from our readers. This priority of the direct to the reflex holds true, not only in respect to the different stages of human life—the childhood and youth of the understanding being chiefly taken up with things of objective contemplation, and not being till its manhood, when the faculty of consciousness is fully developed, that it can best take account of its own processes. But, over and above this, it were better for the mental analyst, even to his latest days, if, ere he entered on those reflex processes by which he is led to his various doctrines, and it may be discoveries, he were beforehand and frequently to describe (*parcourir*) or run over the direct processes which correspond to them. The truth is, that though it be only by looking inwardly, or looking back upon ourselves, that we take cognizance of our various beliefs, these beliefs must be formed, so as to exist, ere they can be recognized or reflected on. But on what ground is it that they are formed? or how is the mind employed when these beliefs arise in it? Not, most certainly, in looking inwardly upon itself, save when it is making a study of its own processes; for in every other science but that of mind do the beliefs proper to them arise in the act of looking to and dwelling upon the subject-matter of these sciences. To get at our mathematical beliefs, we do not look inwardly to the mind, but outwardly to the diagrams of geometry, or to the signs, with their things signified, of the analytical calculus. For our experimental beliefs, at least in things material, we look outwardly and not inwardly. Even in logic, it is not by the study of any inscriptions on the tablet of our nature, that we settle the distinctions between good and bad reasoning. And, to add no more, in theology, although the constitution of the mind, with its adaptation to the surrounding world, forms one of our most illustrious evidences for a God, yet, if there be, as many contend, a direct apperception by us of the Supreme Creator, it were in the act of looking upwardly and objectively to Himself that we should seize upon it, and not by going in quest of it among the recesses of our own psychology. And yet this is the very quarter in which Cousin tells us that he has found it. The following is an extract from one of Cousin's works, as given by Morell:

"'It is by *observation* (he remarks), that with the penetralia of the consciousness, and at a depth to which Kant never descended, under the apparent relativeness and subjectivity of necessary principles, I have succeeded in seizing and analyzing the instantaneous, but veritable fact of the spontaneous apperception of truth, an apperception which, not immediately reflecting itself, passes unperceived in the depths of the consciousness; yet is the real basis of that, which later, under a logical form, and in the hands of reflection, becomes a necessary conception. All subjectivity and reflexivity expires in the spontaneity of apperception. But the primitive light is so pure, that it is unperceived: it is the reflected light which strikes us, but often in doing so, sullies with its faithless lustre the purity of the former. Reason becomes subjective by its connection with the free and voluntary *Me*, which is the type of all subjectivity; but in itself it is impersonal, it does not appertain any more to one than to another, it does not even appertain to humanity as a whole, its laws emanate only from itself.'"—Vol. ii., pp. 388–9.

Now, this spontaneous apperception which Cousin sought after, and thinks that he has seized upon, he has sought for in the place where it is not to be found, till after it has been sensibly realized in the act of looking outward on the object of apperception. He looks for it, and imagines that he has got his first hold of it among the reflections of the psychological tablet within; whereas, if to be had at all, spontaneous as it is, it will be in the primary act of looking direct on the radiance that cometh from the object of contemplation without. And yet, by the same marvellous oversight, does his too faithful and imitative disciple follow up the above extract with this sentence:

"Such is the chief ground on which Cousin repels the latent scepticism of a too subjective philosophy, and such the method by which he proposes to place the lofty authority of reason, as an evidence for objective reality, upon an immovable foundation."

This is the completest example of an intellectual cross-purpose on the part both of Mr. Cousin and Mr. Morell that we ever happen to have met with. It is among the latencies of the subjective that they fancy to have found that evidence of an objective reality which only beams upon us from the objects themselves. It is the consciousness, looking inwardly, which places upon an immovable foundation the lofty authority of the reason that looks outwardly. What becomes of the priority of the spontaneous to the reflective amid these strangely conflicting affirmations? Cousin tells us of the primitive light being unperceived, while it is the reflective light which strikes us. This is the first and only instance we ever heard of, whether in things mental or material, of the reflection being more powerful than the radiance.

We think it is in some of his works he tells us, that we cannot know a thing without knowing that we know it. Even this position might well be questioned. Our knowledge of any object must surely be anterior to our knowledge of that knowledge. The knowledge which is proximate to the object must surely come first, and the knowledge which is more remote from this object, as lying behind the other, must as surely come afterwards. Ere we know of a knowledge, that knowledge must exist, or have been already formed; and so when our consciousness takes cognizance of any belief regarding things apart from the mind, that belief must be anterior to the cognizance which consciousness takes of it, and, therefore, it is a belief generated by some other faculty, and not resting on the authority of consciousness at all. This tallies with the real history of the human mind: for how often, and how long in childhood and youth, and prior to the full development of our consciousness, do we know without knowing that we know, without, at least, thinking that we know, and most certainly without ever taking account of our knowledge. But we shall insist no longer on the erroneousness of this position, yet cannot help remarking, that in the above extract from Cousin there lies involved a position still more flagrantly erroneous. He, there, in effect tells us, that we might know of our knowing, what we do not yet know. He takes from psychology at first hand, that information which psychology can only give at second hand. It is the reason, by his own confession, which is the first informant; and yet its voice is unheard, till echoed back on the ear of the inner-man, from the recess of the consciousness. He has made the primary and the secondary change places. It is his Cartesianism which, in this instance, has misled him; though it is strange, that he who has reasoned so admirably on the distinction between the spontaneous and the reflex, and the priority of the former, and has brought this to bear with such felicity and force on the scepticism of Kant, so as to achieve its entire overthrow—it is strange that he should have fallen into such an error. It is the pervading error of Morell. He, though perhaps himself unaware of it, is Cartesian all over.

It is far otherwise with the primary beliefs of Dr. Reid. These are such, that on the moment of their being simply stated, they are read and recognized of all men—as belief in the reality of an external world, belief in the object of our distinct remembrance, belief in the constancy of nature. These beliefs announce themselves to the consciousness, whereas, in the above instance, it is Mr. Cousin's consciousness which tells him what to believe. This faculty of consciousness, doubtless, has a distinct province of its own; but so also have the faculties of perception, and memory, and judgment; and the beliefs of these latter faculties are just as immediate and original as those of consciousness. It is the office of consciousness to take cognizance of the beliefs which are formed in those provinces, distinct from its own; but it is not consciousness which forms them. These beliefs are formed and felt in the direct exercise of the faculties themselves; and it is after this, not surely before this, that they become the subjects of a reflex cognizance by the consciousness. Whether it be Dr. Reid's perception of an external world, or Mr. Cousin's apperception of a Deity, these must first be felt, and then reflected on. But Mr. Cousin reverses this process. The first discovery he makes of his said apperception is, in the act of searching among the recesses of his own psychology. With him the reflex comes first, and the direct afterwards. It speaks most inauspiciously for this apperception of Cousin, that he has found his way to it by an utter reversal of the right working and order of the human faculties.

And that Morell fully participates in this illusion of Cousin, nay, to a much greater extent than the master whom he loves to honor, is abundantly manifest throughout both his volumes, where he is constantly mixing up consciousness, and the facts of consciousness, as if this faculty had an integral and creative part to perform in them, with those beliefs of which it is only the remembrancer and registrar. He often forgets the wise deliverance of Dr. Reid, that "perception commends our belief upon its own authority," and this anterior to, and apart from consciousness, the proper office of which faculty, is not to originate this belief, not even to ratify it, but simply to record it. "And it were difficult," says Dr. Reid, "to give any reason for distrusting our other faculties, that will not reach consciousness itself." We should have liked, if both Mr. Cousin and Mr. Morell had proceeded more on the views of our Scottish philosopher, in the estimate which he makes of Des Cartes. They would not have made his "Cogito, ergo sum," so much the starting-point of their mental philosophy.

We might now understand, why it is that both these philosophers make such a difficulty of effecting a passage from the subjective to the objective. There was no such difficulty felt by Dr. Reid, for he laid as immediate a hold on one as on the other, and had, therefore, no demand for a passage betwixt them. It is true that he described such a passage, nay, actually struck one out with his own hands—when in the act, and for the purpose of repelling scepticism, he made his appeal from perception to consciousness—not that the latter faculty creates the beliefs of the former, but only depones to them. But this movement of his was from the objective to the subjective, which, after having accomplished, he had no difficulty in finding his way back again. Not so with our two philosophers, who, not for the defence of a sound mental philosophy, but for the primary construction of one, make consciousness their point of departure, as Des Cartes did before them, and are thence groping for an outlet from the subjective to the objective—from their psychology to their ontology. And where do they think that they have found one ?—in a lofty region of transcendentalism, by the stepping-stone of an alleged, but withal a most obscure and questionable apperception,* they arrive at the immediate view of an objective God; whence as from a summit, and by a sort of derivative process, they propose to effectuate their descent to the other doctrines, both of Natural Theology and Mental Science. Our outlet from the subjective to the objective is differently placed from theirs,—on the platform of visible and created things, whence we make our way upward to God, among the realities of His own stable and existent universe. Theirs may be a more sublime, but ours, though an humbler, we hold to be a safer movement, and by a surer pathway.

We have long thought that it might alleviate the mysteriousness, nay, facilitate the study, of mental science, did we proceed more on a felicitous notion of Dr. Thomas Brown—a philosopher of whom, now that we have named him, we have only time to say that both Cousin and Morell hold him in greatly too light estimation. He regards consciousness as but a brief act of the memory. And one does not see why we should not remember our mental states, our emotions for example, and distinguish between them—just as we remember our bodily feelings, so as to distinguish, for example, by memory alone, and after they have passed away, between the pain arising from a blow, or a puncture, or a burn, and thus also between the mental affections, such as those of fear, or grief, or joy, or gratitude. We are quite sure that such a view would mitigate the notion which many have, as if acquaintance with mind were a thing hopelessly beyond the reach of their acquirement. It enables us to dispose of the difficulty alleged by Mr. Hume in the way of all mental or metaphysical inquiries—a difficulty so formidable in the eyes of M. Comte that he founds upon it an argument against the mental philosophy as a thing impossible or null—even that the mind cannot think of two things at once, cannot, therefore, think at one and the same time of an object of contemplation without, and the emotion which it awakens within. And thus, when it turns from the object to the subject, from that which caused the emotion to the emotion itself, the latter, deprived of its needful aliment, even the presence of its counterpart object, vanishes from the inner man, and so eludes every attempt to obtain a view of it. We cease to fear when we cease to think of that which makes us afraid, or to be angry when we cease to think of the provocation. But though we cannot, on

* And this, too, first discovered, not in the light of its own radiance, but in its shadowy reflection among the arcana of our inner nature.

this account, immediately behold the emotion, we can remember it; and, to make this remembrance all the surer and more vivid, the mind can quickly alternate between the object and its emotion, so as to have the acts of memory as short and frequent as we will. This might be all the more necessary when examining our beliefs, than when examining our emotions—seeing that our feeling of the former is greatly more faint and languid than of the latter; and this we conceive to be the actual procedure of our mental analysis when they investigate the phenomena or powers of the human understanding. There is much less than most people imagine of what is called a looking inwardly upon ourselves in the prosecution of these studies. Even in the philosophy of the Absolute—that most appalling and recondite of all themes to a merely British understanding—it is the objective which precedes the subjective. In the controversy, for example, between Cousin and Sir W. Hamilton, whether the idea of the infinite be positive or negative, the first thing which the mind does is, not to introvert or look inwardly, but, as it were, to heave itself outwardly, on space, or upwardly to the immense and illimitable Deity; and then, with instant memory, to take cognizance of its own state while thus employed. Our author, too, ventures, though with becoming diffidence, on the theme which has set these two great thinkers at variance; and we gladly avail ourselves of the opportunity to present our readers with another very interesting specimen of his work. All the three, we have no doubt, looked far more objectively than subjectively, far more outward than inward, when making way to their respective deliverances on this crowning question of the German transcendentalism.

"Here we have three minds standing severally at the head of the respective philosophies of Britain, France and Germany, assuming each a different hypothesis on the subject; while Kant, the Aristotle of the modern world, assumes a fourth. Under such circumstances he must be a bold thinker, who ventures to pronounce confidently upon the truth or error of any one of these opinions. Few, perhaps, in our own country would be inclined to side either with Kant or Schelling; the great point of dispute is most likely to be between Sir W. Hamilton and M. Cousin, that is to say, whether the infinite, the absolute, the unconditioned, be really cognizable by the human reason, or whether it be not; whether our notion of it be positive, or whether it be only negative. And here we freely confess, that we are not yet prepared to combat, step by step, the weighty arguments by which the Scottish metaphysician seeks to establish the negative character of this great fundamental conception; neither, on the other hand, are we prepared to admit his inference. We cannot divest our minds of the belief, that there is something *positive* in the glance which the human soul casts upon the world of eternity and infinity. Whether we rise to the contemplation of the Absolute through the medium of the true, the beautiful, or the good, we cannot imagine that our highest conceptions of these terminate in darkness, in a total negation of all knowledge. So far from this, there seem to be flashes of light, ineffable, it may be, but still real, which envelope the soul in a lustre all divine, when it catches glimpses of *infinite* truth, *infinite* beauty, and *infinite* excellence. The mind, instead of plunging into a total eclipse of all intellection, when it rises to this elevation, seems rather to be dazzled by a too great effulgence: yet still the light is real light, although, to any but the strongest vision, the effect may be to *blind* rather than to illumine. It is not by negations that men are governed; but it is before the idea of eternity and infinity that our fiercest humanity is softened and subdued. Until we are driven from this position by an irresistible evidence, we must still regard the notion of the infinite, the absolute, the eternal, as forming one of our fundamental notions, and one which opens to us the highest field, both for our present meditation and our future prospects."—Vol. ii. pp. 397, 398.

Now, it is precisely thus that we would test the alleged apperception of Cousin, and upon which it is that he claims for the human mind a faculty by which it can take an immediate view or cognizance of the Deity. We should certainly not seek for it in the place where he conceives that it was found by himself—in the deep interior of his own psychology. In the language of Scripture, we should lift up our souls unto God; and seek not into ourselves, but seek after Him if haply we might find Him. It is thus that we tried to accompany Schelling; and unable to see as he saw, cast, at a very early stage, his speculation away from us, long before his cosmogony was so far matured, as that it could be brought to the touch-stone of natural philosophy, and be found by its experiments to be an illusion. The *à priori* theology of Cousin has not yet been carried forward to such an issue, and we wait for the products of its felt or fancied inspiration. It is obvious, both of him and Morell, that, in virtue of this discovery, they feel as if on the eve of a great coming enlargement. Let them try; but meanwhile, it is our own shrewd imagination, that it is marvellously little they will make of it.

But any theological argument which our space will leave room for, we should like to hold with Mr. Morell alone. We cannot, however, take leave of Mr. Cousin without rendering the homage of our grateful admiration to one who, at this moment, holds the balance between the two philosophies of Germany and Scotland. It is true that in his theology he is altogether wrong, though, judging from the general spirit and drift of his speculations, we should say of him, that he is not unhopeful. But what has earned for him our peculiar esteem is his having so nobly asserted the prerogatives of common sense against the sceptical philosophy of Kant. In particular, his manly, and withal, most effectual defence of the reality of space and time, might well put to shame certain of our own *savans*, who, in compliance with this wretched jabber of the school at Königsberg, now speak of both these elements as having no valid significancy in themselves, but as being mere products of idealism, or forms of human thought. In the immediate successors of Kant we can easily forgive this extravagance, as Fichte, of whom we should not have expected, for one moment, that the "common sense" philosophy would ever lead him to give up one iota of his transcendentalism. But although common sense was utterly powerless against it, yet upon one occasion it had nearly given way, when brought into serious conflict with a not uncommon sensibility; for Fichte, as we were pleased to find, though a metaphysician, and in the most abstract form, so far proved himself to be a possessor of our own concrete humanity, as to fall in love. But circumstances forced him to quit for a season the lady of his affections; and, when at the distance of 300 miles, German miles too, he thus writes to her:—"Again left to myself, to my solitude, to my own thoughts, my soul flies directly to your presence. How is this? It is but three days since I have seen you, and I must often be absent from you for a longer period than that. Distance is but distance, and I am equally separated from you in Flaach or in Zurich. But how comes it that this absence has seemed to me longer than usual, that my heart longs more earnestly to be with you, that I imagine I have not seen you for a week? Have I philosophized falsely of late about distance? Oh, that our feelings must still contradict the firmest conclusions of our reason!" Mr. Morell deprecates what he calls the ignoble application of ridicule to philosophy; yet we should not be sorry if, with the possession of such rich materials for the exposure of that intellectual Quixotism into which so many minds in Germany and elsewhere are now running wild, some one having the talents of Butler or Cervantes were to arise, and banish this grotesque and outrageous folly from the face of the earth.

Were it confined to Germany, we should have more toleration for it. But it is now making frequent inroads within our own borders; and we are grieved to find that Mr. Whewell expresses himself as carried by the prestige of the German philosophy and its outlandish nomenclature. We are not even sure if Sir John Herschell be altogether free from it. We shall exceedingly regret if the manly English sense of these great masters in physical science shall prove to have been in the least vitiated by this admixture from abroad. In the face of their high authority, we shall persist in regarding the whole of the intermediate space between ourselves and the planet Uranus as an objective reality; and when we read of this planet "trembling along the line of their analysis," we shall look still further off, or still more objectively, to the space that is beyond it, nay, and shall infer, with all confidence, that there must be a force outside which is disturbing its movements. We are persuaded that common sense prevailed, and their metaphysics were for a time forgotten, when in the glorious discovery of Le Verrier, they beheld the verification both of an objective space and an objective causality.

Altogether it is a wondrous exhibition, and proves most strikingly that high mental power is no guarantee against outrageous error, when one looks to the very opposite effects which the contemplation of space and time had on two such minds as those of Immanuel Kant and Dr. Samuel Clarke. The latter not only ascribed existence to these two elements, but an existence of a much higher character, than to the contingent and variable objects which compose our universe—as self-existence, necessary existence, an existence of which it was not only impossible to conceive the opposite, but of which it was impossible that the opposite could be—on which attributes it was, that he reared his famous *à priori* arguments for the being of a God. Kant, on the other hand, while he admitted the reality in some sort of a phenomenal world, made the very intensity of our belief in space and time his argument, not for going outward or objectively on the things believed, but for turning inward on the subjective mind, and viewed the fixed and ineradicable convictions which have been planted there in no other light than as the necessary laws or forms of human thought. Strange that in very proportion to the strength of our belief, must the object believed be all the more regarded as a nullity, or as having no other existence than in a region of idealism. No one can question the transcendent force of intellect in Kant; but these aberrations of his remind us of the Scripture saying—"If the light that is in thee be darkness, how great is that darkness!" Neither can we deny that both Kant and Samuel Clarke are men of far more gigantic stature than our own Dr. Reid, who, nevertheless, in virtue of his calm, and sober, and reflective judgment, with no higher pretensions than to the common sense which is diffused among all men, had a clearer discernment than either of them, both of the laws and limits of the human faculties. It holds true in the things of science, as well as the things of sacredness, that many things are hid from the wise and the prudent, which are revealed unto babes.

Yet Kant, as if sensible of his errors, by what Cousin terms a noble inconsistency (*inconsêquence*) did much to repair them. For example, he conjured up the Practical Reason, that by means, though it must be confessed, of a clumsy and ill-assorted apparatus, he might compensate for, or rectify the dangerous conclusions of the Pure Reason. And again, as if to caution his successors against any wild excursion into the regions of the imaginative and the ideal, do we meet with the following glorious passage, of which we know not whether most to admire the soundness of the lesson, or the exquisite beauty and appropriateness of the image which he employs for the enforcement of it. It is the rebuke which he pronounces on the impatience of reason, and the utter vanity of all its ambitious efforts, when it seeks across the limits of observational truth, or tries to expatiate beyond the domain of the "*Quid est.*" They wholly misunderstand Kant who think, because of his lofty and arduous speculations, that he undervalues the findings of man on the *terra firma* of our sensible world. On the contrary, he avers with all strenuousness, that human knowledge is bounded by experience.

"The reason," he says, "because of its reach and capacity, and misled by the evidences which it finds of its own power, can see no limits to its passion for knowledge. The buoyant dove, when, with free wing, it traverses the air of which it feels the resistance, might imagine that it would fly still better in the vacuum beyond; and thus Plato forgets and looks slightingly on the sensible world, because it imposes upon his reason such narrow limitations, and so he ventures himself on the wings of his ideas, into the empty space of the pure understanding. He has not remarked that, in spite of his efforts, he makes no progress, for he has no point of support on which to uphold him in his attempt to bear the understanding out of its natural place. Such is the common fatality of reason, when it enters on the walk of speculation: it first raises a superstructure as quickly as it can, but is much too late ere it takes the trouble of ascertaining whether the foundation of it be solid."—*Critic of Pure Reason.*

It is quite refreshing to meet with those places in Kant, where he emerges into the daylight of common sense, and speaks just like one of ourselves. When he makes his transition from the Pure to the Practical Reason, he gives forth a Natural Theology most strikingly accordant in its main lessons and arguments with those which have been delivered for years to large and successive numbers of those youth in Scotland who are in training for the ministry of the Gospel. And really, after reading the masterly criticisms of Cousin upon his categories, and upon the arbitrary lines of demarcation which he has drawn between the reason, and the understanding, and the sensational faculty, one is tempted to put the interrogation—What, after all, in mental philosophy, of the useful and unquestionable, has Kant said, which Dr. Reid did not say before him?

It had been well if Kant had kept closer by Dr. Reid, and well too had the followers of Kant kept closer by their great master. But, after having conducted them to the verge of idealism, he in vain lifted his warning voice against their proceeding further, else we should have been spared the extravagances of Fichte, and Schelling, and Hegel. We cannot now afford the room for a single sentence on any of their systems; but would single out that of Schelling for one brief remark on the outrageous absurdity of the product, and yet notwithstanding, the honest enthusiasm of admiration felt even by the highest minds for the marvellous talent, and withal, lofty, moral, and poetical bearing of the man. Morell speaks of him in the language of endearment; and of his philosophical system, as that "by which the name of Schelling is destined to go down the stream of time to the latest posterity." Nothing can exceed the devout estimation in which he is held by Coleridge; but the most remarkable homage ever rendered to him was by the French Institute, who sat in formal judgment upon his philosophy, and though they sanctioned the adverse deliverance of Mr. Willm, in his memoir of Schelling, yet by their sustained attention to his Critique, and subsequent publication of it, gave ample evidence to the redeeming qualities of a speculation which sets all common sense at defiance, and bears so glaringly the character of utter wildness upon its forehead. Nevertheless, it is patiently reasoned out by the memorialist, most respectfully listened to by the most illustrious body of *savans* in Europe, and at last pronounced upon in the following terms:—

"This doctrine is founded, 1. Upon an illusion. For it takes the process of ordinary generalization for an absolute law of reason; and erects the principle at which generalization stops, into the real and essential principle of things themselves.

"2. Upon a paralogism. For it confounds the order of knowledge with the order of existence.

"3. Upon an exaggeration. For it exaggerates the harmony which exists, or which we naturally affirm between our intelligence and reality, by making it an *identity*, and attributing to reason so absolute an authority, that everything must be as it thinks, from the moment that it thinks it.

"4. Upon an hypothesis. For it is a gratuitous supposition to place all truth in the reason, and thus to equal reason with God."—Vol. ii. pp. 128–129.

We refuse to admit the tabular scheme of Schelling into our pages, but will simply refer to it as given by Morell, vol. ii. p. 106. It virtually implies that the power of thinking is tantamount to the power of creating, and thus that man can think out a universe, down to the minutest and most complicated organisms of the animal and vegetable kingdom. It is the most characteristic specimen we have met with of what the Germans call a construction; and nothing serves more decisively to establish the national differences of mind as well as manners than the simple fact of its unbounded popularity for a season, even among the highest thinkers of one great country, and the earnest discussion of it by the proudest intellects of another—while speaking generally and collectively, we cannot fancy of the English understanding, though sublimed to the uttermost, as bestowing upon it the entertainment of one serious thought, so that a summary rejection would ensue on the very first aspect of it. We have certainly no wish that it should be otherwise; and would rather that all the world should speak of us still, intellectually as well as geographically, as "*Britannos toto orbe divisos*," than that we should ever in the least give in to such monstrous idealism. Yet there must be a charm in the German philosophy lying somewhere else than in its truth, some other inspiration than in the articles of its creed. The gyrations of the noble bird are gazed upon with delight and wonder; but when it gets beyond the limits of our sustaining atmosphere, it then, as Kant hath predicted, is precipitated far out of sight, among the depths and recesses of a viewless infinity.

But we have left far too little room for the special converse that we all along felt desirous of holding with Mr. Morell himself on the subject of theology.

The extract already given by us in our Review, from Morell, vol. i., pp. 239–240, is immediately followed up by the two paragraphs which we now present to the reader.

"Instead, therefore, of entirely separating the investigation of mental from that of all other phenomena, we should here perceive their mutual relations, and learn to gaze upon the universe both of mind and matter as a whole, the one harmonious production of the Infinite Intelligence. In this view of the case we should contemplate man in his mysterious connection with nature, and nature in its relation to humanity, while the last and crowning problem would be to show how they both subsist in God. A system embracing this sweep of investigation, might be termed philosophy in its highest sense.

"Had Reid pointed out this as the ultimate tendency of metaphysical research, we believe that his successors could have built upon such a foundation a noble superstructure of speculative philosophy; but having discouraged this attempt in the outset, his successors have for the most part trodden the path of mere observation, until the science which might soar to the very noblest efforts of the human intellect, and strive to solve the great problems of man, the universe, and their Creator, has dwindled down almost to puerility in the hands of some of its most recent advocates."—Vol. i. p. 241.

It is obvious that our author here contrasts the method in which Natural Theology has been presented by disciples of the Scottish school, since the days of Reid, with that more vigorous and productive method in which he thinks it ought to have been presented. Our reply at present must necessarily be a brief one.*

The first and greatest argument, then, of our Natural Theology, is identical with that of Kant's—the felt supremacy of conscience, which we have long deemed the most influential of all others for upholding the faith of a God throughout the world. It is true that we do not call it the Categorical Imperative, or place it under the head of the Practical Reason, in contradistinction to the Pure Reason of the transcendental philosophy. It is substantially the same argument notwithstanding, and couched by us in surprisingly coincident language with that of Kant and his commentators,—as that a law implies a lawgiver, &c. It must be admitted, however, that we view it as an *à posteriori* argument, by which we pass from the felt experience of a judge within the breast to the inference of a Judge above and over us, who planted it there, being at one in this respect with Bishop Butler, who, as from the regulator in a watch he would infer not only a maker for it but that his purpose in so making it was that it should move regularly,—so from the conscience in a man did he infer the design, and of course a Designer, that man should walk conscientiously. This argument, too, we bring to bear, even as Kant did, on the soul's immortality—along with a second argument, which he also employs, grounded on the boundless aspirations and capacities of the human spirit, seeing that it were a violent anomaly, as being an exception to the universal law of adaptation which runs throughout nature, if creatures endowed as we are, were not provided with a state of conscious existence on the other side of death, in which to expatiate. Such, in its main features, is the Natural Theology of Kant, and such, we add, is the Natu-

* In truth, we could not do full justice to the theme, but in a separate article, at least half as long as the present one, on "The Scottish Natural Theology," to be afterwards followed up by another, where, with express reference to Strauss and to German Rationalism in general, we should like to give forth our views on "The Christian Theology of Scotland."

ral Theology of Scotland, in which, after all, Kant felt himself obliged to take refuge, when, as if by a compensation of errors, he conjured up what he calls the Practical Reason, to repair the mischief, or rather the else irretrievable ruin which his Pure Reason had inflicted on the cause of Theism.

And here we cannot but remark the vast superiority, as it seems to us, of the argument from conscience, to the Cartesian argument for a God, even though advocated by Cousin, and on the ground too of its being an argument that can be felt and recognized by all men. This last and most precious characteristic we have ever regarded, as being, *par excellence*, the property of the argument from conscience, this universal attribute of humanity; but that the other, or argument from contrast, had no pretensions to it. This latter argument proceeds on the postulate that each idea of the human mind suggests its opposite—as the finite suggestive of the infinite, the conditioned of the absolute, the imperfect of the perfect: and that thus every human being, conscious as he must be of his own limited and imperfect nature, is led, by a necessary law of human thought, to the conception of an infinite and all-perfect God. We confess of this argument, —with its additional draught upon us, that the very conception of such a Being is, in itself, the conclusive evidence of His reality,—we do confess to the very slight impression which it makes upon our understanding. Least of all can we imagine that it should have any prevalent or practical effect throughout the species at large—and this though enforced by all the talent and eloquence of Cousin, along with an inimitable gracefulness of illustration, when he pictures forth in some exquisite sentences a religious peasant, strongly reminding us of Cowper's aged female in humble but happy life, with just and elevated faith in the God of the whole universe, though herself "never heard of half a mile from home."

But there is a second great branch of argument in Natural Theology, which, though of far less powerful effect than the former on human consciences, and so far less powerful as an efficient either of religious feelings or religious convictions in the world, is the one on which, at present, we have most to say—it being that on which we hold an adjustment with Mr. Morell to be most urgently called for. We mean the argument for a God, as based on the phenomena and dispositions of the material world. This argument stands in somewhat the same relation to the former, that the External do to the Internal Evidences of Christianity—the strength of the one lying in the credibility of those alleged miracles by which inroad was made on the regularities of nature, and of the other or greatly more influential in the universal manifestation which the subject-matter of Christianity is fitted to make of itself to the consciences of men, and always will make when these consciences are earnest and alive to the realities of the question. We can pursue no further at present this general analogy between the Natural and the Christian Theology —only adverting to their common resemblance, in that each has one argument by which to obtain a hold on the faith of humanity at large; and another, more appropriate to scientific men, and which, if not powerful enough to propitiate their attention to the theme, is at least powerful and strong enough to condemn their summary rejection of it.

But a disciple of the German philosophy should, as much as possible, be spoken with in his own language. "Every event has a cause." This we readily concede to Kant, the great master of that philosophy; nor do we have any quarrel either with the substance or nomenclature of what he tells us, when he says that the words now enunciated form *a synthetic proposition à priori.* But while it is *à priori* that all men believe in a cause for every event, it is only by observation *à posteriori* that they come to know what the cause particular is—though, after this, and by a suggestion *à priori*, they always look for the same effects from the same causes, as well as infer the same causes from the same effects. All men have an original confidence in the stability of Nature's successions; but it is the office of experience to find out what the terms of the succession are—which, when once found out, enable us to say of many a specific event what the cause of it actually and specifically is; as, that heat is the cause of expansion, impulse of motion, injury of resentment, and so of all other ascertained sequences both in the outer world of phenomena and the inner world of sentiment and feeling. These latter propositions, however, belong to a different class from the one that has just been defined by us. They are the *synthetic propositions à posteriori* of Kant.

Even M. Comte himself would allow of such causal successions within the domain of his own positive philosophy; or, if he would object to their being viewed as causal, he would at least allow of such a regularity in the order of succession, as, that from the prior term of a sequence, one might legitimately anticipate its wonted posterior, or from the posterior might infer the prior term that had gone before it. And he is quite right when he makes no difference in this respect between the phenomena of human life or conduct, on the one hand, and the phenomena of inert matter, upon the other—insomuch, that in either of these departments alike, he would, from certain given antecedents, anticipate the same results, or, from certain given results, would infer the same antecedents. For example, should he witness the putting together of any beneficial collocation, as a watch, under process of construction by human hands, where part was added and adapted to part, and all at length to the effect of a very obvious utility, he would have no difficulty, when he next saw a watch, to infer a watchmaker—an artificer of adequate skill and power for the production of such a mechanism. There is nothing in his antipathy to the doctrine of final causes which would at all embarrass or restrain him from such a conclusion—arguing, as he would in any other case of an observed succession, from the consequent, a watch, to the antecedent watchmaker from whom it had sprung. Nay, though he had never seen a watch made, he might still, and with all confidence, have inferred the watchmaker—and this on the strength of his general observation of the way in which such things are originated: And so, though he may be never present at the manufacture of a coach, or a ship, or a house, or a gun, or a steam-engine, he would still most rightfully conclude and on the basis of a sufficient experience, that a designing mind and a designing hand had to do with all these fabrications.

Now, this very conclusion, against which a disciple of Comte would not except in reasoning on the origin of a human or artificial mechanism, a disciple of the Scottish school would regard as equally legitimate and right when reasoning on the first origin of any natural mechanism. Let there be but a beneficial collocation of parts, and he would infer that the hand of a designer had been there—and with an evidence all the more intense in proportion to the number of parts or of independent conditions which entered into the combination. This we hold to be the great *à posteriori* argument which external and visible nature contributes to the evidence for a God—grounded not on the existence, and not even essentially on the laws, but mainly and in chief strength on the dispositions of matter, and from which we infer, that the present economy of things, with its goodly arrangements—its endless variety of manifold, yet all most beneficial adaptations—arose from the fiat of a powerful and presiding intelligence, who willed it into being.

We hold that this argument has been greatly rectified and improved, and put into form, since the days of Dr. Reid. It was a mighty disencumbrance for it to forego all the obscure and unsatisfactory metaphysics which the English theists, at the beginning of the last century, grounded on the mere existence of matter—reasoning from its entity alone to the entity of spirit, and fancying that on this simple step they had found their way to the great anterior cause which gave birth to all things. It was a further concentration of strength to forbear the question of its eternity; and instead of requiring a commencement for the substratum of the universe, to be satisfied, for all the purposes of an effective demonstration, with a commencement for its now subsisting economy. It was even a better intellectual tactics—a retirement from the outworks to the citadel of our argument—when, quitting for a time the consideration of its laws, we made our single appeal to the dispositions of matter, and so could wield the very argument by which we reason from a production of human art to a human artificer, who endows not matter with its properties, but only puts his materials into order and form. The recent discoveries in geology have not only cast a wondrous illustration on this argument, but serve mightily to confirm it. It is when new systems emerge from the wreck of old ones, and from the ruins of a former catastrophe there is built up another modern habitation, and peopled with new races both of animals and vegetables—it is then that we demand the interposal of a God. Whence did these new genera and species come into being? Nature gives no reply to this question; and, though ransacked throughout all her magazines, the secret of these actual and present, and altogether new organisms, is nowhere to be found. These two doctrines, the all but universal faith of naturalists, that there is no spontaneous generation, and no transmutation of the species, are two denials in fact, of nature's sufficiency for the origination of our races, and shut us up unto the faith of Nature's God. It places our argument on firm vantage-ground to say, that were all the arrangements of our existing Natural History destroyed, all the known forces of our existing Natural Philosophy could not replace them.

We are aware of the altogether contemptuous regard which transcendentalism casts upon these things. Its natural habitat is aloft, whence it looks down with utter indifference and scorn on all that takes place in our lower world—whether on the geology so visibly portrayed before our eyes on the face of the globe; or on the theology that would deign to read its characters, and bestow so much as one thought upon its movements. We can therefore scarcely expect even a hearing from it, when we tell of our own satisfaction in the overthrow of an atheistical sophism which threatened at one time the integrity of the *à posteriori* argument, and so put the whole of our Scottish school on their expedients for the defence of it. The truth is, that Hume's argument, grounded on his allegation that the world is a singular effect, always seemed to the metaphysicians of this country the most formidable, or most difficult to deal with, of any that had ever been framed on this side of Atheism—insomuch that both Reid and Stewart betook themselves to the very questionable expedient of inventing a new principle for the purpose of neutralizing it. It is only of late that this sophistry, once so perplexing, and so inadequately met, has been effectually disposed of in another way; and the Natural Theology of Scotland, represented by our author as dwindling into puerility, now stands firm on the basis of vindicated experience—alike safe from the attack of its deadliest enemy, and independent of the frail supports that were rendered by friends in those days of its vaunted manhood.

We expect no sympathy with this vindication at the hands of the transcendentalists. The very name of experience will repel them; nay, create the keenest repugnance in the hearts of those who have vastly greater value for the constructions and excogitations of a German system, than for all which the industry of man can find, or his eye can observe, in the actual constructions of God's own universe.

We confess that our chief value for the experimental argument, is because of its special adaptation to the habitude of those minds which are disciplined in the methods and investigations of Physical Science. For the evidence of theology, whether Natural or Revealed, like the reasoning of Christianity's greatest apostle, has in it something for all men.* It is an evidence which can be carried even within the domain of what Comte terms his positive philosophy, and can there challenge from the sight of the world his belief in a world-maker, for the same principle on which from the sight of a watch he himself would believe in a watch-maker. But this is a quarter in which the metaphysicians of the continent, and Morell among the number (*Morell*, i., 481–485), will tell him that no evidence for a God is to be found—not at least till the glorious spectacle of Nature, teeming to common eyes with all the indices of design and order, shall somehow have been transformed and sublimated into one of their own speculations. Meanwhile these speculations so conflict and alternate with each other—so float and disappear at turns in the whirlpool of debate—so pass onward from hand to hand in successive and ever-shifting transmutations, from the transcendentalism of Kant to the idealism of Fichte, and thence to the still loftier empyrealism of Schelling, and thence to the mysticism of Jacobi, and thence to the nihilism of Hegel—that no wonder if the poor man, bewildered and lost in the turmoil of a thousand controversies and utterly in despair for aught like settlement or repose, should have been tempted to cast the whole theme, with its corollaries or cognate doctrines of an immaterial spirit and supernal God away from him. One cannot say in how far these men are not responsible for the atheism of the boldest and one of the most powerful thinkers whom France has to boast of.

But we confess to a still deeper melancholy in our view of Humboldt—a feeling in which our author seems to share, and this because of the utter destitution of all reference to the Creator in his last work entitled Kosmos; or if he do advert to a first cause, it is to a primordial necessity, and not to the living God. On reading his treatise some months previous to the appearance of Morell's book, we could not help being struck with the total absence of any allusion to the world's Author; but what we felt as most instructive of all, was his own explanation or apology for the want of it—"the wholly objective tendency of his disposition." From other passages which could be cited, it is too obvious that he looks on the theology of his subject as placed at a distance well nigh impassable from the subject itself,—as belonging to a

* 1 Cor. ix., 22.

"higher class of ideas"—as involving him in "the mysterious unresolvable problem of origin" or "the obscure commencement of the history of origination"—as requiring the consideration of "abstract principles, having their foundation in pure reason only;" and upon all which he declines aspiring "to the perilous elevation of a purely rational science of nature," or adventuring on "those depths of a purely speculative philosophy." Altogether, the impression on Humboldt's mind must be that theology is wrapt in transcendentalism; and that he must traverse the mighty gulf of separation between the objective and the subjective ere he can come into contact with it. Now, in point of fact, if he do not need to make this transition in passing from the view of a coach to the inference of a coachmaker, he has little need to make it in passing from the view of those new organisms which each new and successive formation in geology presents to his notice, to the inference of a designing Intelligence who called them into being. It is true that we cannot make either the one inference or the other, without one of Kant's primitive judgments coming into play. But the judgment comes spontaneously; and in the act of forming it there is no necessity for lifting one's eyes from the outward object of contemplation. But herein lies the subtle allusion which operates both on Humboldt's imagination, and on that of the metaphysicians themselves who have done so much to pervert the mind of Germany. He counts it not enough that the primitive or proximate judgment has been evoked, which of itself, though but one step, is a sufficient introduction to the theology of the subject; but that over and above this, he must entertain Kant's judgment of this judgment, or his own reflex judgment thereupon. Now this following up of the direct by the reflex process is wholly uncalled for, but such is the constant subjective habit of these singular people; and it is this which explains, while it vindicates the saying of Goethe in regard to his own countrymen, "that the Germans have the gift of rendering the sciences inaccessible." It is a cruel result when theology is thus made inaccessible. All look back with generous and just indignation to the decretals of that ecclesiastical counsel which compelled Galileo to renounce the true philosophy. We have scarcely less patience for those decretals of the metaphysical school, which, acting with the spell of its authority on such a mind as that of Humboldt, should have deceived him into the notion that the true theology is beyond the reach of his attainment; or that he stands hopelessly and forever debarred from the apprehension of that God over the glories of whose creation he so luxuriates, and this because Nature has withheld from him all talent and all tendency for the subjective!

There is here a grievous misdirection of the view from that place where lies the main strength of our argument and of our cause—a misdirection into which Mr. Morell has himself fallen. For example, our inference from the beneficial collocations of matter to the wisdom of Him who ordained them, is of far too plain and puerile a character to be at all worthy of his entertainment. And what else would he substitute in its place? How is it that he would have us take flight from this humble path of observation, and "soar to the very noblest efforts of the human intellect, and strive to solve the great problems of man, the universe, and their Creator?" Not, it would appear, from aught in the character and properties of man, but from the essence of man; and not from the dispositions of the universe, but from what belongs to the essence of the universe; and not from the attributes of God, as evinced by His works or in His ways, but still from the essence of God. We have really been making it a formal and express effort, to ascertain the starting point of his ontology, or "loftier region of thought," over which he longs to expatiate, and to scale the heights of the Prima Philosophia; and all that we can find, all that he himself alleges, is but these three substrata to come and go upon. Now, though by a fundamental law of the human understanding we believe in a substratum for the Deity, a substratum for man, a substratum for the universe, we cannot, for our lives, imagine what more we know of them than that barely they exist; nor how it is that these three bare entities can be turned, like geometrical definitions, into the germs of reasoning and endless discovery. We fear that they will be of as little avail for progress as the abstract ideas of Plato. However, we again say, let him try; but would further bid our aspiring young philosopher "remember Kant's dove," a saying as brief and sententious, and which it were wholesome and well should it become as memorable, as "remember Lot's wife." We should like that our sanguine and adventurous author had it inwoven on the phylactery of his garment, even as it ought to be on every German toga, and inscribed on the portico of every German university. It might restrain many an Ixionic flight, whereof it is certain that hitherto the monuments or memorials have been far less durable than a pillar of salt—a wreath of attenuated vapor too impalpable for vision. But it is too obvious of Mr. Morell, that he has caught the infection, and that he would fain take wing above the terra firma of experience, nay, beyond the limits of its encompassing atmosphere. We do hope that he will not venture too far. There is much of what is good in him; nor are we without the expectation that, like the bird of Noah, we shall soon have to welcome him back again to the ark in safety—to the commonsense philosophy and puerile theology of Scotland.

And here, for one moment, we would address ourselves to the *seriousness* of Mr. Morell. That theology of which at present he has such fond imaginations, is after all but a theology in prospect. Those inward mysteries of which he speaks, the mysteries of being, and to which he looks so wistfully, with the view of seizing on them, have not yet come within his grasp. And yet he tells us that Natural Theology is the basis of the Revealed, or the basis of Christianity. Which, then, of the natural theologies is it that he means? Is it the Natural Theology which has been already realized, and of which he tells us that it is comparatively worthless? Or is it the Natural Theology still in reserve, and for the completion of which he is now looking forward to the spiritual philosophy of Paris's Eclectic School? Meanwhile, what are we to do with our Christianity? Must we keep it in abeyance, as being a superstructure without foundation, till the great master whom he most reveres shall have given full proof of the inspiration which he claims, and of which he affirms, that it and no other was the inspiration either of prophets in the Old, or apostles in the New Testament?

Had it not been for the danger which lies along the confines of Mr. Morell's speculations (undesigned by himself we have no doubt), we should not have meddled with him. But there is a full call to interpose when the author of a book so fitted to fascinate, and when wrong to mislead, tells the numerous youth of our colleges that hitherto they have only been dealing with superficialities, and have never yet found so much as a door of entry into the recesses and profundities of his inner world. Let them be assured, nevertheless, that with the voice of that conscience which speaks so powerfully in all bosoms, and those glories of a universe patent to every eye, and which shine so palpably around them; and let them further be assured, that in the Bible, that wondrous monument of past ages, with its firm authentic place in history, and its telling power on men's hearts—though unskilled to the end of their days in the idealism of Germany, and in all its categories—let them be nevertheless assured, in the possession of vouchers so ample as these, that both their Natural and their Christian theology are safe.

But, in good truth, he is egregiously wrong, when he speaks of Natural Theology being the basis of Christianity, in the same way that the foundation to a house is of its superstructure, or a premise in argument is of its conclusion. He utterly mistakes the law and nature of this succession. It is true that Natural Theology comes before Christianity, not syllogistically, however, but historically, not in the order of demonstration, but in the order of human sentiment and feeling. The one precedes the other just as the sufferings and anxieties of distress precede the inquiry after relief, and then the actual finding of its efficacy. It is not, however, the felt disease which points to the remedy; but the remedy is offered to the disease, and gives in itself the proof of its own virtues to all who make use of it. In plainer language, the matter proceeds thus: The theology of nature is the theology of conscience; and conscience tells every possessor of it, if not the certainty, at least the probability of a God. And this probability is enough to set men agoing; for, as Butler says with deep and eminently practical sagacity, probability is the guide of life. And so the sense of moral deficiency, the unfailing sense of every earnest spirit, will, without any nice argumentative computation, suggest the instant feeling of at least a probable guilt, a probable God, and a probable vengeance at His hands,—enough to set the whole machinery of human interests, and fears, and disquietudes, into busy operation. It is in the midst of such agitations and doings that Christianity offers itself to the notice of an inquirer; and for the tens or twenties who may seek after its literary and historical evidence, there will at least be thousands who fasten their intent regards upon its subject matter; and who, as the fruit of their moral earnestness and prayers, will be made to behold its divine adaptation to the exigencies of their state, and so to close with it on the strength of those credentials which are properly and independently its own. At the earlier stage of this deeply interesting process, this moral history of the spirit, we can figure to ourselves the peasant so beautifully sketched by Cousin, but at length transformed at a later stage, the stage of her confirmed Christianity, into the peasant of Cowper—the subject of an inspiration different from that of our French philosopher, but which we are not unhopeful, and pray God that he may yet experience, when the Bible, making known to him its marvellous revelations into the psychology of our nature, will draw from him the acknowledgment that verily this book tells us all which is in our hearts, and verily God is in it of a truth.*

The most grievously wrong passage of our author's work, and by which he unknowingly has given the greatest pain to many of his readers, is his Critique on Dr. Abercromby—a man of far higher and holier aim than to create for himself a name in philosophy; and whose writings, by which though dead he yet speaketh, better than all Greek and all Roman fame, are of a character so pure and heavenly, and withal so humble, that the ashes of their truly estimable author, undisturbed by the hand of rude and unsparing violence, should have been suffered to repose in peace.

And though less in fault, he is scarcely less in error, when he fastens the charge of mysticism on Dr. Wardlow, one of the clearest and most logical writers in our day. The mistake into which he falls here is somewhat analogous to that which he commits when speaking of Natural Theology as the basis of Christianity, and only requires to be met by an analogous rectification. It follows not that a perfect system of ethics is discoverable by man, although he might be abundantly capable of recognizing its excellence and truth, when brought to his view by a revelation *ab extra*. Had there been an utter extinction both of conscience and reason in our species, we should have been beyond the pale of all moral reckoning. But there might be enough in man to

* 1 Cor. xiv., 25.

make him responsible for the attention which he gives to Christianity, and yet not enough to make him independent of its disclosures—insomuch that without a Gospel, both its informations and its lessons might have remained hopelessly and forever beyond the reach of his attainment. And this distinction between the two faculties of discovery and discernment is not peculiar to the subject of Theology, but is exemplified in all the sciences.

Mr. Morell, with much to commend and much to be grateful for, in that one so conversant as he is in the philosophy of the continent, should nevertheless lift so intrepid and uniform a testimony on the side of Christianity—has yet been somewhat unfortunate in several of his allusions both to Theology at large, and to certain of its doctrines. Charles Fox once said of a parliamentary acquaintance who had much of the style and manner of cadence of oratory, yet without force and without substance, that he spoke to the tune of a good speech. There is one lengthened passage in Mr. Morell's work, of which we should say throughout, that he reasoned to the tune of a good argument. We refer to his discussion on the question of Liberty and Necessity. Instead of taking the main elements of his ratiocination from the mental phenomena, or from mind itself, which is the truly proper subject of this question, he draws chiefly, not on the philosophy of the subject, but on the history of its philosophy, and makes the determination turn on the respective merits of the schools which took their several parts in this controversy. Now this is greatly too wholesale a style of argumentation for such a topic of inquiry; and, if we may so express it, the elements made use of are of much too bulky and aggregate a description to have that analytic force which is so indispensable to a sound and thorough solution on the matter at issue. He keeps back from us the philosophy of the question, and gives us history instead. Really it were investing the historians of philosophy with a tremendous power, if we must take their dogmata as well as their information—and this on the strength of argument built up of historical materials alone. At this rate M. Comte has just as good a right to found an atheism on what he tells us of the Eras, the theological and metaphysical and positive eras, as Mr. Morell has to found the doctrine of contingency on what he tells us of his Schools. Instead of the slight notice wherewith in half a sentence he dismisses Edwards, we should have liked much better that he had grappled with his arguments. And he has here forgotten to let us know that Leibnitz, though at the head of the rational or spiritual philosophy which he so much admires, was also a Necessarian.* Nevertheless we must

* It is remarkable that Madame de Staël lays claim to Leibnitz as the powerful asserter of Liberty. But the mistake, if mistake it be, is altogether justifiable—for if both he and Edwards were better understood, it would be found, not only that they are the advocates of the only liberty which is at all conceivable, but of the only liberty which can sustain all the activities of human life, as well as all the enforcements and duties of moral obligation.

admit of the whole passage on which we are now animadverting that it is written with great spirit and ability; and that from the beginning to the end of it, he reasons to the tune of a good argument.

But we must now take leave of Mr. Morell; and we desire to do it with the most perfect good humor, as we do with unfeigned respect for his great talents, and gratitude for the instruction that we have received from him. May life and health be long spared to him for the prosecution of his high labors, and for the fulfilment of that expectation regarding him which the promise of this his first appearance so abundantly warrants—as the accomplished combatant of infidelity in its new and coming forms, one of our foremost champions in the sacred cause of Truth and Righteousness.

The question of chief concern to us is—What might be the probable issues of the growing admiration now felt for the philosophical systems of Germany? And first it is of prime importance to remark that much of the admiration thus felt for them is irrespective of their truth. For example, there are many who can speak, and with honest enthusiasm too, of the poetical and comprehensive scheme of Schelling, yet would never once think of admitting it into their creed. And so we read of Fichte that "his singular and commanding address, his fervid eloquence, the rich profusion of his thoughts following each other in most convincing sequences, and modelled with the sharpest precision, astonished and delighted his hearers." Now one can well understand how there might be a series of most convincing *sequences,* a strict logical dependence between step and step in a chain of reasoning, and each step lighted up too with brilliant fancy and deepest moral earnestness—but without a sustaining basis of truth or evidence for the whole. Yet though wanting this, there might still be a glorious symphony for the eye to gaze upon. And accordingly in the University of Jena, Fichte carried all before him. The philosophy of his predecessor, Reinhold, vanished in a moment; and nothing was heard among the students but the cry of *Ego* and *Non-ego* as the new symbols by which the old ones of *substance* and *form* were displaced and superseded. Even Goethe, whom Fichte had before done homage to as the Sophocles of Germany, was carried along on the tide of the then-prevailing fascination, though he still demanded a scientific foundation for a system which otherwise had so much charmed him. There is much to be gathered from the single fact of that intense mutual sympathy, that kindness of spirit, which obtained between these two, living at that time in the same town, and in the occasional enjoyment of each other's society—the one held in honor, for a season at least, as the greatest philosopher; and the other, of more enduring and universal fame, as the greatest poet and dramatist of Germany. The truth is, that the work of each in its own way, the lectureship of the one and the drama of the other, was a sort of theatrical performance, and hung upon with equal, and very much with kindred delight, by the thousands who listened to them. He who dwelt in the romance of sentiment was not further removed from the realities of human life, than he who dwelt in the romance of science was from the realities of truth and nature. Yet both were most wonderfully inspiring and soul-elevating romances, notwithstanding. An excessive love of the fictitious, whether as indulged in the perusal of ordinary or philosophical novels, might be alike injurious to the experimental wisdom of common life, and to the requisite habitudes of thought for the acquirement of a sound and stable philosophy. Yet we are not prepared to say that the occasional recreation of a novel, with the full sense of its being a pure invention and nothing more, will mislead a general reader from the prudentials or the proprieties of our actual and every-day world; nor are we prepared to say that the occasional study of a German metaphysician, with the full sense of his being a baseless speculator and nothing more, will mislead the votary of science from the firm pathway to its best and highest discoveries. Nay, we are not sure but that both might turn out to be improving and beneficial exercises—for that, as a novel on the one hand might, better than the prosaic virtues of familiar and home-bred experience, inspire a purer and nobler style of sentiment; so a speculation on the other, however groundless and unsubstantial in itself, might nevertheless abound in such specimens of logic, and profundity, and marvellous discernment into the inner mysteries of our nature, as both mightily to strengthen the mental faculties, and elevate the aims of science. We do not want to speak lightly of German transcendentalism, and far less of its numerous admirers. On the contrary, we view their passion for it with the same respect that we should a very high species of amateurship. We should reckon the sitters in the gallery, whose strongest relish is for spectacles or the theatricals of sight, to be of a lower grade than the sitters in the pit or the boxes, whose preference is for the theatricals of sentiment. But greatly above both, in our estimation, are they whose higher demand is for what may be termed the theatricals of science; and who, though they do not concern themselves much, if at all, about the truth of its doctrines, yet luxuriate as in their best-loved element, when following in the march of its demonstrations, or soaring upwards to the sublimest height of its ideas.* No wonder that system should follow after

* There is a saying of Lessing's which serves us as a key to these peculiarities of the German character and habit. "If the Almighty held the truth in one hand, and the search after it (*la vérité, et la récherche de la vérité*) in another, it is the latter that I should demand of him in preference." We have all heard of the pleasures of the chase, and how vastly they transcend the felt value of the game. And so we can imagine a far greater delight in the pursuit of truth than in the acquisition of it. It is a high order of sport certainly; but with all respect to these more illustrious sportsmen, we must still hold that the end is better than the means, the landing-place than the way which leads to it, and, at all events, that the truth is too serious and sacred a thing to be thus sported with'

system for the entertainment of such a public, just as drama follows after drama for the lovers of the stage. We refuse to mould our philosophy according to the systems of Germany; but this will not hinder our profoundest veneration for that public in Germany, whose chief enjoyment lies in the regalement of their imaginations and intellects, in the play and exercise of the highest faculties of our nature. In serious and sober earnest, these Germans are the noblest people on the face of the earth. We greatly prefer their taste and value for mental products to the gross utilitarianism of our own land, their Leipsic fair of books to our own broad-cloths and bales of merchandise; and it makes one's old and languid blood beat with the pulse of other days, when we read of their students "warm from the schools of glory," shouting in defiance to each other the watch-word of their respective philosophies, and almost ready to fight in the defence of them. Altogether it marks them as a loftier and more ethereal race; and we rejoice that there should still be one country in the world, uninfected by the breath of our mercantile society, and neither overrun by the frivolities, nor debased by the sordidness of other countries and other climes.

But their great writers have other fascinations besides those of lofty and commanding intellect. Many of them stand forth to us clothed in the virtues of antiquity. Kant has been well designated by Cousin as the Stoic of the 18th century. Of Fichte we are told, that "however extravagant we may consider his theoretical science, yet it is impossible to read his noble sentiments on human duty, and to see them exemplified in his own eventful life, without feeling our moral weakness reproved, and our moral strength invigorated." (*Morell*, ii. 533),—so that the resolute principle and high-minded patriotism of the man may go far with many to redeem his speculative errors. And besides that nobleness of character which awakens in their readers, as it did in their pupils, the admiration that we feel for highest moral chivalry, we must recollect too the graces often of their oratory and grandeur of their imaginations. In the language of Madame de Staël, "we find nowhere but among the German nations the phenomenon of those writers who consecrate the most abstract metaphysics to the defence of systems the most exalted, and who hide a lively imagination under an austere logic." It is not to be wondered then, that with this combination of excellences, they should have kindled such enthusiasm in the hearts of many who did not believe in the dogmata of their creeds, perhaps even did not understand, or at least did not care for them. They are proselytes, not to the philosophy of Germany, but to the living spirit of its authors.

Such, and such precisely, is the proselytism of Mr. Carlyle. He is the champion of Germanism, not in its letter, but in its spirit. We could not, he himself could not, point to one of its dogmata as having aught to do with the inspiration which animates him, and which he has given forth in such marvellous volumes to the world. Could he, for example, tell us what the Articles are, and whether to be found in the Confessions of Schelling, or Hegel, or Fichte, or even Kant, which have caused the fire to burn within him? They are not creeds, but men who are the objects of his idolatry, which, under the name of hero-worship, he renders alike to those of most opposite opinions—as to Luther, and Knox, and Cromwell on the one hand, or with equal veneration to the lofty poets and transcendentalists of Germany upon the other. He is a lover of earnestness more than a lover of truth; and it would not be our counteractive at least, to urge that he should be a lover of truth more than a lover of earnestness. We should rather say that both are best; and would our island only not be frightened from its propriety by the high-sounding philosophy of the continent—neither overborne by its pretensions, nor overawed by its cabalistic nomenclature—would our savans and theologians but keep unmoved on the ground of common sense, and by their paramount demand for evidence at every step, lay resolute arrest on the pruriencies of wanton speculation—then while they rejected all that was unsubstantial and unsound in the dogmata of the transcendental school, it were well that they imported the earnest and lofty enthusiasm of its disciples into the phlegmatic universities and no less phlegmatic churches of our land. We do not need to take down the framework of our existing orthodoxy, whether in theology or science. All we require is that it shall become an animated framework, by the breath of a new life being infused into it. Ours has been most truly denounced as an age of formulism: But to mend this we do not need to exchange our formulas, only to quicken them; nor to quit the ground of our own common sense for baseless speculations; nor to substitute the Divine Idea of Fichte for a personal and living God; nor to adopt for our Saviour a mere imbodied and allegorized perfection, and give up the actual and historical Jesus Christ of the New Testament; nor, finally, to go in quest of a chimerical ontology in upper regions, far out of mortal ken, and for visions of merest fancy there, to renounce either the certainties of our own palpable and peopled world, or the truths which He who dwelleth in the heavens brought down from heaven, because no man can ascend into heaven or tell the mysteries and glories of a place which he never entered.* What we want is that the very system of doctrine which we now have shall come to us not in word only but in power. As things stand at present, our creeds and confessions have become effete; and the Bible a dead letter; and that orthodoxy which was at one time the glory, by withering into the inert and the lifeless, is now the shame and the reproach of all our Churches. If there have been the revival

* John iii. 13.

of a more spiritual philosophy in France or elsewhere, it might well humble us; but this is not exactly the quarter from which we should expect our revival to come. Prayer could bring it down from above; and it is only thus that all which is good in Puritanism, its earnestness without its extravagance, its faith without its contempt for philosophy, its high and heavenly-mindedness without the baser admixture of its worldly politics and passions—it is only thus that the Augustan age of Christianity in England, an age which Mr. Carlyle has done so much to vindicate and bring to light, will again come back to reform our State, and to bless our families. But we must not withhold one part at least of the sketch of this great writer, the whole being one of the most eloquent and masterly that is presented in these volumes.

"In adverting to the philosophy of England, which bears the German stamp upon it, almost every one will immediately recall the name of Thomas Carlyle, a name which stands first and foremost among the idealistic writers of our age. In bringing the works of Carlyle for a moment before our attention, we shall not give any opinion respecting his *theological* sentiments, inasmuch as these lie quite beyond our beat, and have to be judged of before another tribunal, besides that of *à priori* reasoning. Neither do we wish to track his philosophical views to the German originals, from which it is unquestionable that many of them have sprung. In the case of a writer so powerful, so original, and so full of fire and genius, it is a thankless task at best to assign a foreign paternity to the burning thoughts, that we find scattered with no sparing hand almost through every page. That Mr. Carlyle has learned much truth, and added much inspiration to the force of his genius, from the literature and philosophy of Germany, he would himself be the first to own; but his sentiments have not been so much borrowed from these sources, as inspired from them: he has used these philosophers as his familiar companions, rather than as his masters; and instead of sitting at their feet, we should rather say 'that his soul has burned within him, as he has walked with them by the way.'"—Vol. ii., pp. 201, 202.

"Much would we say of Carlyle's earnest appeals on the religion of the age, were we not afraid to venture into so frightful, and, we might almost say, so dangerous a subject; but here, too, we find him uttering his lamentations or his anathemas against the hollow-hearted formalism of Christendom, against the *sham* worship which has taken the place of the undaunted faith and burning love of the prophets and apostles of God. Without distinction of name, of rank, or of popular favor, he tears the mask from the features of hypocrisy, and places again and again, in no very flattering contrast, the pompous, easy, formal, soulless worship that is seen in many a Christian temple, with the Hindoo, the Mohammedan, or even the untutored Indian, who sees God in everything he sees, and hears him in everything he hears. 'Will you ever be calling heathenism a lie, worthy of damnation, which leads its devotee to consecrate all upon its altars, and with a wonder, which transcends all your logic, bows before some idol of nature; while those who, with sleepy heads and lifeless spirits, meet in a framed house, and go over a different act of forms, are the only elect of God? Clear thy mind of cant! Does not God look at the heart?' With a truly Platonic contempt for the material, and as ardent a love for the intellectual, the ideal, the Divine, our author wanders through all the regions of the habits, customs, laws, and institutions of our day, chastening all that is shallow and insincere, and pleading for everything that is earnest and true in human life."—Vol. ii., pp. 204–206.

It is obvious from these extracts, and indeed from all his writings, that they are not the dogmata of Germany which Mr. Carlyle idolizes, but the lofty intellect, the high-souled independence, and, above all, as most akin with the aspirings of his own chivalrous and undaunted nature, the noble-heartedness of Germany. And indeed there is one grand peculiarity for which we would set him down as a direct and diametrical opponent to the philosophy of her reigning schools—and that is the value he ever and anon expresses for facts, his reverence for "great facts," although in the very class of those truths which continentalism would stigmatize as empirical, and reckon with as of immeasurably lower grade than any of the logical results of its own hypothetical speculations.* There lies an immense responsibility on professing Christians, if such men as he, with their importunate and most righteous demand for all the generous and god-like virtues of the Gospel, are not brought to "the obedience of the faith." There must be a most deplorable want amongst us of the "light shining before men," when, instead of glorifying our cause, they can speak, and with a truth the most humiliating, of our inert and unproductive orthodoxy. These withering adjurations of Carlyle should be of use to our churches; and yet most assuredly it is not by grafting the German philosophy on the Gospel of Jesus Christ,—nor yet by overlaying its literal facts or literal doctrines with the glosses and the allegories of German rationalism,—it is not thus that we shall be able to vindicate, far less to magnify, our religion, in the eyes of the world. Without the mutilation of it by one jot or one tittle, we have but to fill and follow up that Gospel, to imbody it entire in our own personal history, turning its precepts into a law, and its faith into a living principle. All the elements of moral grace and grandeur are there—the sublime devotion—the expansive charity—the greatness of soul, inspired not by the visions but the clear and certain views of immortality, and hence the noble superiority to the commonplace objects of a selfish and short-sighted world—the habit of unwearied well-doing, even in the midst of surrounding apathy, or it may be of calumny and injustice—those heaven-born virtues which spring not from earth, but are nurtured by prayer, and descend on the breast of every true believer from the upper sanctuary: And, to crown the whole, the single-hearted loyalty to Him who poured out his soul unto the death for us, and who, Himself the examplar of all righteousness, tells His disciples that He will hold them to be indeed His friends, if they but love one another and keep his commandments

* The distinction between necessary and empirical truths might with all sound philosophy be acquiesced in, were it not for the degrading associations which the term empirical carries along with it—tending to bring down the category of "Quid est" among the lowest, when in fact its rightful place is among the highest objects of human thought. We therefore desiderate another nomenclature for this distinction, as due to the worth, and, we add, to the dignity of experience or of experimental science. Such is the power of imposition that lies in mere words; and we should therefore greatly prefer the classification of *abstract* and *substantive* truths.

—These are the simple and sublime lessons which all the wisdom of all the schools never could have reached, and most certainly can never realize—because only to be sustained on the basis of those Scriptures which "cannot be broken," and of that Word which "passeth not away."

We feel that we have scarcely yet broken ground on the subject of the German philosophy, and more especially of its bearings on the high questions of Natural and Revealed Religion. Nothing, it must be obvious, beyond the general and the introductory can possibly be overtaken within the compass of one Article ; and that for doing full justice to the theme, there should be a succession of Articles—though not more than one of moderate size in each Number of the Review—so as to bestow a piecemeal treatment both on particular authors and particular arguments. It is thus that we should like to obtain distinct and thorough critical estimates, through the medium of some one or other of their writings, of Kant, and Fichte, and Schelling, and Strauss, and above all of Cousin, at whose hands—though himself not altogether unscathed by the transcendentalism which he has done so much to expose—we expect, and indeed have already received most important service, for the re-establishment both of a sounder metaphysics, and of a sound mental philosophy. We happen to know a sufficient number of men in this country, equal, and more than equal, to the accomplishment of what we now desiderate in behalf of this Journal ; and who, would they only give themselves to the task, could make triumphant exposure of the cosmogonies, and, more monstrous still, of the *theogonies*, that have issued, as their original fountain-head, from the school of Königsberg. These men, we understand, in certain subordinate matters of speculation, in some of what may be called the secular parts of their philosophy, are not altogether at one. But this is a difference which in itself, as well as the exhibition of it in these pages, might well be tolerated. Enough for us, if they hold in common that indispensable philosophy, which is either conducive to, or might legitimately co-exist with a sound faith. Enough, if they can join heart and hand against those speculations which would displace from our creed, either a personal and living God, or a Bible which, both in its history and in its doctrines, they hold to be literally true.

Let us proclaim it as the great and distinctive feature that we should wish to see henceforth impressed upon this department of the Journal—the most special service which through its medium we should like were rendered to society—the best and worthiest honor in short to which it can aspire—is that it shall ably acquit itself as a defender of the Christian faith, intact and entire, against those new and unwonted forms of infidelity which are so rife and rampant in our day—whether springing up in our own land, or imported from abroad. And on the subject-matter, as well as the credentials of Christianity, we hope and are persuaded that it will give forth no uncertain sound; but will both be the unflinching advocate of pure Scripture doctrine, and breathe throughout its pages the spirit of a deep-felt and devoted piety.

But as yet we have only spoken of one department in the review—even that which is consecrated to the exposition and defence of a sound Theology, in connection with a sound mental Philosophy and a sound Ethics. We are glad to know that in the high department of Physical Science, it will be supported as heretofore by savants of the first name in the country—while, for the general and miscellaneous reader, every exertion will be made to obtain the best possible contributions on books of history and travels and the fine arts, as well as on the methods and statistics of education. The last of these subjects should ever occupy a prominent place in a work devoted, as this is, to the best and highest interests of society—and more especially to what might be termed the great problem of our day, which is to devise and carry into effect the likeliest means for the permanent amelioration, both as respects their comfort and their character, of the working class in our land.

There are certain topics of an ephemeral character, which are more appropriate for the columns of a Newspaper than for the pages of a Review. And yet these may at times be so closely associated with permanent truth, or be so conducive to the illustration of it, as to claim a rightful place in the higher of these periodicals. Of this we have given recent instances in our discussions both on a Poor-law and on the Corn-laws. To these we should like that a third instance were added, in an Article on the present fearful destitution which has overtaken certain parts of our empire—the most expressive title for which would be "The Political economy of a Famine." We regret the impossibility of such a preparation for the Number now issuing from the press; but though we cannot at present give the reasoning, it may be of more practical importance that we give the results of it. We have already expressed our fears, lest the power and the prolific virtues of Free Trade should be greatly overrated, and accordingly this has already given rise to far too large an expectation of supplies from abroad—an expectation which has deluded the public mind into a false security, and may have perhaps misled the policy of our Rulers, else we might have had, and should have still, *an instant stoppage of the distilleries.* On the other hand, we hold that the evils of a Poor-rate, in corrupting the habits and undermining the independence of the working classes, cannot be overrated. But in an emergency like the present, of palpable, undeniable distress, when human creatures are dying in hundreds before our eyes, all the liberalities of Government (who in this respect are doing nobly), as well as of both public and private benevolence, should be put forth to the uttermost—for the mitigation of a calamity that will soon evince itself to be of ten-fold greater dimensions than have yet come within the reckoning of the community at large, or even of many of our most enlightened philanthropists and statesmen.

In conclusion, let us observe, that, as we disclaim for this Review all partisanship in politics—so with like earnestness do we disclaim for it all sectarianism in things ecclesiastical. We utterly repudiate its being our aim to advance the objects of any one denomination in the Church of Christ, though we shall ever regard it as a high and holy endeavor to advance the objects of the Church Universal. On this sacred theme our alone directory is the Bible, and our alone desire is to speed forward the cause of truth and righteousness in the world.

POLITICAL ECONOMY OF A FAMINE.

1. *Correspondence from July,* 1846, *to February,* 1847, *relating to the measures adopted for the Relief of the Distress in Scotland.*
2. *Correspondence from July,* 1846, *to January,* 1847, *relating to the measures adopted for the Relief of the Distress in Ireland.* (Commissariat Series.)
3. *Do. do. do.* (Board of Works Series.)
4. *Do. from January to March,* 1847. (Commissariat Series.)

(*From the North British Review, May,* 1847.)

We feel as it were somewhat daring to have assumed such a title for our article as "The Political Economy of a Famine," a revolting and unnatural conjunction it will be thought by many; as bringing the severest infliction which can be laid on suffering humanity, bringing it under the inspection and placing it at the disposal of a hard and unfeeling overseer. We adopt the title notwithstanding, and this expressly because we want to make the earliest possible declaration of war against such an imagination. Political economy is no more responsible for the perversities and errors of its disciples than is any other of the sciences. It is true that it is a science, not a sentiment; and that as a science it is conversant with truth alone. It has been variously defined; but let us once take up the view, that its object is to discover and assign the laws by which the increase and distribution of wealth are regulated—surely a fair and competent field of inquiry; and presenting, it may be, a subject in every way as accessible, and as capable of being strictly and fully ascertained, as any other subject of human investigation. Now, surely, Political Economy might be left with all safety, nay often with great advantage, to the accomplishment of this service, without damage or disturbance to the other, and it may be, the higher objects of national policy. We might take her lessons upon wealth, and yet not give in to the false and ruinous principle that wealth is the *summum bonum* of a people. There are other and far greater interests, not to be sacrificed at the shrine of wealth, but to which wealth should be made the subordinate and the tributary. National independence is one of those interests which most men will think is paramount to wealth, and therefore ought to be provided for at the expense of adequate naval and military establishments. National virtue is another of those interests which many men, and ourselves among the number, will also think is paramount to wealth, and ought to be provided for at the expense of good institutions. But, to come nearer the case in hand, the preservation of human life is a far higher object than any which comes within the range of Political Economy; and rather than that so much as one of our fellow-countrymen should perish of hunger, no expense should be spared to prevent a catastrophe so horrible. It is for Humanity to give the word of command in this matter. And yet Political Economy has a word in it too—the word of direction as to how the command can be most fully and effectually executed. We might refuse altogether her authority as a master, and yet avail ourselves to the uttermost of her services as a guide—for in this latter capacity her lessons are invaluable; and it is high time to put a decisive check on those senseless outcries which, both in and out of Parliament, have been lifted up against her. There is no such mal-adjustment in the constitution, whether of man or of things, as that, for the sake of his wellbeing, a violence must be done either to reason or to principle. On the contrary, it will ever be found—that, in like manner as truth and beauty, so truth and benevolence, or truth and all virtue are at one.

And yet scarcely a paragraph can be written on the existing distress without a fling at Political Economy—as if the ills and sufferings of society must be laid at the door of this the most maligned, while perhaps the least understood of the Sciences. And so in how many a newspaper do we read of "the cold maxims of a heartless Political Economy," of the numerous deaths by famine being "holocausts offered at the shrine of Political Economy." "The poor," we are told from Dingle on the 9th of February, "are at the mercy of the famine-mongers, who have advanced the price of meal from three to four shillings, and we have but a small supply even at these prices. Our bakers are making exorbitant profits. It is a pity we have not the same law here as in Turkey, where they are nailed through the ears to their own doors." In like manner, the *Galway Mercury*, after recording a death, goes on to observe that "thus another of our fellow-creatures has been offered up a holocaust to the doctrine of Political Economy, now so much in favor with our Whig rulers." Similar reflections to these occur every day in the Irish newspapers. But to us the far most interesting specimen is that given forth in the verdict of a jury on a coroner's inquest in Dublin, as fully described in Saunders' News-Letter of February 16. The following is a part of that verdict.—"The jury, without entering into any political questions, sincerely deplore that the existing Government, however kindly and well disposed towards this country, should for a single moment adhere to a cold-blooded system of Political Economy, which thus allows famine to invade the very heart of our metropolis, and is rapidly decimating the people throughout the entire island." The verdict closes thus—"In conclusion, the jury, while fully sensible of past exertions, respectfully implore in the name of their fellow-citizens, that the Government will, at all costs, at once adopt comprehensive, energetic, and above all immediate measures, to stay the effects of the famine now ravaging and desolating our unfortunate country."—A most impressive utterance, and in a spirit, too, wherewith one can fully sympathize—given in truly solemn and affecting circumstances, and worthy of all duteous and respectful consideration. We feel inclined to make it the text of our whole Article, though perhaps differing in our views from the right-hearted men who have furnished it; and disposed to think that neither Government nor Political Economy is so chargeable with their country's ills as they seem to apprehend.

We confess our toleration and even our sympathy for such outbreakings as these, when they proceed from the sufferers themselves; but not when uttered, as they sometimes are, within the walls of Parliament. The privations and the high prices, which are sufficiently accounted for by the famine, it might be venial and certainly not unnatural for parties out of doors to charge upon the famine-mongers. But what we can feel the utmost indulgence for, when heard at a public meeting, or given forth from a jury-box, might be a disgrace and utter folly, if spoken in the Senate-house. And yet it is but the other day, when, if the reports might be credited, a distinguished and aspiring statesman could tell, with seeming complacency, of a law by which the dealers in corn, because dealers of course in the miseries of the people, were hung up at their own doors—an invective pardonable enough when uttered, as at Dingle, by a voice from among the dead and dying; but not pardonable, because mischievous and wrong, when thus re-echoed to from the high places of our land. It is certainly not the way to encourage commerce, or to facilitate the diffusion of its blessings, thus to summon up the terrors of Lynch law wherewith to overhang and overbear its operations. We know not in how far the starvation of Ireland might be owing to the dread of such outrages, and to the insecurity attendant on the conveyance of the requisite supplies from one locality to another; but it is our strong persuasion that, with a due liberality on the part of Government, along with a wise and well-principled administration of its grants, not one of these starvations should have occurred. For the explanation of this opinion, however, we must draw on the lessons of Political Economy, against which, so loud is the popular and prevailing cry, that but few will listen to them. As if the famine were not of itself sufficient to account for the present miseries of Ireland, it is this hateful and hated Political Economy which must bear all the blame of them; about as reasonable as when an orator in Conciliation Hall ascribed them all to politics—telling us that it was now the 46th year of the Union, and that such was the state to which that measure had brought their ill-governed country. This might pass in an assembly of demagogues and agitators; but it is truly wretched to hear of such clap-traps in our House of Commons, whether uttered as fetches for popularity, or in sheer ignorance—an ignorance most unseemly among those, who, whether men of wisdom and high talent or not, should at least be men of education.

Let us now endeavor to lay down, with all possible brevity, what we have termed the Political Economy of a Famine.

A famine may be either general, by which we do not mean a famine extending over the whole world, but over a whole country; or it may be local, that is, a famine confined to special parts of the country.

The Political Economy of a general famine might be soon told; and let us accordingly tell it in as few words as we can, that more room might be left for what is specially, and at this particular moment, the matter in hand.

The effect of a scarcity on prices is obvious to all; and even to most men the reason of this effect is alike obvious. The first alarm of it induces an earnest competition among the families for food. There are many other articles of expenditure, the use of which can be greatly abridged, or even might be altogether dispensed with. But to dispense with food is impossible, and neither can the use of it be much abridged, without the feeling of a sore inconvenience. It is thus that a proportion of the money which in ordinary years went to the purchase of other enjoyments, will, in a year of scarcity, be reserved for the purchase of necessaries. In other words, a greater amount of money is brought to market than usual, and this over against a smaller amount of food; and so a rise in its price is the inevitable consequence. It were well if the rationale of this process could be brought clearly and convincingly home to the apprehensions of all men: and so as that we could reconcile the popular understanding to the conclusion which might be drawn from it. In particular it were well if they could be made to see how far the price of an article is the fiat, not of the dealers, but the fiat of the customers; or that such is its price, not because the dealers exacted, but because the customers offered it—insomuch that the collective will of the latter, and not of the former, is primarily and efficiently the cause of prices. It is quite palpable that it is the more intense demand of purchasers which raises prices; and that this calls forth larger supplies, which is the dealer's part of the operation, and has the direct tendency to lower them. All this as being part of the alphabet of their science, is familiar to the economist; nor do we think it impossible to be made as familiar to the people at large. For this reason we have long desiderated that Political Economy should hold a pre-eminent place among the lectureships of a Mechanic School, where instead of a tyrant or a disturber, it would be regarded, and at length become a tranquillizer of the commonwealth.

But not only are high prices in seasons of scarcity a present necessary evil. There is a great ulterior good to which they are subservient. There are few of any pretensions to scholarship or general reading, who are ignorant of Adam Smith's effective illustration upon this subject—when he compares a country under famine to a ship at sea that had run short of provisions, and so had to put the crew upon a short allowance, who although thus for the time being made to suffer, were enabled thereby to live on to the end of the voyage. Such is the precise effect of a high price, when there is a scanty supply of food in the land. It puts the country upon short allowance, by operating as a check upon consumption—when families, that they might get the two ends to meet, are reduced to their shifts and expedients for the economizing of food. Were it not for this salutary restraint, were the inadequate stock of provisions sold off at the usual price, the consumption would go on at its usual rate; and the premature exhaustion of the food on hand, though it should take place only a single month, or even a single week before the coming harvest, would land the country in all the horrors of a general starvation. We are quite sensible how difficult it were to persuade a hungry population, nay how provoking it might be when such a lesson is read out to them in all the pride and confidence of reasoning. The economist would adventure himself on a very serious hazard indeed, were he in all the coolness of his argument to attempt such a demonstration in the hearing of an angry multitude. Nevertheless it is even so, helplessly and necessarily so, in the nature of things and by the constitution of human society. The truth of it is quite palpable within the narrow compass of a ship, however lost sight of on the wider field of a country. Should one or more of the sailors intimidate the store-keeper, and force a larger allowance for themselves, the indignation of the crew, when it became known, would be directed against the purloiner—on whom, perhaps, for the general good, they would carry the Lynch law into effect, and hang him up at the yardarm. Such were the likely proceeding at sea, but on land they would order the matter differently. They would hang the store-keeper—for such the corn-dealer or meal-seller virtually is—who by means of his high prices deals out their short allowances to the people. It is true, it is not their good, but his own gain, that he is looking to all the while. He is but the unconscious instrument of a great and general benefit, which he is not counting on and not caring for. "He meaneth not so." It is the doing of a higher hand, of Him who ordaineth both the laws of Nature and the laws of human society; and who can not only make the wrath of man to praise Him, but who can make even the selfishness of individuals work out a country's salvation. "The foolishness of God is wiser than the wisdom of men."

At the same time there is one important modification of this doctrine, which neither Adam Smith nor almost any other economist has adverted to; and which we state all the more willingly, that it might serve to restrain the unqualified, and sometimes injurious confidence, which is now so generally expressed in the virtues of Free Trade—as if this were to be the grand panacea for all the ills that can befall a country or a country's population. What we refer to is the peculiarities belonging to the necessaries of life, in regard to the degree of variation which their price undergoes, as affected by the variation in the quantity brought to market. The one variation greatly exceeds the other. For example, so small a diminution as one-tenth in the grain of a country would induce a much larger augmentation of its price, so as to make it perhaps one-third dearer than before. The deficiency of a third in the crop would probably more than double the price of grain, while if approaching to one-half, it would infallibly land us in famine prices. It is thus that in articles of prime necessity the price describes a much larger arc of oscillation than does the quantity, or fluctuates far more widely and beyond the proportion of those fluctuations which take place in the supply. And the principle of this is obvious. Men can want luxuries and even comforts; but they cannot want necessaries. They can limit themselves to a much greater extent in the use of the former than in the use of the latter. Should the crop of sugar be deficient by one-third, they could, if they chose, easily put up with one-third less of sugar—so that there might be no rise of price, and the whole loss incurred by the deficiency would fall upon the planters. Should the crops of grain be deficient by one-third, men could not so easily put up with one-third less of bread; and, rather than this, would make a larger outlay for food than usual, so that more money might come into market for less of the article, and, instead of loss, there would be gain to the farmers. It is thus that, generally speaking, the keener competition in years of scarcity for the necessaries of life, causes the deficiency to fall with redoubled pressure on the consumers, who have both less to eat and more to pay for it.

It is not then exactly, and in all cases, true—that the interest of the dealers coincides to the full with the interest of the public; or that the former will take care to sell at prices sufficiently low for there being enough of consumption to carry off their stocks, and so as not to be landed in such a surplus at the end of the agricultural year, as with the supplies of the coming harvest might cause that grain shall be a drug upon the market. The truth is, and on the strength of the principle just explained, that if, instead of reserving a surplus, they had agreed to destroy it, such high prices might have been maintained throughout the year on the reduced quantity brought to market, as that the dealer should be more than indemnified. The elevation of price would more than compensate for the reduction in the quantity—so that could they agree in doing what the Dutch merchants are said to have done with their spiceries, lay aside a certain general surplus to be burned or cast into the sea, it might be greatly more than made up for by the enhanced prices which they would obtain for the remainder. But then the difficulty, or in the corn trade, the impossibility, lies in getting them to agree. What might be effected by a small party of monopolists, is utterly beyond the power of a general combination on the part of dealers spread over a whole empire, and acting without any adequate control or cognizance of each other's operations. Our great security, then, in all our larger markets, and wherever there is enough of competition among parties acting separately, and out of sight from each other, is the difficulty of combination. It is in these circumstances that the doctrine of Free Trade might be practically carried forth in its utmost perfection—and this with the greatest possible advantage to the community at large. The commerce might be left, or to use a still stronger word, might be abandoned with all safety to its own operations. And all which Government has to do is this—refraining from those interferences by which it has so often done mischief—to remove those obstructions which itself may have placed in the way either of arrivals from all parts of the country, or of arrivals from all parts of the world.

Yet there is one important exception, peculiarly applicable to the state of matters at present, and but for this indeed we should not have lengthened out our article by any explanation of it. The argument in favor of Free Trade, and against the interference of Government, requires, not only that there shall be an unshackled competition, *but that there shall be enough of it.* Now there are many places in our land, and more especially in that part of it on which the present calamitous visitation has lighted, where this postulate is altogether wanting—as in sequestered villages, or small and remote islands, where a single meal-shop might suffice for all the customers within its range. Now it is in these circumstances, that one or even a small number of dealers, if but few enough to lay their heads together, could easily so manage as to realize the most unconscionable profits. They have but to impose their own prices, and they have the people at their mercy. It is true they might in this way greatly limit the consumption, to the severe hardship and suffering of all the families, and it may be with some deaths by starvation to the bargain; but although they should thus abridge the sales, they would, if there be truth in our principle, greatly more than make up for this to themselves by an overpassing enhancement of the prices. They might sell one-third less than at a fair price they would have done, but this by a doubling of the price, and so a tripling or quadrupling of their own profits. Yet notwithstanding this cruel monopoly of theirs, we would not just hang them up at their own doors; but, with all deference to the Free Trade principle, should not object if a Relief Committee made free to take the business for a time out of their hands, by importing grain and selling it at the cost prices. This were in the face of all principle in those places where there is enough of competition, both in the retail and wholesale business. But what is at all times sound doctrine for London or Liverpool might in particular emergencies be the very reverse for Owenmore or Tobermory—in the former of which places, we learn from a private source that rice has been selling at 36s. per cwt., when in Dublin it was selling for 24s.; while in the latter, it appears from one of the volumes under review, and on the information of Sir Edward Coffin, that the people were "much gratified with the prospect of obtaining the needful supplies through the intervention of the Government, and at cost price, instead of being obliged to make their purchases at Glasgow or Liverpool, or to pay the exorbitant prices exacted by the few local dealers."—(P. 53 *of Scotch Correspondence*). There is no disparagement in this to the wisdom of the very enlightened Resolutions on the part of the North Leith Parochial Board, when the recommendation was laid before them of laying in stores of provisions; and they very properly decided against it, on the ground "that the saving of the retailer's profits would be nothing to the advantage of their funds." But while very true that the competition in such a place as Leith is a sufficient guarantee against extortion, we believe that what Captain Pole tells us of Skye is just as true,—even that "the dealers there had raised the price of food exorbitantly;" or, as he expresses it in one of those admirable summaries wherewith he closes his letters, that "the market is destroyed locally by the famine prices of the dealers." We therefore fully sympathize with Mr. Rainey, the patriotic owner of the island of Raasay, when he complains that "his people, who are obliged to go to market at Portree, are charged exorbitantly for every article." And hence, too, the Marquis of Lorne, who, fully aware of what the sound Political Economy is on the general question, writes thus to Sir George Grey, the Home Secretary, "That interference with the 'ordinary channels of trade' is in itself objectionable there can be no doubt; but when there is just ground to fear that those channels will not convey to any district a sufficiently accessible supply of food, it becomes one of those cases of necessity which demand extraordinary measures. The fact is that, as regards the most distressed districts of the islands and western coasts, these 'channels of trade' have never been cut."—(*Scotch Correspondence*, p. 26.) The wisdom, therefore, which we have just ascribed to the North Leith Resolutions, does not conflict with the equal wisdom of the Argyleshire Resolutions, in which we find it stated, that "there are localities where, from the great redundancy of population, and great scarcity of food, distance from market, and the nature of the occupation of land, it is practically impossible to command a supply sufficient; that, under these circumstances, Government should be requested to establish stores of food in the localities alluded to, such as Oban or Tobermory, so as to be accessible to proprietors to be purchased by them." Yet what was thus requested and rightly for the Hebrides, was deprecated and just as rightly, for the Shetland isles—where the framers of a truly enlightened memorial tell us that they wanted no interference with the retail dealer, on whom their ordinary supplies depend, because they felt assured "that it may safely be left to mercantile enterprise and competition, to import a sufficient quantity of food at the cheapest rate, provided the means for paying such can be afforded to the people."*—(*Scotch Correspondence*, p. 154.) It is a matter of selection, and dependent on the circumstance of each locality, whether there should be a Government depot or not; and in these islands, as we are afterwards informed, there was no occasion for one, because there was there enough of competition from the frequent interchanges that took place between Lerwick, the capital of the group, and various ports in the south. To point out the exceptions to a doctrine is often a higher effort of discrimination than to understand the doctrine itself. And so we can imagine a number of new-fledged economists in the metropolis parroting over their last gotten lesson of Free Trade, and contending that *in every instance* the supply of what is needed should be left to private speculation and individual enterprise." And we do admit that the general principle is a sound one. Yet we rejoice in the practical good sense which led to the actual instances of a deviation from it in the west of Scotland, and still more throughout Ireland —thus carrying it over a philosophy which has not yet learned to take proper cognizance of its own limits, or to distinguish aright between what are and what are not its legitimate applications.

But we must not linger thus at the threshold; but, keeping in remembrance our allotted limits, enter at once on our main subject, not of a General, but of a Local Famine. This is the character of our present visitation. One-fifth, perhaps one-fourth of our people, now labor under the almost total privation of what constituted their main food. It is not that the other ordinary articles of agricultural produce, besides what themselves eat, are not raised upon their territory. But these are generally sold off; and the price of them reserved for the payment of rent, and the pur-

* Let the reader mark the importance of this last proviso. It is but doing the things by halves to establish depots in such places as Skibbereen or Schull, where, if the food was only to be distributed by purchase, yet the people were not provided with the means of paying for it, they behooved to die in hundreds, although within sight of plenty.

chase of a few indispensable necessaries. In as far as the rent is helped out by the sale of their potatoe-fed pigs, this too has entirely failed them—so that the revenue of the landlords has been greatly impaired while the subsistence of the peasantry has utterly gone. Behold, then, several millions of people thus circumstanced—the great bulk of them in Ireland, with one-quarter or one-third of a million in the Highlands of Scotland—without food and without the money to purchase it.

Meanwhile the rest of our people, amounting to three-fourths or four-fifths of the whole, have been living in the enjoyment of their wonted abundance. We ground this assertion, not on any reckoning of last year's crop, which some contend to have been above and others somewhat beneath an average. We ground it on the palpable fact, that although the price of their staple food be high, the general rate of wages, both throughout England and in the Lowlands of Scotland is proportionally higher. We can find no such record of the wages in different kinds of employment from year to year, as we have of the prices of different kinds of food. Yet though in defect of all arithmetical statements on the subject, we might confidently affirm notwithstanding, that the working-classes, in all those parts of the country where there is but a partial and limited dependence on potatoes, are comparatively well off—we mean comparatively not with our starving Irish or Highlanders, but comparatively with themselves in other and ordinary years. They at this moment, generally speaking, have fully their usual command over the necessaries of life—while no one will deny, that, on ascending upwards in the scale of society, we witness as full a command over its comforts and luxuries; and that in the splendor, and profusion, and varied gratifications of the affluent and higher classes there is no abatement.

These then are the data upon which our question is founded—a territory consisting of two parts, whereof the one, being much the smaller of the two, is famine-stricken to the extent of several millions being in total want both of food and of money to buy it with; and the other, of about four times larger population, is in the full enjoyment of at least its wonted or average abundance. And the question is, In these circumstances can all be kept alive; or by what process of supply and distribution is it possible to avert so dreadful a catastrophe as that a single human creature shall perish of hunger?

This is truly the matter in hand, the first and foremost of all the things which have to be provided for, the instant cry and demand of humanity, admitted and felt in all quarters to be the paramount object, and by none more honestly and intently we believe than by the Government themselves and the leading officials whom they employ. This appears in every page of their published Correspondence, the perusal of which would serve in the mind of every candid reader greatly to mitigate the charges which have been preferred against the heartlessness of our Rulers and the cold-bloodedness of their Political Economy. "The condition of the people in the smaller and more remote islands, who may be overtaken and overwhelmed before their destitution is known or provided for, will require special attention."* "The population must be fed."† "The people cannot *under any circumstances* be allowed to starve."‡ The italics are in Mr. Trevelyan's own hand, whose humanity and intelligence, and the skilful adaptation of whose counsels to the ever varying cases on which his judgment was called for, cannot be too highly appreciated. Into whatever mistakes his constituents may have fallen, or whatever their want of boldness and decision in the encounter with those oppositions to which they may have too easily given way—certain it is, both of him and of them, that their predominant feeling all along has been earnestness for the preservation of human life. To achieve this is, clearly and undoubtedly, what they would if they could, and if they knew but how.

And yet how has the matter actually sped? The number of deaths, and this too in their cruellest and most appalling form, has been quite fearful. We know not, if since the dawn of modern civilization, there has been such a record of starvation in any country within the limits of Christendom. On this distressing subject, it were endless and quite unnecessary to go into detail—although we have by us a very large collection both of newspaper and private informations, thinking at the outset that these might be required to authenticate our statements. Our feeling now is, that in a thing so palpable and notorious, all authentication is quite uncalled for. We have read of the Indian and Chinese famines which carried off their millions; but such tragedies on the great scale, and so near home, have not been realized amongst us for many generations.§ And we feel not merely that

* The Lord-Advocate. † J. R. Macdonald, Esq. ‡ Mr. Trevelyan.

§ With every allowance for newspaper exaggerations, the melancholy evidence is now too palpable to be resisted of their general truth upon the whole. In the large miscellany of extracts with which we have been favored, the one perhaps which has taken the most powerful hold of our memory, is the account of Captain Caffin's visit to Schull. Of all the traits which are given in these numerous discriptions, to us the most painfully affecting is when visitors have been attracted to the miserable cabins by the cries of famishing children inside; and horror is superadded to compassion when, on the occasion of some of these entries into the houses of the dying, we read of the unnatural fights that had been going on between the nearest relatives for the last remaining morsel of food. The details of a recent field of battle covered over with the wounded and the dead, are not so frightful as the details of a famine. Our allotted pace absolutely forbids the introduction of these; but let us present the following from one of the several hundred slips which lie before us.

"*Limerick, Friday, March* 5.
"*County Crown Court.*

"MELANCHOLY INSTANCE OF DESTITUTION.

"William and Margaret Casey, a miserable couple, whose wretched appearance called forth the commiseration of the entire court, were indicted for stealing one sheep, value ten shillings, the property of Arthur Hassett, at Castle Roberts, on the first of March.

our sense of humanity, but that our sense of national honor is affected by it—for the question still recurs, Might these starvations already past have been prevented; or can they yet be prevented for the future, and how?

It might help us to resolve this question, did we imagine the famine to have been of another sort than that by which we have been actually visited—and this with a view to trace the effects of it. Let us conceive then for a moment, not that it had been greater than our present famine in regard to its degree, but that exactly of the same amount, it had only varied from it in regard to its distribution. One can easily figure of this sad scarcity, that without being greater on the whole, it had been more equally spread—or that, instead of being concentrated upon only one of our crops, so as to have nearly destroyed the principal food of one-fourth or fifth of our people, it had been shared among all the crops, and this to the effect that all the staple foods throughout the British islands had been reduced to one-fourth of their usual quantity. At this rate our Irish and Highlanders, instead of having lost nearly the whole of their potatoes, would still have three-fourths left to them—while our Lowlanders would have been obliged to put up with three-fourths of their usual supply of oatmeal, and the English with three-fourths of their wheaten loaves. In other words, instead of an intensely local, we should have had a general famine, of lighter because of equalized pressure over all our population. And this seems to have been very much the state of matters in the severe, yet generally diffused scarcities of 1800 and 1801—the average price of wheat in the latter of these two years having been £5, 19s. 6d. a quarter, whereas at present it has not averaged since November much more than 70s. per quarter; and certain it is, that at the actual rate of wages for the last twelve months, the great majority of our people, throughout the great majority of our land, have not been reduced to the necessity of any hard economical measures, but lived up to their usual rate of sufficiency and fulness. It was quite different at the commencement of this century—when we might with perfect safety affirm that there was an equal deficiency of food upon the whole to what there is at present, but more equally divided, and so borne in like proportion throughout all parts of the country.

Mr. Fleetwood, Clerk of the Crown.—'What say you to this indictment, William Casey, are you guilty or not?' Prisoner.—'We are guilty, my Lord; *two of our children died of starvation, and we had nothing to eat for the other three creatures!* Sir David Roche knows me, my lord.' (Here the prisoners burst into tears, which much affected the learned judge.) Sir David Roche, High Sheriff.—'Indeed, I knew the poor man for many years; and I am sure nothing but the brink of starvation would have led him to be guilty of the act. Two of his children died.' Prisoner.—'They did, my lord, with the hunger.' Mr. Sergeant Stock.—'And where are the other three children—what has become of them?' Both prisoners, in tears.—'We don't know, my lord; maybe they are all dead now!' Sergeant Stock, deeply affected.—'Would you be any service to them, if you were set at large?' Prisoner.—'I would, my lord.' Sergeant Stock.—'Let them be discharged.'"

And thus all were put on their short allowance; and we read of severe privation everywhere, but of starvation nowhere, at least no such wholesale starvation as now makes Ireland—and we might add the whole nation of which Ireland is a part—a spectacle to the world. In 1800 and 1801, the system of fewer and scantier rations was extended over the whole of the ship's company; and at the expense, doubtless, of painful suffering to all, they were all carried through to the end of the voyage, and after much of destitution and distress reached the port in safety. In 1847 there is a different arrangement; and with no greater scarcity on the whole than at the former period, we behold the wonted jollity and abundance along the deck of the vessel, the wonted luxury under the awnings of the quarter-deck or in the officers' cabins—while all those wretched men who have their berths in the forecastle are let to languish and die. Providence equalized the visitation of about fifty years back; and the consequent equality of distribution which laid the necessity of spare living upon all, might be regarded as the effect at once of a direct ordering from God. Providence has laid upon us now, not a heavier visitation than then, but has laid the full weight of it on the distant extremities of our United Kingdom; and left the task of equalization—if there be enough of wisdom and mercy below for the accomplishment of the task—to the ordering of man.

But do the means really exist among us for such an achievement as the preservation of all from death by famine? Have we available resources, notwithstanding the deficiency of our potato crop, for keeping all our people alive? We have no doubt on the subject—resources as great certainly, and we think greater than in 1801, when the universally high prices, far higher in relation to wages than now, put all upon short allowance; and so all were borne through, without those mortalities by starvation, or by diseases consequent on starvation, which are now going on. And what a general short allowance did then, it could do still—and not so short, we believe, as that which was weathered and endured for two years at the beginning of this century. But greater or smaller, it would equalize, or rather it would tend to equalize the pressure over all parts of the country. And the question is, How shall this be brought about? or, By what means, by what method of going about it, can this equalization, or rather this approach to an equalization, be effected?

A certain, and we believe a very large approach, is made to it by spontaneous benevolenee. Such indeed is our faith in the efficacy of this natural provision, that, *in ordinary times*, we could fearlessly confide to it the whole care and guardianship of the poor—we mean not of all the diseased, but of all the merely indigent poor. One of our chief reasons indeed for deprecating the interference of law in this department of human affairs, is, that it tends to supersede and lay an arrest on the otherwise effusive kindness to the destitute of their relatives and neighbors; and it is our honest conviction that on the gradual cessation of the compulsory system by a process which has been often pointed out, an overpassing compensation for the withdrawal of poor-rate allowances would accrue, from the simple restoration to their own proper and original force of those principles in our constitution—the law of self-preservation and the law of compassion,—which have to so great an extent been disturbed in their natural workings by the provisions of a legal and artificial charity. And in this conviction we have been greatly strengthened and confirmed by all that we have read and observed on the subject of the present famines, both in Ireland and the Highlands of Scotland. For, over and above the countless instances of the poor helping the poorer, or of neighbors who had little, sharing their scanty stock with next-door neighbors who had none, till themselves brought down to their last meal—over and above what has taken place, and is still taking place in every little vicinity, where compassion within a right acting distance from its objects, and unable to withstand the spectacles of imploring agony and distress, leads to the noblest sacrifices, and this on the part of men and women in all ranks of society—but, over and above these blissful operations of the home charity, let us contemplate its workings further off, when, instead of neighbor sharing with neighbor, we behold country sharing with country, for that the appeals of suffering humanity, though necessarily becoming fainter and fainter with the lengths to which they are carried, are still found to tell on the hearts and the sympathies of other lands. We speak not only of those broader and more conspicuous streams of liberality which flow from our great metropolitan committees to those places which send forth the loudest cry; but also of those numerous and unseen supplies which are sent through the channels of private correspondence, and are never heard of beyond the parties that are immediately concerned. Why, it is but the other day when an Irish bank was applied to for the facility of suffering any English remittances that came its way, to pass without the usual charge, and it turned out that they had been in the habit of doing so for months, and that through their one office the sum of twenty thousand pounds had been handed over either to the dispensers or receivers of charity. And it is only of late that on a larger scale, the glorious discovery was made of remittances in the same way to the extent of two hundred thousand pounds from Irish emigrants in America to their famishing countrymen. There is a like movement of generosity, and it is most refreshing to be told of it, amongst the Americans themselves—all riveting the confidence that we have ever had in the productiveness and native power of compassion, adequate, as we think, to every fair claim of indigence in ordinary times—insomuch, that with a feeling of perfect security we could leave to its sole guardianship and care those poor of whom our Saviour hath said, that they are always with us, would but a cold and withering legislation keep off its hand, and not overbear the will to do them good.*

But we must not stop longer on this argument. What may suffice in ordinary, clearly will not suffice for the present overwhelming visitation. There is an imperious call for the Government to come forward—and this not to supersede the liberalities of the public, but to superadd thereto the allowances of the State; or rather, for the State to be the principal almoner in such a dire emergency, and its distributions supplemented to the uttermost by the charities of the benevolent. At all events, humanity calls for such allowances as might guarantee in every instance the preservation of life. It is for Political Economy to say, whether there be funds and stores in existence, out of which such allowances can be made; and what were the effect of granting them on the economic state of society at large.

First, then, as to the existence of sufficient stores, we have good *prima facie*, and, to speak our own convictions, a conclusive evidence in the fact, that although there has been an almost total destruction of food in certain parts of our territory, yet, if instead of being thus concentrated, the scarcity had been generalized, all would have been put upon short allowance; but all would have been kept alive—seeing that throughout the whole of this dreary season, as far as it has yet gone, at least three-fourths, we should incline to say four-fifths, perhaps even five-sixths of our population have been averagely fed. Had the present famine been equalized, the country could have weathered it more easily than it did the general famine of 1801. And further, not looking, for the present, to importations from abroad, but looking exclusively at home, the destruction laid upon food last year by the hand of nature, is not equal to the destruction laid upon it every year by the hand of man; so that, could man have been prevailed upon to abstain, for the time, from the work of a destroyer, the whole deficiency might from this source alone have been repaired. Had the distilleries been stopped as they were in 1800 and 1801, and as we believe they would have been now, if the famine, though not greater in amount, had only been general, this, alone, would have gone far to repair the deficiency. If, over and above this, the breweries had been stopped, and so for a season all malting been put an end to, this would have greatly more than covered the deficiency.† A humane and virtuous despotism could and would

* Mark xiv., 7. Our Saviour devolved the care of the poor on the *will* to do them good. The law of England makes that which was left to will a matter of compulsion.

† From M'Culloch's Tables it would appear that duties were charged on malt in 1844, throughout the United Kingdom, to the extent of 37,187,178 bushels, or 4,648,397 qrs. And from a recent memorial of the Scotch distillers, it further appears that the amount of spirits distilled from raw corn is about fourteen millions of gallons, the manufacture of which requres 770,000 quarters of grain, making the whole amount used in breweries and distilleries to be upwards of five millions of quarters, and this exclusive of the quan-

have done it at once. But, as matters stand, Government would demur because of the revenue, and the agricultural interest for its own factitious good would have declaimed against it; and the popular voice in Britain, we fear, has been lifted up in opposition, from a public not themselves goaded on by the agonies of hunger. For ourselves we should have rejoiced had there been a sufficient energy at head-quarters to overrule all this—and not the less but the more, if, by an entire stoppage of the distilleries, the beastly intoxications of Scotland had been suspended. We should even have been glad had the malting of our grain, if not wholly abolished, been at least greatly abridged and limited by a heavier taxation—although we should thereby trench upon the more decorous indulgencies of which the working-classes participate so largely in the beer-shops of England. As it is, what between the class interests of our grandees, and the low and loathsome dissipations of our common people, the cry of famishing millions has been overborne. Altogether, it presents a most piteous and painful contemplation—recalling our old image of the ship, where the full consumption of all sorts of pastry was suffered to go in the cabins, and the full allowance of grog was served out to the sailors on the deck, while the wretched occupiers of the forecastle, perhaps the helots of the company, were left in lingering agony to live or perish as they may.

But there is the semblance of a public interest in one of the considerations which have been just alleged against the stoppage of the distilleries—we mean the damage that would thereby accrue to the revenue. This brings us from the question of *the sufficiency of stores*, to the second question, *the sufficiency of funds*—which latter question, notwithstanding its substantial identity with the former, occupies so distinct and almost exclusive a place in the reasonings of merchants and financiers and practical statesmen, as to require that a separate treatment should be bestowed upon it. And besides, it is in the handling of this question, that we come in sight of the method, the business method, by which the degree of equalization for which we have been contending can at all be effected—that is, by which adequate supplies might have been transferred from one part of the United Kingdom to the other, from the region of comparative plenty to the region of famine, so as to have prevented these horrid starvations; or, in other words, so as to extend that system of short allowance, by which no doubt we should have stinted the livelihoods of all, in itself an evil certainly, but with the greatly overpassing good that we might have saved the lives of all.

tities consumed in illicit distillation. One quarter of grain is understood to be a large allowance for each individual overhead of the population. It should be remarked that the distillation from raw corn is cheifly carried on in England and Ireland, whereas they chiefly distil from malt in Scotland. Altogether, the amount of grain consumed in regular breweries exceeds, by more than three times, the amount consumed in regular or legal distilleries.

Did we continue to discuss this matter in the terms of our first question, we should say, let us share with them of our abundance, and give to these starving creatures the requisite supply of food. But we are now discussing it in the terms of our second question; and we therefore say let us give them the requisite supply of money or means to purchase food. And it is not necessary for our argument, that in every instance the money should be actually put into their hands. It might, when given in the form of wages for work done by the able-bodied. But when in the form of gratuitous charity, it might be given not to the final recipients, but to Relief Committees to be expended for them—because perhaps they choose, and very properly, to grant all their allowances to the destitute in food only. But this is not material to the effect. In either way the same amount of purchasing power would be transferred to Ireland—whether placed in the hands of distributing committees, or of the people themselves. And what we particularly want to impress upon our readers is the effect which this increase of purchasing power must infallibly have upon prices. Say that Ireland is enabled, in virtue of what is done for her, to expend in the course of the year ten millions more than she otherwise could have done, on the purchase of food. Conceive that when Irishmen are left alone, either to live on their potatoes as in ordinary years, or to die for want of them as in this tremendous year of famine—that then the expenditure for food over the United Kingdom is fifty millions; but that when not left alone, when their wants are supplied to the extent of being enabled to come into the food market with ten millions of purchase money—then the whole sum brought to market would instead of fifty be *towards* sixty millions. Let us suppose the full sixty millions; and then there is no power on earth which could restrain the prices from rising, and that in the proportion of fifty to sixty. Let sixty millions of money come in place of fifty into all the food markets of this country, and meet there with but the same quantity of food; and then by an uncontrollable necessity, this is the ratio in which prices behoove to rise. A Government could, in such a state of things, no more prevent an ascent in the price of grain, from 70s. to 84s. a quarter, than it could repeal a law of nature.*

It is thus that, in proportion to the magnitude of our aids to

* The sum of ten millions given to the destitute would not all come back upon the market for the purchase of food—as so much of it would be reserved by them for the purchase of second necessaries. And neither when prices had been raised would the old fifty millions in the hands of the ordinary consumers be expended on grain—for the effect of the now higher price would be to induce a general economy in the use of it. And, besides, so far as importation was induced by the rise of price, this would tend to lessen the rate at which it would advance. Notwithstanding, however, that these various influences must affect the numerical calculation, we trust it is quite palpable that in proportion as we enlarge our grants to the destitute, they must react on the corn market, so as to raise the price of food all the more, and generalize the short allowance in virtue of our now having a greater number of customers to share it with us.

Ireland must be the rise of prices—an evil in itself certainly, but an evil incurred for the sake of a greater good, the preservation of the lives of our people. Had we let them die, we might have retained to ourselves the whole benefit of our own average crops, and at average prices. We might have gruffly refused to share with them of our abundance; and in this way could have kept down prices—an advantage no doubt to us, but no sensible advantage to those millions in Ireland, who, after losing their potatoes, had lost their all; and so, having no money for the purchase of other food, it signified little to them whether the grain was to be had at 50s. or at 70s. per quarter. There was no other remedy for this state of things, than the transfer either of the meat to feed them, or of the money to buy it with. Of these two methods we prefer that Government should take the latter; and after having placed the money there, there was no danger but that the merchants would go in quest of it, and so in time the meat would follow.* It is for this reason that we confess our partiality for much larger and more liberal grants than have been actually voted by Parliament. We had a longing eye, for example, on Lord Bentinck's sixteen millions, though not on his railways, which we could have dispensed with for the present—counting it much better that the money had all been expended, both on the enforcement of their current agriculture, and on the extension of it, that larger breadths of territory might be taken in for the grain crops of the coming harvest. It is thus that the urgent demand of Ireland for food would, in the language of the economists have become an effective demand. But then the inevitable consequences would have been all the larger rise of prices—and so as to stint our people everywhere, but this in order that they should starve nowhere. A most righteous and humane policy we do think—the only expedient by which we could keep off from all parts of our land the horrors of extreme famine—and yet which could not by any possibility be carried into effect without such a rise in the markets, as was sure to bring down all sorts of contumely and execration upon famine-mongers.

And there is nothing so recondite in this process, but that it was felt and complained of by practical men. In a newspaper

* Yet it was well that Government dealt to a certain extent in food, and established their depots in various quarters. Had they but given the money, the meat might have followed *in time*, but in very many places not in due time. Our regret is, that the meat was paraded in these depots before the eyes of the families at Skibereen and Schull; but as these had not the money the meat did not reach them. No wonder at the curses poured by them from their inmost souls on Political Economy. But ere blame can alight anywhere, the question must be resolved, on whom did the obligation lie of furnishing the money? Government bestowed a great deal of money—and with the honest purpose of its descending to the very poorest, but much of it was intercepted by the less poor, and so the poorest were left to die. The Correspondence on which we have bestowed much and earnest attention convinces us, that though Government had enlarged its grants tenfold, the want of preparation and of arrangement and of local agencies was such that in the disorderly scramble of multitudes for the largest possible share of what was going, many in the various fastnesses of Ireland would still have died.

speculation of some months back, the warning was held out, lest by doing too much for Ireland we should be landed in famine prices ourselves. In a recent petition from Blackburn in Lancashire to the House of Lords, the increase of pauperism there and in other parts of England is attributed to "the excessive price of provisions, consequent on the vast drain to Ireland"—a drain, which behooved to be all the greater, the greater our liberalities to Ireland, whether in Government grants, or in the benefactions of private charity. Nay we find one part of Ireland reclaiming against the subscriptions, made in it for the benefit of other parts in Ireland; and we are told that the wealthy in Dublin should leave the care of the poor in the provinces to their own natural protectors, the owners of the land, and should expend all their incomes in Dublin itself for the sake of the traders and shopkeepers there—that "the clear and imperative duty of the residents in Dublin is to expand and not to contract their outlay,"—"to enlarge their expenditure,"—"to spend their money freely,"—for that distress at their own doors would ensue from "a general extinction of innnocent gayeties." It is on some such ground too, that an argument is raised for keeping open the distilleries—for that cows were fed on the refuse of them; and that the citizens of Dublin could not be adequately supplied with milk, unless we consented to the wholesale destruction of food for human bodies by turning it into a poison for human souls. It is thus that in defence of their own near and partial interests, men will strain at a gnat whilst they swallow a camel. And even the distillers themselves, in the stout defence which they make for their own manufacture, can tell us, that doubtless the price of grain is raised by it, but that this is a great public advantage, for that high prices stimulate the importation from abroad—as if because such a supply in consequence of our high prices is good, the supply without such high prices would not be still better. The truth is, that the stoppage of the distilleries, if accompanied by an enlargement of the grants to the destitute, would have effected for them the same double benefit on a large scale, which they obtain on a smaller scale from those benevolent individuals, who retrench the food of their families, and make over the price of that retrenchment to a charitable fund. It is really not possible in such years of scarcity that aught like a general or effectual relief can be made out for the very poorest, without bringing hardship on the less poor than they, and without the burden of sacrifices more or less painful on the community at large. Even in the north of Scotland where the grain was dear, it was right that part of it should be taken away for the supply of those places where the grain was dearer, and still more where the people were in greater want than themselves. It requires a strong as well as a humane Government to repress the outbreakings of local selfishness. Nevertheless it is right they should, because right that one and all in the nation should suffer rather than that any in the nation should starve.

We repeat that the high price of grain is not a good *per se*, but *per se* an evil. And yet, notwithstanding there might be two most valid reasons, why, in times like these, this said high price should gladden the heart of a philanthropist, if he had but the faculty of looking both far enough behind and far enough before him. It might either have been produced as the necessary effect of one good thing which greatly more than compensated the evil, and ought therefore to be rejoiced in; or it might operate as the certain cause of another good thing, which not only more than compensated the evil, but which limited and laid a check upon the increase of it, and ought therefore to be further rejoiced in. But let us explain ourselves, with an earnest request at the same time for the close, even though it should be the painful attention of our readers to what might be felt by many as our dull argument. And first then it had surely been a good thing, if all those wretched creatures who have died of starvation, amounting already by the latest computation that we have faith in to a quarter of a million of human beings, it would surely have been a very good thing had they all been kept alive. But this could only have been done either by giving a requisite amount of food to the people, or of money to buy it with—whether this money was put directly into their own hands, or into the hands, be it of Relief Committees for the destitute, or of paymasters for the able-bodied, and who enforced work in return for it. In whichever of these ways we should have brought no less than four millions of additional customers upon the corn-market—for this is the number, we are credibly told, who in ordinary years would have lived on potatoes alone, but who, this year, deprived of their potatoes, have no other food than grain to subsist upon. And we ask, not at the mouth of Political Economy but at the mouth of common sense, how is it possible that the four millions of additional buyers, not all of course in their own persons but in the persons of their parents or representatives—how is it possible that all these could have come into the market, and with money in hand too for making good their purchases, without a rise of prices? It is true that we could have kept provisions low enough for ourselves, much lower than they are at present, had we just let these people all die off. But we count it greatly better that they should not all die, and better still, if we had so enlarged our liberalities that none of them had died. We observe, at the moment we are writing, that the Irish papers are in a tumult of delight because of the falling markets, while, contemporaneously with this, the deaths by starvation are as frequent as ever. It is very well for those who have any money that prices should fall; but it signifies little to those who have no money at all, whether the Indian meal should be selling at 70s. or 60s. a quarter. Now as we are pleading not for the less poor, but for the very poorest, we confess that rather than lower prices along with numerous starvations, we should like to have higher prices and no starvations. What we want is that the most wretched occupiers of Ireland's lands should be provided with the means of purchasing food, or having it purchased for them—even though it should bring the prices up again. The returning dearness, we most readily admit, were in itself an evil; but if brought about in this way, we should perfectly rejoice in it as the symptom and effect of a greatly surpassing good, in that, though all should suffer, yet none would perish.—Thus much for a high price of grain viewed as the effect of one good thing. But it might, and we may indeed say must, be also the cause of another good thing. Not to speak again of the universal economy which it induces in the consumption of food, so as to cause that our scantier stock than usual shall serve by a sparer maintenance than usual to the coming harvest—let us only reflect on the additions which a high price makes to this stock, by the mighty stimulus it gives to importation. Had any one but watched, as we have done, the progress and fluctuations of the sensitive corn-market in America—not however more tremulous and sensitive there than, by the very nature of the commodity, in all other parts of the world, and observed how constantly and surely every report of falling prices in this country checked the business of exportation, and even led in some instances, to the relanding of its cargoes—had it thus been made palpable to him, that they are our high prices and these alone which have brought and continue to bring the richly-laden flotillas of the New World to our shores —this would have mitigated, it is to be hoped, his invectives against the famine-mongers, and somewhat disarmed his fell and fierce antipathy to the "rogues in grain." But let it again be distinctly understood, that we should like it infinitely better to have the supplies without the high prices; and thus it is that we shall ever mourn over the non-stoppage of the distilleries, as far the least defensible part in the policy of Ministers—even though Dublin should have been thereby stinted in milk for its families, and England been abridged of its beer and brown-stout, and Scotland reft altogether of its mischievous whiskey. It is utterly beyond the endurance of human nerves that these indulgences should have been kept up at their usual rate, or rather for the last twelve-month to a greater excess of dissipation and drunkenness than ever—while Highlanders all the while have been writhing in the agonies of extreme hunger, and Irishmen in thousand have been dying.

They seem to have ordered this matter better in France. We cannot allege aught like precise information on the statistics of the scarcity there—yet the higher price of grain in France than in Britain, a fact in itself most pregnant with inference, is fully in keeping with all that we have heard and all that we conceive of the state of matters there. As first, that there should be a less deficiency than ours—it amounting to a shortness from their usual yearly produce, of forty-five days' consumption, or one-eighth of the whole, whereas ours might be estimated at perhaps one-fifth and certainly not less than one-sixth of the whole—and yet with them a higher price notwithstanding. This might be due in part to theirs being a general, and not as with us a provincial famine; and so an eager competition for food all over, among those who have the means of purchasing—a very different thing truly in its effect on prices, from the cry of distress, however urgent, among those who have not the means. And then the very generality of the famine intermingles to a greater extent, the more with the less needy, and so brings them within a better acting distance, both for the excitement and the exercise of compassion. And last of all more ostensibly, though not perhaps more efficiently than either of these causes in its operation upon prices, is the munificence of the public treasury. As far as the following private letter can be depended on, all these causes have been powerfully at work in France, and might account for the higher prices there.—"Never before, not even during the reign of the cholera, have charity and benevolence been displayed in a manner so spontaneous, so generous, so profuse, so effective. Money is contributed, and relief is administered, not with the character of almsgiving, nor doled out with reluctance and parsimony and accompanied by reproach, but with a liberality truly admirable." "One capitalist here expended, it was said, in charity in 1832 (during the presence of the cholera), £10,000 sterling. His disbursements in this year of suffering, will probably amount to double that sum. This spirit of benevolence, and this energetic observance of its dictates, are, however, and happily, not confined to the wealthy and the great—the whole community participate in them. Even the soldiery divide their rations with the poor. There are no subscription lists, nor newspaper appeals to the beneficence of those who have to give, no stimulus of any kind. Every man gives all that he can afford, and does it as a matter of course, with a good heart, and without ostentation. The consequence of this general movement will be, that few, perhaps none, will perish in France of starvation; that is a great matter; but the struggle to keep up the supply must be gigantic."—It then tells us of the supplies ordered in the ports of the Baltic and the Black Sea, and of the United States; and, what is most instructive of all, of the immensely large orders for flour sent to England. And as the effect of all, we are told that they will have no "deaths by starvation" to register; and that the Government, the capitalists, the clergy, the public, are resolved upon that. It is of a piece with all this information, that we read of the Baron Rothschild's undertaking, in concert with the French Government, to the extent of millions for the importation of food from America. It will perhaps reconcile our own public to high prices, when thus made to perceive that had they been sufficiently high, it would have proved a defence against the exportation of British grain to France, besides enabling us to cope on more equal terms with France in our competition for the grain of other countries. We are aware of the cry that there is to prohibit exportation ; but we should like it better that it were prevented rather than prohibited, and this by the largeness of our home prices, provided it were brought about as in France, by the largeness of our home charities. We should have acquiesced all the more willingly in Lord John Russell's free-trade reply to the demands for prohibition, had he so far enlarged the national grants as to have raised our prices beyond the reach of customers from France. We confess that to put matters right both in Ireland and in our Highlands, we had a longing eye on Lord George Bentinck's sixteen millions, barring his railways—nay could have acquiesced in Mr. O'Connell's thirty millions,* rather than that the whole civilized world should have been so scandalized by the great national outrage upon humanity which has been perpetrated within our own shores.

But we must not be carried away by the first aspect of things. Indeed we should prefer that if possible there were no reckonings with any party for the past, excepting for the practical objects of guidance and safety for the future. Certain it is, that the more we read of this voluminous correspondence, the less are we inclined to lay upon Government the guilt of these starvations. What we shall ever regret, as far the worst of the charges to which they have been exposed is that, whether for the sake of the revenue or in deference to the agricultural interests, they should after such awful tragedies have tolerated that wholesale destruction of human food, which goes on in our distilleries. Yet even this would not have prevented the spectacles of horror that have taken place in Ireland. There were difficulties which all the wealth of the Indies could not have surmounted ; and we must

* Mr. O'Connell, in a letter of February 13th, to Mr. Ray, writes thus—" Parliament is not disposed to go far enough, there will not be sufficient relief given by the Parliament; and it will not be till after the deaths of hundreds of thousands that regret will arise that more was not done to save a sinking nation." Mr. O'Connell's predicted number of deaths has already been fully realized. Yet we cannot be blind to the fact that many not wholly destitute did thrust themselves upon the public works to the exclusion of as many who were altogether without the means of subsistence; and hence a number of the actual starvations. The allowances doubtless were a good deal too small. It was not enough that men should have been kept from dying. They should have been kept from wasting into skeletons. We should therefore have rejoiced in much larger grants, but still cannot rid ourselves of the persuasion, that although they had been increased threefold, still there would have been many deaths by hunger—first from the want of local agencies in Ireland, and secondly from the interception of the supplies by those who were less poor, so as not to reach them who were poorest. See Captain Wynne's Letter, Irish Correspondence, Board of Works Series, Second Part. p. 15.

In Saunders' News-Letter of April 5th, we read that " the 20 per cent. reduction (of the men employed in the public works in the pay of Government) works well, insomuch that it has put off many persons who were able to support themselves." Such men might be looked upon as the causes of the deaths by starvation of those who were excluded from the places which they had no right to occupy. It was very shameful.

take a calm and comprehensive view of these ere we can admit that in France there is either a larger-hearted Government, or a more generous people than our own.

But still we contend that the want of money ought never to have been felt as one of these difficulties. We have already stated our conviction that there was enough of food, even within the limits of the United Kingdom, whereby, though at the expense of a shorter allowance to the whole and the abridgment of certain luxuries, we might have mitigated, to a far greater extent than we have done, those extreme sufferings which have been endured, and are still felt, throughout the famine-stricken parts of our territory. We now affirm with equal confidence, that we could have raised enough of means for the purchase of that food. We do not ourselves think that there is any *natural* necessity for a distinct argument on each of these topics. But the necessity is forced upon us by certain mystifications, or factitious difficulties, which are conjured up to the effect of obscuring the subject. We are told, for example, by Sir Robert Peel, in his opposition to Lord George Bentinck's proposal for raising the sum of sixteen millions, that it could not be done by loan without too violent a disturbing of the money-market—a consideration, we believe, not very well understood by the vast majority of those to whom it was addressed, but all the more fitted on that account to silence them, seeing that the whole mechanism of our Stock Exchange, and monetary system, stands at as great a distance from all ordinary and many superior understandings, as do the very highest themes of high transcendentalism. For ourselves we should have been willing to brave the hazard of disturbing, however violently, the money-market—rather than not have met the exigencies of our present visitation. But there is another and a better expedient, suggested too by Sir Robert himself, and which if fully acted on would help us out of this whole difficulty. When speaking on Lord George Bentinck's motion, and of the deficiency incurred by the outlay on Ireland, he tells us "that he knew no other method of providing for this assumed deficiency (nine millions), except that of making a vigorous effort at direct taxation, to be visited he presumed upon all parts of the United Kingdom." We most sincerely rejoice that he made this suggestion, and still more that it was received with loud cheers by the ministerial side of the House. But could not the same direct taxation which is to make up the deficiency so many months hence, could it not have prevented the deficiency by providing against it beforehand? And if by dint of vigor it can raise the nine millions, can it not by dint of greater vigor raise twenty or thirty millions, if indeed and rightfully called for? We think that it can; and that Great Britain has not aroused herself to an effort at all commensurate to the wants of this awful crisis, or commensurate to her own wealth. Rather than that this should not be done, we would acquiesce in a loan with all its alleged inconveniences and evils; but our clear preference, and for more reasons than we can at present explain, is for direct taxation.

We first observe, then, of these two great rival methods for raising a public revenue—that is, either mediately by a duty upon commodities, or immediately and directly by a tax whether on property or income*—it is obvious that each has its own distinct and peculiar limit. In regard to the former way of it, it is easy to perceive that each addition to the duty lays a further check on the consumption of an article. The dearer that wine is made by taxation, the less of wine will be drunk. It is thus that the wine-tax, with every new addition to the impost, tends to limit more and more the wine-trade till at length it ceases, notwithstanding the higher duties, to be so productive as before. It is at this point that the produce of the tax reaches its maximum, beyond which it cannot be carried without loss to the revenue—so that now the wine-trade is made to yield its uttermost to the National Treasury. But the limit in direct taxation, such as an income tax, shoots greatly ahead of this. It is true that the further it is carried the less will subjects have to spend, and the consumption of every article which can be dispensed with will be all the more restrained. One can imagine in the consequent abridgment which must take place on the use of luxuries, that the consumption of wine might be limited, not merely to the point where it before yielded the greatest possible revenue to the State, but very much within this—nay, that men might cease to drink it altogether, and so the wine-trade be annihilated. It is palpable, however, that as the effect of this process, a greater revenue might accrue to the State than ever—for, over and above all which it ever realized by a tax on the commodity, it, by seizing on the whole price, gets hold not only of that part which furnished the tax, but the natural price of the wine to the bargain. The rapidly intuitive Charles Fox, when himself a Minister of State, had his eye upon this enlargement, and tells us in one of his speeches, that the only limit to the produce of an income-tax, was the reduction of all the families in the land to the necessaries of life—a proposition this, however, which, to be guarded against all exceptions, would require to have some modifications laid upon it, for the statement of which we have no room at present.

But the abridgment, and still more the destruction, of trade,

* We have explained elsewhere our views upon taxation, and the reasons of our preference for a tax on property or income to a tax upon commodities. Our own opinion, and that on grounds altogether distinct from those of the French economists, is that all taxes fall ultimately upon land. It will be very long however before the public will be convinced, or Parliament will act upon this principle. Meanwhile, we hail every approximation to what we deem the optimism of this subject. It would mightily advance the cause, and make direct taxation greatly more popular, were it carried into effect by a small centage on property, rather than by a centage twenty times larger on income—in other words were the tax on property alone, and not at all on income.

which we have represented to be the tendency and effect of direct taxation, carries in it a frightful aspect to many an imagination—as if on the decay and extinction of trade, the whole power and superiority of Britain were to decay and vanish along with it. There is an inveterate delusion here, and yet which a very simple consideration should put to flight. No manufacture, or no trade, yields more for the good of a nation, than just the commodity which it produces, or in which it deals. The wine-trade yields nothing but wine. The whole amount of what the stocking manufacture renders to society is stockings. Our various export commodities, the preparation of which gives employment to so many of our people, contribute nothing more to the public interest than just the import articles which come back in return for them, as oranges, or figs, or India shawls, or tea, or coffee, or rum, or sugar. We are aware that the work of procuring all these things, whether to array with them our persons or to lay them upon our tables, gives rise to a commerce which is dignified with the name of so many interests, as the manufacturing interest, and the shipping interest, and the East or West India interest. But let not the magnificence of these titles impose upon us, or lead us to imagine that any one branch of commerce yields more for the well-being of the community than merely its own articles. But does it not, over and above, afford their maintenance to the people engaged in it? No, it gives them their employment but not their maintenance. This maintenance lies enveloped, not in the article which they produce, but in the price which is paid for it. It comes, as it were, from the other side of the exchange—not from the manufacturers who work up the article, or the traders who bring it to market, but from the customers who pay the price for it. The perpetual tendency is to accredit every particular trade both with its own proceeds and with the returns which they bring; and the most egregious example that can be found of this delusion is in that most mercantile of all politicians, William Pitt, who at the commencement of the revolutionary war prophesied the ruin of France's power from the ruin of her commerce, in the loss of which he could perceive nothing else than the loss of all her means for the payment and maintenance of armies. It was the destruction of her commerce which gave her her armies. She lost by it the luxuries which commerce yields; but the maintenance of the workmen whom commerce employs still remained with her. The effect was to transform millions of artisans and operatives formerly in the pay of individual consumers, into as many soldiers, afterwards in the pay of the state. From the earthquake which ingulfed her commerce, there suddenly sprang forth a host of armed men whom no man could number, who in a few months cleared her territory of all its invaders, and in a few years achieved the subjugation of all continental Europe to the bargain. The levies and conscriptions of France at that period should have taught our statesmen long ago what that is which constitutes the real strength and resources of a kingdom. The lesson we think is now beginning to dawn on the minds of certain of our statesmen, more especially of Sir Robert Peel, who already in a small way has made prosperous trial of vigorous direct taxation, and would recommend for a time at least, the further extension of it, to meet the exigency of our Irish and Highland famines. It is our deep-felt conviction that did Britain but know the might and the magnitude of those resources wherewith Providence has blessed her, she would not so quail and falter and be in sore perplexity before her present visitation. Had she but the full consciousness of her hand of strength, she would put it forth ; and make the grand comprehensive effort so feelingly and forcibly called for by the honest jurymen of Dublin—and, not by one measure only, but by a series of measures, accomplish both the new-modelling of our Highlands, and the reconstruction of Ireland, and this at one tithe of the expense which she has lavished on many of her wars.*

Let us imagine that, among the many things to be yet done for Ireland, there behooved, perhaps for years to come, to be a large importation of food from abroad, and this to provide against the unavoidable deficiencies which must arise from the neglected agriculture of the present year, and which may continue for several years to come ere the difference can be made good between a grain-fed and a potato-fed population. It seems quite clear that without such extraordinary supplies, we shall have again and again to incur the misery and disgrace of those hideous starvations which have scandalized the world—and all the more that they took place in one portion of the United Kingdom, while in the other portions of it the people from high to low were in circumstances for giving full swing, or at least to an extent as great as usual, to all sorts of luxurious and even riotous indulgence. And it seems equally clear that the whole expense of these supplies cannot be left, whether through the medium of grants to the helpless or of wages to the able-bodied beyond the value of their labor, cannot be left on the landlords, without entailing such an amount of ruin upon the order, and filling them with such a sense of despair, as to aleniate from all co-operation, that body of men,

* A direct taxation for the special object of putting Ireland and our Highlands right might be spread over several years of a transition process—just as among our city taxes, there often comes, and for a length of time too, a special charge for improvements—and which continues to be levied till they are all paid for. It were a noble exhibition of Patriotism and public virtue would Parliament venture on such an imposition and the people willingly respond to it. Our own preference would be for the graduation of such a tax and in this way—to lay no tax on any income below £50, and then to tax all above this, not by laying the centage on the whole income, but only upon the excess above £50. Thus a tax of 5 per cent. would amount to 10s. on all who had £60 a year, to 20s. on all who had £70 a year, &c. The produce of such a tax, if wisely administered, might transform both Ireland and the Highlands into prosperous countries in the course of a few years.

through whom alone we can obtain such local agencies, as are indispensable for giving effect to the measures which have yet to be decided on, ere Ireland shall be conducted with safety and general advantage through the difficulties of her present crisis. Let us therefore hope that Government will feel the duty of lending their helping hand in this great national emergency; and that, to be enabled for doing so, they will have recourse to a vigorous direct taxation, both to meet a far larger prospective expense than they have yet contemplated, and to provide for the deficiency of the past expenses which have already been incurred. On the principle that we have just announced, the people of our land are fully able for such an effort and such a sacrifice, provided only that those of them who have more than the necessaries of life to live upon, are able to forego a part of their luxuries. And this we contend is the single, the only inconvenience, that would be suffered, had we only the boldness to face the present exigency in all its magnitude, and the determination by means and measures of commensurate magnitude rightly and fully to dispose of it. The tax-payers would drink less wine than before, in which proportion there behooved to be an abridgment of the wine-trade; but perhaps it will satisfy the worshippers of commerce as our all in all, to be told that in very proportion the corn-trade might be extended; and our alarmists for the shipping interest to be told, that the same, nay a far greater amount of shipping, is required for the importation of grain than of the costlier articles which come to us from abroad. It is demonstrable that in the consequent state of things which would ensue from a heavy direct taxation on all above the working-classes, we should behold as great a population as fully employed and as well maintained as before; and that the whole effect of this altered direction in the expenditure of the country's wealth, were the loss of certain personal indulgences to the higher classes, but with the gain it might be in return for it of nobler objects—as the defence of a country against foreign invasion, or the establishment of a better economy within its borders. We have long advocated the law of primogeniture, and can sympathize with the pleasure and the pride which were felt by Edmund Burke, in the glorious aristocracy of England. But nothing, we are persuaded, would more conduce to the stability of their order—nothing remove further the evil day, when their candlestick shall be taken out of its place—than their willing surrender though but in part of such enjoyments as might well be suspended, to the demands of patriotism and the public weal. This willingness can only have its full expression and effect by the collective voice and through the organ of Parliament. They may provide for the stupendous design of setting up a right economy in Ireland by loans; and we should rather they did, than that Ireland should be left as hitherto to flounder on as she best may. But our own decided preference is for a vigorous and direct taxation.

But ere we carry our proposals any further, let us here advert to the probable effect which the establishment of the Free-Trade system is likely to have for a season on our economists and statesmen. The imagination is, that it will enlarge indefinitely the powers of commerce; and so the tendency in men's minds will be to magnify, we had almost said to deify, commerce all the more—as if it were the primary source and sovereign dispenser of all the blessings which serve to strengthen or enrich a nation. The very famine wherewith we have been visited might serve to correct and sober down these anticipations; and to convince us that commerce is not the fountain-head, but that agriculture is the fountain-head, and commerce but the derivative stream or the derived and dependent reservoir. Even Dr. Smith, notwithstanding his own masterly exposure of the mercantile system, was so far carried away by his favorite principle, the more endeared to him that he himself was its parent and its discoverer, as unduly to exalt at times the prerogatives and powers of merchandise. And yet there is one memorable sentence of his which should help to keep us right—that the great end of all production is consumption. Did we but retain our steady hold of this maxim, and make at all times the right application of it, it would raise us to a higher and more commanding position for a correct survey of the whole question. Commerce would be assigned its true place, if we made our estimate of its importance to turn on the benefit which accrued from the use of his resulting commodities—if we fixed our eye on the *qui bono*, and *terminus ad quem*, of its various processes. It would reduce Political Economy to its just dimensions, so that it should no longer monopolize the whole field of vision, to the subordination or the exclusion of higher interests than its own. We are hopeful that had this consideration been present in the mind of Mr. Trevelyan, it would have saved him from the single error into which we think he has fallen throughout the whole of a correspondence, characterized all along on his part by signal ability and the most enlightened economical views—for then we apprehend that he would not in mere deference to the Free-Trade principle, have advocated as he has done the continuance of distilleries.* On the question—How is it best that our grain should be consumed? Better, we shall ever contend, in a crisis like the present; better in bread to the people, than in liquors for the good cheer of England, or the nauseous dissipation of Scotland, or even in the animal food on which Burke grounds his argument in behalf of distillation. Nay, so far do we carry our views on this matter, we should hold it greatly better that the families in the metropolis of Ireland were put on bread and water, instead of

* Irish Correspondence (Commissariat Series), pp. 106, 107.

bread and milk or bread with butter on it, rather than that families in the provinces should be left without bread altogether. We make every allowance for the want of time and preparation and precise knowledge throughout the year that is past; but it will be an indelible disgrace, if in another year the Irish shall be again left to die in thousands, that the Scotch might luxuriate in spirits, and the English in their potations of beer as usual.

But we must now hasten to a close—yet not surely, it might well be thought, without at least breaking ground on the question—What is to be done for Ireland and the Highlands of Scotland?

And we are not ashamed to confess that at present we have no inclination to do more than break ground upon these questions. It might be a very lengthened process, and one of very many steps or stages, by which to come at last to the establishment of a good permanent economy for either of these countries; and therefore it might be presumptuous and premature to venture on an out-and-out description of the whole of it. But though unwilling, and perhaps unable, to furnish a guide-book for all the thousand miles of this way—yet if perfectly sure, though even of but the first mile, it were doubtless of importance to be told of it, more especially if at the end of this first mile, we shall be in all the better circumstances by the way opening before us as we proceed on it, for ascertaining the ulterior direction of the journey. It is good, nay indispensable, ere we go forth on an expedition for some distant landing place, that we should know what is the right point of departure, and how to make a right outset. The way to be wrong throughout is to make a wrong commencement.

First, then, we should hold it as a good outset principle that the question before us is clearly an imperial one, to be prosecuted and to a great extent carried into effect by imperial means—though to a certain extent by local means also, and this in as great a proportion as might secure the vigilance and helpful cooperation of the landowners, by the interest which they are made personally to feel in their wise and economical administration. We cannot image a worse preparative for any systems of future ameliorations, than to begin either with such acts or such refusals as are fitted to strike despair into the hearts whether of our Highland or our Irish proprietary. Notwithstanding all the ungenerous, and all the flagrantly impolitic abuse that has been heaped upon them, particularly in Ireland, these are the parties on whom we must principally draw for good local agencies, without which Government will be utterly helpless for the right execution of its measures. But how can we expect that they will enter with any heart or hopefulness upon the task, if burdens are to be laid and measures to be adopted, tantamount in their belief to the confiscation of all which belongs to them? To decree such a revolution in property as this were to legalize a wholesale anarchy, and bring all into confusion. The clear wisdom of Government is to gain the confidence and good-will of those who *de facto* are lords of the soil; and this can only be done by convincing them that although it will not give way to indefinite rapacity and clamor, its honest purpose is so to devise and to regulate as that their country shall be worth the living in, and their estates be still worth the having.

We exceedingly lament that this principle has been disregarded, or rather wholly traversed, in the late decisions of Parliament on the subject of an Irish poor-law.* We should have thought that there was enough to be done in devising for the present and pressing exigencies of this awful crisis—how best to provide relief for the destitute, and to enforce the current agriculture of the country, and so to extend it as to compensate for the loss of the potato. Amid such urgent and besetting cares, it seems to us that it was shooting too far a-head, too far into the prospective, to embark in a hasty and hap-hazard legislation, and this too in measures of a permanent character—mixing up these

* The following is the testimony of a most unexceptionable and intelligent witness, to the effect of our new Scottish poor-law in the Highlands. " In regard to the bad feeling on the part of rate-payers towards the poor, the thing is so notorious in Ross-shire, that you are welcome to give me as authority for it to any who ask. I know districts where the poor cottars formerly supported their pauper neighbors most cheerfully, and had the kindest possible feeling towards them, where a day rarely passed without a call from some pauper for food or lodging, and in many situations where the burden from these calls was very great indeed, yet borne without a single thought of complaint. In the same districts, now, when the legal assessment is in force, where it may not amount to 6d. in £1 of rent, these same individuals, who under the old system were contributing perhaps 2s. 6d. for £1 voluntarily, have come to hate the very sight of a pauper, and *curse* them openly and loudly. The very paupers themselves feel the change so much, that I have known some who have insisted on being put off the roll, for no other reason than the hatred shown to them by their former kind neighbors." Had it not been for this recent piece of English legislation, private charity in the Highlands would have flowed more sweetly and productively than it has done in the present distress. We may here state what our preferences would have been had there either been no poor-rate in Ireland; or had the poor-rate been held inapplicable to all cases of destitution which offered, after that the work-houses were filled. These we should have divided into two classes, the able, and the not able to work. The former we would have devolved on a legal fund made up of two-thirds from the Treasury, and one-third from the parties who whether in town or country are made liable for the poor. The fund thus raised would of course be expended on the excess of the wages above the value of the work, that value being paid for by those for whose benefit it was done. The latter class, or the unable to work, we should have devolved on the spontaneous charities of the benevolent, stimulated by an additional allowance from the Government of pound for pound. Such is a very general outline of our scheme; and we should be quite willing, that in what regards the first class, the parties who should support them and the proportions that should fall on each were regulated according to any other process of adjustment which might be deemed more advisable. But we hold it of capital importance that the legal and the voluntary should not be compounded into one sum, and expended jointly on the same objects. Upon this footing the voluntary dwindles into insignificance—whereas if provided with distinct objects of its own, and these devolved upon it wholly, it would rise with the actual necessities which it had been called upon to relieve, and prove itself equal to the task. We have no doubt that under such an arrangement the streams of benevolence flowing in upon the Voluntary Relief Committees from all parts of the empire would have adequately met the destitution in this branch of it. One incalculable benefit of such a division in the work is that it secures most important additions to the agency, and agency of the best sort too for the weak and the helpless—we mean that of ladies.

with measures of immediate necessity. If the object was to compel an instant assessment on the land more commensurate to the existing destitution, could not this have been done by a special and temporary provision, without making a general and enduring change on the state of the Irish poor-law? Or is such a season of perplexity and pressure, when extraordinary visitations should be met by means alike extraordinary—is this the time for building up another system for the ordinary relief of the poor? Better, we do think, that emergencies like the present were met by the operations of some such expedients as did not leave one trace of themselves upon the statute-book. We are sensible of an honest anxiety on the part of rulers that the destitution should be provided for, but provided for with the lowest minimum of allowances from the Treasury. Of this we have had abundant experience in Scotland. Yet we cannot sympathize with the form of the complaint, that so little is doing for us, while so much is doing for Ireland. There is not too much; and it would comport better with the dignity of our great nation, and the amplitude of its resources, that it did a great deal more. Rather than that Ireland should fall into the hands of France, we would readily embark in a war of life or death, though at the expense as in other wars of five hundred millions—yes, and whether by dint of loans or rigorous direct taxation, we could summon into our national coffers every farthing of the money. After this, to speak of its not being a national object, that for a tithe of the sum which has now been specified, we should put Ireland into a right economic condition, or though at the expense of fifty millions spread over a few years, we should enter on that regenerate process by which to transmute our sister country into a prosperous and smiling land.

It is really not the way to govern a country, or to effect for it on extrication from its difficulties, that it shall be left to drift along, the sport and the plaything of merest accidents—for what else but accidents are those extemporaneous measures which are suggested on the spur of an occasion; and then further concocted or modified at random amid the impulses and stormy debates of a popular assembly. Better surely than these were the calm and leisurely and deliberate inquiries of a Parliamentary Commission, vested at the same time with administrative functions, and furnished both with adequate means and adequate powers for the fulfilment of the objects which are intrusted to it.* Such a delegated body should have a large discretion and dictatorship given to it, of defined boundaries no doubt, but still very ample notwithstanding—because with this guarantee for the safety of their pro-

* Of course when we speak of a Commission vested with the discretionary expenditure of money, we suppose the object of this expenditure to be previously defined by Parliament, and a certain maximum sum intrusted for the wise and economical fulfilment of them. It may in the first instance be a Commission of Inquiry.

ceedings, the weight and wisdom of those who had been selected to form it. They in fact should be the most choice men both of Britain and Ireland, not fixed upon because of any eminence they had won in the political arena, whether in or out of Parliament, for economics do not form the vocation of such—neither should we very confidently look for a sound economics at their hand. What we should most desiderate were men in our sister country, of such a type as Lord George Hill and Mr. Hamilton of St. Ernan, and without expressly naming any similar to these of our own country, we should greatly rejoice in a sprinkling of the Friends, those men of primitive worth and withal of careful and conscientious business habits, whose mission to Ireland is one of the noblest achievements in the annals of Philanthropy. These are the very men who in all the outlays and improvements could institute a right composition between the Government and the land owners. The expense on the whole to the State might turn out to be somewhat greater or vastly less than what we have ventured to name; but whether great or little, there is one guiding principle they should never lose hold of—and that is to repress the inordinate expectations both of Irish gentry and the Irish common people, and this on the ground that no people can be effectually helped who will do little or nothing to help themselves. The *terminus ad quem*, in fact, of the whole movement should be to establish an all-sufficiency for the people in their own industry and their own good management. It should be a firm while a merciful regime that is to be exercised over them, under which none of the helpless should be allowed to perish, and none of the able-bodied be exempt from the rule, that "if any will not work neither shall they eat." All rioting against the piece-work on which they might comfortably live, if judged to be better for them than the day's wages on which they might idle and starve—must be vigorously put down. No political economy, however sound, can be of any avail, when there is a weak Government or a worthless people. But we hope better things. We have no taste or sympathy for those tirades against the Irish which in the day of their sore visitation have so disgraced the hostile newspapers of England. Among them are many of the finest and noblest specimens of humanity; and thousands are the hearts and consciences there which will most readily accord with a Government resolved upon their good, though equally resolved not to falter on its path, nor be driven from the right and the reasonable in the accomplishment of its beneficent and well-laid plans. Never was there an opportunity of greater likelihood for those measures which might usher in the future well-being of Ireland. All party and political violence is abated. All factitious grievances are forgotten in the overwhelming grievance that has been laid direct by the hand of God on this sorely stricken people. Now is the time for Britain to step forward; and without the surrender either of authority or wisdom, to acquit herself generously, openly, freely towards Ireland—and by her acts of princely but well-directed munificence to repair the accumulated wrongs of many generations. The chastisements of this dreary period have not been joyous, but grievous; but thus might they be made to yield the peaceful fruits of righteousness to those who have been exercised thereby.

But ere that we bid adieu to the subject for the present, let us be somewhat more specific. They who have read the concluding article of our last Number will have acquired from it some idea of the manifold rectifications and adjustments that must be made, ere the confusion can be unravelled which obtains in the state of landed property throughout Ireland, and in all the tenures by which it is held. We are aware of a commission upon this subject, the report of whose labors, however, we have not yet seen. But the Commission that we would have, should have a great deal more to do than to investigate. It should be furnished with means to aid the disencumbrance of the land. For example it might assist the minor proprietor by loan or otherwise to effect an equitable compromise with those who possess a tenant-right to very small holdings. Or it may help him to emigrate the superfluous families on his estate.* In the course of its statistical inquiries, which cannot be prosecuted too minutely or too thoroughly, other ameliorations will open on its view which with both the power and the will to do good, it might not only suggest but carry into accomplishment. In short, a complete survey, and as complete a study founded upon that survey, should be made of Ireland. Had we known as much a year ago, as we should now set ourselves to learn and might acquire in two or three months, it might have kept us from many errors, and perhaps anticipated all the starvations. In the face of such an argument as this, it were worse than strange, it were shameful, to decline the enterprise, on the score either of its expense or its difficulty. The lives of millions

* We are aware of an apprehension lest a Government Scheme of Emigration subject the country to expense for those who would otherwise emigrate of themselves. But who are they?—families that possess means of their own, and whose abandonment of Ireland is of no advantage to it. The distinction surely is in such instances palpable enough between those who have the means and those who have it not; and they are the latter of course only for whose emigration Government would undertake, in conjunction when possible with those landed proprietors whose estates would be relieved by it either of its squatters or its very small holders. The following is an interesting notice from Saunders' News-Letter of the 5th April. "From the Derry Castle and Burgess estate, Killaloe, 100 poor families, averaging 500 persons, gladly surrendered their small holdings to the proprietor, Francis Spaight, Esq., who this week provided 300 of them a free passage, with sea store for the voyage, on board the Jane Black from Quebec, where they are to be landed free of all charge, with the intention of settling in Canada as farm laborers. The remainder of this cottier tenantry, who grew up as mere squatters on the estate, will follow in other vessels this month, and right glad of the opportunity and conditions for which the poor people express their gratitude."

Such emigration must felicitate the desirable ameliorations which have yet to be made on the system of leases, and we suspect also on the tenures of land. But how sadly a bad measure conflicts with a good one. The ordination of out-door relief in Ireland acts with antagonistic force on the wholesome desire of the people for emigration.

may depend upon it. Ignorance might be pleaded in extenuation; we are willing to entertain it as an excuse for the deaths of last year. Let these be repeated another year, and if from the same cause, our disgrace will be indelible. It was creditable to the science of Government when they overruled the paltry economy which would have laid an arrest on the Trigonometrical Survey. The call is vastly more imperative—the national honor, because the national humanity more loudly demands it—that Government should forthwith set themselves to know the subject with which they are dealing; and however costly or numerous the agencies for carrying forward the work piecemeal from county to county, and from parish to parish, they should from this moment institute and enter with all vigor on the Economical Survey of Ireland.*

Meanwhile we cannot imagine a more egregious impolicy than to have conjured up a new Poor-law for the occasion; or, in order to meet the exigencies of a passing and rare disaster, instead

* See an able and interesting paper by Samuel Ferguson, Esq., on the expediency of taking stock—a lesson as imperative, we should think, at the end of the coming harvest as of the last. We hold him to be perfectly sound on the stoppage of the distilleries, though we demur to his proposal for the prohibition of all exports of food. We prefer the doctrine of Mr. Hancock on the latter of these two questions, yet we cannot acquiesce in the reasoning by which he supports it—a reasoning that, if sound, would be equally valid against the stoppage of the distilleries—a measure that might also be conceived to bring down the prices from 70s. to 50s. a quarter, and so furnish Mr. Hancock with the very same data and guide him to the very same conclusion against the stoppage of the distilleries as against the prohibition of food exports. But to make it available for the relief of the very poorest we must do more than stop the distilleries—we must furnish them with money to purchase the now disengaged food. The mere fall of prices might be a relief to those who can afford to pay 50s. but not 70s. per quarter; but it were no relief to those who have no money at all. Say then that by public works or otherwise they get as much money in their hands as to purchase all the food which the distilleries would have consumed. Then there would have been no fall of prices. The money of these new customers would have had the same elevating effect on the corn-market which the money of the distillers had before. But if they received the same money without any stoppage of the distilleries, then the prices might have risen from 70s to 90s., and the general community would have suffered. Let the distilleries be stopped, then the destitution might be more cheaply relieved and without the burden of a higher price on the classes above them. But let the distilleries not be stopped, then the destitution cannot be relieved without a rise in prices and so a burden on the higher classes. The Government money which went into the pockets of farmers' sons who ought not to have been on the works, and which went to the Savings' Banks—this had no effect in raising prices. Had that money all gone where it was intended, to feed the really destitute and keep them from perishing of hunger, the prices would have risen more than they did, and we should have rejoiced in a rise proceeding from such a cause. Had the distilleries been stopped, and money to purchase the grain now consumed by them been transferred for the relief of hunger, prices would have been unchanged; and the simple unembarrassed question is this—Whether it be better that grain should have been consumed in distilleries, or consumed in the houses and by the families of the destitute? By the way, it must be gratifying to Mr. Trevelyan, who at an early part of the Correspondence reasoned so ably on the benefits of a high price, to observe the practical triumph of his argument in the magnificent importations since of food from America—to a tenfold greater extent than ever Government could have achieved. It remains, however, to be seen whether even these importations will make good an adequate supply for us.

It might perhaps reconcile Mr. Ferguson to a free trade in corn, were he to examine the Liverpool Tables issued from the Corn Exchange there. In one week last month taken at random there were exported from Ireland to Liverpool 381 quarters of wheat; but to balance this, there were exported from Liverpool to Ireland in the same week 4869 quarters.

of a temporary make-shift, to have devised a thing of permanent institution and ordained it to be of perpetual force and operation in all time coming. It was right to set up in every locality of Ireland a gateway of relief for the people from the destitution of this most extraordinary year. But it was not right, it is most grievously and we fear irreparably wrong, to tell the people that this is the very gateway by which they are to seek and to find relief in every future year which lies before them. It is not possible to conceive a likelier expedient for the wholesale initiation of a people into the worst of habits, or for plunging the country *instanter*, and from one end to the other of it, into a universal and inveterate pauperism. Verily, England has not yet gotten her own legislation for the poor into such a state of settlement and perfection as at all entitles her to palm it upon us; or to distemper, as she has done, the social systems both of Scotland and Ireland, by the contention of her own inveterate malady. The method of relief for the present should have been made as peculiar as the emergency itself is peculiar—mainly we hold at the expense of Government, as say in the proportion of two to one; but partly at the expense of the land-owners, and which, if they are not able to pay at the time, should be charged in the form of a mortgage upon their estates. Meanwhile all changes and improvements on the ordinary poor-law should have been kept in abeyance—so that every injurious effect would disappear, after that the special visitation had passed away, and the temporary as well as special apparatus raised to provide for it had been taken down and removed from the eyes of the people.

Nevertheless our proposed Commission should, among their other labors, be tasked with the duty of fully preparing themselves on the question of a Poor-law. And most assuredly if either Ireland or Scotland is to be bettered by their inquiries and lucubrations on such a topic, England will receive a benefit from them also—as little independent as either of these countries of the further lights which experience or principle might cast upon the subject. This is a topic on which we would reserve ourselves for the ample opportunities that will occur for the discussion of it in future Numbers of this work. We would rather append any view or opinion of ours to the Report of a Commission than to the debates of a senate-house; and were men only content to wait the slow processes of diligent investigation, and of earnest patient thought, it would save us from a world of crude legislation in Parliament, as well as of crude and hasty speculation out of doors.

But one word more of this Commission—the only effectual sort of machinery, we do think, if but well put together and well worked, for effecting an extrication from our present difficulties —by leading to the establishment of a right economic state both in Ireland and our own Highlands. We in the first place would have it invested with an ample sufficiency of means, whether present or prospective, and in the conscious possession of these—so as not to shrink as do all our Government officers at present, from every proposal which involves in it the least expenditure of money; but, with the feeling that its vocation is to work out reforms on a large scale, not to be startled by the magnitude of any scheme, or with sensitive alarm to throw it overboard, and without investigation, if at all likely to yield the money's worth for the money bestowed on it. But in the second place, we would have it armed with sufficient resolution and sufficient strength to put down the clamor and the cupidity, and it may be the occasional violence, excited by the imagination of its unbounded resources, and of the facility with which it might give way to every application. We hope that it would soon show itself to have no such facility; and that while conscious of the greatness of its means, it was alike conscious of the great things which it had to do with them. In the third place, we would have it ever to acquit itself as the resolute protector of the most helpless, both against the upper classes on the one hand, and against those of the lower classes who are not so helpless as they,—and this that not a human creature shall perish from want, an object on which the hearts of our rulers have been set from the first, but in which they have been thwarted by difficulties that we trust they will now know how to overcome. And lastly, as the reward of its perseverance in a right and reasonable way, we should calculate that the public respect and the public confidence would at length go along with them, till they arrived at their landing place, the great *terminus ad quem* of their appointment—to relieve the countries on which they operate from the pressure that now lies upon them, and to effect such adjustments between the various orders of society, and more especially between landlords and tenants, as that, raised from the state of beggary and dependence, they might in all time coming be a well-conditioned and self-sustaining people.

There is one question on which grieved and outraged humanity seeks to be appeased, and demands satisfaction. Why is it that, on the one hand, there should be such numerous deaths by starvation, while, on the other, there is such abundance of means, and along with it the most earnest and longing desire that this fearful calamity should be mitigated to the uttermost? Several reasons might be adduced for this most perplexing and piteous phenomenon; but we shall only state two. First, the dispensers of benevolence from without, including Government among the number, are most naturally and justifiably afraid lest the benevolence from within should be at all slackened or superseded, or that in virtue of their interference the operation of home duties and home charities should at all be suspended,—while, on the other hand, there is a mighty, and we should even call it a natural, it may be a pardonable, disposition among the people themselves, to overrate the magnitude of what is doing, or to be done for them from abroad. Between this fear on the one hand, and this delusion on the other, thousands of lives have been sacrificed; and yet we are not prepared to say, but that if the fear had not operated so as to make Government wary in their proceedings, there might not have been ten deaths by hunger, for every one that is now recorded. Let us just imagine that they had made gratuitous distribution of their stores at Schull and Skibbereen; and we have only to conceive the paralyzing effect which the report of this generosity would have had, not on the home charity alone, but on the home and inland trade* of Ireland,—after it had gone abroad that Government, with its inexhaustible treasury and its magnificent depôts, would overtake all and provide for all. There is no Government on earth that possesses the wealth and the power, and above all, the *ubiquity* which might enable it to countervail the mischief of so ruinous a dependence, if it once pervaded, and among all ranks, too, the entire mass of a country's population. But there is a single sentence in the last Report of the Friends, these noble-hearted men of undoubted Christian worth, but of wisdom along with it, which throws a flood of light upon this question. No one will suspect them who went forth months ago on their pilgrimage of charity, and traversed the whole extent of Ireland—none will suspect them of hard-heartedness, or of callous indifference to the sufferings of their fellow-men; and yet let us hear their explanation of the fact, that of the forty thousand pounds which they had raised, augmented if we understand them aright, by twelve thousand more, the sum of twenty-four thousand pounds had been all that was expended—and this while hundreds were dying. "We cannot close this brief Report without expressing the satisfaction that we have in contemplating the proceedings of the Dublin Committee. We believe that if they had hastily distributed the money which had been committed to their charge, it would have been incalculably less useful. Some of those who have contributed money for a time have felt uneasy because their liberality has been husbanded, whilst hundreds of their fellow-creatures were dropping into the grave, but we believe that the larger the acquaintance they have with Ireland, her wants, and her national character, the more reason they will have to rejoice in an intervention of a committee, who, while they have known how to give, have known also how, by withholding for a time, to open the legitimate springs of assistance, which otherwise might have remained sealed, to the necessities of a famishing people." Had all the springs of assistance flowed as they ought, and if the opening of one had not had the effect, as if by some

* In the Longford Journal of January the 16th, we read that in the neighborhood of Castle-town "the report of a Government depot to be established, *kept back the commercial people*, and the whole district is now without food."

sort of moral machinery, of shutting another, the whole even of this stupendous calamity might have been fully overtaken.

The second reason, which we shall only state, without commenting on it, is the want of sufficient local agencies in Ireland—the effect of which is that though adequate funds were raised, they might prove unavailable for the adequate supply and distribution of food, and this over whole breadths of country where, each family living on their own half acre of potatoes, all marketing for victuals was in a great measure unknown. This alone accounts for a great number of the starvations. It is well brought out in an extract given below from a letter of the Rev. F. F. Trench of Clough-Jordan after a visit to the parish of Schull*.

We confess it to be in this last reason especially that we read the prognostication and the omen of future, and perhaps heavier disasters, than ever have yet fallen upon poor unhappy Ireland! It is easy for Parliament to ordain Relief Committees throughout all its localities; but do there exist everywhere materials for their formation, and still more for the vigorous and effectual working of them? Is not there room to apprehend a failure here; and that from this cause alone, unless we become callous—itself the most grievous moral calamity which can befall a nation—we might still continue between this and the coming harvest to be agonized as heretofore by these hideous starvations? It is true that no single Government is responsible for such a want of local agencies, proceeding as it does from a state of society which is the result of the misgovernment of many centuries? But has nothing been done even in our present session of Parliament to aggravate the evil? Whether have they taken the right method to invite or repel the willing co-operation of the most important class, and the best able by their position and influence to lend the readiest and the greatest service in this trying emergency—the landed proprietors of Ireland? Was it the likeliest way for engaging them heart and hand in the work, thus to assimilate, as has been done, the methods of temporary relief with the ordinary and per-

* The date of the letter is March 22, 1847. The following is but a small portion of it—"Take for example the one parish of Schull (and there are many like it). Here there are scarcely any gentry, and none rich. What can one physician do amongst 18,000 people in such a state (and oats for his horse dear)? What can the ordinary number of local clergy do in such an extensive district? They cannot visit one-tenth part of the sick, even if they had horses, and oats to feed them, which some of them have not. Can Dr. Traill be expected to carry meal to the people in the mountains across the pummel of his saddle, as he has done? Can Mr. M'Cabe, the curate, be expected to push in the door and look for a vessel, and wash the vessel previous to putting a drink into it for the sick, who were unable to rise, as he has done? But let there be provided a sufficient staff of fit men to prescribe for the sick, and to place cooked food within the reach of the poor, and I feel confident that the supply of money that the public have proved themselves ready to give would pay for all, and so prevent absolute starvation, and restore health in many instances."

In a subsequent letter of Mr. Trench it appears that his appeal was quite effectual as far as the money was concerned; but the staff of fit men still remained a desideratum. Conceive some hundreds of such localities in Ireland; and we need not wonder if in a country so circumstanced, there should have occurred so many starvations.

manent methods for the relief of the poor in all time coming—and this contemporaneously with the passing of a measure by which to accelerate tenfold the growth and increase of an all-absorbing pauperism? It is not only compelling them to vote away their own money, but to dispose of it so that it shall become the germ of a growing and gathering mischief—a deadly upas, which in a few years will be sure to spread its poison and shed its malignant influences over the whole land. But it is thus that England is ever for imposing on the dependent territories around her, her own wretched poor-law—as if this were the grand panacea for all our moral and social disorders, instead of being what it truly is, a distempering and disturbing influence wherewith to complicate and derange whatever it comes in contact with. It will indeed form a most instructive result, if in France without a poor-law and the disadvantage of higher prices than our own, she come forth of her famine unscathed and without a death—while the enormous destruction of two millions of human beings, now coolly reckoned on as the likelihood in Ireland, shall be held forth to a wondering world, as England's trophy to the wisdom and the efficacy of her boasted legislation.

But with all the blunders of England's legislation, the heart of England is in its right place—bent with full desirousness on Ireland's large and lasting good. We do hope that ere the close of the Parliamentary Session she will make a clear demonstration of her purposes, by the appointment of a Commission that shall at once represent the largeness of her wishes and the largeness of her means—a Commission that will not let down its labors, till it has left and established in both countries, an unfettered proprietary, a secure and leaseholding tenantry; and, best of all, a population in circumstances, should they have the will, to earn a stable sufficiency for themselves by their own prosperous and well-paid industry. In the prospect of blessings such as these, Ireland would forthwith address itself with alacrity and hope to its present duties; and vigorously work even the existing Relief machinery, with all its defects, rather than that the country should sink, and its people die as heretofore in thousands under the burden of their present distress. With the guidance and guardianship of the Holy Providence above, a harvest of good will ensue from this great temporary evil; and Ireland, let us trust and pray, will emerge from her sore trial, on a bright and peaceful career to future generations.

Such are a few of the general views, we fear somewhat confusedly put together, which have been suggested by these interesting volumes of Correspondence between the officials of Government on the subject of the Scottish and Irish famines. The several hundreds of passages to which we had affixed our notanda as the topics of remark and reflection, must all be laid aside for the present, though rich in materials ample enough for two other

Articles on "the Highlands in detail," and "Ireland in detail." Whether these shall ever be forthcoming or not, the subjects certainly will suffer no decline in point of urgency and importance for many months or perhaps years; and on the vista of Irish questions there opens upon our view an argument of as much higher importance than any we have now touched upon, as the moral is higher than the economical or the physical,—what is best to be done for the *education* of a people, using this term in the most comprehensive sense of it, as education both for the present and the future world.

In our dislike to the work of condemnation, we have indicated rather than pronounced our views in regard to the parties on whom the responsibility lies for these starvations in Ireland. It clearly does not lie upon the Government—but partly on difficulties in the state of the country itself, and partly, we grieve to add, on delinquencies of mischievous and extensive operation, on the part both of proprietors and people. We will never give in to any wholesale calumny on either of these classes; but how can we otherwise account for so great a failure of bygone measures of relief, than by a flagrant misconduct somewhere, when we read the following sentences from a Report of the Relief Commissioners just come to hand :—" We feel that as long as the number of the destitute continue to increase as they have done, at the rate of about 20,000 persons per week, and as long as every person sent to the work must be employed, and, no matter how idle, cannot be dismissed, except on account of insubordination or outrage, the overseers, the greater number of whom have been necessarily taken from the surrounding country, are unable, perhaps sometimes unwilling, to enforce regularity or system in works executed by a mass of unskilful, and frequently weak and even dying creatures."

It further appears from Reports and other documents, that all the instructions " which have been from time to time issued, either to reduce the number of persons upon the works, or not to employ persons rated at £6 and upwards, and every other regulation of similar import, have been found utterly inefficacious to check the inordinate increase of persons upon the Relief Works, and that a large proportion of the Relief Committees have recommended for employment upon these works, in considerable numbers, persons having no claim whatever to relief, and have latterly abandoned all attempt to investigate the claim of the applicants."

Well then are the Lords of the Treasury warranted in their conclusion, " that all effectual control over the increase in the number of persons employed, and over the manner in which the work is executed by them, has, for the present, been lost."

In these circumstances we would implore the landed proprietors of Ireland to bestir themselves; and see to it, that there shall be a righteous and well-principled administration of the new methods of relief. Without a patriotic co-operation on their part, and on the part of Ireland generally, all effectual good, whether in the shape of relief or amelioration, will be wholly impracticable."

VALUABLE BOOKS

PUBLISHED BY

ROBERT CARTER & BROTHERS, 285 BROADWAY.

NEW YORK.

Abeel's (Rev. David) Life. By his Nephew, $ 50
Abercrombie's Contest and The Armor. 32mo. 25
Adam's Three Divine Sisters—Faith, Hope, &c. 60
Advice to a Young Christian. By a Village Pastor. With an Introduction by Rev. Dr. Alexander. 18mo. 30
Alleine's Gospel Promises. 18mo. . . . 30
—— Life and Letters. 12mo. . . . 60
Alexander's Counsels to the Young. 32mo. gilt, 25
Ancient History of the Egyptians, Assyrians, Chaldeans, Medes, Lydians, Carthaginians, Persians, Macedonians, &c. 4 vols. 12mo. 2 00
Anderson—The Annals of the English Bible. By Christopher Anderson. Revised, abridged, and continued by Rev. S. I. Prime. 8vo. 1 75
—— The Family Book; or, The Genius and Design of the Domestic Constitution. 12mo. 75
Australia, the Loss of the Brig, by Fire. 18mo. 25
Bagster—The Genuineness, Authenticity, and Inspiration of the Sacred Volume. 12mo. . 60
Baxter's Saint's Rest. Large type. 12mo. . 60
—— Call to the Unconverted. 18mo. . . 30
—— Choice Works. 12mo. 60
Bible Expositor. 18mo. 50
Bickersteth's Treatise on Prayer. 18mo. . 40
—— Treatise on the Lord's Supper. 18mo. 30
Blunt's Undesigned Coincidences in the Writings both of the Old and New Testaments, an Argument of their Veracity. 8vo. . . 1 25
Bogatzky's Golden Treasury. 18mo. . . 50
Bolton (Miss) Memoir, or the Lighted Valley, 75
Bonar's Night of Weeping. 18mo. . . 30
—— Story of Grace. 18mo. 30
—— Morning of Joy, ... 40
Bonnet's Family of Bethany. 18mo. . . 40
—— Meditations on the Lord's Prayer, . 40
Borrow's Bible and Gypsies of Spain. 8vo. 75
Boston's Four-fold State. 18mo. . . . 50
—— Crook in the Lot. 18mo. . . . 30
Brown's Explication of the Assem. Catechism, 60
Bridges on the Christian Ministry. 8vo. . 1 50
—— On the Proverbs. 8vo. 2 00
—— On the CXIX. Psalm. New ed. 8vo. . 1 00
—— Memoir of Mary Jane Graham. 8vo. . 1 00
—— Works. 3 vols., containing the above, 5 00
Brown's Concordance. New and neat ed. 24mo. 20
Do. gilt edge, 30
Buchanan's Comfort in Affliction. 18mo. . 40
—— On the Holy Spirit. 18 mo. 2d ed. . 50
Bunbury's Glory, and other Narratives, . . 25
Bunyan's Pilgrim's Progress. Fine edition, large type, with eight illustrations by Howland. 12mo. 1 00
Do. do. gilt, 1 50
Do. do. close type, 18mo. 50
—— Jerusalem Sinner Saved. 18mo. . 50
—— Greatness of the Soul. 18mo. . . 50

Butler's Complete Works. 8vo. . . . $1 50
—— Sermons, alone. 8vo. 1 00
—— Analogy, alone. 8vo. 75
—— and Wilson's Analogy. 8vo. . . 1 25
Burn's Christian Fragments. 18mo. . . 40
Calvin on Secret Providence. 18mo. . . 25
Cameron's Farmer's Daughter. 18mo. . . 30
Catechisms—The Assembly's. Per hundred, 1 25
Do. with Proofs. 3 00
—— Brown's Short Catechism. Per hund. . 1 25
—— Smyth's Ecclesiastical Catechism. 18mo. 25
—— Willison's Communicant's. 18mo. . 10
—— Key to the Assembly's Catechism. 18mo. 20
Cecil's Works; comprising his Sermons, Original Thoughts on Scripture, Miscellanies, and Remains. 3 vols. 12mo. with portrait, . 3 00
—— Original Thoughts on Scripture, separate, 1 00
Charnock's Choice Works. 12mo. . . 60
Chalmers' Sermons, enlarged by the addition of his Posthumous Sermons. 2 vols. 8vo. with a fine Portrait, ... 3 00
—— Lectures on Romans. 8vo. . . . 1 50
—— Miscellanies. 8vo. 1 50
—— Select Works; comprising the above. 4 vols. 8vo. with portrait, ... 6 00
—— Evidences of Christian Revelation. 2 v. 1 25
—— Natural Theology. 2 vols. . . . 1 25
—— Moral Philosophy, ... 60
—— Commercial Discourses, . . . 60
—— Astronomical Discourses, . . . 60
Christian Retirement. 12mo. 75
Clarke's Daily Scripture Promises. 32mo. gilt, 30
Clark's Walk about Zion. 12mo. . . . 75
—— Pastor's Testimony, ... 75
—— Awake, Thou Sleeper, ... 75
—— Young Disciple, ... 88
—— Gathered Fragments, ... 1 00
—— Experience. By the same author. 18mo. 50
Colquhoun's World's Religion. 18mo. . . 30
Commandment with Promise. By the author of "The First Day of the Week," "Guilty Tongue," &c. With beautiful illustrations by Howland. 16mo. 75
Cowper—The Works of William Cowper; comprising his Life, Letters, and Poems, now first collected by the introduction of Cowper's Private Correspondence. Edited by the Rev. T. S. Grimshaw. With numerous illustrations on steel, and a fine portrait by Ritchie. 1 vol. royal 8vo. . . . 3 00
—— Do. do. sheep, 3 50
—— Do. do. half mor. 4 00
—— Do. do. cloth extra gilt, 4 00
—— Do. do. mor. extra, 5 00
—— Poetical Works, separate. 2 vols. 1 00
Cumming's Message from God. 18mo. . 30
—— Christ Receiving Sinners, . . 30

Cunningham's World without Souls. 18mo. $ 30
Dale—The Golden Psalm; an Exposition of the 16th Psalm. By Rev. Thos. Dale, M.A. 50
Davies' Sermons. 3 vols. 12mo. . . . 2 00
Davidson's Connections. New ed. 8vo. . . 1 50
David's Psalms, in metre. Large type, 12mo. 75
—— Do. do gilt edge, 1 00
—— Do. do. Turkey mor. 2 00
—— Do. 18mo., good type. plain sheep. 38
—— Do. " do. Turkey mor. 1 25
—— Do. 48mo., very neat pocket ed. mor. 25
—— Do. " " " gilt edge, 31
—— Do. " " " tucks, 50
D'Aubigné's History of the Reformation. *Carefully revised*, with various additions not hitherto published. 4 vols. 12mo. half cloth, 1 50
—— Do. " " full cloth, 1 75
—— Do. " " 4th vol. half cloth, 38
—— Do. " " " full cloth, 50
—— Do. " " Complete in 1 vol. 1 00
—— Life of Cromwell. 12mo. . . . 50
—— Germany, England, and Scotland, . 75
—— Luther and Calvin. 18mo. . . . 25
Dick's Lectures on Acts. 8vo. . . . 1 50
Dickinson's Scenes from Sacred History. 3d ed. 1 00
Doddridge's Rise and Progress. 18mo. . . 40
—— Life of Colonel Gardiner. 18mo. 30
Duncan's Sacred Philosophy of Seasons. 4 v. 3 00
—— Life by his Son. With portrait. 12mo. 75
—— Tales of the Scottish Peasantry. 18mo. . 50
—— Cottage Fireside. 18mo. . . . 40
—— (Mrs.) Life of Mary Lundie Duncan, . 50
—— —— Life of George A. Lundie. 18mo. 50
—— —— Memoir of George B. Phillips, . 25
Erskine's Gospel Sonnets. New edition, . 1 00
English Pulpit; a collection of Sermons by the most eminent English Divines. 8vo. . . 1 50
Farr's History of the Egyptians. 12mo. . . 75
—— History of the Persians. 12mo. . . 75
—— History of the Assyrians, Chaldeans, Medes, Lydians, and Carthaginians. 12mo. 75
—— History of the Macedonians, the Selucidæ in Syria, and Parthians. 12mo. . . . 75
Ferguson's Roman Republic. 8vo. . . . 1 50
Fisk's Memorial of the Holy Land. With steel plates. 1 00
Fleury's Life of David. 12mo. . . . 60
Foster's Essays, on Decision of Character, &c. Large type, fine edition, 12mo. . . 75
—— Do. Close type, 18mo. . 50
—— Essay on the Evils of Popular Ignorance 75
Ford's Decapolis. 18mo. 25
Free Church Pulpit; consisting of Discourses by the most eminent Divines of the Free Church of Scotland. 3 vols. 8vo. . . 5 00
Fry (Caroline) The Listener. 2 vols. in one, 1 00
—— Christ our Law. 12mo. 60
—— Sabbath Musings. 18mo. . . . 40
—— The Scripture Reader's Guide. 18mo. . 30
Geological Cosmogony. By a Layman. 18mo. 30
God in the Storm. 18mo. 25
Graham's (Miss Mary J.) Life and Works. 8vo. 1 00
—— Test of Truth, separate. 18mo. . . 30
Green—The Life of the Rev. Ashbel Green, D.D., by the Rev. Dr. Jones, of Philadelphia, 2 00
Griffith's Live while you Live. 18mo. . . 30
Haldane's Exposition of Romans. 8vo. $2 50
Hall (Jos., Bishop of Exeter,) Select Works, 75
Hamilton's Life in Earnest, ... 30
—— Mount of Olives, ... 30
—— Harp on the Willows, ... 30
—— Thankfulness, ... 30
—— Life of Bishop Hall, ... 30
—— The Happy Home. Illustrated, . . 50
—— Life of Lady Colquhoun. With portrait, 75
Hawker's Poor Man's Morning Portion. 12mo. 60
—— " Evening Portion, . . 60
—— Zion's Pilgrim. 18mo. 30
Hervey's Meditations, ... 40
Hetherington's Hist. of the Church of Scotland, 1 50
Hengstenberg's Egypt and the Books of Moses, or the Books of Moses Illustrated by the Monuments of Egypt. 12mo. . . . 75
Henry's (Matth.) Method for Prayer, . . 40
—— Communicant's Companion, . . 40
—— Daily Communion with God, . . 30
—— Pleasantness of a Religious Life, . 30
—— Choice Works. 12mo. 60
Henry (Philip) Life of. 18mo. . . . 50
Hill's (George) Lectures on Divinity. 8vo. . 2 00
—— (Rowland) Life. By Sidney. 12mo. . 75
History of the Puritans in England, and the Pilgrim Fathers. By the Rev. W. H. Stowell and D. Wilson, F.S.A. With 2 steel plates, 1 00
History of the Reformation in Europe. 18mo. 40
Housman's Life and Remains. 12mo. . . 75
Horne's Introduction. 2 v. royal 8vo. half cloth, 3 50
—— Do. 1 vol. sheep, . . . 4 00
—— Do. 2 vols. cloth, . . . 4 00
—— Do. 2 vols. library style, . 5 00
—— (Bishop) Commentary on the Psalms. . 1 50
Howard (John) or the Prison World of Europe, 1 00
Howell's Life—Perfect Peace. 18mo. . . 30
Howe's Redeemer's Tears, and other Essays, 50
Huss' (John) Life. Transl. from the German, 25
Jacobus on Matthew. With a Harmony, . 75
—— Questions on do. 18mo. . . . 15
—— On Mark, Luke, and John, . . .
James' Anxious Inquirer. 18mo. . . . 30
—— True Christian. 18mo. . . . 30
—— Widow Directed. 18mo. . . . 30
Janeway's Heaven upon Earth. 12mo. . 60
—— Token for Children 18mo. . . . 30
Jay's Morning Exercises. 12mo. . . . 75
—— Evening " 12mo. . . . 75
—— Christian Contemplated. 18mo. . . 40
—— Jubilee Memorial. 18mo. . . . 30
Jerram's Tribute to a beloved only Daughter, . 30
Johnson's Rasselas. Elegant edition, . . 50
Key to the Shorter Catechism. 18mo. . . 20
Kennedy's (Grace) Profession is not Principle, 30
—— Jessy Allan, the Lame Girl. 18mo. . 25
Kitto's Daily Bible Illustrations. 4 vols. 12mo. 4 00
Krummacher's Martyr Lamb. 18mo. . . 40
—— Elijah the Tishbite. 18mo. . . 40
—— Last Days of Elisha. 12mo. . . 75
Life in New York. 18mo. 40
Lowrie's Letters to Sabbath School Children, 25
—— (Rev. W. M.) Life. Edited by his Father, 1 50
Lockwood's Memoir. By his Father. 18mo. 40
Luther's Commentary on Galatians. 8vo. . 1 50
Martin's (Sarah) Life. 18mo. 30

Mackay—The Wyckliffites; or, England in the 15th Century, ... $ 75
Martyn's (Henry) Life. 12mo. . . . 60
Mason's Essays on the Church. 12mo. . . 60
—— " on Episcopacy. 12mo. . . 60
Marshall on Sanctification, ... 50
Martyrs and Covenanters of Scotland. 18mo. 40
Malcolm on the Atonement. 18mo. . . 30
McCrindell—The Convent, a Narrative, . 50
McGilvray's Peace in Believing. 18mo. . 25
McGhee on the Ephesians, ... 2 00
McLeod's Life and Power of True Godliness, 60
McCheyne's (Rev. Robert Murray) Works. 2 v. 3 00
—— Life, Lectures, and Letters, separate, 1 50
—— Sermons, separate, ... 2 00
—— Familiar Letters from the Holy Land, 50
McFarlane—The Mountains of the Bible, their Scenes and their Lessons. With four illustrations on steel. 12mo. 75
—— Do. do. extra gilt, 1 25
Meikle's Solitude Sweetened. 12mo. . . 60
Miller's (Rev. Dr. S.) Memoir of Rev. Dr. Nisbet 75
—— (Rev. John) Design of the Church, . 60
Michael Kemp, the Farmer's Lad. 18mo. . 40
Missions, The Origin and History of. By Choules and Smith. With 25 steel plates, 3 50
Moffat's Southern Africa. 12mo. . . . 75
Monod's Lucilla; or, the Reading of the Bible, 40
More (Hannah)—The Book of Private Devotion. Large type, elegant edition, 18mo. . 50
—— Do. do. do. gilt, 75
—— Do. do. small ed. 32mo. 20
—— Do. do. " gilt, 30
Morell's Historical and Critical View of the Speculative Philosophy of Europe in the 19th Century, ... 3 00
Murphy—The Bible Consistent with Geology,
My School Boy Days. 18mo. 30
My Youthful Companions. 18mo. . . . 30
The above two bound in 1 vol. . . 50
Newton's (Rev. John) Works. 2 vols. 8vo. . 3 00
—— Life, separate. 18mo. 30
—— Memoir of M. Magdalen Jasper, . . 30
Noel's Infant Piety. 18mo. 25
North American Indians. Illustrated. 18mo. 50
Olmsted's Counsels for the Impenitent, . . 50
Old White Meeting-House. 18mo. . . 40
Old Humphrey's Observations, . . . 40
—— Addresses, ... 40
—— Thoughts for the Thoughtful, . . 40
—— Homely Hints, ... 40
—— Walks in London, ... 40
—— Country Strolls, ... 40
—— Old Sea Captain, ... 40
—— Grandparents, ... 40
—— Isle of Wight, ... 40
—— Pithy Papers, ... 40
—— Pleasant Tales, ... 40
Opie on Lying. New edition, 18mo. . . 40
Owen on Spiritual Mindedness. 12mo. . . 60
Paley's Horæ Paulinæ. 12mo. . . . 75
Pascal's Provincial Letters. Edited by M'Crie, 1 00
—— Thoughts on Religion. 12mo. . . 1 00
Paterson on the Assemb. Shorter Catechism. . 50
Pike's True Happiness. 18mo. . . . 30
—— Religion and Eternal Life. 18mo. . . 30

Pike's Divine Origin of Christianity. 18mo. $ 30
Philip's Devotional Guides. 2 vols. 12mo. . 1 50
—— Marys, ... 40
—— Marthas, ... 40
—— Lydias, ... 40
—— Hannahs, ... 40
—— Love of the Spirit, ... 40
—— Young Man's Closet Library, . . . 75
Pollok's Course of Time. The most elegant edition ever published; printed on superfine paper. 16mo. with portrait, cloth, . 1 00
—— —— gilt. cloth, extra, ... 1 50
—— —— Turkey morocco, gilt, . . . 2 00
—— —— Small copy, close type, 18mo. . 40
—— Life, Letters, and Remains. By the Rev. James Scott, D.D. With Portrait, 16mo. . 1 00
—— Tales of the Scottish Covenanters. Printed on large paper, uniform with the above. With portrait, ... 75
—— Do. do. small copy, 18mo. 50
—— Helen of the Glen. 18mo. . . . 25
—— Persecuted Family. 18mo. . . . 25
—— Ralph Gemmell. 18mo. 25
Porteus' Lectures on Matthew. 12mo. . . 60
Psalms in Hebrew. Neat miniature edition, 50
Reign of Grace. By Booth, ... 75
Retrospect, The. By Aliquis. 18mo. . . 40
Richmond's Domestic Portraiture. Edited by Bickersteth. New and elegant edition, . 75
—— Annals of the Poor. 18mo. . . . 40
Rogers' Jacob's Well. 18mo. 40
Romaine on Faith. 12mo. 60
—— Letters. 12mo. 60
Rowland's Common Maxims of Infidelity, . 75
Rutherford's Letters. New edition, 8vo. . 1 50
Scott's Force of Truth. 18mo. . . . 25
Scougal's Works. 18mo. 40
Scripture Narratives. By Dr. Belcher. 12mo. 60
Select Works of James, Venn, Wilson, Philip and Jay. Eight complete works in 1 vol. . 1 50
Select Christian Authors; comprising Doddridge, Wilberforce, Adams, Halyburton, à Kempis, &c. With Introductory Essays by Dr. Chalmers, Bishop Wilson, &c. 2 v. 2 00
Serle's Christian Remembrancer, . . . 50
Sinner's Friend. 18mo. 25
Sigourney (Mrs. L. H.) Water Drops. 2d edit. 75
—— The Girl's Book. 18mo., illustrated, . 40
—— The Boy's Book. " " . 40
—— Child's Book. Square, " . 35
Sinclair's Modern Accomplishments, . . 75
—— Modern Society, ... 75
—— Charlie Seymour. 18mo. . . . 30
—— Hill and Valley. 12mo. . . . 75
Simeon's Life, by Carus. With Introductory Essay by Bishop McIlvaine. With portrait, 2 00
Sir Roland Ashton. By Lady Catharine Long, 75
Sketches of Sermons on the Parables and Miracles of Christ. By the author of the Pulpit Cyclopædia. 12mo. 75
Smyth's Bereaved Parents Consoled. 12mo. . 75
Sorrowing Yet Rejoicing. 18mo. . . . 30
Do. do 32mo. gilt, . . 30
Spring (Rev. Gardiner, D.D.)—A Pastor's Tribute to one of his Flock, or Memoirs of the late Hannah L. Murray. With a portrait, . 1 50

Stevenson's Christ on the Cross. 12mo. $ 75
—— Lord our Shepherd. 12mo. . . . 60
Sumner's Exposition of Matthew and Mark, . 75
Suddard's British Pulpit. 2 vols. 8vo. . . 3 00
Symington on the Atonement. 12mo. . . 75
Tacitus' Works translated. Edited by Murphy, 2 00
Tennent's Life. 18mo. 25
Tholuck's Circle of Human Life. 18mo. . 30
Taylor's (Jane) Life and Correspondence, . 40
—— Contributions of Q. Q. New edition, with fine illustrations by Howland, 2 vols. in one, 1 00
—— Original Poems. 18mo. 30
—— Display, a Tale. 18mo. 30
—— Mother and Daughter, ... 30
—— Essays in Rhyme. 18mo. . . . 30
—— Original Poems and Poetical Remains. With 12 fine illustrations by Howland, . 40
—— (Isaac) Loyola; or, Jesuitism in its Rudiments, ... 1 00
—— Natural History of Enthusiasm. 12mo. . 75
—— (Jeremy) Sermons. Complete in 1 vol. . 1 50
Turretine's Complete Works, in original Latin,
The Theological Sketch Book; or, Skeletons of Sermons, so arranged as to constitute a complete body of Divinity. From Simeon, Hannam, Benson, &c. 2 vols. . . . 3 00
Tyng's Lectures on the Law and Gospel. New edition, large type, with a fine portrait, 8vo. 1 50
—— Christ is All. 8vo. with portrait, . 1 50
—— Israel of God. 8vo. enlarged edition, . 1 50
—— Recollections of England. 12mo. . 1 00
Thucydides' History of the Peloponnesian War. Translated by William Smith. 8vo. 1 25
Turnbull's Genius of Scotland; or Sketches of Scottish Scenery, Literature, and Religion. New ed. with 8 fine illustrations, 16mo. 1 00
—— Pulpit Orators of France and Switzerland, with Sketches of their Character and Specimens of their Eloquence. With portrait of Fenelon, ... $1 00
Waterbury's Book for the Sabbath. 18mo. . 40
Whately's Kingdom of Christ and Errors of Romanism, ... 75
Whitecross' Anecdotes on Assem. Catechism, 30
White's (Hugh) Meditation on Prayer. 18mo. 40
—— Believer; a Series of Discourses. 18mo. 40
—— Practical Reflections on the Second Advent. 18mo. 40
—— (Henry Kirke) Complete Works. With Life by Southey. 8vo. 1 50
—— Do. extra gilt, . . . 2 50
Wilson's Lights and Shadows of Scottish Life, 50
—— Do. on large paper, 16mo. with 8 illustrations, from original drawings, by Croome, Billings, &c., engraved by Howland, . . 75
—— Do. do. extra gilt, 1 25
Williams (Rev. John), Memoir of, Missionary to Polynesia. By Eb. Prout. With two illustrations, 12mo. 1 00
Winslow on Personal Declension and Revival, 60
Wylie's Journey over the Region of Fulfilled Prophecy, ... 30
Xenophon's Whole Works. Translated, . 2 00
Young's Night Thoughts. Elegant edition, 16mo. with portrait, ... 1 00
—— Do. do. extra gilt, 1 50

NEW BOOKS.

Blunt's Coincidences and Paley's Horæ Paulinæ. 2 vols. in one, 8vo. . . . $2 00
Brown's, Rev. John, D.D., Exposition of the First Epistle of Peter. 8vo. . . . .
Broken Bud, or Reminiscences of a Bereaved Mother. 16mo. . . . .
Cecil's, Cath., Memoir of Mrs. Hawkes. 12mo.
Cheever, Rev. Dr., Lectures on the Pilgrim's Progress. New edition, 12mo. . . . 1 00
David's Psalms, with Brown's Notes. 18mo. sheep, ... 0 50
Dickinson's, R. W., D.D., Responses from the Sacred Oracles. 12mo. . . . . .
Duncan, Mrs., Children of the Manse. 16mo. 1 00
Do do. Gilt, 1 25
——, Mary Lundie, Rhymes for my Children.
Hooker, Rev. Herm., Uses of Adversity. 18mo. 0 30
——, Philosophy of Unbelief. 12mo. . 0 75
James, J. A., Young Man from Home. 18mo. 0 30
—— Christian Professor. 12mo. . 0 75
Kennedy, Grace, Anna Ross. With six fine illustrations. 18mo. 0 30
Leyburn's, Rev. John, Soldier of the Cross, 12mo. . . . .
Line upon Line. 18mo. 0 30
Lowrie, Rev. John C., Two Years in Upper India. 12mo. 0 75
Matthews, Rev. James, D.D., The Bible and Civil Government. 12mo. . . . $1 00
M'Cosh, Rev. J., The Divine Government, Physical and Moral. 8vo. . . . .
M'Lelland, Prof. Alex., on the Canon and Interpretation of Scripture. 12mo. . . 0 75
New Cobwebs to catch Little Flies. Illustrated.
Pastor's Daughter, by Louisa P. Hopkins. . 0 40
Peep of Day. New edition. 18mo. . . 0 30
Pollok's Tales of the Covenanters. Illustrated edition. 16mo. 0 75
Do. do. Gilt. . . 1 00
Powerscourt's, Lady, Letters and Papers. 12mo. 0 75
Precept on Precept. 18mo. 0 30
Smith, Rev. James, The Believer's Daily Remembrancer, or Green Pastures for the Lord's Flock. . . . . . .
Taylor, Jane, Hymns for Infant Minds. Illustrated. Square. . . . . . .
Waugh, Rev. Alex., D.D., Memoir of, with Selections from his Correspondence, &c., by Dr. Hay and Dr. Belfrage. 12mo. Portrait.
Wilberforce's Practical View. Large type, fine edition. 12mo. . . . . .
Winer's Idioms of the Language of the New Testament. 8vo. 2 50

R. Carter & Brothers have nearly ready the first volume of the "WORKS OF JOHN OWEN," to be completed in sixteen volumes octavo. It is their intention to issue a volume every three months till the whole are issued.

www.ingramcontent.com/pod-product-compliance
Lightning Source LLC
LaVergne TN
LVHW021243110826
845150LV00002B/393

* 9 7 8 1 4 2 5 5 6 1 0 6 2 *